FOREWORD

Shakespeare had a word for it – indeed, as was his practice, he had several words for it. In Henry VI Pt. 2 one of the rabblement said – "The "first thing we do, let's kill all the lawyers."[1]

This cry derived in part, at least, from ignorance. It is in the nature of man to fear what he does not understand. In Ireland, ignorance of the law is compounded by a suspicion and fear that springs from our history. The law, as it touched upon the average Irishman of a hundred years ago, was an instrument of oppression in the enforcement of either the criminal law or of taxation. The average Irishman seldom sought its help because the law was of little use to him; it was administered by the propertied classes for the propertied classes, it was the visible instrument of British rule through its buildings, local symbols of imperial might, and through its Judges and practitioners, garbed in ancient forms of dress and speaking an arcane language. Although the revolutionaries of 1916 proclaimed a republic and the author of the Constitution of 1937 often vouchsafed the State to be such, as it ws proclaimed in 1948[2], the structures, formal approach, and, most regrettably, attitudes of lawyers in Ireland remain English orientated. In a sense, this is not the fault of the lawyers of this generation because they inherited it from the last and the generation before that; but it is the fault of this generation because of a failure to examine and analyse the law, rather than take refuge in an unthinking and uncritical citation of precedent. Forensic forelock touching is as much a part of the cultural cringe that has beset our country as the mimicry of English accents and manners, but it may be more damaging in its long term effects. Whilst no lawyer of the last sixty years can escape his share of blame, some have sought at least to inform the pubic as to some of the intricacies of the legal system but none to the extent that this work seeks to do. Although one is mildly conscious of it at the Bar, it is really since I have sat on the Bench that I have become so aware of the degree to which the citation of precedent is made a substitute for reasoned argument and analysis of principle. Messrs Byrne and McCutcheon in this book, make a valiant effort to examine the doctrine of precedent recognising the vital distinction that it is the reason for the decision that is important, rather than the decision itself; that if the reason be good, it matters not in what Court such reason were used; if the reasoning be defective, then the leather binding of the Law Reports does not give it authenticity or merit. A recent exposure of defective rasoning is to be found in the robust language of Professor Glanville Williams in his article "The Lords and Impossible Attempts, or quis custodiet ipsos custodes?"[3]. In the memoirs of Lord Shandon, of which the type-script is in the King's Inns Library, that worthy did not spare even the great Chief Baron on this score. "There can be no question" he said "that his judgments were held in deserved respect, but his mind was of the type which I dislike though it was one which our legal system necessarily encourages with its slavish adherence to mere precedent. Palles not only had an immense knowledge of case law but his industry was colossal and one might always rely upon Palle's disinterring some forgotten authority which everyone else had failed to discover. Such men remind me of the contrapuntal musicians who by the application of purely empirical rules occasionally produce the most magnificent harmony.

So it was with the Chief Baron. His method was always the same, that of piling up analogy on analogy but often to produce a most logical and coherent result. In the same way he worshipped technicality as if it were a fetish and even when he was fully conscious that the result at which he arrived was imminently unsatisfactory he was unable to burst the bonds of precedent and technicality. He was ably abetted – indeed often inspired in the matter of technicality by his Co-adjutor, Baron Fitzgerald who would subdivide the split hair that his Chief had divided."[4] Strong words indeed, but it is still at times refreshing to be referred to the earlier cases in which Judges appeared to be able to enunciate both principle and decision in a few pages whilst now, armed with the dictating machine gun we sometimes get lost in a sea of words. When the Supreme Court decided *Brogan v. Bennett*[5] in June 1952, the report indicates that judgment was delivered on the day of hearing. The unfortunate Christopher Brogan had believed a pamphlet entitled "T.B. CONQUERED by Mr. J. H. Bennett, Lamagh, Newtownforbes, of Kelly & Bennett, Divining Specialists, Longford. Tel.: Longford 53", and requested some relatives to get in touch with Mr. Bennett who undertook to cure Christopher Brogan and make him fit for work within three months, charging fees of £100 for a rich person and £20 for a poor person, into which category the unfortunate Christopher Brogan fell; as a result, he left Longford tuberculosis hospital and returned home where he took a medicine "prescribed" by Bennett for approximately five weeks and then died. His parents sued for damages for negligence and called evidence from the relatives who had interviewed Bennett, who "produced a bullet on the end of a string, and said he was going to X-ray the patient. He then caused the pendulum to oscillate and pronounced the case to be a fairly bad one. He purported to diagnose the exact percentage of impairment of all the main organs of the patient, and claimed that by means of his pendulum he could diagnose the ailments of a person at the other end of the world". When Kingsmill Moore J., sitting as a Judge of the High Court on Circuit, stated a case for the Supreme Court as to whether he could legally hold that the death of Christopher Brogan was caused by the wrongful acts, neglect, or default of the defendant within the meaning of those words as used in the Fatal Accidents Act, 1846[6], the Supreme Court unanimously, and without hesitation, answered – Yes. With enviable brevity, James Murrnaghan J. said at page 127:—

"There are various kinds of skill which can be exercised. If a person professes to use skill for reward he is liable for negligence in not using that skill . . . The defendant made elaborate claims of power and success. It was not unreasonable for the deceased to believe what he was told and it seems clear that he did believe it and that the defendant failed to fulfil the representations which he made, and he is therefore liable."

Is this much different frm what it took the House of Lords innumerable pages to express in *Hedley Byrne and Company Limited v. Heller and Partners Limited*[7]? You may search, however, the textbooks and find no reference to *Brogan v. Bennett*. Every law student knows what happened to Mrs. Donoghue to the extent, even, of the variety of spellings of her name[8] or whether or not there ever was a snail in the bottle although the way had been identified in *Heaven v. Pender*[9] almost fifty years before.

This excursus on grinding a private axe is a feature of the writing of Forewords to legal textbooks. Partly it derives from a sense of frustration with the ignorance of the general public about the legal structures of the State. The man in the Cabra bus, or, indeed, on the DART has little interest in the law except when it impinges on him directly – obviously in the enforcement of the criminal law and of taxation. His knowledge of the Constitution is mostly one of "rights" and seldom one of "duties". He is not to blame; he is taught nothing of these structures when he is at school or at any level of education unless he takes up the study of the law as an object in itself or as ancillary to some other discipline. The requirement of knowledge of the law in all its aspects is so great that, indeed, those who qualify to practise are often themselves ill equipped to examine and explain the underlying theory – the underlying principle. In this book the authors have set out to pierce that great curtain of ignorance; this book is directed towards the general public as well as to the student and practitioner; it is a book that requires concentration and study; it deserves both; although one may not agree with all of the authors' sentiments, it is right to pay tribute to their energy, research and initiative and, particularly, to their clarity of expression. The law is often the victim rather than the victor in the battle of words. If this book does, as I believe it can, create a more informed body of citizens who will recognise and accept that the law is a two-way traffic, their efforts will have been justly rewarded. If their readers can come to recognise that the Constitution is not merely a document to be quoted and misquoted when the electorate is much exercised about person or family rights, but is also the fundamental law of the State governing our relationships with each other and with the State itself, their achievement will have been great.

[1] Henry VI Pt. 2 – Act IV – Scene II – line 86.
[2] Republic of Ireland Act, 1948.
[3] (1986) Cambridge Law Journal 33.
[4] Memoirs of Lord Shandon – type-script – page 183.
[5] [1955] I.R. 119.
[6] The relevant statute would now be the Civil Liability Act, 1961.
[7] [1964] A.C. 465.
[8] *Donoghue v. Stevenson* [1932] A.C. 562.
[9] 11 Q.B.D. 503.

PREFACE TO THE SECOND EDITION

Three years have elapsed since the appearance of the first edition of this work. We have been encouraged by the supportive comments and well-intended criticisms of our colleagues to produce a new edition. The principal change made has been to divide the book into two parts. Part 1 contains an expanded description of the cardinal features and institutions of the legal system – court structure and procedure, legal personnel, access to the law, remedies, tribunals and adjudicative bodies and the relationship between Irish law and European and international law. Account has been taken of legislative changes made by the Courts (No. 3) Act, 1986, the Courts Act, 1988 and the Courts (No. 2) Act, 1988. We have also, where relevant, made reference to the various reports of the Committee on Court Practice and Procedure. Part 2, which contains materials illustrative of the sources of Irish law and methodological principles employed by Irish lawyers, has been updated to take account of more recent decisions which reflect judicial technique. Whilst it might be overstating the case to suggest that a uniquely indigenous legal methodology has emerged there are indications that Irish courts are more prepared to depart from the practices adopted by their English counterparts, reflected, for instance, in the increasing employment of the schematic approach to statutory interpretation. Moreover, it is evident from *Lawlor v Minister for Agriculture* [1988] I.L.R.M. 400 and *Murphy v Bord Telecom Éireann* [1989] I.L.R.M. 53 that Irish courts are prepared to adapt interpretative principles in order to accommodate the obligations which result from our membership of the European Communities. These developments are considered and we have also expanded the chapter on precedent to consider the *ratio decidendi* of multiple judgment decisions.

In the preparation of this edition we must record our thanks, with the usual exemption from liability for errors and inaccuracies, to Efstratios Konstadinidis and Raymond Friel for reading parts of the manuscript. The secretarial assistance of Marian Healy and Mary O'Brien must also be recorded with gratitude. We are also much obliged to Mr Justice McCarthy for agreeing to the reproduction of his Foreword to the first edition.

ACKNOWLEDGMENTS

The authors and publishers gratefully acknowledge permission to reproduce extracts from the cases in this collection from the following persons and bodies:

The Chief Justice and the President of the High Court, in respect of extracts from unreported judgments

The European Law Centre, in respect of the extract from the Fleet Street Reports

The Incorporated Council of Law Reporting for Ireland, in respect of extracts from the Irish reports

The Irish Times Limited, in respect of the extract from The Irish Times.

The Jurist Publishing Co. Limited, in respect of extracts from the Irish Jurist Reports

The Round Hall Press, in respect of extracts from Irish Law Reports Monthly

CONTENTS

TABLE OF CASES

TABLE OF STATUTES

[*Note*: page references in **bold** type indicate statutory provisions reproduced in full in the text.]

TABLE OF STATUTORY INSTRUMENTS

TABLE OF EUROPEAN COMMUNITY LAWS

TABLE OF INTERNATIONAL AGREEMENTS

TABLE OF CONSTITUTIONAL ARTICLES

[*Note*: page references in **bold** type indicate constitutional articles reproduced in the text.]

Chapter 1

THE NATURE AND DEVELOPMENT OF THE IRISH LEGAL SYSTEM

1. Introduction

This text is titled *The Irish Legal System*, so it may be useful to explain what lawyers understand by 'a legal system.' Most people will have some idea of what a legal system involves, whether from reading newspapers, watching soap operas (American or Irish) or a series such as *Rumpole of the Bailey* on television. Indeed, to understand some films requires an extensive, if arcane, knowledge of law in its many guises. For example, in the film '*Rain Man*', released in Ireland in 1989, the character played by Dustin Hoffman has an extensive knowledge of television schedules, and informs the character played by Tom Cruise that it is 'nine minutes to Wapner' or 'three minutes to Wapner'. This oblique reference to the television programme '*The People's Court*' indicates that everybody is required to have some knowledge of 'the law' even for the purposes of enjoying a film. Much of the information provided by exposure to 'television law' may not be completely accurate, but '*The People's Court*' does indicate that an important aspect of the law is that legal disputes may end up in a court where a judge, or a jury, has the final say on the dispute. The court's verdict means the decision of the judge or jury. This text concentrates to a large extent on the techniques used by judges in arriving at their verdicts because a large proportion of the law is either made by, or applied by, judges. Only in certain cases has a jury an important legal function to perform, and even there the jury can be directed by the judge on the legal rules which apply to the case.

A second important component of a legal system with which most people are familiar is a parliament or legislature in which laws are enacted by elected representatives of the People. The amount of tax which people pay, whether in direct taxes on income or indirect taxes on items purchased, is governed by such laws. As we will also see, judges have an important role in interpreting laws passed by the legislature, and it is important to be aware of the techniques used by judges in this context also.

A third feature of a legal system, which arises from the first two, is the enforcement of legal rules and principles. Parliament may nowadays be the main source of new laws, but these rules are publicly enforced through the courts. In this way, the rules are given operational force and the mechanisms of enforcement are also discussed in this text. Again, most people will be familiar with the idea of a police force, in Ireland the Garda Síochána, whose function is to enforce many criminal laws.

Finally, it is important to be aware of the fact that these rules have a territorial limitation. In general it may be said that the rules of the Irish legal system operate only in Ireland (although this must be modified by reference to our membership of the European Community discussed in Chapter 10). The rules operate in this State, but what is the State? It is, briefly, a territorial area over which the institutions we described above have any power. Inside that territory the Irish National Parliament may make laws which apply in all parts of the State, not just to some of the citizens. That, at least, is the theory of 'the rule of law.' Whether every citizen obeys the law is another matter, but the basis on which all the rules and principles described in this text are founded is that they apply through-out the State.

2. Law As A System of Procedure.

It should be pointed out that the law does not have a monopoly on 'systems', and that modern life requires us all to operate within certain structures in a wide range of activities. An important element in any 'system' is that matters are organised in a certain way, and people who become involved in that system may be required to anticipate how the system will affect them. If a person wishes to become a student in a third level college, she will require some knowledge of the application system which operates in relation to the college or colleges in which she wishes to study. Information as to the points system for different courses and different colleges will be essential in this respect. Of critical importance also is a clear understanding of the method of completing the form distributed by the Central Applications Office (C.A.O.). Where a student fails to complete the C.A.O. form correctly, a place in a college may be lost even though the student may actually have the required points to gain admission to that college. The lesson here is that the system requires those who come into contact with it to comply with certain rules and regulations. In some instances, the system may not be able to cope with a person who, although 'justice' may be on her side, has not complied with the procedure laid down. Sometimes, of course, there may be some way around the problem created by 'the system', but the safer approach is to play by the rules of the system in the first place. To a large extent, this text is an attempt to explain some of the basic rules which apply in the Irish legal system.

To some extent, the purpose of the book can also be explained by using another analogy: how to find your way around a library. Of course, even when you know your way around the library, you may not be familiar with the contents of all the books, but you will at least have dipped into some of them and in time they become easier to digest. This text, therefore, is an introduction to the contents of the system of law which operates in Ireland. It does not provide a list of all the legal rules which exist in Ireland; its primary focus is on the mechanisms by which legal problems may be resolved. But these mechanisms are important, because they are referred to and used by lawyers and others who come into contact with the law. They are, therefore, part of every legal subject which a student might come to study.

Not unlike the C.A.O. system, the legal system is built around many different legal documents. A person who is stopped by a member of the Garda Síochána while cycling to college in the dark without lights on the bicycle may very well receive, some months later, a summons to appear in the District Court to answer a criminal charge. In practical terms, the cyclist might be more concerned that no member of her immediate family discovers that this unhappy event has taken place than in the niceties of the legal basis for all that has happened. And, in relation to most such summonses, there will be very little discussion of legal rules; it is more likely to be a question of appearing in court, apologising, producing a new set of lights for the bicycle and having a relatively small fine imposed. But even in this situation, certain assumptions are made, such as the existence of the Garda Síochána, with apparent powers to stop a person with no lights on their bike, and a District Court where the cyclist is to appear, explain matters and have a fine imposed.

It might be of interest to ask arising from this encounter with the law whether the same system operates in relation to more serious matters. For example, what is the legal procedure which arises in relation to a traffic accident in which a cyclist is paralysed due to the careless driving of another person? And what happens when a person is caught stealing from a private house at night? This text indicates the procedures which should be followed in such cases, such as in which court the incident in question is likely to be resolved. However, this text will not necessarily indicate the legal rules which ultimately resolve, for example, whether the paralysed cyclist is entitled to compensation for the injuries received. That question is a vital one for a lawyer, but it is not the subject-matter of this text. However, some brief mention may be made here of the different kinds of legal rules with which lawyers deal on a regular basis.

3. Law, Rules and Principles.

Lawyers are familiar with many different kinds of rules and principles. One important rule for lawyers is that there is a time limit within which a claim for compensation for injuries received in a road traffic accident must be made. As with the student applying to the C.A.O., if this time limit is not complied with the compensation claim will be prohibited simply because the time limit has expired, and not because of the merits of the case. The relevant legal rule simply requires that claims be brought within a set time, which in cases involving road traffic accidents is, in most cases, three years from the date of the accident. When the three year period has elapsed and no case has been initiated by the injured person, the person who caused the accident may be able to rest easier, from the legal perspective at any rate. If the injured person attempts to seek compensation after the three year period, the other person can claim that the matter is 'statute barred', in other words that the period of limitation for bringing the claim has passed. As we will see in Chapter 2, lawyers should be aware that the rules as to the time limits for different claims are set out in legislation entitled the Statute of Limitations, 1957.

The rules on limitation periods are, to some extent, arbitrary: why three years in some cases and six years in others? While arbitrary in that sense, there is a rationale or principle behind the rule, namely that there should be some finality in relation to matters which can be brought before the courts. This means that, once a certain time period has elapsed from the date of an incident that should be the end of the matter. The rule provides a degree of certainty which would not be present if the finality principle was the only basis for assessing whether a case should be allowed to proceed to court. But in other cases a principle may also be the only basis on which to assess a claim, and this is particularly so with issues arising from the Constitution, which we discuss in detail in Chapter 13. The Constitution states, for example, that all citizens shall be held equal before the law. As we shall see the Constitution is the most important legal document in the State and all other laws must conform with that basic principle of equality. Who is to decide this, and how? Ultimately, it may be a court, and as the cases in Chapter 13 illustrate, certainty as an ideal may in some instances have to be sacrificed.

Assuming, in our example given, that a claim has been initiated within the prescribed time period, the lawyer must also be familiar with a whole range of other rules relevant to the claim for compensation. From the discussion in the first heading of this Chapter it is clear that an important matter is which court the case must be brought in. Both these matters, the limitation period and the appropriate court, may be categorised as procedural rule problems, but there is another vital matter which every lawyer will become concerned with almost from the moment that the case of the injured person is brought to the lawyer. That question is: is the injured person entitled to compensation in the circumstances which have arisen?

This is really the heart of the matter for the lawyer; the lawyer is consulted by the client to obtain an answer to that question. The procedural matters as to what court the case will be heard in and the limitation period which applies are not of prime interest to most lawyers' clients. The lawyer is expected to answer the question: 'what is the law on this'? And the answer which the client expects is not: 'there is a three year time limit on this'. The answer which the client will wish to hear is: 'if it can be proved that the driver of the car was careless, or as we lawyers say "negligent", then you will get compensation which could be in the region of £30,000.' One point to notice here is that lawyers tend to pick their words carefully, so that words and phrases such as 'if' or 'assuming' or 'could be' or 'it depends on the circumstances' or even 'it depends on the judge we get' are a regular feature of legal advice. The reason for this is fairly simple. While the lawyer will have available many legal text books to consult, the client in the office presents a new problem. Unlike the doctor who will treat the client on the basis of knowledge acquired in medical school, the lawyer has a less direct impact, in that the client's case must be processed through a system. The lawyer can only advise and, if required, argue a case; the 'cure' or solution to the client's legal problems may be in other people's hands, such as a judge or jury.

What this text is concerned with primarily is the procedural aspect of law enforcement in the State. When the lawyer receives a particular problem, there may very well be a clear rule which applies to a particular problem, for example, that parking a motor vehcile on a double yellow line in circumstances which have been outlined to the lawyer is a criminal offence. But even here there may be ambiguity or doubt. Was there a time period which was relevant to the offence? Was it a public place? Is there a defect in the documentation which has summoned the person charged to appear in Court? In relation to these questions, there is a combination of two matters which the lawyer is concerned with. First of all, the rule applicable, and secondly the particular circumstances which arise to which the rule is to be applied. As far as the rule itself is concerned, if contained in legislation, there are special rules of interpretation which may be extremely important in order to elucidate its exact meaning, and lawyers are concerned about exact meanings. Thus, the techniques discussed in Chapter 12 are relevant here. And how does that rule, as explained, apply to the situation which arises in the particular case on which the lawyer is giving advice? That is a matter which is discussed in Chapter 11, and is a central feature of the system of law which operates in the State. This text is, therefore, concerned with the techniques which lawyers use in relation to many different areas of law. Sometimes these rules are applied unconsciously by lawyers because their training has taught them to do this. In other situations, the techniques are irrelevant: the rule and its application are clear. But a lawyer's training is geared towards the difficult case, where the rule is unclear or the circumstances which arise now have never been contemplated before. The key is for the lawyer to be able to explain how the established rules can be applied to new situations. And to turn that key requires knowledge of the techniques discussed in Part II of this book. Those techniques are not, however, designed to provide a definitive answer, and indeed even a cursory read of the cases in this book illustrates that judges disagree as to how the techniques apply in given situations. They are, largely, in agreement on the rules and principles, but applying those is a different matter.

It is important at this stage to reiterate our emphasis on the role of the lawyer as being important from a practical point of view. Although this book deals with the operation of the court system and the views of the judges which are quoted in full in Chapters 11, 12 and 13, the lawyer is in practical terms more pivotal in the day-to-day operation of the legal system. The reason for this is simple: not every legal problem will end up in court. The lawyer's function is to act partly as a filter for legal problems, and in order to give the correct legal advice the lawyer must be fully conversant with the way in which a case is likely to be dealt with should it go to court. The lawyer acts, therefore, as a judge once-removed. Based on the lawyer's advice, many cases are settled before they go to Court. In addition as we will see in Chapter 9, litigation in the courts is not the only way in which a legal problem may be resolved; arbitration is an increasingly important process by which such matters may be resolved without the necessity for court adjudication.

4. Law and Legal Persons.

On first thinking about the law, one might ask: 'How does the law affect me or anybody I know?' This is, of course, an important question, and there are many rules of law which affect individuals to a great extent. Much of the criminal law is about preventing individuals from breaking certain rules which are regarded as particularly important. But law also recognises entities which exist 'on paper' rather than as human beings, the most important example being the limited liability company. The company is not a collection of people, but is a legal person with an existence recognised by the law which is quite separate and distinct from the people who may be the moving forces behind the company. The limited liability company is an extremely important vehicle for the conduct of business and in law it is capable of owning property, suing in the courts and being sued by another company or by an individual. So an employee may bring a compensation claim against the company for which he works; this is a claim against the entity and not against the managing director or the board of directors, even though they may be regarded as the real 'owners' by those who deal with the company. It is not possible to deal with company law in the present context, but it is important to bear in mind that the concept of the 'company' as a distinct legal entity is vital to the operation of many rules of law.

5. Criminal and Civil Law.

When a client approaches a lawyer with a problem which involves whether they might be entitled to compensation, this is referred to as a *civil law* problem. Many civil law cases involve seeking compensation, but there are other solutions or remedies which may arise in this context, some of which are discussed in more detail in Chapter 8. For example, if your neighbour keeps six Rotweiler dogs as pets in a small garden and they make a huge noise at night keeping you and your family awake, your lawyer will advise you that you may be entitled to get a court order, called an injunction, to stop the neighbour from keeping the dogs on the ground that in law it constitutes a nuisance. Whether you apply for the injunction is a private matter between you and your neighbour, but there is another aspect to this example which involves the other major category of law, the *criminal law*.

Criminal law consists of a vast array of legal rules ranging from the rule which forbids murder to the law which operates against the cyclist with no light referred to previously. The Rotweiler owner referred to above might also be commiting some criminal offence. What could these examples of criminal law possibly have in common? One common feature is that, where a person is alleged to have committed murder or to have no light on their bike, the process of bringing that person before a court is a matter for some State institution; it is not a private matter, but one concerning the public in general or The People of Ireland. There is some public interest involved which brings the matter into a different category than a purely private dispute. This is not a matter of compensating a victim; it is a case of punishing the offender.

It is at this stage that it is important to mention an important aspect of 'learning the law', which is that distinctions such as those between criminal law and civil law are more complex than at first sight. There is no doubt that there is a clear method of categorising some matters as criminal law matters and others as civil law matters. Where a person is alleged, for example, to have committed murder there is a recognised procedure for bringing that allegation before a court and having the allegation judged by a court, usually a judge and jury, and if the allegation is proved to the satisfaction of the court the person is sentenced to a term of penal servitude for life. It is clear that, in that situation, the purpose of the rule prohibiting murder is to punish the wrongdoer and to deter others from doing the same in the future. Equally, it is clear that, where a person is injured in a road traffic accident and seeks the advice of a lawyer as to compensation, this is a private matter for the injured person. The matter will be brought, if necessary, before a court for the purpose of obtaining compensation for the injured person. The procedure for bringing the civil case to court is, as we will see in Chapter 5, quite different from that in criminal cases. So it can be said that criminal law involves rules of public importance whose purpose, when enforced, is to punish and deter, while civil law involves private disputes which are resolved on the basis of providing some suitable form of compensation to the injured person. Where are the difficulties referred to at the beginning of this paragraph?

Take the murder case first. Is the law in any way concerned with the victims of the crime? The immediate victim is, of course, no longer alive, but what of the surviving family? They may very well be able to claim some compensation against the person convicted of murder. Such claims for compensation were made by the survivors of the attacks of the man referred to as 'The Yorkshire Ripper', but only after it emerged that he might have obtained some payment for agreeing to give his story to a publisher and thus had some money to meet a potential claim. Looking at the traffic accident, the driver of the car who causes a traffic accident may very well be charged by a member of the Garda Siochana with some criminal offence, such as careless driving or dangerous driving, as well as being sued for compensation by the injured person. The point here is that the distinction between criminal and civil law is used simply for the purposes of indicating the different procedures and outcomes which follow from a particular incident. The distinction is not one which gives an exclusive pigeon hole for certain acts; murder is an act which may have both criminal and civil consequences, and it is merely a matter of being able to see the purpose of following one course or another.

One point may be mentioned purely for the purposes of further thought. Consider what happens when a person is injured while working with a panel beating machine which was not properly guarded to prevent injury. It may be that the person will have a good claim for compensation against his employer, assuming that it can be established that the employer was in some way negligent, for instance by failing to guard the machine. The employer may also face a prosecution by an enforcement agency for failing to guard the machine. Assuming part of one of the employee's fingers has had to be amputated as a result of the accident, he may be entitled to up to £100,000 in compensation if he decides to go to Court. If the employer is prosecuted, the maximum fine he can receive in a District Court prosecution is £1,000, the limit set in the Safety, Health and Welfare at Work Act, 1989. Which is the real punishment for the employer in that case? Does this tell you anything more about the punishment/compensation distinction between criminal and civil law?

Finally, it is important to bear in mind that, within the civil law, there are numerous further subdivisions of legal topics which are usually dealt with in separate courses in a law degree. A major distinction exists between what is called the *Law of Torts* and *Contract Law*. Contract law involves the rules and principles which apply in circumstances where two people (including companies) enter into an agreement with an economic content and by virtue of that agreement certain legal obligations arise. The Law of Torts, on the other hand, deals with a wide variety of circumstances in which, apart from contract, one person (including a company) may owe a legal obligation to another where some point of contact arises from those two persons. The rules and principles of negligence, for example, which are discussed in Chapter 11, form an extremely important part of the Law of Torts. Other torts include defamation, employer's liability, trespass, conversion (the civil equivalent, more or less, of theft) and nuisance (which has a very special meaning in law, namely unreasonable interference with another person's enjoyment of property, such as the Rotweiler case referred to above or a fish and chip shop operating at an unreasonable time in a built up area).

Apart from these important topics, there are other subjects which must be studied by the law student and which do not fit neatly into either criminal or civil law, having aspects of both. The *law of evidence* deals with the rules which operate both in criminal and civil cases, and is really a procedural subject, rather than a substantive subject such as the Law of Torts. *Family Law* deals primarily with the civil aspects of family relationships, but some criminal law aspects also arise, such as whether rape within marriage is a criminal offence. *Land Law* is a major area whose subject matter may appear obvious but which extends to all property built on land, and thus deals with the law relating to houses to some extent. These are subjects which form part of the whole of the law which operates in Ireland. While this book does not deal specifically with these areas, many of the cases which will be encountered in Chapters 11 to 13 focus on specific areas within these subjects. This indicates that the rules which are discussed here permeate the whole of the system of rules and principles on which the legal system operates.

6. The Constitution, Independence and the Irish Legal System

Prior to 1922, Ireland was part of the United Kingdom of Great Britain and Ireland, and since 1800 the system of law which operated in Ireland was controlled by the London government, acting through its representatives in Dublin. The Anglo-Irish Treaty of 1921, which was signed by representatives of the Provisional Irish government and the British government, formed the basis for the establishment in 1922 of the Irish Free State, Saorstát Éireann. A Constitution for the Free State was approved as the first piece of legislation passed by Dáil Éireann in 1922, though of course at this stage there had been a bitter split in Ireland about whether the Treaty should have been signed. For some, the Treaty and the 1922 Constitution did not represent full independence, even for the 26 counties which formed the Free State, and for this reason (and others) a new Constitution was drafted and put to the People in a referendum in 1937. That Constitution, Bunreacht na hÉireann, is the document which establishes Ireland as a legal entity, and it is the sole legal basis for the validity of the institutions of State, including the court system, which exists in what the Constitution calls Ireland. For lawyers, therefore, the ultimate source of legal authority in Ireland is the Constitution, and all other laws derive their validity from that relatively short document.

But the 1937 Constitution does not tell the full story of what constitutes Irish law. The 1937 Constitution, and its 1922 predecessor, were not documents which made a complete break with the system of law which existed prior to 1922. It would have been impossible in practical terms to establish a completely new system of legal rules to operate in the new State established in 1922. Thus, while new structures of State, such as a new Parliament consisting of two chambers, Dáil Éireann and Seanad Éireann, and a new court system were established within a very short space of time, the legal rules which were to be applied in the new State were to a large extent those which had been in operation prior to independence. The rule that murder is a criminal offence had been applied in the legal system which operated prior to 1922 and this continued to apply in the Free State and, since 1937, in Ireland. The different departments of government which existed in the Westminster system were also, in effect, transferred to the new regime, although a different title was given to the head of the executive, *An Taoiseach*. At local level, the laws which regulated local authorities, such as county councils and corporations, were also carried over into the new State in 1922. Of great importance also were those rules which regulated the conduct of business, such as the formation of companies. All of these rules were transplanted in full into the new system. This can be gathered from the title of the second Act passed by the Free State Parliament: the Adaptation of Enactments Act, 1922. This Act substituted the relevant names and titles of various institutions and persons who were to carry out the functions formerly assigned to the representatives of the Crown in Ireland, in particular the Lord Lieutenant who was in effect the British Governor of Ireland up to 1922.

It is, therefore, important to bear in mind that events prior to 1922 are relevant in order to understand the system of law which was put in place at the beginning of the life of the Free State. Even today, many of the laws which operate in the State predate 1922 and the court structure which con-tinues to exist can, in some respects, only be understood by reference to English law and its development. It is necessary to move back in time for this purpose and to ultimately arrive back at the Norman Invasion of England in 1066. A number of intermediate steps backward are required, however.

7. The Development of English law in Ireland

It is already clear that the legal history of Ireland is, in some respects, also its political history. From the vantage point of the late 20th Century, it is clear that Ireland was to become a satellite of English control up to in-dependence in 1922. From 1800 onwards, in the wake of the *Act of Union*, English rule in Ireland took the form which was to be the basis for so much violence, failed insurrections and complaints until the granting of independence. During the late 18th Century, there had been an Irish Parlia-ment (Grattan's Parliament), but the Act of Union of 1800 centralised control in London until 1922.

Going further back in time, English rule had been a practical reality only since the 16th or 17th Century, and prior to that date English law and English rule only applied in the area around Dublin known as The Pale where English traders were entitled to operate the King's law. Outside The Pale, native customs and rules, known as the *Brehon Law*, continued to be applied in spite of decrees of the English kings that such rules were contrary to English law and of no effect. The modern phrase 'beyond the Pale' re-flects this point. The native Irish were ruled by local chiefs who came into infrequent contact with the English. The sophistication of the Brehon Law can be guaged from the substantial literature which remains for scholars to discuss.

Before the 16th and 17th Centuries, therefore, English rule in Ireland was a matter of occasional sorties into the hinterland rather than a matter of the type of permanent enforcement of laws which took place in England and Wales. The first, and most infamous perhaps, from the Irish perspec-tive was the 'Norman Invasion of Ireland' of 1170. While the landing of Strongbow (Richard FitzGilbert, Earl of Pembroke) in Wexford may have had immense symbolic significance (leading to the reference to 700 years of oppression), it did not have the immediate effect of transforming Ireland into an English colony. It was, however, the beginning of a process which involved the passing of *Poyning's Act* of 1494, which stated that all laws passed by the English Parliament applied to Ireland, but which did not have full force and effect in Ireland, ultimately, until the passing of the the Act of

Union in 1800. However, as mentioned at the beginning of this section, whatever the position prior to 1800, Ireland was firmly in English control from that date and all laws passed up to then had effect in Ireland from that time; some of them continue to do so. The court system which was established in Ireland during the 19th Century was modelled on the system which had developed in England since the 1066 Norman Conquest, and so from our present vantage point, the court system which existed up to 1922 owed its origins to events in England from the 11th Century onwards, even if Ireland came to inherit that legacy at a relatively late stage. In this respect, Ireland was the first recipient of the English legal system, and so the development of the English system of law must be referred to briefly.

8. The English Common Law

After the Norman Invasion of England in 1066, the conquering kings began the process of extending the king's rule to the outlying areas of the kingdom. One of the most important methods of doing so, after the obvious strength of the army had been used to subjugate the native English, was the use of king's justices, or judges, whose function was to travel throughout the kingdom with the primary function of applying rules laid down by the king. Since the king was the ultimate source of all law at this stage in history, there being no elected parliament to approve laws, it followed that the king's judges had immense power and authority to apply his law throughout the kingdom. This important historical development of the role of judges explains the position of judges within the legal system today.

It is clear from English history, therefore, that it was the judges who were first to apply rules of law within the kingdom. As centuries passed and the English system developed, the judges came to have a central role in the actual development of new legal rules. In effect, the judges came to have delegated to them the king's role in setting out the basic rules of law which were to be applied in the kingdom. These rules, developed by judges and applied by judges, became the core rules of law in England. Collectively, they came to be known as the *Common Law*, and any system of law which is based to a large extent on the development of rules by judges is known as a common law system. By way of contrast, the system of law which developed on the mainland of Europe was and is based on codes of law which contain rules applicable to all types of dispute. This system, called a *Civil Law* system, is based on the ancient Roman and Greek legal systems which were rediscovered by Continental scholars during the middle ages. By this time, however, the English system had developed its own approach. On this historical difference, therefore, the English and continental European legal systems developed in quite different ways.

When the concept of a *parliament* became established in later centuries as a method of curbing the absolute authority of the king and as an alternative source of legal rules—statute law—the judges were very slow to acknowledge that such laws could take priority over the common law rules which had been in existence for many centuries previously. Ultimately, however, the judges accepted that Parliament had full authority to overturn the common law, and that is the position which exists in England today. Parliament, not the monarch, is the supreme and only source of laws, while the function of the judges is to interpret those laws. In Ireland, the 1937

Constitution designates the National Parliament, the Oireachtas, as the sole law-making institution in the State.

It is important to bear in mind, however, that this provision in the Constitution cannot be taken literally, since the common law rules which had been developed prior to independence continue to be applied by the courts in new settings. This means that where legislation has not yet been passed to deal with a particular area of law, the judges continue to be the sole sources of the law to be applied in such situations. And in spite of the increased amount of legislation in recent years a substantial amount of law remains as laid down by judges, before and since independence. One of the points which emerges at various times is that 'judges do not make law; they merely declare it.' That was the ultimate position at which judges operating the common law system had arrived by 1922, and it is, of course, correct in view of the present Constitution. But the judges have the final say in many important instances, as we will see in Chapter 13. As a judge of the United States Supreme Court said at the turn of the century: 'We are under a Constitution, but the Constitution is what the judges say it is.'

9. Common Law and Equity

Common Law has been used up to this in two different settings. Firstly, looking at a legal system externally, in contrast with a Civil Law system, common law indicates a system based on rules developed by judges. Secondly, in contrast with statute law, common law indicates those rules developed by the judges as against those which emanate from a parliament. The third meaning which common law has is by way of contrast with the judge made rules which emanated from the courts of *Equity*, which developed quite separately from the king's common law courts. The background to this particular development in English law was, briefly, as follows.

The system which operated to bring a case to the king's, common law, courts was that a document called a writ was filed with the king's *Lord Chancellor*, who presided over his own department of State. The law developed to a stage that, in order to be allowed to proceed with the case, it was necessary to bring the case within some established form of writ. The Lord Chancellor's department was, in effect, a clearing house for the writs and where a case did not come within one of the established forms the matter could simply not be litigated but might go by way of appeal to the king. Another problem was that the main remedy in the common law courts was an award of compensation. Ultimately, the king delegated the function of hearing such appeals to the Chancellor, with full authority to decide the case according to 'the justice and equity' of the matter. The idea behind this was that the Chancellor could make a decision which was not bound by what was regarded as the rigidity of the common law system of writs.

Ultimately, the Chancellor's Department began to deal with so many of these 'appeals' from the common law courts that it developed into a separate court of law, which became known as the *Court of Chancery*, where rules of equity were applied. The decisions of the Chancellor's Court were once described as being so free of common law rigidity that decisions as to the equity of a case were said to vary according to the length of the Chancellor's foot. This phrase has been handed down the centuries as a mark of disapproval of arbitrary judicial decisions. By the 17th and 18th

Centuries, however, the rules of the equity courts had become well established, and there was very few areas which had not been covered by previous cases which had come to Chancery. If anything, the rules of equity had become just as rigid as the common law which it was developed to modify with flexibility. Ultimately, the Court of Chancery became the dark foreboding place immortalised in Charles Dickens' *Bleak House*, a book which is a mandatory reference in any discussion of Chancery.

Through the historical development of common law and chancery, by the time that Dickens wrote, each set of courts dealt with completely separate areas of law. In general, it could be said that the common law courts dealt with what would be regarded today as commercial law matters such as contracts between businesses and claims for damages. The chancery courts dealt with many issues relating to land, wills and similar areas of law. But the boundaries between the two were never clearcut. By the early 19th Century, the two systems had become so complex to operate that many years could be spent simply litigating which of the two systems was the correct branch of law in which to bring a particular claim. Novels such as *Bleak House* played an important part in highlighting these anomalies in the system, and throughout the 19th Century procedural reforms were introduced which culminated in the enactment at Westminster of the Supreme Court of Judicature Act, 1875, with an equivalent for Ireland appropriately titled the Supreme Court of Judicature (Ireland) Act, 1877.

The effect of this legislation was that the administration of common law and equity was fused into one *unified court system*, in other words that once a case was begun in the new court system the court could apply either the rules of equity or of common law. While this appeared to involve a straightforward administrative tidying up and bringing together of the common law and equity court systems, there is still some confusion over 100 years later as to the precise effect of the 1875 and 1877 legislation. The difficulties which this gave rise to are outside the scope of the present text, but further discussion is contained in Keane, *Equity and the Law of Trusts in the Republic of Ireland* (Butterworths, 1988). It may also be noted that, in recent years, there has been a developing discussion within the courts as to whether the rules of equity should be applied in the type of flexible manner which appeared to be their original purpose. For discussion of this in an Irish context see Brady, 'Trusts, Law Reform and the Emancipation of Women' (1984) 6 *D.U.L.J.(n.s.)* 1.

10. The Irish and the 19th Century Legal System
The early 19th Century saw a marked improvement for the Irish professional classes, the result of increased political pressures. It was only in 1793 that Catholics were admitted to the Bar, one of the first indications of a 'thawing' of the penal laws which had been put into place after the Reformation in the 16th Century. The Catholic Emancipation Act, 1829 permitted entry for Irish Catholics into many positions of importance, including the judiciary. In 1836, the first Irish Catholic was appointed to a senior judicial position in Ireland, but it need hardly be stressed that these changes did little to persuade the representatives of the Irish people that this solved 'the Irish question.' All the important judicial positions continued to be filled from London, and the limited changes of the 19th Century did little to quell the calls for Home Rule, and later complete

independence. It is not possible to provide a complete picture of the position in the 19th Century, but an extremely useful study in this respect is Delany, *Christopher Palles: His Life and Times* (Figgis, 1960), which describes the career of the longest serving Irish judge, and also one of the first Irish Catholics to be appointed to the Bench. It also provides an historical sketch of the legal system in the 19th Century in Ireland. On the exclusion of Catholics from the legal profession see also Kenny, (1987) 25 *Ir. Hist. Stud.* 337.

11. 19th Century Changes in The English Court System

The 1875 and 1877 legislation referred to above established a central court structure, consisting of a *High Court of Justice* with a number of divisions, which amalgamated and rationalised the many different courts which had developed in England over the centuries. The four principal courts which had developed from medieval times (and which gave the title to the main court building in Dublin, the Four Courts) were: (i) the Court of Exchequer, which dealt mainly with Revenue matters, (ii) the Court of Common Pleas, which dealt with civil claims (that is, as opposed to criminal matters), (iii) the Court of King's Bench, which dealt with criminal matters and also issued what were called the prerogative writs (see Chapter 8); and (iv) the Court of Chancery. In addition to these courts, there had developed over the centuries the following specialist courts: (v) the High Court of Admiralty, which dealt with maritime claims; (vi) the Landed Estates Court, which dealt with certain land matters; (vii) the Court of Bankruptcy and Insolvency; (viii) the Court of Crown Cases Reserved, which operated as a type of criminal appeal court before an appeal court as such was established; (ix) the Court of Probate, which dealt with cases arising from wills; and (x) the Court of Matrimonial Causes and Matters. This is not a comprehensive list, but it provides some indication of the complexity which had developed in the system up to the mid 19th Century.

Under the 1877 Act passed for Ireland, the High Court of Justice was to sit in Dublin, and this Court, housed in the Four Courts building, was the principal court for the whole island. The 1877 Act assigned the functions of all the existing courts to the divisions of the High Court which were established by the 1877 Act. Some further refinements were added between 1897 and 1907. To some extent these are of historical interest only, because since independence in 1922 there have been no formal divisions of the High Court, and any judge of the High Court may be assigned to hear any case. In practice, however, the business of the High Court is administered in accordance with the divisions established by the 1877 Act: see Chapter 3. And the legislation which established the court system which operates at present in the State refers to the jurisdiction of the courts which existed prior to independence so that some knowledge of these divisions is required in order to understand the present arrangements. Another reason is that the English court system, while different in many respects from that established by the 1875 Act, still retains a system of dividing the High Court into specialist divisions. And as we will see in later chapters, decisions of English courts continue to be of importance in Ireland. The current divisions of the English High Court are the Chancery Division, the Queen's Bench Division and the Family Division.

Under the 1877 Act, appeals from the High Court could be brought to the *Irish Court of Appeal*, also situated in Dublin, and there was ultimately an appeal to the judicial committee of the *House of Lords* in London, which was and remains the highest court in the English legal system. It may be noted that while the judicial committee of the House of Lords sits in the Parliament building in Westminster it is composed of professional judges as with all other English courts. The judicial committee, as with the House of Lords as a House of Parliament is, however, presided over by the Lord Chancellor who, in modern times, is also a member of the English cabinet. For English courts, the appeal system remains remarkably like that in the 1875 Act, with an appeal from the High Court to the Court of Appeal (sitting in London) with the possibility of a further appeal to the House of Lords, the permission ('leave') of the Lords now being required. There is an alternative method available since 1970 of a direct appeal from the High Court to the House of Lords in some instances.

In addition to the High Court of Justice, there had developed prior to the mid 19th century a number of inferior and local courts which dealt with smaller civil and criminal claims. These courts included the following.

(1) *the Assize Courts*, which heard local criminal trials and civil cases which, in England had not been heard at the High Court in London, and in the Irish version had not been heard in the High Court in Dublin. The judges of the Assize Courts were, in effect, travelling judges of the High Court, which finds a modern echo in the High Court on Circuit (see Chapter 4).

(2) *Quarter and Petty Sessions*. At some time in the development of the court system, judges known as *Justices of the Peace* were appointed to hear many less serious criminal matters, and these Justices sat about four times a year in what were known as *Quarter Sessions*. Ultimately, the business of the courts became such that it was necessary to hold hearings more often and when the Justice sat outside the Quarter Sessions dates, the hearings were known as *Petty Sessions*. These Petty Sessions related primarily to the Justice's function of conducting preliminary hearings for the Assize Courts. If there was enough evidence to justify a trial (*prima facie* evidence), a document known as a 'bill of indictment' would be referred to a Grand Jury, whose function was to decide if the bill was correct in form and whether there was in fact *prima facie* evidence. If they considered that there was, the bill of indictment became an indictment, triable by Petty Jury (which, in spite of its title, was the final decision-making body in the case). The modern manifestation of the Court of Petty Sessions is the District Court and while the present system derives its validity from the present Constitution (see above) the procedures of the District Court in criminal cases are similar to those of the pre-1922 Petty Sessions court. Indeed, the Petty Sessions (Ireland) Act 1851, which outlines some of the procedure for District Court criminal cases, remains in force to some extent (see the discussion in Chapter 4).

Another function which the Justice of the Peace was given was to bind a person over to *keep the peace*. This power, and the fact that the Justices were unpaid and prone to allegations of corruption, made them the focus for much criticism in Ireland in particular. During the 19th Century, in response to these criticisms, the Dublin administration appointed paid Resident Magistrates (immortalised in the Sommerville and Ross *Irish*

R.M. stories) to deal with petty sessions matters outside Dublin. Although in modern days this step might be described as being 'too little, too late', the administration of justice did improve somewhat as a result. And it had at least one lasting effect. The modern petty sessions courts in Ireland are the District Courts presided over by full time Justices who must be former practising lawyers. Thus, the bitter experience of the 19th Century has been remembered to that extent. In England, the magistrates courts are presided over by part-time non-lawyers who are assisted by legally qualified court clerks.

(3) *County Courts* heard small civil cases. The document which was required to begin a case in the County Court was the civil bill, which still forms the basis for claims heard in the Circuit Court today (see Chapters 4 and 5).

12. Independence and Transition

In 1919, all members of the Sinn Féin Party who had been elected to Irish constituencies in the 1918 British general election assembled in the Mansion House in what became known as the First Dáil Éireann. This meeting proclaimed an independent State for Ireland in accordance with the 1916 Proclamation. This was what might be described as the indication to Britain of another insurrection in Ireland and it led to the War of Independence. During the War of Independence the British Government continued to exercise some control in the State and the court structure described above continued to operate. At the same time, however, the Dáil issued a number of decrees which established a separate legal system, including a court structure which operated to some degree between 1919 and 1922. At the time of the establishment of the Free State, therefore, there were two court systems in being, the official British court structure and the Dáil courts.

The Dáil and government which came into existence on the establishment of the Free State decided to abolish the Dáil courts and to carry over the pre-independence court system which had been developed under British rule. In doing so, however, some judges of the Dáil courts were appointed as judges to the courts of the Free State. There was a transitional period between 1922 and 1924 during which time the old system was, in effect, carried on in the new State pending a review of the court structure. The result of this review was the enactment of the Courts of Justice Act, 1924 which established the basic structure of courts that continues to exist today. As indicated in the previous section, the lowest court in the hierarchy, the District Court, which replaced the Justices of the Peace, was comprised of full-time judges who had previously practiced law. The county courts were abolished but effectively were renamed the Circuit Courts. The High Court of Justice replaced the court of the same name which had operated before 1922, though the Court was no longer divided into divisions. The Supreme Court of Justice replaced the Court of Appeal as the final court of appeal in the State. The Court of Criminal Appeal was also established by the 1924 Act. These courts are discussed in more detail in Chapter 4. Finally, it may be noted that the Free State Constitution provided that an appeal could be taken from the Supreme Court to the judicial committee of the Privy Council, which remains in effect the final court of appeal from some former British colonies. This appeal mechanism, which required the permission of the Privy Council itself, was not often used and was in fact abolished by an amendment of the Free State Constitution in 1933.

Chapter 2

SOURCES OF IRISH LAW

1. Introduction

When lawyers speak of sources of law, they mean the sources of the rules and principles of law which exist in a legal system. As we saw in Chapter 1, it is possible to locate three main sources of the legal rules, criminal and civil, which operate in this State. The primary source of law is the 1937 Constitution, Bunreacht na hÉireann. A second source is legislation, statute law, passed by those parliaments which had jurisdiction over Ireland before 1922 as well as the Oireachtas which existed during the Free State and the Oireachtas which operates under the present Constitution. The third source is common law, the rules developed by judges prior to independence and also since 1922. Since this State joined the European Communities in 1972, a fourth source of Irish law has been the law which the Communities have generated, particularly important in the economic area: see Chapter 10.

In addition to what may be called these primary sources of Irish law, there also exist other secondary source material and influences which must be taken into account. Included under this secondary category are textbooks on the law which are used by students and practitioners, including judges. In addition, there are legal journals which comment on the law, both in terms of legal history and contemporary developments. Finally, it is important to bear in mind what intellectual influences have been brought to bear on the development of the legal rules which actually exist today. These rules have not just appeared without any thought, and it is important to understand current rules as well as predict the future shape of the law by having regard to past and present influences.

We now turn to examine in brief these sources of law.

2. Bunreacht na hÉireann.

The 1937 Constitution is a document which was drafted in the years 1935 to 1937 by legal advisers to the then government of the Free State, headed by Éamon deValera. It was a document designed to break free of the perceived connection with former British rule represented by the remnants of the Free State Constitution which had been based on the Anglo-Irish Treaty of 1921. In fact, between 1922 and 1937, the 1922 Constitution had been amended to a considerable degree by means of legislation passed by the Free State Oireachtas. This process of effective emasculation accelerated after 1932 when the Fianna Fáil party formed a government for the first time under deValera's leadership. By May 1936 in fact the amendment process had gone so far as abolishing the Seanad of the Free State, leaving the Free State Dáil as the single chamber of the Oireachtas. Despite these changes, it was felt that a new beginning was needed and this objective was achieved by submitting the text of the new Constitution to the People in a referendum in July 1937. The Constitution came into force on 29th December 1937.

The Constitution, as its Irish name indicates, is the basic law of the State, and all institutions of the State owe their legal validity to it. The Constitution provides for the basic structures of State, divided into three branches of government, the executive or cabinet, the legislature or National Parliament called the Óireachtas and the judicial branch. As indicated in Chapter 4, this tripartite division or *separation of powers* reflects the intellectual basis for the 18th Century revolutions in France and the United States whose central purpose was freedom from arbitrary power. The separation of powers is designed to ensure that no single branch of government retains exclusive powers and that independence of each branch is guaranteed.

Briefly, the separation of powers, as expressed in the Constitution, provides as follows. The primary function of the executive branch of government, headed by An Taoiseach, is to preside over the Departments of State and to implement policy decisions as well as bring forward proposals for legislation. The political head of each Department, the Minister, has the permanent secretariat or Civil Service under his or her control and direction.

The Taoiseach and his Ministers are, under the Constitution, nominated by the members of Dáil Éireann, the House of Representatives chamber of the Oireachtas. They can also be removed by the members of the Dáil. The Constitution does not, however, mention an important practical element in the separation of powers equation: the political party system. Thus, in most situations the party whose leader becomes Taoiseach usually also has a voting majority in Dáil Éireann. Thus, while the Oireachtas has, under the Constitution, the sole power to legislate, in practice it is directed and controlled by the executive whose party strength in the Oireachtas ensures the passage of legislation proposed by the executive. The separation of powers model in the United States allows much more independence for the legislative branch, and the Irish model is very much along Westminster lines in actual practice. The 25th Dáil, which operated from January 1987 to May 1989, was an exception in this respect.

Finally, the judicial branch has the primary function of applying the laws passed by the Oireachtas and in presiding over the public administration of justice.

In addition to establishing the basic structures of State, which involved a continuation of the system which operated since 1922 (including the reintroduction of the Seanad as a second chamber of the Oireachtas), the Constitution includes a number of important provisions guaranteeing basic protection for fundamental human rights, again reflecting the influence of the French and American revolutions. These rights may be enforced through court action and many important such constitutional cases have been brought before the courts since 1937, and more particularly since the 1960s. These aspects of the Constitution are discussed in more detail in Chapter 13. Also in that Chapter is a discussion of the religious influences in the Constitution which play an important role in the process of interpreting the meaning of the rights guaranteed protection by the Constitution.

As to the text of the Constitution itself, it comprises 50 Articles of varying length, some just a short sentence such as Article 7, which reads: 'The national flag is the tricolour of green, white and orange.' Other Articles are complex and lengthy, such as Article 40 which runs to 5 pages in the official version (although the pages are relatively small) and which guarantees protection to a number of specified constitutional rights. And as we will see in Chapter 10, Article 40 is the source for an unlimited number of implied constitutional rights also. Some provisions have been the subject of detailed scrutiny over the years, while others have never arisen for discussion. An example is Article 27 (running to over 4 pages) which provides for a reference of a Bill passed by the Oireachtas to the People for approval in a referendum. Such a referendum has never taken place.

Finally, some brief mention of the formal method of the citation for constitutional provisions. As mentioned, the Constitution is divided into Articles, and some contain further subdivisions which are called sections and subsections. Thus, Article 40 contains six sections, and some of these sections contain a number of subsections. The shorthand citation for Article 40, section 3 is 'Article 40.3'. And the shorthand 'Article 40.3.1°' reads as Article 40, section 3, subsection 1°. The use of the sign ° is unique to the Constitution.

3. Legislation.

Laws passed by a parliament are the second source of Irish law. The various parliaments which have at one time or other had jurisdiction in Ireland are described in Chapter 12. The present National Parliament which functions under the Constitution is the Oireachtas. Article 15.1.2° states that the Oireachtas consists of the President of Ireland and two Houses, namely, a House of Representatives called Dáil Éireann and a Senate called Seanad Éireann. Clearly, the titles of the two Houses of the Oireachtas reflect the influence of the Unites States Constitution. The President of Ireland, however, while the Head of State and commander-in-chief of the Armed Forces does not have the executive powers given to the American President, and the President performs primarily ceremonial and formal functions such as signing into law legislation passed by the Houses of the Oireachtas. The President does, however, have an important power under Article 26 of the Constitution, discussed in Chapter 4.

Article 15.2.1° states that the sole and exclusive power of making laws for the State is vested in the Oireachtas and that no other legislative authority has power to make laws for the State. Article 15.4.1° places an important limit on the law-making function of the Oireachtas by stating that the Oireachtas 'shall not enact any law which is in any respect repugnant to the Constitution or any provision thereof.' Article 15.4.2° goes on to state that any law enacted by the Oireachtas which is in any respect repugnant to the Constitution is invalid. These provisions would, on their own, carry some important political weight but from a legal point of view their importance lies in the effective machinery for their enforcement which is contained in Article 34 of the Constitution. The provisions of Article 34, which are described in detail in Chapter 4, specify that the High Court and, on appeal, the Supreme Court have the power to decide that a law passed by the Oireachtas is invalid because it conflicts with a provision of the Constitution. Many such decisions have been made since the enactment of the Constitution. Finally, as to laws passed prior to the coming into force of the present Constitution (that is, before 29th December 1937), Article 50 of the Constitution provides that such laws continue to have full force and effect '[s]ubject to the Constitution and to the extent to which they are not inconsistent therewith.'

Other limits on the powers of the Oireachtas, as well as the procedures by which legislation is passed through the Oireachtas, are specified in

Article 15 and Articles 20 to 27 of the Constitution. The Constitution also provides that other detailed rules and procedures of the Houses of the Oireachtas may be specified by the members of the Houses. The stages through which a piece of legislation must go before being approved by either House are, for example, laid down in the Standing Orders of both Houses. These are discussed in Chapter 12. Briefly, it may be noted here that while legislation is proceeding through the Oireachtas it is known as a Bill. When it is signed by the President it becomes an Act of the Oireachtas. Thus, the Courts Bill, 1986 (which was introduced to the Oireachtas in 1986) became the Courts Act, 1988 when passed by the Oireachtas. As will be seen, for convenience the year of enactment is added to the Act for ease of identification, as there have been many Courts Acts passed over the years. Note also that a comma is, by convention, inserted after the word 'Act', though this is not a convention which is always adhered to in practice.

4. Modern legislation

Modern legislation, which can be extremely lengthy and technical, is normally broken down into divisions called sections. Sections may be further divided into subsections, paragraphs, subparagraphs and so on. As to the method of citing statutory provisions, 's.2(1) of the Courts Act, 1988' would be an acceptable method of referring to section 2, subsection 1 of the Courts Act, 1988. Other alternatives are outlined in Chapter 12.

Finally, it is important to be aware of a second species of legislation, called secondary (or delegated) legislation. Acts of the Oireachtas are sometimes referred to as primary legislation, and such primary legislation may provide that, in order to implement the basic principles contained in the Act, more detailed laws may be required. The Act will provide in that situation that 'regulations' or 'orders' may be made, usually by the government Minister with responsibility for the area in question, to give effect to the main purpose of the legislation. For example, the Air Pollution Act, 1987 which establishes a framework within which environmental pollution may be controlled in the State provides that regulations may be made by the Minister for the Environment to give effect to a number of different sections in the Act. In this respect the *Air Pollution Act, 1987 (Air Quality Standards) Regulations, 1987* (italicised to indicate the length of their title; this is not a citation convention) specify in detail air quality standards for sulphur dioxide, lead and other substances in accordance with the general power contained in s.50 of the 1987 Act. Secondary legislation is discussed in more detail in Chapter 12.

5. Common Law

As discussed in Chapter 1, the Irish legal system is a common law system, and therefore many of the legal rules which operate today in Irish law were developed originally by judges and these rules are constantly being refined and further explained in cases which proceed through the court system every year. While Article 15.2 of the Constitution, referred to in the previous section, clearly states that the Oireachtas has the sole and exclusive power of making law for the State, the judges play an important role in the manner in which existing laws, including common law rules, are applied in practice. And as already mentioned, the Constitution gives the judges an important role in deciding on the validity of legislation. In addition the

judges have a long established function in deciding the meaning of legislative provisions when there is a dispute as to how the legislation is to apply in
practice. Thus, while the function of the judges in constitutional cases is of
great importance, the vast majority of court time is spent on the application
of common law and statutory rules.

                                                          Ch. 11 118.

6. Precedent and a Common Law System

In the context of the three judicial functions mentioned in the previous
paragraph, namely, questioning the validity of laws having regard to the
Constitution, the interpretation of statutes and the application of common
law rules to particular situations, the judges pay great attention to what has
been decided in a similar case in the past. This deference to previous
decisions of the court is a central feature of a common law legal system, and
is known as the *Doctrine of Precedent*. Precedent provides a framework
within which a judge deciding a case today can place the decision arrived at
within a continually evolving pattern of the law. The precise techniques
used in dealing with past decisions of the courts and applying them to new
situations is something which every lawyer must develop as a basic tool of
the trade. By learning how judges are likely to deal with a particular new
situation a lawyer will be able to provide a client with reasonably reliable
advice as to whether a case should proceed to court. This is relevant both in
criminal and civil cases.

   In Chapter 11, we have chosen one particular instance of the way in
which judges have evolved the law of negligence over the last 50 years.
Negligence is an area of common law, affected now in some areas by important pieces of legislation, in which the judges have explained the circumstances in which compensation may be awarded to a person who has been
injured as a result of the lack of due care of another person. This area of law
forms the core of very many cases which come before the courts, so that an
understanding of the manner in which it has developed is of great practical
importance. Many of the basic principles are now quite clear, but their
application in new situations continues to cause some problems for lawyers,
judges and the litigants whose legal fate they deal with.

   Before leaving this brief introduction to precedent, it is important to
reiterate the historical development of Irish law in this context. As we saw
in Chapter 1, the position on gaining independence in 1922 was that the law
which existed in Ireland in 1922 was, in effect, the law which emanated
from the English system. This is an important point today in Ireland,
because these laws were carried over into the new regime, so that as of 1922
the law administered in Ireland was virtually identical to the law in
England. In many areas, particularly of the common law and important
areas of commercial law such as the law relating to companies, this remains
the position today. The result is that Irish lawyers and judges continue to
refer to decisions of English courts, even though these are now decisions of
foreign courts. Given the similarity of the laws of the two States, this is
almost inevitable. It was accelerated by the absence for many years after
1922 of any textbooks on Irish law, as we discuss below.

   Of course, there were, during the 19th Century and the early 20th
Century, many notable contributions made to the common law by Irish
judges such as Chief Baron Palles (whose judgments most law students will
read at some stage in their study of Irish law), but the point remains that

given the number of cases which are decided in English courts there is an inevitable tug to look at what is being decided in those courts.

7. Precedent and Law Reporting

In view of the importance of precedent in a common law system, it should come as no surprise that the past decisions of judges are regarded as important documents in the law. For the past 200 years in particular, and even earlier, the reasons given by judges for deciding cases were recorded so that these decisions—usually called *judgments*—would be available for later generations of lawyers. Ultimately, a relatively regulated system developed by which the most important judgments were published on a regular basis in book form, known as law reports. The function of recording the decision of a judge is known as *law reporting*, and is of course a vital part of a legal system which is based on precedent. In Ireland, regular series of law reports began to appear in the 1820s, and later a non-profit making organisation, the Incorporated Council of Law Reporting for Ireland, was established and began publishing the semi-official law reports called the *Irish Reports*. A similar organisation had been established for England and Wales. These law reports were called semi-official because the judges were consulted to have the text of their judgments checked before publication.

Nowadays, most of the important judgments of the Circuit Court (to a limited extent), the High Court, the Court of Criminal Appeal and the Supreme Court are delivered some time after the cases have been heard in court—*reserved judgments*—and are in typed format prepared by the relevant secretarial assistants to the different courts and then read out in open court by the judge or judges. Although there is no strict format which must be followed in the layout of these judgments, they generally consist of a narration of the facts of the case as disclosed in the case before the court as well as an explanation of the legal reasons for coming to the conclusion which the judge or judges have reached. The length of judgments varies and obviously depends on the complexity of the legal issues which arise or the practical importance to the development of the law which the decision represents. In this format they are referred to as *unreported judgments*, but many of them will later be printed in the law reports which are published in the State.

It may be noted, however, that at the least from about the 1950s until the early 1980s law reporting in Ireland was in a poor state of health. It would appear that this was due primarily to the extremely small market which existed at the time and to the consequent lack of resources to report all important decisions of the courts. In the mid 1970s an important initiative was taken when it was decided that the unreported typescript judgments of the High Court, Court of Criminal Appeal and Supreme Court should be circulated to third level colleges with law faculties and an annual digest of these judgments (known colloquially as the *Pink Sheets*) was published by the Incorporated Council of Law Reporting for Ireland. This dual attempt to keep track of the decisions of the courts continues to the present and has since been supplemented by other sources such as the monthly digest of cases which appears in the *Irish Law Times*. However, these were clearly not substitutes for a full law reporting service.

Fortunately, in the 1980s the law reporting situation has improved significantly. In 1981, a new series of Irish law reports, *Irish Law Reports*

Monthly, was launched by Round Hall Press. Since then many more important decisions are reported in that series and the longer-established Irish Reports, though some quite important judgments still fall through the net. And the publishers of the Irish Law Reports Monthly have begun to publish previously unreported judgments from before 1981. By 1989, volumes for 1980, 1979 and 1978 had been published, in that order, with the intention of continuing to publish further retrospective volumes. In 1983, the Incorporated Council of Law Reporting for Ireland published a collection of unreported judgments of the Court of Criminal Appeal dating from 1928 to 1978. The collection, now known colloquially as *Frewen* after its compiler, runs to 421 pages of material virtually all of which was unavailable to the legal community.

To revert to the format of a judgment which appears in a law report. In reported form, the law report adds at the beginning of the 'report' a summary of the facts of the case and a summary of the main findings of the court—the *headnote*—together with the names of the lawyers who appeared in the case and in some instances a summary of the legal arguments which were submitted to the court. This is followed by the full text of the judgment as delivered by the judge. While the practice in England is for the judge to be given an opportunity to check the judgment before it is actually reported, this practice is not followed to the same extent in Ireland. The transcript of the judgment as delivered is signed by the judge and this is, in effect, taken to be an indication that the judgment may be reported in that form. Informally, however, law reporters consult on a regular basis with the judges in particular cases. One further difference between the practice which operates in other common law countries, including England, may also be noted. The rule developed that only a law report signed by a barrister, who was present during the case, would be accepted as a true law report. While the report must still be authenticated by a barrister, there is no longer the requirement that the barrister in question should have been present in court when the judgment was delivered or when the case was being argued in court.

8. Standard Citations and References

In civil cases, the parties are known as *plaintiff* and *defendant*. The plaintiff is the party who initiates the civil case and in many instances will be the only party who seeks a remedy, such as damages, from the court. This is not always so, and there are many famous civil cases in which the defendant has successfully obtained a remedy from the courts while the plaintiff's has been dismissed. Thus, in civil cases the designation of one side as the defendant does not indicate that that party is prevented from applying from a remedy in law. This point is further discussed in Chapter 5. The relevance of the plaintiff/defendant distinction in relation to law reports is that a case is given as a title the names of the plaintiff and defendant. Thus, the case in Chapter 11 which deals with a solicitor's obligation under the rules of negligence to a beneficiary under a will is called *Wall v. Hegarty and Callnan*. This indicates to a lawyer that a person called Wall was the plaintiff in a case in which Hegarty and Callnan were the defendants. Some points to note here are: that the parties' names are italicised, that 'v.' (versus) is inserted between plaintiff and defendants, and that only the parties' last names, and not their first names, are given in the title. In Chapter 11 also it can be seen that, immediately after the title of the case, there is an abbreviated reference to the law report in which the full text of the judgment in the case is to be found. The reference is [1980] I.L.R.M. 124. This indicates that the law report of this case is to be found beginning on page 124 of the 1980 volume of the Irish Law Reports Monthly. As to the volume year, the convention is that for some (not all) law reports this is given inside closed brackets. This usually indicates the year of publication of the law report rather than the year in which the judgment was delivered (though in the case of [1980] I.L.R.M. the volume was in fact published in 1986 for reasons explained in the Preface of that volume and almost all the judgments reported date from 1980). Where the legal writer wishes to indicate the year in which the judgment was actually delivered, then this is enclosed in open brackets thus: (1980).

In criminal cases the parties are the *prosecution* and the *defendant*. In serious criminal cases, the prosecution is taken on behalf of the People of Ireland. The method of citation of the case in Chapter 11 in which Shaw was the defendant is, therefore, *The People v. Shaw* [1982] I.R. 1, which indicates that the judgments in the case are reported in the 1982 volume of the Irish Reports beginning at page 1. Because most serious criminal cases are prosecuted on behalf of the People by the Director of Public Prosecutions (see Chapter 5) the case is sometimes also cited as *The People (Director of Public Prosecutions) v. Shaw*, or *The People (D.P.P.) v. Shaw*, either of which reads: 'The People at the suit of the Director of Public Prosecutions versus Shaw.' Prior to 1974 serious criminal cases were prosecuted by the Attorney General, and so the case in Chapter 10 in which O'Brien was the defendant could be cited as *The People (Attorney General) v. O'Brien* or *The People (A.G.) v. O'Brien*. For the sake of brevity and other reasons, we have used the citation *The People v. O'Brien*.

In Chapter 8 we discuss the remedy known as *judicial review*. Prior to October 1986, judicial review was obtained in a manner which made the case instantly recognisable as what was then known as a *State Side* case. The person applying for this remedy was known as the *prosecutor* (or *prosecutrix*) and the person against whom the order was sought was the *respondent*. The case would result in a citation such as *The State (Lynch) v. Cooney* [1982] I.R. 337 (discussed in Chapter 11 also), Lynch being the prosecutor and Cooney being the respondent.

Finally, in family law cases, only the initials of the parties are given to protect the confidentiality of the proceedings. An example is *H v H* [1978] I.R. 138.

There are so many different conventions in relation to the citation of cases that it is only possible to indicate some of them here. In fact, as the previous paragraphs indicate there is a certain amount of choice in relation to citations of cases. In any event there is no requirement that cases be cited in any particular way, and many Irish legal publications have different citation 'in-house' conventions. Some law books published in Ireland ignore even the basic citation conventions, though it must be said that this hardly ever causes confusion as to what law report is being referred to. Adherence to strict conventions of citation may sometimes be regarded as pedantry, such as whether periods are *de riguer* or whether the following would suffice: *Wall v Hegarty and Callnan* [1980] ILRM 124. That, in fact is how the publishers of the law report in question would cite the decision. By way of contrast, in the United States, the more prestigious law journals agreed some years ago to a *Uniform Citation Manual* (popularly called the Blue Book) which has been updated on many occasions since then.

Finally, before leaving law reports it may be useful to pick up the point made at the end of the last section, namely that Irish lawyers and judges have had a tendency to refer to decisions of English courts. This is seen in a practical way by the fact that many Irish lawyers who subscribe to a series of law reports will in all probability subscribe to the best known series of English law reports, the *All England Reports*, published by Butterworths. The decisions reported in the All England Reports, and the semi-official law reports published by the Incorporated Council of Law Reporting for England and Wales, often find their way into the judgments delivered in Irish courts. This is so despite the comments of the independent minded Gavan Duffy J. in *Kirby v. Burke and Holloway* [1944] I.R. 207 (Extract 11.13). And decisions of other common law jurisdictions, which comprise the former British colonies and current members of the British Commonwealth are also cited. Increasingly, therefore, decisions of the courts of the United States (particularly of the United States Supreme Court in constitutional cases), Canada, Australia and New Zealand are referred to as persuasive precedents by Irish lawyers and judges. And, more unusually, decisions of the German, Italian and Cypriot courts were referred to in *Murphy v. Attorney General* [1982] I.R. 241, a constitutional case relating to the taxation of married couples.

All of the above is intended to explain to the law student what is meant when a lawyer asks another lawyer: ‘Is there a case on that?’ The inquiring lawyer means whether there is a precedent in the law reports (or an unreported judgment) which deals with the legal point with which he is currently dealing.

9. Legal Textbooks and Periodicals

In the last 15 years, many important texts have been published on Irish law. Prior to this Irish law students were forced to rely on English textbooks together with additional notes to take account of relevant differences in Irish law. In addition to the historical reasons for this referred to in the previous sections, above, this reliance on English textbooks also inevitably contributed to the tendency in Irish lawyers and judges to refer to decisions of English courts. The Supreme Court judge Mr. Justice Walsh has commented that this reliance on English decisions even applied where there was a relevant Irish decision: see his Foreword to McMahon and Binchy, *Irish Law of Torts* (Professional Books, 1981) The problem was, unfortunately, exacerbated by the fact that many important decisions of the Irish courts were never reported in any series of law reports. The McMahon and Binchy textbook on Torts was a pioneering work in that respect because it uncovered a vast number of important unreported decisions which were virtually unknown to practising and academic lawyers. Of course, uncovering such decisions may create some problems. What if there had been a legal problem which arose in 1979 and which had been dealt with in the Supreme Court in 1966 but its decision had not been reported and was unknown to the lawyers in 1979 and that the problem was resolved in ignorance of the 1966 decision and in direct contradiction of it? There might very well be no remedy for this difficulty.

Despite these possible problems, the arrival of textbooks on Irish law is (or should be) of great practical value to practitioners and law students. It can only help in the creation of a body of law which reflects an Irish perspective. While textbooks are, as mentioned at the beginning of this Chapter, not sources of law in their own right they can have an important influence in the continued development of the law. It may be noted that the old approach to textbooks in the common law was that they were not regarded as of being any *authority* unless the author was deceased. This rule has, however, been relaxed in more recent times, and the question whether a textbook is one of 'authority' is largely irrelevant now. And it is clear from the many references in the decisions of the different courts to the textbooks which have appeared in the last few years that the textbooks by living authors (and most of them are) are regarded with favour by the judges. Of course, it should be noted that the textbooks on English law continue to provide important reference material for Irish lawyers. In addition, textbooks from other countries are sometimes also referred to, particularly those of Commonwealth countries and the United States.

Similar comments may be made in relation to the many periodicals which have begun to appear on a regular basis in Ireland in recent years, though again they are not sources of law as such. The principal law journals which publish material on Irish law are *The Irish Jurist,* the *Dublin University Law Journal* (both published once a year), the *Irish Law Times* and the *Gazette of the Incorporated Law Society of Ireland* (the latter two published monthly). There are also some specialist journals, such as the *Journal of the Irish Society of Labour Law* and the *Criminal Law Journal* (the journal of the Criminal Lawyers' Association). In addition the *Northern Ireland Law Quarterly* publishes much material which is of interest to Irish lawyers. Again, as with textbooks, many Irish lawyers and law libraries subscribe to law journals published in Britain and Commonwealth countries, as well as the United States. As to the use of periodical literature, see for example, *Doyle v. Wicklow County Council* [1974] I.R. 55, *The People v. Shaw* [1982] I.R. 1 and *N.(K.) v. K.* [1985] I.R. 733. And in *Hynes Ltd. v. Independent Newspapers Ltd.* [1980] I.R. 204, 221, Kenny J. made a plea that more periodical literature should be cited to the courts. An important development in relation to Irish legislation was the launching of a series of annotated Irish statutes by Sweet & Maxwell, *Irish Current Law Statutes Annotated*, beginning in 1984. Finally, *ITELIS Ltd*, a subsidiary of the Irish Times Ltd. and Butterworth (Ireland) Ltd., provides a computerised legal data base of Irish case law, in conjunction with the *LEXIS* data base of English, European and United States law.

10. Intellectual Influences
Most law students will at some stage study *jurisprudence*, the philosophy of the law. This is a large subject, with no clear boundaries because it requires the student to examine the whole basis for the way in which legal rules and principles are formulated. One of the first questions that might be asked in a course on jurisprudence is: what is law? This may seem a strange question, particularly as the student might already have studied criminal law, contract law and constitutional law without having had that question posed. But it remains an important question, because it requires the student to examine many issues which lie behind what are sometimes called

the black letter rules of the law. Some of the questions which might be raised would be as follows. Is law merely a set of rules? Is there a difference between rules and principles? Why is the criminal law based on the notion of retribution and punishment? Is there a 'right answer' to every legal problem? Is the death penalty justifiable in any circumstances? Do judges make law? Should judges and lawyers engage in what is described as social engineering? Are judges influenced by their backgrounds? Are they influenced by their political beliefs? Should the judges have the power to declare laws invalid in constitutional cases? Should the law reflect the views of the majority, or have regard to those of the minority within a community? Should law be based on moral principles, reflecting the distinction between right and wrong? Is morality concerned solely with sexual behaviour? Is there a difference between morality and religious beliefs? Should law reflect religious beliefs? Does law reflect religious beliefs? Should law be based on the concept of individual rights? Has the Marxist view of law been influential in Irish law?

It is not possible in the present text to discuss all of these questions, but two important influences may be mentioned.

The first relates to the connection with England until 1922. It is important to bear in mind that the basic structures of this State, including cabinet government, local government, the basic rules of commercial law and criminal law evolved during the 19th Century and were highly influenced by the political debate which took place at that time in England. It must not be forgotten that in the mid-19th Century, England was one of the great world powers, and there was a considerable intellectual contribution to the many reforms which became law at that time. The reorganisation of the court structures, the reform of some aspects of criminal law and the introduction of the concept of the secret ballot in elections to parliament were all major reforms of this time, influenced by the writings of what today would be described as the intelligentsia. And judges developing the common law were not immune from these influences.

A major influence in this respect was the political philosophy of Jeremy Bentham, who developed the concept of *Utilitarianism*. He wrote a treatise which argued that political and legal change should be based on attempting to achieve an increase in the overall welfare (or 'pleasures' as he referred to it) of the community. Bentham's views, and those of other utilitarians and liberals such as John Stuart Mill and Henry Austin, were influential throughout the 19th Century and continue to be so in the development of English political institutions and law. As indicated above, the legislative reforms of the 19th Century are said to have been influenced by the notion of utility. Its close association with efficiency continues to be the basis for discussion in the 20th Century where a new theory called *The Economic Analysis of Law* has developed, based on the writings of the United States lawyer Richard Posner, formerly a Professor of Law and now a senior judge in the United States federal court system.

Given that, as we have already seen, this State took over the apparatus of State which had been developed during the 19th Century, it is important to study utility to get some understanding of the thinking behind what continues to exist in the present legal system. In relation to common law rules, the area of negligence is also appropriate for study in this regard. To what extent does, or should, utility influence the way in which the concept of negligence is applied in practice? Some indications that judges are influenced in this way can be seen in the judgment of Lord Denning M.R. (the highly influential former head—Master of the Rolls—of the civil law Division of the Court of Appeal in England) in *Dutton v. Bognor Regis U.D.C.* [1972] 1 Q.B. 373. In Ireland, similar influences may have led to the outcome in the Supreme Court decision in *Keane v. Electricity Supply Board* [1981] I.R. 44.

A second important influence in Irish law arises from the existence of the 1937 Constitution as the basic law of the State. Included in the Constitution are a number of important Articles which, in effect, incorporate into Irish law much of the theological philosophy behind Judaeo-Christian teaching. This includes the concepts of *natural law* and natural human rights. The Constitution also guarantees, as already mentioned, legal protection for a number of fundamental human rights which reflect the political revolutions of the 18th Century, as well as the concerns of the 20th Century for protection of human rights on a secular, non-religious, basis. These ideas are discussed in more detail in Chapter 13, but it can be said at this stage that the judges have found it difficult to say the least to grapple successfully with all these differing, and sometimes conflicting, notions. In some notable instances, however, they have been immensely successful and it must be said that the Constitution is an area of law in which there is a true original Irish element.

A difficulty which the judges have yet to tackle in this area is the potential conflict between the notion of utility, which as we have seen permeates much of Irish law carried over from before independence, and the concept of individual human rights which is a central part of the Constitution. Jeremy Bentham, the father of utilitarianism, described natural law as 'nonsense' and the idea of natural rights as 'nonsense on stilts.' How legislation and legal reforms based, even partly, on that approach can be reconciled with a basic law which guarantees legal protection for natural human rights has yet to be addressed, but some issues discussed by utilitarians in England have formed the basis for discussion in Irish constitutional cases: see Chapter 13.

Finally, it may be noted that the views of Karl Marx were referred to by McCarthy J. in the Supreme Court decision *Quirke v. Folio Homes Ltd.* [1988] I.L.R.M. 496. Whether the Marxist analysis of the legal system is to become the staple of future Supreme Court decisions is, however, unlikely.

11. Law Reform Generally

We have mentioned above some of the influences on the law. There are, however, many institutional structures which exist in order to ensure that the law, and its administration, are updated on a regular basis. From time to time the government may appoint a Committee to investigate particular areas of law which require investigation for the purposes of recommending changes in the law: see Chapter 9. The government is not, of course, obliged to accept these recommendations or to put forward legislation to the Oireachtas for the purpose of giving effect to these recommendations. Many such reports 'gather dust' in government departments, even those which were regarded as being urgently required at the time. In addition to such committees, a decision of the courts may draw attention to the need for urgent reform. This was the effect of *The State (Clarke) v. Roche* [1986]

I.R. 619, which resulted in the passing within a matter of weeks of the Courts (No.3) Act, 1986 (see Chapter 4). In addition, law reform may result from a commitment given in the course of a general election or a long standing reform which has been promised. Three further permanent institutions may also be mentioned at this juncture.

In 1962 the Minister for Justice established a *Committee on Court Practice and Procedure* with a view to making recommendations as to how the administration of the courts could be updated. Since that time the Committee has produced 20 Interim Reports (the word interim here indicating that the work of the Committee continues), many of which have been implemented in the form of changes in the rules of court or in legislation expanding the jurisdiction of the different courts. Thus, the Courts Act, 1971 implemented the changes in the rights of audience of solicitors recommended by the Committee (see Chapter 3). The Committee is at present chaired by Mr. Justice McCarthy, a Supreme Court judge, and the members of the Committee include lawyers and non-lawyers.

The *Fair Trade Commission*, formerly the Restrictive Practices Commission, was established by the Restrictive Practices Act, 1972. One of its functions is to conduct investigations into any trade or professional practice which might be regarded as restricting free competition or otherwise distorting the market for the consumer. As we will see in Chapter 3, the Commission is at present investigating the legal profession which may well result in some important changes to the present structure of the legal system.

The Law Reform Commission Act, 1975 created the *Law Reform Commission* with responsibility for investigating particular areas of reform and making recommendations as to how the law might be reformed. The Commission is staffed with a number of full-time and part-time researchers. The Commission's first President was Mr. Justice Walsh, the senior ordinary judge of the Supreme Court. The Commission issued a number of important working papers and reports, particularly in the area of family law, only some of which were implemented. A similar fate would appear to befall other similar Commissions in other countries. In 1986, a new President was appointed, Mr. Justice Keane, a High Court judge and author of a number of textbooks on Irish law. A new remit was given to the Commission by the then Attorney General, and the Commission has since been concentrating on many aspects of criminal law which require updating. The system of consultation which the Commission now operates with interested bodies has also been altered. For an explanation of this see Mr. Justice Keane's statement reported in (1987) 5 *I.L.T.* 123. An article indicating some despair on the present pace of law reform in Ireland is Kerr, 'Is there Anybody Out There Listening?' (1983) 1 *I.L.T.* 100, which obviously predated the new terms of reference of the Commission.

Chapter 3

THE LEGAL COMMUNITY

In this Chapter, we discuss the different legal professionals who contribute in different ways to the operation of the Irish legal system. First, we look at the practising lawyers, solicitors and barristers. Second, the place of academic lawyers and third level colleges is examined. Third, the place of the judiciary and court officers is discussed. Fourth, we outline how other professionals may be involved in the legal system. Finally, we outline some changes in the system which might be introduced or considered in the next few years.

THE LEGAL PROFESSION IN IRELAND:
INTRODUCTION

The Irish legal profession is divided into two branches, *solicitors* and *barristers*. As with much of our law, as discussed in Chapters 1 and 2, this division was carried over from the situation which had operated prior to independence in 1922. An important recent study of the legal profession prior to independence is Hogan, *The Legal Profession in Ireland 1789-1922* (Incorporated Law Society of Ireland, 1986).

The distinctions between the branches of the profession as they operate at present are quite significant. One essential starting point is that, in the vast majority of cases, a person with a legal problem must first consult a solicitor for legal advice. A barrister is not permitted to take instructions directly from a member of the public, except in a small number of specific instances which we mention below. And, broadly speaking, the solicitor tends to specialise in legal work which involves the preparation of cases for court rather than for advocacy in court. The barrister is, generally speaking, regarded as specialising in the preparation of cases for court as well as advocacy.

The solicitor is, therefore, in the front line of dealing with the public and for most people their only contact with a lawyer is a visit to the office of the family solicitor in order, for example, to deal with the legal problems related to the sale of a house or the drafting of a will. The local solicitor might also be consulted in relation to a summons regarding a road traffic offence. The picture of the solicitor as dealing solely with conveyancing of property, wills and minor criminal matters is a common one, but not of course entirely accurate because many firms of solicitors provide a high level of legal advice, particularly in the commercial area. But all solicitors share in common the fact that they may do business directly with the public from a high street office. The barrister, on the other hand, does not in general have an individual office or chambers and, as indicated, may generally only give legal advice to a member of the public after receiving instructions from a solicitor.

SOLICITORS

While originally connected to the barrister's branch of the profession, the solicitors ultimately developed to be a distinct branch. The Incorporated

Law Society of Ireland was formed in 1830 for the purpose of securing the independent existence of the solicitors as a branch of the profession. The Solicitors (Ireland) Act, 1898 established for the first time that the Law Society was to have control over the education of students wishing to become solicitors as well as giving it important disciplinary powers over those who qualified as solicitors. The Law Society continues in this dual role under the provisions of the Solicitors Acts, 1954 and 1960.

1. Access

In relation to access to the solicitors' branch of the profession, the Law Society organises, under the provisions of the Acts mentioned, a course of study centred at its headquarters in Blackhall Place, Dublin. The Society requires students to sit an Entrance Examination, consisting of a number of law subjects, before being permitted to proceed to the Society's own examinations. Many of the applicants will have already studied law at third level prior to sitting the Entrance Examination. Having passed the entrance examination and the Society's own examinations the successful candidates are enrolled in the register of solicitors. Some aspects of the Law Society's entrance examination have recently given rise to litigation: *Gilmer v. Incorporated Law Society of Ireland,* High Court, unreported, 31 August 1987 and *MacGabhann v. Incorporated Law Society of Ireland*, High Court, unreported, 10 February 1989. In September 1989, the Law Society in effect discontinued the Entrance Examination for University law graduates.

2. Discipline

As to the disciplinary function of the Law Society, the Disciplinary Committee of the Society may, under the Acts, investigate an allegation of misconduct by a solicitor and it may refer the matter to the President of the High Court. The President may take a number of courses of action, including suspending the solicitor from the roll of practising solicitors. The effect of this is that the solicitor may not practice for the period of the suspension. The President of the High Court also has power to lift the suspension. Under the Solicitors Act, 1954 as originally enacted, the Disciplinary Committee was empowered to take direct disciplinary action, but this power was held to be unconstitutional in *In re the Solicitors Act, 1954* [1960] I.R. 239. The 1960 Act acccordingly transferred the disciplinary function to the President of the High Court.

3. Practice: Non-litigation

In relation to practice as a solicitor, a significant point is that solicitors may form a partnership as a firm of solicitors. Many such firms exist, particularly in the larger towns and cities, but there are also many 'sole practitioners', that is, one person firms. Clearly, there are advantages in having a partnership and the larger firms are capable of providing a high level of expert advice to their clients. As to the type of work done by solicitors there are no express limits as to what areas of law in which they may practice. As indicated above, the drafting of wills and conveyancing are important areas for many solicitors. Indeed, under s.58 of the Solicitors Act, 1954 solicitors enjoy what is generally described as a 'conveyancing monopoly'. What this means is that a solicitor is the only professional person who may check the legal title to land. The result is that a solicitor is required in relation to all land transactions, which includes the sale of houses. There is, of course, no legal prohibition on a purchaser checking that everything is in order in relation to the house being purchased, but in practice most purchasers would prefer to have the matter checked by a professional adviser. In any event, since many house purchases are with the aid of a mortgage from a building society or other financial institution the quirement of having a solicitor is usually insisted on. In light of the Fair Trade Commission investigation of the legal profession (see below) and an earlier report which recommended removal of the 'monopoly' (following a similar move in Britain) there are likely to be changes in this area at some time in the near future.

In addition to these areas of practice, the larger firms are, for example, involved in the flotation of companies on the stock exchange, engaging tax advisers for clients and many other areas of commercial law.

4. Practice: Litigation

As indicated above, many solicitors do not become engaged in advocacy, except in relation to some cases, civil and criminal, in the lower courts. In relation to proceedings in the High Court and Supreme Court in particular, the tendency is for solicitors to instruct a barrister (counsel) to appear in court. Indeed, this also occurs quite frequently in relation to cases in the Circuit Court and District Court. The solicitor's primary function in such circumstances is to prepare the papers in the case for the court hearing. This will include, in a civil case for example, writing on behalf of the client to the firm of solicitors for the other party in the case and obtaining reports from expert witnesses, such as medical consultants and engineers. The solicitor also liaises with the barrister in relation to what is required at the court hearing.

Since the enactment of the Courts Act, 1971 solicitors have the same right to appear in any court, including the High Court and Supreme Court, as barristers. Prior to the 1971 Act this right, called the right of audience, was severely limited, but the Committee on Court Practice and Procedure (as to which see Chapter 2), in its 13th Interim Report published in 1971, recommended that full rights of audience be given to solicitors. The Courts Act, 1971 was enacted as a consequence. In fact very few solicitors take full advantage of the right of audience, though in many instances they appear in the High Court and Supreme Court in relation to preliminary matters re-lating to a case and this has proved extremely convenient. Most of the advocacy and arguing of full cases remains with barristers, however, with a few notable exceptions.

5. Chief State Solicitor

Since the State is involved in much litigation, whether criminal or civil, there is a requirement of a permanent solicitor to represent the State and to instruct barristers on the State's behalf. This is the function of the *Chief State Solicitor*, who is a civil servant. In addition to the Chief State Solicitor, solicitors in private practice are appointed to appear at local level on behalf of the State, and are referred to as County State Solicitors.

BARRISTERS

The barristers branch of the profession is generally also known collectively as The Bar. Individually, they may be referred to as barristers or counsel. Thus, in the extracts from judgments in Chapters 11 to 13 below, the reader may find the judge stating something such as: 'Counsel for the plaintiff has submitted. . . ' The Bar is usually regarded as the senior branch of the profession, though like the solicitors branch it has gone through many changes over the centuries, so its precise roots are difficult to trace. Unlike the solicitors branch the Bar is not regulated by statute. Again the English influence is important in this context. Originally, Inns of Court were established in London for the purpose of providing, amongst other things, for the education of those who wished to practice as advocates. A similar institution, the Honourable Society of King's Inns, was established in Dublin and it remains the body which provides post-graduate legal training for those who wish to practice at the Bar, in a system parallel to the Law Society. As indicated, however, the King's Inns does not operate under legislation and the precise position in relation to access to the Bar requires further explanation.

1. Access

Students with law degrees or other acceptable degree are not at present required to sit an entrance examination in order to proceed to the examinations provided in King's Inns, which is situated in Henrietta St. (or fronting onto Constitution Hill, depending on your approach route) in Dublin. The Honourable Society of King's Inns at one time appeared to operate under Royal Charter granted in 1792, but this, it appears, was later revoked. The King's Inns therefore operates at present as a voluntary society, under the control of what are called the Benchers of the Honourable Society of King's Inns. These Benchers include a number of the judiciary as well as senior members of the Bar. The Benchers exercise ultimate control over the courses of education provided by the Honourable Society. When a student has successfully completed the course of studies prescribed by King's Inns she is 'called to the Bar' in the Supreme Court, located in the Four Courts building Dublin, in the presence of the Chief Justice and, generally speaking, other members of the Supreme Court bench. She then signs the roll of members of the Bar which is also located in the Four Courts.

2. The Law Library

The call to the Bar means that the person is admitted to practice as a barrister-at-law, or *junior counsel*. A significant feature of the Bar in Ireland is that barristers may not join together to form groups or 'chambers' of barristers as is the practice in England. Instead, most members of the Bar practice from what is called, simply, the *Law Library* which is located in the Four Courts building in Dublin. Here, the barristers are provided with accommodation and access to legal textbooks, subject to an annual membership fee. The Four Courts building houses all the major courts in the State, including the High Court, Court of Criminal Appeal and Supreme Court as well as some other courts. The location of the Law Library is, therefore, ideally suited to the needs of the Bar. Not all members of the Bar practice from the Four Courts. Many barristers practice around the country ('on circuit'). Most barristers who practice in the

Cork area in fact have chambers in Cork city, though generally these are not shared with other members of the Bar.

3. Mode of Dress

A further difference between the two branches of the profession relates to the mode of dress of a member of the Bar. In court, a barrister must wear a wig, usually made of horsehair, as well as a black gown over dark dress. The barrister's shirt, or blouse, has, generally speaking, a winged collar and, in place of a tie, the barrister wears a white band. These requirements are matters of convention rather than legal requirement at the Bar and were carried over from the practice which existed prior to independence. The requirement that barristers dress in this way does not apply in relation to sittings of the courts outside of the legal terms (as to which see below).

4. Instructions and Fees

A barrister is, as indicated above, usually required to receive instructions from a solicitor. This rule applies invariably to litigation. There are, however, some exceptions to this general rule, including appearing in the Employment Appeals Tribunal (as to which see Chapter 9). One consequence of receiving instructions through a solicitor is that the solicitor is also responsible for ensuring that the barrister's fees are paid. The convention which follows is that a barrister may not sue for fees due, though this convention has never been put to the test in recent times, and most barristers rely on a good relationship with their instrucuting solicitors to ensure collection of fees.

5. Junior Counsel and Senior Counsel

A distinction exists within the Bar between *junior counsel* and *senior counsel*. A senior counsel is, generally speaking, a member of the Bar of some years standing. The general rule is that a barrister will practice for a number of years as a junior counsel before deciding to become a senior counsel. The functions of a junior counsel include the drafting and preparation of pleadings (see Chapter 5) as well as conducting some cases in court, generally in the lower courts though not exclusively so. The senior counsel's functions, on the other hand, include scrutiny of draft pleadings which have been prepared by a junior counsel (called 'settling' pleadings) as well as the conduct of some of the more difficult legal cases in the High Court and Supreme Court. There are a number of conventions which developed over the years as to the circumstances in which junior and senior counsel would be retained in a case. An important rule is that, in the vast majority of cases, a senior counsel may not appear in a case unless a junior counsel is also retained in the case. In addition, for example, the practice developed in civil claims for personal injuries (colloquially called 'running down' cases because of the number of road traffic accidents involved) that one junior and two senior counsel would be retained by each side. This rule was subject to some criticism and since the passing of the Courts Act, 1988 (which also provided that High Court personal injuries cases should no longer be decided by a jury; they are now decided by a judge alone) the practice in many cases is to retain one junior and one senior counsel.

The exact progression from junior to senior counsel is not a simple matter of automatic 'promotion' after a specified number of years. It should be borne in mind that many eminent practitioners decide not to become senior counsel. Some of the eminent junior counsel who practice at the Bar continue as 'juniors' into their 70s and 80s. Once a barrister decides to become a senior counsel, he or she applies to the Chief Justice, but the actual appointment is made by the government. There are no set rules for applying to become a senior counsel, though it may be said that no member of the Bar applies unless they are 'qualified' to do so, in other words that they have achieved sufficient prominence within the profession that the application will be granted. The process of becoming a senior counsel is also referred to as 'taking silk.' This is a reference to the fact that in court a senior counsel wears a black silk gown, as opposed to the black gown which a junior counsel wears. Finally, collectively, junior barristers may be referred to as the 'Outer Bar' while senior counsel may be referred to as the 'Inner Bar.'

6. Advocacy and the Bar

The general picture of barristers is of great orators and in many instances the most eminent practitioners are indeed extremely persuasive advocates and speakers. This may be particularly important in cases heard before juries where the barrister is expected to 'tug the jury's heartstrings.' But apart from those barristers who specialise in criminal cases and also the civil cases which tend to receive a large degree of publicity (and which form the basis for most films or television series on the law) the reality of practice at the Bar is that much time is spent on 'paperwork', in other words the preparation of pleadings in anticipation of a court hearing. Given that the vast majority of cases in which a barrister receives instructions are settled before a court hearing, the true position is that advocacy plays a relatively low part in the normal work of the practitioner. Of much greater practical importance is the ability to give advice on a legal problem and to draft documents which will begin the process of accelerating the satisfactory settlement of the legal problem presented, whether through a court hearing or otherwise. Some important thoughts on advocacy were, however, provided by the present Chief Justice, Mr. Justice Finlay, in his address to Blackhall Place students entitled 'Criminal Defence Advocacy' (1981) 1 *Crim. Law Journal* 1 and his 1986 address at Fordham University School of Law entitled 'Advocacy: Has it a Future?' which was published as a *Supplement* to the December 1986 issue of the *Irish Law Times*.

Ireland has, of course, produced well-known and brilliant advocates, including Daniel O'Connell and Sir Edward Carson, and it may be no coincidence that both were also well-known and successful politicians. The mixture of law and politics as a career continues to the present, a feature of most countries. And Ireland has also produced its quota of publications about life at the Bar, some of which may contribute to a somewhat unbalanced view of the barrister's life. The classic in this area is Maurice Healy's *The Old Munster Circuit*, originally published in the early part of this Century but regularly reprinted, most recently by Mercier Press. It contains a wealth of 'legal folklore' from the late 19th and early 20th Century. From recent times, Rex Mackey's *Windward of the Law* (W.H. Allen, 1965) contains a similar collection of anecdotes. This book—written by one of the most eminent of present day criminal law practitioners—is, unfortunately, out of print and is a collector's item much sought after in second hand book shops.

7. Discipline

The general conduct of the members of the Bar is controlled by a non-statutory body, called the General Council of the Bar of Ireland. The Council, which is elected annually by the members of the Bar, issues to each member a Code of Conduct which, again, may be amended from time . to time by the members of the Bar. Where a barrister is found by the Bar Council to be in breach of the Code of Conduct, he may be liable to expulsion from the Law Library. In addition, he may be reported to the Benchers of the King's Inns who have the ultimate disciplinary sanction of disbarment.

8. The Attorney General

The Attorney General is, by Article 30 of the Constitution, the legal adviser to the government. He is appointed by the President of Ireland on the nomination of the Taoiseach. The Attorney is, by convention, always a member of the Bar and a senior counsel. Generally speaking the Attorney is also drawn from the ranks of the practising Bar, though in 1977 Professor John Kelly was appointed Attorney General. Professor Kelly had indeed practised at the Bar during the 1960s but had for many years been Professor of Jurisprudence and Roman Law in University College Dublin as well as being a member of Dáil Éireann. The Attorney General is also what is called the leader of the Bar, in other words he ranks as the most senior member of the bar. This is largely a ceremonial position. While there is no rule requiring the Attorney to cease private practice while acting as Attorney, this has in fact happened in recent years. As legal adviser to the government, the Attorney General scrutinises all draft legislation which it proposes to bring before the Oireachtas, and is in effect the head of the Office of the Parliamentary Draftsman. In addition, he is the representative of the State in constitutional actions and in this regard his function is to argue to uphold the constitutionality of any challenged legislation. In some instances the Attorney himself has argued such cases in the High Court and Supreme Court but in the majority of cases other senior counsel are chosen to appear in Court on his behalf. Prior to 1974, all serious criminal offences were prosecuted by the Attorney General, but since then this function has, in most instances, been transferred to the Director of Public Proscutions (see Chapter 5). Finally, in 1987 the Attorney General was given a new function in relation to the scrutiny of extradition requests, by the Extradition (Amendment) Act, 1987. A detailed account of the history and role of the Attorney General is Casey, *The Office of the Attorney General in Ireland* (Institute of Public Administration, 1980).

THE UNIVERSITIES

Most solicitors and barristers who qualified in the past 20 years hold a law degree from one of the universities in the State. This was not always the case, and until the 1960s the state of law schools in Ireland was less than satisfactory. It was only in the 1960s, for example, that the universities increased the number of full time law lecturers to a level which was capable of offering a law degree in the form in which it is recognised today. Up to that time, and continuing to the end of the 1960s, many of the lecturers were practitioners who split their time between the universities and the courts.

Because of the state of the law schools for much of this Century, many of
the senior practitioners of the law—solicitors, barristers and judges—hold
general university degrees such as a B.A. and/or M.A. followed by the
training provided by the Law Society or King's Inns as the case may be.
Whether this was an advantage or a disadvantage is a matter of debate, and
there is no doubt that many of the important decisions given by Irish judges
in the last 30 years were from judges whose university education was much
broader from some recently qualified practitioners.

The result of the change to full-time staff in the universities has been
significant. As indicated, many students now follow a path from law degree
through to professional qualification, although there are also a number who
take a general degree followed by a Diploma in Legal Studies course which are
provided by the many other third level colleges who prepare students for the
professional courses. But the university law school sector has certainly increased in size and importance in recent years. Apart from the more professional contribution to legal education which has resulted from this, there has
been an increased level of publications on Irish law and much of this has been
generated by the university sector. As indicated in Chapter 2, there was a
dearth of such publications up to the 1970s, and the transformation in this respect has, broadly speaking, brought further increased knowledge for practitioners as well as for students who are required to read these indigenous texts.

THE JUDICIARY

Since the foundation of the State, the courts in permanent operation have
been the District Court, the Circuit Court, the High Court and the Supreme
Court. Although there are very few judges by comparison with the number
of lawyers, both practising and academic, the judiciary have the final say on
many areas of legal development. It is the judges of the High Court and
Supreme Court in particular who deliver judgments on important areas of
law and which are then included in the law reports for the use of the present
and future generations of lawyers. These judgments therefore give an air of
permanency to the work of a judge. While some practitioners may obtain
great satisfaction from arguing a case well in court or achieving a satisfying
result for a client, only the judge can make a permanent mark on the law in
the sense of writing a judgment which is relied on in future cases. For this
reason, many eminent practitioners aspire ultimately to becoming a judge,
particularly of the High Court or Supreme Court. This is so even though
practice is, in most instances, much more remunerative than a judicial
salary. Nonetheless, 'going on the Bench' remains the ultimate goal, a
point which is illustrated by the calibre of practitioners who have become
judges in Ireland over the years. It would be foolish to suggest, however,
that all members of the judiciary are equally capable or courteous or concerned about the development of Irish law, but the general rule is that the
best of the legal profession aspire to judicial office and that the contribution
of some Irish judges to the law has been significant and illuminating.

Although it may be an obvious point at this stage of the text, it is important to note that a central aspect of the administration of justice is that the
courts sit in public. This is enshrined in Article 34 of the Constitution (see
Chapter 4, below), and again reflects the reaction to the injustice of the In-
quisition and the infamous Star Chamber court.

1. Appointment, Qualifications, Retirement

Article 35.1 of the Constitution provides that all the judges of the courts established under the Constitution shall be appointed by the President of Ireland. The effect of Article 13.9 of the Constitution is that the President makes such appointments on the advice of the government, and this means that the government has the primary power in this respect. Article 36 states that the detailed provisions as to appointment, remuneration and retirement shall be regulated in accordance with law.

The formal qualifications for appointment are set out in the Courts (Supplemental Provisions) Act, 1961 and they vary according to the Court to which a judge is to be appointed. Beginning with the District Court, s.29 (2) of the 1961 Act states that a practising barrister or solicitor of not less than ten years' standing is qualified for appointment as a District Court justice. In relation to the Circuit Court, s.17(2) of the Act provides that only barristers of at least ten years' standing are qualified. Finally, in relation to the High Court and Supreme Court, s.5(2) of the Act states that only barristers of 12 years' standing may be appointed. From this it is clear that only practicing barristers of the relevant years standing are qualified to be appointed to the Circuit, High or Supreme Courts. To that extent, therefore, virtually all the important judgments which develop the law are written by judges who were formerly practicing barristers.

As to retirement of judges, for the District Court the retirement age is, under s.30(1) of the 1961 Act, 65 but under the Courts of Justice (District Court) Act, 1949 a Justice may be continued in office on a year to year basis until the age of 70. For a Circuit Court judge, s.18 of the 1961 Act states that the age of retirement is 70 years. And, by way of variety, the age of retirement for High Court and Supreme Court judges, 72, is set out in s.12 of the Courts of Justice Act, 1924. While these retirement ages are higher than those which apply in most occupations with a retirement age, a retirement age for judges of the higher courts did not exist prior to independence and was a novelty introduced by the Courts of Justice Act, 1924. In England, retirement ages for judges of the High Court and above were not introduced until the 1950s.

Some mention may be made of the conventions which operate side by side with the formal legal qualifications set out in the Courts (Supplemental Provisions) Act, 1961. One important convention is that in most instances, only senior counsel are considered for appointment to the High Court and Supreme Court. And indeed many of the appointments to the Circuit Court are from the ranks of the inner Bar also. And while the legislation refers to 10 and 12 years' practice, in most instances those appointed to the Bench have considerably longer experience, and the average age of judges on appointment would be in the mid 50s. There have been some notable exceptions, such as Mr. Justice Walsh who was appointed as a judge in his early 40s. Another practice is that once a judge is appointed to the Circuit Court there is hardly ever any 'promotion' to any of the higher courts. An exception to both of these conventions was Mr. Justice McWilliam, who was first appointed to the Circuit Court at a time when he was a junior counsel, though an extremely eminent practitioner. He was then appointed to the High Court in 1977, where he made many important contributions to the development of Irish law. This progression is, as indicated, somewhat unusual. There is a greater tendency, however, for judges appointed to the

High Court to be considered for later appointment to the Supreme Court on the retirement of a Supreme Court judge, but no clear rules exist in this respect either and many recent appointments to the Supreme Court have been made directly from the ranks of senior counsel. Finally, in practice the Attorney General plays an important part on behalf of the government in the 'sounding out' process which is necessary when a vacancy falls due in the courts and he also has "first refusal" of any judicial vacancy.

2. Independence, Remuneration, Removal

Article 35.2 of the Constitution provides that all judges shall be independent in the exercise of their judicial functions, reflecting the separation of powers concept which forms a central part of the structure established by the Constitution. Article 35.5 buttresses this in a practical way by providing that the remuneration of a judge shall not be reduced during the period of office held. The withholding of a judge's salary by a government which was unhappy with the decisions of the judiciary was a course of action which has been adopted in history to limit independence. No attempt would be likely in Ireland in the present climate. However, Article 35.5 did arise for discussion in *O'Byrne v. Minister for Finance* [1959] I.R. 1. There, the widow of Mr. Justice O'Byrne, who had been a judge of the High Court and later the Supreme Court from 1926 to 1954, claimed that subjecting a judge's salary to income tax was in conflict with Article 35.5. This claim was, however, rejected in the Supreme Court, by a 3-2 majority of the judges. The three judges in the majority stated that Article 35.5 must be read with Article 35.2 as protecting the independence of the judges from governmental interference. In this light, to require a judge to pay income tax like other citizens could not be described as an attack on judicial independence. The salaries of the judges are fixed from time to time by legislation. The levels as of July 1989 ranged from £65,798 for the Chief Justice, down to £33,897 for a District Justice: see *The Irish Times,* 29 July 1989.

Article 35.4 of the Constitution provides that a Supreme Court or High Court judge shall not be removed from office except for what it terms 'stated misbehaviour or incapacity'. Such removal can only take place after resolutions calling for the judge's removal have been passed by Dáil Éireann and Seanad Éireann. On notification of such resolutions by the Taoiseach to the President of Ireland, the President must, by an order signed by him with the Presidential seal attached, remove from office the judge to whom they relate. No resolutions proposing the removal of a judge have ever been presented to the Dail or Seanad, so that the provisions of Article 35.5 have never been considered, for example, as to the meaning of misbehaviour or incapacity.

Although the Constitution does not require a resolution of the Houses of the Oireachtas for removal of Circuit Court judges or District Justices, this is in fact provided for by the s.39 of the Courts of Justice Act, 1924 (Circuit Court judges) and s.20 of the Courts of Justice (District Court) Act, 1949, which provides that they 'hold office by the same tenure as the judges of the Supreme Court and the High Court.'

One of the consequences of the relatively privileged position of the judiciary under the Constitution, and under most other legal regimes, is that the judges do not generally become involved in public controversy, even where they have been subjected to considerable criticism. Up to recent times, indeed, it was unusual for judges to give interviews to the different media. This has changed to some extent, indicating that the judiciary is not immune from the media age. Thus, in 1987 the President of the High Court, Mr. Justice Hamilton, agreed to appear on a television series, '*Open File*', in which, as an influential public figure, he was subjected to questions by a two person panel, one a lecturer in law in University College Dublin and the other a journalist. Such a programme would have been unthinkable ten years ago. Another significant event was the public discussion which emerged arising from a judicial inquiry conducted into what became known as the 'Kerry Babies' Case. The judge who conducted that inquiry, Mr. Justice Lynch, responded to comments which had appeared in the current affairs magazine *Magill*: see the March 1986 issue of *Magill*. In former times, the judiciary's response to public criticism would be to either ignore the matter, to bring a claim for defamation against the publication, or initiate contempt of court proceedings (as to which see Chapter 8). It is interesting to note, therefore, that the judiciary would appear to be prepared nowadays to engage in public debate where necessary, even though this may have the less comfortabe result of subjecting them to greater scrutiny. This is likely to be beneficial in the long run.

The performance of the judiciary and the court system has, in fact, always been subjected to public scrutiny. Dickens' *Bleak House*, already mentioned in Chapter 1, is a classic example of the use of fiction as polemic. In addition, from time to time non-fiction has appeared dealing, usually, with criminal trials in the courts. One may be recommended as a modern version of the 'Notable Trials' variety. This is Deale, *Beyond any Reasonable Doubt?* (Gill and Macmillan, 1971), written by the well-known and highly respected Mr. Justice Kenneth Deale, a long-time Circuit Court judge who was also a High Court judge for a short time until his death. Two books were generated by what became known as the 'Sallins Train Robbery case' of the 1970s, Dunne and Kerrigan, *Round Up the Usual Suspects* (Magil, 1984) and Joyce and Murtagh, *Blind Justice* (Poolbeg, 1984), both of which were written by journalists drawing on the official transcripts in the case. Going further back to 1970, what was known as the Arms Trial was dealt with in two very different books. The first is Tom McIntyre's *Through the Bridewell Gate* (Faber & Faber, 1971) which captures some of the underlying atmosphere of court proceedings. The second is Kelly, *Orders for the Captain?* (published by the author, 1971) an account of the trial written by one of the defendants, all of whom were acquitted by the High Court jury. This second book provides useful background information. Unfortunately both these books are long out of print. The background to the important constitutional case *Crotty v. An Taoiseach* [1987] I.R. 713 (see Chapter 10) is provided in the account of the plaintiff *A Radical's Response* (Poolbeg, 1988).

Finally, on a more down-to-earth note, Nell McCafferty's, *In the Eyes of the Law* (Ward River Press, 1981) is a collection of her articles on the Dublin District Court written for the Irish Times during the 1970s. The descriptions of the people who come into contact with the law at this level of the criminal justice system reflect some of the real problems of a legal system. A small passage from Chapter 1 of *In the Eyes of the Law* may provide a flavour of the essays:

The gowns and wigs may imply majesty, though they too are faded and torn sometimes. The Dublin District Courts themselves have the trappings of sadness . . . Within the court itself, no room. Three hard benches, and the unlucky ones line the walls. It gets too hot, too cold, too stuffy, too noisy, too quiet. Even the gardai don't know how to use the microphones. The Justice is irritated. Justice is flawed. The solicitor arrives late. Justice is delayed. The lists are long and the bailsmen have to come back next day. People don't know what to do and other people are too busy to help them. Tempers flare, spirits flag, and the long hopeless grind grinds on.

Around in the High Court, planning permission is debated in leisure and the dignity befitting high finance.

The conditions described there might be thought to reflect a bad day in Dickensian times, but in 1989 conditions in Kilmainham District Court in Dublin were such that the sitting Justice announced that she was not prepared to continue court business in a building with rat infestation. And this over a decade after the High Court ordered the Minister for Justice to comply with statutory obligations in relation to the maintenance of courthouses: see *The State (King) v. Minister for Justice* [1984] I.R. 169 (decided in 1975).

3. Numbers and Hierarchy
Article 36 of the Constitution provides that the number of judges shall be regulated in accordance with law. In this discussion we begin at the top of the hierarchy of courts, the Supreme Court.

(a) Supreme Court
S.1(2) of the Courts (Establishment and Constitution) Act, 1961 provides that the Supreme Court shall be constituted by the Chief Justice, who is the president of the Court and head of the judiciary, and not less than four ordinary judges. The number of judges may be increased by legislation but s.4 of the Courts (Supplemental Provisions) Act, 1961 which fixes the number of ordinary judges at four has never been amended. However, the Law Reform Commission Act, 1975 provides that, where a judge of the Supreme Court is appointed President of the Law Reform Commission the number of ordinary judges of the Supreme Court shall be five. From 1975 to 1985, Mr. Justice Walsh, a Supreme Court judge, was the President of the Law Reform Commission and so the number of ordinary Supreme Court judges for that time was five. On the appointment of a new President of the Law Reform Commission in 1986 (see below) the Court continued to consist of six judges in all. In November 1988, Mr. Justice Henchy resigned to take up the position of Chairman of the Independent Radio and Television Commission, established by the Radio and Television Act, 1988. Since then the Supreme Court has reverted to the 'normal' position of comprising five judges.

An important feature of the Supreme Court is that it is a *collegiate court*, in other words it always consists of a number of judges, not just one. From this point of view it is different from the other courts discussed below (but note that the Court of Criminal Appeal and Special Criminal Court, discussed in Chapter 4, are also collegiate courts). Being a collegiate court presents a number of interesting issues which should be briefly noted. Since the common law convention is that each judge on a collegiate court is entitled to express a view on the legal issues arising in a case, this means that in a Court with five judges, a case may be decided by the views of three of the judges sitting. We have already seen in fact that this was the case in *O'Byrne v. Minister for Finance* [1959] I.R. 1, referred to above.

There has been no analysis made of the way in which the Irish Supreme Court arrives at its decisions. It is known, however, that the judges of the Court meet to discuss cases after they have been argued in Court. The contents of such discussions as may take place between the judges remain confidential, but it is clear from reading judgments delivered in the Supreme Court that draft judgments are circulated by the judges to their colleagues prior to the date when the judgments are delivered in open Court: see for example the judgments in *Norris v. Attorney General* [1984] I.R. 36 (Extract 13.7) where Mr. Justice McCarthy quotes extracts from the other judgments which had just been delivered. This clearly required advance circulation. However, as already stated, very little is known about this process. Perhaps it would be harmful to the decision-making process if any details were to emerge as to what occurs between the judges of the Supreme Court.

In his Foreword to McMahon and Binchy, *A Casebook on the Irish Law of Torts* (Professional Books, 1983), Mr. Justice Walsh, the senior ordinary judge of the Supreme Court, suggests that the decision-making process of collegiate courts 'should be studied under the rubric of small group sociology.' Such studies have been a common feature of the law schools of the United States of America for very many years. They have begun to be employed in relation to the English legal system in recent years also. The process has yet to take hold in Ireland, though this may change with the increased numbers of full-time law faculties referred to above. A preliminary step on the road was Professor Bartholomew's, *The Irish Judiciary* (Institute of Public Administration, 1971), which reflects the writer's American background and sociological approach. No similar study has been published since Professor Beth's work. It may be noted, by way of comparison, that the United States Supreme Court is seen as being part of the political as well as the legal landscape in that country to an extent which is not the case in relation to the Irish High Court and Supreme Court. This has meant that the United States Supreme Court has been subjected to considerable scrutiny, most notably and publicly in Woodward and Bernstein's *The Brethern* (Secker & Warberg, 1979), an account of the 'inside' workings of the Supreme Court from 1969 to 1975. Such an account in the Irish context is unlikely. A more traditional, and highly informative, judicial biography is Golding, *George Gavan Duffy* (Irish Academic Press, 1982).

In most important cases, the Supreme Court sits as a five judge Court. Articles 12 and 26 require that when the Court performs its functions under those provisions (as to which see Chapter 4), the Court must consist of not less than five judges. And s.7(3) and (4) of the Courts (Supplemental Provisions) Act, 1961 provide that the Court shall also be comprised of five judges in cases involving the validity of a law having regard to the Constitution. But s.7(4) also provides that in any other case the Chief Justice may direct that the Court shall consist of three judges. This usually happens in relation to preliminary matters before the Court, where the case does not involve a general point of legal importance or where there is a shortage of available judges for some reason. The President of the High Court (see below) is, under s.1(3) of the Courts (Establishment and Constitution) Act, 1961, *ex officio* (that is by virtue of the office) an additional judge of the Supreme Court. And under s.1(4) of that Act the Chief Justice may request a High Court judge to sit as an additional judge of the Supreme Court for a particular case. Finally, the Supreme Court always sits in the Four Courts building in Dublin.

(b) High Court

S.2(2) of the Courts (Establishment and Constitution) Act, 1961 provides that the High Court shall be constituted of the President of the High Court (who is the second most senior judge in the State after the Chief Justice) and such number of ordinary judges as may from time to time be fixed by law. The ordinary number of judges was fixed at not more than six judges at that time by s.4(2) of the Courts (Supplemental Provisions) Act, 1961 but has increased since then so that the present maximum number of ordinary judges is 15, which was fixed by the Courts (No. 2) Act, 1981. The Courts Act, 1985 allows for a further judge to be appointed but that when the next vacancy after 2nd April 1987 occurs the maximum permissible number of ordinary judges would revert to 14. No vacancy has, up to the time of writing, occurred since 2nd April 1987, so the 1985 Act still applies. In addition, the Law Reform Commission Act, 1975 provides that where a High Court judge is appointed President of the Law Reform Commission, an additional High Court judge may be appointed. In 1986, Mr. Justice Keane, a High Court judge, was appointed to that position in succession to Mr. Justice Walsh. As at present, therefore, the maximum permissible number of ordinary judges is 16 (including Mr. Justice Keane). When a vacancy occurs next, the maximum number of ordinary judges will be 15, and if another person (other than a High Court judge) is appointed President of the Law Reform Commission the position will be as set out in the Courts (No.2) Act, 1981. Finally, the Chief Justice and the President of the Circuit Court are both *ex officio* judges of the High Court under s.2(3) and (4) of the Courts (Establishment and Constitution) Act, 1961.

In most cases, a High Court judge sits either alone or with a jury to decide a case. A jury is required in all criminal cases and in certain civil cases: see Chapter 4. In some instances, the President of the High Court may direct that a panel of three judges shall sit to hear important cases. In this situation the panel of judges is known as a *Divisional High Court*, a description which derives from the pre-independence situation where judges of the different divisions of the High Court would be asked to sit as a panel (*en banc*). Article 40.4 of the Constitution provides that a Divisional Court may sit in cases of inquiries into the validity of a person's detention in custody. An example of this was *The State (Murray) v. McRann* [1979] I.R. 133. A Divisional Court was also convened for *Crotty v. An Taoiseach* [1987] I.R. 713, the constitutional case in which the Single European Act was challenged (see Chapter 10).

The High Court ordinarily sits in Dublin, in the Four Courts building, but on two occasions each year, High Court judges (as well as such Supreme Court judges as may be assigned) sit in various venues around the country to hear appeals from the Circuit Court. This is known as the High Court on Circuit.

(c) Circuit Court

S.4(2) of the Courts (Establishment and Constitution) Act, 1961 provides that the Circuit Court shall comprise the President of the Circuit Court and such number of ordinary judges as may be fixed from time to time. The Courts Act, 1985 fixes the maximum number of ordinary judges at 15. However, s.14 of the Courts of Justice Act, 1936 empowers the Minister for Justice to appoint 'temporary' Circuit Court judges, over and above the maximum permitted by the 1961 Act. In 1988, there were two such Circuit Court judges: see the *Law Directory 1989*, published by the Incorporated Law Society of Ireland. A Circuit Court judge sits alone to hear cases, except in those cases where the Court hears serious criminal cases when a jury trial is required: see Chapter 4. The President of the Circuit Court sits in Dublin and there are a number of Circuit Court judges permanently assigned to the Dublin area. But the other judges are assigned to different *Circuits* of the country. At present there are seven such Circuits: Cork, Eastern, Midland, Northern, South East, South West and Western. Each Circuit usually incorporates a number of towns in which the Circuit Court judge sits on dates specified in advance on a yearly basis. The towns in which the judge for the Eastern Circuit sits, for example, are: Athy, Drogheda, Dundalk, Kells, Naas, Trim and Wicklow. This division of the Circuit Court's jurisdiction into different areas is a feature shared with the District Court.

(d) District Court

S.5(5) of the Courts (Establishment and Constitution) Act, 1961 provides that the District Court shall be comprised of the President of the District Court and such number of other judges, called Justices of the District Court, as may from time to time be fixed by law. The Courts Act, 1977 fixes the present maximum number of Justices at 39. However, as with the Circuit Court the Minister for Justice is empowered under s.51 of the Courts of Justice Act, 1936 to appoint temporary Justices. In 1988, there were four such temporary Justices: see the *Law Directory 1989*.

A Justice of the District Court always sits alone, there being no circumstances in which a jury is required. The President of the District Court sits in Dublin, and as with the Circuit Court, some of the Justices are assigned to the Dublin area while others are assigned to specific District Court areas throughout the country. There are at present 23 such District Court areas. A helpful list of these areas and the towns they serve is also provided in the *Law Directory 1989*.

4. Mode of Address and Notation

Brief mention will be made of the statutory requirements as to addressing a judge and the manner of noting a judge's name. This is, to some extent, a companion to correct citation of names of cases and law reports. The correct mode of address of a judge should, however, be regarded as somewhat more serious.

(a) Judges of the High Court and Supreme Court. S.10 of the Courts of Justice Act, 1924 states that the mode of address is to be prescribed by rules

of court. The Rules of the Superior Courts, 1986 specify, in Order 119, rule 1, that the judges shall be addressed by their respective titles and names and that they may be referred to as 'The Court.' In fact, when counsel appear in Court they generally use one of two alternative modes of address. The first is 'The Court', as in the 1986 Rules, giving rise to: 'If the Court pleases'. Alternatively, in the course of argument the judge might be addressed as 'My Lord' or 'Your Lordship.' This is, incidentally, also the mode of address chosen by the first, and currently only, woman High Court judge, Miss Justice Carroll. When writing a High Court or Supreme Court judge's name, the following is correct: 'Mr. Justice McCarthy' or 'McCarthy J.' (note that the latter reads as 'Mr. Justice McCarthy' and not 'McCarthy Jay', although this latter form has been known to creep into even the most punctilious lawyer's vocabulary!). When addressing a High Court or Supreme Court judge directly, but not in court, the correct mode of address is: 'Judge Griffin', but, perhaps confusingly, when introducing a judge the method is: 'Mr. Justice Griffin.' Thus, at a public meeting, the person who proposes a vote of thanks might say: 'I would like to thank on your behalf Mr. Justice Hederman for his presence this evening' and then turn to the judge and state to him directly 'Thank you Judge Hederman.'

Special notations exist for the Chief Justice and President of the High Court. 'The Chief Justice, Mr. Justice Finlay' is usually noted as follows: Finlay C.J. And 'The President of the High Court, Mr. Justice Hamilton' is usually noted thus: Hamilton P.

(b) Judges of the Circuit Court. The President of the Circuit Court, as an *ex officio* judge of the High Court, is referred to as the President of the Circuit Court Mr. Justice Roe, or Roe J. The mode of address in Court of all the Circuit Court judges is stipulated (pursuant to the power in s.38 of the Courts of Justice Act, 1924) in O.3, r.2 of the Rules of the Circuit Court, 1950 as 'A Thiarna Bhreithimh' or 'My Lord.' In written form and in addressing them outside court, they are referred to as 'Judge'.

(c) District Justices. The President of the District Court is referred to as the President of the District Court, Justice Macklin. The mode of address in Court is, under Rule 3 of the District Court Rules, 1948, 'Justice', and this is also the correct mode of address outside court.

COURT ADMINISTRATION

The judiciary represent the public face of the court system, but it falls to the officers of the different courts to administer the system which exists. In the courtroom itself, the judges of the Circuit, High and Supreme Courts are assisted by the court *registrar* (in the District Court called the *Clerk*) whose functions include the drawing up of the formal court orders which represent the official record of the decision for the purposes of the parties in the case. This formal order is what is presented by one party to any other person to prove in law that a particular decision was made in the case by the Court. The judge will, of course, be required to approve the wording of an order but, in most cases, it is the registrar who is responsible in the first place and may well liaise personally with the lawyers for the two parties to ensure that the wording of the order reflects their understanding of the decision of the judge.

Behind the public courtroom setting, the administration of the courts also proceeds in accordance with the basic structures established in the 19th Century. In the High Court, the Central Office is responsible for the receipt and cataloguing of most pleadings which are presented in order to initiate and continue court proceedings (see Chapter 5 on pleadings). The administrative head of the Central Office is called the *Master of the High Court*. The Master performs some quasi-judicial functions in relation to court procedure, some of which were expanded by the Rules of the Superior Courts, 1986. These functions include the granting of judgment in cases in which a claim for a sum in default of a loan is made, for example, by a bank and there is no defence to the claim or no real defence. In addition, the Master is empowered to ensure that before cases are sent to the High Court in special summons cases (see Chapter 5) the legal documentation is correct (or as it is usually termed that 'the papers are in order.').

In addition to the Central Office there are specialist units, or offices within the High Court system. These include the Probate Office (wills), the Office of the Official Assignee in Bankruptcy, the Examiner's Office (with responsibility for many chancery matters, including company law cases), the Office of the Wards of Court (responsible for those persons whose affairs are administered by the Court after an application to Court based on their own inability to look after their own interests) and the Taxing Master's Office (with important functions regarding the assessment of litigation fees: see Chapter 7).

In the Circuit Court, the system is administered through *County Registrars* who also have considerable administrative back-up teams. In the District Court, as mentioned Court clerks are responsible for the administrative side of the court system. The jurisdiction and functions of the different court offices are governed by the provisions of the Court Officers Acts, 1926 to 1961, as well as the different rules of court.

Finally, it may be noted that the Rules of the Superior Courts, 1986 fix four terms for the sitting of the High Court, Court of Criminal Appeal and Supreme Court. The *Michaelmas Term* runs from the first Monday in October to the 21st December; the *Hilary Term* begins on 11th January and ends two weeks before Good Friday; the *Easter Term* runs from the Monday after Easter week and ends on the Thursday preceding Whit Sunday; and the *Trinity Term* begins on the Wednesday following Whitsun week and ends on 31st July. The period between 31st July and the first Monday in October is called the *Long Vacation*. Similar terms operate for the Circuit Court, but the District Court sits for much longer terms, generally the same as for other public institutions.

JURIES

Where a jury sits in cases, they have the final say in the outcome of the case, guided by the legal rulings of the judge: see Chapter 5. The origin of the jury in the common law system may be regarded as something of an historical accident, but its place in Irish law is enshrined in Article 38 of the Constitution insofar as serious criminal cases is concerned. It may also be said that the rules of evidence which developed over the years in relation to civil and criminal law owe something to the fact that the judges did not wish to have anything resembling prejudicial evidence being heard by a group of people who were not legally qualified and who may not, in earlier centuries, have been entirely literate. Nonetheless, the rules of evidence which continue to exist in the Irish legal system today may be justified on different grounds now, including perhaps studies on the impact of prejudicial material even on lawyers trained, supposedly, to reject the effects of such prejudicial material.

In relation to the composition of the jury, it was, strangely, one of the last institutions of State to be fully democratised. Under the Juries Act, 1924, membership of the jury panels was open only to property (land) owners, and the level of property required varied from one county to the next. In its 2nd Interim Report, published in 1965, the Committee on Court Practice and Procedure recommended that jury service be available to all adult citizens, including women (though the minority report contains a dissent regarding married women which reads rather peculiarly today). Unfortunately, the Report was not acted on, but in *deBurca v. Attorney General* [1976] I.R. 38, the Supreme Court held that the 1924 Act was unconstitutional. The Juries Act, 1976 now provides that jury members are to be drawn from the electoral roll, and this has resulted in an increasing number of young people and women forming the juries which sit in criminal and civil cases.

In a civil High Court jury action (as to which see Chapter 4), the verdict may, under the Courts of Justice Act, 1924 by reached by a majority of nine of the twelve members. In criminal cases, both in the Circuit Court and High Court the Criminal Justice Act, 1984 introduced majority verdicts for the first time. The Act provides that a jury verdict in a criminal case may be given where ten of the members are agreed on the verdict. Special safeguards are built into the 1984 Act requiring the trial judge for example to be satisfied that the jury has considered the case for a reasonable period of time, and not less than two hours. And the majority verdict does not apply in relation to offences carrying the death penalty; these still require a unanimous verdict. See *The People v. Kelly* [1989] I.L.R.M. 370.

Apart from juries drawn for Court service, a jury may be called under the Coroners Act, 1962 in relation to the holding of an inquest into a death. The jury may be selected in the much more informal manner of asking members of the public who are passing in the street outside the Coroner's Court whether they would be prepared to sit.

OTHER PROFESSIONALS

As mentioned at the beginning of the Chapter, other professional persons may also be deeply involved in the operation of the law. Engineers and architects may require detailed knowledge of, for example, patent and copyright law and many textbooks are written for that audience. In addition, however, such professionals may serve as specialist arbitrators in hearings conducted under the Arbitration Acts, 1954 and 1980 (see Chapter 9).

Other professionals such as accountants are likely to have more detailed knowledge of the practical operation of certain areas of law than even some barristers who specialise in particular areas. Accountants are likely to be familiar with the details of the Income Tax Act, 1967 and other revenue legislation, as well as some aspects of company law. For this reason, they will also be given a good grounding in the basic principles of law associated with those areas of legislation in their university degrees and professional courses.

CHANGES IN THE PRESENT SITUATION

1. The Legal Profession

In recent years, a number of different problems and issues have been identified in relation both to access to the legal profession and the organisation and structure of the profession itself.

On access to the legal profession, the following issues have arisen. What is, and should be, the role of the university sector in relation to the profession? Is there a need to adapt university law syllabi to reflect to a greater degree the vocational needs of law students? Or is the professional training a matter for the Law Society and King's Inns? Is there a quota system in operation in the Law Society or King's Inns which restricts the number of students attempting to gain access to either professional schools? Should there be a quota system? Are the standards set by either the Law Society or King's Inns at the correct level?

On the structure of the legal profession itself, one of the perenniel questions has been whether there is a continuing justification for the separation into the two branches. Should the distinction between solicitors and barristers be abolished? Should the solicitors' conveyancing monopoly be abolished? Do other practices exist within the profession which contribute to excessive costs in litigation? Is it appropriate that solicitors are excluded from being appointed as judges of the Circuit, High and Supreme Courts?

It is clear that these questions raise fundamental questions about the legal profession, and it is not surprising, therefore, that a formal inquiry has been held to investigate and report on virtually all these matters. In 1986 the Minister for Industry and Commerce requested what is now called the Fair Trade Commission (then called the Restrictive Practices Commission) to conduct an inquiry into the legal profession under the provisions of the Restrictive Practices Act, 1972. The Commission held a number of meetings with various interested bodies, including the universities and both branches of the profession, with a view to assessing the position. In early 1989 it appeared from media reports that the Commission would be presenting its final report by the end of the year. This may still be possible, but at the time of writing (June 1989) the Commission had been asked to conduct an inquiry into the petrol industry in Ireland and it appears that this may postpone the drafting of the report on the legal profession.

Another complicating feature of the situation is that in early 1989, the British Lord Chancellor, Lord Mackay, published consultative documents (Green Papers) in relation to the reorganisation of the legal profession in Britain. While these proposals clearly do not have immediate relevance to the Irish position, it is felt that Lord Mackay's initial proposals, which were modified in the July 1989 White Paper, will become the focus of discussion in Ireland. And the deep hostility to some of the proposals which had been expressed by the different interested bodies in Britain may also provide an advance indication of the possible response to any far-reaching proposals which the Fair Trade Commission might make in the Irish context. It is clear, therefore, that in the coming years the shape and composition of the legal profession in Ireland will be the subject of considerable debate.

2. The Judiciary

The functions of the courts inevitably change from time by time by virtue of changes in the jurisdiction and business of the different courts in accordance with the Courts Acts which are passed by the Oirechatas from time to time. In addition, however, there have been from time to time some concerns expressed as to the method of appointment of judges which, under the Constitution, ultimately rests with the government of the day. It has been suggested, for example, that a Commission, including present members of the judiciary, be appointed to make recommendations as to new appointments. This suggestion would appear to be similar to the system for appointments to the higher grades of the civil service, but it should be borne in mind that there is little prospect of such a system being introduced in the near future. Another suggestion made in recent years is the establishment of an intermediate civil court of appeal interposed between the High Court and the Supreme Court. The purpose would be to take some of the burden from the Supreme Court which it would appear is unable to cope with the increased workload of recent years. This suggestion has been put forward in public by the present Chief Justice, Mr. Justice Finlay, and is discussed by Hogan in Duncan (ed.) *Laws and Social Policy* (D.U.L.J., 1987). It would appear that such a court may be established by the government which was elected in 1989. Also in the context of the Supreme Court, the Committee on Court Practice and Procedure, in its 11th Interim Report published in 1970, made some important comments on what is still, broadly, the current procedures of the Court, with many recommendations for changes. These included the possibility of appointing legal research assistants (law clerks) along lines similar to those which exist in North American courts, particularly the United States. No fundamental changes have been made on foot of this Report, though as indicated it remains an extremely useful account of current practice.

3. Court Officers

In recent years the Department of Justice has indicated that legislation to update the current position of court officers was being prepared. While such legislation was not presented when the 25th Dail was dissolved in May 1989 for the general election it is likely that such legislation will be forthcoming within a short time.

4. Women in the Law

One of the striking features of the last few decades for most professions has been the emergence of women as major contributors, particularly in those professions such as the law which were once the preserve of men. In terms of the numbers of women solicitors and, more particularly, barristers the changes in the last 15 years have been considerable. In the Bar, women have become significant contributors to branches of the law, such as criminal law, which were virtually all-male preserves until recently. Thus, it is no longer possible to state that women lawyers only practice, say, in family law or chancery law. This development is bound to have a further impact in the courts within the next few years, and a significant factor here are the increasing number of women senior counsel. This has implications for the complexion of the judiciary in future years. At the time of writing, there are no women judges in the Supreme Court, there is one woman High Court judge, there are no women Circuit Court judges and there are four women District Justices.

Chapter 4

THE COURT SYSTEM

INTRODUCTION

In Chapter 1, we described the evolution of the court system to the position as of the creation of the Irish Free State in 1922. In this Chapter, we describe the present jurisdiction of the courts in civil and criminal matters. We describe the manner in which a court is chosen to hear a case in the first instance; clearly it is important to know which court should hear a particular type of case. This aspect of court jurisdiction is known as the original (or first instance) jurisdiction of the courts. In this discussion, both the civil and criminal jurisdiction of the courts, where appropriate, will be described. In Chapter 6, we describe the appellate jurisdiction of the courts. The courts currently in operation in the State are:

1. The District Court.
2. The Circuit Court.
3. The High Court.
4. The Special Criminal Court.
5. The Court of Criminal Appeal.
6. The Supreme Court.

THE LEGAL BASIS FOR THE COURTS' JURISDICTION

1. The 1922 Constitution of the Irish Free State

The Constitution of the Irish Free State which was enacted as a Schedule to the Constitution of The Irish Free State (Saorstát Éireann Act, 1922, the first Act passed by the Free State Dail included, in Articles 64 to 72, important provisions dealing with the court structure to be established in the new State. When the 1937 Constitution was later brought into effect by referendum of the people, the provisions regarding the courts were modelled to a large extent on those contained in the 1922 Constitution. As we will see below, the 1937 Constitution required the establishment of a new court system, but again the courts of the 1937 Constitution, for all practical purposes, are similar to those of the Free State.

Because of the broad similarity between the 1922 and 1937 Constitutions in this respect, we will outline the relevant provisions of the 1937 Constitution only. Apart from the names of the courts, the 1922 Constitution has had another important impact on the current court structure. In pursuance of the 1922 constitutional provisions, the Courts of Justice Act, 1924 was passed to establish the different courts and to describe their functions. Many of these basic provisions were carried over into the court system established under the 1937 Constitution, so that in the description below of the powers and functions of the courts today there are a number of references to the 1924 Act.

2. The 1937 Constitution

As mentioned in Chapter 2, the Constitution of Ireland of 1937, Bunreacht na hÉireann, is the ultimate source of all legal authority within the State. The Constitution, in Articles 34 to 37 (which are headed 'The Courts'), provides a broad outline regarding the structure of the court system, and in terms of legal validity whatever structures exist must conform to the basic framework established by the Constitution. Article 38 (which is included under the heading 'Trial of Offences') also contains provisions regarding the operation of criminal courts in the State.

Article 34.1 states that:

> 'Justice shall be administered in courts established by law by judges appointed in the manner provided by this Constitution, and, save in such special and limited cases as may be prescribed by law, shall be administered in public.'

This simple provision lies at the heart of the functions of the courts in Ireland. What follows in the remainder of Article 34 through to Article 37 puts some flesh on this basic proposition, which implies that 'justice' cannot be administered in any place except in a court which has been established in accordance with the Constitution, presided over by a properly appointed judge, and that usually the courts should be open to the public.

While Article 34.1 is a short provision, it signifies that the Irish Constitution has adopted the principle that the administration of justice must be assigned to a separate arm of government, in accordance with the doctrine of the separation of powers which was central to the American and French revolutions of the 18th Century. Given Ireland's historical connections with these two great revolutions, it is hardly surprising that the Constitution should reflect the philosophical basis of those similar struggles. In the next section, some of the difficulties associated with this important provision are considered. The remainder of Articles 34 to 37 should be mentioned at this stage, however, because they give an indication of the framework around which legislation in relation to the courts must be built. Among the elements of this structure are the following:

(i) The courts shall comprise courts of first instance and a court of final appeal (Article 34.2).

(ii) The courts of first instance shall include a High Court and the court of final appeal shall be called the Supreme Court (Article 34.3.1° and Article 34.4.1°).

(iii) The courts of first instance shall also include courts of local and limited jurisdiction with a right of appeal as determined by law (Article 34.3.4°).

(iv) The High Court shall have full original jurisdcition in all matters, civil and criminal (Article 34.3.1°). This point is considered below.

(v) The Supreme Court, presided over by the Chief Justice, shall have appellate jurisdiction from all decisions of the High Court, subject to such exceptions as may be prescribed by law (Article 34.4.2° and 34.3.3°).

(vi) The High Court and, on appeal, the Supreme Court shall have the power to determine whether laws are invalid due to their being in conflict with the Constitution, and no law can be passed prohibiting the Supreme Court from hearing an appeal from the High Court in a constitutional case (Article 34.3.2° and 34.4.4°).

(vii) Judges appointed to the High Court and Supreme Court shall subscribe to a declaration to carry out duly and faithfully that office and to uphold the Constitution (Article 34.5.1°).

(viii) All judges shall be appointed by the President acting on the advice of the government (Article 13.9 and 35.1).

(ix) All judges shall be independent in the exercise of their judicial functions, subject only to the Constitution and the law (Article 35.2).

(x) Judges of the High Court and Supreme Court can only be removed from office for stated misbehaviour or incapacity, and only after resolutions passed both by Dáil Éireann and Seanad Éireann calling for removal (Article 35.4).

(xi) Judges' remuneration cannot be reduced during the time they hold office (Article 35.5).

(xii) Subject to the foregoing, a number of matters relating to the courts may be regulated by law, including the number of judges of the different courts, remuneration, age of retirement and pensions, as well as 'the constitution and organisation of the . . . Courts, the distribution of jurisdiction and business among the . . . Courts and judges, and all matters of procedure' (Article 36).

(xiii) Nothing in the Constitution may be invoked to invalidate the exercise of limited functions of a judicial nature, other than in criminal matters, by a body or person authorised by law to exercise such functions, even though such person or body is not a judge or court appointed under the Constitution (Article 37). This provision was inserted to validate the functions of bodies such as the Land Commission (since abolished) which exercised extensive powers under legislation. Some doubts were expressed in the course of the case *M. v An Bord Uchtála* [1977] I.R. 287 whether the orders of the Adoption Board, An Bord Uchtála, were protected by this provision. In order to avoid any doubt about the legal validity of adoption orders the provision was amended so that An Bord Uchtála was expressly protected.

(xiv) In relation to criminal cases, Article 38 sets out an important code of procedure, as follows.

   (a) no person shall be tried on any criminal charge save in due course of law (Article 38.1);

   (b) minor offences may be tried by courts of summary jurisdiction (Article 38.2);

   (c) special criminal courts may be established by law in the circumstances which are discussed later in the Chapter (Article 38.3);

   (d) military tribunals may be established to deal with offences committed by persons subject to miltary law, as well as deal with a state of war or armed rebellion (Article 38.4.1); and

   (e) except in the case of trials of minor offences or trials before special criminal courts or military tribunals, no person shall be tried on any criminal charge without a jury (Article 38.5).

3. Public Sittings and Exceptions

Article 34.1 clearly provides that the courts must, usually, sit in public, subject to exceptions specified by law. This general requirement of public sittings has been mentioned briefly in Chapter 3. S.45 of the Courts (Supplemental Provisions) Act, 1961 provides for a number of cases in which justice may be administered otherwise than in public. These are:

(1) applicatons of an urgent nature for *habeas corpus*, bail, prohibition or injunction;

(2) matrimonial causes and matters (that is, family law matters);

(3) lunacy and minor matters (the wardship jurisdiction of the High Court);

(4) proceedings involving the disclosure of a secret manufacturing process.

There are a number of other statutory provisions which allow for hearings in private (*in camera*): see Kelly, *The Irish Constitution*, 2nd ed. (Jurist, 1984) pp. 258-260. See also *In re R. Ltd.*, Supreme Court, unreported, 2 May 1989.

4. The meaning of 'administration of justice'

What is the 'administration of justice'? This is not just an interesting academic question bearing no relation to ordinary day-to-day problems in the court system. The courts have found it difficult to provide an analysis of the concept of administering justice which can apply to all situations. To an extent, the judges have a general set of guidelines which have been given from time to time as indicators of what constitutes the judicial power, but there is no definitive test and the judges have tended to prefer an approach by which each individual problem is looked at as it presents itself rather than laying down a governing principle. Among the decisions over the years have been: in making an exclusion order against a greyhound trainer, Bord na gCon was not exercising a judicial power (*McDonald v. Bord na gCon (No.2)* [1965] I.R. 217); in deciding whether to acquire land compulsorily, Bord na Mona was not exercising a judicial function (*O'Brien v. Bord na Mona* [1983] I.R. 255); in striking a solicitor off the roll of solicitors, the Incorporated Law Society was exercising a judicial function (*In re the Solicitors Act, 1954* [1960] I.R. 239).

It should be noted that where a body other than a judge exercises a judicial function, that tribunal acts in violation of the Constitution, and its decisions are by definition invalid. In the case of solicitors, the solution was that the Incorporated Law Society is still given the basic disciplinary function over solicitors but that any decsion to strike a person off the roll would have to be made by the High Court; this approach, contained in the Solicitors Act, 1960, has been repeated in, for example, ss.38 to 40 of the Dentists Act, 1985.

A similar change in procedure, on this occasion relating to the courts themselves, arose as a result of the decision in *The State (Clarke) v. Roche* [1986] I.R. 619. It was held in that case that the then system for issuing Road Traffic Act summonses in the District Court was invalid because it was in conflict with Article 34.1 of the Constitution. The system in operation at that time was that summonses were issued under the control of a District Court Clerk. Under s.10 of the Petty Sessions (Ireland) Act, 1851, as interpreted by the courts, the Clerk then had to be 'satisfied' that the summons was in the correct format. In other words the Clerk had to be satisfied that the summons appeared to be a valid call to the accused person to attend court to answer the criminal charge contained in the summons. The Supreme Court decided in the case that the Clerk's function, in having to decide whether the summons was valid, amounted to the 'administration of justice'. The Court concluded that, since only judges appointed under the Constitution were entitled to 'administer justice' under Article 34.1 of the Constitution, the system that existed at the time was invalid.

There are a number of important consequences which this decision had. First, it meant that many thousands of summonses under the Road Traffic legislation, for example, those relating to driving with an excess of alcohol, were declared invalid. Indeed, it proved impossible to issue new, valid, summonses in these cases as the six month time limit for their issue (set out in the 1851 Act) had, by then, expired. Second, because of the importance of ensuring that summonses would in future be issued in accordance with the Constitution, the Courts (No.3) Act, 1986 was passed by the Oireachtas immediately after the Supreme Court gave its decision in *The State (Clarke) v. Roche*. The 1986 Act altered the procedure for issuing summonses. It retained the use of District Court clerks, but under the new system the clerks are not required to make any judgment as to whether the summonses being issued are correct, in the sense that they no longer make any decision as to whether the summons outlined a criminal offence. All the clerk does now is to process the summons as an administrative matter; the decision-making in relation to it is now performed by a District Justice, a judge appointed in accordance with Article 34.1 of the Constitution. Thus, even though the system has not changed in any substantial way, it is sometimes important to pay scrupulous attention to the forms of procedure.

Finally, it might be noted that between 1937 and the time of the *Clarke* case, many hundreds of thousands of summonses had been issued in a way that was in conflict with the Constitution. Why was a case not brought on this point in 1938 or 1958 or 1968? And what is the legal status of all those 'invalid' summonses? The first question is relatively easy to answer: sometimes it might not have occurred to lawyers to argue that particular point. Another possible reason is that it is only since the early 1960s that many cases based on the Constitution have been brought and so in earlier years the judges may not have been ready or willing to entertain what might appear to be a technical point without much merit. The short answer is, therefore, that times change, and it is important to bear in mind that the law does not stand still. As to the second question, this is discussed in more detail in Chapter 13, below. But the short answer to this difficult question is that all the summonses issued under the old system, while clearly invalid, will not be overturned because the passage of time, and various other factors, have made them immune from legal challenge.

5. The Position of the High Court and Supreme Court

A significant feature of Articles 34 to 36 of the Constitution is that they refer specifically to the High Court and Supreme Court. No other courts are mentioned by name. Article 34.2 states that the courts 'shall comprise Courts of First Instance and a Court of Final Appeal.' Article 34.3.1° states that the courts of first instance:

'shall include a High Court invested with full original jurisdiction in and power to determine all matters and questions whether of law or fact, civil or criminal.'

The next subsection, Article 34.3.2°, states that:

'the jurisdiction of the High Court shall extend to the validity of any law having regard to the provisions of this Constitution, and no such question shall be raised (whether by pleading, argument or otherwise) in any court established under this or any other Article of this Constitution other than the High Court or the Supreme Court.'

Article 34.4.1° states: 'The Court of Final Appeal shall be called the Supreme Court.' And Article 34.4.3° provides that:

'The Supreme Court shall, with such exceptions and subject to such regulations as may be prescribed by law, have appellate jurisdiction from all decisions of the High Court . . .'

These provisions are important for a number of reasons. First, by mentioning the High Court and Supreme Court by name the Constitution appears to be affording these two courts special status. This is confirmed by Article 34.4.2°, which makes the High Court and Supreme Court the constitutional courts in this State. Both the High Court and, on appeal, the Supreme Court are empowered to decide on the validity of laws passed by the Oireachtas, as to which see Chapter 13, below. But the specific reference to the courts in the Constitution is significant in another way. Neither the High Court or Supreme Court could be abolished by law unless the relevant provisions of the Constitution were themselves repealed. Thus, the reference in the Constitution gives a permanence to those courts which other courts established by statute cannot claim. This has a further knock on effect.

The High Court and Supreme Court can claim to exercise their power by virtue of the Constitution; this provides them with a stature similar to that of the King's (or Queens's) courts under the system which operated in Ireland prior to 1922. The High Court which operated in that system did so with the authority of the monarch, and was for that reason said to possess certain 'inherent' powers. In other words, by virtue of being the King's (or Queen's) Court, the High Court prior to 1922 was regarded as having certain powers over and above those actually conferred by law. The special mention which the High Court and Supreme Court receive in the Constitution puts them on the same footing as the pre-independence courts. And so judges of the High Court and Supreme Court will occasionally refer to the 'inherent' jurisdiction of the High Court or Supreme Court as a basis for making a decision which might not fit into an already established approach.

The same kind of inherent powers simply cannot be claimed by judges of the other courts which were listed at the beginning of this Chapter. They are also provided for by the Constitution, but in a less direct manner. They are mentioned in Article 34.3.4° as follows

'The Courts of First Instance shall also include Courts of local and limited jurisdiction with a right of appeal as may be determined by law.'

Quite clearly, whatever courts are set up in accordance with this provision their powers cannot approach those already set aside for the High Court and Supreme Court. Again the comparison with the pre-1922 position is useful. There were, as seen in Chapter 1, many courts in existence prior to independence under the High Court, all of them established by legislation to perform particular, limited functions. The same may be said of the courts envisaged by the 1937 Constitution: under the High Court and Supreme Court there may exist different lower courts with local and limited powers. And Article 34.3.1° had already provided that the High Court could have full powers in all matters, civil and criminal. The distinction could not be sharper. Whether talking about the local and limited courts prior to 1922 or those contemplated by the 1937 Constitution, judges have often referred to such courts as 'creatures of legislation', indicating that such courts only have powers to the extent that they are actually granted by statute. For the local and limited jurisdiction courts, there is no possibility of having inherent powers.

6. A New Court System

Other issues arise from the apparently simple provisions of Article 34.1 of the Constitution. Many of these are more appropriately dealt with in a full course on Constitutional Law. There is, however, one matter which must be mentioned at this stage. In a Supreme Court decision, *The State (Killian) v. Minister for Justice* [1954] I.R. 207, the Court concluded that the correct meaning of Article 34.1, where it referred to 'courts established by law', was that such courts would have to be established as from the coming into force of the Constitution itself. In other words, the Court considered that the Constitution envisaged a fresh establishment of a court system. The Supreme Court pointed out that the Constitution itself contained a provision, Article 58, which allowed for the continuance of the court system which operated under the 1922 Constitution of the Irish Free State, so there was no possibility of an immediate collapse of the legal basis for the courts which did exist. Nonetheless, the decision in *Killian* came as something of a shock, though no doubt very few people, including lawyers, regarded the decision as catastrophic.

In any event, the Courts (Establishment and Constitution) Act, 1961 was passed to regularise the position and 'establish' the court system envisaged by Article 34.1. To a large extent, however, this short Act merely carried forward the existing court system which had been created pursuant to the provisions of the 1922 Constitution by the Courts of Justice Act 1924. At the same time as the 'new' court system was established the opportunity was taken to pass legislation to update and clarify different functions of the courts. This Act, the Courts (Supplemental Provisions) Act, 1961, contains detailed provisions on the current jurisdiction of the courts. But to provide a full picture of the courts' jurisdiction it is necessary to reach both back and forward in time. The reason for this is that, in the first place, both of the 1961 Acts refer back to previous legislation conferring functions on the different courts; the older legislation must, therefore, be consulted before a full picture can be obtained of the position in 1961. And as for reaching forward from 1961, a number of significant amendments have been made to the jurisdiction of the courts since that time.

Does the 1961 Act make a significant difference? Arguably, it should because the courts in operation prior to the 1961 Act were 'transitory' courts under Article 58 of the Constitution. This might, for example, justify the present courts treating the decisions of the pre-1961 courts as having less force as precedents than decisions of the courts established under the 1961 Act. They might do that, but for pragmatic reasons it is not done in fact: see for example the judgment of Henchy J. in *The State (Lynch) v. Cooney* [1982] I.R. 337 (Extract 11.11). There are other, more difficult, problems which arise in this context, such as whether the Supreme Court which operated prior to the 1961 Act was entitled to hear references of Bills from the President under Article 26 of the Constitution: see the discussion in Kelly, *The Irish Constitution*, 2nd ed. (Jurist, 1984) p. 149. This issue has not, however, been addressed in any decision of an Irish court.

As it would be almost impossible, and mind-numbingly tedious, to provide comprehensive treatment of all statutes which affect the courts' jurisdiction, a description of the principal legislative provisions follows. It should be realised, however, that the general framework thereby established, is supplemented by many statutes which confer jurisdiction in individual instances on particular courts. We provide some examples of such legislation for illustrative purposes.

THE COURTS' ORIGINAL JURISDICTION

In relation to civil cases, the original jurisdiction of the different courts is allocated on two different bases. First, there are general monetary limits set for the lower courts in relation to the amount of compensation (which lawyers refer to as damages) which they can award. Second, jurisdiction is also allocated in terms of the subject matter which the different courts may deal with. As regards criminal cases, the issue is primarily a matter of allocating less serious crimes to the lower courts while the higher courts are allocated the more serious offences.

1. The District Court

The District Court was established by s.5 of the Courts (Establishment and Constitution) Act, 1961. The District Court is a unitary court, in the sense that it is presided over by the President of the District Court who has complete administrative control over the assignment of district justices throughout the State: see also Chapter 3.

However, in keeping with the requirements of Article 34.3.4° of the Constitution, the District Court is a court of local and limited jurisdiction. Both 'local' and 'limited' are important. The District Court is a local court in the sense that a District Justice has responsibility for a particular District Court area, and has no legal authority to act outside that geographical location. The areas and districts for which each Justice is responsible are designated from time to time pursuant to s.26 of the Courts of Justice Act, 1953 (carried forward by s.32 of the Courts (Supplemental Provisions) Act, 1961 and amended by s.16 of the Courts Act, 1971).

As to being limited, the District Court is limited in dealing with civil cases both in relation to the amount of damages it may award and also in relation to the legal subject matter with which it may deal. In relation to criminal cases, Article 38.2 of the Constitution limits the court to dealing with minor offences, and as a direct consequence the penalties which the Court may impose are also limited. The discussion on p. 55, above, of the District Court as a 'creature of statute' should be borne in mind in this context. The simple rule is that the District Court's jurisdiction is restricted to whatever has been expressly given it by legislation; there is no inherent jurisdiction of the District Court. Finally in this context, s.13 of the Courts Act 1971 states that the District Court 'shall be a court of record'. *A court of record* is one which is regarded as having certain minimum powers in civil and criminal cases, and the classification of courts into courts of record and courts 'not of record' is one which is not, strictly speaking, relevant in the light of the 1937 Constitution; the classification is a remnant from the pre-independence court structure. Nonetheless, for the avoidance of doubt, s.13 of the Court Act 1971 confirms that the District Court is rightly entitled to be conferred with the relatively extensive jurisdiction which it now enjoys. However, it must be remembered that the validity of the Court's jurisdiction rests, ultimately, on compliance with the 'local and limited' requirements of Article 34.3.4° of the Constitution.

The District Court: Civil Cases

The general jurisdiction of the District Court is conferred by ss.77 and 78 of the Courts of Justice Act, 1924, carried forward by s.33 of the Courts (Supplemental Provisions) Act, 1961, and extended from time to time, most recently by the Courts Act, 1981?(The principal areas of jurisdiction for the District Court are as follows:

(i) *General.* In cases of contract and tort and in cases of ejectment for non-payment of rent, the Court can award damages not exceeding £2,500. This limit was set by s.6 of the Courts Act 1981, and involved a substantial increase in the Court's jurisdiction. But even here, the Court's jurisdiction is limited, because it is precluded from dealing with any claim involving defamation, false imprisonment or malicious prosecution. These kinds of cases have been reserved for the higher courts since the District Court was established by the Court of Justice Act, 1924.

(ii) *Licensing.* Up to the passing of the Courts (No.2) Act, 1986, it was compulsory for the holder of an intoxicating liquor licence to renew the licence each year in the District Court, even where there was no objection to the renewal. Since the passing of the 1986 Act, the District Court now only hears cases where there is an objection on some ground to the licence renewal. SP. EX. ORDERS

(iii) *Family law.* Under the Family Law (Maintenance of Spouses and Children) Act, 1976, as amended by s. 12 of the Courts Act, 1981, the District Court is empowered to award maintenance to a spouse up to a maximum of £100 per week and to a maximum of £30 per week per child. The effect of Part IV of the Status of Children Act, 1987 is that the same rules as to maintenance now apply regardless of whether the parents of the child are married.

(iv) *Miscellaneous.* The District Court is given jurisdiction to deal with cases under the Hire-Purchase Acts, 1946 to 1980 and the Hotel Proprietors Act, 1963, again with limits of £2,500 as to the amount of damages which may be awarded.

The District Court: Criminal Cases

The jurisdiction of the District Court in criminal matters can be divided into two parts. First of all it acts as a 'clearing house' for serious criminal cases, through the preliminary examination procedure. Secondly, it can hear in full what can generally be categorised as less serious criminal offences. Two comments can be made about the cases which the District Court actually hears. First, while they are, generally speaking, less serious they constitute, in weight of numbers, the largest portion of criminal cases heard in the State and so the District Court is the busiest criminal court in the country. Second, the powers of the District Court are limited under the

Constitution, by virtue of Article 38 of the Constitution, which requires that serious criminal charges should, in general, be heard in a court consisting of a judge and jury. As we have seen in Chapter 3, the District Court is a judge-only court; it is a court of summary trial.

(i) *Preliminary Examination.* Most serious criminal cases must be brought before the District Court in the first instance. These cases cannot proceed to full trial in the higher courts until they have been through the preliminary examination stage provided for in the Criminal Procedure Act, 1967. This procedure is examined in Chapter 5.

(ii) *Minor offences.* Article 38.2 of the Constitution states: 'Minor offences may be tried by courts of summary jurisdiction.' Generally speaking, the legislation which has conferred criminal jurisdiction on the District Court limits its power to ordering a fine of up to £1,000 and/or twelve months imprisonment. This maximum limit has been set by reference to a number of decisions of the High Court and Supreme Court given in the light of Article 38.2 and the meaning to be attached to the word 'minor'. Among the decisions dealing with this provision are those of the Supreme Court in *Conroy v. Attorney General* [1965] I.R. 411 and *The State (Rollinson) v. Kelly* [1984] I.R. 248. The kinds of offences with which the District Court deals with in this light include, for example, most offences under the Road Traffic Acts, 1961 to 1978 (including parking offences, speeding, and driving with an excess of alcohol) as well as the less serious offences under the Misuse of Drugs Acts, 1977 and 1984 (such as possession of scheduled drugs where there is no evidence of intention to supply others).

In relation to minor offences alleged against persons under the age of 16, the District Court is described in s.80 of the Courts of Justice Act, 1924 as 'The Children's Court'. This provision states that the District Justice assigned to deal with accused persons under the age of 16 may deal with the case 'in such manner as shall seem just'. This allows more flexibility than in cases involving an accused over the age of 16. But it may be noted that s.80 does not apply where the Justice is faced with 'charges which by reason of their gravity or other special circumstances he shall not consider fit to be . . . dealt with' under s.80.

Finally, in the European context, it may be noted that virtually all prosecutions for breaking European Community law, as implemented in Irish statutory regulations, come before the District Court. This is because the Irish regulations create minor offences only: see further Chapter 10, below.

(iii) *Indictable Offences specified in the Criminal Justice Act, 1951.* The Schedule to the 1951 Act, as amended by the Criminal Procedure Act, 1967 and the Criminal Law (Jurisdiction) Act, 1976, specifies certain offences which, although they could be tried on indictment in one of the higher criminal courts, can be dealt with in the District Court if two conditions are satisfied. The kinds of offences mentioned include, for example, indecent assault, offences under the Larceny Acts, 1861 and 1916 and obtaining goods by false pretences. To be tried in the District Court, a number of steps must be followed.

First, the District Justice must be satisfied that the offence is one fit to be tried summarily. This requires the Justice to examine the factual circumstances relating to the particular (alleged) crime and then to decide whether those circumstances make the offence a minor or a non-minor offence. The Justice is entitled to change his mind in the course of hearing the case, even after he has originally decided that the matter can be dealt with summarily: see *The State (O'Hagan) v. Delap* [1983] I.L.R.M. 241 and *Feeney v. Clifford*, [1988] I.R. 499.

The second step is that the accused must be informed of the right to have the case tried before a jury, and that the accused does not object to having the case tried in the District Court. In this context, the accused will most likely be aware of the fact that if the case is heard in the District Court the maximum penalty which may be imposed will be twelve months' imprisonment and/or a fine. Generally speaking, the maximum sentence possible in a higher court is substantially greater.

Third, in some instances the consent of the Director of Public Prosecutions is required in addition to the first two steps mentioned above. Sometimes consent is only required where there is damage to property over a certain limit. An example of where the consent is required without reference to any property damage is assault with intent to resist arrest, an offence under s.38 of the Offences against the Person Act, 1861. In relation to demanding money with menaces (blackmail), an offence under s.29 of the Larceny Act, 1916, the Director's consent to summary trial in the District Court is required (in addition to the two steps mentioned above) where the money demanded exceeds £200.

A list (up to date to early 1983) of indictable offences, including those triable summarily, is contained in Appendix H of Ryan and Magee, *The Irish Criminal Process* (Mercier, 1983).

(iv) *Under the Extradition Act 1965*, the District Court is empowered to decide at first instance whether a request for extradition should be granted. Where it is granted, the Court may designate the point of departure at which custody of the person is handed over to the requesting State.

2. The Circuit Court

The Circuit Court was established by s.4 of the Courts (Establishment and Constitution) Act, 1961. Like the District Court, the Circuit Court is a unified court presided over by the President of the Circuit Court; and it is also a local and limited jurisdiction court within the meaning of Article 34.3.4° of the Constitution. Again, the Court is only empowered to deal with those matters which have been expressly assigned to it by legislation. It is also, pursuant to s.21 of the Courts (Supplemental Provisions) Act, 1961, a court of record.

The Circuit Court: Civil Cases.

(i) *General.* In general, the Circuit Court has the same jurisdiction, in terms of subject matter, as the High Court; that is the effect of s.22 of the Courts (Supplemental Provisions) Act, 1961. There is no limit to the jurisdiction of the Circuit Court in relation to contract or tort cases. This has the effect, for example, that the Circuit Court is empowered to hear cases of defamation and false imprisonment which are outside the jurisdiction of the District Court. But a practical limit on the Circuit Court's jurisdiction is the monetary limits set from time to time, most recently in the Courts Act, 1981. But, as we will see below, the Circuit Court can be conferred with an unlimited jurisdiction by consent of the parties. In civil cases, the Circuit Court consists of a judge sitting alone, Circuit Court civil juries having been abolished by the Courts Act, 1971.

(ii) *Monetary*. The monetary limit specified by the Courts Act, 1981 is £15,000, but under s.48 of the Courts of Justice Act, 1924 the parties to a Circuit Court action can, if both of them consent, confer unlimited jurisdiction on the Court. This consent must be in writing and in the form prescribed for this purpose by the Rules of the Circuit Court, 1950.

(iii) *Land*. In relation to issues involving title to land, the Court has jurisdiction where the poor law valuation does not exceed £200.

(iv) *Equity Suits*. In relation to cases involving the dissolution of a partnership, the partition or sale of land, specific performance and injunctions (all of which are usually called equity matters or equity suits), where the subject-matter does not exceed £15,000 or include land of a poor law valuation greater than £200.

(v) *Landlord and Tenant*. Since the enactment of the Courts of Justice Act, 1924, the Circuit Court has dealt with landlord and tenant cases on an exclusive basis. For example, all claims for new leases, whether business or private, are assigned to the Circuit Court under the Landlord and Tenant (Amendment) Act, 1980. This jurisdiction applies regardless of the amount of rent payable or the value of the property in question.

(vi) *Malicious Injuries*. A similar exclusive jurisdiction for the Circuit Court arises from the Malicious Injuries Acts, 1981 and 1986. Up to 1986, the Circuit Court heard many thousands of cases each year in which owners of property sought compensation from local authorities for damage to their property if it was caused maliciously. The cost to local authorities was enormous. Under the Malicious Injuries (Amendment) Act, 1986, a claim may now only be made where the damage is caused in the course of a riot or arising from the activites of an unlawful organisation or an organisation advocating the use of violence related to Northern Ireland. The 1986 Act has, therefore, led to a large decrease in the number of malicious injuries cases in the Circuit Court.

(vii) *Intoxicating Liquor*. Under the Intoxicating Liquor Acts, the Circuit Court is, again, given exclusive jurisdiction to grant (or refuse) applications for new intoxicating liquor licences. This is not affected by the provisions of the Courts (No.2) Act, 1986 which, as we saw above, has limited the jurisdiction of the District Court in relation to renewals of licences.

(viii) *Family law*. Under the Courts Act, 1981, the Circuit Court was given new power to hear cases involving judicial separation (divorce *a mensa et thoro*) as well as in relation to maintenance and other family law matters. While the intention of the 1981 Act seemed to be to have all such cases heard in the Circuit Court, it was decided in the High Court in *R. v. R.* [1984] I.R. 296 that the High Court itself retained a concurrent jurisdiction in relation to these areas of law by virtue of the provisions of Article 34 of the Constitution referred to in the previous section. This resulted in many such cases being heard in the High Court, while others were assigned to the Circuit Court.

Under the Judicial Separation and Family Law Reform Act, 1989, the Circuit Court will be known as the 'Family Court', and new procedures designed to make the court atmosphere more suitable to such cases are due to be introduced when the 1989 Act becomes fully operational. The effect of *R. v. R.*, however, would appear to be that the High Court will still retain jurisdiction in this area. And, as discussed in the next section dealing with the High Court, *R. v. R.* clearly casts a constitutional shadow over the legislation conferring exclusive jurisdiction on the Circuit Court relating to landlord and tenant and malicious injuries. However, these powers remain in operation unless they are successfully challenged in the High Court.

The Circuit Court: Criminal Cases

The significant feature of the Circuit Court as a criminal court is that it consists of a Circuit Court judge and a jury. Given the requirements of Article 38.5, referred to above, the Circuit Court is entitled to hear serious criminal cases.

S.25 of the Courts (Supplemental Provisions) Act, 1961 provides that the Circuit Court is entitled to hear all indictable cases which the High Court (the Central Criminal Court) may hear. But exempted from this were a number of serious criminal offences, specified in s.25(2) of the 1961 Act. These reserved offences, which only the Central Criminal Court is entitled to hear, are: (i) treason (an offence defined by Article 39 of the Constitution, with some further details being dealt with in the Treason Act, 1939); (ii) offences under ss.2 or 3 of the Treason Act, 1939, namely encouragement or misprision of (concealing knowledge of) treason, respectively; (iii) offences under ss.6, 7 or 8 of the Offences against the State Act, 1939, namely, offences relating to the usurpation of the functions of government, obstruction of government and obstruction of the President, respectively; (iv) murder, attempt to murder or conspiracy to murder; (v) piracy; and (vi) offences under the Genocide Act, 1973.

Finally, a comment in relation to rape and other serious sexual assaults. At present these cases are dealt with in the Circuit Criminal Court. If the Criminal Law (Rape) (Amendment) Bill, 1988 is enacted these offences will in future be tried in the High Court (the Central Criminal Court). This will be done on foot of the recommendations of the Law Reform Commission *Report on Rape* (1988) as a measure of the seriousness of the offences.

A first reading of s.25 of the 1961 Act might indicate that many serious criminal offences, such as manslaughter and rape, could be tried in the Circuit Court. However the position was more complicated because prior to the Courts Act, 1981, it was permissible for an accused person to apply for a transfer of a trial from the Circuit Court to the High Court, and such transfer was mandatory when requested. Many such transfers were granted in practice. This right of transfer was abolished by s.31 of the Courts Act, 1981. These provisions were held to be constitutionally valid in *Tormey v. Ireland* [1985] I.R. 289 (Extract 13.3) and *The State (Boyle) v. Neylon* [1986] I.R. 551.

The position now is that where, for example, an accused person is due to be charged in the Circuit Court outside Dublin, an application for transfer to the Circuit Court sitting in Dublin may be made, but transfer to the High Court is not possible. The effect is that, since 1981, the provisions of s.25 of the 1961 Act may now be relied on as reflecting exactly what happens in practice, namely that the High Court only hears the 'reserved' offences, while the Circuit Court hears all other serious indictable offences.

3. The High Court

The High Court was established by s.2 of the Courts (Establishment and Constitution) Act, 1961. Bearing in mind the provisions of Article 34.3.1° referred to above, the Constitution has invested the High Court with powers over and above those given to the lower courts. This reflects the position of the High Court prior to independence as a court possessing inherent powers, and as having substantial supervisory functions in relation to the inferior courts. While Article 34.3.1° appears to give the High Court 'full original jurisdiction in and power to determine all matters and questions whether of law or fact, civil or criminal', this has not generally been taken quite as literally as it appears. Thus, the lower courts can be given functions over certain matters, as described in the preceding sections—otherwise there would be no point in having other courts, and the Constitution itself envisages such other courts. However, Article 34.3.1° has been interpreted to have a two-fold effect in this regard.

First, Article 34.3.1° has the effect that the High Court cannot be prevented from having some role, such as on appeal or by way of its traditional supervisory functions under what is now the procedure for judicial review (see Chapter 8 below). For discussion of this see, for example, *Tormey v. Ireland* [1985] I.R. 289 (Extract 13.3).

Second, there is some doubt as to whether a lower court can validly be given exclusive jurisdiction over an entire subject-matter. In relation to the provisions of the Courts Act, 1981, which appeared to give the Circuit Court exclusive jurisdiction in certain family law cases, it was decided in *R. v. R.* [1984] I.R. 295 that the High Court still retained its 'full' jurisdiction under Article 34.4.1°. Taking account of these difficulties, therefore, the jurisdiction of the High Court is as provided for in legislation, subject to whatever the Constitution, by implication, has additionally (or concurrently, bearing in mind the decision in *R. v. R.* [1984] I.R. 296) been reserved to the High Court. This reality is even reflected in s.8 of the Courts (Supplemental Provisions) Act, 1961, which states that the Court shall have 'such original and other jurisdiction as is prescribed by the Constitution'; and then s.8 goes on to specify that the High Court is invested with such jurisdiction as was vested in the former High Court under the Courts of Justice Act, 1924. What follows, therefore, is what is generally understood in practice to be the current jurisdiction of the High Court.

The High Court: Civil Cases

In civil cases, the High Court usually consists of one judge only. Since the passing of the Courts Act, 1988, juries sit only in High Court civil actions for defamation, false imprisonment and malicious prosecution. Prior to the 1988 Act, juries also sat in personal injuries civil actions.

(i) *General.* The effect of the Courts Act, 1981 is that the High Court is the appropriate court to hear cases involving claims for damages of £15,000 and over (subject to the unlimited consent jurisdiction of the Circuit Court). There is no legislation which has set an upper ceiling on the damages which may be awarded by the High Court. The result is that, for example, most of the serious personal injuries cases are heard in the High Court. As well as such personal injury cases, most business contract cases will be heard in the High Court as the consequences of breaking business contracts will usually involve a loss of over £15,000.

(ii) *Constitutional cases*. As mentioned earlier in this Chapter, Article 34.3.2° conferred on the High Court the exclusive function of determining the constitutional validity of legislation. No other court, other than the Supreme Court on appeal from the High Court, may make such a determination.

(iii) *Companies*. The Companies Act, 1963 has designated the High Court as the court with exclusive jurisdiction in relation to matters arising from the operation of the Act.

(iv) *Bankruptcy.* Similarly the Bankruptcy Act, 1988 continues the long standing position of the High Court as the court which deals exclusively with bankruptcy cases, regardless of the amount involved.

(v) *Chancery*. Under s.24 of the Courts of Justice Act, 1924, as carried over by s.8 of the Courts (Supplemental Provisions) Act, 1961, the types of cases, particularly those associated with land, which were dealt with in the Chancery Division of the High Court prior to independence continue to be dealt with in the High Court. In practice, while there are no divisions within the High Court, such chancery matters are channelled in administrative terms quite separately from other cases and will be heard by judges whose expertise lies in this area. Company law cases are also dealt with by the High Court chancery judges. It should be remembered that the Circuit Court has some limited jurisdiction in this chancery also.

(vi) *Wardship.* S.9 of the Courts (Supplemental Provisions) Act, 1961 devolved onto the High Court the jurisdiction in relation to 'lunacy and minor matters' formerly exercised by the Lord Chancellor of Ireland and the Lord Chief Justice of Ireland. S.9 provides that this jurisdiction is usually exercised by the President of the High Court. This involves conferring the status of a ward of court onto a person of unsound mind or a minor (that is, a person under 18 years of age: see the Age of Majority Act, 1985) whose property requires administration by the High Court.

The High Court: Criminal Cases

Like the Circuit Court, the High Court consists of a High court judge and jury when it sits as a criminal court, so that consequently it is entitled, in accordance with Article 38.5, to hear serious criminal cases. The effects of the Courts (Supplemental Provisions) Act, 1961 and subsequent legislation has already been outlined in the section dealing with the Circuit Court, so it is not necessary to repeat those provisions. Briefly, the effect is that the High Court now deals with only a limited category of criminal matters, such as treason and murder and, if the Criminal Law (Rape) (Amendment) Bill, 1981 is enacted, rape and other serious sexual assaults.

There is one important point as to the title of the High Court when hearing criminal cases. S.11 of the Courts (Supplemental Provisions) Act, 1961 states that the High Court exercising its criminal jurisdiction 'shall be known' as the Central Criminal Court. This designation is in keeping with the pre-independence position by which the principal criminal court in Ireland was known as the Central Criminal Court (as is the position in England at present where its Central Criminal Court is also known by the place where it sits, the Old Bailey). In practice the High Court as a criminal court is always referred to as the Central Criminal Court, whether being referred to in newspaper reports or by other judges: see for example *Travers v. Ryan* [1985] I.L.R.M. 343. But in *The People v. Bell* [1969] I.R.

24, Walsh J. pointed out that the Constitution had given the High Court one name, whether dealing with civil or criminal matters. Thus, the title 'Central Criminal Court' may in fact be an invalid title for the High Court, but it remains at the least its colloquial title.

4. The Special Criminal Court

The title 'Special Criminal Court' provides two clues as to the nature of particular court. In the first place it is a court which functions in relation to criminal trials only. As to its being 'special', the Court derives its legal basis from Article 38.3 of the Constitution. Article 38.3.1° states:

'Special courts may be established by law for the trial of offences in cases where it may be determined in accordance with such law that the ordinary courts are inadequate to secure the effective administration of justice, and the preservation of public peace and order.'

And Article 38.3.2° states: 'The constitution, powers, jurisdiction and procedure of such courts shall be prescribed by law.' The relevant law enacted in accordance with Article 38.2 is Part V of the Offences against the State Act, 1939. This provides for the establishment of special criminal courts where the government issues an order specifying that it is satisfied that the ordinary courts are inadequate to secure the effective administration of justice and the preservation of public peace and order. This formula is taken verbatim from Article 38.3 of the Constitution. Part V of the 1939 Act also provides for the matters referred to in Article 38.3.2° of the Constitution, namely the composition of the court as well as providing for the detailed procedures by which it is to operate.

One of the important features of the 1939 Act as far as special criminal courts is concerned is that it is possible to have cases transferred from the ordinary criminal courts, that is, the District Court, the Circuit Court and the High Court. This can be effected in one of two ways.

First, the 1939 Act provides that certain lists of offences may be specified as offences in relation to which the ordinary courts are always to be deemed inadequate within the terms of Article 38.3.1° of the Constitution. These offences are referred to as 'scheduled offences', and the government is entitled to compile a list of such offences by statutory instrument. The current list of scheduled offences, contained in the Offences against the State (Scheduled Offences) Order, 1972, are: (a) any offence under the Malicious Damage Act, 1861; (b) an offence under s.7 of the Conspiracy and Protection of Property Act, 1875; (c) any offence under the Explosive Substances Act, 1883; (d) any offence under the Firearms Acts, 1925 to 1971; and (e) any offence under the Offences against the State Act, 1939 itself.

Even where an offence is not a scheduled offence, however, such as murder, an individual trial may be transferred to a special criminal court where the Director of Public Prosecutions issues a certificate stating that in his opinion the ordinary courts are inadequate to secure the effective administration of justice and the preservation of public peace and order. Once such a certificate is issued the case must be transferred by the ordinary court to a special criminal court. The courts have indicated that they will be extremely reluctant to invalidate such a transfer even where the accused person claims he has no connection with any terrorist type organisation: see *Savage v. Director of Public Prosecutions* [1982] I.L.R.M. 385 and *Judge v. Director of Public Prosecutions* [1984] I.L.R.M. 224.

Special Criminal Courts do not exist on a permanent basis; as noted they only come into existence when a government order has been made bringing into effect Part V of the Offences against the State Act, 1939. Such an order has been made on two occasions. The first was at the outset of World War II in 1939. The special criminal courts continued to operate until 1946, when in effect they ceased to function, though the government order bringing Part V of the 1939 Act was not actually revoked. And the special criminal courts were revived in 1961 and 1962 to deal with a number of offences connected with what was termed the I.R.A. 'border campaign' of that time. In 1972, a new government order was issued bringing Part V of the 1939 Act into force, and a single special criminal court was established. That court has continued to operate since that date dealing with cases primarily connected with subversive activities and those connected with criminal acts related to Northern Ireland.

The present Special Criminal Court differs in a number of respects from the previous manifestations of World War II and the early 1960s. Apart from the fact that there has only been a need to have one such court at a time, the most significant difference is its composition. The 1939 Act permits the government to appoint officers of the Defence Forces to sit as judges of a special criminal court. But since 1972, the Special Criminal Court has always consisted of judges of the ordinary courts, whether sitting or retired. This must, to some extent, be attributed to the growing awareness that where a person is being charged with an ordinary criminal offence then the least that should be required of the tribunal which is to determine the matter is that it be composed of legally qualified persons. A panel of 9 judges is available to the government to appoint from time to time to sit, when required, to hear cases in the Special Criminal Court. Each time the Court sits it is comprised of three judges, consisting of one High Court judge, one Circuit Court judge and one District Justice. The High Court judge presides. As mentioned, any of these three might either be a sitting or retired judge or Justice as the case may be.

It is arguable that this basic composition of the present Special Criminal Court has rendered it proof from constitutional challenge. Nonetheless, there have been numerous such challenges, all of which have been unsuccessful. Two related to the Court when previously established: *In re MacCurtain* [1941] I.R. 43 and *The People v. Doyle* (1943) 77 I.L.T.R. 108. In relation to the present Court see *In re the Criminal Law (Jurisdiction) Bill, 1975* [1977] I.R. 129, *Eccles v. Ireland* [1985] I.R. 545 and *McGlinchey v. Governor of Portlaoise Prison*, High Court (Divisional), unreported, 14 and 17 December 1987 and 13 January 1988, Supreme Court, 29 July 1988.

5. The Supreme Court

The Supreme Court was established by s.1(1) of the Courts (Establishment and Constitution) Act, 1961. Primarily the Supreme Court is an appeal court, as can be seen from Chapter 6, below. There are, however, two provisions of the Constitution which allow for the Court to hear matters at first instance.

Firstly, Article 12.3.1° states that where the President of Ireland is to lose office by virtue of permanent incapacity, this must be established to the satisfaction of the Supreme Court consisting of not less than five judges. This issue has never arisen for decision since 1937.

However, the other first instance function of the Supreme Court has been of more practical importance. Pursuant to Article 26 of the Constitution, the President of Ireland may, after consultation with the Council of State, refer a Bill passed by both Houses of the Oireachtas to the Supreme Court which is required to pronounce on whether the Bill, or any provision of the Bill, is repugnant to the Constitution. The President is prohibited by Article 26.3.1° of the Constitution from signing into law any Bill which is held in any respect repugnant to the Constitution.

For the purpose of an Article 26 reference, the Court must consist of at least five judges. The decision of a majority of the judges shall be, Article 26.2.2° provides, the decision of the Court and this provision also states that the decision is to be pronounced by one judge from the majority and that no other opinion whether it is assenting or dissenting is to be disclosed. On the difficulties of a collegiate decision, see Chapters 3 and 11.

There have been eight references to the Court to date under Article 26 of the Constitution: *In re the Offences against the State (Amendment) Bill 1940* [1940] I.R. 470 (not repugnant); *In re the School Attendance Bill 1942* [1943] I.R. 334 (repugnant); *In re the Electoral (Amendment) Bill 1961* [1961] I.R. 169 (not repugnant); *In re the Criminal Law (Jurisdiction) Bill 1975* [1977] I.R. 129 (not repugnant); *In re the Emergency Powers Bill 1976* [1977] I.R. 159 (not repugnant); *In re the Housing (Private Rented Dwellings) Bill 1981* [1983] I.R. 181 (repugnant); *In re the Electoral (Amendment) Bill 1983* [1984] I.R. 268 (repugnant); and *In re the Adoption (No.2) Bill 1987* [1989] I.L.R.M. 266 (not repugnant).

It should be remembered that, while the Article 26 reference procedure has proved useful, the vast majority of constituional cases have arisen where an individual citizen has brought a case to the High Court alleging that legislation, or some other instrument, or even the activity of private citizens, is acting in contravention of the rights contained in the Constitution. Thus the Article 26 procedure remains, and will remain, by comparison relatively underused as far as the development of constitutional law is concerned. One reason for this is that where the Court upholds the constitutionality of the legislation under review, that renders the legislation immune from further constitutional challenge at any time in the future. This builds in a degree of inflexibility which is not regarded as appropriate.

Chapter 5

COURT PROCEDURE

In this Chapter we outline some of the basic rules of procedure which are set out in rules of court and some conventions of practice. The basic requirement of the law is that before a case may proceed to Court certain documents must be drafted and filed in Court and given to the other party to the court proceedings. This basic requirement of advance notice from one side to the other applies in both civil and criminal cases but the precise mechanisms by which this is achieved is substantially different in both areas of the law. It is thus important to distinguish between the two.

CIVIL PROCEDURE

In civil cases it is important for both sides to be fully informed of the basic outline of the legal case being made by the other side so that there can be no complete suprises when and if the case comes to court. This is achieved by the mechanism of requiring both sides to furnish written summaries of their cases to other. These summaries are called *pleadings.* It is as well to note immediately that there is a major difference between these pleadings and what is sometimes called pleading on behalf of a client. Pleadings are the bread and butter of a barrister's legal work, and they are written documents drafted on the basis of extremely old rules and requirements to state with great care the claim being made by the plaintiff or defendant. It was once the case that even the slightest fault in the pleadings could result in a case being dismissed by a court. This result can still occur on occasion and the fear of such a calamitous result for a client has resulted in barristers taking an ultra cautious approach to the wording of pleadings. The result is that the pleadings are written in language which might appear more at home in the late 19th Century but that language is based on the notion that erring on the side of caution is the better course than attempting to draft pleadings which are a delight to read.

For example, take the case of a personal injuries action in which the initial pleadings were filed in Court two years and six months after the accident to which they relate. If the barrister has failed to state a basic legal ground on which the case either stands or falls the matter may be thrown out of court. But the defect may not be discovered until, say, a year later, that is three and a half years after the accident. It will then be impossible to recommence proceedings because the relevant time limit under the Statute of Limitations, 1957 has expired (see Chapter 1). The result of this possible fear is, as mentioned, that the pleadings tend to be over-inclusive documents which attempt to cover every possible ground on which the plaintiff or defendant might have a cause of action.

It may also be noted here that the requirements of the rules of court differ from one court to another. The most complex rules of court so far as all aspects of procedure and pleadings are concerned are those which apply in the High Court and Supreme Court. These are the Rules of the Superior Courts, 1986. The requirements for the Circuit Court, set out in the Rules of the Circuit Court, 1950, are significantly less complex, while those for the District Court, contained in the District Court Rules, 1948 do not set out pleadings requirements as such at all. Each of these sets of rules are secondary legislation enacted under different enabling statutes. The other point to make is that substantial changes are made from time to time in the rules of court in the light of new insights into problems which have come to light in litigation or where new legislation has been enacted to deal with a particular problem.

We will provide in what follows a brief description of the course of civil proceedings in the High Court. This should not be taken in any way as a definitive account of a typical High Court case, but is simply designed to indicate the kind of language which appears in pleadings which, as indicated above, is a staple of the practice of law and must become familar to any practising lawyer.

Under the Rules of the Superior Courts, 1986 (which in essence update but continue in force the system of practice which had developed in the court system by the end of the 19th Century), there are three basic forms of initiating documents for the broad range of civil cases which are dealt with by the High Court. These documents are all give the title *summonses*. In addition the 1986 Rules provide for initiating documents called *petitions*, which are used in relation to family law matters and also company law matters. Yet another form of procedure is provided for in relation to seeking orders for judicial review (see Chapter 8). For present purposes, we will concentrate on the summonses only.

The first of the initiating documents is called the *Summary Summons*, which is the appropriate document used in relation to claims for what is called a liquidated sum of money. This means a sum of money which can be readily calculated. A typical case in which a summary summons may be issued is where a bank claims that, on default of a loan given by the bank, a customer owes a certain sum of money. Obviously, there may be complex calculations as to the rate of interest payable in order to calculate the precise sum owing on the date when the case comes to Court, but once the sum can be calculated by reference to rates of interest which were agreed when the loan was taken out, then the Summary Summons procedure is the appropriate initiating document in the High Court.

The second form of initiating document is the *Special Summons*, which is used primarily for legal disputes relating to land, for example, a claim by a building society that, on foot of a mortgage on which a person has defaulted the building society is entitled to possession of the property. These special summonses will be dealt with by what are, in effect, the Chancery judges of the High Court. Although as indicated in Chapter 1, the divisions of the High Court were abolished on the passing of the Courts of Justice Act, 1924, the administrative arrangements within the Court system still exist by which such cases are directed towards particular judges who deal on a regular basis with these areas of law.

Finally, the third major initiating document in the High Court is the *Plenary Summons*, which is used, in effect, in relation to all other cases which are not appropriate for either a summary or special summons; it is the residual catch all form of High Court Summons. The Plenary Summons is used, for example, in relation to any claim which it is anticipated requires a full hearing requiring oral evidence under oath. It is also used where the amount of damages claimed cannot be reduced to a liquidated sum of money. Thus, the many thousands of personal injuries actions which take up much of the time of the High Court in civil matters are plenary summonses cases. This is because, although an experienced barrister, whether junior or senior, may have an accurate estimation of the amount of compensation which would be reasonable for, say, a severe back injury or a partial limb amputation, there is no definitive system for calculating in advance the precise sum of money which should be awarded in damages. Other plenary summonses cases would include defamation claims. It is the Plenary Summons procedure which we will use as an example of the pleadings system.

When a barrister receives instructions in relation to a personal injuries action, it is clear that the plenary summons procedure is the appropriate path to take. The first document must be filed by the plaintiff in the action and invariably the plaintiff is the person who has been injured. The example we will use is of a person who has been injured in the eye by fragments of glass from an abrasive wheel (which is a rotating wheel used to grind metals and other materials such as glass) while working for a company which manufactures glass. The barrister will, as indicated, know that this injury is quite serious and, although the medical prognosis for the employee may not be fully known at the time the barrister is first instructed, it will be regarded as in most cases being sufficiently serious to warrant being brought in the High Court. In other words, the barrister will make an estimation that the level of damages which might be received by the employee would be over £15,000, the level set by the Courts Act, 1981 as the basic minimum level for the High Court (see Chapter 4). This estimation will be made on the basis of an assumption that the employee was not at all to blame for the accident in question.

The first document in the Plenary Summons procedure is the plenary summons itself, which includes blank spaces into which are inserted the parties' names and a brief outline of the claim being made by the plaintiff. This brief outline is referred to as the *General Indorsement of Claim.* The relevant outline for our example might be as follows:

> The Plaintiff's Claim is for Damages for Personal Injuries Arising from the Breach of Duty of the Defendant his servant or agents.

This may seem a relatively uninformative list of information but it is merely the first stage in what becomes later an increasingly complex and, sometimes, long drawn out process. The Plenary Summons itself consists of three standard form pages, the basic contents of which are set out in the Rules of the Superior Courts, 1986, in Appendix A. The first page of the Plenary Summons is as follows:

THE HIGH COURT

19   No. [Official Number]

Between   Raymond Byrne   Plaintiff

and   McCutcheon Glass Company Limited   Defendant

To the defendant [Name] of [Address]

This plenary summons is to require that within eight days after the service thereon upon you (exclusive of the day of such service) you in person or by solicitor do enter an appearance in the Central Office, Four Courts, Dublin in the above action; and TAKE NOTICE that, in default of your so doing, the plaintiff may proceed therein, and judgment may be given in your absence.

BY ORDER, Thomas A. Finlay,

Chief Justice of Ireland,
the day of one thousand nine hundred and

N.B.—This summons is to be served within twelve calendar months from the date hereof, and, if renewed within six calendar months from the date of the last renewal, including the day of such such date, and not afterwards.

The defendant may appear hereto by entering an appearance either personally or by solicitor at the Central Office, Four Courts, Dublin.

It may be noted that the Summons is, in effect, a call by order of the Chief Justice to the defendant to answer the claim by the plaintiff in the case. This form of initiating document has medieval roots, because it reflects the form of the old writs issued in the Lord Chancellor's Department, issued in those days of course on the authority of the monarch. That is, indeed, the form of summons which continues to operate in England to the present day.

The official number which appears at the top of the plenary summons is important administratively. It identifies the case for the court officials who receive any further pleadings which are delivered in the case as well as identifying the case should it proceed to court hearing. The plenary summons is brought to the Central Office of the High Court in the Four Courts, usually by the solicitor for the plaintiff and, if it appears to be in the correct format set out in the 1986 Rules, it will be accepted by the officials of the High Court Central Office. The plenary summons will then be given its official court number and the fact that a plenary summons has been issued will be entered in the Central Office records. These records include sufficient space to record any subsequent pleadings. Once the summons has been entered in the Central Office records, it is officially stamped, in accordance with the requirements of the 1986 Rules. It then becomes an official court document which may be served on the defendant. In fact the original summons is retained by the court officials, and the plaintiff's solicitor will serve on the defendant what is called a certified copy of the original summons.

The second page of the plenary summons contains the space for the general indorsement of claim, in the form of the indorsement given above. In addition, there must be filled in on this part of the summons the information that the summons was served on the defendant, usually at his residence, or in this case where a company is being sued as employer, at its registered place of business. It also contains a space for the insertion of the place of residence of the plaintiff and where court documents in response to the summons may be served.

The filing of the plenary summons has a great significance for the law on the limitation period for bringing claims to court. If a plenary summons is correctly issued under the three year limitation period for personal injuries actions, then this is the crucial date for the Statute of Limitations, 1957. The 1957 Statute does not require that the case comes to hearing before a court within 3 years; all that is required is that the plenary summons is issued within that time.

Once the plenary summons is duly issued and then served on the defendant, it is up to the defendant to respond. As the first page of the plenary summons indicates there is an obligaton to enter an *appearance* within eight days of being served with the documents. In fact this requirement is not an absolute obligation and in many instances an appearance might not be entered for a number of weeks. If the plaintiff attempted to obtain a decision from the High Court nine days after serving a plenary summons on the defendant the Court would be most unlikely to grant such judgment without giving the defendant an opportunity of defending the case. In fact many of the time limits specified in the 1986 Rules for various stages of the court procedure are not adhered to, and it is usually a year or even longer before all the relevent documents are served on both sides so that the stage is reached when the case is ready for hearing.

As indicated, in response to the plenary summons, the defendant must enter an appearance. The Appearance is a very brief document which is, quite simply, an instruction to the Court that an appearance should be entered for the defendant and that the defendant intends to defend the claim brought. The appearance also usually indicates the solicitor representing the defendant and the address at which further pleadings may be served, usually the solicitor's office. The claim is then back in the plaintiff's hands.

The next document to be filed by the plaintiff is, usually, the *Statement of Claim* which provides in much more detail the circumstances surrounding the accident which is the subject matter of the case. The Statement of Claim is in a standard format as with the Plenary Summons, but in this instance the amount which must be filled in by the plaintiff is considerably greater. The relevant part which a barrister will draft would, in our example, be something along the following lines.

THE HIGH COURT

[Title and Parties as in the Plenary Summons]

1. The plaintiff, maintenance fitter, resides at 2 Sunnybank Terrace, in the City of Dublin.

2. The defendants are a limited liability company having their registered place of business at 23 Glass Lane, in the City of Dublin.

3. On or about the 23rd day of May 1989, the plaintiff suffered severe personal injury, loss, distress and damage while working at an abrasive wheel in the premises of the said defendants when he was struck in the eye by a fragment of glass which projected from the said abrasive wheel.

4. At the time of the said accident the plaintiff was the servant or agent of the said defendants, acting in the course of his employment.

5. The said personal injury, loss, distress and damage were caused solely by virtue of the breach of duty, including statutory duty, of the defendants, their servants or agents in or about the care, management and control of the said premises and more particularly the said abrasive wheel.

PARTICULARS OF PERSONAL INJURY

[In this portion of the Statement of Claim the barrister would insert information as to the extent of the eye injury which would be gleaned from the medical reports obtained by the plaintiff's solicitor. This could be in the form of a number of points relating to the immediate impact of the glass fragments, the extent to which this affected the eye immediately as well as some indication as to the prognosis. In addition, the particulars might add: 'Further adverse sequelae cannot be ruled out', a phrase which allows for subsequent medical information.]

PARTICULARS OF SPECIAL DAMAGE

[In this section the plaintiff will insert those items such as medical expenses and loss of earnings to date which are available. Some aspects of these claims may, however, be left over for further detailing later in the proceedings.]

PARTICULARS OF BREACH OF DUTY

[In this section the barrister will include the details of the manner in which it is alleged that the employer was in breach of some obligations which are owed by an employer to an employee in respect of safety in the workplace. The relevant legal rules may be found in the Employer's Liability Chapter of a book on the Law of Torts. The particulars might be as follows:]

The defendants, their servants or agents, were in breach of duty in that:
1. They failed to provide the plaintiff with a place of work which was reasonably safe in all the circumstances.
2. They failed to provide the plaintiff with plant and machinery which was reasonably safe in all the circumstances.
3. They failed to provide the plaintiff with a system of work which was reasonably safe in all the cirumstances.
4. They failed to provide the plaintiff with co-workers who were in the all the circumstances reasonably competent.
5. They exposed the plaintiff to a danger of which they knew, or ought reasonably to have known.
6. They exposed the plaintiff to danger from the said abrasive wheel of which they knew or ought reasonably to have known.
7. They failed to provide the plaintiff with any, or any adequate, training or supervision in relation to the use of the said abrasive wheel.
8. They were in breach of statutory duty and in particular of the provisions of the Safety in Industry Acts, 1955 and 1980 and the Safety in Industry (Abrasive Wheels) Regulations, 1982.

In the premises, the plaintiff claims damages in Negligence for severe personal injury, loss, distress and damage.
And the plaintiff claims costs.
And the plaintiff claims damages pursuant to the Courts Act, 1981.

[The names of counsel for the plaintiff
will appear here.]

As will be seen, the language of the Statement of Claim is careful, to what might appear to be an excessive degree. The reader may see many different aspects of this, so they need not be pointed out here. It is, however, the particulars of negligence which may be focused on in particular. The reader may notice a certain degree of overlap between the eight different paragraphs of the Statement of Particulars. The point here is that the barrister will wish to ensure that this aspect of the statement of claim is particularly comprehensive, even at the expense of being over-inclusive. In this context, particularly having regard to the Statute of Limitations, 1957, it is better to be sure than sorry.

It may be noted also there is a reference to legislation, both primary and secondary in claiming a breach of duty. The Safety in Industry Acts, 1955 and 1980 are to factories what the Road Traffic Acts, 1961 to 1984 are to motor car travel. The primary purpose of the legislation is to prevent accidents in the factory context by setting down standards which, if broken, may result in a prosecution of the employer in question. But, an employee who is injured in an accident which may be attributed to a failure to observe a statutory provision may also be able to claim compensation in such circumstances. Again, breach of statutory duty is a subject matter dealt with in texts on the Law of Torts, but the barrister will be aware that in relation to factories most of the provisions of the 1955 and 1980 Acts, and the regulations made under them, may be used in personal injuries claims (in other words, are actionable).

In response to the statement of claim, the defendants' approach may become more complex. One possible step is for the defendants to file a pleading known, simply, as the *Defence.* But they may not be happy with several aspects of the plaintiff's Statement of Claim. A defendant is entitled, under the Rules of the Superior Courts, 1986 to seek further information from the plaintiff in respect of the claim being made. This is called seeking *further and better particulars* of the claim and is an almost automatic procedure in personal injuries actions. The format of the claim for particulars is, usually, a letter to the solicitors for the plaintiff which lists the points in respect of which more detail is required. For example, the precise circumstances of the incident in which the glass fragment struck the plaintiff may be sought; the details of medical expenses, if these are not specified; and the precise provisions of the 1955 and 1980 Acts and of the 1982 Regulations in respect of which the defendants are alleged to be in breach. Having received satisfactory replies to these queries (in the absence of which the matter may be brought by way of motion to the High Court for a judge to determine whether the replies were in fact adequate) the defendants may then file a Defence in response to the Statement of Claim. This may be along the lines over.

THE HIGH COURT

[Title and name of Parties as in Plenary Summons]

DEFENCE

1. The alleged accident the subject matter of these proceedings did not occur in the manner alleged or at all.

2. The defendant denies that the premises are a factory within the meaning of the Safety in Industry Acts, 1955 and 1980, as alleged or at all.

3. The defendant denies that the plaintiff was injured in the manner alleged, or at all.

4. The defendant denies that the plaintiff suffered the alleged or any personal injury, loss, distress or damage as a result of the alleged accident or at all.

5. The defendant denies that it was by itself, its servants or agents or any of them guilty of the alleged or any negligence, breach of duty or breach of statutory duty as alleged or at all or in or about the matters alleged or at all.

6. Each and every particular of negligence and breach of duty including breach of statutory duty as alleged against the defendant its servants or agents is denied as if the same was herein set out and traversed seriatim.

7. If the plaintiff suffered the alleged or any personal injury, loss, distress or damage, which is denied, the same was not caused or contributed to as a result of any negligence or breach of duty or breach of statutory duty on the part of the defendant or any of its servants or agents.

8. The plaintiff was guilty of contributory negligence.

The above Defence indicates even further perhaps the somewhat stilted style of prose in which the Bar must engage, at least in written form. A cardinal rule of a Defence in civil proceedings is that each and every claim by the plaintiff must be denied. If the case goes to court, the plaintiff will then be obliged to prove each of the allegations contained in the Statement of Claim. If the defendant does not deny a particular claim made by the plaintiff, this is regarded as having been admitted by the defendant. Thus, the sense of 'overkill' by the defendant in the above instance. Note also that the defendant goes on the offensive at the end of the defence by claiming that the plaintiff was guilty of contributory negligence. Again, should the case proceed to hearing, the defendant will be allowed to argue that, even if as employer they were in breach of some obligation to the plaintiff then some action of the plaintiff, such as lack of due care, may at least allow the defendant to be held less than 100% responsible in terms of the amount of compensation payable.

In certain other cases also the defendant may go on the offensive to an even greater extent. For example, in a dispute over the sale of a car the plaintiff might be the seller who brings a claim for breach of contract against the buyer for non-payment. The buyer might not only put in a defence to such a claim but might also *counterclaim* against the seller on the basis that the car was defective causing the buyer to pay a certain sum in renting another car. If the defendant's case is believed in court, the defendant may be awarded damages in the sum of the cost of renting the other car, as well as dismissing the plaintiff's claim. This indicates that the defendant may, in a civil case, turn the tables completely.

When the parties have served all the pleadings which they consider necessary on each other it is said that the *pleadings have closed* and the case is now ready to be placed in the list of cases for which dates for hearing may be assigned in order of priority. On a regular basis the list of cases which are due for hearing on a specified date or dates are published in a document called the *Legal Diary*, which is published on a daily basis while the High Court is sitting. This Diary is posted up in the Law Library of the Four Courts where the Bar may consult it. Some members of the Bar and many of the larger firms of solicitors subscribe to the Legal Diary in order to keep themselves informed of forthcoming cases in which they are involved. In relation to the time period between the closing of pleadings and receiving a date for hearing, there was, in the early 1980s, a substantial time lag due to the large number of cases due for hearing. It might have taken perhaps 18 months after pleadings had closed for a case to receive a date for hearing. The period is much shorter at present, however, and a case will most likely be given a date for hearing within 6 months of the pleadings closing, and sometimes even within 6 months.

The above example of pleadings have dealt only with the Statement of Claim and Defence in a High Court plenary summons action. It by no means provides a comprehensive view of what the pleading process may involve or the length of time spent prior to a case coming to hearing in relation to the presentation of evidence for either side. In addition to the Statement of Claim and Defence, parties may wish to serve on each other further pleadings. Thus, where in a particular case a completely new issue is raised in the Defence, the plaintiff may serve on the defendant a *Reply*. And in response to the Reply, the defendant may issue a *Rejoinder*. This could be followed by a *Surrejoinder* from the plaintiff, and the process could, conceivably, continue on indefinitely. However, in most cases the Reply will mark the close of pleadings.

There are many other pre-trial remedies available to either side in a civil High Court action. As mentioned previously, a party may apply, for example, to Court where there has been failure to comply with some time limit specified by the Rules of the Superior Courts, 1986, such as in failing to enter an appearance within eight days from service. But, as also indicated, the Court is unlikely to enter judgment in favour of the plaintiff without giving the defendant an opportunity of putting the other side of the case and explaining the delay. There are many occasions in the course of a case proceeding through the court system in which such applications will come before the Court. These are always brought by way of motion to the Court, and must be on notice to the other side in the case. In most cases, these motions involve one side being given a specific period of time within which to, for example, file in the Central Office a Defence or Reply to a Notice for Particulars.

One important pre-trial remedy may be mentioned briefly, however. Subject to certain exceptions, either party is entitled under the Rules of the Superior Courts, 1986 to obtain possession of documents within the control of the other party. This process is known as the *discovery of documents*. In some instances this may simply amount to the exchange of originals which were in the possession of each party and there will be no dispute as to the scope of discovery. But over the years there have been many examples of cases in which documents obtained by discovery ('discovered' being used in a somewhat unusual manner in this context) have been the key to success in a case. As indicated there are limits to what may be sought on discovery. For example, any communications from a legal adviser which were obtained by one party at a time when court proceedings were either contemplated or were already started are absolutely privileged from discovery. In addition, one party cannot simply come to court on a fishing expedition, claiming that the other side has unnamed documents which would help the applicant's case; the discovery must be in relation to either a named document such as a letter or there must be some, even limited, basis on which something concrete can be identified. Up to the time of the 1986 Rules discovery could only be obtained by one party from another party to the proceedings, but now discovery may be obtained from a person who is not involved in the court proceedings provided that that non-party has relevant information. For an example, see *Tromso Sparebank v. Beirne (No.2)*, [1989] I.L.R.M. 257 (Extract 11.8).

There are other pre-trial remedies which are also available to either party in High Court civil proceedings, such as interrogatories, which it is not possible to deal with in this context.

The procedure in civil cases in the Circuit Court is, as indicated earlier, somewhat less complex than in the High Court, bearing in mind the fact that the Court tends to deal with cases of less monetary value, even if they may very well be important for those involved in the case. The basic originating document in the Circuit Court is the *Civil Bill*, which as we saw in Chapter 1 was the document used in the County Courts prior to 1922. The Civil Bill contains the equivalent of the High Court Statement of Claim from the plaintiff. In response, the Circuit Court Rules, 1950 provide for the defendant filing a Defence, which is in similar terms to the High Court Defence. There is no further provision for pleadings in the Circuit Court.

In the District Court, the originating document is called the *Civil Process*, and it usually contains a brief description of the claim made by the plaintiff. There is no provision in the District Court Rules, 1948 for any pleadings as such, and certainly not a defence. However, in practice, many solicitors will issue what amounts to a Defence by way of formal letter to the plaintiff. The lack of any formal pleading system in the District Court reflects the fact that in 1924 when it was established it heard cases of an extremely small nature. Since the ceiling on awards was lifted to £2,500 by the Courts Act, 1981, however, this lack of formality has created some problems in relation non-consumer type cases which are dealt with in the District Court and some changes to the present system would appear appropriate.

CRIMINAL PROCEDURE

There are two essential forms in which a criminal case comes to trial. The first method, used for relatively less serious criminal cases, is by way of *summons*. The second method, used in relation to more serious offences is by way of *indictment*. The categorisation system for criminal offences is a number of centuries old, and has not been updated as yet. One category of offences are *felonies*, which originally carried the death penalty. The other category of offence is the *misdemeanour.* In general, felonies are the more serious offences though of course many of them no longer carry the death penalty in the State. And, again, in general misdemeanours are the less serious type of offences. But this is not always the case, and a careful study of criminal procedure as a subject in itself is required before the correct mode of prosecution is chosen. Murder is a felony at common law, but for example assault occasionming actual bodily harm is a misdemeanour under common law and s.47 of the Offences against the Person Act, 1861 while assault with intent to rob is a felony under s.23 of the Larceny Act, 1916 (as amended by s.5 of the Criminal Law (Jurisdiction) Act, 1976).

To complicate the categorisation somewhat, in recent years where new criminal offences are created, they are not usually categorised as felonies or misdemeanours. Instead, the penalties attaching to the offence are specified by reference to whether the charge is brought by way of indictment or by summons. This mirrors the introduction in Britain in 1968 of the concept of an 'arrestable offence', an offence which carried a possible sentence of imprisonment of five years and for which a member of a police force could arrest without warrant. Although the 'arrestable offence' has not been introduced in Irish Law, much of the recent criminal law legislation is based on the five year period. An example is the Criminal Justice Act, 1984, which introduced new detention powers in respect of arrests for offences carrying five years imprisonment. The penalties on indictment are, necessarily, greater than on a summary prosecution. This arises from the fact that trial on indictment usually takes place before a jury, as required by Article 38 of the Constitution (see Chapter 4).

The initiation of many less serious crimes is a matter for a member of the Garda Síochána, for example under the Road Traffic Acts. Other minor offences created by legislation may be prosecuted by other regulatory authorities, for example local authorities in relation to the Local Government (Water Pollution) Act, 1977 or the Minister for Labour in relation to pay legislation.

In relation to a summary prosecution, the procedure is relatively straightforward. A summons is issued by a person authorised by legislation, usually a District Court Clerk on application by a member of the Garda Síochána, against the person alleged to have committed the offence, for example, driving a motor vehicle with an amount of alcohol in excess of that permitted under s.49 of the Road Traffic Act, 1961, as amended by s.10 of the Road Traffic (Amendment) Act, 1978. The summons contains the allegation of the offence together with information as to the registration number of the vehicle, the owner of the vehicle (who, if the driver, is also the person charged) and the date and location of the alleged offence. This summons is then the basis for the charge being brought to Court. There may be other evidence, such as the results of the test conducted by the Medical Bureau of Road Safety on the urine or blood sample which must be provided by the driver of the vehicle under the Road Traffic Acts. The summons is, however, the basic document on which the criminal trial in the District Court will take place.

As to trials on indictment the procedure is more complex. As indicated in Chapter 3, the prosecution is in the hands of the *Director of Public Prosecutions.* The office of the D.P.P. was created by the Prosecution of Offences Act, 1974. Up to that time prosecutions in serious cases were initiated by the Attorney General. It was felt, however, that an independent officer was required to discharge these functions, similar to the situation in England where the same office had been established in the 1940s. The Attorney General, however, retains some functions in relation to some cases such as under the Official Secrets Act, 1963. And the Director's functions may be transferred back to the Attorney at any time.

The reasons behind the decisions of the Director as to whether to prosecute are never made public in relation to individual cases, although the general principles are, basically, twofold. First, is there, on the evidence presented to the Director by the Garda Síochána, evidence to indicate that a conviction is likely? It may be noted that the Director does not play any investigative role as such and is dependent on the Gardaí in this regard. The second factor is whether the public interest lies in favour of a prosecution. These are, usually, factors which run together but in some instances the public interest may militate against a prosecution even where there is some evidence that a conviction is likely. The Director's decision is, as the law stands at present, final in relation to whether to prosecute and no successful private prosecution has ever been successfully taken in Ireland in recent years.

Once the decision is made to prosecute, the normal procedure is that a District Justice conducts a *preliminary examination* under the provisions of 27/A. the Criminal Procedure Act, 1967. Before the case leaves the District Court and is sent forward for trial in the relevant court of trial, the prosecution must provide to the defence all the evidence on which the prosecution intends to prosecute the defendant. All this material, colloquially called the *Book of Evidence*, is required under the terms of s.6 of the Criminal Procedure Act, 1967. It includes a statement of the charges, a list of the witnesses it is proposed to call at trial and their statements and a list of exhibits, if any. In the District Court the defence is entitled to cross-examine any prosecution witness but in many instances this does not take place, for tactical reasons, and any examination is left to the trial itself. The accused person is, usually, entitled to bail under the decision in *The People v. O'Callaghan* [1966] I.R. 501, thus being free up to the time of the trial.

The form of most indictments is specified in the Criminal Justice (Administration) Act, 1924, which simplified to a great extent the procedural requirements regarding an indictment. The Act also provides that defects in the indictment may be remedied at any time provided that this does not cause an injustice to the defendant.

The indictment is usually headed 'The People (at the suit of the Director of Public Prosceutions) v. [the person charged]' and then states the Court of trial. The indictment then states that '[The accused] is charged with the following offence[s]'. The core of the indictment then specifies the different offences, or counts, which are charged. Each count is in two parts: the *statement of the offence* and the *particulars of the offence*. The statement of the offence describes the offence in relatively straightforward language. For example, it might be: 'Assault with intent to rob, contrary to s.23 of the Larceny Act, 1916, as amended by s.5 of the Criminal Law (Jurisdciton) Act, 1976.' Where the offence is one created by statute it is necessary to specify the legislation, as amended if appropriate. The particulars of the offence then sets out the circumstances in which it is alleged that the defendant committed the offence, but these particulars are not always as specific as the particulars in a civil pleading. In the above example, the date and place of the assault and the allegation that there was an intent to rob may be specified as having taken place on a particular date, but in the case of murder, the precise date may be unknown so that the particulars may state 'on a date unknown'. This is an acceptable form of particulars.

PROCEDURE IN COURT

The system of law which operates in common law countries is an *adversarial* system. This means that the judge in a case plays the role of impartial referee between two sides in the contest which takes place in the courtroom. The two sides, and their lawyers, play what has been described as a 'mutually antagonistic role', but this simply means that each side presents and argues its side; there are rarely any 'antagonistic' theatricals.

The basis for any court hearing, whether civil or criminal, is the requirement that evidence to the Court must be given under oath. This is, of course, the requirement in most legal systems, and its origins reflect the religious basis of much of our law. The oath originally had both a spiritual and temporal aspect, but in recent times the temporal aspect is more important. Giving false evidence under oath constitutes the crime of perjury and although prosecutions and convictions for perjury are relatively rare they still constitute as much of a deterrent as any other criminal sanction.

To a great extent also, the adversarial system, and the common law, has long regarded *oral testimony* as being of high value in relation to proving a particular assertion (usually stated as being of high probative value). The reason for this lies in the fact that the oral testimony is tested in court, the judge (and where relevant the jury) will have an opportunity to see the reaction of the witness and to test the veracity of the evidence given on that basis. Thus, oral testimony is of crucial importance. Nonetheless, there are many instances in which written sworn evidence is used in Court proceedings.

These written sworn pieces of evidence are referred to as *affidavits*. In civil cases in particular, they are used as the basis for many preliminary applications to Court. For example, a motion for discovery of documents will be supported by an affidavit ('grounded on an affidavit' is the usual phrase) which sets out in relatively simple language the basis for the application to Court. The affidavit is actually sworn in the presence of a person called a Commissioner for Oaths, who in Dublin is usually also a solicitor, and once this is done the document is admissible as evidence in Court. A slightly different mechanism is available for non-contentious evidence in criminal proceedings. Ss.21 and 22 of the Criminal Justice Act, 1984 provide for proof of certain matters by way of *formal statement* and *formal admission*. It should be noted that these statements and admissions are not sworn statements and they do not relate in any way to the admission of confessions as evidence. They relate only to matters which are accepted as correct by both prosecution and defence. Such a system does not, however, operate in civil proceedings. Thus, even a witness whose evidence is accepted by both sides may be required to attend in Court to formally prove certain matters in order to satisfy the rules of evidence.

Apart from the circumstances indicated above in which written evidence may be admissible, the normal rules of evidence of most important issues in dispute is to require <u>oral evidence</u>. In a civil case, the witnesses for the plaintiff are called to give evidence by the plaintiff's counsel or solicitor as the case may be. After examination by the plaintiff's lawyer (which is called examination-in-chief), the witness for the plaintiff may then be <u>cross-examined</u> by the lawyer appearing for the defendant. Similar procedure operates in relation to the witnesses for the defendant, if any. In civil cases it is quite common for the two sides to give evidence, but the procedure in criminal cases is governed to a large extent by the operation of the *presumption of innocence*, another central feature of the common law system of criminal justice.

The <u>presumption of innocence</u> is the practical expression of the *accusatorial* nature of the common law criminal justice system (and is in a sense the twin to the adversarial aspect of the system). Under the accusatorial approach (as opposed to the *inquisitorial* system of Civil Law systems), the State may accuse a person of having committed a crime but it <u>must prove that case by</u> independently gathered evidence which the State possesses and without resorting to evidence from the defendant. This is modifed somewhat by allowing the State to rely on incriminating statements (colloquially called confessions) which were made by the accused person to, for example, a member of the Garda Síochána while the accused was in custody under a lawful arrest.

Under the accusatorial system, the presumption of innocence means that the <u>defendant is entitled to refuse</u> to give evidence in a criminal trial and, at the end of the evidence for the prosecution, the case may go to the jury who must make a decision without reference in some instances to the defendant's version of events. The <u>defendant is entitled to be acquitted by the</u> jury if the State has failed to prove its case *beyond a reasonable doubt*. This means that even if the jury considers that the State has made a case which requires some explanation from the defendant, the defendant is still entitled to be found not guilty if there is a reasonable doubt in their mind. It may be noted that in a Civil Law system operating the inquisitorial system, the accused person may be asked a number of questions by the investigating judge which the accused person is obliged to answer. While this is quite different from the posititon in Irish law (though see the point relating to the use of confessions, above), it is not accurate to state that the inquisitorial system operates a presumption of guilt.

In a civil action in Ireland the burden of proof is not beyond a reasonable doubt, but on the *balance of probabilities*. This means that the plaintiff or defendant is entitled to succeed in the case if either prove their case on the basis that their version is more probable than not. In other words in a civil case the trial court (whether a judge or a jury) is entitled to find for one party on the basis of what would appear to be the most plausible version of events, even if there is no absolutely 'right' version. In a criminal case, on the other hand, the trial court must be absolutely clear on the guilt of the accused person before a guilty verdict can be brought in.

JUDGE AND JURY

Finally, a comment on the function of the judge and jury in civil and criminal cases. As seen in Chapter 4, juries in civil cases are quite unusual since the passing of the Courts Act, 1988, only being retained in a limited number of High Court cases. In criminal cases, the jury is present in serious trials in the High Court (the Central Criminal Court) and the Circuit Court. The judge's function in a jury trial is to conduct the trial according to law, ensuring that no inadmissible evidence is introduced and that the lawyers do not break any of the procedural rules which apply. In addition, the judge's function is to direct the jury on points of law which arise. In civil cases, it may be to explain to the jury what amounts to defamation in law, while in a criminal case it may be to explain the ingredients of murder so that they can arrive at a verdict which conforms to that rule whether it is a guilty or not guilty verdict. At the end of the case in a civil or criminal case, the judge will also summarise the evidence given in the Court case and indicate to the jury its obligation to arrive at a verdict in accordanaec with the evidence and not on the basis of any impression they might have obtained from any other source. In summary, therefore, the judge rules on the law while the jury gives the verdict in the case.

However, the role of legal arbiter may amount to allowing the judge the full decision even where there is a jury. For example, in a civil case, if the judge considers that there is no basis on which the jury could find for the plaintiff he may withdraw the case from the jury and enter judgment for the defendant. The plaintiff can, of course, appeal such a decision. Once the judge allows the case to go to the jury, he cannot, however, instruct them to find for the plaintiff; that is for the jury. In the criminal trial, the equivalent rule allows the judge to withdraw a case from the jury and direct them to find the accused not guilty, where the judge has arrived at the conclusion that no jury could reasonably convict. The prosecution may appeal this decision in a High Court criminal trial, but it appears that no re-trial can be ordered (see *The People v. Quilligan (No. 2)* [1989] I.L.R.M. 245). Otherwise the not guilty verdict in such a situation will stand. Once the judge decides to let the case go to the jury he cannot direct the jury to find the accused guilty; that is a matter for the jury. Whether particular judges in fact move a jury in a particular direction, in civil or criminal cases, is a matter of some comment by practitioners, and obviously hard evidence on this is difficult to come by. However, there have been some instances in which the Court of Criminal Appeal has overturned convictions which appear to have resulted from overly robust directions by the trial judge.

In the large number of cases where there is no jury, of course, the judge is both the legal arbiter and the person with the responsibility to arrive at the verdict. And it is precisely this function which a judge performs in delivering judgments which law students must become familiar with in their studies.

Chapter 6

THE APPELLATE JURISDICTION OF THE COURTS

In Chapter 4 we described the jurisdiction of the courts when dealing at first instance with civil and criminal matters. It is, however, also a feature of the court system that the decisions of a court may be appealed to a higher court. That characteristic, namely appeal to a higher court, is basic to the current arrangements. While there is no such notion as an appeal from one High Court judge to another it is possible, as we will see below, that a re-trial (whether in civil or criminal matters) has virtually the same final out-come. But the essence of operating the appeal procedure involves bringing the matter to a higher court.

The forms of appeal may be divided into two general types. First, there are some instances where either party may seek to have the case, whether it is civil or criminal, reheard in full in a higher court.

This is called a hearing *de novo*, and as its name signifies this form of appeal involves a complete rehearing of the case to the extent that it is as if the first hearing in the lower court had not taken place at all. In other words, the hearing *de novo* is conducted as if the case was a first instance hearing. There may, however, be some limits on the appellate court's powers as will be seen below. The second form of appeal is an *appeal on a point of law*. This is a more limited form of appeal, and involves a resolu-tion by the higher appeal court of some issue of law rather than a complete rehearing of the entire case. We will see below that such an appeal can take different forms.

Two important and connected points must, however, first be made in relation to the functions of an appellate court when hearing an appeal on a point of law. It is clear that a complete rehearing must be different in certain respects to a hearing on a point of law. The difference is in relation to the finding of facts made by the court whose decision is under appeal. Take, for example, the conduct of an appeal to the Supreme Court on a point of law. The procedure here is that the Supreme Court does not hear any witnesses. Instead, the Court is given a *transcript* of the evidence as taken by the stenographer at the High Court hearing. In civil cases, it is a matter for the parties whether to retain a stenographer, but this is in-variably done in any litigation which might involve an appeal. In criminal cases, a stenographer is present in all cases. In examining the transcript the Supreme Court will, of course, be able to ascertain whether the findings of fact made by the High Court have some foundation in the evidence which was given. But once there is a foundation in the evidence given, the Supreme Court will not generally interfere with the findings made in the lower court.

The rationale for this has been explained on many occasions, but primarily it arises from a matter mentioned at the end of Chapter 5. This is that the trial court will have had an opportunity to see the witnesses give their evidence and to detect the nuances of human reaction to examination and cross-examination which may not be apparent from a transcript, such as a hesitation in answering a particular question. The Supreme Court will, therefore, leave intact what are called the *primary findings of fact*. There is, however, another category of findings which the Supreme Court does have certain control over; these are what are called *secondary findings*. These are the findings of the High Court which arise by way of inference from the primary findings, and they do not depend on an assessment of the witness' candour in giving evidence. For example, the trial judge might decide to believe the evidence of a particular witness. This is, in effect, a primary finding which will not be interfered with by the Supreme Court, even if there was other evidence available to challenge that witness' account. But the trial judge may draw a particular inference from the evidence which has been given and the Supreme Court may consider that this inference is not warranted in the circumstances. In that situation, this secondary finding can be overturned and the Supreme Court is entitled to arrive at a different finding. This was the position in *Hanrahan v. Merck Sharpe & Dohme Ltd.* [1988] I.L.R.M. 629, where the Supreme Court applied principles set out in *Northern Bank Finance Corp. Ltd. v. Charlton* [1979] I.R. 149.

THE DISTRICT COURT

Being at the lower end of the court system, the appellate functions of the District Court are quite limited. They are confined to hearing appeals regarding the exercise of statutory powers by various persons. It is difficult to categorise such appeal functions since they tend to involve the boundary between criminal and civil law.

For example, s.20 of the Fire Services Act, 1981 empowers a fire authority (which is usually under the control of a local authority) to serve what the Act describes as a 'fire safety notice' on the owner of a potentially dangerous building, which the Act defines as a building likely to be a source of injury were a fire to occur in it. The notice can prohibit the use of the building to which it relates. Failure to observe the contents of the fire safety notice is a criminal offence under s.4 of the 1981 Act and can be tried summarily in the District Court. But apart from the criminal aspect of the matter, an owner on whom such a fire safety notice has been served may appeal to the District Court. On such appeal, the District Justice can either confirm or annul the fire safety notice. For discussion of the functions of the District Court in such an appeal see *Transactus Investments Ltd v. Dublin Corporation* [1985] I.R. 501. Similar appellate functions are conferred on the District Court by other safety legislation, such as the Safety, Health and Welfare at Work Act, 1989.

CIRCUIT COURT

Circuit Court: Civil Appeals

The Circuit Court is empowered to conduct a full re-hearing—a hearing *de novo*—of a case heard in the District Court, under s.84 of the Courts of Justice Act, 1924. This right of appeal is available both to plaintiff and defendant. The power of the Court to award damages is, however, limited to that of the District Court.

The importance of such a complete re-hearing may be illustrated as follows. Where, for example, at the hearing of the case in the District Court one witness for the plaintiff failed to turn up or did not give convincing evidence the appeal to the Circuit Court may allow that non-appearance or unconvincing testimony to be remedied. In the Circuit Court, the defendant is not entitled to say to the witness 'But you did not turn up to give evidence in the District Court' or 'Your evidence in the District Court was much less convincing.' In effect, both parties are provided with an opportunity to present their cases afresh. Other circumstances in which the Circuit Court conducts a full rehearing is in relation to appeals from the Employment Appeals Tribunal, under the Unfair Dismissals Act, 1977, and in tax cases from the Appeal Commissioners, under the Income Tax Act, 1967.

In addition, the Circuit Court is empowered to hear appeals from certain other adjudicative decisions. Under s.16 of the Abattoirs Act, 1988 the Court is empowered to hear appeals from the refusal of the Minister for Agriculture and Food to grant an abattoir licence.

Circuit Court: Criminal Appeals

In criminal matters, the Circuit Court may also conduct a full rehearing, but the general rule is that this is only where there has been a conviction in the District Court. S.18 of the Courts of Justice Act, 1928 (as amended by s.24 of the Criminal Justice Act, 1951) provides that such appeals only arise where a conviction has been made in the District Court, so that in the event of an acquittal there cannot, in general, be an application by the prosecution for a rehearing of the case in the Circuit Court (but note there is a possibility of an appeal on a point of law to the High Court, discussed below). S.18 also allows for an appeal against sentence by the convicted person.

S.18 of the 1928 Act sets out the general rule in this respect, but in some instances special provision is made for appeals by the prosecution from an acquittal. This arises more frequently with respect to what might be termed 'regulatory' offences prosecuted by administrative agencies rather than 'ordinary' offences. For example, s.45 of the Safety in Industry Act, 1980 was enacted to allow precisely for this, because s.111 of the Factories Act, 1955 (which deals with appeals from prosecutions under the Act) had been interpreted as not allowing such an appeal. To the same effect see s.52 of the Safety, Health and Welfare at Work Act, 1989. It may be noted that, on appeal from the District Court, the Circuit Court does not consist of a judge and jury; the Circuit Court judge alone hears the case.

HIGH COURT

High Court: Civil Appeals

(i) Full rehearings

Where a case has been initiated in the Circuit Court, either party may appeal that decision to the High Court for a full rehearing of the case, that is, an appeal *de novo*: s.38 of the Courts of Justice Act, 1936. The decision of the High Court in such cases is, under s.39 of the 1936 Act, final. But before the High Court judge reaches a final verdict in a *de novo* appeal from the Circuit Court, either party may apply for an appeal to the Supreme Court on a point of law. The High Court judge may allow such an appeal to proceed and, if he does, the High Court proceedings will stand adjourned.

Specific provision is made in certain matters for appeals *de novo* to the High Court. For example, under the Trade Marks Act, 1963 the High Court may hear appeals from determinations of the Controller of Patents,

Designs and Trade Marks as to whether to register a trade mark. On such appeals, the High Court has precisely the same powers and functions as the Controller, in other words this amounts to a special form of appeal *de novo*. S.57 of the 1963 Act allows the High Court judge to determine the matter without being bound by any evidence given to the Controller. S.57(4) of the 1963 Act provides that the decision of the High Court is final and not appealable, but this is subject to s.57(5) which permits an appeal to the Supreme Court by leave of the High Court. Thus, there is no appeal to the Supreme Court as of right.

The position of the High Court in relation to appeals from the Controller in a patent case is slightly different. Under the Patents Act, 1964, the High Court is again empowered to conduct a full re-hearing from a refusal of a patent by the Controller. A further appeal to the Supreme Court is not governed by the need to obtain leave from the High Court judge. Instead, s.75(7) of the 1964 Act specifies certain instances in which an appeal may be brought, and specifies others in which no appeal may be brought.

(ii) Appeals on a point of law

Under s.52(1) of the Courts (Supplemental Provisions) Act, 1961, the High Court is empowered to hear appeals on a point of law from the District Court where either party requests of the District Justice what is referred to as a '*case stated*'. This form of appeal on a point of law generally takes place at the end of the hearing in the District Court, but it can be applied for at an earlier stage, and if so it is known as a consultative case stated. Both parties agree, in writing, on the facts as found by the District Justice and then formulate an issue of law for determination by the High Court. This document, the 'case stated', is then usually presented to the District Justice who is required to sign it. In form, the document itself appears as if it has been drafted by the Justice because it is written in the first person. The document is lodged in the High Court and the parties argue the point of law arising in the High Court and the judge determines the issue by answering the question posed in the case stated, which can generally be done in the form of a yes or no answer. The case may then be transmitted back to the District Court for final determination in accordance with the answer given by the High Court. A further appeal to the Supreme Court on a point of law may also be brought from the High Court, but only with the leave of the High Court judge: s.52(2) of the 1961 Act.

High Court: Criminal Appeals

The only appellate function which the High Court performs in criminal cases is by way of hearing a case stated from a decision of the District Court (except where the District Court is conducting a preliminary examination in an indictable offence). The procedure is precisely the same as in civil cases, and both the prosecution and the defence may apply, under s.52 of the Courts (Supplemental Provisions) Act, 1961, for a case stated; and a further appeal to the Supreme Court is also subject to the leave of the judge.

In this context it is notable that the prosecution can apply for a case stated even where the District Justice has entered a not guilty verdict in favour of the defendant. If the case stated to the High Court results in a finding that the District Justice erred on a point of law, the result is that the case is transmitted back to the District Court for what amounts to a second trial of the same issue.

COURT OF CRIMINAL APPEAL

As its name signifies the Court of Criminal Appeal performs a specialist function, namely, that of hearing criminal appeals. The Court was established by s.3 of the Courts (Establishment and Constitution) Act, 1961. In accordance with s.12 of the Courts (Supplemental Provisions) Act, 1961, it carries over the appellate functions given to the Court of Criminal Appeal which was established by the Courts of Justice Act, 1924. The Court hears appeals from those courts which conduct trials on indictment. At present, therefore, it is the appellate court for the Circuit Court (s.63 of the Courts of Justice Act, 1924), a special criminal court (s.44 of the Offences against the State Act, 1939) and the High Court (the Central Criminal Court) (s.31 of the Courts of Justice Act, 1924).

In accordance with s.3(2) of the Courts (Establishment and Constitution) Act, 1961, the Court of Criminal Appeal is composed of one Supreme Court judge (the Chief Justice or other Supreme Court judge nominated by the Chief Justice) and two judges of the High Court (nominated by the Chief Justice). The Court sits only when required to dispose of business, generally speaking about once every week during the legal term. Given the provisions of s.3(2) of the 1961 Act, the composition of the Court can change from one week to the next, depending on the availability of the different judges of the High Court and Supreme Court.

The Court of Criminal Appeal deals with a number of different matters, but two areas constitute the majority of its work.

First, a person convicted on indictment in the Circuit Court, High Court (Central Criminal Court) or a special criminal court may appeal that conviction to the Court of Criminal Appeal either where the trial judge grants (or trial judges grant, in the case of a special criminal court) a certificate of leave to appeal or the Court of Criminal Appeal itself grants such a certificate on a refusal by the trial judge: ss.31 and 63 of the Courts of Justice Act, 1924 and s.44 of the Offences against the State Act, 1939. In essence the appeal against conviction is on the basis that the trial court made some error of law in making a finding of guilt.

Certificates of leave to appeal are rarely granted by the trial court for the reason that, in the case of the Circuit or High Court the trial judge would, by granting a certificate, be in some sense casting doubt on the correctness of the verdict reached by the jury (in the case of a conviction in a special criminal court the reasons for not granting a certificate are even clearer). Thus, most cases heard by the Court of Criminal Appeal are from refusals by the trial court of a certificate of leave to appeal. As with any appeal involving points of law, both the prosecution and defence lawyers will argue the relevant legal points involved in the appeal, but the nomenclature used in Court of Criminal Appeal hearings is a little confusing.

The convicted person is referred to as the 'applicant', rather than the appellant. The reason for this is that the full hearing in the Court of Criminal Appeal is in fact, in accordance with s.36 of the 1924 Act, an application for leave to appeal. In fact nothing of substance turns on this point. If, having heard the legal points raised, the Court of Criminal

Appeal decides that the conviction was wrong in law, the Court will 'allow the application for leave to appeal, treat the hearing of the application as the appeal and allow the appeal.' A *lacuna* in the Court's powers was filled by the Courts of Justice Act, 1928 when it was granted the power to order a re-trial where it had allowed an appeal.

The second form of appeal which the Court hears is appeals against sentence. In such cases the Court is asked to assess whether the sentence imposed by the trial court was within the range of sentences deemed appropriate to the particular crime and the particular convicted person.

A person applying to the Court of Criminal Appeal has the choice of appealing: (a) against conviction and sentence or (b) against conviction only or (c) against sentence only. Where an appeal against conviction only is made the Court of Criminal Appeal may not interfere with the sentence given in the trial court: *The People v. Earls* [1969] I.R. 414. In relation to convictions against sentence, the Court does not usually increase the sentence imposed in the trial court, though on occasion it has done so. From the convicted person's point of view, of course, the purpose of such an appeal is to have the sentence reduced and that outcome is certainly more common than an increased sentence.

The Court of Criminal Appeal also deals with other matters connected with appeals, such as whether to grant a legal aid certificate for the appeal in accordance with the Criminal Justice (Legal Aid) Act, 1962. The Court may also admit a person to bail his or her appeal is pending.

THE SUPREME COURT

The Supreme Court is, as required by Article 34.4.1°, the court of final appeal in the State. This is not to say that all decisions of the lower courts can be appealed to the Supreme Court, as Article 34.4.3°, discussed above, also makes clear. What can be said is that the Supreme Court is, with the exception of the two cases referred to in Chapter 4, a court of appeal which usually does not hear evidence and in all cases hears appeals on points of law only. In exceptional circumstances, however, the Court may be prepared to admit new evidence on the appeal: see *B. v. B.* [1975] I.R. 54 (decided in 1970) and *The People v. Lynch* [1982] I.R. 64 (Extract 11.10).

Supreme Court: Civil Cases
(i) *From the District Court.* It is possible for a case begun in the District Court to reach the Supreme Court, in two different ways, both requiring leave of the High Court. First, where a District Court decision has been appealed for a *de novo* hearing in the Circuit Court, the case may be appealed from the Circuit Court by way of case stated to the High Court. From here, a further appeal on a point of law may take place, but only by leave of the High Court judge, whose decision is final: s.38 of the Courts of Justice Act, 1936. The second method is where the High Court has heard a case stated from the District Court, the High Court judge may grant leave to appeal to the Supreme Court pursuant to s.52 of the Courts (Supplemental Provisions) Act, 1961. Again this appeal is not available as of right; the High Court judge must grant leave, and there is no appeal against a refusal.

(ii) *From the Circuit Court.* Again there are two possible routes. Where a case has begun in the Circuit Court, that Court may state a case for the opinion of the Supreme Court: s.16 of the Courts of Justice Act, 1947. Secondly, if a case begun in the Circuit Court has been appealed for a *de novo* hearing in the High Court, the High Court may grant leave to appeal to the Supreme Court by way of case stated on any point of law arising on the appeal: s.39 of the Courts of Justice Act, 1936.

(iii) *From the High Court.* In relation to cases commenced in the High Court, either party may appeal to the Supreme Court on a point of law: s.25(2) of the Courts (Supplemental Provisions) Act, 1961. In cases involving damages, the appeal may involve the issue of liability (for example whether an employer was in breach of the duty of care to employees in the circumstances which arose) or the issue of *quantum* (whether the amount of compensation awarded was correct). The Supreme Court's function in an appeal as to *quantum* is limited to deciding whether the amount was within an acceptable range of damages; if so then the appeal is dismissed even if the Supreme Court might, as a court of trial (looking at the matter *res integra*), have awarded less (or more). The Supreme Court has complete power, however, in relation to the issue of liability, which is a 'pure' issue of law.

Where the Supreme Court allows the appeal, it may order a re-trial of the action in the High Court, which would normally be presided over by a different High Court judge. In effect, therefore, a successful appeal to the Supreme Court results in a hearing *de novo* in the High Court. Where the Supreme Court considers that the *quantum* of damages awarded in the High Court was excessive, it may, instead of ordering a re-trial on the issue, assess the correct level of damages itself. This is regarded as being part of the inherent jurisdiction of the Supreme Court under Article 34.4.3° of the Constitution in hearing appeals from the High Court: see *Holohan v. Donohoe* [1986] I.R. 45.

Finally, pursuant to Article 34.4.4° of the Constitution, no law may be enacted which would limit the Supreme Court's jurisdiction to hear appeals from the High Court in constitutional cases.

Supreme Court: Criminal Cases

(i) *From the Court of Criminal Appeal.* The most common way in which criminal appeals are heard in the Supreme Court is in relation to appeals which have been dismissed by the Court of Criminal Appeal, that is, appeals by the defendant. The Court of Criminal Appeal itself, the Director of Public Prosecutions or the Attorney General may, under s.29 of the Courts of Justice Act, 1924, grant to the convicted person a certificate of leave to appeal to the Supreme Court where it is certified that 'a point of law of exceptional public importance' arises in the case and that it is desirable in the public interest that the opinion of the Supreme Court be taken on that point. Examples have been the *mens rea* required in order to convict a person of capital murder (*The People v. Murray* [1977] I.R. 360), the extension of time for applying for leave to appeal to the Court of Criminal Appeal (*The People v. Kelly* [1982] I.R. 90) and the admissibility of confessions obtained from a person while in Garda custody (*The People v. Kelly (No.2)* [1983] I.R. 1). There is no method of appeal from the refusal of such a certificate.

(ii) *Reference by D.P.P.* Under s.34 of the Criminal Procedure Act, 1967, the Director of Public Prosecutions may appeal on a point of law to the Supreme Court arising out of a trial on indictment in which the accused person was found not guilty. This form of appeal is without prejudice to the outcome of the trial, so that even if the Supreme Court finds that there was an error of law in the trial, the person found not guilty cannot be placed on trial for a second time.

(iii) *From the High Court.* Although the appeal by certificate under s.29 of the 1924 Act is in a sense an indirect form of appeal from the Circuit Court and High Court and a special criminal court, the Supreme Court has, by virtue of Article 34.4.3° of the Constitution, the power to hear appeals from the High Court exercising its original criminal jurisdiction. In other words the Supreme Court can hear appeals directly from the Central Criminal Court. This appeal procedure was first acknowledged by the Supreme Court as recently as 1975, that is over 50 years after the establishment of the Court of Criminal Appeal, in *The People v. Conmey* [1975] I.R. 341. (As to the precedent value of this case see Chapter 11.) In *The People v. O'Shea* [1982] I.R. 384 (Extract 13.4), the Supreme Court held that, where a person had been found not guilty in the Central Criminal Court, the prosecution could appeal the aquittal to the Supreme Court.

The issue of ordering a re-trial did not arise in that case because, having allowed the Director of Public Prosecutions to argue the appeal the Supreme Court found that the acquittal in that case had been correct in law. But in *The People v. Quilligan* [1987] I.R. 495, the Supreme Court found that the aquittal of the two accused had been made on the basis of an error of law, and the Court granted an order to the Director allowing the appeal. However, in *The People v. Quilligan (No.2)* [1989] I.L.R.M. 245, the Supreme Court, by a 3-2 decision, held that a re-trial should not be ordered in this case. Only two of the judges (Henchy and Griffin JJ.) held that re-trials should never be ordered. The third judge in the majority, Hederman J., merely decided not to order a re-trial in this particular case. So the matter is not yet finally resolved one way or the other. It may be noted that because this jurisdiction arises under Article 34.4.3° of the Constitution, it would be possible for legislation to remove this form of appeal mechanism. While it appeared that such removal was to have been included in the Criminal Justice Act, 1984 (see Kelly, *The Irish Constitution*, 2nd ed, p.338), the final version of the Act made no reference to the point.

(iv) *From the District Court.* As in civil cases, where the High Court has heard a case stated from the District Court in a criminal matter, the High Court may grant leave to appeal to the Supreme Court on a point of law: s.52 of the Courts (Supplemental Provisions) Act, 1961.

(v) *From the Circuit Court.* Again, as with civil cases, the Circuit Court may refer a point of law by way of case stated to the Supreme Court in a criminal trial. This however happens rarely because of the disruption involved in stopping a criminal trial after a jury has been empanelled to hear the case.

Chapter 7

ACCESS TO LAW

One of the most controversial topics in recent years has been the extent to which the old maxim about access to the law remains true. According to this maxim 'The law, like the Ritz Hotel, is open to all.' Is access to law limited to those who can afford it? This is an important question, because no matter how well a law student is familiar with the law, it may be that such rules and principles as exist will not apply in practice. It has been the tradition of the legal profession to provide some services free of charge. The question which arises is, firstly, whether this provides for all the situations in which a person wishes to bring a case to court and, secondly, whether the State is under an obligation to provide free legal aid and advice to all citizens so that they will not be at a disadvantage when they appear in Court. The provision of legal aid and advice in this State has developed to quite a considerable extent since 1922, but there are still many difficulties which stand in the way of a person having access to the courts through a lawyer. There is, of course, nothing to stop a person appearing in Court in person without the benefit of a lawyer. Many judges are accustomed to providing assistance to such persons in the presentation of cases, but ultimately the assistance of a lawyer may be what is really required. In addition to the provision of lawyers we will also consider, briefly, the cost of going to law in terms of court fees and payment of legal fees. In relation to access to a lawyer, it is necessary to deal with access in criminal and civil cases separately.

ACCESS TO LEGAL AID IN CRIMINAL CASES

Prior to 1962, a person accused of a criminal offence could only expect to be provided by the State with the assistance of a lawyer where the charge carried the death penalty. In all other cases the defendant was required to instruct a lawyer of his or her choice. And even in capital cases, it was not uncommon for the defendant to be represented by junior counsel while the prosecution was represented by senior and junior counsel. The Criminal Justice (Legal Aid) Act, 1962 changed the picture in this respect to a substantial degree. The 1962 Act introduced a system whereby in relation to all serious criminal cases a District Justice could assess whether an accused person was unable, by reason of lack of means, to afford the services of a lawyer. If the Justice made such an assessment, then legal assistance, in the form of a solicitor and counsel would be assigned to appear on behalf of the accused person. It should be remembered that, by virtue of the wording of the 1962 Act, there is no right to legal representation in all cases, only those which are relatively serious. This excludes, for example, those cases in which it is determined that the 'gravity' of the offence is not deemed of such importance as to require legal assistance. Thus, the District Justice is given a substantial discretion in this respect.

The system has developed since 1962, although from time to time there have been indications that it has not been working in a manner which was satisfactory to the members of the legal profession who specialise in criminal work. The most recent difficulty arose in 1988 to 1989 in relation to the prompt payment of fees. A comprehensive review of the 1962 Act up to 1977 is provided by the *Report of the Criminal Legal Aid Review Committee* (the Tormey Report) (Prl.9986).

An important development in the operation of the 1962 Act came with the decision of the Supreme Court in *The State (Healy) v. Donoghue* [1976] I.R. 325, in which the Court took the view that for serious criminal matters the Constitution required the State to provide an accused person with legal representation. The Court was, of course, considering this point in the context of the existing operation of the 1962 Act, but it made the point that in applying the Act a District Justice had to bear in mind that the Constitution required legal representation. In this way, legal aid in criminal cases cannot be seen merely as a statutory dispensation by the State.

In other criminal-related areas, the Attorney General operates a special scheme outside the 1962 Act, in relation to applications for judicial review, formerly the State Side orders, which are discussed in Chapter 8. The scheme, by which the Attorney General will meet the costs of legal representation in judicial review matters where the High Court determines that legal representation is required, was first announced in the course of an application by a convicted prisoner challenging the legality of his detention: see *Application of Woods* [1970] I.R. 154 (decided in 1967). Since 1976, as indicated, the scheme has been extended to all judicial review applications in criminal cases.

ACCESS TO LEGAL AID IN CIVIL CASES

Much more controversial, however, is the position in regard to legal aid by the State in civil matters. In *O'Shaughnessy v. Attorney General*, High Court, unreported, 16 February 1971, the argument that the Constitution required civil legal assistance as of right was rejected by O'Keeffe P. It must be remembered that this decision predated the Supreme Court judgment in *The State (Healy) v. Donoghue* [1976] I.R. 325. In any event, of more significance was the establishment in 1969 of the Free Legal Advice Centres (F.L.A.C.), which was composed of law students who established centres to which members of the public could go to seek advice on a wide range of legal problems, including housing, social welfare and family law. The centres were staffed on a purely voluntary basis, but in many instances practising lawyers would be available to provide backup as well as to bring proceedings to Court on the basis that only the stamping fees (see below) would be met either by the client or from F.L.A.C. funds.

F.L.A.C. continues to exist and to provide services to the public but its other primary aim was to press for the introduction of a State scheme of legal aid and advice in civil cases. In 1974, the then government appointed a Committee under the Chairmanship of Mr. Justice Denis Pringle to make recommendations for the introduction of a scheme of civil legal aid. This Committee reported in December 1977: *Committee on Civil Legal Aid and Advice, Report to Minister for Justice* (Prl.6862). No further steps were taken by the government, but at this time it had already been brought before the institutions of the Council of Europe for allegedly being in breach of the European Convention on Human Rights (as to which see Chapter 10). In 1979, in a decision of the Court of Human Rights, *Airey v. Ireland* (1979) 2 E.H.R.R. 305, the Court found Ireland to be in breach of the Convention to the extent that it did not provide Mrs. Airey with reasonable access to legal representation in proceedings for a judicial separation in the Irish courts.

As a result of the *Airey* decision, the government introduced a non-statutory scheme for civil legal aid in December 1979: *Scheme of Civil Legal Aid and Advice* (Prl.8543), which has been amended from time to time since then. Under the scheme, a Legal Aid Board was established to administer the scheme and a number of Law Centres were established around the country staffed by fully qualified lawyers to provide legal advice as well as to prepare court cases for members of the public who are unable to retain their own lawyers.

Some brief comments may be made on the scheme. Firstly, it is not a statutory scheme, although this was recommended by the Pringle Committee in its Report in 1977. In addition, the scheme is confined, in effect, to family law cases and there are a substantial number of areas of law which are completely outside the terms of the scheme. Finally, it has been argued that the scheme is substantially underfunded and that the State is not meeting its obligations in accordance with the spirit of the *Airey* case. A critical review of the Scheme as operated is provided by Whyte, 'And Justice for Some' (1984) 6 *D.U.L.J. (n.s.)* 88 and *The Closed Door; A Report on Civil Legal Aid Services in Ireland* (F.L.A.C., 1987).

COURT FEES

One of the significant cost factors in litigation is the requirement that stamp duty must be paid on all pleadings and other court documents. The precise rates of stamp duty are set from time to time by amendments to the rules of courts. The fees are substantial, however, and while they represent a relatively low percentage of the full cost of going to court they may represent a disincentive for those who are unable to avail of the current system of civil legal aid. It is important to stress the civil cases, as the availability of legal aid in criminal cases obviates the necessity to consider this cost factor in criminal matters. It was for this reason that the Committee on Court Practice and Procedure, in its 17th Interim Report published in 1972, recommended the abolition of all court fees on the basis that such fees may be unconstitutional as being an unreasonable bar on the right of access to the courts. The Committee also made, however, some other recommendations in relation to how court fees could be reduced. It is apparent from the above, however, that the main recommendation of the Committee, namely abolition of all fees, was not carried through. In many instances, therefore, the question still remains whether such fees constitute an unconstitutional bar to access to the courts. The fees continue, however, on the basis that the State requires some method of funding the quite large administration involved in the court structure.

LEGAL COSTS

A final direct cost of litigation are the fees which must be paid to the lawyers involved in civil and criminal cases. In serious criminal cases, of course, where the accused cannot afford to retain legal representation of his own, the costs of both the prosecution and defence are borne by the

State. And in those civil cases to which the 1979 Legal Aid Scheme applies, again the State may be bearing the cost of the plaintiff's and/or defendant's lawyers. An important initial point is that at common law it is illegal to charge *percentage contingency* fees. This means that a solicitor or barrister is not entitled to ask a client to agree to give a percentage of the fee if the client is successful. Such arrangements are lawful in the United States, but not in Britain or Ireland. Some 'no foal, no fee' arrangements are, however, in a different category, and many solicitors and counsel are prepared to take on a case on the basis that the client has a reasonable prospect of successs in the litigation. Where the solicitor or barrister takes on a case on the basis that no fee will be charged if the case is unsuccessful, they are perfectly entitled to obtain payment where they are successful. As we will see, however, the fees are, in fact paid by the unsuccessful party in those circumstances, but they may never in any event be calculated on the basis of a percentage of the damages awarded.

Where either or both parties must retain legal advice of their own, the position is as follows. In criminal cases, it is unusual that the Court will award costs to either side. Where the prosecution is successful and the defendant is found guilty, the State will still be required to pay its own costs. The defendant will also have to pay his or her legal advisers' fees. In some cases where the defendant is acquitted, the trial judge has a discretion to award costs against the State, in other words the State will be required to pay its own lawyers as well as the defendant's legal advisers: see *The People v. Bell* [1969] I.R. 24. In a District Court criminal case, costs may never be awarded against a member of the Garda Síochána who has taken a prosecution, and this special exemption has been held to be constitutionally valid: see *Dillane v. Attorney General* [1980] I.L.R.M. 167.

In civil cases the position is relatively simple and is governed by the rule that 'costs follow the event'. This indicates that in a civil case the successful party, whether plaintiff or defendant, is normally entitled to costs, that is, that the costs will be borne by the losing party. An unsuccessful plaintiff is, therefore, required to pay not only his own lawyers but also the lawyers for the defendant who has successfully defended the action.

While this rule is relatively straightforward, some modifications may be noted. A defendant in an action in which the plaintiff is seeking, say, damages for personal injuries in the High Court, may be advised that the plaintiff would receive something in the region of £20,000 from the Court. The defendant may, therefore, be advised to offer £15,000 to the plaintiff to settle the case. This sum may be formally *lodged* with the Accountant attached to the Four Courts and is then available to the plaintiff for acceptance. If the case goes to hearing and the plaintiff is awarded less than £15,000, then the plaintiff, although successful, is not entitled to costs. It may be noted that the existence of the lodgment cannot be notified in advance to the judge hearing the case. (In the Circuit Court the existence of the lodgment may be notified but not its amount.) It is, therefore, of great importance for the plaintiff to 'beat the lodgment', and, of course, the lodgment is a strong motivating factor in the settling of many cases.

The second point to note about costs awarded in civil actions is that these costs relate to the direct cost of litigation, called 'party and party' costs. They would include all the barrister's fees as well as the fees involved in securing the attendance of witnesses and the solicitors fees directly connected with the litigation. But they do not include what are called 'solicitor and client' costs, those costs which a solictior may consider were required in the interests of the client but which may not have been strictly necessary for the case. These costs may have to be borne by the client out of the damages received in the case.

Thirdly, in relation to certain actions in which the State is involved, particularly constitutional cases, the Court may require the State to pay costs even to the unsuccessful plaintiff: see the discussion in *Attorney General (S.P.U.C. Ltd) v. Open Door Counselling Ltd.* [1987] I.L.R.M. 477, 503 (not in fact a case involving the State).

Fourthly it may be noted that, where the unsuccessful plaintiff is an individual, the successful defendant will find it quite difficult to obtain costs because the individual is unlikely to have readily available assets, unlike a company. In such cases, the successful defendant will, therefore, still be required to pay its legal advisers.

Finally, there is an important point on the actual amount of fees which may be charged. The direct litigation fees payable to solicitors are regulated by statute, while all those payable to barristers are not regulated as such but are, usually, based on a scale of fees which are agreed from time to time by the General Council of the Bar of Ireland. Bar fees can, however, vary from one counsel to the next. The point, however, is that a lawyer cannot charge any fee and be paid that exact sum. If there is a dispute between the parties to litigation as to the correct level of fees, either party is entitled to have the matter referred for determination by a court officer whose function is the setting of the correct level. In the High Court, this function is performed by an officer of the Court called the Taxing Master. The basis on which costs are assessed are discussed in *Irish Trust Bank Ltd. v. Central Bank of Ireland*, High Court, unreported, 4 March 1976 (Extract 11.5), which indicates that there is also an appeal from the decision of the Taxing Master to the High Court, and from there to the Supreme Court. The function is performed by the County Registrar in the Circuit Court.

SMALL CLAIMS COURT

There have been calls in recent years, particularly from the Consumers' Association of Ireland (a voluntary group which monitors consumer laws) for the introduction of a small claims court system, similar to that introduced in Britain. Under such a system, members of the public would be entitled to litigate small legal disputes in an informal forum where legal formalities are waived and all necessary documentation would be filled in by the administrators of the court system. It might be argued that the District Court performs such a function at present, but it still remains the preserve of the legal profession. A true small claims court would be very similar to Judge Wapner's Court.

Chapter 8

REMEDIES AND ENFORCEMENT

In this Chapter we examine a number of different remedies and enforcement mechanisms which are available in civil cases. Criminal cases represent a different problem, as the direct end result of a criminal prosecution is either a conviction or acquittal of the accused person. We will, however, examine judicial review, which is available as a remedy both in criminal and civil matters. We firstly outline those remedies which are available in civil cases, then we discuss judicial review. Finally, we outline some of the different enforcement mechanisms to ensure compliance with court orders.

CIVIL REMEDIES

1. Damages.

Monetary compensation, called damages by lawyers, is the single most common form of remedy available in the court system. Where a person has received personal injuries, it may not be possible to repair an injured limb, and this is in any event outside the compass of the law. Nor does the law permit any application of the 'eye for an eye' maxim, even where it is found that a wrong has been intentionally done. The basic rule which applies in relation to the award of damages is that the sum awarded is to be a compensatory amount which places the injured person in the position she was, so far as money can do so, before the legal wrong was committed.

This rule applies whether the wrong alleged was a tort or a breach of contract. However, the details of the exact amount of damages which can be awarded may differ between breach of contract and other cases, but there has been an increasing tendency for judges to treat the different categories as being the same so far as possible: see for example *Hickey & Co. Ltd. v. Roches Stores Ltd.* [1980] I.L.R.M. 107, at pp.118-120. This is a particular problem where the claim being made is one which arises both from contract and tort, as where a client sues his solicitor: see *Finlay v. Murtagh* [1979] I.R. 249 (Extract 11.15). On the overlap between contract and other areas of liability see Phillips, 'The Concurrence of Remedies in Contract and Tort' (1977) 12 *Ir. Jur. (n.s.)* 234.

As already mentioned, the purpose of awarding damages is compensatory and not punitive, bearing in mind in particular the overall purpose of the civil law as opposed to criminal law. In exceptional circumstances, however, an extra sum of money, over and above the sum necessary to compensate the person who has suffered the wrong, may be awarded as a mark of the court's particular disapproval of the wrongdoer's conduct. Such exemplary damages are, however, usually, relatively modest: see for example *Kennedy v. Ireland* [1987] I.R. 587. For a discussion of this area, see McMahon and Binchy, *Irish Law of Torts*, 2nd ed. (Butterworths, 1989).

Damages in constitutional cases pose particular difficulties, some of which are discussed in Cooney and Kerr, 'Constitutional Aspects of Irish Tort Law' (1981) 3 *D.U.L.J. (n.s.)* 1 and *Kearney v. Minister for Justice* [1986] I.R. 116.

Under s.22 of the Courts Act, 1981 a court awarding damages of £150 or more may also order the payment of interest on all or part of that sum from the date of the cause of action to the date of the judgment.

2. Injunction

The injunction was a remedy developed by the courts of equity to prevent one party from acting in such a way as to interfere with the rights of another. Thus, a person who complains that another person has trespassed on his land may not be satisfied with the damages remedy which was available in the common law courts. The trespasser may, for one thing, not have any assets to meet the award of damages. The injunction is an order which simply states that the trespasser is to cease and desist from all acts of trespass.

The injunction is a remedy which is available at the different stages of civil proceedings and may also take many different forms. In relation to the forms of the injunction, it may be used to prevent some future action which the applicant fears; this is referred to as a *quia timet* injunction. The injunction may be either positive or negative, in other words it may order a person to do something which they are not doing or prohibit them from doing something which is prohibited. The positive form of injunction is called the *mandatory injunction* and could, for example, be directed at a builder who is not building in accordance with the specifications agreed to in a building contract. The negative form of injunction, called a *prohibitory injunction*, could be used in the case of the alleged trespasser referred to above.

An injunction, once awarded after a full court hearing, may last in perpetuity, that is for all time. This is referred to as a perpetual injunction. But not all situations require a permanent injunction of this nature and, indeed, many situations are of such urgency that to wait for a full court hearing would make the obtaining of a perpetual injunction pointless. For example, where a former employee of yours has become an employee of a rival company it may be pointless for a lawyer to advise you that in two years time, when the case may come to court, the employee may be ordered by injunction not to pass on any trade secrets to the new employer. At that stage the secrets will have been passed and you may be out of business. Something more immediate is needed. The solution is to apply for an *interlocutory injunction*.

The procedure adopted is that proceedings are instituted seeking a perpetual injunction against the former employee as well as, perhaps, damages for loss of business. Immediately this is done you may then apply to court for an interlocutory injunction by which the former employee may be prevented from passing any information to the new employer until the full case is heard. The basis on which such interlocutory injunctions are granted is by reference to two tests. The first is whether the applicant has made out a *stateable legal case* in relation to obtaining the final remedy, the perpetual injunction. This requires the applicant to persuade the court that it has a reasonable chance of being ultimately successful in the proceedings, not necessarily that it will definitely be successful. The second test is that the *balance of convenience* must be in favour of granting an injunction. This requires the Court to consider what would be the position if, on the one hand, an injunction is granted and the court decides at the final hearing that the employer was not entitled to the perpetual injunction, and, on the other hand, to look at the situation if the interlocutory injunction is not granted but the court decided at the final hearing that the employer is entitled to a perpetual injunction. On both these tests, the court usually awards an interlocutory injunction to preserve the position of the parties (the *status quo*) until the full hearing of the case. The weighing of these factors was considered by the Supreme Court in *Campus Oil Ltd. v. Minister for Industry and Energy (No.2)* [1983] I.R. 88.

The interlocutory injunction must be applied for on notice to the other party, but even this may create difficulty in some instances. In a case where a plaintiff is alleging fraud, for example, it may be necessary to obtain a remedy to freeze the assets of a defendant for fear that the defendant may remove these assets from the State to make it impossibile to enforce, for example, a court order for damages. In such circumstances, the plaintiff may apply without notice (*ex parte*) to the appropriate Court to obtain an *interim injunction*. Courts do not readily grant such injunctions since they have not been made with the benefit of hearing both sides. However, in the exceptional circumstances outlined above, the court might grant the interim injunction to operate for, say, two days, at the end of which both sides must present arguments as to why the interim injunction should either be discharged or else converted into an interlocutory injunction.

The type of injunction referred to in the fraud example above is called a *Mareva* injunction (named after one of the first English cases in which it was considered, *Mareva Compania Naviera S.A. v. International Bulk-carriers S.A.* [1975] 2 Lloyd's Rep. 509) which may take the form of an order to a bank to maintain the amount of money in a specified bank account above a certain level pending the outcome of the action taken by the plaintiff. On the principles to be applied in a *Mareva* case, see *Powerscourt Estates v Gallagher* [1984] I.L.R.M. 123. A similar type of emergency remedy is the *Anton Piller* Order, which allows one party to take documents and other items from a named premises; such orders have been used, for example, in relation to video piracy cases brought by video manufacturers. This type of order is named after one of the first English cases in which the order was considered, *Anton Piller K.G. v. Manufacturing Processes Ltd.* [1976] Ch. 55. Such an order should be distinguished from discovery orders, discussed in Chapter 5.

Finally it may be noted that where interlocutory injunctions are granted, the person to whom they are awarded must give an undertaking that, in the event that the Court finds at the full hearing of the case that such relief should not have been granted, appropriate damages will be payable to the person against whom the injunction was granted.

The interlocutory injunction, it may be noted, has proved somewhat controversial as a method of restraining picketing on premises where a trade dispute is in existence. In effect, such injunctions may be used to prevent any picketing which would interfere with the business of the employer with whom the trade dispute exists by preventing picketing of the entrance to the premises. For a discussion see Kerr and Whyte, *Irish Trade Union Law* (Professional Books, 1985), Chapter 11.

3. Specific Performance

This is another equitable remedy which was developed to give a more effective remedy than damages in the context of an allegation of failure to perform a contract. Specific performance is on order requiring the person in breach of contract to perform it according to the terms agreed. The order, being equitable is also discretionery, and there are a number of requirements which must be met before it will be ordered. Damages must be an insufficient remedy and in addition there must have been no undue delay or other matter which might disentitle the applicant to the remedy. In addition, there are certain types of contracts for which the remedy will not, usually, be granted. These include contracts of personal service, such as employment contracts. The reason for this is that the courts will not grant an order which appears to force a person to provide their labour against their will, as this would smack of slavery. The remedy of specific performance is, however, a particularly valuable remedy in relation to contracts for the sale of land. On the development of the remedy see Wylie, *Irish Conveyancing Law* (Professional Books, 1978), Chapter 12.

JUDICIAL REVIEW

Applications for *judicial review*, *State Side* applications until 1986, are the successors to the *prerogative writs* which were issued by the English monarch and directed at the lower, inferior, courts and other tribunals as a method of ensuring compliance with certain basic requirements of the common law. The prerogative writs could only be issued by the Court of King's Bench, and this common law tradition was carried on after independence when the jurisdiction to grant the State Side orders was vested in the High Court. O.84 of the Rules of the Superior Courts, 1986 made substantial changes to the procedure in applications for these orders, now called applications for judicial review. Nonetheless, the titles of the former State Side orders remain in the 1986 Rules, and the main changes are, as mentioned, on the procedural side. The four types of prerogative writs which were developed by the common law courts were as follows:

1. *Certiorari*: this order is used to quash the decision of a lower court or tribunal which has been found to have acted outside its powers: see, for example, *The State (Pine Valley Developments Ltd.) v. Dublin County Council* [1984] I.R. 407.

2. *Mandamus*: this is directed to a tribunal ordering it to fulfil a lawful obligation which it is not carrying out: see for example *The State (King) v. Minister for Justice* [1984] I.R. 169.

3. *Prohibition*: this is directed at a court or tribunal preventing it from exercising its powers, either completely, or until certain conditions have been met: see *The State (O'Connell) v. Fawsitt* [1986] I.R. 362 for an example of a complete ban by way of prohibition as a result of delay in prosecuting in a criminal case.

4. *Habeas Corpus*: this is the remedy which orders production of the body of a person who is alleged to be unlawfully imprisoned. Of the four remedies developed by the common law, only the *habeas corpus* remedy may have been affected to any substantial extent by the passing of the Constitution. The reason for this is that Article 40.4 of the Constitution provides for a remedy for investigating the lawfulness of detention. For this

reason, the old common law remedy of *habeas corpus* may be obsolete, though judges have continued to use the Latin phrase when referring to an Article 40.4 application for release. In this particular respect, the judges have not, however, always been consistent. For a case in which Article 40.4 was noted as having affected the old remedy see *Cahill v. Governor of the Curragh Military Detention Barracks* [1980] I.L.R.M. 191, 201.

It may be noted here briefly that the courts do not regard judicial review as a form of appeal from the lower tribunal. It is, in effect, an attack on what is termed the jurisdiction of the tribunal to hear the matter in dispute. For example, if judicial review is sought in relation the decision of An Bord Pleanála (see Chapter 9) to grant planning permission to a particular company, the applicant for judicial review will not be allowed to apply for *certiorari* simply by arguing that the Bord was lawfully entitled to have refused planning permission. *Certiorari* will only be granted where the Bord has completely misunderstood the entire legal basis for its power to make a decision in the matter, for example, by failing to hear certain parties before deciding the case or ignoring completely a fundamental legal provision which was relevant to the case. The types of errors of law for which a Court will, and those for which it will not, grant judicial review are, however, not altogether clear and this is an area of law which is in a constant state of flux and change. *cf. Scott & Ors v An Bord Pleanála + Arcon Mines 29/11/94 S.C.*

The changes made by the 1986 Rules were based largely on the Working Paper of the Law Reform Commission *Judicial Review of Administrative Action: The Problem of Remedies* (1979). The Rules now allow, for example, a more straightforward application procedure, similar to the system which was introduced in Britain some years earlier. The application for judicial review is in two stages. The first, *ex parte* stage, involves an application to a High Court judge for leave to proceed, where the applicant sets out the grounds on which relief is being sought. This application is granted if the judge considers that the case discloses some ground for claiming relief, though no decision is made at this stage as to whether the applicant is likely to be ultimately successful. The applicant must then serve notice on the other party, called the respondent. The second stage involves both parties arguing whether, for example, an order for *certiorari* should issue. One of the major changes introduced by the 1986 Rules was that the Court may award damages on judicial review, something which the common law had held was not available with such applications. One reason for this approach of the common law was that judicial review was regarded as, and still is, a public law remedy, not to be used in private law disputes where damages would be more appropriate. A private dispute could be resolved, for example, by means of an injunction. Again, this is another aspect of judicial review which requires close attention because the boundaries between public and private law are being eroded as changes such as those in the 1986 Rules are implemented in practice. For fuller discussion of this see Hogan and Morgan, *Administrative Law* (Sweet & Maxwell, Irish Law Texts, 1986).

ENFORCEMENT MECHANISMS

Where a person obtains an order for specific performance or injunction, or even damages, what is the position when the person against whom the

Egan J. concluded that substantial grounds had not been made out to contending that the decision was invalid. Supreme Court; Irish Times 23 Jan. 95.

order is directed decides not to obey the order? And what happens where a person refuses to hand over possession of property in respect of which a court order to that effect exists?

1. Contempt of Court

Where a court order is disobeyed, a person is in contempt of court. This form of contempt is referred to as *civil contempt* to distinguish it from *criminal contempt*, which we mention below. Where a civil contempt occurs it is a matter for the person who obtained the court order which has been disobeyed to bring this to the attention of the court in question. The judge may then order that the person in contempt (the contemnor) be brought before the Court (attached for contempt). When the person comes before the Court he or she may decide to obey the Court order, but if not the judge will order that the person be lodged in prison 'until he doth purge his contempt.' The effect of this somewhat alarming power is that the person in question must remain in prison until he or she is prepared to come before the Court to apologise and to undertake to obey the Court order in the future. Until that is done the person may not be released under any circumstances, except by order of the Court. It is a term of imprisonment unlike any other, therefore. It has no time limit and there is no parole. It has been described as coercive, but not punitive in the sense in which a sentence of imprisonment for a crime is: see *Keegan v. deBurca* [1973] I.R. 223.

Criminal contempt, referred to above, is somewhat different. It is a criminal offence in the same category as other criminal offences in that it carries a definite term of imprisonment. It consists of any act which is calculated (that is, intended) to bring the administration of justice into disrepute. There is a problem in describing the distinction between criminal and civil contempt in that some acts may be both. For example, a failure by a witness to give evidence when called and ordered to do so by a Court may be regarded as civil contempt (refusal to obey a court order) and a criminal contempt (act calculated to bring the administration of justice into disrepute). Although the refusal to give evidence might seem to be more a civil than a criminal contempt it is invariably treated as a criminal contempt. Thus, a person who refuses to obey a direction in court is likely to be sentenced to a period of imprisonment for contempt, at the end of which the person is released without the requirement to obey the Court direction: see for example *In re O'Kelly* (1974) 108 I.L.T.R. 97. Finally, although the sentence for criminal contempt is for a definite period, there is no legislation specifying the maximum term; contempt of court law in Ireland is purely common law, and the judges have the power to sentence a person to, say, 40 years imprisonment for contempt, even though such a sentence is extremely unlikely. The procedure for initiating a criminal contempt may be through the D.P.P. in the normal manner as described in Chapter 5, but contempt was developed originally by the courts themselves and they may still initiate an arrest, try the person and impose sentence without any of the normal procedures involved in a criminal prosecution. Even here, however, the Constitution may have changed the common law position. In *The State (D.P.P.) v. Walsh* [1981] I.R. 412, the Supreme Court indicated that a jury trial might be required in some instances of contempt, and that the courts should be reluctant to initiate a prosecution without the intervention of the D.P.P.

2. Order for Sale of Land

Perhaps one of the least practical methods of enforcing a court order is the court order for the sale of land, particularly farm land. The 19th Century evictions remain a vivid memory for many people and where land is placed for auction by court order there have been many occasions in which no bids have been made. In such circumstances, the reality of, for example, a bank attempting to recover a debt in relation to land is that an arrangement is usually made by which the land is sold or auctioned without being categorised as a court sale, even though an order for sale may have been obtained on foot of a possession order on default of a bank loan.

3. Enforcement of Court Orders Acts, 1926 and 1940

These Acts, amended by the Courts (No.2) Act, 1986, allow the District Court to require a person in default of a money order to make payments in accordance with a schedule of payments arrived at by the Court after an assessment of the defaulter's means. If the defaulter continues to default on such payments then he may be attached for contempt and lodged in prison for such failure. It may be noted, however, that no person can be sent to prison for inability to pay a debt, but only for wilful refusal to pay a debt within the person's means. There are, therefore, no longer any debtor's prisons in the sense which Dickens described and which, indeed, were one of the first purposes for which prisons were constructed.

TRIBUNALS AND ADJUDICA

Many tribunals and other bodies exist to deal with spe
In this Chapter, we do not provide a comprehensive li
and bodies, but we list a number to provide an idea of the e
matter with which they deal. Of the tribunals discussed the
tribunals which must act judicially. This indicates that, though the
courts and are not, therefore, exercising the judicial power under Art
of the Constitution, they must act in accordance with basic rules of p
cedure. At common law these were called the rules of natural justice and
this phrase continues to be used, although some judges refer to these procedural requirements as the obligation to provide fair procedures in
accordance with Article 40.3 of the Constitution. In any event, the requirement is that these tribunals exercise their powers in accordance with procedures which, although less formal than those in a court of law, require that
the tribunal (a) be unbiased (*nemo judex in causa sua*) and (b) give both sides
an opportunity to be heard (*audi alteram partem*). Apart from such
procedural rules, these bodies are liable to correction by the High Court in
accordance with the judicial review procedure discussed in Chapter 8.

1. Arbitrations

There are an increasing number of situations in which a legal dispute
which cannot be settled between parties is referred by the parties to an
arbitrator whose function is to perform the kind of adjudicative function
which is usually assigned to a Court. The Arbitration Acts, 1954 and 1980
set out much of the procedural and legal requirements relating to a reference to arbitration. Such arbitration may arise automatically from the terms
of a contract which includes an arbitration clause. These clauses are found
increasingly in many commercial contracts such as holiday contracts, building contracts, insurance contracts and the like. Three main reasons appear
to exist for the increased use of arbitration: the possibility of a speedy
decision; a hearing conducted by an expert in the field in question, such as
an engineer or architect; and a hearing conducted in private.

Under s.5 of the Arbitration Act, 1980 where such an arbitration
clause appears in a contract any attempt to bring court proceedings without referring the matter to arbitration must be stayed by a Court where
the other party to the contract applies for such a stay. Under the Arbitration Act, 1954, the Court had a discretion as to whether to grant a stay,
but s.5 of the 1980 Act has severely limited this discretion. See for
example *O'Mahony v. Lysaght* [1988] I.R. 29 and *MacCormac Products
Ltd v. Town of Monaghan Co-Op. Ltd.* [1988] I.R. 304 (both judgments
of O'Hanlon J.).

In addition the Supreme Court has indicated, in *Keenan v. Shield Insurance Co. Ltd.* [1988] I.R. 89 that the courts are not likely to interfere with
the findings of an arbitrator because of the importance of encouraging this
alternative to litigation. Nonetheless, the arbitration hearing must comply
with the basic rules of procedure required by natural justice and Article
40.3 of the Constitution as well as the requirements of the 1954 and 1980
Acts.

...ation may be an alternative
...sessment of Compensation)
...for the determination of the
...is compulsorily acquired by,
...nt purposes e.g. road widen-
...in property arbitration and the
...similar procedure was intro-
...nt) Act, 1985 in relation to land

...e procedure under which inquests
...ury must be summoned to issue a
...igh the procedure which operates in
...an ordinary court—to the point of
...severely limited by the 1962 Act as to
...be reached which would in any way
...ninal law sense. Thus, it would not be
possible to mak... ...l killing. Nor could a finding of suicide
be made by the jury or c... ...is was decided by O'Hanlon J. in *The State (McKeown) v. Scully* [1986] ı.R. 524.

3. Labour Law: Employment Appeals Tribunal and Labour Court

The Employment Appeals Tribunal, established by the Unfair Dismissals Act, 1977 as the successor to the Redundancy Appeals Tribunal, hears cases in which an employee claims that he or she has been unfairly dismissed by an employer. The 1977 Act provides some meaning to the concept of 'unfair dismissal' by stating that a person is deemed to have been unfairly dismissed unless there were substantial grounds justifying the dismissal. And it also specifies that an employer may dismiss on grounds relating, for example, to the competence of the employee. The Tribunal is, generally speaking, comprised of three people, one lawyer and a representative of an employer organisation and a trade union. A comprehensive analysis of the law on unfair dismissal is provided by Redmond, *Unfair Dismissals Law in the Republic of Ireland* (Incorporated Law Society, 1982).

In spite of its title, the Labour Court is, in fact, a less formal tribunal than the E.A.T. The function of the Labour Court is primarily to provide a forum for the settlement of disputes which might require the arbitration of a specialist tribunal which can mediate between the employer and employees. The recommendations of the Labour Court are not automatically binding on either party. However, in particular instances the parties may decide in advance of a Labour Court hearing that the recommendations will be accepted and implemented by both sides. Attached to the Labour Court are Rights Officers who may be used to assist in the settlement of disputes also.

4. Revenue Matters

Under the Income Tax Act, 1967 the Appeal Commissioners are empowered to hear appeals from an assessment of tax which has been made by an Inspector of Taxes in relation to either an individual taxpayer or a company. The Appeal Commissioners constitute a type of internal appeal mechanism, because they are actually officers within the Revenue Commissioners itself. However, they are also independent of the collection system and on many occasions they find that the taxpayer is not liable to the tax assessed. As appears from Chapter 6, above, there is also an appeal mechanism available from the Appeal Commissioners to the court system.

In addition, on the collection side County Registrars and, in Dublin, Sheriffs are empowered under the 1967 Act to seize property belonging to a taxpayer where the taxpayer is in default on payment of tax which has been lawfully levied by an inspector of taxes. See *Weekes v. Revenue Commissioners* [1989] I.L.R.M. 165 (Extract 12.14).

5. Social Welfare

Under the Social Welfare (Consolidation) Act, 1981, where an individual is refused a particular allowance or benefit under the social welfare legislation an appeal may be made to an Appeals Officer within the Department of Social Welfare. Unlike the situation with respect to taxation matters, however, there is no direct appeal mechanism from an Appeals Officer to the court system. However, an aggrieved person may apply for judicial review where for example it is alleged that the procedures adopted were unfair or that the Department was not applying the law properly. See for example *The State (Kershaw) v. Eastern Health Board* [1985] I.L.R.M. 235.

6. Planning Matters

The Local Government (Planning and Development) Act, 1976 established a planning appeals board, An Bord Pleanála, with power to hear appeals from either the granting or refusing of planning permission. The procedures which must be adopted in appealing to An Bord Pleanála are set out in the Local Government (Planning and Development) Rules, 1977. On this area see O'Sullivan and Shepherd, *A Sourcebook on Planning and Development Law in Ireland* (Professional Books, 1984, and 1987 Supplement).

7. Valuation Tribunal

The Tribunal was established by the Valuation Act, 1988. The Tribunal's function is to hear applications in relation to the rateable valuation which has been placed on property by a local authority. Rateable valuation means the sum specified by a local authority as the basis for calculating the rates which the local authority may charge as a property tax in order to provide at least part of the services, such as water and sewage, which a business has come to expect of a local authority since the early part of the 19th Century. The Tribunal, in effect, took over the functions of the Circuit Court which up to then heard all appeals from local authority valuations. Given that history it is not surprising, perhaps, that the procedures in the Tribunal are similar to those in a courtroom and that in many instances counsel are retained to appear before the Tribunal.

8. Criminal Injuries Compensation Tribunal

This Tribunal was established by a scheme which was introduced by the government in 1974, and amended a number of times since then. The scheme is not a statutory scheme and the government has complete control over the terms of the scheme as they may decide from time to time. In fact in 1986 the government decided, in order to reduce expenditure, to limit severely the scope of the scheme. Until 1986, a person who received personal injuries as a result of a criminal act could apply to the tribunal for compensation of the same order which would be received in a court action. The changes introduced to the scheme in 1986 by the government resulted in a victim only being entitled to compensation provided that the injuries resulted from a riot or from the activites of an illegal organisation or from other violence associated with Northern Ireland. Similar changes were also made by the Malicious Injuries (Amendment) Act, 1986 in relation to property damage, where compensation may be claimed from local authorities. On the duties of the Tribunal see *The State (Hayes) v. Criminal Injuries Compensation Tribunal* [1982] I.L.R.M. 210 and *The State (Creedon) v. Criminal Injuries Compensation Tribunal* [1988] I.R. 51.

9. Tribunals of Inquiry

Under the Tribunals of Inquiry (Evidence) Acts, 1921 and 1979, the government may, by order, establish a tribunal of inquiry to investigate a particular matter which is of particular difficulty. The tribunal thus established has powers similar to those of a court and in most instances they have, in recent years, been chaired by a High Court judge. These tribunals may also be given power to make recommendations in relation to the matter under investigation, for example, as to whether any change in the law is required. An example of such an inquiry was that in relation to the Fire at the Stardust in Dublin in 1981, which sat for 122 days, with legal representation including junior and senior counsel and which resulted in a Report of over 600 pages: *Report of the Tribunal of Inquiry on the Fire at the Stardust, Artane, Dublin* (1982, Pl.853).

10. Ministers

Virtually every government Minister is empowered to make decisions which must be exercised judicially. For example, where the Minister for Agriculture decides whether to grant a licence to a person to conduct business as a livestock mart, the decision must be made in accordance with fair procedures: see *East Donegal Co-Op. Ltd v. Attorney General* [1970] I.R. 317 (Extract 12.1) Of course, many policy decisions of a Minister do not come under this heading, such as how much government money should be allocated to assisting the mart industry.

11. Disciplinary Tribunals

We have seen how, in relation to the legal profession (see Chapter 3) certain disciplinary tribunals have the power to make decisions in respect of individuals which may have an extremely important effect on that person's professional life. Such tribunals are quite common and they also must conform with the rules of fair procedures.

12. Other Tribunals

In some instances, the government may establish tribunals or commissions which make an investigation of a partiuclar subject without necessarily being required to conduct an inquiry which is of a judicial nature. Thus, the Ó Briain Committee established in the 1970s by the government to make recommendations in relation to Garda Custody (1978, Prl.7158) was not one which heard evidence in the same way in which a tribunal established under the Tribunals of Inquiry Acts would. The Ó Briain Committee heard evidence in the sense that it received submissions from interested parties but it did not act as a court-like tribunal.

Other examples of such government commissions or tribunals include the *Commission on Social Welfare* (1986, Pl.3851) and the *Commission of Inquiry on Safety, Health and Welfare at Work* (1983, Pl.1868). The latter Commission may be regarded as much more of a success than some others since its main proposals were incorporated in the Safety, Health and Welfare at Work Act, 1989, whereas many of the recommendations of other commissions are unlikely to be implemented in full. This is so even though these commissions may be regarded as official in the sense that its members would have been appointed by the relevant government Minister of the day.

Chapter 10

EUROPEAN AND INTERNATIONAL LAW

On behalf of the State the government has acceded to a number of international agreements and treaties with other governments. These have had an impact on Irish law, to a greater or lesser extent, depending on the treaty or agreement in question. Article 29.6 of the Constitution provides that no international agreement shall be part of Irish law except as may be determined by the Oireachtas. This is in conformity with the general principle that agreements between States, that is between their governments, do not create any legal rights for the individual citizens of those States. That, in effect, is international law, the law between States, which is not part of domestic law unless and until it is made so by domestic legislation. As far as international agreements are concerned, therefore, they tend to operate quite separately from the domestic legal system of the government who might accede to them.

There is one major exception to this rule of international agreements, and this involves the treaties which established the European Community of which Ireland became a member in 1973. We will discuss in this Chapter the effect of membership of the Community on Irish domestic law. In addition we will discuss the impact of other international organisations of which Ireland is a member, some of which also have a less direct impact on Irish law.

EUROPEAN COMMUNITY LAW

1. The Constitution and Community Law

The simple point to be made in relation to European Community Law is that it is also domestic Irish law. It is important, therefore, to be clear as to what is meant by European Community Law. Article 29.4.3° of the Constitution provides the starting point. This provision was inserted into the Constitution after its terms were approved in the 1972 referendum by which the State was authorised by the People to join what was commonly called the 'Common Market' or 'the E.E.C.' In fact the amendment to the Constitution which was approved in 1972 authorised the State to join three Communities, the European Coal and Steel Community (E.C.S.C.), the European Economic Community (E.E.C.) and the European Atomic Energy Community (Euratom). Each of these three Communities had been established in the 1950s by way of treaties which had been signed by the governments of six continental European States which had been devastated by World War II, including France, Germany and Italy. The purpose of the E.C.S.C., for example, was to ensure that by combining the economic development of the coal and steel industries in a common purpose there would never again be any need for what amounted to economic wars between France and Germany which had been part of the causative factors in World War II. The E.E.C. was designed to ensure that, so far as possible, customs barriers between the States would be removed so that there would be free movement of goods and services and workers between the States and ultimately that a 'Common Market' in goods would be established. Finally Euratom was to ensure that the nuclear industry would be developed primarily for commercial purposes. 3.

The treaties which established these Communities were, however, from the beginning different from other treaties between States. Complex secretariats with executive powers, answerable to Ministers from the member States, were established. Assemblies were established for each Community with some powers also. Finally, a Court of Justice was established to oversee implementation of the treaty obligations. The texts of the treaties were also different from other international agreements, and they indicated that the provisions as to free movement of workers were to take priority over the internal domestic laws of the member States. The Communities must be seen as the culmination of efforts by European statesmen to establish different forms of institutions to prevent a recurrence of World War II, some of which had foundered in the early 1950s. The three Communities amounted to an arrangement which was acceptable and which could be developed over time.

By the 1960s, the Communities had developed to such an extent that single institutions for all three had been established. At this time, Britain and Ireland renewed applications for membership, and lengthy negotiations culminated in the signing of the three treaties in 1972. By this time, the European Communities had developed to the extent that its effect on Irish law was clear. The Court of Justice of the European Communities had stated quite clearly, in *Costa v. E.N.E.L.* [1964] E.C.R. 74, that Community law created a completely new legal order which was superior to domestic laws of the member States. Where there was any conflict, Community law must take priority and domestic law was secondary. This was, of course, a reversal of the usual position of agreements made by States. It created a dual problem for Irish law.

First, legislation would be required to make the treaties which established the Communities part of Irish law. This was achieved by the passing of the European Communities Act, 1972. The second problem lay in the Constitution itself. The Constitution remains the paramount domestic law in the State, and any provision of the Constitution would take priority in this State over, for example, the European Communities Act, 1972. The Constitution required to be amended, therefore.

In addition to permitting Ireland to join the European Communities, Article 29.4.3° also provided that no provision of the Constitution could be invoked to invalidate any acts 'necessitated' by membership of the Communities, or to prevent any European Community law from having full force and effect in Irish law. In effect, therefore, Article 29.4.3° brought the Constitution into line with the requirements of the Communities.

The effect of the constitutional amendment, therefore, was that European Community law became part of domestic Irish law in accordance with the timetable which had been agreed in the negotiations by the government. It introduced into Irish law a huge amount of what might be described, broadly, as commercial and economic law. And, significantly for the Irish court system, it established that the Court of Justice of the European Communities was from that time onwards the final court of appeal in relation to matters which came within the competence of the European Communities. The effect of joining the Communities was, therefore, to cede to some extent the sovereignty of the State in relation to certain areas of law, and to create a new level of law which takes priority over some aspects of the Constitution. As Henchy J. stated in the Supreme Court decision *Doyle v. An Taoiseach* [1986] I.L.R.M. 693, Community law 'has the paramount force and effect of constitutional provisions.'

It is not possible to discuss in depth the effect of European Community law in Ireland. At a very fundamental level, however, it has resulted in massive injections of funds into the agricultural sector of Irish life in particular and it has resulted in the passage of an enormous amount of legislation through the Oireachtas as well as by way of secondary legislation. Apart from the enormous effect on the agricultural sector, membership has resulted in the passage of important legislation on companies law; recognition of professional qualifications; competition law; employemnt law, particularly in the area of equality; social welfare law; as well as having an increasingly important impact on how the Oireachtas may raise taxes through revenue legislation. For the purposes of this text, however, the main focus is on the arrangements which have been made at Community and national level to implement these changes. What follows, therefore, is an outline of the European Community legal system, which operates in parallel with each domestic legal system of the member States.

When reading this outline, it should be clear that many of the procedures which are used at Community level to implement its basic rules in domestic law are different from those which operate in a common law system. This arises from the fact that the original member States of the Communities all have Civil Law legal systems. In fact, of the current twelve member States, only two, the United Kingdom and Ireland, have common law systems. This, of course, presents some unusual problems of technique with which Irish judges have found some difficulty. Some of these are referred to in the discussion of *Murphy v. Bord Telecom* [1989] I.L.R.M. 53 (Extract 12.15). There are other areas in which Community law has made a significant impact on the extent to which Ireland remains a common law system. Only time will tell, however, whether the development of the European Community will lead to a single legal system for the member States of the Community.

2. The Institutions of the Community

The following are the main Community institutions.

(a) *The Commission*. This is the embryonic government of the Community. The members of the Commission, 17 in all, are appointed by their governments for a four year full time term, and the headquarters is permanently in Brussels, in the Berlaymont Building. The head of the Commission is called the President. Each of the Commissioners is given a particular area of responsibility, just like government Ministers. The present Irish Commissioner is Ray McSharry former Minister for Finance in Ireland, and whose area of responsibility is Agriculture Policy. The Commissioners are each backed up by the permanent civil servants of the Community, also in Brussels, and the Community civil service is divided into 20 Directorates-General. The main function of the Commission is to initiate proposals as to how the basic principles set out in the Treaties are to be implemented in practice. This involves the Commission forwarding proposals to the governments of the member States for decisions by the

Councils of Ministers. And the Commission must also forward proposals to the Parliament of the Community. Having heard comments from these other institutions the Commission may then reformulate the proposals, and this process can take a long time, depending on the political sensitivities involved in, for example, prices for agricultural produce. The ultimate decision in most situations, however, rests with the Councils of Ministers.

(b) *The Councils of Ministers.* There are a number of different Councils, such as the Council of Agriculture Ministers, the Council of Transport Ministers, and so forth. What happens is that, for example, each Agriculture Minister in each of the member States of the Community is kept briefed on developments from the Commission in relation to agriculture proposals. Our Minister for Agriculture and Food would get his departmental officials to deal with these and respond to Commission proposals. On a regular basis, meetings of all the Agriculture Ministers take place in Brussels to discuss these proposals with the Commissioner responsible for Agriculture and a final decision may be made. It is the Council of Ministers who have the final say on whether a particular proposal goes through, for example, on how much is to be spent on milk production in the Community. And in matters of vital national interest to one country, its Minister can refuse to consent to a decision on which all other Ministers are agreed (this is usually referred to as the veto). This means that for many decisions there is a requirement of unanimity in the Council for a decision to be made. In some areas since the Single European Act was approved (see below), decisions can be taken by a majority vote, but the veto still remains in some areas.

In certain areas the Council has delegated day-to-day implementation to the Commission, such as in relation to competition policy. This delegation of power has included the power to impose fines on individuals or companies for breaking Community law rules on competition. And once the Council has made a decision on the agriculture budget, for example, the Commission has the task of ensuring that the correct payments are made. In addition, twice a year there is a meeting of the heads of government, called the European Council (or, more colloquially, the Summit). This has been used increasingly as a forum for making decisions, for example after an Agriculture Minister had used a veto at a Council of Ministers meeting.

(c) *European Parliament.* Formerly called the Assembly, the Parliament is still in third place as far as power is concerned, but catching up. Up to 1979, its members (M.E.P.s) were nominated by the parliaments of the member States. Since 1979, the members have been elected directly by the people, in elections usually held on the same day throughout the Community. This has had a psychological effect in support of calls by the M.E.P.s for more powers; there are also many more full time members than formerly. Committees of the Parliament monitor developments and have produced influential reports which have resulted in real changes in the direction of the Community; the Parliament has become less of a talking shop. In the early 1980s, the Parliament exercised its only real power, which is to block the budget proposed by the Commission (the Councils of Ministers can do this as well, of course). The Parliament also has power to dismiss the Commission, but this drastic power has never been used. This can be explained by the fact that the Parliament cannot dismiss an individual

Commissioner only: it must be the entire Commission. The Commission must consult the Parliament on all proposals and must attend Parliament on a regular basis to explain its decisions. This is similar to Irish government Ministers being required to answer questions in Dáil Éireann.

(d) *Court of Justice*. The Court has power to interpret the provisions of the Treaties establishing the Community. Its decisions are binding on all courts in the Community, including the Irish Supreme Court. This is, as noted above, a requirement of Community law, which is superior to domestic (national) law. It should also be noted, however, that this superiority only applies to the areas of law with which the European Community is concerned. There are many areas of the Constitution which are unaffected by membership such as the prohibition on divorce in Article 41 of the Constitution. Many cases which come before the Court of Justice originate in the courts of the member States. For example a person might be charged with an offence in the District Court for breaking some Community law on, say, fishing quotas. The District Court can refer any point of Community Law to the Court of Justice under Article 177 of the Treaty of the E.E.C. This is discussed below. Cases can also be brought by the Council or Commission against the governments of the member States or against one of the institutions of the Community for failure to implement a Community law. This form of case will involve the Court making a final judgment on the matter in dispute. The Court has power to impose fines in this situation.

3. The Form of Community Laws

Procedures for implementing Community law were set out in the treaties establishing the three Communities. These are as follows.

(a) *Regulations*. The Council of Ministers has the ultimate power to approve Community Regulations, which immediately become law in the member States. The prices given by the Community for surplus agricultural produce is specified in a Community Regulation approved each year by the Council of Agriculture Ministers based on the proposals worked out in consultation with the Commission and Parliament.

(b) *Directives*. This is the form of law most used to achieve harmonisation of laws across the Community. Because of the different systems of law which exist in the 12 member States (and this is especially so with the two common law systems since the United Kingdom and Ireland joined) it was felt that immediately enforceable Regulations would be inappropriate to achieve the harmonisation or approximation of laws in the member States. Thus, the drafters of the original Treaties felt that the mechanism of a Directive would be more appropriate. The basic purpose of the Directive is set out in its text and this must be implemented by the member States, but the wording of the Directive does not have to be followed to the letter. This provides the flexibility. A Directive must be approved by the Council as with a Regulation, but it usually specifies a date, say, 3 years into the future, by which time it must be implemented by the member States. So a Directive approved in 1988 might not have to be implemented until 1991. After that deadline has passed, however, the Council or Commission might bring a case before the Court to force its introduction by the defaulting member State. In fact many countries fall behind, and are gently persuaded to implement as soon as possible. The advantage of the Directive is that the precise method by which it is implemented is left to the member State. Some directives, even when they have not been implemented by a member State, in fact become law once the deadline passes (become 'directly applicable'). This means they become enforceable in the courts of the member States including the Supreme Court in Ireland. This applies to Directives which confer rights on individuals: see for example the Directive on Equal Pay discussed in *Murphy v. Bord Telecom* [1989] I.L.R.M. 53 (Extract 12.15). Some Directives are in fact worded in such a way they are not directly applicable.

(c) *Decisions.* The Commission's decisions in relation to a particular company breaking competition laws of the Community apply only to that company. But these decisions may also be followed up by a fine, sometimes of millions of ECUs, the European Unit of Currency, which does not in fact exist as a separate currency. It is possible to appeal to the Court of Justice against these fines, but many of them have been upheld by the Court.

(d) *National laws.* Regulations made by the Councils of Ministers generally become law in the member States without any further steps being necessary. Directives, as we saw, do need to be implemented by domestic legislation in most cases. Under s.3 of the European Communities Act, 1972, these implementing laws can take the form of secondary legislation, that is, Irish statutory instruments signed by the appropriate Minister. For example, the European Communities (Major Accident Hazards of Certain Industrial Activities) Regulations, 1986 were signed by the Minister for Labour to implement a June 1982 Directive. The 1986 Regulations (not to be confused with Council regulations, discussed above) ran to 79 typed pages, so they are an important piece of law regarding the safety precautions which must be taken in certain chemical installations. Between 20 to 30 (sometimes more) such statutory instruments are signed into law each year, but of course they do not need to be debated in the Oireachtas like Acts; they become law 'at the stroke of a pen'. And (as if to confuse a little more) some laws implementing Directives have been implemented by Act of the Oireachtas, for example, the Companies (Amendment) Act, 1982.

(e) *Court Decisions.* The Court of Justice decisions are, of course, important; they are discussed above. And courts of the member States are also decisions which will become increasingly important as time progresses; but a decision of a German court interpreting Community law would not be binding on an Irish court.

4. The Irish Courts and Community Law

On the procedural level, Article 177 of the Treaty of Rome, which established the E.E.C. (and which in practical terms is the most important Community from Ireland's perspective) permits a form of case stated to the Court of Justice of the European Communities from any Irish court or other tribunal which is required to deal with a Community law problem. This enables the Irish court or tribunal to obtain the advice of the Court of Justice in order to enable the domestic Court or tribunal to reach a decision in accordance with the correct view of Community law. Many such references have been made, one of which resulted in the High Court decision in *Murphy v. Bord Telecom* [1989] I.L.R.M. 53 (Extract 12.15).

However, by virtue of the nature of European Community law itself, each domestic tribunal is empowered to apply the decisions of the Court of Justice even without the need for a reference, so that all the decisions of the Court of Justice in relation to any area of Community law are binding precedents which must be followed in the domestic courts. This is specifically provided for in the European Communities Act, 1972. The discussion of precedent in Chapter 11 should be read, therefore, with this is mind. On the factors which are relevant in deciding whether to refer a question under Article 177 or to apply existing Court of Justice decisions, see the judgment of Barrington J. in *Irish Creamery Milk Suppliers Association Ltd. v. Ireland* (1979) 3 J.I.S.E.L. 66. Once a Court or tribunal has made a decision to refer the case to the Court of Justice, the reference must go ahead and not even the Supreme Court will interfere. That is the effect of *Campus Oil Ltd. v. Minister for Industry and Energy* [1983] I.R. 82.

In relation to legislation, some important points also arise. As *Murphy v. Bord Telecom* indicates, judges may be more prepared to apply new approaches to statutory interpretation where Community law is involved. There is a more fundamental matter. Pursuant to the European Communities Act, 1972, Community law may be introduced into Irish law by means of secondary legislation, that is, statutory instruments signed by a relevant Minister which do not require to be passed through the Oireachtas. This has never been challenged in Irish law, the question which might arise being, perhaps, whether this arrangment is 'necessitated' by membership of the Communities. If not, of course, the legislative power of the Oireachtas under the Constitution might require that such laws be approved by the Oireachtas. Another feature of the 1972 Act is that where secondary legislation approved under its provisions creates criminal penalties, as most of them do, they may only be prosecuted by way of summary trial, which of course results in a limit on the penalties which may be imposed for such offences, regardless of gravity.

5. The Single European Act

In the early 1980s, it was acknowledged that the achievement of the basic aims of the three Communities had become stalled, partly because of the political arrangements which had been made during the 1960s requiring unanimity in decisions of the Councils of Ministers. After a number of years of debate between the Member States, the Single European Act (S.E.A.) was signed in 1986. The S.E.A. provides for a number of important amendments to the Treaties of the three Communities with the purpose of accelerating towards a Single European Market by the end of 1992. To this end, over 300 Community laws are required and provision for some majority voting in the Council was introduced as an important requirement to achieve the deadline set. In addition to these changes in Community institutional procedures, the S.E.A. introduced a new lower court level under the Court of Justice to act as a clearing house for cases, with the Court of Justice to act, in effect, as the final court of appeal in Community law matters. Finally, Title III of the S.E.A. introduced provisions dealing with European Political Co-Operation, which in effect was a formalisation of the existing arrangements by which the Community member States would agree common positions on foreign policy matters, though in view of Ireland's declared policy of neutrality this co-operation excludes military aspects of European defence.

In December 1986, the Oireachtas passed the European Communities (Amendment) Act, 1986 to give effect in Irish law to the provisions of the S.E.A. But before the government had deposited the formal instruments of ratification in Rome, as required by the S.E.A. itself in order for it to come into effect, the High Court, in *Crotty v. An Taoiseach* [1987] I.R. 619, granted an interlocutory injunction to prevent ratification of the S.E.A. The interlocutory injunction could hardly have been granted in more dramatic circumstances. Barrington J. heard legal argument in his home on Christmas Eve 1986 and delivered judgment after only a short adjournment to consider the matter. A Divisional High Court (Hamilton P., Barrington and Carroll JJ.) later upheld the validity of the 1986 Act and held it had no function in relation to Title III of the S.E.A. While the first part of this was upheld on appeal to the Supreme Court, the Court held, by a majority of 3-2 (Walsh, Henchy and Hederman JJ.; Finlay C.J. and Griffin JJ. dissenting) that the provisions of Title III were unconstitutional. This necessitated a referendum to amend the Constitution to add a new provision to Article 29.4.3°, authorising the State to sign the S.E.A. This was approved by the People in the May 1987 referendum, and the S.E.A subsequently came into force. Since then, many of the steps required to bring about the Single Market have been put in train. The S.E.A. has resulted in references to the European Community (E.C.) rather than to the European Communities.

A comprehensive analysis of the effect of Community law is contained in McMahon and Murphy, *European Community Law in Ireland* (Butterworths, 1989). Finally, it may be noted that the Irish Centre for European Law was established in 1988 in response to the need to provide information as to the effects of the S.E.A., and the Centre has published a number of important monographs on aspects of Community law.

COUNCIL OF EUROPE

The Council of Europe was one of the first institutions established after World War II as an attempt to prevent the mass violation of human rights which had occurred during the war. One of the first major initiatives of the Council of Europe was to draft the Convention for the Protection of Human Rights and Fundamental Freedoms in 1950. In fact Seán MacBride, the late Nobel and Lenin Peace Prize winner, was involved in the drafting, of the Convention and Ireland ratified the Convention in 1950.

A central part of the Convention was the establishment of a mechanism for enforcement of its terms against the member States. This mechanism is by way of complaint, which may be made by an individual citizen or a member State of the Council to the European Commission of Human Rights (not to be confused with the Commission of the European Community) which is situated in Strasbourg, France. If the complaint of breach of the Convention is deemed to be well-founded the Commission may bring the matter to the European Court of Human Rights. The decision of the Court is a final determination of the matter and is binding on the member State to whom it is directed. Indeed the first case brought to the Court was *Lawless v. Ireland* (1961) 1 E.H.R.R. 25. And in a case brought by the Irish government against the British government, the Court found that police procedures in Northern Ireland in the early 1970s constituted inhuman and degrading treatment contrary to the Convention: *Ireland v. United Kingdom* (1978) 2 E.H.R.R. 25. In *Airey v. Ireland* (1979) 2 E.H.R.R. 305 Ireland was found to be in breach of the Convention in failing to provide Mrs. Airey with access to legal advice to take separation proceedings in an Irish court: see Chapter 7.

There are a number of limits which may be noted in relation to the Convention. First, member states of the Council are not obliged to accept the jurisdiction of the Commission or Court. Second, even where the jurisdiction of the Court is accepted, a member State may decide to notify the Council that it intends, in effect, to ignore a decision by derogating from the relevant provision of the Convention. This step is somewhat unusual, but derogation may also take place where it is anticipated that a domestic law is likely to be regarded as being in breach of the Convention. Third, the decisions of the Commission or Court are only binding on the member State to whom they are directed. Finally, under Article 29.6 of the Constitution, the Convention is not part of Irish domestic law and is thus not relevant in any court proceedings in Ireland.

These last two points were significant in relation to *Norris v. Attorney General* [1984] I.R. 36 (Extract 13.7). As we will see in Chapter 13, the plaintiff in that case challenged the constitutional validity of ss.61 and 62 of the Offences against the Person Act, 1861. The case was dismissed in the High Court in 1980. In 1981 the Court of Human Rights ruled that these sections, which were at that time still in force in Northern Ireland, were in conflict with the provisions of the Convention on Human Rights: *Dudgeon v. United Kingdom* (1981) 4 E.H.R.R. 149. In the Supreme Court in *Norris*, the Court decided in April 1983 by a majority of 3-2 that ss.61 and 62 of the 1861 Act were not unconstitutional. In the course of the majority judgment in *Norris,* O'Higgins C.J. pointed out that the ruling in the *Dudgeon* case was not relevant to a decision on the constitutional validity of the sections. This was a correct statement of the law, though as Henchy J., one of the dissenting judges pointed out, the sections appeared to be doomed in view of the *Dudgeon* ruling.

This was confirmed, though not until over five years later, when the Court of Human Rights ruled that ss.61 and 62 of the 1861, as they operated in Ireland, were in conflict with the Convention: *Norris v. Ireland* (judgment of 26 October 1988). While the experience in the *Norris* case indicates that the Convention can prove to be a difficult law to implement in practice, it must be remembered that the mechanisms established under the Convention predated the establishment of the European Communities. Thus any enforcement mechanism was a new departure at the time, and the role of the Court of Human Rights has, in general, been significant particularly since the 1970s when its workload began to increase dramatically.

In addition to the Commission and Court, the Council of Europe established a Parliamentary Assembly and Committee of Ministers which also have certain important powers. The Committee has, for example, adopted recommendations some of which have found their way into domestic law. They are of course by no means binding on the member

States, though they are influential and one such recommendation was even referred to by Barron J. in *Hand v. Dublin Corporation*, High Court, unreported, 28 October 1988.

Apart from the Convention on Human Rights a number of other Conventions have been signed since 1950 under the auspices of the Council. These include the European Social Charter (1961), the European Convention on Social Security (1972), the European Convention on the Legal Status of Migrant Workers (1977) and the Convention for the Protection of Individuals With Regard to the Automatic Processing of Data (1982). The Data Protection Act, 1988 implemented the latter Convention in Irish law.

Finally, although there are 21 member States of the Council of Europe while there are only 12 members of the European Community, there is considerable overlap between the membership. All the member States of the Community are member States of the Council of Europe, and this fact led the Court of Justice of the European Communities to state that the basic principles underlying the Convention of Human Rights could be relevant to the interpretation of the Community treaties: see McMahon and Murphy, *supra*, at pp.132-137. A further indication of the connection is that, since 1987, the official logo of the European Community has been 12 stars in a circle against a blue background. This is very similar to the Council of Europe logo.

OTHER INTERNATIONAL AGREEMENTS

As indicated at the beginning of this Chapter, agreements made between governments do not usually create rights or entitlements within the domestic laws of the signatory States. Membership of the European Community and the Council of Europe are, therefore, exceptions to this general rule. Thus, membership of the United Nations Organisation or the General Agreement on Tariffs and Trade (G.A.T.T.) would not appear to create any rights in Irish law except insofar as the Oireachtas passes legislation giving effect to some obligation of membership of those organisations. After the *Crotty* case, referred to above, however, some doubts were expressed as to the scope of the decision, and whether certain international agreements were invalid by virtue of the Supreme Court decision in that case. In particular, worries were expressed in relation to the 1985 Anglo-Irish Agreement. The Agreement's validity was upheld by Barrington J. in *McGimpsey v. Ireland* [1989] I.L.R.M. 209, but at the time of going to print this decision was under appeal to the Supreme Court.

Other organisations of which the State is a member include the Organisation for Economic Co-Operation and Development (O.E.C.D.) and the International Labour Organisation (I.L.O.). Many of the Conventions signed by the government under the auspices of the latter organisation have become law in domestic legislation.

For general discussion of international law and its operation in Irish law see Symmons, 'The Criminal Law (Jurisdiction) Act 1976 and International Law' (1978) 13 *Ir. Jur. (n.s.)* 36 and Connelly, 'Non-Extradition for Political Offences' (1982) 17 *Ir. Jur. (n.s.)* 59.

Chapter 11

THE DOCTRINE OF PRECEDENT

OVERVIEW

It should by now be obvious that the distinctive feature of a common law system, such as the Irish legal system, is that courts are required to follow earlier decisions of a similar nature. The purpose of this is to ensure a consistent application of the law. Since common law systems, unlike their civilian equivalents, lack the textual basis of an authoritative code their rules are essentially unwritten. Instead, those rules are to be found in the decisions of courts which are charged with the task of applying them. As a result judicial decisions are a source of law, loosely called "case law", to which lawyers have recourse. In this respect, if courts were allowed a discretion as to whether to follow an earlier case the perceived danger is that different courts would identify and apply different rules. That is not to say that judges would exhibit favouritism, but the risk is that through the application of different judicial standards conflicting and contradictory rules might emerge. Thus, to ensure consistency the practice developed whereby courts followed earlier relevant decisions. The practice has become so prevalent that its correctness is now beyond dispute and can be considered to be the principal rule of judicial decision-making in common law systems. In seeking consistency two objectives of justice are pursued. The first is that the law is applied equally, as similar cases are treated similarly. The other is that the law becomes certain and one can determine in advance the legal quality of a proposed course of action. Those who are subjected to a regime of regulation are entitled to know that which is required of them. One of the hallmarks of authoritarianism is that one is uncertain of the laws which governs one's conduct.

However, when we speak of following cases it should be realised that the process is neither simple nor mechanical. On the contrary, it is complicated and involves the use of skills and techniques which are acquired through exposure to, and experience of, the methods and devices employed by courts. In one sense no two cases are similar, in that each case presents a unique set of circumstances which differentiates it from any other. The task of the courts is to identify cases which can be considered to be similar and to reach similar conclusions in those cases. To this extent courts enjoy a discretion as they are in essence required to place cases in conceptual categories from which the legal issues involved are analysed. But once two cases are placed in the same category, and thus deemed to be similar, the expectation that earlier cases be followed, encapsulated in the principle of *stare decisis*, strives to ensure consistency of application. In this respect the doctrine of precedent establishes a methodology within which relevant legal principles are extracted from earlier decisions and are developed and expanded through their application in later cases.

Access to reliable documents which accurately report judicial decisons is essential to the effective operation of a system of precedent. The decisions of earlier courts are to be found in law reports. A report usually contains the judgment or judgments delivered, a synopsis of the arguments of counsel and a headnote, or abstract, which is prepared by the reporter, who by convention is a practising barrister. For this reason newspaper reports which are written by journalists, though illustrative, are not considered to be authoritative. Before being reproduced in the law reports the judgments are corrected by the judges who delivered them and it is the corrected text which is authoritative. The headnote is not part of the case, but is prepared principally for the purposes of reference; it allows the reader to know at a glance the contents of the case. It is important to realise that the headnote is not law, nor is it an authoritative interpretation of the decision. The two series of law reports which are currently published in Ireland are the Irish Reports, published by the Incorporated Council of Law Reporting for Ireland, and the Irish Law Reports Monthly, which are published commercially. The Irish Reports enjoy a "semi-official" status and are preferred to the Irish Law Reports Monthly where a conflict arises between the two. Since March 1989 these have been supplemented by the Irish Times Law Reports which are published each Monday in the *Irish Times*. Whilst the latter merely contain synopses of the judgments delivered they may be cited in court as they are reported by practising barristers. To these reports must be added a number of series which are no longer published, principal amongst them being the Irish Law Times Reports and the Irish Jurist Reports. As the number of reported cases in this country runs into thousands, if not tens of thousands, locating the appropriate case law can be a time-consuming and cumbersome exercise. To this end recourse is had to Digests of Cases, which contain abstracts of cases, and enable the reader to locate the relevant cases on a particular topic and allow him or her to trace the subsequent history of any given case. Due to lack of resources, amongst other things, it is not possible to report all cases in this country. Accordingly, the superior courts have adopted the practice of circulating unreported judgments, which consist of the judicially corrected version of the judgment delivered in the case, to the principal law libraries in the country. However, they do not contain the arguments of counsel nor are they accompanied by a headnote. The advantage of this practice is that it provides lawyers with the complete jurisprudence of the Irish courts and makes decisions available before they are eventually, if ever, reported. The traditional paper-based sources have recently been supplemented by a legal database, ITELIS, which allows subscribers access to a wide range of legal materials. ITELIS contains all Irish reported cases since 1950 and a selection of unreported judgments since 1985 as well as an extensive selection of English, Commonwealth, American and European materials.

Although we have spoken so far of courts being expected to follow earlier decisions it should not be assumed that a court is required to follow every relevant decision which preceded it. A distinction is drawn between *binding authority* and *persuasive authority*. A court is required to follow the former, but in respect of the latter it enjoys a discretion as to whether or not it should adopt the decision. The principal rule which has emerged is that a court must follow the prior decisions of courts superior to it in the judicial hierarchy. This rule is so well established that it has rarely been questioned, in this jurisdiction at least. In addition, a court is generally expected to follow the earlier decisions of courts of coordinate, or equal, jurisdiction. The latter is not an inflexible rule and courts, on occasion, have declared themselves to be free to depart from their own earlier decisions. On the other hand, a court is not bound by the decisions of an inferior court.

Likewise, Irish courts are not bound by the decisions of foreign courts, as that would amount to a derogation from Irish sovereignty. However, the decisions of both inferior and foreign courts are of persuasive authority and so may be followed at the option of the court. As we have noted in Chapter 2 the decisions of foreign courts are regularly cited in and adopted by Irish courts, especially where there is an absence of relevant Irish authority.

When a court is said to be bound by an earlier decision it does not follow that everything which the earlier court said is binding. Although judges do not adopt a uniform format when writing their judgments, a number of elements may be identified in each judgment. There will be a recitation of the facts of the case coupled, if necessary, with comments on and an evaluation of the evidence which was adduced by the parties. A discussion and analysis of the relevant law will follow, and finally the law will be applied to the facts of the case. The part of the judgment which is binding is called the *ratio decidendi.* For present purposes it can be defined as being the reason for the decision; it consists of the relevant principle of law applied to the facts of the case. Other statements of law which are contained in the case are called *obiter dicta*. They are not of direct relevance to the decision and, consequently, are not binding. They are, however, of persuasive authority and may be adopted at the option of the later court.

Several terms ought to be explained at this stage. When an appeal is successful the appellate court is said to have *reversed* the inferior court. The effect is that the decision of the lower court is replaced by that of the higher court and the party who initially lost the case now finds that he or she has won. When an appellate court in a later case considers the earlier decision of a lower court to be erroneous it may *overrule* that decision. Its effect, however, is prospective only in that it does not affect the position of the parties to the earlier case. In other words by overruling a case a court states that it is not to be followed in the future. Courts rarely resort to overruling decisions, preferring instead to *distinguish* them. A decision is said to be distinguished when a later court decides that, for one reason or another, it is not relevant to the case before it. A case might be distinguished because the later court discovers a material factual difference between the two cases or because different legal issues are involved. In essence, the subject matter of the two cases is perceived to differ and they are placed in separate conceptual categories. However, in practice, the effect of distinguishing a case can be equivalent to overruling it. By distinguishing it, a court can confine an earlier case to a very precise situation such that it becomes marginal and of limited importance. It will state that the decision was confined to its particular facts and is of no assistance in other cases. Moreover, if one court distinguishes a particular decision other courts might be more prepared to do likewise. In some cases a court might have reached a decision in ignorance of a relevant statutory provision or binding authority. In that event the decision is said to have been reached *per incuriam*. The consequence is that no valid proposition of law is established by the decision and a later court is not bound to follow it. Where it appears that a court decided a point without its being specifically argued or mentioned in the judgment it is said to have been decided *sub silentio* and, once again, a later court is not required to follow it. A difference of judicial opinion is evident on the question of a judge considering a point which was not specifically addressed in counsel's argument. In *G v An Bord Uchtala* [1980] I.R. 32 Walsh J. spoke of the right to life and the constitutionality of certain decisions which were made by the Adoption Board. His brethren expressly reserved their opinions on those points as they had not been the subject of argument. Likewise O'Higgins C.J. and Griffin J. did not join McCarthy J. in commenting on the appropriate judicial evaluation of foreign cases in *Irish Shell Ltd. v Elm Motors Ltd.* [1984] I.R. 511 (Extract 11.7). Similar difficulties which were presented by the question of direct appeals from the Central Criminal Court to the Supreme Court in *The People v Shaw* [1982] I.R. 1 (Extract 11.9) and *The People v Lynch* [1982] I.R. 64 (Extract 11.10) are discussed by Casey (Extract 11.12).

STARE DECISIS IN IRISH COURTS

As stated earlier the principle of *stare decisis* reflects the expectation that earlier cases be followed. To this end a hierarchical framework is established within which the authority of prior decisions can be determined. The principal rule is that an inferior court must follow the earlier decisions of superior courts. Thus, the High Court must follow the Supreme Court and the Circuit Court must follow both the High and Supreme Courts. This rule is so well settled that it has seldom been questioned by an Irish court. Thus, in *The State (Harkin) v O'Malley* [1978] I.R. 269 O'Higgins C.J. observed that Gannon J., in the High Court, was bound to follow an earlier Supreme Court decision which the Court then overruled on the grounds that it was erroneously decided and, also, was a *per incuriam* decision. Unlike the position in which the House of Lords has found itself in the past—see, for instance, *Cassell & Co. Ltd. v Broome* [1964] A.C. 1027—the Supreme Court has rarely had to reprimand the High Court for failure to follow one of its decisions. The only recent case in which this has occurred is the marginally reported decision in *McDonnell v Byrne Engineering Co. Ltd. Irish Times*, October 4, 1978 (Extract 11.1).

The related question of whether a court should follow its own earlier decisions has been in issue in Irish courts over the past twenty-five years or so. The Supreme Court has decided in *The State (Quinn) v Ryan* [1965] I.R. 110 (Extract 11.2) and *Attorney General v Ryan's Car Hire* [1965] I.R. 642 (Extract 11.3) that it is not absolutely bound by its earlier decisions. The judgments in those cases show that, whilst in general the Supreme Court will follow its own decisions, it reserves a freedom to depart from them where there are "compelling reasons". *Stare decisis* is now considered by the Court to be a policy, not an inflexible rule. It should be noted that when those cases were decided the House of Lords was considered to be strictly bound by its earlier decisions, a position which was relaxed some years later: see *Practice Note* [1966] 1 W.L.R. 1234. But although the Supreme Court has declared its freedom to depart from its earlier decisions it is clear that it will do so with reluctance. That the desire to maintain "judicial order and continuity" is strong is evident in Henchy J.'s judgments in *The State (Lynch) v Cooney* [1982] I.R. 337 (Extract 11.11), *Mogul of Ireland Ltd. v Tipperary (North Riding) County Council* [1976] I.R. 260 (Extract 12.17) and *Hynes-O'Sullivan v O'Driscoll* [1989] I.L.R.M. 349 and the dissenting judgment of Griffin J. in *Doyle v Hearne* [1987] I.R. 601 (Extract 11.4). However, it appears from the judgments of Henchy J. in *Hamilton v Hamilton* [1982] I.R. 466 and McCarthy J. in *Doyle v Hearne* that the Court when composed of five judges will more readily reconsider the decision of a three judge Supreme Court.

The High Court is not considered to be absolutely bound by its previous decisions. However, in *Irish Trust Bank Ltd. v Central Bank of Ireland* High Court, unreported, 4 March, 1976 (Extract 11.5) Parke J. manifested a reluctance to depart from an earlier High Court decision. He felt that unless an earlier decision could be clearly shown to have been wrongly decided a court of coordinate jurisdiction should follow it; the decision not to follow it should normally be made by an appellate court which enjoys the power to overrule it. It should be noted that whilst Parke J. was considering *stare decisis* in the High Court much of the language of his judgment was in more general terms, in that he referred to "courts of first instance" and "courts of equal jurisdiction" and did not confine his comments specifically to the High Court. In *Walsh v President of the District Court and D.P.P.* [1989] I.L.R.M. 325 Murphy J. remarked that his decision to depart from an earlier High Court decision was reached with "considerable hesitation". Again he emphasised the desirability of maintaining the convention of following decisions of courts of coordinate jurisdiction but felt compelled by a Supreme Court decision to depart from the earlier High Court case. The Court of Criminal Appeal has also declared its freedom to depart from its earlier decisions. In *The People v Moore* [1964] Ir. Jur. Rep. 6 (Extract 11.6) the Court accepted the practice adopted by its English counterpart in *R v Norman* [1924] 2 K.B. 315.

Some questions have arisen as to the status of pre-1961 Irish decisions and pre-1922 decisions of the House of Lords. With respect to the former, although Article 34 of the Constitution deals with the courts, it was conceded in *The State (Killian) v Minister for Justice* [1954] I.R. 207 that the text of that Article envisaged their being established by statute. As noted in Chapter 4 this was achieved by the Courts (Establishment and Constitution) Act, 1961. Whilst the courts thus established are identical to the earlier courts, technically they are new courts and decisions of the pre-1961 courts are not decisions of those courts. That point was adverted to by Walsh J. in *The State (Quinn) v Ryan* [1965] I.R. 110 (Extract 11.2) and was elaborated on by Kingsmill Moore J. in *Attorney General v Ryan's Car Hire Ltd.* [1965] I.R. 642 (Extract 11.3), where he was of the view that a pre-1961 decision of the Supreme Court, to the effect that it should adopt a rigid practice of *stare decisis*, could not bind the "new" Supreme Court. In contrast, Henchy J in *Mogul of Ireland v Tipperary (North Riding) County Council* [1976] I.R.260 (Extract 12.17) considered that neither pre- nor post-1961 decisions should be overruled unless they were clearly shown to be erroneous. He was unprepared to overrule a 1949 decision of the Supreme Court which, had the matter been previously undecided, he would have decided the other way. And in *The State (Lynch) v Cooney* [1982] I.R. 337 (Extract 11.11) the same judge expressed similar views regarding pre-1961 decisions.

Prior to independence in 1922 the House of Lords was the court of final appeal for Ireland and, accordingly, Irish courts were bound by its decisions. After 1922 the question was whether those decisions still bound the Irish courts. In *Exham v Beamish* [1939] I.R. 336 Gavan Duffy J. suggested that only those decisions which had been accepted as being part of Irish law *before* 1922 were binding. On the other hand, Maguire C.J. and Black J. in *Boylan v Dublin Corporation* [1949] I.R. 60 and Murnaghan J. in *Minister for Finance and Attorney General v O'Brien* [1949] I.R. 91 considered all pre-1922 decisions to be binding. In the light of the subsequent relaxation by the Supreme Court of the practice of *stare decisis* it can be presumed that those decisions are no longer to be considered to be binding. Indeed, it is interesting to note that in *Attorney General v Ryan's Car Hire Ltd.* [1965] I.R. 642 (Extract 11.3) the Supreme Court refused to follow its earlier decision in *Minister for Finance and Attorney General v O'Brien.* This issue was also touched on by McCarthy J. in his judgment in *Irish Shell Ltd. v Elm Motors Ltd.* [1984] I.R. 511 (Extract 11.7). In a similar vein, Davitt P., in *Attorney General v Simpson* [1959] I.R. 105, 129, rejected the submission that an advice of the Privy Council in an Australian appeal, given before Irish appeals thereto were abolished, bound the Irish courts.

A court is not bound to follow the decisions of inferior or foreign courts. However, those decisions are of persuasive authority and may be followed at the option of the court. Decisions of other common law countries are frequently cited and adopted by Irish courts, particularly where there is no Irish authority governing the issue in question. Given the origin of the Irish legal system and the traditional links between the two systems it is not surprising to find that English decisions are the most commonly cited foreign decisions. But that is not to suggest that those decisions should be adopted uncritically by Irish Courts. In *Irish Shell Ltd. v Elm Motors Ltd.* [1984] I.R. 511 (Extract 11.7) McCarthy J. criticised an observation by Costello J. that English decisions should be followed unless they were shown to be erroneous. More recently however, in *Tromso Sparebank v Beirne (No. 2),* [1989] I.L.R.M. 257 (Extract 11.8), Costello J. again stated that an Irish court should be reluctant to refuse to follow a firmly established principle in English law. In recent years Irish courts have been willing to have recourse to decisions of other jurisdictions. In constitutional matters the courts pay special attention to American decisions as the constitutions of both countries bear broad similarities and are rooted in similar legal ideologies. Where the decisions of different jurisdictions lead to different conclusions an Irish court is not bound to prefer any particular line of authority and may choose to adopt one or other or neither; see, for example, *The People v Dwyer* [1972] I.R. 416 and *In re Keenan Brothers Ltd.* [1985] I.R. 401. The status of foreign decisions was considered by McCarthy J. in *Irish Shell Ltd. v Elm Motors Ltd.* [1984] I.R. 511 (Extract 11.7). Finally, it should be noted that where there is an absence of earlier relevant decisions the courts occasionally refer to recognised textbooks and learned articles; see *Kirby v Burke and Holloway* [1944] I.R. 207 (Extract 11.13), *The People v Lynch* [1982] I.R. 64 (Extract 11.10) and *Hynes Ltd. v Independent Newspapers Ltd* [1980] I.R. 204.

Extract 11.1

McDONNELL v. BYRNE ENGINEERING CO. LTD

Supreme Court (O'Higgins C.J., Griffin and Kenny JJ.)
October 3, 1978
Irish Times October 4, 1978

The Supreme Court yesterday set aside an award of £100,205 and costs by a High Court jury to a nine-year-old Dublin boy, James McDonnell, Lower Gardiner Street Flats, who suffered a severe head injury on June 12th, 1973, when part of a mobile scaffolding tower collapsed on him at Railway Street, Dublin. The Court directed a new trial but did not award the costs of the appeal to the defendants in the action, who had appealed the amount as being excessive. The action had been taken on behalf of the boy by his mother, Mrs Elizabeth McDonnell. The defendants were Byrne Engineering Co. Ltd., Jervis Lane, Dublin. The action had been heard before Mr Justice Murnaghan and a jury on November 15th and 16th last. Special damages had been agreed at £205 and the jury had assessed general damages at £100,000. Judgment for £100,205 and costs had been entered in favour of the boy. The jury had been asked only to assess general damages.

The Chief Justice, Mr Justice O'Higgins, giving the judgment of the Supreme Court yesterday, said that the trial judge had been expressly asked to divide the question on damages, so that the jury would be asked to consider damages in relation to pain and suffering up to the trial, and to consider them separately for the future. The trial judge declined to do so. The matter was considered by the jury as one question. "This question to the jury was not in accordance with the correct procedures nor in accordance with the appropriate legal procedures," said the Chief Justice. "The jury verdict was a verdict which was subject to some incapacity."

It seemed to him, said Mr Justice O'Higgins, having regard to all the evidence and to the history of this young boy following the injury that the amount was excessive. He was expressing his own view and that of his colleagues that the verdict, in the circumstances, could not stand. The Court, he said, had come to the conclusion that it would not be appropriate to fix damages. Accordingly the plaintiff's claim should go back to the High Court for assessment in another trial.

The Chief Justice said that under the Constitution, the Supreme Court was the final court of appeal. As such, it had the duty, when necessary, to declare what legal principles should apply to cases that were reviewed by the Court. Where necessary it had the duty to lay down guidelines for all courts and all judges as to the manner in which such cases were to be tried. It was equally the duty of all other courts and judges to follow directions as to law and procedures as given by the Supreme Court.

The Chief Justice said that in relation to trial by jury in claims for damages for personal injury where future loss of earnings and pain and suffering were involved, the Supreme Court had, over the years, expressed certain views which were most recently stated in the Supreme Court decision of *Carroll* v. *Clare County Council* [1975] I.R. 230. In that judgment, he said, Mr Justice Kenny had stated that it was highly undesirable that a jury should be asked to award damages for the period up to the trial and for the future, under one heading, as one. He said it was essential that there should be separate questions in relation to the matter. The Chief Justice said that following this clear and concise statement it became the duty of all judges trying such cases to follow this directive.

"It is with real concern that this Court notes that despite being asked by counsel to leave the question on damages in accordance with the directions of this court, the trial judge, Mr Justice Murnaghan, expressly refused to do so. Not only did he refuse to do so, but he has indicated it is his intention to disregard this in other cases." The Chief Justice continued: "This Court will not permit this situation to continue and will insist that its directions be respected and obeyed."

Unfortunately, said the Chief Justice, the only way this could be done was by means of its jurisdiction on appeal to review and set aside. "This jurisdiction will be used," he added. "It should be made known that any verdict in damages arrived at as a result of procedures which this Court has condemned will, on that account alone, be in danger of being set aside." This would be because of the views expressed by the Supreme Court . . . because the award would not have been obtained in accordance with due course of law.

In this case when counsel for the plaintiff, in accordance with what was stated in *Carroll* v. *Clare County Council*, had asked that the question be left in the appropriate form, counsel for the defendants remained silent. "Directions on law, directions in relation to procedures and directions in relation to their obedience must be the common concern of all litigants," added the Chief Justice.

Mr Justice Griffin and Mr Justice Kenny were the other members of the Court.

Extract 11.2

THE STATE (QUINN) v RYAN [1965] I.R. 110

The prosecutor was arrested on foot of an English warrant and his immediate removal to England was sought under the provisions of s. 29 of the Petty Sessions (Ireland) Act, 1851. He challenged the constitutionality of that section, which had been upheld in two earlier Supreme Court decisions, *The State (Dowling) v Kingston* [1937] I.R. 699 and *The State (Duggan) v Tapley* [1952] I.R. 62. It was argued on behalf of the respondent that the Court was bound by those decisions. In holding the section to be unconstitutional, the Supreme Court declared its freedom to depart from a strict adherence to *stare decisis*.

Walsh J.

. . . It has been urged upon this Court on behalf of the Attorney General and on behalf of the respondents that these sections have already been held to be not inconsistent with the Constitution of Saorstát Eireann in *The State (Dowling)* v. *Kingston (No. 2)* [1937] I.R. 699 and not inconsistent with the provisions of the present Constitution in *The State (Duggan)* v. *Tapley* [1952] I.R. 62. It has been further urged that these decisions are binding upon this Court. It is unnecessary in this case to explore the consequences of the fact that this Court is not the Court which decided either of those cases; this Court was established in 1961. It is also unnecessary to express any final view upon the constitutionality of subjecting this Court (as distinct from all other Courts set up under the Constitution) to the rule of *stare decisis*. Neither is it necessary to discuss in detail the question of whether in the case of a Court of final appeal *stare decisis* can ever be anything more than judicial policy, albeit strong judicial policy. However, in view of the implications in the submissions advanced in this Court on behalf of the Attorney General and of the respondents it must be clearly stated, though one would have hoped it should not have been necessary to do so, that this Court is the creation of the Constitution and is not in any sense the successor in Ireland of the House of Lords. The jurisdiction formerly enjoyed by the House of Lords in Ireland is but part of the much wider jurisdiction which has been conferred upon this Court by the Constitution. I reject the submission that because upon the foundation of the State our Courts took over an English legal system and the common law that the Courts must be deemed to have adopted and should now adopt an approach to Constitutional questions conditioned by English judicial methods and English legal training which despite their undoubted excellence were not fashioned for interpreting written constitutions or reviewing the constitutionality of legislation. In this State one would have expected that if the approach of any Court of final appeal of another State was to have been held up as an example for this Court to follow it would more appropriately have been the Supreme Court of the United States rather than the House of Lords. In this context it is not out of place to recall that in delivering the judgment of the Supreme Court in *In the Matter of Tilson Infants* [1951] I.R. 1 Mr. Justice Murnaghan stated, at p. 32:—"It is not a proper method of construing a new constitution of a modern state to make an approach in the light of legal survivals of an earlier law."

So far as the provisions of the Constitution itself bear upon the place of *stare decisis* in constitutional cases the provisions of section 3, sub-section 3, of Article 34, which is an amendment to the Constitution as enacted by the People, appear to me to clearly indicate that it is only in the case of a law or a provision of a law, the

Bill for which had been referred to the Supreme Court by the President under Article 26 of the Constitution, that there is no longer jurisdiction in any Court to question the constitutional validity of that law or that provision of that law. It has been submitted on behalf of the Attorney General and the respondents that this amendment to the Constitution was designed only to meet a possible argument that because it was a Bill which *had been* approved by the Court that the law when enacted would be open to challenge again once it was signed by the President and that it was to be inferred from this provision that the Constitution impliedly imposed the rule of *stare decisis* in respect of constitutional cases. In my view this contention is quite unsustainable and it would be strange indeed if the Constitution in making such an express provision for Bills only would leave unexpressed but to be inferred a provision in similar terms applicable to Acts. To my mind the absence of such an express provision is an indication that the People in enacting this Constitution and the Oireachtas in amending it within the period limited by the transitory provisions of the Constitution, which have since expired, had no intention of creating by inference only a situation in which a decision of this Court upon the interpretation of the Constitution could be altered only by way of a national referendum for the purpose of amending the Constitution. Far from being daunted by this formidable but inescapable conclusion arising from their submissions counsel for the Attorney General and for the respondents urged that this was the position envisaged by the Constitution. Having regard to the express provision of the Constitution I have no hesitation in rejecting the submissions which lead to such a conclusion. This is not to say, however, that the Court would depart from an earlier decision for any but the most compelling reasons. The advantages of *stare decisis* are many and obvious so long as it is remembered that it is a policy and not a binding unalterable rule . . .

Extract 11.3

THE ATTORNEY GENERAL AND THE MINISTER FOR DEFENCE v RYAN'S CAR HIRE LTD. [1965] I.R. 642

A member of the Air Corps was seriously injured due to the negligence of the defendants' employee. During his recovery his wages were paid by the plaintiffs and he was maintained for some time in a military hospital at their expense. His action against the defendants was compromised. The plaintiffs issued a civil bill in which they claimed damages to the amount of wages paid to the injured party and the medical expenses which they incurred. The claim was based on the action *per quod servitium amisit* which allowed an employer to recover damages in respect of losses suffered through injury to his or her "servant". The issue for the Supreme Court to decide was whether a member of the Defence Forces is a "servant" for the purposes of the action. In deciding in the negative the Court refused to follow two of its earlier decisions, *Minister for Finance and Attorney-General v O'Brien* [1949] I.R. 91 and *Attorney-General and the Minister for Posts and Telegraphs v C.I.E.* (1956) 90 I.L.T.R. 139. The extract from Kingsmill Moore J.'s judgment deals with the status of *stare decisis* in the Supreme Court and reiterates the points made in *The State (Quinn) v Ryan* [1965] I.R. 110 (Extract 11.2).

Kingsmill Moore J.
. . . The first question, then, is whether this Court is to accept and lay down the principle that it is to be bound irrevocably by an earlier decision, the so-called rule of "*stare decisis*." The merits and demerits of this rule have been widely canvassed

and there is no consensus of opinion among academic jurists or serving judges. The practice of Courts of ultimate resort varies, the United States Supreme Court and the ultimate Courts of most European countries and of Canada, South Africa and Australia holding themselves free, where they think requisite, to refuse to follow an earlier decision; while the House of Lords, somewhat uncomfortably, abides by the principle laid down by Lord Halsbury in *London Street Tramways Co.* v. *London County Council* [1898] A.C. 375, that a decision of the House on a question of law is conclusive and binds it in all subsequent cases until (if ever) it is upset by legislative enactment. Not all the Law Lords have been content to be confined within the strait-jacket of an earlier case. Lord Denning has broken loose (*London Transport Executive* v. *Betts* (*Valuation Officer*) [1959] A.C. 213, 247; *Ostime* v. *Australian Mutual Provident Society* [1960] A.C. 459, 489; *Close* v. *Steel Company of Wales* [1962] A.C. 367, 388). Lord Reid clearly strains at the bonds (*London Transport Executive* v. *Betts* (*Valuation Officer*) at pp. 213 and 232; *Midland Silicones Limited* v. *Scruttons Limited* [1962] A.C. 466, 475–7). Lord Wright would like the House of Lords to have the same freedom as the United States Supreme Court: 8 Camb. L. J. 144. In *R.* v. *Taylor* [1950] 2 K.B. 368 Lord Goddard, giving the judgment of a Court of Criminal Appeal, consisting of seven judges, refused to follow the decision of an earlier Court of Criminal Appeal where the subsequent Court unanimously considered the former decision to be wrong and where an accused person had been sentenced and imprisoned on the assumption that such earlier decision was correct. In *The State* (*Quinn*) v. *Ryan* [1965] I.R. 70, Mr. Justice Walsh in his judgment, to which the other members of the Court assented, refused to accept "*stare decisis*" as universally binding in constitutional cases, adding, at p. 127:—"This is not to say, however, that the Court would depart from an earlier decision for any but the most compelling reasons. The advantages of *stare decisis* are many and obvious so long as it is remembered that it is a policy and not a binding, unalterable rule."

This Court is a new court, set up by the Courts (Establishment and Constitution) Act, 1961, pursuant to the Constitution and it is free to consider whether it should adopt the rule which prevails in the House of Lords or any of the less restrictive rules which have found favour in other jurisdictions. It seems clear that there can be no legal obligation on this Court to accept "*stare decisis*" as a rule binding upon it just because the House of Lords accepted it as a rule binding upon their Lordships' house. A decision which only purported to affect the House of Lords could not, by virtue of Article 73 of the Constitution of 1922, have been carried over into our law so as to bind the Supreme Court set up by that constitution; and if that Supreme Court in fact adopted the rule (as it would seem to have done in *Attorney General and Minister for Posts and Telegraphs* v. *Coras Iompair Eireann* 90 I.L.T.R. 139) any such determination could only bind that Court and would not under Article 50 of our present Constitution be binding on the new Supreme Court created by Article 34, 4, of our present Constitution and the Courts (Establishment and Constitution) Act, 1961.

Mr. Kenny has properly drawn a distinction between the general principle of following precedent and the strict rule of *stare decisis*. The law which we have taken over is based on the following of precedents and there can be no question of abandoning the principle of following precedent as the normal, indeed almost universal, procedure. To do so would be to introduce into our law an intolerable uncertainty. But where the Supreme Court is of the opinion that there is a compelling reason why it should not follow an earlier decision of its own, or of the Courts of ultimate jurisdiction which preceded it, where it appears to be clearly wrong, is it to be bound to perpetuate the error?

If it could safely be assumed that all members of a Supreme Court were perfectly endowed with wisdom and completely familiar with all branches of law, to treat their judgments as infallible would need but little justification. Judicial modesty has refrained from putting forward such a claim and to most jurists such a Court appears a Platonic rather than a practical ideal. Lord Halsbury in the *London Street Tramways*

Case [1898] A.C. 375 takes his stand on more pragmatic grounds:—". . . what is that occasional interference with what is perhaps abstract justice as compared with the inconvenience—the disastrous inconvenience—of having each question subject to being re-argued and the dealings of mankind rendered doubtful by reason of different decisions, so that in truth and in fact there would be no real final Court of Appeal."

This argument from inconvenience would come more suitably from the mouth of an executive official than from that of a judge. The plea that "it is expedient that one man should die for the multitude" must always be met uncompromisingly by a judge with the words, "I find no fault in this just man," and he must not falter in his determination. However desirable certainty, stability, and predictability of law may be, they cannot in my view justify a Court of ultimate resort in giving a judgment which they are convinced, for compelling reasons, is erroneous. Lord Halsbury himself was forced to make some modification. Faced with the hypothesis that a case might have been decided in ignorance of the existence of some relevant statutory provision or in reliance on some statutory provision which was subsequently discovered to have been repealed, he suggested that it would not be a binding authority because it was founded on a mistake of fact. The same reasoning would be applicable if the decision were given in ignorance of an earlier authority of compelling validity. Where a point has been entirely overlooked, or conceded without argument, the authority of a decision may be weakened to vanishing point. In my opinion the rigid rule of *stare decisis* must in a Court of ultimate resort give place to a more elastic formula. Where such a Court is clearly of opinion that an earlier decision was erroneous it should be at liberty to refuse to follow it, at all events in exceptional cases. What are exceptional cases? I have already given some examples of cases which I would consider exceptional, but I do not suggest that these close the category and I do not propose to attempt to make a complete enumeration. It is sufficient to consider whether the present case should fall within the exception . . .

Extract 11.4

DOYLE v HEARNE [1987] I.R. 601

Pursuant to s. 16 of the Courts of Justice Act, 1947 a case was stated by the Circuit Court for the opinion of the Supreme Court. A preliminary issue arose as to whether the Court could entertain the case as all the evidence which might fall to be considered by the Circuit Court had not been adduced. In holding by a majority (Finlay C.J., Walsh and McCarthy JJ., Henchy and Griffin JJ. dissenting) that the case stated did lie, the Court refused to follow its earlier decisions to the contrary in *Corley v Gill* [1975] I.R. 313 and *Dolan v Corn Exchange* [1975] I.R. 315. The extract from the dissenting judgment of Griffin J. reflects a preference for a stricter policy of *stare decisis* whilst that of McCarthy J. suggests that a full Court may review decisions of a Court composed of three judges.

Griffin J.

For the reasons stated by Henchy J in his judgment, I agree that the Circuit Court judge had no jurisdiction to state the case submitted by him to this Court and that therefore this Court has no jurisdiction to entertain it. That conclusion is in line with the decisions of this Court in *Corley v Gill* [1975] I.R. 313 and *Dolan v Corn Exchange* [1975] I.R. 315, in which four of the then members of the Court (O'Higgins CJ, Henchy J, Griffin J and Kenny J) reached the same conclusion. Mr Fennelly SC has invited this Court to reconsider those two cases and to overrule them, notwithstanding that they have been followed and applied in a number of cases in which the Court has refused to entertain a case stated until all the acts have been found. The most recent of such cases was *D.P.P. v Gannon* Supreme Court, unreported, 3 June 1986 to which Henchy J has referred in his judgment.

In my opinion s. 16 of the Courts of Justice Act, 1947, was correctly construed in those cases and they should be followed in the instant case.

Quite apart from the question of the correctness of that construction, I believe that stating a case at the conclusion of the evidence makes good sense. It must be borne in mind that s. 16 is concerned with a case stated from the Circuit Court. Unlike the High Court, (except perhaps in some criminal cases tried with a jury) the Circuit Court judges sitting throughout the country habitually hear and determine several cases on each sitting day. Once a case is listed for hearing on a particular day all the witnesses must attend and be available to give evidence on that day. If during the hearing of a case by the Circuit Court judge an application is made to have a case stated to this Court before the evidence is completed, far from being more convenient and less costly to the parties to state the case at that stage, as was alleged and submitted on the hearing of this appeal, it is in my view very much less convenient and far more expensive to accede to the application at that stage. All the expenses of having the witnesses in attendance would by then have already been incurred and would have to be discharged in any event. Further, if the case is stated, and is answered by this Court at a time when the evidence has not been completed, it may very well be that at the resumed hearing another application may be made to have a different or further question of law determined by this Court. In my view, it is unquestionably more desirable that *all* the questions of law which may arise in any given case in the Circuit Court should be determined at the one time, and this can be assured only when the case is stated at the conclusion of the evidence.

Although the question decided by *Corley v Gill* and *Dolan v Corn Exchange* was, in the result, mainly a procedural one, a more fundamental question which arises is whether this Court *should* overrule those two cases. The right of this Court to depart from the policy of *stare decisis* and to decide not to follow one of its previous decisions is now well established. It was first recognised in *State (Quinn) v Ryan* [1965] I.R. 70, but in that case it was emphasised that the Court would not "depart from an earlier decision for any but the most compelling reasons". A short time later, in *Attorney General v Ryan's Car Hire Ltd*, [1965] I.R. 642 it was stated by Kingsmill Moore J, delivering the Judgment of the Court, at p. 654 that:

> . . . the rigid rule of *stare decisis* must in a Court of ultimate resort give place to a more elastic formula. Where such a Court is clearly of opinion that an earlier decision was erroneous it should be at liberty to refuse to follow it, at all events in exceptional cases.

The right to overrule a previous decision was expressed in even more restrictive terms in *Mogul of Ireland Ltd v Tipperary (N.R.) County Council* [1976] I.R. 260. That was also a consultative case stated under s. 16 of the Courts of Justice Act, 1947, and, as in the present case, the question was whether the court should accept or overrule a previous interpretration of a statutory provision. The Court (O'Higgins CJ, Walsh J, Budd J, Henchy J and Griffin J) unanimously refused to overrule the earlier decision. O'Higgins CJ (Walsh J concurring) said at p. 269:

> When a court does pronounce on the meaning of a statute and thereby defines the law, a court of review ought not to pronounce this definition incorrect merely because a contrary view as to the statute's meaning is also possible.

Henchy J (Budd J and Griffin J concurring) on the same topic said at p. 272:

> a balance has to be struck between rigidity and vacillation, and to achieve that balance the later Court must, at the least, be *clearly* of opinion that the earlier decision was erroneous. In *Attorney General v Ryan's Car Hire Ltd* the judgment of the Court gave examples of what it called exceptional cases, the decisions in which might be overruled if a later Court thought them to be clearly wrong. While it was made clear that the examples given were not intended to close the

category of exceptional cases, it is implicit from the use in that judgment of expressions such as 'convinced' and 'for compelling reasons' and 'clearly of opinion that the earlier decision was erroneous' that the mere fact that a later Court, particularly a majority of the members of a later Court, might prefer a different conclusion is not in itself sufficient to justify overruling the earlier decision.

So far as I have been able to ascertain, there is no case in which a previous decision of this Court was overruled by other than a unanimous decision of a court of five.

A similar approach would appear to have been adopted by the House of Lords. In *Reg. v National Insurance Commissioners, Ex parte Hudson* (also referred to as *Jones v Secretary of State*) [1972] A.C. 944, in which the House was invited to reconsider an earlier decision (referred to in the speeches as *Dowling's* case, and reported at [1967] 1 A.C. 725) it was held by Lord Reid, Lord Morris of Borth-y-Gest, Lord Pearson and Lord Simon that the certainty of the law will be impaired unless the practice of the House to reconsider previous decisions is used sparingly, and that the practice should only rarely be invoked in cases of the construction of statutes or other documents.

In *Fitzleet Estates Ltd v Cherry* [1977] 1 W.L.R. 1345, in which an earlier decision of the House was unsuccessfully challenged, Viscount Dilhorne in dealing with the importance of precedent as providing a degree of certainty upon which individuals can rely in the conduct of their affairs said at p. 1350:

> That certainty would in my view be impaired if, where there had been a decision by a majority, the House permitted the matter to be reopened and re-argued before a differently constituted House with the possibility that a majority in that House preferred the view of the minority in the decided case. If this House acceded to such an application it would open the door to a similar application in years to come to restore the view of the majority in the first decision on the ground that the majority when the question had been re-argued, had erred.

Can it be said that there are the 'most compelling reasons' to depart from the earlier decision of *Corley v Gill* and *Dolan v Corn Exchange*? Can it be said that the construction of s. 16 accepted by four members of the Court as composed in 1975, followed by a full Court (Finlay CJ, Henchy J, Griffin J, Hederman J and McCarthy J) in *D.P.P. v Gannon*, and still accepted by at least two members of the Court, is 'clearly wrong'? Can it be said that the instant case is an 'exceptional case' as envisaged by the Court in *Attorney General v Ryan's Car Hire Ltd*? In my opinion, the answer to each of these questions should be "no".

For the foregoing reasons, I would refuse to entertain this case stated.

McCarthy J.

I agree with the conclusion of the Chief Justice. I recognise that in *Corley v Gill* [1975] I.R. 313 in a case where no evidence had been called, in effect, the court would not entertain a moot. Indeed, the words of O'Higgins CJ in this context are important:

> When the matter came before this Court, I queried the jurisdiction of the Circuit Court judge to state a Case under s. 16 of the Act of 1947 where no evidence had been adduced before him, and the Court rose for 15 minutes to enable counsel to consider the point. (at p. 314)

The decision not to entertain the case must be read in that light. There is nothing to indicate the nature of the argument made on behalf of either side.

In *Dolan v Corn Exchange* [1975] I.R. 315 determined on 4 December 1975 although argued before the hearing in *Corley v Gill*, with the court constituted of different personnel, in a case stated by a judge of the High Court hearing a Circuit Appeal, the essential decision was that there could not be more than one case stated under s. 38 of the Courts of Justice Act, 1936. It is clear, however, that the reasoning in the majority judgment (Henchy J) was founded upon the requirement that the order of adjournment pending the determination of the case stated was to be at the end of all of the evidence, whilst reserving the right 'where events render it necessary in the interests of justice, to hear further evidence or legal argument so as to ensure that his judgment or order will be soundly based, in law and in fact.' Walsh J dissented, as I understand it, for the reasons set out at pp. 321 and 322.

Reference is made to *Corley and Gill* in the judgment of Henchy J in *The State (Harkin) v O'Malley* [1978] I.R. 269. Whilst O'Higgins CJ delivered a separate judgment he expressed agreement with the views of Henchy J as did the other three members of the Court. In *Harkin's* case, the full Court expressly decided that an earlier decision (*People (Attorney General) v Doyle* (1964) 101 I.L.T.R. 136) of this Court was, *per incuriam*, incorrectly decided. Henchy J said:

> *Doyle's* case was decided without any mature consideration. The judgment was given on the day the case was argued. Counsel who argued the case do not seem to have directed the Court's attention to the application of s. 6(3) of the Act of 1924. Had they done so, a different judgment would have been given. The decision was clearly given *per incuriam*. (at p. 287)

Some of these criticisms might, indeed, be levelled against *Corley's* case and, indeed, to the argument as reported in *Harkin's* case itself. *The State (Cahill) v The President of the Circuit Court* [1954] I.R. 128 was referred to in the course of argument in *Doyle's* case (the Registrar's note is evidence of this). The real question in issue in *Harkin* (pace the Chief Justice) (at page 280) was whether *Doyle* insofar as it appeared to support the prosecutor's contention was an authority to be followed; the Chief Justice concluded no. Henchy J added a further reason, based on *Corley's* case, that this Court in *Doyle's* case had no jurisdiction to entertain the Case Stated because the evidence had not concluded. There is nothing to indicate that this point was ever argued, no more, indeed, that it excited much argument in the hearing of the present appeal. I do not, however, look upon *Harkin's* case as bearing directly upon the issue presently arising in the instant appeal. In *D.P.P. v Gannon* Supreme Court, unreported, 3 June 1986. I queried the application of *Corley's* case in a criminal matter; the section does not differentiate between civil and criminal matters.

In *Wexford Timber v Wexford Corporation And Others* (1952) 88 I.L.T.R. 137 the Supreme Court of Justice entertained and ruled upon a Case Stated pursuant to s. 36(3) of the Act of 1936 on the hearing of a Circuit Appeal at a stage in the trial when, it is clear from the intrinsic evidence of the report, the evidence may not have concluded. The decision of the Supreme Court was that, on the facts as found on the evidence to date the applicants were not entitled to succeed. This is an instance of what was not argued not being decided. Perusal of the reports in both *Corley* and *Dolan*, as well as experience of the instant appeal, do not suggest that that situation has been significantly altered. In each case it appears that the issue as to whether or not the court should entertain the Case Stated was raised by the court itself.

For example, nowhere can I find any indication of the following argument:

In a District Court Criminal Appeal, the appellant applies to the Circuit judge, at the end of the prosecution's evidence, that he should rule that there is no evidence to sustain a conviction. Important questions of law may well arise on such a submission; the Circuit judge may consider he should seek the guidance of this Court in that regard. The appellant is entitled to press for such a course; is he to be met with the absolute answer that the judge cannot do so until the evidence is concluded leaving the appellant with the option of giving no evidence or being forced into giving evidence which may, of itself, be the very evidence that would convict him? Such a construction appears to me in circumstances that are by no means uncommon, to produce a clear injustice. It is true to say that an accused tried on indictment may be faced with a like problem when he seeks to have a verdict of not guilty entered by direction at the end of the prosecution case; if he fails in his application, he then must determine whether or not to go into evidence. The circumstances of a jury trial, however, render it impossible, in practical terms, to state a case in the course of such a trial. This was not the exact issue in *The People (Attorney General) v McGlynn* [1967] I.R. 232 where the evidence had concluded and the accused had been given in charge of the jury, but the reasoning would appear to be in *pari materia*.

In *Hamilton v Hamilton* [1982] I.R. 466 Henchy J (at 484) stated:

> In *Tempany v Hynes* [1976] I.R. 101 I expressed the opinion that a purchaser, whether he has paid part of the purchase price or not, becomes the equitable or beneficial owner of the whole estate. That view, however, did not prevail in that case. Mr Justice Kenny (with whom the Chief Justice concurred) considered that the equitable or beneficial estate becomes vested in a purchaser only to the extent to which the purchase price is paid. Unless and until a different conclusion is reached by a full Court, that majority opinion must be taken to be the law.

I do not take this expression of opinion as being one that invited reconsideration of and possible disagreement with any particular triumvirate of this Court, but it lends support to the view that decisions of this Court constituted of less than its full complement may be reviewed.

Much time and labour have been spent in considering the issues that arise in this case; I confess that I would think that the court would be better otherwise engaged than in resolving, at such length, what is no more than a procedural matter. For my part, I am content to leave it to the Circuit judge and, *a fortiori*, a High Court judge hearing Circuit Appeals, to determine the time, having heard evidence, at which he will state a case for the Supreme Court.

Extract 11.5

IRISH TRUST BANK LTD. v CENTRAL BANK OF IRELAND
HIGH COURT, UNREPORTED, 4 MARCH, 1976

In this case Parke J. was asked to review an assessment of costs, or taxation which is its technical term, by the Taxing Master. In particular, he was urged not to follow an earlier High Court decision *Dunne v O'Neill* [1974] I.R. 180. He followed that decision and in the extract outlines his reasons for so doing.

Parke J.

[His Lordship outlined the facts of the case and continued]

However, in respect of all the items relating to counsel's fees a general proposition was advanced on behalf of the plaintiffs that I should follow and apply the principle laid down by Gannon J. in *Dunne v O'Neill* [1974] I.R. 80 which was cited to the Taxing Master in the course of the taxation. The Taxing Master in the course of his report and subsequently counsel on behalf of the defendants have argued with great force that this principle is erroneous and based upon a disregard or misunderstanding of a large number of previous authorities.

The principle which is stated in slightly different form in different parts of the judgment may I think be fairly summarised as follows. It is the duty of the Taxing Master to assess the amount which he should allow on a party and party taxation in respect of disbursements by solicitors for counsel's fees and that the standard which he should adopt in measuring these amounts is to ascertain what a reasonable and prudent practising solicitor would consider proper to offer to a suitable counsel in order to obtain his services in the particular case in question. In order to do this he must not only rely upon his own experience as a solicitor but must keep himself informed as to the current practice of solicitors and counsel. At page 189 the learned judge says:

> It is no part of the function of the Taxing Master on taxation of costs, or of the Court on a review of the taxation, to examine the nature or quality of the work done by or required of counsel or to assess, by measurement of fees, the value of counsel's work. The sole matter with which the Taxing Master is concerned in respect of the items which are the subject matter of this application is whether to allow in whole or in part the disbursements made by the solicitor in the course of his practice in respect of fees to counsel retained by him in an action in accordance with the rules relating to party and party taxation.

After a quotation from the judgment of Sullivan M.R. in *Robb v Connor* (1875) I.R. 9 Eq. 376 (one of the cases referred to by the Taxing Master in the present case and counsel for the defendants) the learned judge continues:

> Because these items are disbursements made by a solicitor in the course of his practice in respect of fees to counsel retained by him on his client's behalf, the amounts of the disbursements should be assessed on the basis of what a practising solicitor who is reasonably careful and reasonably prudent would consider a proper and reasonable fee to offer to counsel. This standard does not involve any presumption in favour of particular fees allotted by a solicitor to counsel of his choice, but it does involve having due regard to the changes in what the practising solicitor considers to be reasonably derived from his day to day and year to year experiences in the course of his practice.

This principle is challenged by the Taxing Master who devotes ten pages of his report to a review of a large number of cases and quotations from their judgments and says on pp. 20 and 21 of his report:

> I am at a loss therefore to reconcile the dicta of the Honourable Mr. Justice Gannon as contained in the judgment of the learned judge in the hereinbefore mentioned case of Nicholas Dunne and James O'Neill in the light of the several above recited cases, Rules of Court and the long established practice of the Taxing Masters.
>
> Accordingly it seems to me that the overwhelming weight of authority confirms the judicial discretion which is vested in a Taxing Master and his right but not only his right but his duty to measure, settle or adjudicate upon counsel's fees and other fees charges and disbursements appearing in a Bill of Costs for taxation.

I think it might be said that the propriety of a Taxing Master reporting to a judge of the High Court that another judge of that Court was wrong in law is very much open to question. The situation would have been even more anomalous had this case, as it might very well have done, come on for hearing before Gannon J. Be that as it may I have no doubt that this portion of the Taxing Master's report provided a useful and well researched brief for counsel on behalf of the defendants.

Mr. O'Neill on behalf of the defendants urged me that I should not follow or apply the principles quoted from the judgment of Gannon J. I fully accept that there are occasions in which the principle of *stare decisis* may be departed from but I consider that these are extremely rare. A Court may depart from a decision of a Court of equal jurisdiction if it appears that such a decision was given in a case in which either insufficient authority was cited or incorrect submissions advanced or in which the nature and wording of the judgment itself reveals that the judge disregarded or misunderstood an important element in the case or the arguments submitted to him or the authority cited or in some other way departed from the proper standard to be adopted in judicial determination. It is clear that none of these elements can be detected in *Dunne v O'Neill* or the judgment therein delivered. Mr. O'Neill does not in fact contend any such thing but his argument rests solely on the fact that the decision is contrary to previous authorities and that I am therefore not obliged to follow it. Whatever may be the case in Courts of final appellate jurisdiction a Court of first instance should be very slow to act on such a proposition unless the arguments in favour of it were coercive. If a decision of a Court of first instance is to be challenged I consider that the appellate Court is the proper tribunal to declare the law unless the decision in question manifestly displays some one or more of the infirmities to which I have referred. The principle of *stare decisis* is one of great importance to our law and few things can be more harmful to the proper administration of justice, which requires that as far as possible lay men may be able to receive correct professional advice, than the continual existence of inconsistent decisions of Courts of equal jurisdiction. The present case affords an interesting example of what ought to be avoided. Mr. Mackey appeared for the applicants in *Dunne v O'Neill*. Not only are his arguments set out in detail in the judgment but they are adopted and made part of the *ratio decidendi* in a manner in which counsel is seldom gratified to experience. Mr. Mackey appeared for the plaintiffs in the present case and it would be an ironic comment on the state of the law if counsel could find his arguments adopted and applied in one Court and yet be told in another Court of equal jurisdiction that they were fundamentally wrong and inconsistent with the authorities.

I find nothing to convince me that the judgment of Gannon J. shows such disregard or inconsistency with previous authorities to justify me in departing from it. Although the report is scanty in information as to the authorities cited by counsel it is clear from a perusal of the judgment that almost all of the cases cited to me in argument and set out in the Taxing Master's report were considered by the learned judge. Indeed many of the passages relied upon by Mr. O'Neill and cited in the Taxing Master's report are also cited and relied upon by the learned judge. I therefore take the view that the only grounds upon which I could properly be asked to descend from or fail to follow *Dunne v O'Neill* have not been established to my satisfaction.

I would like, however, to make it clear that I have not formed this view merely as a reluctant adherent to the doctrine of *stare decisis*. My decision is not in the words of Bowen L.J. "a sacrifice made upon the altar of authority": *Montague v Earl of Sandwich* 32 Ch. D. 525 at p. 549. I think that the argument on behalf of the defendants suffers from two disabilities. The discretion conferred upon the Taxing Master in the exercise of his functions is a judicial discretion and is therefore not unfettered. Where for example Order 99 R. 37 (10) uses the expression "as the Taxing Master shall in his discretion think fit and reasonable" it is not in my view correct to argue as Mr. O'Neill did that this ousts the discretion of the Court on review so as to leave the matter entirely in the hands of the Taxing Master. Such a discretion would be unlimited and if exercisable in determining a party's right to legal indemnity as to costs would probably by unconstitutional. The Taxing Master's discretion is a judicial discretion and is therefore exercisable only in accordance with judicial principles. In my view these principles must be determined by the High Court and what Gannon J. was doing was prescribing the proper principles to be applied in deciding the proper disbursements to be allowed in respect of counsel's fees. No doubt he did this in a manner not theretofore to be found in any decided case but the challenge to his right so to do leads to what I consider to be the second infirmity in the argument mainly. This is a disregard of the difference between the Rules of the Superior Courts 1962 and those previously in force which is so carefully analysed by Kenny J. in *Lavan v Walsh (No. 2)* [1963] I.R. 329. This is specifically relied upon by Gannon J. at p. 191.

For these reasons I propose to apply the principles laid down by Gannon J. in *Dunne v O'Neill* [1974] I.R. 180. Although the point did not arise in that case it seems to me that the same principle should apply to the right and duty of a solicitor in seeking the advice or in briefing counsel.

[Parke J. proceeded to review individually the items in dispute, applying the principles set out in *Dunne v O'Neill*]

Extract 11.6

THE PEOPLE v MOORE [1964] Ir. Jur. Rep. 6

The applicant for leave to appeal had been convicted of dangerous driving causing death. He made a statement in which he admitted that prior to the incident he had been drinking. His counsel sought to have references to his drinking excluded on the grounds that that evidence was not relevant to the offence with which he was charged. The trial judge admitted the statement in evidence but instructed the jury to leave the question of drinking out of their considerations. The Court of Criminal Appeal, in dismissing the application, refused to follow its earlier decision in *The People v O'Neill* [1964] Ir. Jur. Rep. 1. The extract from the Court's judgment deals with *stare decisis* in the Court of Criminal Appeal.

Davitt P.

. . . There remains the question whether we are bound to accept and apply the principle enunciated in *O'Neill's case* even though we differ from it to the extent which we have indicated. We have not been referred to, nor are we aware of, any case in which the question whether this court is bound to follow its previous decisions has arisen. Mr. Hederman, on behalf of the Attorney General, cited the case of *R. v. Norman* [1924] 2 K.B. 315 in which the Court of Criminal Appeal in England expressly over-ruled its previous decision in *R. v. Stanley* [1920] 2 K.B. 235. In *Stanley's* case the Court consisted of the usual number of three judges; in *Norman's Case* there was a full court of thirteen, four of whom dissented. The constitution of the Court of Criminal Appeal in England is not dissimilar from ours; and its jurisdiction is much the same as ours except that they cannot direct a new trial where they reverse a conviction. An appeal lies from them to the House of Lords in the same circumstances as an appeal lies from us to the Supreme Court. This Court, as at present constituted, certainly claims no jurisdiction to *over-rule* the decision in *O'Neill's case*. We are, however, encouraged by the decision in *Norman's case* to take the course which we now propose to adopt. We are not unmindful of the principle of *stare decisis* and of the desirability of having uniformity in judicial decisions interpreting the law. We think, however, that the interests of justice will best be served by giving effect to our own opinions, even though they differ from some of those expressed in *O'Neill's case*, and allow the questions involved to go to the Supreme Court for final decision. We accordingly dismiss the present appeal against conviction and sentence; but, as we are of opinion that our decision involves two questions of law of exceptional public importance, and that it is in the public interest desirable that an appeal should be taken to the Supreme Court, we will certify accordingly. The two questions are: (a) Whether the principle enunciated in *O'Neill's case* viz. that on a charge of dangerous driving evidence that the accused person had taken alcoholic drink should be excluded unless there is evidence that his driving was in fact affected by it, is correct in law; and (b) if not, whether we were free to give, or ought to have given effect to our own opinion.

[Note: the applicant abandoned his appeal to the Supreme Court]

Extract 11.7

IRISH SHELL LTD. v ELM MOTORS LTD. [1984] I.R. 511

The defendants entered into an agreement with the plaintiffs by which, *inter alia*, they agreed to sell the plaintiffs' products exclusively. The plaintiffs sought and were granted an interlocutory injunction, by Costello J. in the High Court, which compelled the defendants to abide by the terms of the agreement. On appeal, the Supreme Court affirmed the order of the High Court. The judgment of McCarthy J. is interesting in a number of respects. In upholding the decision to grant the injunction he disagreed with Costello J.'s analysis of the law governing interlocutory injunctions. Moreover, he took issue with Costello J.'s suggestion that English decisions ought to be followed by Irish courts unless they were shown to be erroneous. O'Higgins C.J. and Griffin J. concurred in his judgment but expressly reserved their opinions on the latter point.

McCarthy J

. . . In referring to the observations cited from *Kerr on Injunctions, Halsbury's Laws of England* and the *American Cyanamid* case, I pause to draw attention to the observations of the learned trial judge in his relatively lengthy judgment after his analysis of the English case law in *Esso Petroleum Company Ltd v Harper's Garage (Stourport) Ltd* [1968] A.C. 269, *Cleveland Petroleum Co Ltd v Dartstone Ltd* [1969] 1 W.L.R. 116, and *Amoco Australia Pty Ltd v Rocca Bros. Motor Engineering Co Pty Ltd* [1975] A.C. 561, the latter being a decision of the Judicial Committee of the Privy Council. I do not necessarily agree or disagree with the analysis made by the learned trial judge but I deem it proper to comment on his observation that 'the High Court in this country is not, of course, bound to follow the decisions and judgments to which I have referred if there are compelling reasons for rejecting them'. I do not believe that the true inference from this observation is that, in the absence of compelling reasons for rejection, the High Court in this country is bound to follow decisions and judgments of the House of Lords, the Court of Appeal in England, or the Judicial Committee of the British Privy Council, but lest any such view should be entertained I would unequivocally deny the existence of any such principle or the propriety of any such practice. Of the decisions of these courts decided prior to 1922, it is proper to say that they are part of the corpus of jurisprudence and law that was taken over on the foundation of Saorstát Eireann being the laws in force in Saorstát Eireann at the date of the coming into operation of the Constitution of the Irish Free State (Saorstát Eireann), subject to that Constitution and to the extent to which they were not inconsistent therewith. Similarly Art. 50 of the Constitution provides:

1. Subject to this Constitution and to the extent to which they are not inconsistent therewith, the laws in force in Saorstát Eireann immediately prior to the date of the coming into operation of this Constitution shall continue to be of full force and effect until the same or any of them shall have been repealed or amended by enactment of the Oireachtas.
2. Laws enacted before, but expressed to come into force after, the coming into operation of this Constitution, shall, unless otherwise enacted by the Oireachtas come into force in accordance with the terms thereof.

Art. 50 was stated by Kingsmill Moore J in *The Educational Company of Ireland Ltd v Fitzpatrick (No. 2)* [1961] I.R. 323 as 'carrying forward statutes or law into our corpus juris' but this view has been questioned by Walsh J (with whom O'Higgins CJ agreed) in *Gaffney v Gaffney* [1975] I.R. 133 where he said: 'Contrary to what appears to have been the view of Kingsmill Moore J I do not think that Art. 50 refers to any law other than statute law, and in my view the text of Art. 50 makes that clear'. Walsh J may well have been echoing the observations of Gavin Duffy J in *Exham v Beamish* [1939] I.R. 336 where he stated:

As a matter of practice, we constantly refer to judgments in the English Courts and such judgments, as every lawyer will recognise, have often proved to be of great service to us; but let us be clear. In my opinion when Saorstát Eireann, and afterwards Eire, continued the laws in force, they did not make binding on their courts anything short of law. In my opinion, judicial decisions in Ireland before the Treaty, and English decisions which were followed here, are binding upon this Court only when they represent a law so well settled or pronounced by so weighty a juristic authority that they may fairly be regarded, in a system built up upon the principle of *stare decisis*, as having become established as part of the law of the land before the Treaty; and to bind, they must, of course, not be inconsistent with the Constitution. In my opinion, this Court cannot be fettered in the exercise of the judicial power by opinions of very different courts under the old regime, unless those opinions must reasonably be considered to have had the force of law in Ireland, so that they formed part of the code expressly retained. If, before the Treaty, a particular law was administered in a way so repugnant to the common sense of our citizens as to make the law look ridiculous, it is not in the public interest that we should repeat the mistake. Our new High Court must mould its own *cursus curiae*; in so doing I hold that it is free, indeed bound, to decline to treat any such absurdity in the machinery of administration as having been imposed on it as part of the law of the land; nothing is law here which is inconsistent with derivation from the People.

Whilst observations of judges of the former Supreme Court in *Boylan v Dublin Corporation* [1949] I.R. 60 and *Minister for Finance v O'Brien* [1949] I.R. 91, appeared to support the view that decisions of the House of Lords upon law common to England and Ireland given before the coming into operation of the Constitution of 1922 are a binding force in our courts, in my view the decision of this Court in *Attorney General v Ryan's Car Hire Ltd* [1965] I.R. 642 and *The State (Quinn) v Ryan* [1965] I.R. 70, wherein the rigidity of the principle of *stare decisis* was denied, must now call into question the binding force of any such pre-1922 decision. Since 26 July 1966, the House of Lords has recognised that too rigid adherence to precedent may lead to injustice of a particular case and also unduly restrict the proper development of the law. It stated its right, while treating former decisions of the House as normally binding, to depart from a previous decision when it appears right to do so. *Practice Note* [1966] 1 W.L.R. 1234. Such a statement of principle by the House of Lords inevitably makes even weaker any case for following the decisions of that House whether they are in cases before or after 1922. There are many other jurisdictions like to our own where the *corpus juris* includes the common law—the United Stated, Canada, Australia, New Zealand and so on. These are nations where, in addition, there are written and, consequently rigid Constitutions, unlike that of the United Kingdom. Whilst the judgments in cases decided in the English Courts at all levels, will on a great many occasions prove convenient and, indeed, convincing statements of principle and attractive arguments in favour of such principles, they are no more than that and must be examined and questioned in the light of a jurisprudence whose fundamental law is radically different in its denial of a supremacy of parliament and its upholding of three co-equal organs of government, the legislature, the executive and the judiciary. In no sense are our courts a continuation of or successors to the British Courts. They derive their powers from a Constitution enacted by the people and would, in my view, find more appropriate guidance in the decisions of courts in other countries based upon a similar constitutional framework than in what at times appears to be an uncritical adherence to English precedent, which, itself, appears difficult to reconcile from time to time; see *Pirelli General Cable Works v Oscar Faber & Partners* [1983] 1 All E.R. 65. Within the relatively narrow confines of the instant appeal, it is to be noted that the *American Cyanamid* case, appears to have departed from an existing requirement of 'probable success' and to substitute for it that of there being a serious issue to be tried.

Extract 11.8

TROMSO SPAREBANK v BEIRNE (No. 2) [1989] I.L.R.M. 257

In an action, *inter alia*, for damages for fraud and negligent misrepresentation Costello J. had to consider a number of pre-trial motions for discovery of certain documents. In respect of certain of the documents the plaintiffs claimed that they were privileged on the grounds that they were obtained for the purpose of supplying them to their legal advisers in order to obtain legal advice. Costello J. considered a number of conflicting English authorities on the point and ordered discovery. However, the extract from his judgment suggests that an Irish court ought to adopt English cases, the authority of which is not in doubt.

Costello J.
. . . Privilege is claimed for these documents and in support of that claim reliance is placed on a statement in the White Book, 1988 Ed. Paragraph 24-5-10, and the decision of the Court of Appeal in England on which the statement in the White Book is based. The statement is to the effect that original or copy documents obtained or prepared by a party for the purpose of obtaining a solicitor's advice in view of pending or anticipated proceedings are privileged. The cases on which that statement is based are *The Palermo case* (1883) 9 P.D. 6 and *Watson v Cammell Laird & Co* [1959] 1 W.L.R. 702. The Defendant submits that the principle in the White Book is too wide and that the decisions which established it should not be followed. The Defendant submits that no privilege should attach to copies of documents which themselves are not privileged, even if the copies were obtained for the purpose of obtaining legal advice. In support of these submissions Mr Cooke has referred me to the views of Lord Denning M.R., in *Buttes Gas Oil Co. v Hammar (No. 3)* [1981] Q.B. 223 at 244. In the course of his judgment the Master of the Rolls referred to the two decisions to which I have referred and the principle which is to be extracted from them:

> If the original document is privileged (as having come originally into existence with the dominant purpose aforesaid), so also is any copy made by the solicitor. But, if the original is not privileged, a copy of it also is not privileged—even though it was made by a solicitor for the purpose of the litigation: see *Chadwick v Bowman* (1886) 16 Q.B.D. 561. There are some cases which appear to give a privilege to copies on their own account, even when the originals are not privileged. They range from *The Palermo* (1883) 9 P.D. 6 down to *Watson v Cammell Laird & Co. (Shipbuilders and Engineers) Ltd.* [1959] 1 W.L.R. 702. But these cases are suspect. They were adversely commented on in the Sixteenth Report of the Law Reform Committee on Privilege in Civil Proceedings (1967) (Cmnd. 3472). Since *Waugh's case* [1980] A.C. 521 it is open to us to reconsider them. In my opinion, if the original is not privileged, neither is a copy made by the solicitor privileged. For this simple reason, that the original (not being privileged) can be brought into court under a subpoena duces tecum and put in evidence at the trial. By making the copy discoverable, we only give accelerated production to the document itself. This was pointed out by Winn L.J.'s Committee in the Report of the Committee on Personal Injuries Litigation in July 1968 (Cmnd. 3591), para. 304.

In reply to the views of the Master of the Rolls, Mr Kelly, on behalf of the Plaintiff Bank, referred me to a recent decision in *R. v Board of Inland Revenue, Ex Parte Goldberg* [1988] 3 All E.R. 248, which expressly disapproved of the comments of the Master of the Rolls.

In this situation what should the attitude of the High Court in Ireland be? I think the High Court should be slow to refuse to follow a principle established in English

Law since 1883. But if high legal authority in England questions the validity of the principle so that it appears it may well be changed either by judicial decision of the courts or by the legislature, then it seems to me that the Irish Court is justified in not following it should it consider it erroneous.

The conclusion I have come to is this: I can see no reason why legal professional privilege should apply to the copy documents with which this case is concerned. Legal professional privilege primarily exists so that a litigant can have recourse to his legal advisers in circumstances which enable him to have complete confidence that the communications made to him and from him will be kept secret. It is well established that this privilege extends to documents which come into existence after litigation is commenced, either for the purpose of obtaining or giving legal advice (see: *Anderson v Bank of British Columbia* (1876) 2 Ch. 644 at 649). But I cannot see that the protection of the interests of a litigant requires the privilege to be extended to copies of documents which came into existence prior to the contemplation of the litigation, documents which are themselves not privileged and which the other side could probably inspect as a result of a third party discovery order and which they could have produced at the trial pursuant to a subpoena duces tecum. The rules of court are designed to further the rules of justice and they should be construed by the court so that they assist the achievement of this end. If inspection of documents cannot conceivably injure the interests of one party and may well assist the other to ascertain the true facts of the case prior to trial I do not think that the Court should put a gloss on the rules which would prevent this result and so I will order inspection of the documents referred to in section A. . .

THE *RATIO DECIDENDI* AND *OBITER DICTUM*

As has been already stated not every part of an earlier decision must be followed by a later court. In the course of a judgment it is not unlikely that the judge will canvass and consider a number of propositions of law, some of which bear on the point in question and others of which are tangential thereto. The discussion of law in which the judge engages will typically set out reasons in support of accepting certain arguments and drawing a particular conclusion. In this respect the reasoning operates to justify the decision and to establish that it has been reached in accordance with the pre-existing law. Once decided a case becomes authority for a certain proposition of law and the part which is binding is called the ratio decidendi. Briefly stated it can be defined as the reason for the decision. A proposition of law contained in the judgment which is not binding is termed *obiter dictum* (*obiter dicta* being the plural). It is unusual for a court expressly to state the *ratio decidendi* of its decision, preferring instead to leave it concealed in its reasoning. This does not reflect a judicial predilection for obfuscation but rather a desire not to hinder or fetter future courts. A court is concerned with deciding the particular case before it and not potential future cases, which will be the task of later courts. Discovery of the *ratio decidendi*, therefore, is largely a matter of interpretation for later courts. It must be emphasised that when a court searches for the *ratio decidendi* of an earlier decision it is looking for the rule or principle which underlies the decision and for which the decision is authority. The task is essentially one of classifying statements of law as being *ratio decidendi* or *obiter dictum*. In this context, it should be realised that judges infrequently employ the expression "*ratio decidendi*" and more often speak of the "rule" or "principle" which is contained in the earlier decision. In this respect the terms are largely synonymous and are used interchangeably. Given the nature of the exercise no precise formula for the extraction of the *ratio decidendi* has evolved, it being a matter of art rather than science. Despite that, several points can be made.

1. Ratio decidendi is based on the facts of the case

Because courts decide actual cases, and not moot points, the *ratio decidendi* is based on the facts of the case rather than on any hypothetical set of circumstances. It is the rule which was applied as limited by those facts. A court's discussion of the case is normally confined to the actual facts and a decision, by its very nature, concerns those facts and no others. This is sometimes reflected in the observation that a case is authority only for that which it decides. Unfortunately this does not provide the simple solution which at first sight it might suggest. Every case can be read as presenting an individual set of facts which will never be repeated. Details such as the identity of the parties, the time and location of the event, and the event itself are unique to the particular case. However, to read cases in such a narrow manner would be so restrictive as to destroy the system of *stare decisis*. No two cases would be alike and, in consequence, no decision would bind any other. But as it is authority for a particular proposition of law it is necessarily implicit that a case is capable of being applied beyond its own particular facts. It follows that courts are required to identify similarities and dissimilarities between cases and to adjudicate accordingly. Thus, if adequate reasons cannot be found to justify distinguishing the instant case from the earlier case the latter must be followed.

In general, therefore, the individual details of a case do not limit its scope. For instance, the fact that the victorious plaintiff in the earlier case was injured by a car does not, of itself, preclude that case from being applied to a case which involves injury caused by atrain. The function of the later court is to identify the categories into which the earlier court sought to place the particular individual facts. When the court decides that the earlier case is a relevant authority which must be followed it is placing the different sets of individual facts in the same category. To draw on the example already used, if the court in the case involving injury by the train decides that it is bound by the earlier case involving the car it, in effect, states that for the purposes of the rule there is no difference between a car and a train. In other words, the *ratio decidendi* of the earlier case allows recovery whether the injury is caused by a car or by a train. Thus, one must realise that facts can be stated at different levels of generality. It is in the identification of the appropriate level that the *ratio decidendi* is discovered. The agent of harm in the example under discussion can be described variously as a car, a motorised vehicle, a mechanical vehicle, a vehicle which might or might not be mechanical or a tangible thing. In equating, or indeed differentiating, cases the court selects a level of generality to apply to instant case. The irrelevance of certain factual differences will be obvious to all. For instance, injury caused by a Ford is not perceived to differ from injury caused by a Rolls Royce. However, diverse factors might enter into consideration when one asks whether injury caused by a car is to be equated with that caused by a runaway horse, a leakage of chemicals or the carelessness of a surgeon. The answer will depend on the level of generality which is selected. In searching for the appropriate level the later court is attempting to identify the rule which was invoked in the earlier decision.

And that, in turn, requires the court to examine the earlier decision with a view to determining how it was reached.

2. Relevance of Reasoning and Arguments

When it examines an earlier case the later court is looking for indications in the judgment as to the rule which was invoked. The earlier court will usually have commented on the individual facts concerned and have defined the category which it had in mind. However, that in itself is not conclusive as the later court might ignore the stated category and redefine it. This is particularly so where the category has been drawn in especially broad, or narrow, terms. Thus, although the earlier court might have spoken of the agent of harm as being a tangible thing, the later court might decline to employ that level of generality, saying that the earlier case concerned a car or a vehicle and not tangible things in general. In so explaining the earlier decision the later court is, to an extent, refashioning its *ratio decidendi*. The earlier court will also have considered any relevant cases which preceded it. For instance, the court concerned with the injury caused by a car might have felt itself bound by, and followed, a precedent involving injury caused by a galloping horse. In that instance the category would have to include both galloping horses and cars and the appropriate level of generality is thereby defined, in part at least. The question which the later court will face is whether the new agent of harm, a train, falls into that category. In other words, it will have to identify, for the purposes of the rule, the characteristics which are shared by galloping horses and cars and determine whether a train possesses those properties. Again, the later court will examine the earlier judgments in its attempt to ascertain the nexus between them. It might be that those cases indicate that galloping horses and cars are dangerous objects which are likely to cause serious personal injury and which should be kept under control. If that is the common characteristic identified by the court it is probable that a train, which also is a dangerous object, would come within the rule. But, by the same token, injury caused by a stationary horse might be distinguished as the latter does not possess the degree of danger shared by the other objects.

This, of course, is to assume that the earlier courts will have commented on the categories which they had in mind. It is, however, not uncommon that a court will confine its discussion of the case to the particular facts. This, in part at least, is motivated by a desire to restrict consideration of the legal issues to the case in hand and a wish not to engage in speculation which is thought to be the more suitable subject of future litigation. In this respect, the later court is left to interpret the earlier court's silence. Thus, the later court might conclude that nothing has been said in the earlier case which prevents its application to the new case. That silence can be so construed is appreciated by McCarthy J. in his judgment in *Ó Domhnaill v Merrick* [1984] I.R. 151, 167 where he expressed his disagreement with certain propositions which had been advanced in argument ". . . lest my silence on the topics might be considered to denote agreement . . .". Equally, a court might rely on the silence of its predecessor to exclude application of the precedent to the new case, saying that there is no indication in the earlier case which suggests that it should apply to the later.

The earlier court's discussion of the relevant law will also indicate the rule which it had in mind. That court will have considered cases which preceded it and will have subjected them to the same form of analysis to which it will be subject in later cases. That analysis of earlier cases and the evaluation of their scope and effect will be taken into account by the later court in its efforts to discover the *ratio decidendi*. The earlier court will have expressed its reasons for choosing to follow, or not to follow, a preceding case, thereby stating a relationship between the two which indicates the rule which was applied. This is to state the rule in a somewhat oblique manner, but occasionally a court will state clearly the rule which it intends to apply. However, even where that occurs it does not determine the issue. The later court might not accept the stated rule as being the *ratio decidendi* of the earlier decision. The court might state that the purported rule was too broad for the particular decision and that a less expansive rule would have sufficed. Likewise, if the rule is expressed in narrow terms, which would suggest that the later case lies outside its scope, the court might conclude that the rule was so expressed as a particular application of a more general rule.

It has been noted that the *ratio decidendi* of a case is based on its actual facts rather than on a hypothesis. A further characteristic is that a decision rests on the arguments which were advanced in the case. It is said that a point not argued is a point not decided. For instance, a claim based on contract does not provide a binding rule in respect of tortious liability. The *ratio decidendi* of that case consists of some rule which forms part of the law of contract, not the law of torts. A further decision in a case on the same facts will be necessary to arrive at a binding rule which governs liability in tort. Once again, when this matter is being considered the later court will have to examine the judgment in the earlier case in order to discover the basis on which the earlier case was decided. And in *Re Hetherington* [1989] 2 All E.R. 129, 133 Browne-Wilkinson V.C. stated that a court is not bound by a proposition the correctness of which was assumed by the earlier court without its having been specifically considered. A related feature, which has already been observed, is a *per incuriam* decision. That is one which has been made in ignorance of a relevant statute or binding authority and, in consequence, is not itself binding. Although the earlier court will, in all probability, have thought that it was reaching a binding decision its ignorance of the earlier law deprives it of that quality. A relevant point has not been argued and, therefore, has not been decided.

So far our consideration of this topic has been predicated on the assumption that a case consists of one judgment which advances one reason for the decision reached. Matters are more complicated where a judge advances several reasons in support of the decision or where a number of judgments are delivered. In respect of the former, it has been stated by Budd J. in *Brendan Dunne Ltd. v FitzPatrick* [1958] I.R. 29, 45 that where a judge states two reasons for the decision both are part of the *ratio decidendi*. Thus, to return to our example of the injury caused by a car, were the court to hold the car owner liable on the grounds that a car is a dangerous object *and* that its situation on the highway increases the risk of injury to other users of the highway the *ratio decidendi* would include both those factors. This rule would incorporate injuries caused by cars and by runaway horses as both share the characteristics identified in the judgment. But it would exclude injury caused by trains as the latter do not pose additional threats to highway users.

3. Ratio Decidendi and Multiple Judgments

Special considerations apply with regard to multi-judge courts, such as the Supreme Court and less frequently a Divisional Court. Where one judgment attracts the concurrence of the other members of the court or where a majority of the judgments delivered agree on the reasons for the decision few additional problems are created. The reasoning which attracts the unanimous, or at least majority, support of the court would form the basis of the *ratio decidendi*. However, where the court is unanimous but different reasons are advanced, none of which attracts the support of a majority, two possible approaches exist. One is that the *ratio* would consist of the sum of the reasons advanced. Thus, if two judges opt for reason A and one each for reasons B, C, and D the *ratio* of the case would consist of reasons A, B, C, and D. The difficulty with this approach is that it results in the selection of the narrowest possible *ratio* which accommodates all the judgments delivered. This would come close to stating that the case is an authority only for that which it decides and it would lack a binding quality except in identical cases. With this in mind Cross, in his article "The *Ratio Decidendi* and a Plurality of Speeches in the House of Lords" (1977) 93 *L.Q.R.* 378, presents an alternative approach which is probably closer to actual judicial practice. He suggests that one should think of the case as comprising of a number of *rationes decidendi* and select that which can be said to attract the support of a majority. Therefore, if reasons A and B are not mutually incompatible but are inconsistent with reasons C and D the *ratio* would embrace A and B. But it should be recognised that this approach is of little avail in the, fortunately rare, case where five judges advance five separate and incompatible reasons. In that event, a later court is very much left to its own devices and can select any of the five different *rationes* or, indeed, a sixth of its own invention.

As Cross notes, dissenting judgments can be relevant when it comes to ascertaining the *ratio decidendi*. It is all too tempting to ignore those judgments in the, possibly mistaken, belief that they shed no light on the subject. Dissents can be relevant for several reasons. A dissent might be based on a different interpretation of the evidence or a different evaluation of legal issues which the case presents but nevertheless support the propositions of law advanced by the majority. Moreover, in some cases the majority might agree on the result but for conflicting reasons and recourse must then be had to the dissenting judgments. This can be illustrated by an example where three reasons, A, B and C, are advanced in the judgments. The majority is composed of two judges who opt for reason A and one who opts for reason B but expressly disapproves of reason A. The dissidents advance reason C and also express their disapproval of reason A. The third judge of the majority also expresses his support of reason C but considers it inapplicable in the instant case. In this event it is difficult to conclude that reason A is the *ratio* of the case as three judges, the two dissidents and one member of the majority, have voted against it. Nor can the *ratio* be said to be based on reason B as it enjoys the support of only one judge, namely the third majority judge. Thus, the available alternatives are that the *ratio* is based on reason C or that the case possesses no discernible *ratio* and is merely authority for that which it decided. But the first alternative presents the difficulty of elevating the reasoning of a dissident minority into the *ratio* of the case and it would seem that we are left with the second.

Another example which is considered by Cross also concerns a case where there is a three-to-two majority. Two judges opt for *ratio* A, one for *ratio* B and the two dissidents opt for *ratio* C, but this time each of the judges in the majority expresses disapproval of *ratio* C. In that event, Cross suggests that *ratio* A is the *ratio* of the case. *Ratio* B is not that of the case as it is supported by only one judge and *ratio* C having been condemned by three judges could not be the *ratio* of the case. However, this approach does not reflect recent judicial practice in the Supreme Court. In *The People v O'Shea* [1982] I.R. 384 (Extract 13.4) it was held that the prosecution may appeal to the Supreme Court from an acquittal in the Central Criminal Court. In the course of the judgments two members of the majority, O'Higgins C.J. and Walsh J., suggested that the Court could order a retrial in the event of a successful appeal (*ratio* A) whilst the remaining member of the majority, Hederman J., reserved his opinion on that question (*ratio* B). The two dissenting judges, Finlay P. and Henchy J., held that the prosecution does not enjoy a right of appeal (*ratio* C). On Cross's analysis part of the *ratio* of *O'Shea* is that the Supreme Court may order a retrial following a successful prosecution appeal. But in *The People v Quilligan and O'Reilly (No. 2)* [1989] I.L.R.M. 245 the Court had to consider that very issue. Henchy J., writing for the majority, observed that only two of the judges in *O'Shea* supported that proposition and concluded that the point was still undecided. The majority proceeded to hold that the Court does not possess the power to order a retrial consequent on a successful prosecution appeal. In effect, the majority in *Quilligan and O'Reilly (No. 2)* held that the remarks of the two majority judges, which we have labelled *ratio* A, are not part of the *ratio* of *O'Shea*. Two alternative conclusions can be drawn from this. One is that the Court in *Quilligan and O'Reilly (No. 2)* misinterpreted the *ratio* of *O'Shea* and, applying Cross, ought to have adopted the remarks of O'Higgins C.J. and Walsh J. The other is that Cross's analysis does not reflect the position in Ireland and that the most that can be said is that *O'Shea*—and any case like it—is authority only for that which it decided. Any wider proposition which might be thought to flow from the decision is not part of the *ratio* and, therefore, not binding. To the extent that discussion of the *ratio decidendi* is descriptive, in that it attempts to focus on actual judicial practice, it would seem that the latter alternative is to be preferred.

A final point about multi-judge decisions concerns the infrequent case where the court divides evenly. This can occur when one of the judges dies during the course of the hearing or must absent himself for some other unavoidable reason. Where an appellate court divides evenly the decision of the lower court stands. But the problem of determining the *ratio* in such an event remains. It would be tempting to select the reasoning of the judges who voted to dismiss the appeal as their judgments prevailed. But that would be to allow an external event, which inadvertently deprived the court of the ability to form a majority, shape the *ratio* of the decision. A solution which was proposed by Ó Dálaigh C.J. in *Rexi Irish Mink Ltd. v Dublin County Council* [1972] I.R. 123, 130 is that in such a case the question of law is still undecided and the later court has to determine which of the two views suggested should be adopted.

4. Significance of Obiter Dicta

As we noted earlier, a statement of law which is not binding is called an *obiter dictum*. It consists of anything said by the earlier court which is not considered to be directly relevant or essential to the decision. However, although an *obiter* is not binding it does not lack significance as it possesses persuasive authority. It can be adopted or followed at the option of the later court. The weight, or value, of an *obiter dictum* depends on a variety of factors, including the court in which it was delivered, the judge who delivered it and its closeness to the instant case. It is not unusual for a statement which was obiter in one case to form the *ratio* of a subsequent case. In effect, the later court adopts the statement and bases its decision on it. Thus, in *The State (Raftis) v Leonard* [1960] I.R. 381, 419 Murnaghan J. followed two pre-1922 decisions, which he was otherwise reluctant to do, as they had been approved of, *obiter*, by the Supreme Court in *Walsh v Minister for Local Government* [1929] I.R. 377. He did not feel free to adopt his own interpretation as the views of the Supreme Court should, in his opinion, be ". . . given the weight of an opinion of the Court and, as such, an acceptance that the law was as stated therein." On the other hand, it should be noted that the classification of a statement of law as being *obiter* can be contentious. In some cases a court's declaration that an earlier judicial opinion is *obiter* frees it from following what might otherwise be thought to be binding. This, in essence, is what occurred in *The People v Shaw* [1982] I.R. 1 (Extract 11.9) where Griffin J. argued that the remarks of Walsh J. in *The People v O'Brien* [1965] I.R. 142, which had been followed in a number of cases, were *obiter*. In this respect, a cynic could be led to the conclusion that the attribution of that status to a proposition of law is nothing more than a device to evade the application of a statement of law which the court dislikes.

5. Evolution of Principles

So far we have been considering how the *ratio decidendi* of an earlier decision can be discovered and it has been suggested that it is principally a matter for the later court. In this respect, the expression "*ratio decidendi*" can be understood in two senses. The first is a description of the manner in which the court arrived at its decision. The second is a proposition of law for which the case is an authority. The two are related. When a later court attempts to extract a binding proposition from an earlier case it examines the reasoning of the earlier court. The rule which is divined from the earlier case is the product of the reasoning in that case. As more cases are decided the rule becomes more detailed and, in effect, the courts are engaged in the process of adding flesh to what initially was a skeletal rule. Rules are not static but evolve through the course of litigation.

Thus, the operation of the system of precedent does not result in the stagnation of rules. The process of adjudication as much involves law creation as it does law application. The system possesses a flexibility which requires later courts to make choices. The later court must select a binding proposition from a range of canvassed alternatives. As those choices are made rules are defined and redefined, their scope being expanded and contracted. This is not to say that later courts are presented with unrestricted choices or that the process results in a form of judicial anarchy. Whilst a case might present choices, the freedom of the later court is constrained by parameters set by the reasoning in the earlier case from which the relevant legal principle is extracted. If, in categorising that principle, the court makes unreasonable distinctions or is irrational in its analysis it runs the risk that its decision will be ignored. For instance, were a court to ignore the earlier case on the grounds that it governed injuries caused by a Rolls Royce and not by other cars it would not be followed in later cases—we would all agree that the manufacture of the car which caused injury is immaterial to a rule which governs injuries caused by cars. By identifying similarities and placing cases in the same category the law develops through a process of reasoning by analogy, a point which was acknowledged by Costello J. in *D v C* [1984] I.L.R.M. 173, 189. Moreover, although courts, by interpreting cases, can revise rules they are not entitled to ignore precedents or, where binding, to overrule them. A court must accept the rule which has been determined in earlier cases and is permitted to define its scope in a manner which is reasonable and not spurious or arbitrary. Developments in new cases must be consistent with earlier cases and the pattern which emerges is one of the law gently ebbing and flowing rather than of sudden tempestuous alterations which depend on the whims of particular judges.

When we speak of the law evolving gradually it must be realised that its development does not follow a planned or predetermined course. In exercising choice courts select the directions in which the law should develop. The system of precedent operates to channel that development within certain constraints. The necessity to follow earlier cases ensures that new developments can be accommodated within the pre-existing law. Thus, a court's reasoning is both retrospective and prospective. In the former sense the court attempts to justify a new decision as being consistent with the old law. It invokes earlier cases in support of its decision. In this context *stare decisis* operates as a standard by which to evaluate the legitimacy, or permissibility, of new decisions. A decision which is perceived as being unwarranted by preceding cases will itself be rejected in later cases. But at the same time, the court's reasoning is prospective in that it contains a set of options from which later courts will choose. And later courts will repeat the exercise when they come to consider the legal issues which are raised by the decision. Thus, as old questions are settled new ones are raised and the process continues unabated, surviving as the central feature of our legal system.

Extract 11.9

THE PEOPLE v SHAW [1982] I.R. 1

In *The People v O'Brien* [1965] I.R. 142 the Supreme Court considered the question of the exclusion of illegally obtained evidence from criminal trials. Stolen goods were found in the appellant's house which had been illegally searched, the search warrant having incorrectly stated the address. The Court held that the evidence was admissible as the illegality was "inadvertent". The Rule invoked by three judges (Kingsmill Moore, Lavery and Budd JJ.; Ó Dalaigh C.J. and Walsh J. dissenting on this point) was that illegally obtained evidence could be excluded at the discretion of the trial judge. But where the illegality amounts to a breach of the accused's constitutional rights Walsh J., with the concurrence of his fellow judges, stated that the evidence thereby obtained must be excluded except in "extraordinary excusing circumstances".

The question arose again in *Shaw*. The appellant was arrested one night and detained for nearly three days whilst the Gardaí attempted to discover the whereabouts of a young woman whom he was believed to have kidnapped. During this time he made a statement in which he admitted to having kidnapped, raped and murdered her and he took the Gardaí to the places in which she had been held. In the normal course of events he should have been brought before a court within a reasonable time, which in this case would have been the morning after he was arrested (see *Dunne v Clinton* [1930] I.R. 366; *The People v Walsh* [1980] I.R. 294). The question was whether his extended detention was illegal and, therefore, a breach of his right to personal liberty, which is guaranteed by Article 40.4 of the Constitution. In the event, a majority of the Court (Henchy, Griffin, Parke and Kenny JJ.) held that the detention was lawful as the appellant's right to personal liberty was limited by the victim's right to life which the Gardaí, at the time, were attempting to vindicate. Walsh J. considered the detention to be illegal but was satisfied that there was an "extraordinary excusing circumstance" which justified the admission of the evidence.

The Court also took the opportunity to review *The People v O'Brien* and the extracts from the judgments of Walsh and Griffin JJ. reflect different interpretations of that decision. Henchy and Parke JJ. concurred with Griffin J. and Kenny J. delivered a judgment which was in similar terms. It should be noted that, strictly speaking, the discussion was unnecessary as the decision of the Court rested on the assumption that *O'Brien* was applicable. A further point arose which is included in the extracts. In *The People v Conmey* [1975] I.R. 341 the Supreme Court expressed the view that an appellant could appeal directly from the Central Criminal Court to the Supreme Court. This was challenged by Griffin J. who considered that view to be *obiter*. Walsh J., however, was of the opposite opinion.

Walsh J.

. . . I feel that I should elaborate a little upon my reference to *The People (Attorney General)* v. *O'Brien* [1965] I.R. 141 as, from time to time, there appears to be some confusion as to what the case decided. As I had the advantage of being a member of the Court which gave that decision, I feel that I am in a position to deal with it. The case and the decision dealt primarily with two matters concerning the admissibility of evidence. The first was the question of the admissibility of evidence which was obtained illegally but where the illegality did not amount to an infringement of a constitutional right of the accused person. The second point was the question of the admissibility of evidence obtained by illegal methods which constituted infringements of the accused's constitutional rights. With regard to the first point, the majority of the Court decided that evidence obtained illegally could be admissible at the discretion of the judge, whereas the minority members of the Court took the view that such evidence was always admissible provided that it was relevant and probative. With regard to the second point, the basic proposition was that an objection to the admissiblity at a criminal trial of evidence obtained or procured by the State, its servants or agents, as a result of a deliberate and conscious violation of the constitutional rights of the accused person must be upheld, subject to certain exceptions. This general proposition was contained in my own judgment and was agreed to by all the members of the Court. I expressed the view that an exception to this general rule would be where "extraordinary excusing circumstances" existed and I gave three examples, namely, the imminent destruction of vital evidence, the need to rescue a victim in peril, and also evidence obtained by a search which was incidental to and contemporaneous with a lawful arrest, though made without a valid search warrant. I said that, in addition to these "extraordinary excusing circumstances", evidence obtained without a deliberate and conscious violation of an accused's constitutional rights was not inadmissible by reason only of the existence of a violation of his constitutional right. In other words, accidental and unintentional infringements of the Constitution would not be sufficient to exclude such evidence.

It is important to emphasise that "extraordinary excusing circumstances" and "accidental and unintentional infringement of the Constitution" are quite separate matters. Kingsmill Moore J. in his judgment accepted the general proposition and also agreed that there might be certain "extraordinary excusing circumstances" which would warrant the admissibility of such evidence, but he preferred not to attempt to enumerate such extraordinary excusing circumstances by anticipation. He also expresssly agreed that an accidental and unintentional infringement of the Constitution would not normally exclude evidence so obtained. His disinclination to attempt to enumerate all the cases which might amount to excusing circumstances was shared by all the members of the Court. He was thus leaving open the question of what could amount to extraordinary excusing circumstances and he was not prepared to enumerate them by anticipation. He took the view that circumstances of cases vary so widely that it would be a matter for the discretion of the trial judge to decide whether or not the circumstances which were pleaded in excuse of the violation of the constitutional right in question were such as to amount to "extraordinary excusing circumstances." The examples of these given in my own judgment were simply illustrative and did not claim to be exhaustive.

O'Brien's Case was examined recently by this Court in *The People* v. *Walsh* [1980] I.R. 294 and the views I now express were the views of the Court in that case. It is also necessary to emphasise that nothing in the admissibility rule renders lawful what was and is unlawful. By definition the question of admissibility arises only because there was an illegality.

I might add that there is nothing whatever in *O'Brien's Case* to suggest that the admissibility of the evidence depends upon the state or degree of the violator's knowledge of constitutional law or, indeed, of the ordinary law. To attempt to import any such interpretation of the decision would be to put a premium on ignorance of the law. The maxim *ignorantia legis neminem excusat* does not permit an intentional and deliberate act or omission to be shorn of its legal consequences. It is appropriate to point out that the opinion of this Court on a similar subject was expressed as follows at p. 134 of the report of *The State (Quinn)* v. *Ryan* [1965] I.R. 70:—

> A belief, or hope, on the part of the officers concerned that their acts would not bring them into conflict with the Courts is no answer, nor is an inadequate appreciation of the reality of the right of personal liberty guaranteed by the Constitution.

To hold otherwise would be to hold what to many people would be an absurd position, namely, that the less a police officer knew about the Constitution and, indeed, of the law itself, the more likely he would be to have the evidence which he obtained in breach of the law (and/or the Constitition) admitted in court. If such indeed were the position, it could well lead to a demand that the interests of equality of treatment should permit an accused person to be allowed to be heard to the effect that he did not know that the activity of which he was charged, and which has been proved against him, amounted to a breach of the criminal law. In *The People* v. *Madden* [1977] I.R. 336 the learned Chief Justice said at p. 347 of the report:—

> The court of trial appears to have sought an element of wilfulness or *mala fides* in the conduct of the Garda officer and, not finding such, to have concluded that the deprivation of constitutional rights was not deliberate and conscious. In the

view of this Court to adopt that approach is to misunderstand the decision in *O'Brien's Case* and, accordingly, to err in law. What was done or permitted by Inspector Butler and his colleagues may have been done or permitted for the best of motives and in the interests of the due investigation of the crime. However, it was done or permitted without regard to the right to liberty guaranteed to this defendant by Article 40 of the Constitution and to the State's obligation under that Article to defend and vindicate that right.

In the result the evidence was held to he inadmissible and the defendant Madden was set free . . .

. . . In conclusion I wish to say a few words concerning the decision of this Court in *The People (Attorney General)* v. *Conmey* [1975] I.R. 341. It had not originally been my intention to mention that case at all as it was never mentioned in the course of this hearing nor, indeed, has it any relevance whatever to it. However, as it appears that one or more members of the Court wish to avail of this occasion to express a view on it, I feel I cannot let the matter pass without comment.

The decision of the Court in that case was to the effect that an appeal lay directly from a decision of the Central Criminal Court (which is the High Court exercising its criminal jurisdiction) to this Court by virtue of the provisions of Article 34 of the Constitution. In that case the applicant applied to this Court for an extension of time to lodge a notice of appeal to the Court and, for the purpose of deciding that matter, it was necessary to consider whether or not an appeal did lie to this Court from the Central Criminal Court. The applicant had already brought an appeal to the Court of Criminal Appeal pursuant to s. 31 of the Courts of Justice Act, 1924. That appeal had been dismissed and he had been refused a certificate pursuant to s. 29 of the Act of 1924 to enable him to appeal to this Court. A majority of the members of the Court expressed the view that an appeal did lie to this Court from the Central Criminal Court and that it had not been restricted or regulated by any legislation enacted since the coming into force of the Constitution. The Court also held that the Court of Criminal Appeal, being a statutory appellate court of limited jurisdiction, enjoyed a concurrent jurisdiction with this Court within a limited area and that, when its jurisdiction within that area had been invoked, the matter under appeal was then completely exhausted and no further appeal could be taken to this Court, save by virtue of the provisions of s. 29 of the Act of 1924. If, however, the concurrent jurisdiction of the Court of Criminal Appeal had not been invoked, then the matter would not have been exhausted and an appeal would lie directly to this Court. Therefore, the Court, being of opinion that there was nothing left to determine as the applicant's appeal had been fully disposed of and that there was no basis for enlarging the time, decided that the application for enlargement of time should be dismissed. Two members of the Court, while not expressly dissenting from the views of the majority, expressly reserved their opinion on the general question of a direct appeal from the Central Criminal Court to this Court. They expressed the view that the applicant, having taken the course of appealing to the Court of Criminal Appeal, had exhausted the *statutory* remedies available to him and that, if an appeal did lie to this Court, such an appeal would be an alternative and not an addition to the statutory right of appeal to the Court of Criminal Appeal. They took the view that, having exercised that statutory right, it was not open to the applicant to claim to exercise *in addition* thereto a constitutional right of direct appeal to this Court.

The question is now being raised as to whether the decision of the majority of the Court may be disregarded as being simply an *obiter dictum*. I do not think that any judge would wish any statement which he might have made casually and as mere *obiter* to be treated as necessarily being an authority on the subject in question. However, when, as in *Conmey's Case*, a fundamental issue is elaborately and substantially argued and the Court thinks it necessary for the purpose of the case to make an exhaustive and deliberate examination of the law and of the relevant constitutional provisions and, in the result, to state the law, the authority of such a statement of the law cannot be got rid of simply by claiming that it was not really necessary for the actual decision of the case. As was shown in the judgments of the majority of the Court it was necessary, both in fact and in law, to resolve the issue for the purpose of their decision. This the judgments clearly demonstrate. Of course, some members of any court may from time to time be less than happy with some particular decision, but any such feeling cannot acceptably warrant either ignoring the decision so elaborately argued and decided or treating it as only "a remark by the way."

Griffin J.

. . . The jurisdiction of the Court of Criminal Appeal to grant a certificate of leave to appeal to this court is conferred by s. 29 of the Courts of Justice Act, 1924, as applied by s. 48 of the Courts (Supplemental Provisions) Act, 1961. A certificate under that section is the only statutory means whereby a person convicted on indictment may appeal to this Court. In *The People (Attorney General) v. Conmey* [1975] I.R. 341 there are to be found *dicta* to the effect that a person who is convicted on indictment in the Central Criminal Court can appeal directly to this Court, but (as I said in my judgment in that case) I consider those dicta to have been *obiter*. Because the attention of the Court in that case was not directed to the application to the suggested appellate jurisdiction of certain constitutional provisions (for example Article 40, s. 1) and of other authorities, the opinion expressed in those dicta may be thought to have been reached *per incuriam* or *sub silentio*. Therefore, I consider it to be an open question whether an appeal lies to this Court from any conviction on indictment save by means of s. 29 of the Act of 1924. However, this dictum itself is *obiter*, because the point was not argued in this case. I must reserve for an appropriate case, in which the Director of Public Prosections will be *legitimus contradictor*, my considered opinion on this point . . .

. . . The ruling made by the trial judge in this case, and the judgment of the Court of Criminal Appeal, proceeded on the basis that the test of admissibility of the questioned statements was, first, whether each was a statement taken in deliberate and conscious violation of the appellant's constitutional rights and, secondly, if so, whether it should nevertheless be held admissible because of extraordinary excusing circumstances. Because the trial, the hearing in the Court of Criminal Appeal, and the appeal in this Court all rested on the assumption that that represented the correct test of admissibility, this judgment has ruled on the certified point of law on the same basis.

That, however, does not mean that I or those of my brethren who join in this judgment accept that that test of admissibility is the correct one. That test derives from certain dicta enunciated in some of the judgments of this Court in *The People (Attorney General) v. O'Brien* [1965] I.R. 142 and it has been applied in a number of subsequent cases. It needs to be said, however, without in any way questioning the correctness of the actual decision given in *O'Brien's Case*, or in any of those other cases in which the same test was applied, that the ambit of the question certified for the decision of this Court in *O'Brien's Case* did not lend itself to the pronouncement of any binding statement of the correct test to be applied when a ruling is required as to whether an allegedly incriminating statement by an accused should be admitted in evidence. As I hope to show, the test for the admissibility of such statements, in so far as it was propounded in *O'Brien's Case*, was in terms which went beyond the issue presented to the Court in that case; it therefore lacks the authoritativeness that it would possess if it were a necessary element of the *ratio decidendi* of that decision.

The facts in *O'Brien's Case* were simple in the extreme. The Gardaí hoped to find stolen goods in the house at No. 118 Captain's Road, and they needed a warrant to search that house. By mistake they received a warrant to search No. 118 Cashel Road. In ignorance of the mistake, they used the faulty warrant to search No. 118 Captain's Road and they found certain stolen articles there. In the subsequent trial (for housebreaking and for receiving those stolen articles) of the two accused, who were brothers and who resided at No. 118 Captain's Road, objection was taken on their behalf that evidence of the finding of those articles was not admissible because of the defective warrant. That objection was disallowed and the accused were convicted. On the hearing in the Court of Criminal Appeal of their application for leave to appeal, the same objection was taken and it was again disallowed; but the Court of Criminal Appeal granted a certificate under s. 29 of the Courts of Justice Act, 1924, which allowed the accused to pursue their objection in this Court.

In essence, the point certified was whether evidence of stolen goods discovered in an accused person's home by the use of a search warrant which was inadvertently illegal was admissible, notwithstanding the guarantee in Article 40, s. 5, of the Constitution that "the dwelling of every citizen is inviolable and shall not be forcibly entered save in accordance with law." Kingsmill Moore J. (who gave the majority judgment of this Court) framed the question, as follows, at p. 150 of the report:— "Is evidence procured by the Guards in the course of, and as a result of, a domiciliary search, unauthorised by a search warrant, admissible in subsequent criminal proceedings?"

The Court unanimously held that such evidence was admissible notwithstanding the irregularity of the warrant and the illegality of the search on foot of it which brought to light the stolen goods. Indeed, the point was so clear to Lavery J. (who agreed with the majority judgment of Kingsmill Moore J.) that he was prepared to dismiss the appeal by saying, at p. 148:—"If a judge were to hold inadmissible the evidence in question in this case, or in any comparable case, his ruling would, in my opinion, be wrong to the point of absurdity and would bring the administration of the law into well-deserved contempt."

It will be noted that, because *O'Brien's Case* was concerned only with the admissibility of evidence as to *goods* found in pursuance of the use of a defective search warrant, the scope of its facts did not admit of any authoritatively binding decision as to the test or tests for the admission in evidence of *statements* of an inculpatory nature made by an accused. The latter evidence is evidence emitted by, or extracted from, the accused and, as such, requires to be tested for admissibility primarily by the manner in which the accused was led, or came, to produce a confessional or inculpatory statement which the prosecution wishes to adduce in evidence against him. The same considerations do not necessarily apply when the question is whether testimony as to real evidence (*i.e.*, material objects other than statements) should be received. The essential difference is that a statement does not exist until the accused himself makes it.

The limitation imposed by the question before this Court in *O'Brien's Case*, and the essence of the answer given to it by the majority, were expressed as follows by Kingsmill Moore J. at p. 161 of the report:—"It would not be in accordance with our system of jurisprudence for this Court to attempt to lay down rules to govern future hypothetical cases. We can do no more than decide the case now before us, and to lay down that, in future cases, the presiding judge has a discretion to exclude evidence of facts ascertained by illegal means where it appears to him that public policy, based on a balancing of public interests, requires such exclusion." Had the judgment of Kingsmill Moore J. gone no further, *O'Brien's Case* would probably never have been relied on, in the way it has been, as an authoritative source for the test as to the admissibility of evidence as to confessions or admissions.

However, because Mr. Justice Walsh in his minority judgment thought it proper to deal with the certified question on a broader basis, Kingsmill Moore J. added the following at the end of his judgment at p. 162 of the report:—"Mr. Justice Walsh, in the judgment which he is about to deliver, is of opinion that where evidence has been obtained by the State or its agents as a result of a deliberate and conscious violation of the constitutional (as opposed to the common law) rights of an accused person it should be excluded save where there are 'extraordinary excusing circumstances,' and mentions as such circumstances the need to prevent an imminent destruction of vital evidence or rescue of a person in peril, and the seizure of evidence obtained in the course of and incidental to a lawful arrest even though the premises on which the arrest is made have been entered without a search warrant. I agree that where there has been such a deliberate and conscious violation of constitutional rights by the State or its agents evidence obtained by such violation should in general be excluded, and I agree that there may be certain 'extraordinary excusing circumstances' which may warrant its admission. I would prefer, however, not to attempt to enumerate such circumstances by anticipation. The facts of individual cases vary so widely that any hard and fast rules of a general nature seem to me dangerous and *I would again leave the exclusion or non-exclusion to the discretion of the trial judge.*" (Italics supplied).

Apart from the fact that Kingsmill Moore J. elsewhere in his judgment warns that judicial pronouncements of a general nature must be read *secundum materiam subjectam*, it is clear from the extracts I have cited that the *ratio decidendi* of *O'Brien's Case* goes no further than to lay down that when real evidence has been procured by illegal means, it falls within the discretion of the trial judge to decide whether public policy, based on a balancing of public interests, requires that such evidence be excluded. The specific and narrow issue involved in the case prevented its decision from being a vehicle in which to convey an authoritative and binding ruling on the test for the admission in evidence of oral, written, or other forms of statements tendered as confessions or admissions.

Since the admissibility of such statements is directly in issue in this case, I think it proper and desirable to express an opinion as to the correct approach to the question of the admissibility of such statements. Before such statements are admissible, two conditions must be satisfied by the prosecution.

The primary requirement is to show that the statement was voluntary, in the sense in which that adjective has been judicially construed in the decided cases. Thus, if the tendered statement was coerced or otherwise induced or extracted without the true and free will of its maker, it will not be held to have been voluntarily made. The circumstances which will make a statement inadmissible for lack of voluntariness are so varied that it would be impossible to enumerate or categorize them fully. It is sufficient to say that the decided cases show that a statement will be excluded as being involuntary if it was wrung from its maker by physical or psychological pressures, by threats or promises made by persons in authority, by the use of drugs, hypnosis, intoxicating drink, by prolonged interrogation or excessive questioning, or by any one of a diversity of methods which have in common the result or the risk that what is tendered as a voluntary statement is not the natural emanation of a rational intellect and a free will. As to the present case, there is no question but that the questioned statements were made voluntarily.

Secondly, even if a statement is held to have been voluntarily obtained in the sense indicated, it may nevertheless be inadmissible for another reason. Because our system of law is accusatorial and not inquisitorial, and because (as has been stated in a number of decisions of this Court) our Constitution postulates the observance of basic or fundamental fairness of procedures, the judge presiding at a criminal trial should be astute to see that, although a statement may be technically voluntary, it should nevertheless be excluded if, by reason of the manner or of the circumstances in which it was obtained, it falls below the required standards of fairness. The reason for exclusion here is not so much the risk of an erroneous conviction as the recognition that the minimum of essential standards must be observed in the administration of justice. Whether the objection to the statement be on constitutional or other grounds, the crucial test is whether it was obtained in compliance with basic or fundamental fairness, and the trial judge will have a discretion to exclude it "where it appears to him that public policy, based on a balancing of public interests, requires such exclusion"—*per* Kingsmill Moore J. at p. 161 of the report of *O'Brien's Case* [1965] I.R. 142. This is a fairer and more workable test than a consideration of whether the questioned statement complies with specific constitutional provisions, because most of the criminal trials in this State are held in courts (the District Court, the Circuit Court and the Special Criminal Court) which, in terms of their judicial personnel, judicial experience and vested jurisdiction, are not designed for constitutional interpretation or for the balancing of constitutional rights, or for the preferment of one invoked constitutional provision over another.

The test of basic fairness, based on a due consideration of the rights of the accused coupled with the requirements, in the interests of the common good, of the prosecution, superimposed on the need for voluntariness, has the merit of ensuring, if the judicial discretion is correctly exercised, that an accused will not be wrongly or unfairly convicted out of his own mouth.

Applying those two tests to the facts of the present case, the elucidation I have given earlier in this judgment of the circumstances in which, and the purpose for which, the questioned statements were taken shows that both those tests were satisfied. Therefore, I would dismiss this appeal.

Extract 11.10

THE PEOPLE v LYNCH [1982] I.R. 64

The question of the admissibility of unconstitutionally obtained evidence and the decision in *The People v O'Brien* [1965] I.R. 142 arose again in a differently constituted Supreme Court in this case. The appellant was convicted of murder on the basis of a statement which he made following twenty-two hours' interrogation. He argued that the statement was obtained in breach of his right to personal liberty. The Supreme Court allowed his appeal on the basis that the statement had been obtained "oppressively" and should have been excluded by the trial judge in the exercise of his discretion. The Court felt unable to deal with the question of the alleged breach of the appellant's right to personal liberty, as certain vital issues of fact concerning his alleged detention had not been put to the jury. [It should be noted that this aspect of the decision has subsequently been departed from by the Court in *The People v Conroy* [1986] I.R. 460 where it was held that these matters should be determined by the judge alone]. However, both O'Higgins C.J. and Walsh J. considered the decision in *O'Brien* and Griffin J.'s judgment in *The People v Shaw* [1982] I.R. 1 (Extract 11.9). Kenny J. concurred in the result on the basis that he believed it to be consistent with the majority judgments in *Shaw*.

The question of direct appeals from the Central Criminal Court to the Supreme Court also arose again. O'Higgins C.J. and Walsh J. reiterated the view stated in *The People v Conmey* [1975] I.R. 341 that such appeals could be brought by virtue of Art. 34.4.3 of the Constitution. Kenny J. assumed for the purposes of the case that a direct appeal could be brought but declined to express a definitive opinion on the matter as he considered that he had not heard full argument on the point. This issue was finally resolved by the Supreme Court in *The People v O'Shea* [1982] I.R. 384 (Extract 13.4).

O'Higgins C.J.

The appellant was tried in the Central Criminal Court before Mr. Justice D'Arcy and a jury on the charge of having murdered Vera Cooney. The trial lasted 13 days and resulted in the appellant's conviction and the passing upon him of the mandatory sentence of penal servitude for life. Against this conviction the appellant has appealed directly to this Court. In so doing, the apellant exercised a right which is conferred by Article 34, s. 4, sub-s. 3, of the Constitution which expressly provides:—"The Supreme Court shall, with such exceptions and subject to such regulations as may be prescribed by law, have appellate jurisdiction from all decisions of the High Court . . ." The Supreme Court is the court of final appeal mentioned in Article 34, ss. 2 and 4. The Central Criminal Court is the name applied to the High Court when exercising its criminal jurisdiction in relation to the trial of offences, and a verdict given in that court by a jury on the trial of an indictable offence is a decision of that court.

The present Court of Criminal Appeal was established by s. 3 of the Courts (Establishment and Constitution) Act, 1961. By s. 12 of the Courts (Supplemental Provisions) Act, 1961, there was vested in it all jurisdiction which had been vested in, or which was capable of being exercised by, the former Court of Criminal Appeal. That jurisdiction included a power to hear appeals by persons convicted on indictment before the Central Criminal Court. That power was conferred by s. 31 of the Courts of Justice Act, 1924, which section was (in effect) re-enacted to apply to the new Court of Criminal Appeal. None of these statutory provisions, however, purport to except or to limit or affect the existing appellate jurisdiction of the Supreme Court under Article 34, s. 4, sub-s. 3, of the Constitution.

Accordingly, despite the establishment of the Court of Criminal Appeal and the provision for appeals to it from the Central Criminal Court, there continues to exist also a right to appeal from all decisions of the Central Criminal Court directly to the Supreme Court. However, a person who, having been convicted before the Central Criminal Court, appeals to the Court of Criminal Appeal thereby exhausts his right of appeal (see [1975] I.R. 341) unless a certificate is granted by that court under s. 29 of the Courts of Justice Act, 1924.

The right to appeal directly to the Supreme Court from decisions of the Central Criminal Court will continue to exist until such time as appropriate legislation is passed delimiting the Supreme Court's appellate jurisdiction in accordance with Article 34, s. 4, sub-s. 3, of the Constitution. Such legislation could not contravene the prohibition contained in Article 34, s. 4, sub-s. 4, against excepting from the appellate jurisdiction of the Supreme Court cases which involve questions as to the validity of any law, having regard to the provisions of the Constitution. Accordingly, even if legislation were introduced for the express purpose of excepting from the Supreme Court's appellate jurisdiction appeals from the Central Criminal Court, such legislation could not extend to, or affect, cases involving such questions.

In this case the appellant has exercised this right to appeal directly to this Court. This Court has entertained his appeal and, in exercise of its jurisdiction to do so, has unanimously allowed it. The matter is listed to-day to enable reasons for this decision to be given . . .

. . . In view, however, of the wide range of argument advanced, it seems to me that something should be said of a general nature with regard to the admissibility of evidence which is alleged to have been obtained irregularly in the course of a Garda investigation, such as took place in this case. In the first place it should be accepted that such an investigation is conducted on behalf of the State and that there is a direct public interest in its success. Equally important, however, is the fact that every such investigation takes place in a democratic State which is subject to the Constitution and to the laws which operate thereunder. There is always a public concern that criminals should be brought to justice and a public interest that the rights of the individual citizen, which the Constitution guarantees, will be protected.

Most Garda investigations, certainly of major crimes, involve a painstaking search for clues, the following up of leads, the questioning of many people who may be able to add to the information available and so help in bringing those responsible to justice. Often in such investigations the Gardaí, for one reason or another, do not get the co-operation and assistance which they seek and require. Moreover, they are frequently confronted with an organised conspiracy to shield the culprit, to hamper the investigation and generally to defeat the ends of justice. In so far as they are faced with such problems and have to overcome such difficulties, they are entitled to the sympathy and understanding of both the general body of the public and of judges who preside at subsequent trials. Sympathy for, and understanding of, difficulties is one thing: to excuse irregular means which have been adopted because of those difficulties, in order to secure evidence at a trial, is quite another. I use the word "irregular" deliberately in order to comprehend both methods or means which under our legal system are illegal in the sense that they offend the ordinary common or statute law and also such methods or means which offend and violate the Constitution.

In countries which do not possess a written constitution the word "illegal" is sufficiently wide to cover both technical and minor breaches of the common law and serious and deliberate interferences with the accepted civil rights of citizens. In such countries it is possible to lay down a general policy which can be applied to all situations in which illegality of any kind is used in the securing of evidence. In England the general rule is that such evidence will not be excluded merely on the grounds that it was obtained by illegal means, if it is relevant and not otherwise inadmissible: *Kuruma* v. *The Queen* [1955] A.C. 197; *Noor Mohamed* v. *The King* [1949] A.C. 182 and *Harris* v. *Director of Public Prosecutions* [1952] A.C. 694. Nevertheless, it is recognised in England that, even if relevant and otherwise admissible, such evidence may be excluded if the judge, in exercising his discretion, thinks its admission would be unfair to the accused. In Scotland the leaning of the courts is in the opposite direction. There the view is that such evidence ought not to be admitted unless what was done can be excused on the grounds of urgency, inadvertence, mistake, the minor or technical nature of the illegality involved, or on some such other similar ground: *Lawrie* v. *Muir* [1950] S.C. (J.) 19; *McGovern* v. *H.M. Advocate* [1950] S.C. (J.) 33. Despite the difference in policy, the position is that the courts of both England and Scotland are free to, and do, regard in the same light all evidence obtained by illegal means irrespective of the nature of the illegality. Illegality is, in the one case, ignored except in circumstances of unfairness to the accused and, in the other, regarded as fatal to the admission of the evidence unless the methods used can be excused.

Where, however, there exists a written constitution which guarantees rights to citizens and prohibits specified acts and conduct in violation of such rights, quite different considerations must apply. In countries governed by a written constitution one may expect the judges, by their oath and office, to be bound to uphold the constitution and its provisions and to do so on all occasions in the courts in which they preside. In the United States the Federal Supreme Court has established in a series of decisions a rule strictly excluding evidence obtained in breach of constitutional provisions: *Weeks* v. *United States* (1918) 232 U.S. 383; *Mapp* v. *Ohio* (1961) 367 U.S. 643 and *Terry* v. *Ohio* (1968) 392 U.S. 1. In the last-mentioned case Warren C.J. explained the reason at page 13 of the report in the following words:—

> Courts which sit under our Constitution cannot and will not be made party to lawless invasions of the constitutional rghts of citizens by permitting unhindered governmental use of the fruits of such invasions. Thus in our system evidentiary rulings provide the context in which the judicial process of inclusion and exclusion approves some conduct as comporting with constitutional guarantees and disapproves other actions by state agents. A ruling admitting evidence in a criminal trial, we recognize, has the necessary effect of legitimizing the conduct which produced the evidence, while an application of the exclusionary rule withholds the constitutional imprimatur.

It was exactly this question which was considered by this Court under certificate from the Court of Criminal Appeal in *The People (Attorney General)* v. *O'Brien* [1965] I.R. 142. In that case the judgment of Kingsmill Moore J. (which had the approval, in one of two respects, of a majority of the Court, and, in the other, of the entire Court) has always been regarded as laying down two clear principles to be applied in considering the admission of evidence irregularly obtained. The first of these principles is that evidence obtained as a result of a deliberate and conscious violation of the Constitution should be excluded unless there is some extraordinary excusing circumstance which warrants its admission. The second principle is that, in relation to evidence obtained by illegal means which fall short of a violation of constitutional rights, the presiding judge has a discretion to exclude such evidence where it appears to him that public policy, based on a balancing of public interest, requires such exclusion. Since 1965 these principles have been applied in a large number of cases, of which I will only mention the most recent: *The People* v. *Madden* [1977] I.R. 336; *The People* v. *O'Loughlin* [1979] I.R. 85 and *The People* v. *Walsh* [1980] I.R. 294.

Recently, however, in the course of his judgment in *The People* v. *Shaw* [1982] I.R. 1, Mr. Justice Griffin questioned the application of the *ratio decidendi* of *O'Brien's Case* to statements of an inculpatory nature made by an accused. He pointed out, as was the fact, that the disputed evidence in *O'Brien's Case* consisted of property found in premises which had been entered without a lawful warrant. He contrasted such "real evidence" with the evidence of a statement which is, in his words, "evidence emitted by, or extracted from, the accused and, as such, requires to be tested for admissibility primarily by the manner in which the accused was led, or came, to produce a confessional or inculpatory statement which the prosecution wishes to adduce in evidence against him." He then suggested that the proper and appropriate test as to the admissibility of such statements, whether the objection be on constitutional or other grounds, should be whether they were obtained in compliance with basic or fundamental fairness and that, in this respect, the trial judge should have a discretion to exclude where the public interest requires such exclusion. I fear that I cannot agree with these views, either in relation to the ambit of the decision in *O'Brien's Case* or in relation to the generality of the test which he suggests for the admission or exclusion of statements. I do not think that any such test could ever be applied in circumstances which involve a deliberate and conscious breach of constitutional rights.

While the facts of *O'Brien's Case* related to the discovery of stolen goods as the result of an entry made pursuant to a defective warrant, the point of law raised thereon and certified to the Supreme Court for clarification in the public interest under s. 29 of the Courts of Justice Act, 1924, was of a much wider ambit. That point of law concerned the admissibility of evidence as to the property discovered following an illegal search, and also the question of the admissibility of evidence obtained in direct violation of the Constitution—since the house has been entered without lawful authority. On a reference of a point of law of exceptional public importance under s. 29 of the Act of 1924, in my view it is proper that this Court should give as much assistance as possible in clarifying the law and should not regard itself as imprisoned within the particular facts upon which the point referred is first raised. In my view, this was the manner in which the Supreme Court approached the point of law which it had to consider in *O'Brien's Case*.

An examination of the judgment of Kingsmill Moore J. in *O'Brien's Case* indicates that the Court considered the general question of the admissibility of evidence obtained by illegal means and also a similar question in relation to evidence obtained as a result of a direct violation of the Constitution. It is true that the admission of incriminating statements as such was not considered, except as coming within the general category of evidence obtained by irregular means. The reason for this is easy to see in that such statements generally fall to be excluded on the grounds that they are not voluntary. The Court was divided as to the admissibility of evidence obtained by illegal, as opposed to unconstitutional, means; but it was unanimous "that where evidence has been obtained by the State or its agents as a result of a deliberate and conscious violation of the constitutional (as opposed to the common law) rights of an accused person it should be excluded save where there are 'extraordinary excusing circumstances' . . ."—*per* Kingsmill Moore J. at p. 162 of the report. In relation to the admissibility of the particular evidence in that case, which was obtained both illegally and in breach of the Constitution, Kingsmill Moore J. added:—"This case is not one of deliberate and conscious violation, but of a purely accidental and unintentional infringement of the Constitution."

I must say I cannot see anything either in the point of law considered, or in the judgments delivered, in the *O'Brien's Case* which confines or which should confine the principles there enunciated to property or "real evidence." Those principles were applied to an incriminating statement in *The People* v. *Madden* and were approved, as of general application, in *The People* v. *O'Loughlin* and *The People* v. *Walsh*. In any event, even if the *O'Brien's Case* did not effectively decide that statements obtained as a consequence of a deliberate and conscious violation of the constitutional rights of an accused should be excluded except in the circumstances mentioned, it seems to me that such a proposition must be accepted. It does not seem to me possible for any judge, except in such special circumstances as occurred in the *Shaw Case*, to countenance or endorse a deliberate violation of the Constitution by the admission of a statement obtained as a consequence of the violation. It is probable that, in any event, the vast majority of such statements would be excluded on other grounds; but this is not the point. I do not see that any discretion is possible.

Once the Constitution has been violated for the purpose of securing a confession, the fruits of that violation must be excluded from evidence on that ground alone. Nor can it be said that the matter can safely be left to a decision on fairness or the voluntary nature of the statement. In *The People* v. *Madden* the statement was held to be voluntary at the trial, although it was secured by a violation of constitutional rights. It could be that the deprivation of liberty, contrary to the express provisions of the Constitution, would in itself lead to a voluntary confession of guilt by an accused. If such a confesssion were ever admitted in evidence because it was voluntary or because it was fairly taken, or for any other reason then, in the words of Warren C.J., the Courts would "be made party to lawless invasions of the constitutional rights of citizens by permitting unhindered governmental use of the fruits of such invasions." I cannot accept that such a result could ever be permissible under the Constitution.

Walsh J

. . . I now come to the question of the illegalities involved in the making of these "admissions." As has been set out in the judgment of the Chief Justice, it is now a well-established principle in our jurisprudence that evidence, including statements, obtained by illegal means which amount to a violation of constitutional rights of an accused person is not admissible under any circumstances, save where there are "extraordinary excusing circumstances" or where the infringement is purely accidental and unintentional. This subject is fully and excellently treated by Mr. Peter Charleton, a member of the Bar, in his article (Improperly Obtained Evidence and the Constitution) at p. 180 of the October, 1980, issue of the Gazette of the Incorporated Law Society of Ireland. That issue of the Gazette was not published until December, after the judgments in *The People* v. *Shaw* [1982] I.R. 1 had been prepared.

The reasons of public policy which require exclusion of such evidence have been fully dealt with in the judgment which has just been delivered by the Chief Justice; they are also to be found in the judgments in *The People (Attorney General)* v. *O'Brien* [1965] I.R. 142 The Chief Justice has found it necessary to refer to the judgment of Mr. Justice Griffin in *The People* v. *Shaw*. There are passages in that judgment which would appear to suggest that the principles underlying *O'Brien's Case* and those now, and previously, enunciated by the Chief Justice are not applicable to statements made by an accused person. The judgment of Kingsmill Moore J. in

O'Brien's Case contains nothing to support such a view. As has been stated by the Chief Justice, the point in question was one of principle and was not dependent upon the nature of the evidence. For this purpose there is no distinction between what has been referred to as "real evidence," like an article, and an admission or a statement. The governing legal principle is quite clear. If I may adapt Lord Dunedin's famous reference to the "fallacy of the similarity of facts," it appears to me that to allow a distinction on the basis of the difference between "real evidence" and other evidence would be to base a distinction on the fallacy of the dissimilarity of facts. It was not submitted in *Shaw's Case*, nor was it the subject of any argument addressed to the Court, that *O'Brien's Case* did not apply to statements or admissions made by an accused person. As will be seen from the judgment of Mr. Justice Griffin, the question was whether or not there existed excusatory circumstances which would permit the admission of the statements within the principles enunciated in *O'Brien's Case*. In the passage cited by him from the judgment of Kingsmill Moore J., at p. 162 of the report of *O'Brien's Case*, the reference in the penultimate sentence of the passage cited to "such circumstances" is to the immediately preceding "extraordinary excusing circumstances"—as is quite clear from the text itself. That was also decided by this Court in *The People* v. *Walsh*. [1980] I.R. 294 In the last sentence of the passage cited, the reference by Kingsmill Moore J. to the "discretion of the trial judge" is made solely in relation to the discretion to decide if, on the facts of the individual case, there exist "extraordinary excusing circumstances." The use of the word "again" clearly indicates that Kingsmill Moore J. was not speaking of illegally obtained evidence where the illegality did not amount to a violation of constitutional rights (which he had already dealt with) but of the cases where it did. The last four sentences on p. 162 of the report make it abundantly clear what was in the judge's mind. They also make clear that *O'Brien's Case* was initiating an important principle of law in a field which, up to then, had been undefined in our law.

The breadth of the decision and the underlying principle in *O'Brien's Case* may also be gauged by the approach of Kingsmill Moore J. to the question of evidence obtained as a result of gross personal violence or methods which offend against the essential dignity of the human person. At p. 150 of the report he said:—

> To countenance the use of evidence extracted or discovered by gross personal violence would, in my opinion, involve the State in moral defilement.

In this context the constitutional dimension is also recognised in *Shaw's Case*. Speaking of statements which have been voluntarily made, Mr Justice Griffin said:—

> . . . and because . . . our Constitution postulates the observance of basic or fundamental fairness of procedures, the judge presiding at a criminal trial should be astute to see that, although a statement may be technically voluntary, it should nevertheless be excluded if, by reason of the manner or of the circumstances in which it was obtained, it falls below the required standards of fairness.

That passage imports this constitutional safeguard into the relations between the police and a suspect as well as to the judicial process. The guarantee of fair procedures contained in the Constitution is to be found in Article 40 which is the Article which also deals with unlawful detection and unconstitutional deprivation of liberty.

It is important to recall that the District Court and the Circuit Court, which deal with the great bulk of criminal trials in the State, are courts set up under the Constitution. Like their brethren in the Supreme Court and in the High Court, each judge of the Circuit Court and of the District Court is obliged by Article 34, s. 5, of the Constitution to make and subscribe in open court to the solemn and sincere promise that he will uphold the Constitution and the laws. Therefore, the judges of the District Court and judges of the Circuit Court are not dispensed from, or expected to overlook, their constitutional obligation to uphold the Constitution in the discharge of their constitutional and legal function of administering justice. It would be most incongruous if they were to apply a general test of basic fairness because the Constitution requires it, and not to rule on questions of the admissibility of evidence obtained as a result of breaches of the constitutional rights of the accused. The judicial obligation is to uphold all of the Constitution. It should also be borne in mind that members of the Garda Síochána are required by the Police Forces Amalgamation Act, 1925, to make a solemn declaration of obedience to the Constitution.

The real points in *Shaw's Case* were the voluntary character of the statements and the question of whether or not there existed excusatory circumstances which would permit the admission of the statements within the principles enunciated in *O'Brien's Case*. The factual basis which had to be examined was whether the evidence was sufficient in law to prove the existence of excusatory circumstances. The conflict was whether there existed a reason to believe that the life of one of the girls might be saved. If that was established as a question of fact, then the case clearly came within extraordinary excusatory circumstances referred to in both the judgment of Kingsmill Moore J. and my own judgment in *O'Brien's Case*; see, in particular, my reference (at p. 170 of the report) to "the need to rescue a victim in peril." No valid distinction can be drawn between a statement or an admission obtained by reason of the unconstitutional deprivation of an accused's liberty and any other type of evidence so obtained. As has been so often pointed out, it is the protection and upholding of the Constitution which is the dominant consideration and not the preferment of one type of evidence over another.

In the present case the appellant had already spent 22 hours in garda stations before he made any incriminating admission. The trial judge's finding was that he was in detention under arrest as from 12 noon on the 20th September, 1976, which was approximately two hours before the first incriminating admission was made. However, all the circumstances surrounding his presence in the garda station prior to that from the time he arrived there on the 19th September appear to indicate that he was not free to leave. These have been fully set out by the Chief Justice in his judgment and I do not propose to repeat them. But, like the Chief Justice, I am also of the opinion that the evidence points coercively to the fact that he was under arrest in the sense that he was not at liberty to leave the station and, as he had not been brought before a peace commissioner or a District Court within a reasonable time, his detention had already become illegal and, therefore, unconstitutional under Article 40 of the Constitution by the time any "admission" was made.

Extract 11.11

THE STATE (LYNCH) v COONEY [1982] I.R. 337

S. 31(1) of the Broadcasting Act, 1960 allows the Minister for Communications to make orders prohibiting R.T.E. from broadcasting certain matters "where he is of the opinion" that those matters would promote or incite crime or undermine the authority of the State. The Minister made an order which prevented R.T.E. from broadcasting party political broadcasts on behalf of Sinn Fein.

The prosecutor was a Sinn Fein candidate in the general election of February 1982. He sought an order of certiorari quashing the Minister's order on the grounds that s. 31 violated the guarantee of free speech contained in Article 40.6.1 of the Constitution and, alternatively, that it was *ultra vires*. In the High Court O'Hanlon J. held s. 31 to be unconstitutional on the grounds that the Minister's "opinion" is not susceptible to judicial review, thereby exceeding the limitations on free speech permitted by the Constitution.

The Supreme Court, in a judgment delivered by O'Higgins C.J., held that the section is constitutional but that orders made thereunder are reviewable. In separate judgments the Court further held that the order in question was not *ultra vires*. The judgment of Henchy J. is interesting for its analysis of earlier relevant cases and the view that what was *obiter* in one case, *In re the Offences against the State (Amendment) Bill, 1940* [1940] I.R. 470, became part of the ratio decidendi of a later case, *In re Ó Laighléis* [1960] I.R. 93.

Henchy J.

At the most, two questions require to be answered in this appeal. The first question is whether it was correctly determined in the High Court that, apart from the issue of invalidity under the Constitution, certiorari does not lie to quash the order made on the 9th February, 1982, by the first respondent (being the Minister for Posts and Telegraphs) under s. 31, sub-s. 1, of the Broadcasting Act, 1960 (as amended) directing Radio Telefís Éireann (the Authority) to refrain from broadcasting any matter which is "(*a*) a broadcast, whether purporting to be a political party broadcast or not, made by, or on behalf of, or advocating, offering or inviting support for, the organisation styling itself Provisional Sinn Féin, (*b*) a broadcast by any person or persons representing, or purporting to represent, the said organisation." It is only if the answer given by the High Court judge to that question is affirmed on the same basis, and an order of certiorari is denied on that basis, that the second question would arise; for it is a sound and well-established practice that, where the relief sought may be granted on a ground which does not involve a decision as to the constitutionality of a statutory provision, the issue of constitutionality should be left undecided.

If the impugned order were quashed for the being *ultra vires* for any of the reasons set out in the second schedule to the conditional order of certiorari, a ruling on the plea that s. 31, sub-s. 1, of the Act of 1960 (as amended) is unconstitutional would be plainly unnecessary for the disposition of this case. If, however, certiorari does not lie to quash the impugned order for being *ultra vires*, the second question would arise, *i.e.*, does it lie with the prosecutor to contend successfully that s. 31, sub-s. 1, of the Act of 1960 is invalid for being repugnant to the Constitution? If such a plea were to prevail, then the impugned order would be quashed at the behest of the prosecutor not because the Minister exceeded the law-making power delegated to him but because the statutory delegation itself is repugnant to the Constitution.

As to the first question, the High Court judge held that the impugned order was not open to challenge on the ground of *ultra vires*. He so held because the Minister is empowered to make such an order when he is "of the opinion that the broadcasting of a particular matter or any matter of a particular class would be likely to promote, or incite to, crime or would tend to undermine the authority of the State." The judge felt compelled by judicial authority to hold that the purely personal and exclusively subjective element connoted by the words "of the opinion" meant that, when the Minister has formed the type of opinion mentioned in the section and has then issued (as he did in this case) an order based on such opinion, the order could not be invalidated by the Courts by reason of any defect in the process by which the Minister reached his opinion. The judge seems to have accepted the argument put forward on behalf of the Minister that, no matter how unreasonably or unwarrantedly the Minister's opinion was formed, it was the Minister's opinion and, as such, by reason of its unqualified subjectivity, was beyond the scrutiny of the Courts.

However, it is right to point out that the judge said that it is only when "the Minister was bona fide in forming the necessary opinion" that the Courts are debarred from testing the validity of the order on the ground of reasonableness. That qualification would seem to undermine the logic of the approach adopted by the judge for, if the good faith of the Minister in making the order is open to consideration by the Courts, it would be difficult to justify the exclusion from judicial scrutiny of all or any of the other matters which could be said to be necessary for the formation by the Minister of a valid opinion of the kind specified in the section.

Some of the most erroneous and insupportable opinions may be formed in good faith. For example, they may derive from a genuine misapprehension or misapplication of necessary legal or factual considerations and, thereby, be outside the implied range of the statutory delegation to a Minister of the specified law-making power. In such a case, where the impugned opinion is not simply one that a court disagrees with (or thinks impolitic or unwise) but is shown to be vitiated by an improper exercise of the law-making process necessarily implied in the delegation, it would seem to be an abrogation by a court of its constitutional function if it deemed itself powerless to intervene merely because the opinion was formed in good faith. If the opinion relied on in a particular case is shown by a duly qualified litigant to be outside the scope of the delegation, it would be strange if a court which is empowered to pronounce on the validity of subordinate legislation on the ground of *ultra vires* were to be bound to withhold a finding of invalidation notwithstanding that the root of the invalidity was an *ultra vires* opinion.

It appears from the judgment under appeal that the reason why the judge held that, apart from factors arising from the Constitution, the Minister's opinion was excluded from judicial review was because the judge felt bound to follow a statement to that effect in the judgment of the then Supreme Court in *In re the Offences Against the State (Amendment) Bill, 1940* [1940] I.R. 470. If that statement could be said to be part of the *ratio decidendi* of that judgment, I would agree that the doctrine of *stare decisis* would have obliged the judge to follow it—even though the Supreme Court which gave that judgment was the Supreme Court which was empowered to function as such under the transitory provisions of the Constitution of Ireland, 1937, and was not the Supreme Court which was required by Article 34, s. 1, of the Constitution to be established by law and which was eventually so established by the Courts (Establishment and Constitution) Act, 1961. The maintenance of judicial order and continuity would support such a conclusion.

However, I do not consider that the statement relied on could be said to be part of the *ratio decidendi* of that decision of the former Supreme Court. The reference by the President of Ireland to the Supreme Court of the Bill in question was deemed necessary because of the decision of Gavan Duffy J. in 1939 in *The State (Burke)* v. *Lennon*. [1940] I.R. 136 In that case Gavan Duffy J. ordered the release by habeas corpus of an internee who was being detained under Part VI of the Offences Against the State Act, 1939; the judge made the order primarily because, in his opinion, Part VI of the Act of 1939 was repugnant to the Constitution. Part VI had contained a provision (s. 54) whereby the Government was empowered in certain emergency circumstances to bring that Part of the Act into operation by making and publishing a proclamation to that effect. The Government had made and published such a proclamation. Part VI had also provided (s. 55, sub-s. 1) as follows:—

> Whenever a Minister of State is satisfied that any particular person is engaged in activities calculated to prejudice the preservation of the peace, order, or security of the State, such Minister may by warrant under his hand order the arrest and detention of such person . . .

Section 55, sub-s. 3, of the Act of 1939 provided:—

> Every person arrested under the next preceding sub-section of this section shall be detained in a prison or other place prescribed in that behalf by regulations . . . until this Part of this Act ceases to be in force or until he is released

under the subsequent provisions of this Part of this Act, whichever first happens.

In *The State (Burke)* v. *Lennon* [1940] I.R. 136 the person on whose behalf an application was made for an order of habeas corpus was in internment under a warrant made by a Minister under sub-s. 1 of section 55. In the course of his judgment, in which he held Part VI of the Act of 1939 to be unconstitutional, Gavan Duffy J. said at pp. 151-2 of the report:—

> Fifthly, I am of opinion that indefinite internment under Part VI of the Act is indistinguishable from punishment for engaging in the activities in question, and I consider that the decision of a Minister of State to order the arrest and internment of a man under s. 55 is equivalent to a judgment pronounced against the internee for his dangerous activities. These considerations are . . . sufficient to show that the authority conferred on a Minister by s. 55 is an authority, not merely to act judicially, but to adminster justice and an authority to administer criminal justice [*in breach of Article 37*] and condemn an alleged offender without charge or hearing and without the aid of a jury . . . consequently a law endowing a Minister of State, any Minister, with these powers is an invasion of the judicial domain and as such is repugnant to the Constitution . . . If my analysis of the Minister's statutory duty is accurate, the document which the Act calls a warrant is really a combination of a conviction, an order to arrest and a warrant of committal.

As the report shows, when the respondents brought an appeal to the Supreme Court from that decision, the Supreme Court held that an appeal did not lie. In what was apparently an effort to circumvent this impasse, the Government introduced the Offences Against the State (Amendment) Bill, 1940, and it was passed by both Houses of the Oireachtas. When the Bill was presented to the President of Ireland for signature he, in exercise of the power vested in him by Article 26 of the Constitution, referred the Bill to the Supreme Court for a ruling as to its constitutionality. Since the Bill amounted essentially to a repeal and re-enactment of the condemned Part VI of the Act of 1939, the reference under Article 26 was a method whereby, in substitution for the appeal which had been held not to lie against the decision of Gavan Duffy J. in *The State (Burke)* v. *Lennon* [1940] I.R. 136, the opinion of the Supreme Court could be obtained as to whether Gavan Duffy J. had been correct in ruling Part VI of the Act of 1939 to be unconstitutional. Possibly to justify the enactment of the Bill as an amendment, the text of the Bill differed in a few minor respects from that of Part VI of the Act of 1939. The main difference was that under the Bill a warrant of internment could issue "whenever a Minister of State is of opinion" that the proposed internee is engaged in the specified activities, whereas under the condemned Part VI the warrant could issue whenever a Minister "is satisfied" that the proposed internee is engaged in those activities.

A study of the judgment of Gavan Duffy J. shows that, even if s. 55, sub-s. 1, of the Act of 1939 had used the words "is of opinion" instead of "is satisfied," he would still have found Part VI to be unconstitutional. I say that because it is clear from that judgment that it was the effect of the ministerial warrant (which was held to be "an authority, not merely to act judicially, but to administer justice and an authority to administer criminal justice") and not the mental element leading to the making of the warrant that was the foundation of the opinion of Gavan Duffy J. that Part VI of the Act of 1939 was unconstitutional. Indeed, it might well be contended that if s. 55, sub-s. 1, of the Act of 1939 had used the words "is of opinion"—thus connoting a laxer and more arbitrary level of ministerial assessment—Gavan Duffy J. might very well have treated those words as an *a fortiori* reason for his finding of unconstitutionality.

Upon the hearing of the reference by the President, the Supreme Court rejected the argument that the Bill was unconstitutional. In doing so, the Court set aside the conclusion of Gavan Duffy J. that, in making and issuing a warrant for detention, the Minister of State was administering justice within the meaning of Article 34; it rejected the argument that the impugned provisions created a criminal offence; and it dismissed the contention that those provisions fell short of the guarantees as to personal rights contained in Article 40. In short, the Supreme Court overthrew the conclusion of Gavan Duffy J., as well as the rationale for that conclusion, as to the *effect*, in the constitutional perspective, of the making and issuing of a warrant of detention. In neither decision was the adjudicative process, whereby the Minister of State decided in that case to make and issue a warrant, a crucial element. Each decision would have reached the conclusion actually reached, whether the impugned provisions used the expression "is of opinion" or the expression "is satisfied."

It is true, however, that in *In re the Offences Against the State (Amendment) Bill, 1940* [1940] I.R. 470 the Supreme Court expressed itself (p. 479) as follows in the course of its decision:—

> The only essential preliminary to the exercise by a Minister of the powers contained in s. 4 [*i.e., as to the making and issue of a warrant of detention*] is that he should have formed opinions on the matters specifically mentioned in the section. The validity of such opinions is not a matter that could be questioned in any Court.

On a perusal of the judgment as a whole, I am satisfied that the opinion expressed in that quotation was purely *obiter*. It is a parenthesis which has no necessary connection with either the conclusions or the reasoning of the judgment. It is no more than a passing remark, superfluous to the disposition of any of the reported submissions of counsel in the case. On the application of any of the tests for distinguishing *obiter dicta* from that which is part of the *ratio decidendi* of a case, I would deem that by-the-way observation to be *obiter*. Therefore, it has not the authority of a binding precedent.

I regret, therefore, that I cannot agree with the conclusion reached in the decision under appeal in this case, *i.e.*, that the judgment given by the then Supreme Court is a conclusive authority for the proposition that the expression "is of opinion" does not permit of a judicial review of the opinion actually formed, so as to determine whether it was legally valid or not. Considering the commendable speed with which this case was dealt with in the High Court, one might excuse counsel for not having directed the judge's attention to a binding decision on the point, *i.e.*, the decision of the then Supreme Court in *In re Ó Laighléis* [1960] I.R. 93. It is less understandable why, despite the fact that counsel on each side had an opportunity to file written submissions for the purpose of the appeal, this Court's attention has not been directed by counsel to that case, either in the written submissions or in the course of the argument. Notwithstanding that lapse, however, once the case has come to our notice it has to be considered for the purpose of overruling or approving its decision on this point.

The *Ó Laighléis Case* came before the Supreme Court on appeal from a decision of the High Court to the effect that Ó Laighléis, who was being held in internment pursuant to a warrant made by the Minister for Justice under s. 4 of the Offences Against the State (Amendment) Act, 1940, was not entitled to be released by habeas corpus. The appeal by the internee was dismissed. While not questioning the bona fides of the Minister for Justice in making and issuing the warrant, counsel for Ó Laighléis submitted that, as the internee had averred in his affidavit that he was not engaged in illegal activities at the time of his arrest, he was entitled to question the validity of that Minister's opinion. The Court ruled otherwise. In doing so it quoted (at p. 130) and applied the dictum, *supra*, appearing at p. 479 of the report of the judgment of the Court in *In re the Offences Against the State (Amendment) Bill, 1940* [1940] I.R. 470, which dictum states that the validity of such opinions cannot be questioned in any court. What was merely *obiter* in the 1940 case thus became part of the *ratio decidendi* in the *Ó Laighléis Case*. The question, then, is whether that ruling should be still adhered to. In my opinion, it should not. It should be overruled in exercise of the power of this Court to do so as stated in *The Attorney General* v. *Ryan's Car Hire Ltd.* [1965] I.R. 642 and in *Mogul of Ireland* v. *Tipperary (N.R.) County Council* [1976] I.R. 260.

While it might be argued that the opinion of the then Supreme Court expressed in those decisions of 1939 and 1957 was part of what was then current judicial thinking, that could not be said if the same opinion were expressed to-day. Decisions given in recent years in this and other jurisdictions show that the power of the Courts to subject the exercise of administrative powers to judicial review is nowadays seen as having a wider reach than that delimited by those decisions of 1939 and 1957. The more recent decisions in this and other jurisdictions—I do not cite them because counsel have not referred to them—show that there is good foundation for the conclusion stated in de Smith's Judicial Review of Administrative Action (4th ed. p. 326) as follows:—"As we have already observed, nowadays the courts will not readily be deterred by subjectively worded statutory formulae from determining whether acts done avowedly in pursuance of statutory powers bore an adequate relationship to the purposes prescribed by statute."

I conceive the present state of evolution of administrative law in the Courts on this topic to be that when a statute confers on a non-judicial person or body a decision-making power affecting personal rights, conditional on that person or body reaching a prescribed opinion or conclusion based on a subjective assessment, a person who shows that a personal right of his has been breached or is liable to be breached by a decision purporting to be made in exercise of that power has standing to seek, and the High Court has jurisdiction to give, a ruling as to whether the precondition for the valid exercise of the power has been complied with in a way that brings the decision within the express, or necessarily implied, range of the power conferred by the statute. It is to be presumed that, when it conferred the power, Parliament intended the power to be exercised only in a manner that would be in conformity with the Constitution and within the limitations of the power as they are to be gathered from the statutory scheme or design. This means, amongst other things, not only that the power must be exercised in good faith but that the opinion or other subjective conclusion set as a pre-condition for the valid exercise of the power must be reached by a route that does not make the exercise unlawful—such as by misinterpreting the law, or by misapplying it through taking into consideration irrelevant matters of fact, or through ignoring relevant matters. Otherwise, the exercise of the power will be held to be invalid for being *ultra vires*.

Because the prescribed opinion or other conclusion is necessarily subjective, there may be cases where it would be difficult, if not impossible, to subject to scrutiny the reasoning or the thought processes of the person or body exercising the power. That, however, is not the position in this case. The Minister has unveiled in his affidavits all the factual material on which he brought his mind to bear, together with the reasoning by which he formed his opinion. Having considered all those matters, I am satisfied that not only was that opinion formed in good faith and justified by the facts but that an opinion to the contrary would have been perverse. For the uncontroverted evidence showed that Sinn Féin, the party on whose behalf the prosecutor was putting himself foward as a candidate at the general election, is an integral and dependent part of the apparatus of the Provisional I.R.A., an illegal terrorist organisation which, by both its avowed aims and its record of criminal violence, is shown to be committed to, amongst other things, the dismantling by violent and unlawful means of the organs of State established by the Constitution. Therefore, the Minister was fully justified in his opinion that a broadcast by, or on behalf of, or in support of, Sinn Féin (commonly, if inaccurately, referred to as Provisional Sinn Féin, because of its closeness to the Provisional I.R.A.) would, in the words of the section, "be likely to promote, or incite to, crime or would tend to undermine the authority of the State."

[Henchy J went on to hold that the prosecutor had standing to challenge the validity of the section under which the order had been made].

Extract 11.12

(From Casey *Criminal Appeals: the Confusion Persists* (1981)
16 Ir. Jur. 271)

. . . This judicial controversy is unusual, and does not appear to have any parallel in the earlier case-law of the Supreme Court. Further, the techniques employed are curious. It is perfectly understandable that the *Shaw* majority—three of whom did not sit in *Conmey's* case—should wish to reconsider that decision. And it can hardly be thought inappropriate that, even by way of *dictum*, they should serve advance notice of their desire to do so. But, with respect, it seems very odd to stigmatise the majority conclusion of *Conmey's* case as *obiter* . . . only on the most restrictive view could it be so considered; I might add that I know of no precedent in the common-law world for the adoption of so restrictive an approach.

The desire to categorise the *Conmey* majority's conclusion as *obiter* is most interesting from the standpoint of judicial psychology. As is well known, the Supreme Court has power to overrule its own previous decisions (as well as those of its predecessors as final courts of appeal). And the present court has indicated that it is quite prepared to invoke this power in constitutional cases, as it has already done in others. But the court nonetheless seems to prefer to eschew overruling, and to rely instead on traditional, less direct methods to avoid following its earlier decisions. Thus in *State (Harkin)* v. *O'Malley* [1978] I.R. 269 the court was at pains to show that *People (A.G.)* v. *Doyle* (1964) 101 I.L.T.R. 136 was not binding because (a) it was given without jurisdiction, and (b) it was a decision *per incuriam*.

It is doubtful, however, whether such an oblique approach is available in regard to *Conmey's* case. It can scarcely be categorised as a precedent *sub silentio*, since that term is employed only where a point appears to have been decided, though without argument or specific mention in the judgment(s). Nor can it properly be regarded as a decision *per incuriam*; this refers only to decisions given in ignorance of a statute or previous case in point. In *Morelle Ltd.* v. *Wakeling* [1955] 2 Q.B. 379 the English Court of Appeal declined to extend the *per incuriam* rule to cases in which the argument was not as full as it might have been. Now it is into this cateogry, if any, that *Conmey's* case falls, since a number of relevant points do not appear to have been raised. Among these are: that "no appeal against acquittal" was so familiar a principle in 1937 that the Constitution must be taken to have assumed its continuance in force; that for the Supreme Court to enter a conviction in an appeal against acquittal would deny the accused the jury trial required by Article 38.5; and that a Constitution which guarantees equal protection should not be construed so as to subject one class of acquitted defendants to a form of double jeopardy. These considerations would justify reconsidering *Conmey's* case and, perhaps, overruling it; but they cannot justify anything short of this . . .

PRECEDENT IN ACTION: AN EXAMPLE

In order to put what has already been examined in context and to place it on a somewhat more understandable basis it is helpful to see how a particular rule has developed through a series of cases. The area which we have chosen is the law governing the liability in tort of professional persons, such as doctors, solicitors and accountants. This is an area which has occupied the attention of the Irish courts for the past decade or so and will, no doubt, continue to do so for many years to come. But first, some background explanation is required.

In 1932 the House of Lords, by a three-to-two majority, delivered a landmark decision in *Donoghue v Stevenson* [1932] A.C. 562 in which it was held that a consumer, who was injured as a result of eating a contaminated food product, could sue the manufacturer in negligence. The decision is significant in that it established that the existence of a contract between the plaintiff and defendant was not necessary in order to maintain an action in negligence. In the course of his speech Lord Atkin enunciated his now-famous neighbour principle:

> The rule that you are to love your neighbour becomes in law: You must not injure your neighbour and the lawyer's question: Who is my neighbour? receives a restricted reply. You must take reasonable care to avoid acts or omissions which you can reasonably foresee would be likely to injure your neighbour. Who then, in law, is my neighbour? The answer seems to be persons who are so closely and directly affected by my act that I ought reasonably to have them in contemplation as being so affected when I am directing my mind to the acts or omissions which are called in question.

But despite the broad terms in which that principle was expressed Lord Atkin also formulated the somewhat narrower proposition that:

> . . . a manufacturer of products which he sells in such a form as to show that he intends them to reach the ultimate consumer in the form which they left him, with no reasonable possibility of intermediate examination, and with the knowledge that the absence of reasonable care in the preparation or putting up of the products will result in injury to the consumer's life or property, owes a duty to the consumer to take reasonable care.

Some years later the Irish High Court had to consider the identical question in *Kirby v Burke and Holloway* [1944] I.R. 207 (Extract 11.13). Although the Court reached the same conclusion as the House of Lords it did not adopt *Donoghue v Stevenson*, but preferred to rely on first principles. Subsequently, however, Irish courts have accepted that *Donoghue v Stevenson* is applicable in Ireland.

Whilst *Donoghue v Stevenson* [1932] A.C. 562 dealt with the relatively narrow issue of the liability of a manufacturer, Lord Atkin's neighbour principle has been adopted and developed by later courts, and it now applies to a wide range of categories beyond that of defective products. In general, courts have focused on that principle and used it as a guide to the development of the tort of negligence: see, for instance, *Home Office v Dorset Yacht Co. Ltd.* [1970] A.C. 1004; *Anns v London Borough of Merton* [1978] A.C. 728; *McNamara v Electricity Supply Board* [1975] I.R. 1; *Keane v Electricity Supply Board* [1981] I.R. 85. By using it as a guide the courts have tended to avoid categorising the neighbour principle as either *ratio* or *obiter*. The development of the tort of negligence can be traced in any reputable textbook such as McMahon and Binchy, *The Irish Law of Torts* (2nd ed. Dublin, 1989) and Salmond and Heuston, *The Law of Torts* (London, 1987). Of the myriad of articles which *Donoghue v Stevenson* has generated we might, somewhat selectively, recommend Heuston, "*Donoghue v Stevenson* in Retrospect" (1957) 20 M.L.R. 1, Smith and Burns, "*Donoghue v Stevenson*—the Not So Golden Anniversary" (1983) 46 M.L.R. 147 and Stapleton, "The Gist of Negligence" (1988) 104 L.Q.R. 213, 389.

With regard to professional liability, the House of Lords, in *Hedley Byrne & Co. Ltd. v Heller and Partners Ltd.* [1964] A.C. 465, overruled *Candler v Crane, Christmas & Co.* [1951] 2 K.B. 164 and extended

Donoghue v Stevenson [1932] A.C. 562 to negligently performed services, where there was a contractual relationship or a relationship "equivalent to contract" between the plaintiff and defendant. Liability would arise where the defendant was aware that the plaintiff relied on his or her skill and competence. In essence, the principle applies where the plaintiff is dependent on the defendant's expertise or specialist knowledge. The decision in *Hedley Byrne* was adopted by the Irish High Court in *Securities Trust Ltd. v Hugh Moore & Alexander Ltd.* [1964] I.R. 417 (Extract 11.14). The general principle has been applied to the case of a solicitor who neglected to initiate litigation within the statutory limitation period (see *Finlay v Murtagh* [1979] I.R.249—Extract 11.15), a solicitor whose neglect in preparing a will caused a potential beneficiary to be deprived of a bequest under that will (see *Wall v Hegarty and Callnan* [1980] I.L.R.M. 124—Extract 11.16) and a solicitor whose neglect resulted in a client losing a deposit paid in respect of the purchase of property (see *Desmond v Brophy* [1985] I.R. 449—Extract 11.17).

The standard of care which a professional person must exercise was considered by the Supreme Court in *O'Donovan v Cork County Council* [1967] I.R. 173. In general, it is sufficient that the defendant adopted the approved practices of the profession provided, however, that those practices are not themselves defective. The matter was stated by Walsh J. in the following terms [1967] I.R. 173, 193:

> A medical practitioner cannot be held negligent if he follows general and approved practice in the situation in which he is faced: see *Daniels v Heskin* [1954] I.R. 73, and the cases referred to therein.
>
> That proposition is not, however, without qualification. If there is a common practice which has inherent defects, which ought to be obvious to any person giving the matter due consideration, the fact that it has been shown to have been widely and generally adopted over a period of time does not make that practice any the less negligent. Neglect of duty does not cease by repetition to be neglect of duty.

Roche v Peilow [1985] I.R. 232 (Extract 11.18) provides an example of an approved professional practice which the Supreme Court considered to be inherently defective. However, it should be realised that the mere fact that the defendant made, what in retrospect emerges to be, a mistake does not render him or her liable. In *Park Hall School Ltd. v Overend* [1987] I.R. 1 it was held that, given the uncertain state of the relevant law at the time, the defendant solicitors were not necessarily negligent when they made an erroneous assumption regarding the validity of a transaction in which their clients were involved.

Extract 11.13

KIRBY v BURKE AND HOLLOWAY [1944] I.R. 207

A woman bought some jam which was subsequently eaten by members of her family, but not by her. The jam was contaminated and those who ate it became ill. They brought and action against the vendor and the manufacturer of the jam. The action against the vendor was dismissed, but damages were awarded against the manufacturer. An interesting feature of the decision is that although the plaintiffs cited *Donoghue v Stevenson* [1932] A.C. 562 in support of their claim Gavan Duffy J. refused to follow it and decided the case on first principles instead.

Gavan Duffy J.

[His lordship outlined the facts of the case and continued]

I have now to consider whether the law sustains the claim of the plaintiffs to make the manufacturer liable for the unpleasant consequences to them of eating his jam. The defendant manufactures a common article of food, jam, made from fruit of the particular season; he then distributes it for sale by retail grocers to members of the public; he intends it to be sold as food for human consumption and bought as food for human consumption. Before sending it out he pots the jam and places waxed paper over it, closes the pot with a cover and packs it in a coloured cellophane wrapper, with the result that the jam, when sold over the counter, will be taken to be (as it is meant to be) in the condition in which it left the factory, and that the purchaser will have no reasonable opportunity to examine the contents for any visible defects; and a manufacturer must know, as a matter of ordinary experience, that a housewife, the probable purchaser, does not usually, on opening the pot at home, begin by scrutinising the contents for signs of corruption; why should she?

A particular pot of jam turns out to be unwholesome, when bought, and injurious to the consumers, and the question at once arises on what principle is the alleged liability of the maker, who intended no injury and made no contract with the consumers, to be determined? The inquiry involves the ascertainment of the foundation, upon the authorities, of liability for tort at common law.

In 1869, an Irish Court, following English decisions, held on demurrer that, in the absence of fraudulent misrepresentation, the law could give no redress against the manufacturers to a man (the purchaser's servant) injured by the explosion of a boiler in a steam engine, upon an allegation that the boiler was unsafe by reason of negligence in its construction: *Corry v Lucas* I.R. 3 C.L. 208. The confusion and conflict in later cases in England left the basis of liability in tort at common law so uncertain that at the time of the Treaty nobody could find in case law any sure guide to the actual legal position, and I have no Irish decision to guide me.

I am thus thrown back upon first principles in the endeavour to ascertain where the line is drawn at common law between conduct resulting in unintended hurt which entails liability for damage, and conduct resulting in unintended hurt which entails no liability.

In the quandary produced by the baffling inconsistencies among the pre-Treaty judicial pronouncements, I turn from the Courts to one of the outstanding juristic studies of the nineteenth century, "The Common Law" by Oliver Wendell Homes, afterwards Mr Justice Holmes of the Supreme Court of the United States. The work was published in London in 1887. The law which I apply to this case is taken from his penetrating Lectures III and IV on torts and the theory of torts.

That master of the common law shows that the foundation of liability at common law for tort is blameworthiness as determined by the existing average standards of the community; a man fails at his peril to conform to those standards. Therefore, while loss from accident generally lies where it falls, a defendant cannot plead accident if, treated as a man of ordinary intelligence and foresight, he ought to have foreseen the danger which caused the injury to his plaintiff.

Applying that norm to the facts, I have to inquire whether a man in the position of the defendant, making jam for the public to eat, is bound, according to the standards of conduct prevailing among us, to take specific precautions against the danger, to the hurt of customers, of infection to his jam from external causes before it finally leaves his factory; or, more exactly, though he may not have anticipated the precise injury that ensued to the plaintiffs from infection, was he bound, in conformity with those standards, to safeguard his jam from access by flies, as notoriously ubiquitous as they are notoriously dirty, during the interval between the moment when the jam is poured into a jam pot after boiling and the moment, three or four days later, when the jam pot is finally enveloped for sale and sent out? I answer this question, as I believe a jury of practical citizens would answer it, in the affirmative, because our public opinion undoubtedly requires of a jam manufacturer that he shall take care to keep flies out of his jam. Any novice would foresee that a fly might get in, given the chance, and I have already found as facts that the defendant failed to take adequate precautions and that the buyer was in no way at fault.

On the facts of the case now before me, there is no question of remoteness of damage. The test, as Holmes J. puts it, is whether the result actually contemplated was near enough to the remoter result complained of to throw the peril of that result upon the actor. The plaintiffs are therefore entitled to succeed.

The much controverted "Case of the Snail in the Bottle", while leaving subsidiary questions open, has settled the principle of liability on a similar issue finally against the manufacturer in Great Britain. But the House of Lords established that memorable conclusion only twelve years ago in *Donoghue v Stevenson* [1932] A.C. 562, by a majority of three Law Lords to two, "a Celtic majority", as an unconvinced critic ruefully observed, against an English minority. Where lawyers so learned disagreed, an Irish judge could not assume, as I was invited to assume, as a matter of course, that the view which prevailed must of necessity be the true view of the common law in Ireland. One voice in the House of Lords would have turned the scale; and it is not arguable that blameworthiness according to the actual standards of our people depends upon the casting vote in a tribunal exercising no jurisdiction over them. Hence my recourse to the late Mr Justice Holmes. His classic analysis supports the principle of Lord Atkin and the majority. And to that principle I humbly subscribe . . .

Extract 11.14

SECURITIES TRUST LTD. v HUGH MOORE & ALEXANDER LTD. [1964] I.R. 417

A shareholder in the defendant company held the shares on trust for the plaintiff company. The defendant company was unaware of this arrangement. The shareholder applied to the defendant company for a copy of their Memorandum and Articles of Association. The copy delivered contained an error, on the basis of which the plaintiff company bought shares in the defendant company at a price above their market value. The investment was lost when the defendant company was wound up. The plaintiff company sued for damages for negligent misrepresentation.

Davitt P.

[His lordship outlined the facts of the case and went on to consider the plaintiffs' claim]

In their statement of claim they aver that they applied for a copy of the Memorandum and Articles of Association through their agent, Mr. Anderson, and were supplied with the one containing the printers' error. They claim that by reason of the negligent misrepresentation of the defendant Company they were induced to purchase the 850 Preference Shares at a price exceeding their market value and have thereby suffered damage. The substantial defences raised in the defendants' pleadings are: that the copy of the Memorandum and Articles supplied to Mr. Anderson were not supplied to him as agent for the plaintiff Company; that the defendant Company owed no duty to the plantiff Company to supply them with an accurate copy of the Memorandum and Articles; that there was no negligence on their part; and that the plaintiff Company did not suffer the alleged or any damage; or, alternatively, that the damages claimed are too remote.

The law to be applied in this case is not in controversy. It would appear that the proposition that innocent (i.e. non-fraudulent) misrepresentation cannot give rise to an action for damages is somewhat too broadly stated, and is based upon a misconception of what was decided by the House of Lords in *Derry* v. *Peek* 14 App. Cas. 337. Such action may be based on negligent misrepresentation which is not fraudulent. This was pointed out in *Nocton* v. *Lord Ashburton* [1914] A.C. 932, particularly in the speech of Haldane L.C. At page 948 he says:—"Although liability for negligence in word has in material respects been developed in our law differently from liability for negligence in act, it is none the less true that a man may come under a special duty to exercise care in giving information or advice. I should accordingly be sorry to be thought to lend countenance to the idea that recent decisions have been intended to stereotype the cases in which people can be held to have assumed such a special duty. Whether such a duty has been assumed must depend on the relationship of the parties, and it is at least certain that there are a good many cases in which that relationship may be properly treated as giving rise to a special duty of care in statement." It was apparently considered in some quarters that such a special duty could arise only from a contractual or fiduciary relationship. In *Robinson* v. *National Bank of Ireland* [1916] S.C. (H.L.) 150 Haldane L.C. was at pains to dispel this idea. At page 157 he said:—"The whole of the doctrine as to fiduciary relationships, as to the duty of care arising from implied as well as express contracts, as to the duty of care arising from other special relationships which the Courts may find to exist in particular cases, still remains, and I should be very sorry if any word fell from me which would suggest that the Courts are in any way hampered in recognising that the duty of care may be established when such cases really occur."

The proposition that circumstances may create a relationship between two parties in which, if one seeks information from the other and is given it, that other is under a duty to take reasonable care to ensure that the information given is correct, has been accepted and applied in the case of *Hedley Byrne & Co. Ltd.* v. *Heller and Partners Ltd.* [1964] A.C. 465, recently decided by the House of Lords. Counsel for the defendant Company did not seek to dispute the proposition. He submitted, however, that the circumstances of this case created no such special relationship.

Sect. 18, sub-s. 1, of the Companies (Consolidation) Act, 1908, provides:— "Every company shall send to every member, at his request, and on payment of one shilling or such less sum as the company may prescribe, a copy of the memorandum and of the articles (if any)." At the time that Mr. Anderson made his request to the secretary of the defendant Company for a copy of their Memorandum and Articles of Association he was a shareholder. The plaintiff Company had not then been registered as owner of any shares. He was a member of the defendant Company; his Company was not. The position was that he was entitled to receive a copy of the Memorandum and Articles; his Company was not. He was entitled to receive it personally *qua* member; he was not entitled to receive it *qua* agent of the plaintiff Company. In these circumstances I must, I think, conclude that the copy was requested and supplied, in accordance with the provisions of s. 18, sub-s. 1, of the Act, by the defendant Company to Mr. Anderson personally and not as agent for the plaintiff Company. It seems to me that there was no relationship between the parties in this case other than such as would exist between the defendant Company and any person (other than Mr. Anderson) who might chance to read the copy supplied to him; or, indeed, between that Company and any member of the community at large, individual or corporate, who chanced to become aware of the last sentence in Article 155 of the defective reprint of the Memorandum and Articles. It can hardly be seriously contended that the defendant Company owed a duty to the world at large to take care to avoid mistakes and printers' errors in the reprint of their Articles. In my opinion, counsel is correct in his submission that in this case the defendant Company owed no duty to the plaintiff Company to take care to ensure that the copy of the Articles supplied to Mr. Anderson was a correct copy. For these reasons there must, in my opinion, be judgment for the defendant Company.

Extract 11.15

FINLAY v MURTAGH [1979] I.R. 249

The plaintiff engaged the defendant to act as his solicitor in proceedings which he sought to institute against a third party. The defendant neglected to bring the proceedings within the statutory limitation period and, consequently, it became time-barred. The issue in this case was whether the plaintiff could sue in tort for negligence or whether he was confined to suing for breach of contract. The Supreme Court (O'Higgins C.J., Henchy, Griffin, Parke and Kenny JJ.) unanimously held that an action in tort would lie for the negligence of a solicitor.

Henchy J.

. . . There has been no decision of this Court on the point at issue but we have been referred to three decisions of the High Court. In *McGrath* v. *Kiely* [1965] I.R. 497 the client sued his solicitor for negligence and, alternatively, for breach of contract in failing to show due professional care in the preparation of an action for damages for personal injuries. The claim was pursued in court as one for breach of contract and no effort was made to pursue the claim in negligence. The parties agreed to treat the solicitor's default as a breach of contract. Therefore, that case throws no light on the present problem.

The second case, *Liston* v. *Munster and Leinster Bank* [1940] I.R. 77, was an action by the personal representative of a customer of the bank against the bank for damages for negligence, for conversion, and for money had and received. The issue being whether the entire cause of action arose out of a contract, in which case notice of trial by a judge without a jury would be appropriate, or whether it lay partly in tort, in which case the notice of trial that had been served specifying trial by a judge with a jury would have been correct. In holding that the claim was partly for breach of contract and partly for conversion, O'Byrne J. applied the following test which had been laid down by Greer L.J. in *Jarvis* v. *Moy, Davies, Smith, Vanderell & Co.* [1936] 1 K.B. 399 at p. 405 of the report:—

> The distinction in the modern view, for this purpose, between contract and tort may be put thus: where the breach of duty alleged arises out of a liability independently of the personal obligation undertaken by contract, it is tort, and it may be tort even though there may happen to be a contract between the parties, if the duty in fact arises independently of that contract. Breach of contract occurs where that which is complained of is a breach of duty arising out of the obligations undertaken by the contract.

The third High Court case to which we were referred is *Somers* v. *Erskine* [1943] I.R. 348. There the question was whether an action commenced by a client against a solicitor for negligence, and sought to be continued against the solicitor's personal representative, had abated with the solicitor's death as an action in tort, or whether it survived his death as an action in contract. In an unreserved judgment Maguire P. applied the same test as was applied by O'Byrne J. in *Liston* v. *Munster and Leinster Bank,* and held that the client's claim was essentially one in contract rather than in tort and that, therefore, the claim had survived the solicitor's death. In my opinion, the conclusion that an action by a client against a solicitor for damages for breach of his professional duty of care is necessarily and exclusively one in contract is incompatible with modern developments in the law of torts and should be overruled. In my view, the conclusion there reached does not follow from a correct application of the test laid down by Greer L.J. in the *Jarvis Case*.

The claim made by the plantiff in the *Jarvis Case* was one by a client against stockbrokers "for damages for breach of contract arising out of the defendants' relationship with the plaintiff as stockbrokers and client." Therefore, it is clear that the action was one for breach of contract, at least in form. But the particulars given in the writ show that the substance of the complaint was that the stockbrokers had departed from the specific instructions given by the client. Therefore, the cause of action arose from the breach of a particular binding provision created by the parties, and not from any general obligation of care arising from the relationship of stockbroker and client. The nub of the matter was that the stockbrokers had defaulted on a special personal obligation which was imposed by the contract. They could not have been made liable otherwise than in contract and the court held correctly that the claim was "founded on contract" in the words of the statute which was being applied.

The test adumbrated by Greer L.J., which commended itself to O'Byrne J. in *Liston* v. *Munster and Leinster Bank* and to Maguire P. in *Somers* v. *Erskine*, correctly draws a distinction between a claim arising out of an obligation deriving from, and owing its existence to, a personal obligation undertaken pursuant to a contract (in which case it is an action in contract) and a claim arising out of a liability created independently of a contract and not deriving from any special obligation imposed by a contract (in which case an action lies in tort). The action in tort derives from an obligation which is imposed by the general law and is applicable to all persons in a certain relationship to each other. The action in contract is founded on the special law which was created by a contract and which was designed to fit the particular relationship of that contract. As I understand it, therefore, the test propounded by Greer L.J. does not support the conclusion reached by Maguire P. that, because the contract of retainer implies a duty of professional care and skill and because a default in that duty has occurred, the cause of action lies exclusively in contract.

It has to be conceded that for over a hundred years there has been a divergence of judicial opinion as to whether a client who has engaged a solicitor to act for him, and who claims that the solicitor failed to show due professional care and skill, may sue in tort or whether he is confined to an action in contract. In *Somers* v. *Erskine* (and in some English cases) it was held that the sole cause of action was the solicitor's failure to observe the implied term in the contract of retainer that he would show due professional skill and care. It is undeniable that the client is entitled to sue in contract for breach of that implied term. But it does not follow that the client, because there is privity of contract between him and the solicitor and because he may sue the solicitor for breach of the contract, is debarred from suing also for the tort of negligence. Since the decision of the House of Lords in *Hedley Byrne & Co. Ltd.* v. *Heller & Partners Ltd.* [1964] A.C. 465 and the cases following in its wake, it is clear that, whether a contractual relationship exists or not, once the circumstances are such that a defendant undertakes to show professional care and skill towards a person who may be expected to rely on such care and skill and who does so rely, then if he has been damnified by such default that person may sue the defendant in the tort of negligence for failure to show such care and skill. For the purpose of such an action, the existence of a contract is merely an incident of the relationship. If, on the one side, there is a proximity of relationship creating a general duty and, on the other, a reliance on that duty, it matters not whether the parties are bound together in contract. For instance, if the defendant in the present case had not been retained for reward but had merely volunteered his services to the plaintiff, his liability in negligence would be the same as if he was to be paid for his services. The coincidence that the defendant's conduct amounts to a breach of contract cannot affect either the duty of care or the common-law liability for its breach, for it is the general relationship, and not any particular manifestation such as a contract, that gives rise to the tortious liability in such a case: see *per* Lord Devlin in the *Hedley Byrne Case* at p. 530 of the report.

A comprehensive survey of the law governing the liability of a solicitor to his client in negligence is to be found in the judgment of Oliver J. in *Midland Bank* v. *Hett, Stubbs & Kemp* [1979] Ch. 384, in which it was held that the solicitor's liability in tort exists independently of any liability in contract. That conclusion, which was reached at first instance and with which I agree, may be said to be reinforced by dicta in the judgments of the Court of Appeal in *Batty* v. *Metropolitan Realisations Ltd* [1978] Q.B. 554 and *Photo Production Ltd.* v. *Securicor Ltd* [1978] 1 W.L.R. 856.

On a consideration of those cases and of the authorities mentioned in them, I am satisfied that the general duty of care created by the relationship of solicitor and client entitles the client to sue in negligence if he has suffered damage because of the solicitor's failure to show due professional care and skill, notwithstanding that the client could sue alternatively in contract for breach of the implied term in the contract of retainer that the solicitor will deal with the matter in hand with due professional care and skill. The solicitor's liability in tort under the general duty of care extends not only to a client for reward, but to any person for whom the solicitor undertakes to act professionally without reward, and also to those (such as beneficiaries under a will, persons entitled under an intestacy, or those entitled to benefits in circumstances such as a claim in respect of a fatal injury) with whom he has made no arrangement to act but who, as he knows or ought to know, will be relying on his professional care and skill. For the same default there should be the same cause of action. If others are entitled to sue in tort for the solicitor's want of care, so also should the client; that is so unless the solicitor's default arises not from a breach of the general duty of care arising from the relationship but from a breach of a particular and special term of the contract in respect of which the solicitor would not be liable if the contract had not contained such a term. Thus, if the client's instructions were that the solicitor was to issue proceedings within a specified time, or to close a sale by a particular date or, generally, to do or not to do some act, and the solicitor defaulted in that respect, any resulting right of action which the client might have would be in contract only unless the act or default complained of falls within the general duty of care owed by the solicitor.

The modern law of tort shows that the existence of a contractual relationship which impliedly deals with a particular act or omission is not, in itself, sufficient to rule out an action in tort in respect of that act or omission. For instance, in *Northern Bank Finance Corporation Ltd.* v. *Charlton* [1979] I.R. 149 it was unanimously held by this Court that a customer of a bank can sue the bank for the tort of deceit where the deceit arises from fradulent misrepresentations made by the bank in the course of carrying out the contract between the bank and the customer. The existence of a contract, for the breach of which he could have sued, did not oust the customer's cause of action in tort.

Therefore, I conclude that where, as in the instant case, the client's complaint is that he has been damnified by the solicitor's default in his general duty of care, the client is entitled to sue in negligence as well as for breach of contract. In the plaintiff's statement of claim, after reciting his accident and his retainer of the defendant as the solicitor to prosecute his claim for damages in respect of it, the plaintiff pleads that the defendant "negligently failed to issue proceedings on behalf of the plaintiff in respect of the accident aforesaid within the time limited by the Statute of Limitations, 1957." That was intended to be, and is, a claim in negligence. Such being the case, by virtue of the provisions of s. 94 of the Courts of Justice Act, 1924, as amended, the plaintiff was entitled to service notice of a trial by a judge and jury. Mr. Justice D'Arcy was correct in refusing to set aside the notice of trial so served. I would dismiss this appeal.

Griffin J.

. . . A solicitor holds himself out to the client who has retained him as being possessed of adequate skill, knowledge and learning for the purpose of carrying out all business that he undertakes on behalf of his client. Once he has been retained to pursue a claim for damages for personal injuries, it is the duty of the solicitor to prepare and prosecute the claim with due professional skill and care. Therefore, he is liable to the client in damages if loss and damage are caused to the client owing to the want of such skill and care on the part of the solicitor as he ought to have exercised.

Mr. Kinlen, for the defendant, contends that the duty owed by a solicitor to his client under his retainer is a duty which arises *solely* from the contract and excludes any general duty in tort; he submits that this action is one founded upon contract, in which event the plantiff would not be entitled to have the action tried by a jury. Mr. Walsh, for the plaintiff, submits that, apart from the duty which arises from contract, there is a general duty to exercise skill and care on the part of the solicitor, for breach of which he would be liable in tort if damage is suffered by the client as a result of the want of such skill and care. He submits that, as one claiming damages for negligence, this action is properly a claim in tort, in which case the plaintiff is entitled as of right to have the action tried before a judge and jury pursuant to s. 94 of the Courts of Justice Act, 1924, as amended.

There is abundant, if somewhat conflicting, authority on the question in England, and in argument we were referred also to two Irish cases in which the question arose.

In *Groom* v. *Crocker* [1939] 1 K.B. 194 the Court of Appeal in England had to consider whether the mutual rights and duties of a solicitor and his client were regulated by the contract of employment alone, and whether the solicitor was liable in tort. It was there held that the contract of employment regulated the relationship and that the solicitor was not liable in tort. In the course of his judgment, Sir Wilfred Greene M.R. said at p. 205 of the report:—

> In my opinion, the cause of action is in contract and not in tort. The duty of the appellants was to conduct the case properly on behalf of the respondent as their client. . . . The relationship of solicitor and client is a contractual one: *Davies* v. *Lock* (1844) 3 L.T. (O.S.) 125; *Bean* v. *Wade* (1885) 2 T.L.R. 157. It was by virtue of that relationship that the duty arose, and it had no existence apart from that relationship.

Scott L.J. at p. 222, having set out the duty of a solicitor, said that the tie between the solicitor and the client is contractual and that no action lies in tort for the breach of such duties. MacKinnon L.J. put the position succinctly at p. 229 where he said:—"I am clear that this is a claim for damages for breach of contract . . ."

After that unanimous decision of the Court of Appeal, it was generally accepted in England, at least until very recently, that the liability of a solicitor to his client was contractual only and that he could not be sued in tort either in the alternative or cumulatively. The case has been almost universally followed and applied there since it was decided; see, for example, *Bailey* v. *Bullock* [1950] 2 All E.R. 1167; and Hodson and Parker L.JJ. at pp. 477 and 481 respectively of the report of *Hall* v. *Meyrick* [1957] 2 Q.B. 455; *Cook* v. *Swinfen* [1967] 1 W.L.R. 457. At p. 510 of the report of *Clark* v. *Kirby-Smith* [1964] Ch. 506 Plowman J. said:—"A line of cases going back for nearly 150 years shows, I think, that the client's cause of action is in contract and not in tort: see, for example, *Howell* v. *Young* (1826) 5 B.&C. 259 and *Groom* v. *Crocker*". In *Heywood* v. *Wellers* [1976] Q.B. 446 James L.J. said at p. 461 of the report:—"It is well known and settled law that an action by a client against a solicitor alleging negligence in the conduct of the client's affairs is an action for breach of contract: *Groom* v. *Crocker*." However, in that case Lord Denning did say at p. 459 that *Groom* v. *Crocker* might have to be reconsidered, and in *Esso Petroleum* v. *Mardon* [1976] Q.B. 801 at p. 819 of the report he "ventured to suggest" that that case, and cases which relied on it, are in conflict with other decisions of high authority which were not cited in them—decisions which show that, in the case of a professional man, the duty to use reasonable care arises not only in contract but is also imposed by the law apart from contract and is, therefore, actionable in tort; it is comparable to the duty of reasonable care which is owed by a master to his servant or vice versa; it can be put either in contract or in tort. In *Midland Bank* v. *Hett, Stubbs & Kemp* [1979] Ch. 384, on which the plaintiff relied strongly, Oliver J., in a judgment in which he examined exhaustively all the leading cases on the subject of a solicitor's liability, held that a solicitor was liable in tort quite independently of any contractual liability.

In *Somers* v. *Erskine* [1943] I.R. 348 the client sued his solicitor for damages for negligence in the discharge of his professional duty to the client. The solicitor died after the action was commenced and one of the issues which then arose was whether or not the cause of action had survived against his executrix. It was held by Maguire P. that the action was in substance founded in contract and that, in considering whether an action is founded on contract or on tort, the court must look not merely at the form of the pleadings but at the substance of the action and decide whether it is founded on contract or tort. He adopted and applied the following passage from the judgment of Greer L.J. in *Jarvis* v. *May, Davies, Smith, Vandervell and Co.* [1936] 1 K.B. 399 (a claim against a stockbroker) at p. 405 of the report:—"The distinction in the modern view, for this purpose, between contract and tort may be put thus: where the breach of duty alleged arises out of a liability independently of the personal obligation undertaken by contract, it is tort, and it may be tort even though there may happen to be a contract between the parties, if the duty in fact arises independently of that contract. Breach of contract occurs where that which is complained of is a breach of duty arising out of the obligations undertaken by the contract." That passage had been accepted and approved by O'Byrne J. in *Liston* v. *Munster and Leinster Bank* [1940] I.R. 77. Applying that test, the learned President held that the substance of the client's claim was the breach of a duty arising out of an obligation created by contract, and said that he found it difficult to dissociate that duty from the contract. Counsel for the defendant in that case had urged that the duty which was alleged to have been broken was merely the ordinary common-law duty, the breach of which constituted negligence, *i.e.*, the duty to take reasonable care in the particular circumstances; but the President held that the duty arose out of a contractual obligation only.

I have had the advantage of reading in advance the judgment of Mr. Justice Henchy and I agree with him that Maguire P. did not correctly apply the test laid down by Greer L.J. in the *Jarvis Case*. I agree with the analysis made by Mr. Justice Henchy of the passage quoted from the judgment of Lord Justice Greer.

The only other Irish case cited in argument was *McGrath* v. *Kiely* [1965] I.R. 497 in which the client sued a surgeon and a solicitor, founding her claim for damages on both negligence and breach of contract. In the course of the hearing before Mr. Justice Henchy it was conceded on behalf of the client that the liability sought to be imposed on each of the defendants arose *ex contractu*, so that the question of the liability of the defendants in tort was not argued and did not fall to be decided.

In *Somers* v. *Erskine* [1943] I.R. 348, the learned President was not prepared to accept that, in the case of a solicitor, there was a general duty to use reasonable care imposed by the law quite apart from contract. He took the view that because there was a contractual relationship between the solicitor and the client, and a liability in contract for breach of the duty owed to the client, there was no duty in tort. Counsel for the defendant had cited the passage in Bevan on Negligence (4th ed. at p. 1384) that states:—"A solicitor is liable for negligence both in contract and in tort. He is liable in contract where he fails to do some specific act to which he has bound himself. He is liable in tort where, having accepted a retainer, he fails in the performance of any duty which the relation of solicitor and client as defined by the retainer imposes on him." Authorities to support that proposition were not cited; if they had been cited, it is likely that the President would have come to a different conclusion. The law is concisely and clearly summed up in a few sentences in the well-known passage in the speech of Viscount Haldane L.C. in *Nocton* v. *Ashburton* [1914] A.C. 932 at p. 956 of the report:—"My Lords, the solicitor contracts with his client to be skilful and careful. For failure to perform his obligation he may be made liable at law in contract or even in tort, for negligence in breach of a duty imposed on him." See also what was said by Tindal C.J. in *Boorman* v. *Brown* (1842) 3 Q.B. 511, (1844) 11 Cl. & Fin. 1 in the Court of Exchequer Chamber at p. 525 of the report and by Lord Campbell in the House of Lords at p. 44 of the report of the appeal. It is to be noted that these cases also were not cited in *Groom* v. *Crocker*, or in the cases which followed it, and that the failure to do so led to the criticism of these cases by Lord Denning in *Esso Petroleum* v. *Mardon*. In my opinion, the President was wrong in holding that the liability of the solicitor to the client was solely in contract. *Somers* v. *Erskine* should not be followed.

Quite apart from the fact that *Somers* v. *Erskine* was decided without the citation of relevant authorities and on an incorrect application of the test laid down by Greer L.J. in the *Jarvis Case*, the decision is inconsistent with developments in the law of tort since the case was decided. It is now settled law that whenever a person possessed of a special knowledge or skill undertakes, quite irrespective of contract, to apply that skill for the assistance of another person who relies on such skill, a duty of care will arise: see the speech of Lord Morris of Borth-y-Gest at p. 502 of the report of *Hedley Byrne and Co. Ltd.* v. *Heller & Partners Ltd.* [1964] A.C. 465 At p. 538 of the report Lord Pearce said:—"In terms of proximity one might say that they are in particularly close proximity to those who, as they know, are relying on their skill and care although the proximity is not contractual." See also Lord Hodson at p. 510 and Lord Devlin at p. 530 of the report. Where damage has been suffered as a result of want of such skill and care, an action in tort lies against such person, and this applies whether a contractual relationship exists or not. This doctrine applies to such professional persons as solicitors, doctors, dentists, architects and accountants. Although in the *Hedley Byrne Case* the claim was in respect of a non-contractual relationship, the statements of the Law Lords were general statements of principle, and it is clear from their speeches that they did not in any way mean to limit the general principle and that their statements were not to be confined to voluntary or non-contractual situations.

Therefore, where a solicitor is retained by a client to carry out legal business (such as litigation) on his behalf, a general relationship is established, and "Where there is a general relationship of this sort, it is unnecessary to do more than prove its existence and the duty follows "—*per* Lord Devlin at p. 530 of the report of the *Hedley Byrne Case*. If, therefore, loss and damage is caused to a client owing to the want of such care and skill on the part of a solicitor as he ought to have exercised, there is liability in tort even though there would also be a liability in contract. Even if the relationship between the solicitor and the client was a non-contractual or voluntary one, the same liability in tort would follow.

In my opinion it is both reasonable and fair that, if the issues of fact are such that he would be entitled to succeed either in contract or in tort, the plaintiff should be entitled to pursue either or both remedies; there can be nothing wrong in permitting the plaintiff, who is the injured party, to elect or choose the remedy which to him appears to be that which will be most suitable and likely to attract the more favourable result.

In my judgment, the plaintiff in the instant case has a good cause of action in tort as well as in contract and is entitled to sue in respect of either or both remedies since he has suffered loss and damage as a result of the negligence of the defendant, as the plaintiff's solicitor, in failing to institute proceedings within the time limited by the Statute of Limitations, 1957. Accordingly, the plaintiff is entitled as of right to have his action tried before a judge and jury, and Mr. Justice D'Arcy was correct in so deciding. Accordingly, I would dismiss this appeal.

Extract 11.16

WALL v HEGARTY AND CALLNAN [1980] I.L.R.M. 124

The plaintiff was named as executor and a beneficiary under a will which was prepared on behalf of the deceased by the defendants, a firm of solicitors. The will was insufficiently attested and, on discovering the flaw, the next of kin challenged the validity of the will. The plaintiff had to concede that the will was invalid. He sued the defendants for negligence. In essence, his claim was one that the defendants owed him, as a potential beneficiary under the will, a duty to take care in its preparation.

Barrington J.

. . . At the hearing it was decided that I should defer the question of the quantification of the plaintiff's loss until I had first dealt with the substantial issue of whether a solicitor retained by a testator to draw up his will owes any duty to a legatee named in the will to ensure that the will and the legacy are valid.

There is no doubt the he does owe a duty to a testator to show reasonable care and to exercise professional skills appropriate to a solicitor in ensuring that the testator's wishes are carried out. But if a legacy fails, the testator and his estate may suffer little or no damage. The legatee may suffer substantial damage but may have no right of action against the solicitor. The testator's estate may have a right of action against the solicitor in contract or in tort, but may be entitled only to nominal damages.

The plaintiff, in his statement of claim, pleads that a solicitor retained by a testator to prepare a will owes a duty to an executor and beneficiary named in the will to ensure that the testator's benevolent intentions in respect of the executor and beneficiary are not frustrated through lack of reasonable care on the part of the solicitor. At paragraph 7 of the statement of claim, he pleads:

> The defendants and each of them as solicitors for William Wall, deceased, were obliged at all material times to conduct the affairs of the deceased in such manner as would ensure and protect the best interests of the plaintiff as the person named as his executor by the deceased and as a beneficiary under his said will and of all persons entitled to benefit from, or concerned with, the will of the deceased, which said duty the defendants failed to discharge.

Traditionally, English law did not regard a solicitor as owing any such duty to a legatee named in a testator's will and, so far as I am aware, the law of Ireland was no different in this respect. A passage which appears on p. 184 of the 1961 edition of Cordery's *Law Relating to Solicitors*, puts the matter as follows:

> Since the solicitor's duty to his client is based on the contract of retainer, he owes no duty of care to anyone other than his client, save where he is liable as an officer of the court.

The chief authority relied on, in support of that proposition was *Robertson* v. *Fleming* (1861) 4 Macq. 167. That was a decision of the House of Lords in a Scottish case. It is arguable that the central question in that case was whether an issue which had been settled in the Second Division of the Court of Session properly raised the question of fact in dispute between the parties. But it is also arguable that this question of fact would have been irrelevant if a solicitor owed a duty, not only to his client, but also to the person for whose benefit his services had been retained. In any event, as Sir Robert Megarry has stated in the recent case of *Ross* v. *Caunters* [1980] Ch. 297, at p. 304, the dicta, whether they were of the *ratio* or not, are clearly of high authority.

In that case, Lord Campbell L.C. rejected in the strongest possible terms the suggestion that a solicitor retained by a testator might owe any duty to a legatee who was a stranger to him. In a passage which appears at p. 177 of the report, he says:

I never had any doubt of the unsoundness of the doctrine, unnecessarily (and I must say unwisely) contended for by the respondent's counsel, that A employing B, a professional lawyer, to do any act for the benefit of C, A having to pay B, and there being no intercourse of any sort between B and C,—if through the gross negligence or ignorance of B in transacting the business, C loses the benefit intended for him by A, C may maintain an action against B, and recover damages for the loss sustained. If this were law, a disappointed legatee might sue the solicitor employed by a testator to make a will in favour of a stranger, whom the solicitor never saw or before heard of, if the will were void for not being properly signed and attested. I am clearly of opinion that this is not the law of Scotland, nor of England, and it can hardly be the law of any country where jurisprudence has been cultivated as a science.

While Lord Campbell was in a minority in other aspects of the case, it would appear that a majority of his colleagues agreed with him on this point.

However, since *Robertson* v. *Fleming* was decided, there have been two major advances in the law, material to the consideration of the present question. First was the development of negligence as an independent tort and the line of authority running from *Donoghue* v. *Stevenson* [1932] A.C. 562 to *Hedley Byrne & Co. Ltd.* v. *Heller & Partners Ltd.* [1964] A.C. 465. In particular was the famous passage in Lord Atkin's speech in *Donoghue* v. *Stevenson*, where he stressed the duty to take reasonable care to avoid injuring one's neighbour, and went on to inquire:

Who, then, in law is my neighbour? The answer seems to be persons who are so closely and directly affected by my act that I ought reasonably to have them in contemplation as being so affected when I am directing my mind to the acts or omissions which are called in question.

Lord Atkin went on to stress that the concept of "neighbour" did not include merely persons in close physical proximity to the alleged tortfeasor; but also, all such persons as stood in such direct relationship with him, as to cause him to know that they would be directly affected by his careless act: see [1932] A.C. 562, at p. 580.

The second important legal development which has taken place since *Robertson* v. *Fleming*, is that it is now finally established, so far, at any rate, as the law of Ireland is concerned, that a solicitor owes two kinds of duties to his client. First, is his duty in contract to carry out the terms of the retainer. Second is a duty in tort to show reasonable professional skill in attending to his client's affairs. It is clear that this duty in tort arises simply because he is purporting to act as a solicitor for his client and is independent of whether he is providing his professional services voluntarily or for reward: see the judgment of the Supreme Court in *Finlay* v. *Murtagh* [1979] I.R. 249 and also the judgment of Oliver J. in *Midland Bank* v. *Hett, Stubbs & Kemp* [1979] Ch. 384.

The Supreme Court in *Finlay* v. *Murtagh* was merely dealing with a net point of law as to whether a solicitor owed a duty to a client in tort as well as in contract, but it is quite clear that the Court, in holding that he did, derived the duty from the proximity principle outlined by Lord Atkin in *Donoghue* v. *Stevenson*. For instance, the following passage appears in the judgment of Kenny J. (at p. 264):

The professional person, however, owes the client a general duty, which does not arise from contract but from the 'proximity' principle (*Donoghue* v. *Stevenson* [1932] A.C. 562 and *Hedley Byrne & Co. Ltd.* v. *Heller & Partners Ltd.* [1964] A.C. 465) to exercise reasonable care and skill in the performance of the work entrusted to him. This duty arises from the obligation which springs from the situation that he knew or ought to have known that his failure to exercise care and skill would probably cause loss and damage. This failure to have or to exercise reasonable skill and care is tortious or delictual in origin.

Indeed, Henchy, J., in a passage in his judgment, appears to anticipate the situation which has arisen in the present case. He says (at p. 257):

> The solicitor's liability in tort under the general duty of care extends not only to a client for reward, but to any person for whom the solicitor undertakes to act professionally without reward, and also to those (such as beneficiaries under a will, persons entitled under an intestacy, or those entitled to benefits in circumstances such as a claim in respect of a fatal injury) with whom he has made no arrangement to act but who, as he knows or ought to know, will be relying on his professional care and skill. For the same default there should be the same cause of action. If others are entitled to sue in tort for the solicitor's want of care, so also should the client.

Since the decision of the Supreme Court in *Finlay* v. *Murtagh*, the specific question which arises in the present case arose for consideration in the English High Court in the case of *Ross* v. *Caunters* [1980] Ch. 297.

In that case, the testator instructed solicitors to draw up his will to include gifts of chattels and a share of his residuary estate to the plaintiff, who was his sister-in-law. The solicitors drew up the will naming the plaintiff as legatee. The testator requested the solicitors to send the draft will to him at the plaintiff's home where he was staying, to be signed and attested. The solicitors sent the will to the testator with a covering letter giving instructions on executing it, but failed to warn him that under section 15 of the Wills Act, 1837, attestation of the will by the beneficiary's spouse would invalidate the gift to the beneficiary. The plaintiff's husband attested the will which was then returned to the solicitors who failed to notice that he had attested it. In fact, prior to the execution of the will, the testator had, in correspondence, raised with his solicitors, the question "Am I right in thinking that beneficiaries may not be witnesses?" The solicitors unfortunately did not answer this question which clearly provided them with an opportunity to warn the testator that the spouse of a beneficiary should not be a witness either.

The testator died two years after the execution of the will. Some time later, the solicitors wrote to the plaintiff informing her that the gifts to her under the will were void because her husband had attested it. The plaintiff brought an action against the solicitors claiming damages for negligence for the loss of the gifts under the will. Sir Robert Megarry V.-C., after an exhaustive analysis of the authorities, held that she was entitled to succeed.

In the present case, [counsel for] the plaintiff has relied strongly on *Ross* v. *Caunters*. [Counsel for] the defendants has drawn the distinction that in *Ross* v. *Caunters* there was a valid will—only the bequest was invalid—whereas in the present case there was no valid will. He has also stated that I should not, by following *Ross* v. *Caunters*, extend the traditional boundaries of the law of negligence in this country. However, it appears to me that the decision of the English High Court in *Ross* v. *Caunters* was already anticipated by the decision of our own Supreme Court in *Finlay* v. *Murtagh* and, for my own, part, I find the reasoning of Sir Robert Megarry in *Ross* v. *Caunters* unanswerable.

I do not think that the fact that there was a valid will in *Ross* v. *Caunters* and that there is not a valid will in the present case is a material distinction. The question is whether the testator's solicitor owes any duty at all to the named legatee. If he owes such a duty and if the legacy fails because of his failure to observe it, it is immaterial whether the gift fails because of a defect in the words granting the legacy or because of a defect in the will itself.

I fully accept the reasoning of Sir Robert Megarry that in a case such as the present, there is a close degree of proximity between the plaintiff and the defendant. If a solicitor is retained by a testator to draft a will, and one of the purposes of the will is to confer a benefit on a named legatee, the solicitor must know that if he fails in his professional duty properly to draft the will, there is considerable risk the legatee will suffer damage. To use Sir Robert's words, his contemplation of the plaintiff is "actual, nominate and direct."

Likewise, I accept Sir Robert's reasoning that there can be no conflict of public policy in holding that a solicitor has a duty to take care in drafting a will, not only to the testator but also to a named legatee in the will. There is no possible inconsistency between the duty to the testator and the duty to the legatee. Recognising a duty to a legatee tends to strengthen the chances that the testator's wishes will in fact be properly expressed in the will. The two duties march together.

The authorities are, as I said, analysed by Sir Robert Megarry with consummate ability in his judgment in *Ross* v. *Caunters*, and it would be otiose for me to repeat here the exercise which he has carried out in his judgment. Suffice it to say that I am satisfied on the basis of the decision in *Finlay* v. *Murtagh* that a solicitor does owe a duty to a legatee named in a draft will, to draft the will which such reasonable care and skill as to ensure that the wishes of the testator are not frustrated and the expectancy of the legatee defeated through lack of reasonable care and skill on the part of the solicitor.

If a solicitor owes any duty to a named legatee, then it is quite clear that the solicitor in the present case has failed to show the appropriate care and skill. It is unnecessary to labour the point. The case has been frankly met. No effort has been made to defend what was done, except to say that the defendants owed no duty to the plaintiff.

To turn now, to the question of the plaintiff's loss. [Counsel for the defendants] has suggested that the plaintiff had no more than a *spes*. His loss, it is suggested, is too remote to be taken into consideration by the law. I cannot accept this. The testator died without revoking his purported will. Had, therefore, the will been validly drawn, the plaintiff would have received his bequest of £15,000. There might, of course, be circumstances in which the plaintiff would suffer no loss. There might, for instance, be an earlier and valid will under which the plaintiff would receive financial benefits of equal value. The testator's estate might have been insolvent and the plaintiff might have received nothing even if the will had been valid. Or the will might have been invalid on some other collateral ground in respect of which the solicitor had no responsibility. I understand that none of these factors apply to the present case though the defendants have asked for formal proof of the value of the testator's estate, and they are clearly entitled to this before the plaintiff's loss is finally quantified.

Apart from that, the plaintiff has suffered loss in that he got involved in legal proceedings to have the will upheld. It appears to me that a solicitor who draws up a will in which an executor is named and which on its face appears to be in order, must foresee or anticipate that the executor will or may attempt to have the will admitted to probate. It is clearly the proper thing for the executor to attempt to have the will admitted to probate so that the testator's wishes may be upheld. It therefore appears to me that ordinary costs incurred by the executor, prior to being put on notice of any irregularity, in having the will admitted to probate, flow naturally from the solicitor's lack of care and are recoverable against him. In this respect there may be a distinction between the position in the present case and the position in *Ross* v. *Caunters*. There it was held that legal costs incurred by the plaintiff in investigating her own claim against the solicitor, were not recoverable as damages against the defendants. They were recoverable as costs, if at all. The present question is quite distinguishable. We are not dealing here with costs incurred by the plaintiff investigating his own claim. We are dealing with costs incurred by him in upholding the will at a time when he had every reason to believe that the will was a valid one. It appears to me that this item of loss could also be recovered on a different basis. After the testator's death, the defendants sent to the plaintiff a copy of the testator's will without drawing to his attention a fact (which someone in the firm must have known) that while the testator's signature appeared on the face of the will, to have been properly attested it had not in fact been properly attested. Even therefore, if the plaintiff's loss in getting involved in legal proceedings to prove the will did not flow directly from the original carelessness in drafting the will on the principles of *Donoghue* v. *Stevenson,* it appears to me that the loss would still be recoverable because of the fact of the circumstances in which the will was sent to the plaintiff on the principles of the *Hedley Byrne Case* [1964] A.C. 465.

Apart from the foregoing there appears to me to be another heading under which the plaintiff is entitled to recover damages. Had the will been valid, the plaintiff would, in the normal course, have been entitled to interest on his legacy at the conclusion of the executor's year at the rate which the law allows, there being no express provision for the payment of interest on legacies in the will. Whether the plaintiff would have been entitled to recover interest in the circumstances of the present case, however, where he, himself, was the executor is a matter on which I would like to hear further argument.

Under these circumstances I propose to adjourn the case for the assessment of damages (if any) under these three heads.

Extract 11.17

DESMOND v BROPHY [1985] I.R. 449

The two plaintiffs independently retained the first defendant as solicitor to act for them in the purchase of two flats. They informed him of their concern that deposits paid by them would not pass to the builders until completion of the flats. Both believed that he would arrange matters so that the deposits would not pass to the builders until completion of the flats. The first defendant sent their deposit cheques to the builders' solicitors, intending that they hold them as stakeholder rather than as agent for the builders. He did not make this clear to the builders' solicitors who, in accordance with custom and their instructions, endorsed the cheque in favour of their clients. Before the contract was signed the builders went into liquidation and the plaintiffs lost their deposits. They sued the first defendant for negligence. The builders' solicitors were joined as defendants, by order of the Master, and the plaintiffs made an alternative claim against them for the return of the deposits as monies had and received. The claim against the second defendants was dismissed.

Barrington J.

[His lordship outlined the facts of the case and continued]

. . . For many years the Incorporated Law Society had been aware of the practice of builders demanding and receiving booking deposits and of the risks which purchasers who paid such booking deposits were running. The Solicitors' Gazette for January/February 1977 (Vol. 71, p. 17) contained an item under the heading "Purchasers at risk on Deposits" where the problem was discussed. This item contained the following paragraph:—

> The purpose of this memorandum is to emphasise to solicitors the importance of putting on record to their clients the risks which they are taking. Clients in our experience are under the mistaken impression that once the monies are paid to a solicitor or through a solicitor they have the full protection as if their own solicitor was a stakeholder. It does, of course, seem quite unfair that the purchasers should be at risk in this way as while transactions like this might be a commercial risk to the builder, it could hardly be so described from the point of view of the purchasers.

A similar warning was issued by Mr. Wylie at paragraph 10.133 of his book on Irish Conveyancing Law.

Mr. Brophy cannot be faulted for not being aware of these dangers. He discussed them with his clients and took what he considered to be proper steps to protect his clients against them. The question is whether these steps were reasonably adequate to protect his clients' interests . . .

. . . [Counsel] on behalf of Messrs. P. C. Moore & Co., [the builders' solicitors] referred to a passage in Wylie's Irish Conveyancing Law which appears on p. 466 of the book at paragraph 10.066. The passage reads as follows:—"If the deposit is not paid to the vendor personally, the question arises as to what is the capacity of the third party who receives it. The general law recognises two basis capacities in such a case, namely, receipt as *agent* for the vendor and as *stakeholder*. The significance of the distinction is this. If the deposit is paid to the vendor's agent, e.g., his auctioneer or solicitor acting in that capacity, the agent is liable to pay it to the vendor on demand. He must also account to the vendor for any interest earned or other profit made from the deposit. If the sale falls through, the purchaser can sue the vendor only, not the agent, for recovery. The advantage from the vendor's point of view is that he can demand the deposit immediately and use it, e.g., in connection with some other transaction such as the purchase of a new house. It has been suggested that there are dangers in this from the purchaser's point of view in that, if the vendor suddenly goes bankrupt and the deposit has been spent by him, the purchaser may have difficulty in recovering it. On the other hand, it is settled that, if the deposit is paid to the vendor's agent, the purchaser has a lien on the vendor's land for its return, and in this respect the purchaser is better off than he would be if the deposit were paid to a stakeholder."

This passage appears to reflect the law as stated by Mr. Justice Kenny in his judgment in *Leemac Overseas Investment Ltd.* v. *Harvey* [1973] I.R. 160. In a passage which appears at p. 164 Mr. Justice Kenny states:—

An auctioneer who receives a deposit as stakeholder has been said to be the agent for the vendor and the purchaser. *Harrington* v. *Hoggart* (1830) 1 B. & Ad. 577 dealt with the issue whether a stakeholder was liable for the interest earned on the deposit, but in the course of his judgment Lord Tenterden said at p. 586 of the report:—'A stakeholder does not receive the money for either party, he receives it for both; and until the event is known, it is his duty to keep it in his own hands.' Similar language was used by Lord Justice Brown in *Ellis* v. *Goulton* [1893] 1 Q.B. 350 at p. 352 of the report:—'When a deposit is paid by a purchaser under a contract for the sale of land, the person who makes the payment may enter into an agreement with the vendor that the money shall be held by the recipient as agent for both vendor and purchaser. If this is done, the person who receives it becomes a stakeholder, liable, in certain events, to return the money to the person who paid it. In the absence of such agreement, the money is paid to a person who has not the character of stakeholder; and it follows that, when the money reaches his hands, it is the same thing so far as the person who pays it is concerned as if it had reached the hands of the principal'.

At p. 469 of his book Mr. Wylie deals with deposits paid to solicitors and estate agents. In the case of a solicitor he puts the matter as follows:—"Again in the absence of a contrary agreement, a deposit paid to the vendor's solicitor is treated as paid to him as the vendor's agent rather than as a stakeholder." In the case of a deposit paid to an estate agent he puts the matter as follows:—"In the case of a sale by private treaty, it is usual that the 'deposit' received by a house or estate agent will be a pre-contract deposit, and it would seem, in the light of recent authorities, that as a general principle this should not be regarded as being received as agent for the vendor, in the absence of express authority conferred by the latter. At most, therefore, the 'agent' should be regarded as receiving such a deposit as a stakeholder."

In *Sorrell* v. *Finch* [1977] A.C. 728 it was held that, in the absence of special agreement, a pre-contract deposit paid by a prospective purchaser to an estate agent was not received by the estate agent with the implied or ostensible authority of the prospective vendor. In such circumstances the purchaser was at all times until contract the only person with any claim or right to the deposit monies and he could reclaim them on demand from the estate agent. [Counsel], on behalf of Mr. Brophy, relied on this case and also referred to *Burt* v. *Claude Cousins & Co.* [1971] 2 Q.B. 426 and to the notes on the decision in *Rayner* v. *Paskell & Another* and *Regina* v. *Pilkington* which are appended to the report of *Burt* v. *Claude Cousins & Co.* in Volume 2 of the Queen's Bench Reports for 1971 (see p. 429). He also referred to *Barrington* v. *Lee* [1972] 1 Q.B. 326.

All of these were cases of deposits paid to estate agents and [counsel for Mr. Brophy] has attempted to apply the reasoning to preliminary deposits paid to solicitors in a pre-contract situation or on the basis that the deposit is paid "subject to contract". [He] relied, in particular, on the dissenting judgment of Lord Justice Denning in *Burt* v. *Claude Cousins & Co.* [1971] 2 Q.B. 426 which judgment was approved of by the House of Lords when they overruled *Burt* v. *Claude Cousins & Co.* in *Sorrell* v. *Finch* [1977] A.C. 728.

In his judgment in *Burt* v. *Claude Cousins & Co.* [1971] 2 All E.R. 611 Lord Justice Denning distinguishes three situations in relation to a deposit. One is where a deposit is received "as agent for the vendor", another is where a deposit is received "as stakeholder" and a third is where nothing is said. It may be significant that in the first two cases Lord Justice Denning refers to "an estate agent or a solicitor" but in the third case he refers only to an estate agent. Referring to the third case he says at p. 615:—

> If an estate agent, before any binding contract is made, asks for and receives a deposit, giving the receipt in his own name without more, the question arises: in what capacity does he receive it? As agent for the vendor? or as stakeholder? I cannot believe that he receives it as 'agent for the vendor', for, if that were so, the estate agent would be bound to pay it over to the vendor forthwith, and the vendor alone would be answerable for its return. That cannot be right. Seeing that no contract has been made, the vendor is not entitled to a penny piece. If the estate agent should pay it over to the vendor, he does wrong; and if the vendor goes bankrupt, the estate agent is answerable for it.

It seems to me doubtful if this kind of reasoning can be applied to the case of a solicitor. But, more important, I do not think that the present case can be resolved by such general considerations. I think the same applies to evidence which the court received concerning the practice of some solicitors who act for builders and whose practice, in the absence of clear instructions, is guided by admirable considerations of what they consider to be fair as between their builder clients and prospective purchasers in relation to the payment of booking deposits. In the present case [the builders] had formulated a clear policy in relation to booking deposits and stage payments. These deposits and payments, whether received by the estate agent or the solicitor, were to go to the builder and the solicitor had no authority to accept these deposits except as agent for the builder. The fact that these deposits would go to the builder was explained by Mr. Lynch to [the plaintiffs] when they first showed interest in buying the flats.

[The plaintiffs] understood this and it was because they did not like it that they consulted Mr. Brophy. Mr. Brophy intended to bring about a situation where Messrs. P. C. Moore & Co. would hold the deposit and the first stage payment "as stakeholders" and not as agents for the vendor. It would have been very easy for him to say, in his first letter, that the deposits were being paid to Messrs. P. C. Moore as stakeholders. Unfortunately, he did not do this.

In each case Mr. Brophy's letter sending the cheque for the initial deposit was in similar terms. The question is whether this letter was sufficient to put Messrs. P. C. Moore & Co. on notice that the deposit was being paid to them as stakeholders and not in accordance with what they knew to be their instructions from their clients and their clients' general course of business. In my view it was not sufficient, in the circumstances of the case, to put them on notice that the deposit was being tendered on special terms. It is possible that an extremely careful solicitor would have written back to Mr. Brophy asking him precisely what he meant but I do not think it is reasonable, in the circumstances, to fault Messrs. P. C. Moore for not raising such a query. It appears to me that they correctly interpreted their own clients' instructions in paying the deposit over to them and that the letter was not sufficient to put them on notice that the deposit was being tendered on the basis that they were to be stakeholders.

When the first stage payment was made by Mr. Brophy on the 11th January, 1980, he made clear that he was paying it on the same terms as those set out in his letter of the 5th November, 1979. Again I do not think the letter was sufficient to put Messrs. P. C. Moore on notice that the deposit was being paid to them as stakeholders.

It is always unfortunate when, as in the present case, the court has to decide which of two innocent persons must bear a loss. I do not think there was any lack of concern on the part of Mr. Brophy for his clients' interests but unfortunately, in this case, it appears to me that he did not show reasonable professional skill in defending those interests and the clients as a result, are at a loss.

In the circumstances I hold that the plaintiffs are entitled to recover against Mr. Brophy the loss which they have suffered. In the case of Miss Desmond the capital loss is £8,000 and in the case of Miss Boyle £3,000.

As this was a commercial transaction I think also that the plaintiffs should be entitled to interest on their money from the time when Messrs. P. C. Moore informed Mr. Brophy that a receiver had been appointed over [the builders].

This, it appears to me, is the time when Messrs. P. C. Moore & Co. would have returned the deposits had they been holding them as stakeholders. Section 22 of the Courts Act, 1981, was not in force at that time. Interest will accordingly be payable from the date of the coming into operation of s. 22 of the Courts Act, 1981, at the rate of 11% per annum.

Extract 11.18

ROCHE v PEILOW [1985] I.R. 232

The appellants engaged the respondent solicitors to act for them in the purchase of a new house from a building company. The latter had created an equitable charge in favour of a bank on the land on which the house was to be built. The charge was registered in the Companies' Office but not in the Land Registry. When they came to investigate title the defendants made the usual Requisitions on the Title, but they did not make a search in the Companies' Office. Only such a search would have disclosed the existence of the charge.

The building company went into liquidation, by which stage the appellants had paid £8,000 towards the purchase price. The liquidator was prepared to complete the contract, but the bank was unprepared to release the charge unless paid £6,000. The appellants sued the respondents alleging that they were negligent in that they failed to discover the existence of the charge in favour of the bank. The respondents denied that they were negligent as they had followed the approved practice of the profession. The Supreme Court (Walsh, Henchy, Griffin, Hederman and McCarthy JJ.) held that the respondents were negligent.

Walsh J.

. . . The appellants have alleged that the respondents were negligent and in breach of their contract with the appellants for not discovering the mortgage by making the appropriate searches in the Companies' Office and of warning them of this additional risk. The appellants had already paid the builders £8,000 on foot of their building contract when the builders went into liquidation which followed a resolution of the shareholders of the building company on 18 October 1974 when it was resolved that the company be wound up. The lease had not yet been executed. The company was, through its liquidator, eventually compelled to grant a lease of the premises to the appellants but that, of course, was not valid as against the Lombard and Ulster Bank. The bank was and is willing to release the site upon payment to them of £6,000, but not otherwise. In default of such payment they are apparently prepared to recover the property from the appellants and, of course, with it would go the house which has now been built upon it.

The respondents, in answer to the claim in negligence, have stated that they acted in accordance with the normal practice of solicitors in these matters, that is to say not to make all the necessary inquiries until the time for granting the lease had arrived. It appears that there is no general practice of pre-contract searches by solicitors in advising purchasers with regard to the purchase of houses provided by a system of a building contract to be followed by a lease. The question in this case is whether such a common practice has such inherent defects that they ought to be obvious to any person giving the matter due consideration.

It is clear from the evidence given by solicitors, including the respondents in this case, that this particular risk was well known to them and that they appreciated that in cases where money was being paid out during the course of a building contract if the site was not already secured it would be lost in the event of the insolvency or liquidation of the builder. In a case where no money was being paid out on foot of a building contract until completion then the risk would, to a very large extent, be diminished, even though in the event of loss of the site the purchaser might be very disappointed and might indeed suffer damage. While in a case such as the present one it could well be that the appellants, even if they were made aware of the risk, might have elected to go on but the fact is that they were not made aware of it and so it is idle to speculate on what they might have done if they had become aware of it. In this transaction appellants' position was fraught with very grave risks. The first one was that pointed out by their solicitor, namely that by making periodic payments during the course of the building they were liable to lose it all if the builder went bankrupt or went into liquidation or, alternatively, they might be able to mitigate their loss by getting somebody else to complete the building. There was ample evidence that the appellants were fully aware of this risk and accepted it. The second risk in their situation was the question of the site itself. They were not warned of this and the question is whether the respondents' failure to discover the mortgage and to pass the information on to the appellants was negligence on the part of the respondents. In my view it was.

It is quite clear on the evidence in the case that this method of financing building was well known to solicitors and they also knew the risks inherent in it. In a case where the builder was a limited company, as well as making a search in the Land Registry it would also be clearly necessary to make a search in the Companies' Office. It may well be that the general practice of solicitors not to make these searches until the time has arrived for completion was based upon the experience that in most cases nothing goes wrong. However, that practice does not obviate the risk clearly inherent in such a practice. The whole object of a search is to discover these matters and no solicitor can permit his client to purchase lands or to commit himself irrevocably financially in the purchase or development of lands unless he has first of all ascertained whether or not the land is free from encumbrances. If it is not he must bring the fact to the notice of his client and allow the client, after proper advice to decide whether or not he should take the risk of accepting the transaction with the risk posed by the existence of the encumbrance.

In his judgment the learned President of the High Court cited a passage from the decision of this Court in *O'Donovan v Cork County Council* [1967] I.R. 173. In my view the last paragraph of that passage governs this case. The learned President in deciding against the appellants relied upon a passage in an English judgment, *Simmons v Pennington & Son* [1955] 1 W.L.R. 183. In that case the vendor had purchased shop premises in 1922. They were then being used as a shop and had been used ever since then. The premises, however, were subject to a restrictive covenant imposed by an indenture of 1870 under which their user was restricted to use for residential purposes. When the premises were put up for sale in 1951 the vendor in the conditios of sale stated:

> This property is sold subject the restrictive covenant as to user and other matters contained in a deed dated 29th September 1870 . . . as far as the same are still subsisting and capable of taking effect, and the purchaser shall in the conveyance to him covenant to observe the same in so far as aforesaid and to indemnify the vendor in respect thereof. A copy of the said restricted covenant may be inspected . . . and the purchaser whether he inspects the same or not shall be deemed to purchase with full notice thereof.

The purchaser bought the premises at the auction and signed the contract of purchase. He made requisitions and one of them was the following:—

> Is the property or any part thereof subject to any covenant or agreement restrictive of the user or enjoyment thereof or otherwise? If so has the same been duly observed or performed?

The answer given to the vendor's solicitor to that was:

> Yes. See special condition No. 7. There appeared to have been breaches of the covenant as to user but no notice of breach has been served.

The purchaser's solicitors then wrote to the vendor's solicitors stating that the purchaser had not been informed before the sale that there was a restrictive covenant which restricted the use of the property to that of a private dwellinghouse and the purchaser was not prepared to complete and requested that the stakeholder should be instructed to return the deposit. This was refused and in the meantime the property, which was not insured by either party, was very badly damaged by fire. In the case which followed Denning L.J. expressed the view that the answer to requisition No. 14 was a fatal mistake in that it enabled the purchaser to get out of his bargain and that he was thus entitled to cancel the contract forthwith. He also held, however, that he was satisfied that the solicitors who gave the response were not negligent and expressed the view that the restrictions were in all probability obsolete but nevertheless the solicitors could not assert categorically that they were. The requisition to which the answer had been given was described as "a stock requisition" but the answer given was, in the view of the learned judge, not a negligent answer. The Court of Appeal went on to hold that it was ill luck that the words which the solicitors used instead of protecting their client amounted to repudiation of the contract but that was not the solicitor's fault. It could not have been reasonably anticipated, the Court thought, that such a repudiation would flow from the answer to the requisition and that they had acted in accordance with the general practice of conveyancers. The Court went on to observe that no ill consequence had ever been known to flow from the answer. In the result, the Court held that the solicitor was not guilty of a breach of duty to his client. A number of observations may be made about that particular case. The first is that the conditions of sale were not particularly candid and the second is that it could scarcely be regarded as negligence to give a truthful answer to a requisition. It may well have been thought that a solicitor might not reasonably foresee that telling the truth in what was a stock answer to a stock question would fail to satisfy a purchaser. However, in my view, the case is totally different from the present case. The risk in the present case cannot be neutered by describing it as a stock risk. It is a very substantial and real risk. The fact that it was frequently undertaken does not in any way diminish the danger to which it gives rise. The consequences of the risk materialising could not be said to be unforeseeable when the evidence in this case indicates that it was a well known risk and the consequences were obvious if it should materialise. In my view, the decision in *Simmons v Pennington & Sons* is not applicable.

I have had the advantage of reading the judgments delivered by the then President of the High Court in *Taylor v Ryan* (delivered 10 March 1983) and the judgment of Mr. Justice Murphy in *Dermot C. Kelly & anor v Finbarr J. Crowley* (delivered 5 March 1985). The principles enunciated in those cases confirm, in my view, that the respondents were guilty of a failure in the duty they owed to the appellants to the extent that they were negligent in law. I would therefore set aside the order of the High Court and remit the case to the High Court for the purpose of having damages assessed.

Henchy J.

When the plaintiffs engaged the defendants to act as their solicitors in the purchase of a house, they were entitled to believe that their interests would be protected by the defendants with the degree of care to be expected from a reasonably careful and competent solicitor. That duty of care may be said to arise either as a matter of contract, by reason of an implied term to that effect in the contract of retainer, or alternatively, as an aspect of the tort of negligence arising out of the proximity of the relationship between solicitor and client: see *Finlay v. Murtagh* [1979] I.R. 249.

In deciding whether the plaintiffs are entitled to succeed in their claim for damages for want of reasonable care on the part of the defendants, it is necessary to underline certain features of the house purchase in question. The house had yet to be built. The site of the house was one of a number of sites which were being developed by a building company. Those sites were contained in Folio 58474 of the Register of Freeholders for Co. Cork and the registered owner was the building company. The building company were to build a house on one of those sites for the plaintiffs for the sum of £9,450. That sum was to be paid in instalments payable at different stages of the building of the house, namely £1,000 as a booking deposit, £2,500 at first floor, £2,000 at roof-plate level, £2,500 at internal plastering and £1,450 on completion. In conjunction with that building agreement, the building company agreed to grant a 999 years lease of the house when it was completed.

The plaintiffs instructed the defendants to act as their solicitors in connection with the transaction before they entered into any written contract with the building company. The contract to build the house was executed by the parties on the 19th February 1973 and the agreement to grant the lease was executed on the same date. The plaintiffs' plea of negligence rests on the complaint that before they bound themselves contractually, the defendants as their solicitors should have made a search in the Companies' Office to ascertain if a charge on the site had been registered by the building company under the Companies Act, 1963. If such a search had been made it would have shown that the building company had given a charge to a Bank, by deposit of title deeds, on the lands on Folio 58474 to secure all moneys due by the building company to the Bank. Had that position been thus disclosed, the defendants would doubtless have informed the plaintiffs that the Bank were equitable mortgagees and have warned them of the perils involved in making stage payments to the building company, who had not the beneficial title and against whom there would be no effective redress in case of insolvency.

In ignorance of the Bank's interest in the site, the plaintiffs executed the building agreement and the agreement for a lease. The defendants investigated the title in the normal way by serving requisitions on title. Neither the replies to the requisitions nor the certified copy of the Folio disclosed the charge in favour of the Bank. Only a search in the Companies' Office would have brought to light that charge, and such a search was not made.

Meanwhile, the plaintiffs proceeded to make the stage payments required by the building contract. They had paid stage payments totalling £8,000 when the building company became insolvent and went into liquidation. While the liquidator was eventually prepared to grant the plaintiffs the lease contracted for, such a lease is valueless because the equitable estate is vested in the Bank as a result of the charge, and the Bank are not prepared to release the site from their charge unless they are paid £4,000.

The present claim by the plaintiffs against the defendants for damages for negligence and/or breach of contract rests on the contention that the financial loss incurred by them in connection with the attempted purchase of this house was caused by the defendants' failure to search for and discover the charge in favour of the Bank. In particular they complain that before they were allowed by the defendants to enter into contractual relationship with the building company the defendants should have ascertained the Bank's interest in the site and warned the plaintiffs of the financial risk involved in proceeding with the transaction when the building company had not an unencumbered title.

I have no doubt that the financial disaster that has befallen the plaintiffs may be said to result from the defendants' failure to discover and bring to their notice, before the contract, the existence of the Bank's charge. The real question is whether that failure amounts to negligence by the defendants as solicitors.

The general duty owed by a solicitor to his client is to show him the degree of care to be expected in the circumstances from a reasonably careful and skilful solicitor. Usually the solicitor will be held to have discharged that duty if he follows a practice common among the members of this profession: see *Daniels v. Heskin* [1954] I.R. 73 and the cases therein referred to. Conformity with the widely accepted practice of his colleagues will normally rebut an allegation of negligence against a professional man, for the degree of care which the law expects of him is no higher than that to be expected from an ordinary reasonable member of the profession or of the speciality in question. But there is an important exception to that rule of conduct. It was concisely put as follows by Walsh J. in *O'Donovan v. Cork Co. Co.* [1967] I.R. 173, 193:

> If there is a common practice which has inherent defects, which ought to be obvious to any person giving the matter due consideration, the fact that it is shown to have been widely adopted over a period of time does not make the practice any the less negligent. Neglect of duty does not cease by repetition to be neglect of duty.

The reason for that exception or qualification is that the duty imposed by the law rests on the standard to be expected from a reasonably careful member of the profession, and a person cannot be said to be acting reasonably if he automatically and mindlessly follows the practice of others when by taking thought he would have realized that the practice in question was fraught with peril for his client and was readily avoidable or remediable. The professional man is, of course, not to be judged with the benefit of hindsight, but if it can be said that if at the time, on giving the matter due consideration, he would have realized that the impugned practice was in the circumstances incompatible with his client's interests, and if an alternative and safe course of conduct was reasonably open to him, he will be held to have been negligent.

I consider it to be beyond doubt that it was inimical to the plaintiffs' interests for the defendants to allow them to enter into contractual relations with the building company, and in particular to bind themselves to make stage payments, without first making a search in the Companies' Office which would have shown that the beneficial owner of the site was the Bank. Because of the defendants' default in that respect, the plaintiffs were left open to disappointment and financial disaster if, as happened, the building company proved to be unable to discharge their indebtedness to the Bank. As the evidence in the High Court showed, in not making that search the defendants were following a conveyancing practice common at the time among solicitors. However, adherence to that practice can avail as a defence only if it be shown that a reasonable solicitor, giving consideration at the time to the interests of the client, would have justifiably concluded that a search in the Companies' Office was unnecessary or undesirable. Having regard to the fact that no undue delay, expense or difficulty was involved in making such a search, and bearing in mind that financial disaster of the kind actually sustained by the plaintiffs was reasonably foreseeable by the defendants as a risk for the plaintiffs, I consider that, notwithstanding that the defendants in not carrying out a search were conforming to a practice widespread at the time in the profession, they were nevertheless wanting in the duty of care owed by them to the plaintiffs. It is to avoid detectable pitfalls of the kind that beset the plaintiffs that prospective puchasers engage solicitors to act for them.

I would allow the plaintiffs' appeal and remit the case to the High Court for the assessment of damages.

Chapter 12

INTERPRETATION OF LEGISLATION

INTRODUCTION

Legislation consists of documents which are enacted by a legislative organ in a manner which is prescribed by a constitutional formula. In other words it is the product of a legislative process. The document, called a statute or an Act, is a source of law, in that its text is law. Delegated or secondary legislation consists of documents enacted by organs which are authorised to do so by the legislative organ. Like legislation such documents constitute a source of law. Much of what is to be said of legislation applies with equal force to delegated legislation, and for the purposes of this chapter the term "legislation" includes "delegated legislation".

The process of legislating connotes the activity of deliberate law making. Unlike adjudication its primary concern is the creation of rules which will apply to future events. In this respect, the process is prospective and abstract—it establishes standards to be adopted in cases which have yet to occur. However, it should be realised that some statutes regulate past events, although this tends to be an exception to the general practice. In contrast, adjudication is retrospective and concrete, being concerned with the resolution of past events according to pre-existing rules. Nevertheless, as we have seen in the preceding chapter, the adjudicative process does possess a creative dimension—common law is often referred to as "judge made" law. But the creative character of adjudication differs significantly from that of legislation. Common law rules emerge from their being identified from an existing body of law and applied by the adjudicator to the dispute which he or she is charged with resolving. The creative scope afforded to a judge is constrained by the pre-existing law and, in this respect, is incidental to the adjudicative function. On the other hand, legislators are not so constrained, being confined only by the constitutional formula which confers a legislative capacity on them. Thus, despite their both being creative the general distinction between legislation and adjudication is based on their respective functions, that of the former being law-making and that of the latter being law-application.

The principal characteristic of legislation is that it reduces rules to a written and fixed verbal form. A legislative rule is stated in an inflexible manner and no linguistic variations can be substituted. This contrasts with common law rules which, as has been seen, are unwritten and unfixed, in that a variety of verbal formulae can, with equal accuracy, be employed to state them. A judge's articulation of a rule in the course of a decision is but an explanation or approximation of the rule. An example will demonstrate this characteristic of legislation. The prohibition on "drug pushing", contained in s. 15(1) of the Misuse of Drugs Act, 1977, is stated thus:

> Any person who has in his possession, whether lawfully or not, a controlled drug for the purpose of selling or otherwise supplying it to another in contravention of regulations under section 5 of this Act shall be guilty of an offence.

The section cannot be stated in any other verbal form and an alternative statement of the rule can only amount to an explanation of it. It should, however, be noted that the rule stated in s. 15(1) also contains an unwritten element. It is sufficient to note at this stage that the common law defences of insanity and infancy apply to the offence. Thus "any person" does not include lunatics or children under the age of seven. This theme shall be returned to later in the chapter.

2) A second characteristic of legislation is that rules tend to be stated in a precise rather than a general form. This is not a universal characteristic and some legislative rules are stated in general terms. However, that does not detract from the general observation. Several factors contribute to this characteristic. The subject matter of many, if not most, statutes is such that detailed provisions are required; this is especially true of statutes dealing with economic and social matters. For instance, a tax statute, to be workable, must specify precisely the details of the tax which is to be levied. To state the subject matter in general terms would result in a degree of vagueness and doubt which could undermine the purposes of the tax. Moreover, the desire for certainty in the law, whereby those who are affected by it are in a position to know exactly that which is required of them and to plan their activities accordingly, contributes to the relative precision of statutes. Related to this is an attempt by the legislature to provide for every eventuality which might arise or, in other words, to cover all conceivable loopholes. A further factor is an element of mistrust of the judiciary on the part of the legislature. If judges could be fully trusted, in the sense that their decisions would accord with the legislative preference, legislators could compose statutes in more general terms, secure in the knowledge that the courts would decide doubtful cases in the desired manner. On the other hand, some statutes are expressed in comparatively general terms, leaving their detailed operation to be supplied by judicial interpretation. This is achieved by the use of open-ended phrases such as "in the opinion of the court" or "reasonable". A point which should be made is that laws which exist in documentary form need not necessarily by stated in precise terms, the law maker being free to employ general terms. The degree of precision employed will depend largely on the subject matter of the statute.

In Ireland, as we noted in Chapter 2, the legislative organ is the Oireachtas, established by the Constitution of 1937. Legislation is passed by both Houses of the Oireachtas, the Dáil and the Seanad, and is signed into law by the President. Although most Bills, as proposed statutes are called, may be initiated by any member of either House, in virtually all cases they are initiated in the Dáil by the Government minister who has responsibility for the subject matter in question. In recent years, however, the Government has initiated a number of Bills in the Seanad, a measure necessitated by the demands placed on Dáil time. The passage of a Bill through the Dáil occurs in five stages. At the first stage the minister responsible obtains the permission of the Dáil to circulate the Bill. At the second stage the general provisions of the Bill are debated. At the third, or committee stage, the details of the Bill are debated clause by clause. Any amendments and alterations to the Bill's provisions are usually made at this stage. The fourth stage is the report stage and the fifth is the final stage. Again amendments may be made at either of these stages, but they tend to be of a technical nature designed to "tidy up" the Bill. Having been passed by the Dáil the Bill goes through a similar process in the Seanad. However, if a Bill is either rejected by the Seanad or passed with amendments with which the Dáil disagrees Article

23 of the Constitution provides that the Dáil may, within one hundred and eighty days, pass a resolution which deems the Bill to have been passed by both Houses. In this respect, the Dáil enjoys the power to overrule the Seanad. When a Bill is passed by both Houses it is sent to the President for signing, on the occurrence of which it becomes law and is called an Act of the Oireachtas.

Although a statute is enacted by the Oireachtas it will not have been drafted by its members. The task of drafting is left to a Parliamentary draftsman, a lawyer who specialises in legislative drafting. Parliamentary draftsmen are civil servants attached to the Office of the Attorney General. The draftsman is instructed as to the contents and objectives of the proposed legislation and he or she, in effect, converts those instruction into a legally intelligible form. Thus, the draftsman who was asked to draft a prohibition on "drug pushing" developed the offence of possession of controlled drugs for the purpose of sale or supply, contained in s. 15(1) of the Misuse of Drugs Act, 1977.

1. What does a statute contain?

In Ireland statutes are published in both the English and Irish languages. Both texts appear side by side in the published version of the statute. A statute has a short title, by which it is generally known, and a statutory number. For instance, the Misuse of Drugs Act, 1977 is the short title, its statutory number being Number 12 of 1977. A statute also has a long title which appears at the head of the document in which it is contained. The long title of the Misuse of Drugs Act, 1977 is:

AN ACT TO PREVENT THE MISUSE OF CERTAIN DANGEROUS OR OTHERWISE HARMFUL DRUGS, TO ENABLE THE MINISTER FOR HEALTH TO MAKE FOR THAT PURPOSE CERTAIN REGULATIONS IN RELATION TO SUCH DRUGS, TO ENABLE THAT MINISTER TO PROVIDE THAT CERTAIN SUBSTANCES SHALL BE POISONS FOR THE PURPOSES OF THE PHARMACY ACTS, 1875 TO 1962, TO AMEND THE PHARMACOPOEIA ACT, 1931, THE POISONS ACT, 1961, THE PHARMACY ACT, 1962, AND THE HEALTH ACTS 1947 TO 1970, TO REPEAL THE DANGEROUS DRUGS ACT, 1934 AND SECTION 78 OF THE HEALTH ACT, 1970 AND TO MAKE CERTAIN OTHER PROVISIONS IN RELATION TO THE FOREGOING. [16th May 1977]

The long title states in very general terms the purpose and object of the statute. In the example given it can be seen that the object is to deal with dangerous and harmful drugs and to amend various earlier statutes accordingly. The date which appears at the conclusion of the long title is that on which the Bill was signed by the President. Thus, the Misuse of Drugs Act, 1977 became law on the 16th of May 1977. However, it should be noted that a statute might not come into effect until a later date, which is called the *date of commencement*. This might be stated expressly in the statute or the statute might give a minister power to bring the Act into force at any time, or within, or not before a stated time. For example, s. 43(2) deals with the commencement of the Misuse of Drugs Act, 1977:

Subsection 1 of this section and section 41(2) of this Act shall come into operation on the passing hereof and the other purposes and provisions shall come into operation on such day or days as may be fixed therefor by any order or orders of the Minister [for Health] either generally or with reference to any particular such purpose or provision and different days may be so fixed for different such purposes and different such provisions of this Act.

Thus it can be seen that, with the exceptions of ss. 41(2) and 43(1) which came into force immediately, the effective operation of the Act was delayed until the the appropriate order was made by the Minister. Moreover, the Minister was given power to bring either the whole Act or selected parts thereof into operation at a later date. The Act was eventually brought into operation by the Misuse of Drugs Act, 1977 (Commencement) Order, 1979. A variant on the formula used in s. 43(2) is contained in s. 2 of the Succession Act, 1965 which deals with the commencement of that Act thus:

This Act shall come into effect on such day, not earlier than the 1st day of July, 1966, as the Minister [for Justice] by order appoints.

In this case it can be seen that the Minister was given power to bring the entire Act into force, but not before the specified date. That Act was brought into effect by the Succession Act, 1965 (Commencement) Order, 1966. One reason for delegating the power of commencement to a minister is to allow the necessary financial and administrative changes to be made before the legislation is brought into force.

It should be noted that in both the examples given the respective ministers are given a power to bring the Act into force but were not expressly obliged to do so. In this context the decision of the Supreme Court in *The State (Sheehan) v The Government of Ireland* [1987] I.R. 550 is instructive. S. 60(1) of the Civil Liability Act, 1961 makes local authorities liable for injuries suffered through their failure adequately to maintain public roads. However, s. 60(7) provides that the section "shall come into operation on such day, not earlier than the 1st day of April, 1967, as may be fixed therefor by order made by the Government." At the time of the proceedings no such order had been made and the prosecutor sought an order of mandamus directing the Government to so order. In rejecting his claim the Court noted that the wording of the section is enabling, or permissive, rather than mandatory. The only limit imposed was that the provision could not come into effect before the specified date and the Government's discretion is not otherwise fettered. The absence of limiting words such as "as soon as convenient" or "as soon as may be" confirmed the Court's view that the power is unlimited. It can be concluded, therefore, that unless express limits are imposed on the power to order the date of commencement of an Act the person so empowered is not obliged to bring the statute into force. This, in effect, allows a minister to postpone indefinitely the implementation of Acts passed by the Oireachtas, subject only to the infrequently used device of parliamentary accountability. Moreover, in *Sheehan* Finlay C.J. and Griffin J. reserved their opinions on the questions whether a court could direct the making of a commencement order either generally or where the implementation of the legislation would impose a burden on the public finances. Thus, the judicial power to order the implementation of legislation is not assured and it is conceivable that the Supreme Court in a future case will hold that it lacks such power.

The principal subdivision of a statute is a section. Sections are further subdivided into subsections and paragraphs. In general, a section deals with one point while subsections elaborate on or supplement the main point of the section. To return to an example used earlier, the prohibition on the possession of drugs for sale or supply is contained in subsection 1 of section 15 of the Misuse of Drugs Act, 1977. Subsection 2 of the section deals with evidence in relation to the possession of drugs. For references purposes a provision of a statute can be cited thus:

Misuse of Drugs Act, 1977 section 16(1)(c)(i)

This refers to section 16, subsection 1, paragraph c, subparagraph i. Frequently "s." is used as an abbreviation for "section" and "subs." for "subsection". Some statutes are divided into parts, which consist of a number of sections which deal with a general topic. Division into parts is common in Acts which deal with a large general subject and makes the Act less cumbersome. For instance, the Succession Act, 1965 consists of twelve parts. In some cases an Act will contain one or more Schedules which appear at the end of the document. A Schedule, in effect, is an appendix which contains material which is too unwieldy to list in the main body of the Act. The Misuse of Drugs Act, 1977 has one Schedule which lists controlled drugs, of which there are in excess of one hundred and twenty. The Succession Act, 1965 has two Schedules. The first sets out the rules as to the application of a deceased's assets and the second lists earlier legislation which is affected by the Act, whether repealed, amended or otherwise altered.

An Act contains an arrangement of sections at the start. This states briefly the subject matter of each section and it operates as a list of contents. This brief listing is repeated in the margin beside the main body of the Act, section by section, and in that context is referred to as marginal notes. Marginal notes sometimes contain a reference to an earlier statute or common law rule which is affected by the section. For example, the marginal note to s. 124 of the Succession Act, 1965 reads, in part, "New. Overrules *Rice v Begley* [1920] 1 I.R. 243." By scanning the margin a user can quickly locate the provision sought. However, s. 11(g) of the Interpretation Act, 1937 provides that marginal notes are not part of the text of the statute and may not be considered in relation to its interpretation.

2. Finding the law
An initial problem faced by someone searching for the legislative provisions on a particular subject is that they are not necessarily to be found in one Act. In many cases the relevant provisions are contained in a number of statutes, sometimes supplemented by ministerial orders or other species of delegated legislation. The problem is aggravated in this jurisdiction by the fact that Acts of a number of different parliaments are in operation. Acts of the old English Parliament (pre-1707), of the old Irish Parliament (pre-1800), of the British Parliament (1707-1800), of the Parliament of Great Britain and Ireland (1801-1922) and the Oireachtas of the Irish Free State (1922-1937) apply in Ireland along with Acts of the Oireachtas (post-1937). Matters are further complicated by the fact that many pre-1922

statutes which have subsequently been repealed in Britain, but not in Ireland, are not published by the Stationery Office thereby making access to them more difficult. Another source of difficulty is that the text of a section might not actually be found in the statute of which it is part. Frequently statutes amend, alter or repeal earlier provisions. However, the text of those earlier provisions remains unaltered as statutes are not reprinted to take account of subsequent changes. A relatively straightforward example is provided by the offence of robbery which is contained in s. 23 of the Larceny Act, 1916. That section was replaced by s. 5 of the Criminal Law (Jurisdiction) Act, 1976. But it is the old unaltered version of s. 23 which appears in the Larceny Act, 1916. Thus, to locate the offence prohibited by the 1916 Act one must consult the 1976 Act. As the number of operative statutes runs into thousands the difficulty of researching the applicable legislative provisions on a particular topic can be appreciated. Someone who seeks to rely on a provision must check to see whether, and to what extent, it has been affected by later legislation. The task of researching legislation requires much time, resources and enthusiasm. It is somewhat lightened by having recourse to the Index of Statutes, which has currently been updated to 1985, and Humphreys, *Index of Statutory Instruments 1922-1986* (Dublin, 1988).

Periodically the Oireachtas attempts to alleviate the problem by enacting statute law revision legislation to clear the statute book of its deadwood. Such legislation repeals those statutes which have become obsolete and are of no practical effect. However, it is usual expressly to provide that the revision does not affect any existing rules or principles; see *The State (Dixon) v Martin* [1985] I.R. 106. The most recent such effort in Ireland is the Statute Law Revision Act, 1983. However, statute law revision is only a partial solution as old statutes which are still in operation are left untouched. A second method of alleviating the problem is by enacting either *consolidating* or *codifying* legislation. A consolidating Act is one which reenacts all the relevant provisions on a particular subject in one statute, making, at most, only minor amendments to the existing law. A codifying statute is one which enacts in one statute all the relevant provisions on a topic, often making major changes to the existing law. The Larceny Act, 1916 is an example of the former, while the Succession Act, 1965 is an example of the latter. Although such legislation helps to reduce the bulky and cumbersome nature of the statute book, it is of limited assistance. Due to the time and effort involved in its drafting and preparation such legislation tends to be infrequent. Thus, part of a lawyer's skill involves the ability to extract relevant provisions from a diverse range of legislative sources. Bringing statutes up to date is probably still best achieved by the use of a pair of scissors and paste!

3. The task of interpretation

Once enacted, the task of interpreting a statute falls primarily on the courts. It should be noted, however, that a number of others bodies, agencies and officials might be involved in the interpretation of the legislation. They include civil servants and administrative agencies charged with the function of implementing the legislation, tribunals involved in its application and lawyers and other specialists who advise clients affected by the legislation. To an extent these non-judicial bodies will lend to their interpretation a perspective which is not necessarily shared by the courts. For example, a lawyer or accountant who advises a client on a new tax statute will look at it from the client's perspective and the interpretation canvassed will be coloured accordingly; the adviser in that case will attempt to interpret the statute in a manner which minimises the client's liability. By the same token, a civil servant who has the function of collecting the new tax might wish to maximise the client's liability, especially if the former was involved in drafting the statute and views its provisions expansively. But although the interpretations of different persons might be influenced by their different perspectives, account must be taken of the likely interpretation which will be adopted by the courts. The courts are the ultimate interpreters of legislation and, therefore, their probable response to the statute operates as a parameter within which other bodies will interpret it. Because the courts have the last word on the subject, an interpretation by another agency will in part amount to a prediction of their decision.

The stated objective of the courts is to discover "the intention of legislature". In this respect, the exercise is one of unravelling the meaning which the Oireachtas expected the words to bear. However, to an extent the phrase is devoid of meaning. It is pointless to speak of the intention of a group of people in the sense that the group had a collective intent. One can hardly say that the all the members of the Oireachtas intended the statute to bear one meaning to the exclusion of all other possibilities. The reality is that most members will not, in all probability, have considered the meaning of the statute. Moreover, of those who did consider the matter it is conceivable that they had different intentions in mind and, indeed, the variety of intentions might not be available in reliable form. The intention of the minister who introduced the Bill, and who, therefore, was most closely associated with its drafting, cannot be ascribed to the Oireachtas—amendments to the Bill might have been made during its passage through the Oireachtas despite opposition from the minister. Thus, as a concept "the intention of the legislature" is meaningless and can best be regarded as a linguistic device which states the nature of the task of interpreting legislation. It points to a constitutional arrangement which governs the relationship between the legislature and the judiciary. It recognises that the function of legislating is given to the Oireachtas and that that function should not be undermined by the courts. The intention of the Oireachtas is expressed in legislation and the courts are required to give effect to that duly expressed intention. Thus, it conveys the idea that the principal constraint on statutory interpretation is that the courts are required to act in a manner which does not usurp the legislative function.

In interpreting legislation the courts are guided by several rules, or canons, of interpretation, which are supplemented by a number of presumptions and maxims which exist in respect of linguistic usage and subject matter of the statute. The canons of interpretation are not rules in the sense that the courts are absolutely bound to apply any or all of them. They are better regarded as general principles which guide the function of interpretation—they reflect different approaches which can legitimately be adopted by the courts. But amongst those approaches the choice of which one to adopt is, ultimately, a matter of choice for the courts. Traditionally, the options open to the courts have been expressed in the form of three rules of interpretation: the *literal rule*, the *golden rule* and the *mischief rule*. The literal rule was thought of as being the primary canon of interpretation.

Briefly stated, it required the court to attribute to a word its ordinary, literal and commonplace meaning. If the literal rule led to an absurdity the court was permitted to have recourse to the golden rule, by which it could interpret the word in its context in order to avoid the absurdity. The mischief rule allowed the court to examine the pre-existing common law in order to determine the defect, or mischief, which the statute was designed to remedy. The statute was interpreted in a manner which was sufficient to deal with that defect, and in this respect the rule, unlike the former two, was teleological. Whether, and to what extent, the canons of interpretation survive in those forms is open to question. But however they might be stated two principal issues remain: how expansive the task of interpretation should be and whether account should be taken of the statutory context and purpose as opposed to reading the words in isolation. A further device which has been developed by the Irish courts is the *presumption of constitutionality*. The presumption will be treated later in the chapter and it is sufficient to note here that it merits separate consideration.

While the canons of interpretation which are currently invoked by the courts might be differently stated, and indeed are better regarded as approaches rather than "rules", the nature of statutory interpretation is essentially the same. It should be borne in mind that often the application of the different canons will lead to different results. The task of the courts is to determine which is the most appropriate result. To this extent the courts enjoy a choice, but one which is circumscribed by the canons themselves. If a literal interpretation does not produce an absurd conclusion it will prevail. It is only where the literal interpretation leads to an absurdity that the courts have the option of looking to the statutory context and purpose and adopting a modified, non-literal meaning. Despite those constraints the courts enjoy a wide measure of freedom as it is they who determine when the literal meaning leads to an absurdity and when it is justifiable to depart from the literal meaning. Thus, the task of interpretation frequently becomes an exercise in selecting what is considered to be the most suitable of a number of possible interpretations.

Before considering the canons of interpretation some preliminary issues should be disposed of. The first is that interpretation is governed by the *Interpretation Act, 1937*. The Act does not set out general principles of interpretation, but it does contain rules and definitions which are of general application. Second, words used in a particular statute might be defined for the purposes of the statute in an interpretation section. For instance, s. 1 of the Misuse of Drugs Act, 1977 contains definitions of twenty-five words and phrases which appear in the Act. Moreover, words and phrases might be defined for a particular part or section of an Act. Thus, when faced with interpreting a provision recourse must be had to the Interpretation Act, 1937 and the interpretation section, if any, of the Act in which the provision appears. With this in mind it is now possible to consider the principal canons of interpretation which are used in Irish courts.

THE PRESUMPTION OF CONSTITUTIONALITY

It is presumed that all statutes passed by the Oireachtas are constitutional until the contrary is established. Moreover, it is also presumed that all powers and procedures created by the statute will be exercised in a manner which accords with the dictates of the Constitution. This is based on an assumption that when the Oireachtas enacts legislation that it intends to abide by the provisions of the Constitution. The basis to, and effect of, the presumption were articulated by the Supreme Court in *East Donegal Co-operative Livestock Mart Ltd. v Attorney General* [1970] I.R. 317 (Extract 12.1). It is also presumed that statutes passed by the Oireachtas of the Irish Free State accord with the Constitution under which they were enacted. Apart from amounting to an assignment of the burden of proof in cases where the validity of a statute is challenged, the presumption has a bearing on the interpretation of post-1937 statutes. Those statutes must, where possible, be interpreted in a manner which would render them constitutional. Thus, where a court is faced with two reasonable interpretations one of which would result in the statute bearing a constitutional meaning, and the other of which would render the statute unconstitutional, the former must be adopted. In this respect, the presumption is a binding rule, unlike the other canons of interpretation which will be examined, as can be seen in *Quinn v Wren* [1985] I.R. 322 (Extract 12.2) and *In re J.H.* [1985] I.R. 375 (Extract 12.3). It should, however, be realised that the interpretation of a word need not necessarily be confined to the meaning which it bears in the Constitution, provided that a different meaning does not lead to the statute's being unconstitutional. Thus, in *Jordan v O'Brien* [1960] I.R. 363 (Extract 12.4) the word "family" in the Rent Restrictions Act, 1946 was given a wider interpretation than that which it bears in Article 41 of the Constitution.

Extract 12.1

EAST DONEGAL CO-OPERATIVE LIVESTOCK MART LTD. v ATTORNEY-GENERAL
[1970] I.R. 317

The Livestock Marts Act, 1967 controls the business of selling animals at auction. The Act establishes a system by which marts may operate only on licence issued by the Minister for Agriculture. The Act confers on the Minister the power to grant or refuse to grant licences, to attach conditions to licences and to revoke a licence if the holder is guilty of an offence under the Act. The plaintiffs brought an action in which they claimed that the Act infringed the Constitution. Apart from a provision which allowed the Minister to exempt particular individuals from its operation, the Supreme Court held the Act to be constitutional. In the course of its judgment the Court considered the presumption of constitutionality and its effect on statutory interpretation.

Walsh J.
. . . It is now necessary to consider the submissions made in respect of the provisions of the Act itself. As this Act was passed subsequent to the coming into force of the Constitution, the Act is a law contemplated by the provisions of Article 34, s. 3, sub-s. 2, of the Constitution: see *The State (Sheerin)* v. *Kennedy* [1966] I.R. 379. It is important to bear in mind the differing approaches that a court must make when dealing with Acts passed before the coming into force of the Constitution and those passed subsequent to that event. The approach in the former case was formulated in the judgment of Mr. Justice Walsh in *The State (Quinn)* v. *Ryan* [1965] I.R. 70, 125

and assented to by the other judges who were then members of the Court. In all such cases the Court's declaration is made pursuant to the provisions of Article 50 of the Constitution and the question is not whether the Act is valid but rather whether it was carried over into law on the coming into force of the Constitution. In testing the validity of Acts of the Oireachtas which were passed since the coming into force of the Constitution, the approach is that laid down by this Court in *McDonald* v. *Bord na gCon* [1965] I.R. 217. It was pointed out in that case that there was a presumption of constitutionality operating in favour of all such statutes and it was stated at p. 239 of the report that "one practical effect of this presumption is that if in respect of any provision or provisions of the Act two or more constructions are reasonably open, one of which is constitutional and the other or others are unconstitutional, it must be presumed that the Oireachtas intended only the constitutional construction and a Court called upon to adjudicate upon the constitutionality of the statutory provision should uphold the constitutional construction. It is only when there is no construction reasonably open which is not repugnant to the Constitution that the provision should be held to be repugnant." It should be pointed out that the term "repugnant" in that quotation is used in its general sense and that the more precise term would have been "invalid having regard to the provisions of the Constitution." As a term of art the term "repugnant" in the Constitution is confined to cases arising under Article 26.

Therefore, an Act of the Oireachtas, or any provision thereof, will not be declared to be invalid where it is possible to construe it in accordance with the Constitution; and it is not only a question of preferring a constitutional construction to one which would be unconstitutional where they both may appear to be open but it also means that an interpretation favouring the validity of an Act should be given in cases of doubt. It must be added, of course, that interpretation or construction of an Act or any provision thereof in conformity with the Constitution cannot be pushed to the point where the interpretation would result in the substitution of the legislative provision by another provision with a different context, as that would be to usurp the functions of the Oireachtas. In seeking to reach an interpretation or construction in accordance with the Constitution, a statutory provision which is clear and unambiguous cannot be given an opposite meaning. At the same time, however, the presumption of constitutionality carries with it not only the presumption that the constitutional interpretation or construction is the one intended by the Oireachtas but also that the Oireachtas intended that proceedings, procedures, discretions and adjudications which are permitted, provided for, or prescribed by an Act of the Oireachtas are to be conducted in accordance with the principles of constitutional justice. In such a case any departure from those principles would be restrained and corrected by the Courts.

The long title and the general scope of the Act of 1967 constitute the background of the context in which it must be examined. The whole or any part of the Act may be referred to and relied upon in seeking to construe any particular part of it, and the construction of any particular phrase requires that it is to be viewed in connection with the whole Act and not that it should be viewed detached from it. The words of the Act, and in particular the general words, cannot be read in isolation and their content is to be derived from their context. Therefore, words or phrases which at first sight might appear to be wide and general may be cut down in their construction when examined against the objects of the Act which are to be derived from a study of the Act as a whole including the long title. Until each part of the Act is examined in relation to the whole it would not be possible to say that any particular part of the Act was either clear or unambiguous . . .

Extract 12.2

QUINN v WREN [1985] I.R. 322

The extradition of the plaintiff to England on a charge of obtaining money by deception contrary to the Theft Act, 1968 (Eng.) was ordered. He admitted the offence but claimed that he committed it on behalf of the Irish National Liberation Army, of which organisation he was a member. Accordingly, he argued that the offence was a "political offence" or an "offence connected with a political offence" and that by virtue of s. 50 of the Extradition Act, 1965 he could not be extradited. He also argued that were he returned to England he would be tried for a political offence, namely being a member of a proscribed organisation contrary to the Prevention of Terrorism (Temporary Provisions) Act, 1976 (U.K.). His claim was rejected by the High Court and, on appeal, by the Supreme Court. In his judgment Finlay C.J. relied on the presumption of constitutionality to interpret s. 50 so as to exclude organisations whose purposes include the destruction of the Constitution. Hederman J. delivered a somewhat less expansive concurring judgment. Henchy, Griffin and McCarthy JJ. concurred in the judgments delivered. The Court has subsequently confirmed this decision in *Russell v Fanning* [1988] I.L.R.M. 333.

Finlay C.J.

This is an appeal brought by the plaintiff against the dismissal by Gannon J in the High Court of his claim for an order directing his release pursuant to s. 50 of the Extradition Act, 1965.

By order of the District Court dated 19 December 1983 it was directed that the plaintiff should be delivered into the custody of a member of the London Metropolitan Police Force for conveyance to Horseferry Road Magistrates Court, London, on a warrant charging him with an offence contrary to s. 15(1) of the Theft Act 1968, the particulars of the offence being that he 'did, by deception, with a false pretence made with intent to defraud, dishonestly obtained £600 cash, from Barclay's Bank by falsely pretending that National Westminster Travellers Cheques No. 5-05302602-614 were a good and valid order, with the intention of permanently depriving the said Barclay's Bank of the said property'. The offence thus charged was held in the order of the District Court to correspond with the offence under the law of the State created by s. 6 of the Forgery Act, 1913.

No question has arisen with regard to the form of this order nor with regard to the validity or completeness of the documentation leading up to the making of it.

The plaintiff's claim is that the offence with which he is charged is either a political offence or an offence connected with a political offence within the meaning of those words contained in s. 50 of the Act of 1965 or, in the alternative, that there are substantial reasons for believing that the plaintiff will, if removed from the State under the Act, be prosecuted or detained for a political offence within the meaning of s. 50(2)(b) of the Act of 1965.

The Facts

The proceedings were heard on affidavit and the plaintiff's claim for relief was based on his own affidavit, the facts deposed to in which were not contested by any other evidence. These facts have been neatly and briefly summarised in the judgment of Gannon J delivered on 15 November 1984; no question has arisen as to the accuracy of that summary or of the findings of fact thus made in the High Court and the facts so found relevant to the issues arising on this appeal are as follows:

1. He committed the offence to which the warrant relates.

2. At the time of committing the offence he was a member of the Irish National Liberation Army otherwise I.N.L.A.

3. The I.N.L.A. is a proscribed organisation.

4. He committed the offence on the instructions of the I.N.L.A.

5. The nature of the offence and the manner in which and place where it was to be committed was determined by the I.N.L.A.

6. He gave the money obtained by him in the commission of the offence to a person believed to be a fellow member of the I.N.L.A.

7. The purpose of the offence was to obtain in this criminal manner money for use by the I.N.L.A.

8. He had committed a number of similar offences while a member of I.N.L.A. on the instructions and with the co-operation of other members of the I.N.L.A.

9. He did not commit this or any of these offences for his own benefit and all moneys thus obtained by him were so obtained for the use of and given to the I.N.L.A.

10. The I.N.L.A. has need of and uses such money to 'fund their campaign'.

11. The campaign of the I.N.L.A. is: "The aims and objectives of this organisation are the establishment of a thirty two county workers' republic by force of arms and, *inter alia*, a military campaign against the forces of the Crown within the six counties of Northern Ireland, and the United Kingdom and elsewhere".

The other material evidence was firstly contained in an affidavit of Florence O'Donoghue, a barrister, of the English Bar and also of the Irish Bar, who deposed that as a matter of law the Irish National Liberation Army was a proscribed organisation, proscribed under s. 1 (3) of the English statute entitled the Prevention of Terrorism (Temporary Provisions) Act 1976, which made provision for the conviction and punishment of persons who belonged or professed to belong to proscribed organisations. Jeraine Dickin Olsen, barrister-at-law, of the English Bar, and an Assistant Director of Public Prosecutions in England, deposed that the Director of Public Prosecutions in English law had a right to intervene in a private prosecution for the purpose of offering no evidence, having previously given an undertaking that the defendant would not be prosecuted for his part in a particular offence and that she had a right, pursuant to the statute establishing the Office of Director of Public Prosecutions in England, to do any act or thing which the Director is required or authorised to do, and undertaking in pursuance of that right that the plaintiff would not be put on trial in any part of England or Wales in respect of an offence or offences under s. 1 of the Prevention of Terorrism (Temporary Provisions) Act 1976. A further affidavit of John Christopher Barnes, a Detective Inspector serving with the Central Cheque Squad, New Scotland Yard, London, deposed to the fact that the offences with which the plaintiff is charged and in respect of which his delivery was sought on warrant, are offences punishable irrespective of the motive of the person's political activities and that there was no question of those offences being prosecuted only because they might be related to the aims of a political party.

The Law
In the course of the submissions made to the court, the court was referred to the decision of *Bourke v The Attorney General* [1972] I.R. 36, *McGlinchey v Wren* [1982] I.R. 154 and *Shannon v Fanning* [1985] I.R. 569.

From these decisions certain conclusions relevant to the instant case arise, which are:

(1) There has not been any comprehensive or complete definition of political offence for the purposes of the law of extradition.

(2) Whilst it is possible and of assistance to identify factors which should be assessed in reaching a decision as to whether any particular offence is or is not a political

offence, it is probably neither possible nor desirable to attempt a precise or comprehensive definition. As was stated by O'Higgins CJ in *McGlinchey v Wren* the court must form an opinion on the facts of each particular case whether the offence in question can properly be described as political.

(3) Historically the purpose of the inclusion in any extradition statute, convention or treaty of an exemption for persons charged with political offences evolved from the concept of political asylum, or to put the matter in another form, is to prevent a political refugee from being unjustifiably surrendered to his political enemies.

The task of the court, therefore, in this as in all similar applications under s. 50 of the Act of 1965 is to interpret the words 'political offence' contained in that statute and to apply that interpretation to the facts as found in any particular case and the inferences raised by them.

The Act of 1965, having been passed since the coming into force of the Constitution, the first and fundamental rule which governs that interpretation is that it must be presumed that the Oireachtas intended an interpretation which will not offend any express or implied provision of the Constitution: see *McDonald v Bord na gCon* [1965] I.R. 217 and *East Donegal Co-Operative Livestock Mart Ltd v The Attorney General* [1970] I.R. 317.

The plaintiff states that he committed the offence charged for the purposes of the I.N.L.A., the aims and objectives of which are the establishment of a 32 county workers' republic by force of arms. The achievement of that objective necessarily and inevitably involves the destruction and setting aside of the Constitution by means expressly or impliedly prohibited by it: see Articles 15.6 and 39. To interpret the words 'political offence' contained in s. 50 of the Act of 1965 so as to grant immunity or protection to a person charged with an offence directly intended to further that objective would be to give to the section a patently unconstitutional construction. This Court cannot, it seems to me, interpret an Act of the Oireachtas as having the intention to grant immunity from extradition to a person charged with an offence the admitted purpose of which is to further or facilitate the overthrow by violence of the Constitution and of the organs of State established thereby.

Whilst there exists other grounds on which the plaintiff's claim may fail including those contained in the careful judgment of Gannon J in the High Court I rest my judgment on this constitutional principle. I am, therefore, satisfied that the plaintiff has not established:

(a) that the offence with which he is charged is, within the true meaning of s. 50 of the Act of 1965, a political offence;
(b) that such offence is connected with a political offence or that there are substantial grounds for believing that the request for extradition has been made for the purpose of prosecuting him for a political offence or an offence connected with a political offence.

In these cirumstances I find myself in agreement with the decision of Gannon J and would, therefore, dismiss this appeal.

Hederman J.

I agree that this appeal must be dismissed. The plaintiff has raised no question either with regard to the statutory formalities of the request or with regard to the sufficiency of the evidence to sustain the charge laid against him. The appeal turns entirely on a claim that the offence charged is either a political offence or an offence connected with a political offence within the meaning of the provisions of the Extradition Act, 1965.

The submissions addressed to this Court by both sides on this aspect of the case involve references to the decisions of this Court in three cases—*Bourke v The Attorney General* [1972] IR 36, *McGlinchey v Wren* [1982] IR 154 and *Shannon v*

Fanning [1985] I.R. 569. These cases do not, of course, exhaust the full body of case law which is relevant to the subject. *Bourke's* case, however, does draw attention to the fact that the Extradition Act, 1965 constituted Ireland's ratification of the European Convention on Extradition 1957, to which this State was a party. Both the Convention and the Act incorporate the concept of a political offence and the concept of an offence connected with a political offence. In fact *Bourke's* case was decided on the latter concept.

It is evident from the relevant case law in all common law countries at least, and in other countries with different legal systems, that the concept of 'political offences' embraces both absolute and relative political offences. Admittedly there does not appear to be in Irish law, or in any common law country, any exhaustive definition of 'political offence' in the law of extradition. Nor indeed is there any uniform international practice in extradition law. It is true that the history of extradition law shows that the exemption for persons charged with either absolute or relative political offences, or offences connected with political offences, evolved from the concept of political asylum, but the evolution of the concept of the political offence followed a consistent pattern in common law countries. In non common law countries the evolution has differed somewhat from country to country. But it is of interest to note that the European Convention on Extradition embraced one common law country, namely Ireland, several civil law countries and a number of Scandinavian countries. The United Kingdom, the only other common law country in Europe, did not ratify the Convention.

While in some circumstances it may be of assistance to identify particular factors which might be assessed in reaching a decision (as appears to be done in some civil law countries), as to whether a particular common offence is or is not a political offence, I agree with the Chief Justice that it is probably neither possible nor desirable to attempt any 'comprehensive definition'.

When faced with the question of whether any particular common offence is or is not a relative political offence the task of the court centres on the identification of the circumstances in which it could be so regarded or be regarded as an offence connected with a political offence, as indeed was stated by O'Higgins CJ in *McGlinchey v Wren* [1982] I.R. 154.

The admitted objective of the organisation referred to in the present case is by force of arms or other violent means to overthrow the Government established by the Constitution. This is clearly in violation of Article 39 of the Constitution. The law of this State, to remain in conformity with the Constitution, cannot give immunity from extradition for persons engaged in such activities. The mere fact that such organisation may seek to dignify itself by the use of the word 'army' in its title, is not, in my view, sufficient in itself to bring within the contemplation of Article 15 (6) of the Constitution. I do not say there may not be circumstances in which this type of illegal organisation might not fall within the terms of Article 15 (6), but in the present case there is no evidence whatsoever as to where the self-styled army was raised and maintained, if at all.

Because of the provisions of Article 39 of the Constitution I must hold that the plaintiff's claim to motivation for acting as he so did, takes the offence charged outside the meaning of political offence or offence connected with a political offence as set out in the Extradition Act, 1965. I also agree that it has not shown that there are substantial grounds for believing that the request for extradition has been made for the purpose of prosecuting him for a political offence or an offence connected with a political offence.

Extract 12.3

IN RE J.H. [1985] I.R. 375

The natural mother of a girl placed her for adoption, believing at the time that it was in the child's best interests. She subsequently married the child's natural father and refused to consent to the making of an adoption order in favour of the adopting parents. The latter applied to adopt the child and issued proceedings under the Adoption Acts 1952-1974 to dispense with the natural mother's consent. The natural parents applied to have the child's birth re-registered pursuant to the Legitimacy Act, 1931. They also brought proceedings under the Guardianship of Infants Act, 1964 in which they claimed custody of the child. S. 3 of that Act provides that in cases of this nature the court should regard "the welfare of the infant as the first and paramount consideration". "Welfare" is defined in s. 2 as comprising "the religious and moral, intellectual, physical and social welfare of the infant". The High Court refused to grant an order dispensing with the natural mother's consent, but granted custody to the adopting parents on the grounds that it would be in the child's best interests. Both sets of parents appealed to the Supreme Court. The Court remitted the custody issue to the High Court, but considered the interpretation of s. 3.

Finlay C.J.

The infant in the title named, who is a girl, was born on 25 September 1982 to M. C. (hereinafter called the mother) who was then unmarried. The father of the infant was M. C., also in the title named, whom I will hereinafter refer to as the father. At the time of the birth of the infant the mother and father were not married thought both were free to marry. The infant was cared for by her mother for a week after her birth in the hospital in which she was born. The mother then arranged for her to be placed in foster care. She visited her whilst in such care from time to time.

On 18 November 1982 the mother signed a consent for the placement of the infant for adoption. On 22 December 1982 the infant was placed with K. C. and A. C. (hereinafter called the adopting parents) with a view to being adopted by them. The infant has remained in the custody and care of K. C. and A. C. since that time.

In the beginning of the month of December 1983 the mother withdrew her consent to the adoption of the infant by communicating in writing to An Bord Uchtála.

On 26 March 1984 the mother and father of the infant were married. The adopting parents issued proceedings in the High Court, by special summons on 7 February 1984 seeking, *inter alia*, an order pursuant to s. 3 of the Adoption Act, 1974, authorising An Bord Uchtála to dispense with the consent of the natural mother to the making of the adoption order and seeking a further order granting custody of the infant to them pursuant to the provisions of that Act.

After compliance with the usual procedures of giving notice to the mother of the infant these proceedings came on for hearing before Lynch J and were at hearing on 6 and 7 June 1984 and on 12 July 1984. Judgment was reserved and was given by Lynch J on 10 August 1984. On 7 June 1984 in the course of the hearing the learned trial judge firstly made an order adding the father as a party to the proceedings and, secondly, made an order adding An tArd Cláraitheoir as a party and restraining him, pending the determination of those proceedings, from re-registering the birth of the infant under the provisions of the Legitimacy Act 1931.

On 10 August 1984 Lynch J made an order refusing the claim of the adopting parents for relief pusuant to the provisions of the Adoption Act, 1974 and also continuing the order restraining An tArd Cláraitheoir from re-registering the birth of the infant until after the expiration of a period of 21 days from the date of the perfection of that order. From the judgment delivered by him at that time it is clear that the grounds for this refusal, and the only grounds, were a finding that the father of the infant had not agreed to the placing of the child for adoption and that having regard to the provisions of s. 21 of the Adoption Act, 1964, and s. 3 of the Adoption Act, 1974, the court had no jurisdiction to make an order under s. 3 of the Act of 1974.

On 22 May 1984 the parents had issued a summons under the Guardianship of Infants Act, 1964, claiming custody of the infant and naming the adopting parents as the defendants. The adopting parents issued a summons on 21 June 1984 under the Guardianship of Infants Act, 1964, claiming custody of the infant. These last two proceedings were heard in the High Court on 20, 21 and 24 September 1984 and judgment was reserved. On 15 October 1984 judgment was delivered by Lynch J and custody of the infant was awarded to the adopting parents with rights of access to the parents.

By a further order, dated 17 October 1984, Lynch J continued the order restraining An tArd Cláraitheoir from re-registering the birth of the infant pending the appeal against the decision of the High Court in the summons under the Adoption Acts.

From these decisions of the High Court the adopting parents appealed against the decision refusing their application for an order under s. 3 of the Adoption Act, 1974 and the parents appealed against the order granting custody under the Act of 1964 to the adopting parents, and also against the order restraining An tArd Cláraitheoir from re-registering the birth of the child.

Issues on the Appeal

Upon the hearing of these appeals the adopting parents did not pursue their appeal against the refusal of their application under s. 3 of the Adoption Act, 1974. Whilst conceding that the consequential confirmation of the order made by Lynch J on 10 August 1984 should lead to the discharge of his order dated 17 October 1984 continuing the restriction on the re-registration of the birth of the infant, counsel on behalf of the adopting parents wished not to consent to the removal of that restriction on the grounds that it was possible in the event of the adopting parents being successful in upholding the decision of Lynch J with regard to the custody of the child made on 15 October 1974 that they could persuade the parents to abstain from re-registering the child and to give consent to its adoption.

In short, the issue which arose on the appeal by the parents against the order granting custody of the infant to the adopting parents was as to whether the learned trial judge had applied the right test having regard to the fact that they are now married; that the infant is now their legitimate daughter and has that status even before re-registration of its birth.

In the course of his judgment, on 15 October 1984, Lynch J held that the issue before him must be determined in accordance with s. 3 of the Guardianship of Infants Act, 1964, regarding the welfare of the infant as the first and paramount consideration, and that on the evidence the way in which he could give effect to that Section was by asking and answering the question: 'Is there anything really worthwhile to be gained for the child by transferring her from the adopting parents to the parents?' This question, in the course of his judgment, he answered in the negative by reason of a finding that the risk of long-term psychological harm to the infant arising from its separation from the custody and care of the adopting parents with whom it had been continuously living for almost two years at the date of his judgment was sufficiently proximate to outweigh contrary factors likely in the future to arise from its continued custody by adopting parents, such as the fact that it was the legitimate child of the parents; that they had a right to be involved in and make decisions concerning its education and that it would have Succession Act rights against its parents but not against its adopting parents. On behalf of the adopting parents it is contended that this was the correct legal test to apply and that the conclusions of facts on its application are supported by the evidence. This submission was largely based on an assertion that, in the absence of a challenge to the constitutional validity of s. 3 of the Act of 1964 when applied to the case of a legitimate child, which has not been made in this case, s. 3 must be given its clear and literal meaning. On behalf of the parents it was submitted that, having regard to the constitutional rights of the infant as a member of a family provided by Articles 41 and 42 of the Constitution, s. 3 must be construed as meaning, in the case of a legitimate child, that its welfare as defined in the Act must be deemed to be best served by being in the custody of its own parents and of its family unless it is established that there are compelling reasons why its custody should be found elsewhere. In this context reliance was placed on the fact that the family of which the infant is a member now consists not only of the parents but of a child born to them since the hearing in the High Court, who is another daughter.

The Law

In the course of the submissions before this Court, the following cases were referred to:

> *G v An Bord Uchtála* [1980] I.R. 32.
> *In re J. an Infant* [1966] I.R. 295.
> *J v C* [1970] A.C. 669.
> *J v D* Supreme Court 1977 No. 26, 22 June 1977.
> *M v An Bord Uchtála* [1977] I.R. 287.
> *In re O'Hara* [1900] 2 I.R. 232.
> *The State (Williams) v Markey* [1940] I.R. 421.
> *W v W* High Court 1976 No. 308 Sp (Ellis J) 21 April 1980.

Having considered these decisions and the relevant provisions of the Constitution I have come to the conclusion that the principles of law applicable to this case are as follows.

1. The infant being the child of married parents, now legitimised, has in addition to the rights of every child, which are provided for in the Constitution and which are identified by O'Higgins CJ in *G v An Bord Uchtála* [1980] I.R. 32, at p. 56, rights under the Constitution as a member of a family which are:

(a) to belong to a unit group possessing inalienable and imprescriptible rights antecedent and superior to all positive law (Article 41.1);

(b) to protection by the State of the family to which it belongs (Article 41.2);

(c) to be educated by the family and to be provided by its parents with religious, moral, intellectual, physical and social education (Article 42.1).

2. The State cannot supplant the role of the parents in providing for the infant the rights to be educated conferred on it by Article 42.1 except 'in exceptional cases' arising from a failure for moral or physical reasons on the part of the parents to provide that education (Article 42.5).

3. The Act of 1964 must, if possible, be given an interpretation consistent with the Constitution: *East Donegal Co-Operative Marts Ltd v Attorney General* [1970] I.R. 317; *McDonald v Bord na gCon* [1965] I.R. 217.

In the case, therefore, as this case is, of a contest between the parents of a legitimate child, who with the child constitute a family, within the meaning of Articles 41 and 42 of the Constitution, and persons other than the parents as to the custody of the child, it does not seem to me that s. 3 of the Act of 1964 can be construed as meaning simply that the balance of welfare as defined in s. 2 of the Act of 1964 must be the sole criterion for the determination by the court of the issue as to the custody of the child or, to put the matter in another way, that it is a case as would be the situation in a contest between the parents of a legitimate child as to which of them should have general custody where the court could or should determine the matter upon the basis of the preferred custody, having regard to the welfare of the child as defined in s. 2 of the Act.

A child of over two years of age, as this infant is, in the dominant or general custody of persons other than its parents and continuing in such custody against the wishes of its parents, cannot be said to enjoy the right of education by its family and parents granted by Article 42.1 of the Constitution, and no additional arrangements as were indeed put in train in this case by the orders of the High Court for access by its parents to the child or participation by them in the decision-making processes concerning its education could alter that situation. Furthermore, notwithstanding the presumption of validity which attaches to the Act of 1964 and the absence of a challenge in these proceedings to that validity, the court cannot, it seems to me, as an organ of the State supplant the right to education by the family and parents which is conferred on the child by the Constitution unless there is established to the satisfaction of the court a failure on the part of the parents as defined in Article 42.5 and 'exceptional circumstances'.

I would, therefore, accept the contention that in this case s. 3 of the Act of 1964 must be construed as involving a constitutional presumption that the welfare of the child, which is defined in s. 2 of the Act in terms identical to those contained in Article 42.1, is to be found within the family unless the court is satisfied on the evidence that there are compelling reasons why this cannot be achieved or unless the court is satisfied that the evidence establishes an exceptional case where the parents have failed to provide education for the child and to continue to fail to provide education for the child for moral or physical reasons.

This interpretation of the provisions of the Act of 1964 gains support from the decision of the High Court in the case of *In re J, an Infant* [1966] I.R. 295 and in particular from the judgment of Henchy J, then a judge of the High Court, in that case, where, at p. 308 he stated:

> Having regard to the inalienable right and duty of parents to provide for the education of their children, and their right in appropriate cases to obtain custody of the children for that purpose, I consider that s. 3 must be interpreted in one or other of the following ways: first, by regarding it as unconstitutional, or, secondly, by reading it in conjunction with Articles 41 and 42 as stating, in effect, that the welfare of the infant in the present case coincides with the parents' right to custody.

It also finds support from the conclusions of Ellis J in *W v W* High Court 1976 No. 308 Sp. 21 April 1980. In *G v An Bord Uchtála* [1980] I.R. 32 Walsh J, dealing with the provisions of s. 3 of the Act of 1964, stated at p. 76 as follows:

> The word 'paramount' by itself is not by any means an indication of exclusivity; no doubt if the Oireachtas had intended the welfare of the child to be the sole consideration it would have said so. The use of the word 'paramount' certainly indicates that the welfare of the child is to be the superior or the most important consideration, *in so far as it can be, having regard to the law or the provisions of the Constitution applicable to any given case.* (Emphasis supplied).

In *J v D* Supreme Court 1977 No. 26, 22 June 1977, the judgment of O'Higgins CJ clearly indicates that he laid it down that a consideration of the welfare of the child, as defined in s. 3 of the Act of 1964, was a sufficient reason to refuse custody to the father who was the sole surviving parent of the children concerned. The judgment also contains specific findings that the father had been guilty of conduct which, having regard to the provisions of ss. 14 and 16 of the Act of 1964 would in any event have disentitled him to custody. Such findings go close to equating with a finding, though the matter is not dealt with in the judgment, of an exceptional case where, for moral or physical reasons, the parent has failed in his or her duty to provide for the education of the child and in which the State can accordingly intervene to provide for that care and education by other means. Insofar, however, as that judgment may be construed as clearly indicating that in the case of legitimate children, paramount consideration of their welfare as defined in the Act of 1964 can be applied as the sole test without regard to the provisions of Articles 41 and 42 of the Constitution, I must, respectfully, refuse to follow it.

Having regard to my view of the appropriate principles to be applied, namely, that the test of compelling reasons why the welfare of the child cannot be secured to it in the family unit and by the parents was not applied by the learned trial judge in the court below and was not present to his mind in the careful judgment which he delivered, I consider that notwithstanding the litigation that has already occurred and the importance from the point of view of all the parties, including the infant, of a speedy and final determination of its future, the case should be remitted to Lynch J in the High Court, further to be considered by him either on the evidence as its exists or on such further evidence as he may consider material in accordance with this test. I would, therefore, allow the appeal of the parents and direct the further trial of this issue before Lynch J in the High Court.

I would dismiss the appeal of the adopting parents against the order refusing them relief under s. 3 of the Adoption Act, 1974 which was not pursued by them in this Court, and having regard to that decision I am satisfied that the order restricting the re-registration of the birth of the child must be set aside.

Extract 12.4

JORDAN v O'BRIEN [1960] I.R. 363

The Rent Restrictions Act, 1946 provided for a scheme by which certain tenants were guaranteed security of tenure and their rents were controlled accordingly. S. 39 of the Act allowed members of a deceased tenant's "family", who resided with him at the time of his death, to retain possession of the premises. The question in this case was whether a sister of the deceased was a member of his "family". In Article 41 of the Constitution the term "family" is confined to parents and children. In an earlier case, *McCombe v Sheehan* [1954] I.R. 183, Murnaghan J. held that "family" should bear the same meaning in both the Act and the Constitution. In the instant case the issue was stated for the opinion of the Supreme Court. In holding that "family" in the Act bore a wider meaning than the same expression in Constitution, the Court pointed to the different purposes of the Act and the Constitution. Although the Rent Restrictions Acts were subsequently held to be unconstitutional in *Blake v Attorney General* [1982] I.R. 117 because they infringed owners' property rights, the case is of interest as it demonstrates that a word in a statute is not necessarily limited to the meaning which is attributed to it in the Constitution.

Lavery J.

This is a case stated by Mr. Justice Murnaghan for the opinion of this Court under s. 38, sub-s. 3, of the Courts of Justice Act, 1936.

The action was by ejectment civil bill on the title to recover possession of premises, no. 14 William Street, Galway. The facts are found in the Case. They need not be stated at length. It is sufficient to set out that Michael J. O'Brien was the contractual tenant under a tenacy agreement made on the 23rd May, 1903, and that by virtue of a notice to quit served in 1942 his contractual tenancy was determined and he became, and continued till his death on the 15th April, 1952, a statutory tenant.

The defendant, his sister, claims to be his successor as statutory tenant by virtue of s. 39, sub-s. 3, of the Rent Restrictions Act, 1946.

The house has been for at least 50 years what may be called, without pre-judging the issue, the family home of the mother, brothers and sisters of the deceased statutory tenant, who respectively lived with him until, in the case of the mother, her death in 1907, and in the case of the brothers and sister, other than the defendant, till they left the home to embark on their several careers, leaving the statutory tenant and his siter, the defendant, alone in the premises. This history of the family and their tenancy of the property is not, I think, irrelevant to the answer to be given to the question posed in the Case.

This question is:—Whether on these findings of fact the defendant is entitled to retain possession of the premises upon the death of the statutory tenant, Michael J. O'Brien, her brother, by virtue of the provisions of s. 39, sub-s. 3 of the Rent Restrictions Act, 1946? Sect. 39, sub-s. 3, provides that on the death of the statutory tenant of controlled premises—I summarise—leaving a wife him surviving who was residing with him at the time of his death she shall be entitled to retain possesion under the same terms and conditions (sub-clause (*a*)); if leaving no wife so residing such member of the statutory tenant's family so residing, or, where more than one such, such one as may be agreed upon or selected by the Court in default of agreement shall be entitled to retain possession as aforesaid (sub-clause (*b*)).

If the statutory tenant was a woman the same provisions are to have effect with respect to husband and family as to a wife and family of a statutory tenant being a man.

Otherwise the interest of the statutory tenant shall determine (sub-clause (*d*)).

The issue in the present case is therefore whether the defendant is a member of the statutory tenant's family residing with him at the time of his death. The condition as to residence is satisfied and is not in controversy.

Mr. Kenny for the landlords submits that the word, "family," includes only children or grandchildren and, perhaps, adopted children—either legally or informally adopted. It is unnecessary to consider anything more than the broad proposition that brothers and sisters are not included. It does not arise for decision whether nephews or nieces by blood or marriage, cousins or other remoter relatives, or even parents, are capable of being admitted as members of the family.

Mr. Justice Murnaghan in *McCombe and Another* v. *Sheehan and Another* [1954] I.R. 183 decided that the word, "family," had the narrow meaning—said to be the primary meaning—contended for by Mr. Kenny. That case can be distinguished from the present as the relationship of the claimant to the deceased statutory tenant was that of niece by marriage but the learned Judge based his decision on the general principle and naturally, therefore, he felt that in this case he should follow his own decision, but being asked to state a case for this Court he has done so.

In giving judgment in *McCombe's Case* the learned Judge said he was unable to adopt the meaning given to the word, "family," in a series of English decisions because—I summarise—Article 41 of the Constitution, undoubtedly, in his opinion, attributed to the word the meaning, parents and children. He held that where a word is used in a statute such word, unless the contrary intention appears, must bear the same meaning as it does when used in the Constitution.

I will accept, without deciding, that the word as used in the Constitution does mean parents and children and does not include other relationships. Certainly the Constitution has primarily in mind the natural unit of society—parents and children—which it protects.

I mention in passing—without expressing any opinion thereon—that the word might well include—and the protection be afforded to—a family where the children were adopted either legally or informally, or even to a unit where both parents being dead an elder brother and sister undertake the care, maintenance and education of younger members of the "family"—a situation not at all uncommon.

However, in my opinion it is sufficient to say that the purpose of the Constitution in this Article and in Article 42 is wholly different from the purpose of s. 39 and the sections of the earlier Acts which it replaces and I do not find the ground of the decision of the learned Judge convincing though it has some force. There are several decisions of Mr. Justice Shannon, President of the Circuit Court, in which he accorded the benefit of the section to successors other than children and one at least in which he recognised that a sister could succeed (*Healy and the Provincial Bank of*

Ireland Ltd. v. *Armstrong* [1949] Ir. Jur. Rep. 18 and I myself, rightly or wrongly, in an unreported case admitted a cousin as successor (*Margaret Murphy* v. *John and Kathleen O'Keeffe*, 21 March, 1952, at Cork). Mr. Justice Black, in a case of *O'Sullivan and Sons* v. *O'Mahony* [1953] I.R. 125, accepted that a niece was a member of the family. In none of these cases was what may be called the constitutional point raised. But there are also several English cases—as Mr. Justice Murnaghan has recognised—which give a less restricted meaning to the word than parents and children and the legislation in Great Britain is for all material purposes indistinguishable from ours. Notably, there is the case of *Price* v. *Gould and others* (1930) 143 L.T. 333, where Wright J. admitted a family relationship of brother and sister for the purpose of succession. This case was decided in 1929 and has never been dissented from and appears to have been approved by the Court of Appeal in *Langdon* v. *Horton* [1951] 1 K.B. 666 by at least one member of the Court, Lord Justice Singleton.

These cases are not of binding authority on any Court in this country but where one finds parallel legislation, over a number of years, obviously they afford a valuable guide as to the intention of the Legislature when enacting the statute of 1946, presumably with knowledge of the existing law both in Great Britain and in this country.

But the provision in question was not new in 1946. The Increase of Rent and Mortgage Interest (Restrictions) Act, 1920, s. 12, has a similar provision. I need not quote it. This Act applied to Ireland but as Dail Eireann had repudiated the jurisdiction of the British Parliament it was at pains to enact a Decree on the 11th March, 1921—the Increase of Rent and Mortgage Interst (Restrictions) Decree, 1921, which contains a similar provision, viz., clause 12(1)(*g*).

The Increase of Rent and Mortgage Interest (Restrictions) Act, 1923, has a similar provision. All these Acts preceded the enactment of the Constitution and the argument apparently is that words which had been used in a series of Acts *in pari materia* are to be given a different meaning because of the sense in which it is said they are used in the Constitution. I ask myself can it be said that the Constitution of 1937 effected an alteration of the Act of 1923 which remained in force till 1946.

Sect. 39, sub-s. 3, makes provision specifically for the case of a wife or husband. It is unnecessary therefore to consider these cases as coming under sub-clause (*b*). This means that on the submission made, this clause only applies to children. If that were so the word, "child," or "children" or, perhaps, "issue" would most certainly have been used. Mr. Kenny drew attention to certain differences between the Act of 1946 and the earlier Acts. He mentioned 1, the husband of a deceased statutory tenant being a woman is now provided for as the wife of a statutory tenant being a man was previously. Before this Act the husband in such a case could only come in as a member of the family. Now he is given a paramount claim;

2, Mr. Kenny says there now is an emphasis on "the linking of the spouses" and their children;

3, He says that it having been decided in *Pain* v. *Cobbe and others* (1931) 146 L.T. 12 in England that there could be only one succession, a decision followed by Mr. Justice Shannon and other judges, the Act of 1946 permits a series of successions; and

4, Finally, he refers to the structure of the section.

I recognise these differences but I cannot see how any of them bear on the question of construction before us.

As I have said I have only to consider the relationship of brother and sister. In the circumstances of this case I think that the defendant and her deceased brother were members of a family and that that family was his family. The position would, I think, be the same if the sister had been the statutory tenant and had died leaving her brother. Other relationships, I am inclined to think, might come within the meaning of the word in certain circumstances but we cannot now decide that.

I do not think that every brother and sister, even residing together, must necessarily come within the section. For example, if a statutory tenant were an inn-keeper and a brother or sister had rooms in the house for which they paid the usual charges it might be that they might not be considered to be residing with the statutory tenant. I mention this only so as to make it clear that I do not intend to lay down a universal rule. A joint home between unmarried brother and sister is very usual in this country and I would answer the question put in the case, "Yes."

I would like to say that the Court got every assistance from counsel and also to refer to a most informative article in 90 I. L. T. and S. J. 217, entitled:—"When a Tenant Dies . . ."

Kingsmill Moore J.

This Case Stated raises a net question on which there have been conflicting decisions. Is the sister of a deceased statutory tenant a "member of the statutory tenant's family" within the meaning of those words as used in s. 39, sub-s. 3 (*b*), of the Rent Restrictions Act, 1946? The plaintiffs in the suit are landlords who have issued an ejectment on the title to recover premises which were occupied by the late Michael J. O'Brien as a statuory tenant at the date of his death in April, 1952. The defendant is the sister of Michael O'Brien who was resident with him at the date of his death, and she claims to retain possession by virtue of the provisions of s. 39, sub-s. 3, of the Act of 1946. The relevant portions of the sub-section are as follows:—

"On the death of the statutory tenant of controlled premises the following provisions shall have effect:—

"(*a*) in case the statutory tenant leaves him surviving his wife, who was residing with him at the time of his death, she shall be entitled to retain possession of the premises under the same terms and conditions as the deceased statutory tenant;

"(*b*) in case the statutory tenant does not leave a wife so residing, such member of the statutory tenant's family so residing or, where there is more than one such member, such one of them as may be agreed upon between them or as may be selected by the Court in default of agreement shall be entitled to retain possession as aforesaid;

"(*c*) in case the statutory tenant was a woman paragraphs (*a*) and (*b*) of this sub-section shall have effect with respect to her husband and family as they have effect with respect to the wife and family of a statutory tenant being a man."

Somewhat similar provisions were contained in s. 1(*b*) of the Increase of Rent and Mortgage Interest (Restrictions) Act, 1923, where it is enacted that "the expression 'tenant' includes the widow of a tenant dying intestate who was residing with him at the time of his death, or, where a tenant dying intestate leaves no widow or is a woman, such member of the tenant's family so residing as aforesaid as may be decided in default of agreement by the Court."

Identical provisions to those in the 1923 Act are to be found in s. 12, sub-s. 1(*g*), of the British Increase of Rent and Mortgage Interest (Restrictions) Act, 1920, which was law in Ireland until the passing of the 1923 Act.

The object of all three Acts was to preserve the possession of the spouse or a member of the family of a deceased tenant living with the tenant at the date of death, though the two earlier Acts gave protection where the tenant was a con-tractual or a statutory tenant, and the 1946 Act confined the protection to cases where the tenant ws a statutory tenant. What is common to all three is that the privilege of retaining possession is given to the spouse or "member of the tenant's family residing with him at the time of his death." In this respect the statutes are "*in pari materia.*"

There is no definition of family, a word which has a variety of meanings. It is used in a narrow sense to denote children, e.g., "Have you a family?," in a wider sense to denote ascendants and descendants in a direct line, and in a still wider sense to in-clude collaterals. It may also include adopted children and relations by marriage. It may even include the servants of the household. Among those various possible meanings the courts have had to pick their way and the decisions have not been uniform. In *McCombe and Another* v. *Sheehan and Another* [1954] I.R. 153 Mr. Justice Murnaghan held that "family" included only parents and children, while in *Murphy* v. *O'Keeffe* (unreported) Mr. Justice Lavery held that a third cousin was included. In *Butler* v. *McCormick* 63 I.L.T.R. 176 a grandchild was held to be included and in *O'Byrne* v. *Byrne* 72 I.L.T.R. 65 Mr. Justice Shannon was apparently prepared to include a niece, if he had been satisfied that she was resident with the deceased tenant at the time of his death. In *Toomey* v. *Murphy* [1949] Ir. Jur. Rep. 17 Mr. Justice Murnaghan held there must be some blood relationship, while on the same day in *Brock* v. *Wollams* [1949] 2 K.B. 388 an English Court decided that persons *in loco filii* were entitled to be regarded as "members of the tenant's family." At the date of the passing of the Act there was an express English decision to the effect that brothers and sisters were included in the words, "members of the tenant's family": *Price* v. *Gould and others* (1930) 143 L.T. 333. I think that the framers of the Act must be assumed to have been familiar with this decision, and other decisions such as *The Workingman's Benefit Building Society* v. *Flanagan* [1939] Ir. Jur. Rep. 90 and *Tandy* v. *Bamford* (1928 Estates Digest 216) which did not confine the meaning of "members of the tenant's family" to "children" but included nieces and nephews. If they desired to confine the right of retaining possession to spouses, parents and children nothing was easier than to say so in clear terms. Instead the wide and vague expression, "members of the tenant's family," is retained. To my mind it must have been intended to include in that expression relations other than parents and children. What may be the perimeter of such extension it is not necessary now to decide. It may be wide enough to include third cousins as Mr. Justice Lavery thought, or so limited as to exclude first cousins, which was the view expressed in *Langdon* v. *Horton* [1951] 1 K.B. 666. It may, or may not, include relations-in-law and persons *in loco filii*. But if we are to include anyone other than parents and children, as I think is clearly intended, we must admit the next closest relation, that of brothers and sisters.

It seems to me that Mr. Justice Murnaghan may have been correct in saying, as he did in *McCombe's Case*, that "family" in Article 41 of the Constitution means "parents and children": but where a word has a number of recognised meanings the use of it in one such meaning in the Constitution does not seem to me to warrant any presumption that the same meaning is to be given to it in a statute which is not *in pari materia*.

In my opinion the defendant is entitled to retain possession of the premises as being one of the family of the statutory tenant residing with him at the date of his death.

THE CANONS OF INTERPRETATION

As stated earlier, the task of the courts when interpreting statutes is to give effect to the "intention of the legislature", which is discovered in the words used by the legislature in the statute. Canons of interpretation, which outline general approaches to be adopted, are employed by the courts in the exercise of that task. The principal canon was outlined by Henchy J. in *Inspector of Taxes v Kiernan* [1981] I.R. 138 (Extract 12.5). It is that the words be given their ordinary, or where appropriate their technical, meaning taking account of the context in which they appear. It is to this canon that the courts have first recourse and it can be considered to be a modern statement of the literal rule. In this respect, as was explained in *McGrath v McDermott* [1988] I.R. 258 (Extract 12.6), the courts may not add words to the statute, even where to do so would result in a more equitable interpretation, since that would amount an invasion of the legislative domain. It is important to note that, while the court concentrates on the ordinary or literal meaning of the particular provision, the word or phrase in question is not viewed in isolation. The context in which it appears has a bearing on the meaning to be attributed to it. In this respect the nature of the legislation and its subject matter can be relevant to the manner in which it is interpreted. Reference was made earlier to s. 15(1) of the Misuse of Drugs Act, 1977 where it was stated that the defences of infancy and insanity would apply. That is not expressed in the Act, which is silent on the matter, but those defences apply by virtue of the general principles of criminal responsibility which were developed at common law. Unless the contrary is stated or is suggested by its context, penal statutes are interpreted in a manner which is consistent with those general principles. Thus, the phrase "any person" will be interpreted to exclude children under the age of seven and lunatics. The point is that although the Act is silent on the issue, the fact that it is a penal statute leads to that interpretation. The literal approach has a special application in two instances. The first is where the words are legal terms of art, in which case they bear that meaning rather than their ordinary colloquial meaning—see *Minister for Industry and Commerce v Pim Brothers Ltd.* [1966] I.R. 154 (Extract 12.7). The second is where the statute is directed to a particular class, rather than the public at large, in which case the words are attributed the meaning which would be understood by that class—see *Minister for Industry and Commerce v Hammond Lane Metal Co. Ltd.* [1947] Ir. Jur. Rep. 59 (Extract 12.8)

Where the application of the literal approach leads to an "absurdity" the courts have recourse to alternative approaches. Where an absurdity would arise the courts reject the literal interpretation and attribute to the words a secondary, modified meaning which they are capable of bearing. In the past, those approaches were known as the golden rule, where the provision was looked at in its wider statutory context, and the mischief rule, where the perceived defect of the pre-existing common law was examined. In the last decade or so the courts have avoided using those terms, preferring to invoke what is called a schematic or teleological approach, the classic articulations of which are to be found in the judgments of Henchy J. in *Nestor v Murphy* [1979] I.R. 326 (Extract 12.10) and Murphy J. in *Lawlor v Minister for Agriculture* [1988] I.L.R.M. 400 (Extract 12.11). In the latter case Murphy J. indicated a willingness to adopt this approach when interpreting domestic legislation which is based on obligations imposed by European Community law. This stance was also adopted, in somewhat different circumstances, in *Murphy v Bord Telecom Eireann* [1989] I.L.R.M. 53 (Extract 12.15). When the schematic approach is invoked a court examines the general purpose and scheme of the statute. In ascertaining the statutory purpose the court may examine the long title to the Act, its subject matter and the pre-existing law which it was designed to alter—see *Minister for Industry and Commerce v Hales* [1967] I.R. 50 (Extract 12.9), *Charles McCann Ltd. v Ó Cúlachain* [1986] I.R. 197 (Extract 12.13), *Weekes v Revenue Commissioners* [1989] I.L.R.M. 165 (Extract 12.14). Once the statutory purpose is identified the provision in question is interpreted in a manner which is consistent with it and which avoids the absurdity. In this respect, the courts, in effect, read words into the provision. Thus, in *Frescati Estates Ltd. v Walker* [1975] I.R. 177 (Extract 12.16) the word "applicant", in the Local Government (Planning and Development) Act, 1963, was interpreted to refer to a person who applies with the consent of the owner, despite the Act's being silent on the question of owners' consent.

The invocation of the schematic approach is premised on the court's having concluded that an absurdity would result from the literal interpretation. But there is no clear or concrete definition of what constitutes an absurdity. Various broadly synonymous expressions which are employed by the courts to justify the adoption of a non-literal meaning are little more definite. The schematic approach is adopted where the literal meaning is said to be repugnant, to render the statute unworkable or meaningless or to be grossly unreasonable. On the other hand, the mere fact that the literal meaning would lead to an unfair, unreasonable or inequitable result is insufficient to warrant its rejection. Something more is required and an absurdity is considered to arise where the literal interpretation leads to a conclusion which, it is thought, could not have been intended by the Oireachtas. It is this factor, the failure to give effect to the assumed intention of the Oireachtas, which justifies the invocation of the schematic approach. Thus, whilst ordinarily the modification by the courts of statutory language is considered to be a usurpation of the legislative function, such modification is permissible where it is done to implement the "true" or "real" intention of the Oireachtas. Nevertheless, the identification of an absurdity leaves an element of discretion to the courts and, to this extent, they are in the position of exercising choice. What to one court is considered to be absurd might not be so viewed by another. For instance, in *Rafferty v Crowley* [1984] I.L.R.M. 350 (Extract 12.12) Murphy J. refused to adopt the schematic approach and read an exception into the definition of "prior mortgage" in the Building Societies Act, 1976 on the grounds that if the Oireachtas intended to create that exception it could easily have done so. But the same reasoning could have been adopted by the Supreme Court in *Nestor v Murphy* [1979] I.R. 326 (Extract 12.10) where it invoked the schematic approach and exempted certain conveyances from the prior written consent requirement of the Family Home (Protection) Act, 1976—if the Oireachtas wished to exempt those conveyances it could easily have done so. The point is that the element of choice which is left to the courts could have led to both those cases having been decided the other way. To this extent, the interpretation of legislation, despite its purpose being to give effect to the legislative expression of choice, possesses a creative dimension not unlike the position which pertains in respect of common law decision making. Ultimately the decision to prefer one approach to the other is a matter of choice which is based on the judicial perception of the legislative intention which motivated the statute.

In some instances legislation might have been preceded by earlier legislaiton on the same point. If the words in the earlier legislation have been repeated in the later, that can lead the court to conclude that no change in the law was envisaged by the Oireachtas. If a change in the law was desired it could be expected that different language would have been used. Thus, decisions on the meaning of a particular word in one statute can determine the meaning to be attributed to the same word when used in a later statute in a similar context. But the statutory context must be similar, a point made by Henchy J. in *The State (Sheehan) v The Government of Ireland* [1987] I.R. 550, 562 where he stated that ". . . in construing a particular statutory provision no provision of another statute may be used as an aid or a guide unelss that other statutory provision is in *pari materia,* that is forming part of the same statutory context." Thus, in *Mogul of Ireland Ltd. v Tipperary (North Riding) County Council* [1976] I.R. 260 (Extract 12.17) s. 1 of the Malicious Injuries (Ireland) Act, 1853 was interpreted in the light of s. 135 of the Grand Jury (Ireland) Act, 1836 as both form part of the same legislative scheme. Reference was made earlier to consolidating and codifying legislation. It is presumed that a consolidating statute is not intended to change the law and, thus, is interpreted accordingly. No such presumption applies in respect of codifying legislation. Finally, it should be noted that a decision on the interpretation of a particular provision is binding. The application of *stare decisis* to statutory interpretation was considered by the Supreme Court in *Mogul of Ireland Ltd. v Tipperary (North Riding) County Council* [1976] I.R. 260.

Extract 12.5

INSPECTOR OF TAXES v KIERNAN [1981] I.R. 117

During a particular tax year the respondent, Kiernan, engaged in intensive pig production on his land by buying, fattening and selling the animals. He was assessed for income tax under the provisions of s. 78 of the Income Tax Act, 1967 which applied to an occupier of land who was a "dealer in cattle". The effect of that assessment was to make him liable for a greater amount of tax than he would otherwise pay. The issue was whether "cattle" includes pigs. The Circuit Court held in the affirmative. A case was stated for the opinion of the High Court which held that pigs were not "cattle". The Inspector of Taxes appealed to the Supreme Court.

Henchy J.
    The respondent taxpayer was assessed for income tax for the years 1965-6 and 1966-7 under r. 4 of Case III in schedule D of the Income Tax Act, 1918; and for the year 1967-8 under s. 78 of the Income Tax Act, 1967. Those two statutory provisions are not materially different. For either or both of them to apply to the respondent, it would be necessary to show that in the years in question he was "a dealer in cattle or a dealer in or a seller of milk." The inspector of taxes held that the respondent was "a dealer in cattle" because his principal farming activity on a holding of 27 acres was intensive pig production. In fact, when the appeal from the inspector's assessment came before the Circuit Court in November, 1969, it was found that the taxpayer kept an average of 2,000 to 2,500 pigs on this small farm. He bred no pigs on the land. He simply bought them, fattened them and sold them. It was on that basis that the inspector assessed the respondent for the years in question as "a dealer in cattle."
    The respondent's appeal against the assessments was heard in the Circuit Court in November, 1969, when the Circuit Court judge affirmed the assessments, having held that the word "cattle" included pigs and that the respondent was "a dealer in cattle." Being dissatisfied with that ruling, the respondent required the Circuit Court judge to state and sign a Case for the opinion of the High Court . . .
    . . . In the High Court Mr. Justice McWilliam ruled, *inter alia,* that "cattle" did not include pigs. If that ruling is correct, it renders the other questions in the Case Stated redundant. Therefore, I shall address myself in the first place to that ruling.
    There is no doubt that, at certain stages of English usage and in certain statutory contexts, the word "cattle" is wide enough in its express or implied significance to include pigs. That fact, however, does not lead us to a solution of the essential

question before us. When the legislature used the word "cattle" in the Act of 1918 and again in the Act of 1967, without in either case giving it a definition, was it intended that the word should comprehend pigs? That the word has, or has been held to have, that breadth of meaning in other statutes is not to the point. A word or expression in a given statute must be given meaning and scope according to its immediate context, in line with the scheme and purpose of the particular statutory pattern as a whole, and to an extent that will truly effectuate the particular legislation or a particular definition therein. For example, s. 1 of the Towns Improvement (Ireland) Act, 1854, defines the word "cattle" as including "horse, mare, gelding, foal, colt, filly, bull, cow, heifer, ox, calf, ass, mule, ram, ewe, wether, lamb, goat, kid, or swine." Unlike such an instance, the question posed here is whether the word "cattle" includes pigs in a taxing Act where the word is left undefined.

Leaving aside any judicial decision on the point, I would approach the matter by the application of three basic rules of statutory interpretation. First, if the statutory provision is one directed to the public at large, rather than to a particular class who may be expected to use the word or expression in question in either a narrowed or an extended connotation, or as a term of art, then, in the absence of internal evidence suggesting the contrary, the word or expression should be given its ordinary or colloquial meaning. As Lord Esher M.R. put it in *Unwin* v. *Hanson* [1891] 2 Q.B. 115 at p. 119 of the report:—

> If the Act is directed to dealing with matters affecting everybody generally, the words used have the meaning attached to them in the common and ordinary use of language. If the Act is one passed with reference to a particular trade, business, or transaction, and words are used which everybody conversant with that trade, business, or transaction, knows and understands to have a particular meaning in it, then the words are to be construed as having that particular meaning, though it may differ from the common or ordinary meaning of the words.

The statutory provisions we are concerned with here are plainly addressed to the public generally, rather than to a selected section thereof who might be expected to use words in a specialised sense. Accordingly, the word "cattle" should be given the meaning which an ordinary member of the public would intend it to have when using it ordinarily.

Secondly, if a word or expression is used in a statute creating a penal or taxation liability, and there is looseness or ambiguity attaching to it, the word should be construed strictly so as to prevent a fresh imposition of liability from being created unfairly by the use of oblique or slack language: see Lord Esher M.R. in *Tuck & Sons* v. *Preister* (1887) 19 Q.B.D. 629 (at p. 638); Lord Reid in *Director of Public Prosecutions* v. *Ottewell* [1970] A.C. 642 (at p. 649) and Lord Denning M.R. in *Farrell* v. *Alexander* [1975] 3 W.L.R. 642 (at pp. 650-1). As used in the statutory provisions in question here, the word "cattle" calls for such a strict construction.

Thirdly, when the word which requires to be given its natural and ordinary meaning is a simple word which has a widespread and unambiguous currency, the judge construing it should draw primarily on his own experience of its use. Dictionaries or other literary sources should be looked at only when alternative meanings, regional usages or other obliquities are shown to cast doubt on the singularity of its ordinary meaning, or when there are grounds for suggesting that the meaning of the word has changed since the statute in question was passed. In regard to "cattle", which is an ordinary and widely used word, one's experience is that in its modern usage the word, as it would fall from the lips of the man in the street, would be intended to mean and would be taken to mean no more that bovine animals. To the ordinary person, cattle, sheep and pigs are distinct forms of livestock.

It was submitted on behalf of the appellant that it should be borne in mind that the Act of 1967 is a consolidating Act and that the Act of 1918 is also a consolidating

Act which incorporated, *inter alia*, the Income Tax Act, 1842, which contained an almost identical provision for persons who were dealers in "cattle." Accordingly, it was contended, the prevalent meaning of the word in 1842 is the meaning that should be applied for the purposes of the Acts of 1918 and 1967, and it was submitted that there were grounds for believing that at that time the word had a wider usage and meaning which would comprehend pigs. However, as has been pointed out by Mr. Justice McWilliam in his judgment in the High Court, a consideration of the definition of the word "cattle" contained in the edition of the Oxford Dictionary published at the end of the 19th century clearly confirms the meaning as restricted to bovine animals. Therefore, I would so construe it in the context in question here.

Reliance was also placed on behalf of the appellant on the decision of Atkinson J. in *Phillips (Inspector of Taxes)* v. *Bourne* [1947] K.B. 533 who there held that the word "cattle" in the Act of 1918 included pigs. It was submitted that that decision was a precedent which should be followed by this Court in interpreting the provisions of the Act of 1918 and those of the Act of 1967; it was also contended that the Court should hold that, in enacting the Act of 1967, the legislature endorsed the meaning given to the word "cattle" in that decision.

Any principle to the effect that, in interpreting a statute, a court should presume that the legislature when enacting it was aware of, and was endorsing, judicial decisions concerning previous statutory use of the same expression in the same context is subject to considerable qualification: see *R.* v. *Bow Road Justices* [1968] 2 Q.B. 572 where Lord Denning M.R. (at p. 579) quotes from what he said in *Royal Court Derby Porcelain Co. Ltd.* v. *Russell* [1949] 2 K.B. 417 at p. 429 of that report:

> I do not believe that whenever Parliament re-enacts a provision of a statute it thereby gives statutory authority to every erroneous interpretation which has been put upon it. The true view is that the court will be slow to overrule a previous decision on the interpretation of a statute when it has long been acted on, and it will be more than usually slow to do so when Parliament has, since the decision, re-enacted the statute in the same terms. But if a decision is, in fact, shown to be erroneous, there is no rule of law which prevents it being overruled.

In my respectful opinion, *Phillips (Inspector of Taxes)* v. *Bourne* was wrongly decided. I have not been able to discover any reported case in England or in Ireland in which it was approved or followed. As Atkinson J. himself indicated in the judgment, he reached his decision by relying heavily on the wide meaning that had been attributed by the courts to the word "cattle" in other statutes but, as I have pointed out, that is not a reliable approach to the specific problem of interpretation that he was confronted with. The scope of a word in one statute may be no guide to the true meaning of that word in another statute.

I would answer the first question in the Case Stated by ruling, as did Mr. Justice McWilliam, that "cattle" in the relevant statutory provisions does not include pigs. Regardless, therefore, of the scope of the word "dealer," the respondent taxpayer was not "a dealer in cattle." The remaining questions in the Case Stated are thereby rendered otiose, so I would reserve a reply to them for a case in which such further questions require to be answered.

Extract 12.6

McGRATH v McDERMOTT [1988] I.R. 258

Taxpayers entered into a series of transactions which involved the purchase and disposal of shares in certain companies. The purpose of the transactions was to enable the taxpayers to become "connected" with the companies so that they could claim allowable losses under the Capital Gains Tax Act, 1975. While the transactions were not "shams", their sole purpose was tax avoidance and no real losses were incurred by the tax-payers. It was argued that the transactions should be regarded as "fiscal nullities" and should be disregarded for tax purposes. In rejecting that argument the Supreme Court adopted a literal reading of the Act and refused to read words into it. Henchy, Griffin and Hederman JJ. concurred in Finlay C.J.'s judgment while McCarthy J. delivered a separate concurring judgment. Subsequent to this decision s. 86 of the Finance Act, 1989 has introduced anti-avoidance provisions.

Finlay C.J.

This is an appeal by the Inspector of Taxes from the order dated 31 July 1987 made by Carroll J on a case stated to the High Court by the Commissioners for the special purposes of the Income Tax Acts. By that order it was adjudged that the Appeal Commissioners were wrong in law in determining that the respondents herein ('the taxpayers') were not entitled to an allowable loss as claimed for capital gains tax purposes in respect of gains assessed for the year 1981/1982.

As appears from the case stated, each of the taxpayers had in the year 1981/1982 entered into a series of transactions which were identical as a scheme, although the amounts involved differed, and it was agreed that the decision in law in one case accordingly ruled all three cases. The case of the first-named taxpayer was chosen to be the subject matter of the individual findings in the case stated. Those relevant to the issues arising on this appeal may thus be summarised:

(1) The series of transactions was avowedly a tax avoidance scheme and had no other purpose;

(2) The steps taken were real as distinct from sham transactions;

(3) The scheme which is fully set out in the case stated involved:

   (a) the purchase for £110 sterling from Caversham Trustees Ltd of 110 preference shares in Parapet Holdings Ltd, which purchase made the taxpayer connected for tax purposes with that company;

   (b) the purchase from that company for £900 sterling of the entire issued ordinary share capital of a company named Garfish Investments Ltd, which shares were subject to an option to purchase in favour of the holders of the preference shares in Parapet Holdings Ltd;

   (c) the sale of these shares in Garfish Investments Ltd at their true market value of £900 sterling to a company named London Law Securities Trustees Ltd;

   (d) the sale of the preference shares in Parapet Holdings Ltd at their true market value of £110 sterling to London Law Securities Trustees Ltd.

(4) The taxpayer had no connection with Caversham Trustees Ltd or London Law Securities Trustees Ltd other than that arising in connection with these transactions.

(5) Having regard to the assets and liabilities situation of Garfish Investments Ltd at the time of the purchase of the shares in it, if the provisions of s. 12 and s. 33 of the Capital Gains Tax Act, 1975 ('the 1975 Act') are applicable to these transactions, there was an allowable loss calculated in accordance with s. 33(5) of that Act in the sum of IR £1,341,484. The expenses for legal and financial advice which were paid before the purchase of the shares exceeded the sum of £1,010 sterling paid in total for the shares.

In the course of their decision leading to the stating of the case the Appeal Commissioners found that the Revenue were unable to show that this scheme had not been effectively carried through and that it did not achieve its purpose. They further decided that it should be disregarded taxwise as totally artificial and fiscally a nullity producing neither a gain nor a loss.

Carroll J in her reserved judgment held that the so-called doctrine of 'fiscal nullity' was not part of Irish law and that on the facts of this case the court should not intervene to render inapplicable the statutory provisions which on their face appear to apply to these transactions on the basis, as was contended, of the absence of a 'real loss'. With that decision, and the reasoning by which it was reached, I find myself in full agreement.

The statutory provisions

The relevant provisions of the Act of 1975 are as follows:

> Except as otherwise expressly provided, the amount of a loss accruing on a disposal of an asset shall be computed in the same way as the amount of a gain accruing on a disposal is computed. (s. 12(1))

> This section shall apply where a person acquires an asset and the person making the disposal is connected with him (s. 33(1))

> In a case where the asset mentioned in subsection (1) is subject to any right or restriction enforceable by the person making the disposal, or by a person connected with him, then (the amount of the consideration for the acquisition being, in accordance with subsection (2), deemed to be equal to the market value of the asset) that market value shall be—(a) what its market value would be if not subject to the right or restriction, as reduced by—(b) the market value of the right or restriction or the amount by which its extinction would enhance the value of the asset to its owner, whichever is the less:

> Provided that if the right or restriction—
> (i) is of a nature that its enforcement would or might effectively destroy or substantially impair the value of the asset without bringing any countervailing advantage either to the person making the disposal or a person connected with him,
> (ii) is an option or other right to acquire the asset, or
> (iii) in the case of incorporeal property, is a right to extinguish the asset in the hands of the person giving the consideration by forfeiture or merger or otherwise,
> that market value of the asset shall be determined, and the amount of the gain accruing on the disposal shall be computed, as if the right or restriction did not exist. (s. 33(5))

The market value of an asset coming within the provisions of s. 33(5)(ii) is not its true or real market value but one artificially calculated by ignoring the existence of a restriction or right as defined. The amount of the gain accruing on the disposal of such an asset is computed at a figure which is artificial and may not coincide with the real or any gain. There being no express provision to the contrary contained either in the Act of 1975 or in any other statute, the amount of loss accruing on the disposal of an asset coming within the provisions of s. 33(5) of the Act of 1975 is similarly to be computed at a figure which is artificial and may not coincide with the real or any loss.

In my view these consequences follow the plain and unambiguous meaning of the statutory provisions which I have quoted.

It is, however, contended on behalf of the appellants that this Court should introduce into the application of these statutory provisions a rule or principle which renders them inoperative unless the taxpayer can establish a real loss. It is with some hesitation conceded on their behalf that it is difficult to avoid the logical conclusion that a similar precondition would have to apply to the computation of a gain under the subsection. Such a principle, it is suggested, would be justified by the general undesirabiilty and unfairness of tax avoidance and by the necessity for the courts to look on such schemes with disfavour.

It is contended that such a development of judicial intervention has recently occurred in England, particularly instanced by the decision of the House of Lords in *W.T. Ramsay Ltd. v I.R.C.* [1982] A.C. 300 and *Furniss v Dawson* [1984] A.C. 474.

A similar approach, it is submitted, is to be found of longer standing in the United States of America, exemplified in particular by the decision of the United States Supreme Court in *Knetsch v United States*, 364 U.S. 361 (1960) and of the Federal Court of Appeals in *Goldstein v C.I.R.*, 364 F. 2d 734 (1966).

It is clear that successful tax avoidance schemes can result in unfair burdens on other taxpayers and that unfairness is something against which courts naturally lean.

The function of the courts in interpreting a statute of the Oireachtas is, however, strictly confined to ascertaining the true meaning of each statutory provision, resorting in cases of doubt or ambiguity to consideration of the purposes and intention of the legislature to be inferred from other provisions of the statute involved, or even of other statutes expressed to be construed with it. The courts have not got a function to add to or delete from express statutory provisions so as to achieve objectives which to the courts appear desirable. In rare and limited circumstances words or phrases may be implied into statutory provisions solely for the purpose of making them effective to achieve their expressly avowed objective. What is urged upon the Court by the appellants in this case is no more and no less than the implication into the provisions of either s. 12 or s. 33 of the 1975 Act of a new subclause or subsection providing that a condition precedent to the computing of an allowable loss pursuant to the provisions of s. 33(5) is the proof by the taxpayer of an actual loss, presumably at least co-extensive with the artificial loss to be computed in accordance with the subsection.

In the course of the submissions such a necessity was denied but instead it was contended that the real—as distinct from what is described as the artificial—nature of the transactions should be looked at by the Court, and that if their real nature was examined, the section could not apply to them.

I must reject this contention. Having regard to the finding in the case stated that these transactions were not a sham, the real nature, on the facts by which I am bound, of this scheme was that the shares were purchased and the purchaser became the real owner thereof; that shares were sold and the vendor genuinely disposed thereof and that an option to purchase shares really existed in a legal person legally deemed to be connected with the person disposing of them. In those circumstances, for this Court to avoid the application of the provisions of the 1975 Act to these transactions could only constitute the invasion by the judiciary of the powers and functions of the legislature, in plain breach of the constitutional separation of powers.

Such an approach appears to me to be entirely consistent with the decision of the former Supreme Court in *Revenue Commissioners v Doorley* [1933] I.R. 750 and with the decision of this Court in *Inspector of Taxes v Kiernan* [1981] I.R. 117.

Apart from the special constitutional rights vested in Dáil Éireann in regard to taxation legislation in their character as Money Bills, the acceptance by the Oireachtas of its special powers and duties in regard to tax legislation, with particular reference to the desirability of preventing the success of tax avoidance schemes, is exemplified (as was pointed out by counsel for the taxpayer) by the fact that since 1973 there have been 8 Finance Acts containing chapters especially headed with the words 'anti-avoidance' or similar words.

Not only am I quite satisfied that it is outside the functions of the courts to condemn tax avoidance schemes which have not been prohibited by statute law, but I would consider it probable that such a role would be undesirable even if it were permissible. It is the Revenue Commissioners (whose advice is available to the Oireachtas in enacting taxation legislation) who have the practical expertise and experience to know the most likely types of avoidance to be anticipated and prohibited, and most importantly of all, the predictable consequences and side-effects of the terms of any prohibiting enactment.

In some jurisdictions such as Canada and Australia general statutory provisions against tax avoidance have been enacted, which in cases to which they apply would, of course, affect the interpretation of specific provisions of taxation laws. In the absence of any such general provisions in our law, there are no grounds for departing from the plain meaning of these sections.

I would accordingly dismiss this appeal.

Extract 12.7

MINISTER FOR INDUSTRY AND COMMERCE v PIM BROTHERS LTD [1966] I.R. 154

The Hire Purchase and Credit-Sale (Advertising) Order, 1961 governed advertisements which offered goods for sale by way of hire purchase or credit-sale agreement. Such advertisements were to contain certain specified information. The defendants attached an advertisement to a coat which was displayed for sale in their premises. If the Order applied to the notice it was deficient in a number of respects. The issue was whether the display amounted to an "offer" for sale. A case was stated for the opinion of the High Court.

Davitt P.

. . . It is to be noted that the only requirement imposed by the Order in the case of an advertisement which relates to goods *available* for sale by way of hire-purchase agreement or credit-sale agreement, as distinct from one which relates to goods so *offered* for sale by such means, is that it should include a statement of the price at which the goods may be purchased for cash.

In the Case Stated, 1964, No. 118 S.S., the relevant facts as stated are as follows:—the defendants, Messrs. Pim Brothers Ltd., are a limited liability company incorporated here who carry on the business of retailers of divers goods at their premises in South Great George's Street, Dublin. By far the greater part of their trading is done by way of hire-purchase and credit-sale agreements. On the 25th January, 1963, they displayed in their premises a notice attached to a coat indicating that the cash price of the coat was 24 guineas, and that weekly payments in respect thereof were 5s. 10d. The defendants were the persons responsible for the notice. The learned District Justice found that the placing of the notice on the coat was a display of an advertisement; that if it was an advertisement to which the Order applies it failed in a number of respects to comply with the provisions of the Order. He found, however, that it was impossible from an examination of the advertisement to determine whether by its terms it necessarily related to goods offered or available for sale by means of one or other of the following kinds of transaction, that is to say, by way of hire-purchase agreement or by way of credit-sale agreement. He held accordingly that the advertisement was not one to which the Order applies and dismissed the summons. As his conclusions appeared to be somewhat ambiguous the case was remitted to him to answer the following questions:—

"1. Is the said advertisement an advertisement relating to goods offered or available for sale by way of hire-purchase agreement?

"2. Is the said advertisement an advertisement relating to goods offered or available for sale by way of credit-sale agreement?

"3. If you are unable to answer these questions, answer accordingly.

He replied as follows:—

"1. The said advertisement was not an advertisement relating to goods offered for sale by way of hire-purchase agreement. I cannot say whether it was an advertisement relating to goods available for sale by way of hire-purchase agreement.

"3. The said advertisement was an offer to treat for the sale of goods with an indication that credit facilities, not specified, would be available to a purchaser."

If the advertisement was one relating to goods available for sale, whether by way of hire-purchase agreement or by way of credit-sale agreement, it would be one to which the Order applies; but it would comply with the provisions of the Order in as much as it includes a statement of the price at which the coat could be purchased for cash. What the defendants were really charged with was displaying an advertisement relating to goods *offered* for sale, by way of hire-purchase agreement or credit-sale agreement, which failed to include certain statements required by the Order. Before one could determine whether the advertisement related to goods offered for sale by way of hire-purcahse agreement or to goods offered for sale by way of credit-sale agreement one would have to decide whether it related to goods offered for sale at all; in other words, whether the advertisement constituted an offer by the defendants to sell the coat. In one sense it could be described as an offer to sell. In popular terms the coat could properly be said to be on offer to the public. In the strictly legal sense, however, the advertisement was merely a statement of the cash price at which the defendants were prepared to sell the goods, with an indication that certain credit facilities, the exact nature of which were unspecified, would be available. This would not constitute an offer to sell which could be made a contract of sale by acceptance: *Harvey* v. *Facey* [1893] A.C. 552. This appears to have been the view taken by the learned District Justice and to be the real ground of his decision to dismiss. If the expression, "offered for sale," in Article 6 (1) of the Order is to be construed in the strict legal sense, then the learned District Justice was clearly correct in his decision. In my opinion, it should be so construed. Apart from any other consideration the distinction made in the Order between advertisements relating to goods offered for sale and goods available for sale, a distinction which does not appear in the relevant sections of the statute, indicates, to my mind, that the expression, "offered for sale," as used in the Order should be construed in its strict legal sense. In the case of Case Sated No. 118 it was essential to prove that the coat was offered for sale in this sense. The learned District Justice was not satisfied that this had been established; and in my opinion he was correct in the view he took.

If he could have been satisfied that the coat had been offered for sale in this sense he would have then had to decide whether or not it had been offered for sale by way of hire-purchase or credit-sale agreement. Before the Order can be contravened and an offence committed, the goods must be offered for sale by one means or the other. If the position were that he was satisfied that they were offered for sale by one means or the other, but that he could not say which, it may be that he would not be entitled to dismiss the summons since it would be clear to him that the Order had been contravened and an offence committed. A similar position, no doubt, sometimes arises where it is clear that a person found in possession of recently stolen goods has either stolen them or received them knowing them to have been stolen, and a Court or a jury is in doubt as to which is the true explanation of his possession. In such circumstances it may be that the Court or jury is not bound to acquit but can select which explanation they consider the more appropriate, and convict accordingly. In this case, however, it is, I think, clear that the learned District Justice, if he could have been satisfied that the goods had been offered for sale, would not have been satisfied that they had been offered for sale by way of hire-purchase or credit-sale agreement; and here again he would in my opinion have been correct in his view.

Extract 12.8

MINISTER FOR INDUSTRY AND COMMERCE V HAMMOND LANE METAL CO. LTD.
[1947] Ir. Jur. Rep. 59

Art. 3 of the Emergency Powers (Scrap Lead)(Maximum Prices) Order, 1945 established a maximum price for "scrap lead". The appellants were convicted of selling lead above the maximum price. It appeared that the lead sold by them was known in the scrap trade as "battery lead". The Circuit Court was asked whether "scrap lead" should be given its ordinary meaning or that attributed to it by the scrap trade.

Judge Shannon.
The question for my determination is whether Article 3 of the Emergency Powers (Scrap Lead) (Maximum Prices) Order, 1945, should be construed in its ordinary acceptation or its acceptation in the particular trade to which the Order was, in my opinion, intended primarily to apply. If I accept Mr. O'Keeffe's submission I would hold the commodity in question to be "scrap lead". There is no doubt that it is "scrap" and that it is in the main "lead". I think the submission on behalf of the defendants is correct, and that I should look at the aims of the Order and consider the people to whom it was meant to apply. The Order was meant to apply to a particular trade and the control of certain sales in that trade. I must have regard to the meaning of words as accepted by that trade. The commodity in this sale was invoiced as "battery lead". There is a distinction in the trade between the meaning of "scrap lead" and "battery lead", and in view of that distinction I hold that the defendants did not sell "scrap lead". The appeal must be allowed and the summons dismissed.

Extract 12.9

MINISTER FOR INDUSTRY AND COMMERCE V HALES [1967] I.R. 50

The provisions of the Holidays (Employees) Act, 1961 required employers to allow their "workers" certain holidays and to make payments in respect of those holidays. S. 3(1) of the Act defined "worker" as being "any person of the age of fourteen years and upwards who is employed" with certain exceptions. S. 2(1) defined "employ" as "employ under a contract of services" and cognate words were to be interpreted accordingly. S. 3(3) allowed the Minister to make regulations which provide that "any person or any class or description . . . of persons shall be deemed to be a worker for the purposes of this Act." The Minister by regulation (S.I. No. 139 of 1963) provided that wholetime insurance agents who were paid by commission and who were engaged under contracts for services should be deemed to be "workers" for the purposes of the Act, thereby bringing them within its scope and entitling them to paid holidays.

The defendants, who were trustees of the Royal Liver Friendly Society, were prosecuted for an alleged failure to pay holiday pay to one of their agents to whom the Regulation applied. The defendants contended that the Regulation was ultra vires. The prosecution sought to adduce evidence that s. 3(3) was inserted into the Act so that the Minister could bring insurance agents within its terms. A case was stated for the opinion of the High Court. The Court, by a majority with Butler J. dissenting, held for the defendants.

The judgment of Henchy J. dealt with the interpretation of the Act, on which turned the validity of the Regulation. The concurring judgment of McLoughlin J. which dealt with the use of external material in the interpretation of the Act appears in Extract 12.20.

Henchy J.

This test case comes before us on a consultative Case Stated. The District Justice seeks the guidance of the Court as to whether he is entitled to enter convictions on two summonses brought by the Minister for Industry and Commerce (whom I shall call the Minister) against the trustees of the Royal Liver Friendly Society (which I shall call the Society). The first summons (as amended) in effect charges the Society with failing to allow annual leave to Joseph Patrick Fitzsimons, one of its agents, during the employment year 22nd July, 1963, to the 22nd July, 1964 as required by s. 10 of the Holidays (Employees) Act, 1961, contrary to ss. 11 and 19 of the Act (as I shall call it). The second summons (as amended) in effect charges the Society with failing to pay Mr. Fitzsimons a sum equivalent to twice his normal weekly wage in respect of his annual leave for that year of employment, as required by s. 10 of the Act, contrary to ss. 18 and 19 of the Act.

The legal relationship for the purposes of this case between Mr. Fitzsimons and the Society appears clear from the facts found by the District Justice and the documents furnished to this Court. In the month of July, 1960, Mr. Fitzsimons applied in writing to the Society for appointment as a whole-time agent. His contract of appointment was executed on the 20th July, 1960, and it provided *inter alia* that he would diligently and to the best of his ability devote his attention to the business of the Society for the purpose of collecting premiums and securing good healthy lives for assurance pursuant, and subject to, the rules and regulations of the Society. It also provided that the conditions set forth in the form of his appointment, together with the rules and regulations of the Society for the time being and from time to time, should apply as if they were incorporated in the contract of appointment. Mr. Fitzsimons was remunerated on a commission based on the amount of premiums he collected. He also received bonuses, the amount of which, in most instances, depended on the premiums collected. His average weekly income as agent came to approximately £15 15s. 0d. It appears that Mr. Fitzsimons was allowed to carry out his duties as agent at times of his own choice. No control was exercised over him as to when he performed his duties as agent and he was never asked by the Society about the hours worked by him. In other words, it would seem that, subject to complying with the terms and conditions of his contract of appointment, he was his own master as to when he carried out his duties of collecting premiums on existing policies and seeking new business. In these circumstances it is clear that Mr. Fitzsimons was engaged not on a contract of service but on a contract for services; see *Graham* v. *Minister for Industry and Commerce* [1933] I.R. 156 and *O'Brien* v. *Tipperary Board of Health* [1938] I.R. 761; and for specific authority that an agent in Mr. Fitzsimons's situation has not a contract of service and is an independent contractor, see the judgment of Sellers J. in *Co-Operative Insurance Society* v. *Richardson* [1955] C.L.Y. 1365. In fact, counsel for the Minister conceded, both in the District Court and here, that Mr. Fitzsimons was engaged under a contract for services.

The importance of this interpretation of the contract lies in the fact that the right to annual leave and holiday pay was granted by the Act only to persons employed under a contract of service or a contract of apprenticeship: see s. 10 and the definition of "employ" and cognate words in s. 2 of the Act. Since neither of these types of contract fits the relationship between Mr. Fitzsimons and the Society, it is clear that neither summons would be sustainable if the Act stood alone. But s. 3, sub-s. 3, of the Act empowered the Minister to extend the benefits of the Act to persons other than those specifically benefited by the Act. In reliance on that power, the Minister on the 22nd July, 1963, made the Holidays (Employees) Act, 1961 [Section 3(3)]

Regulations, 1963. I shall refer to those Regulations (S.I. No. 139 of 1963) as the Regulations. The prosecution of the Society (through its trustees) was founded on the contention that the effect of the Regulations was to make Mr. Fitzsimons entitled to annual leave and holiday pay as if he were given those rights by the Act itself, and that the Society was in default in both respects. The defence is, first, that the Regulations are void as being *ultra vires* the Act and, secondly, that, whether the Regulations be *ultra vires* or not, the Society in fact gave Mr. Fitzsimons his statutory annual leave and holiday pay. I shall deal with the second of these defences first.

If the Regulations are valid and effective to cover Mr. Fitzsimons, it is clear from s. 10 of the Act and Reg. 5 that his entitlement to annual leave in the employment year in question was at most to fourteen consecutive whole holidays, including two Sundays, at such time as Mr. Fitzsimons thought fit. It was found as a fact by the District Justice that in the employment year in question Mr. Fitzsimons took and was allowed to take two weeks holidays. It was conceded to this Court in the course of argument by counsel for the Minister that this was not less than his statutory entitlement. Accordingly, I hold that the complaint in the first summons has not been made out and that this summons must be dismissed.

The contention of the defence that Mr. Fitzsimons was given his statutory holiday pay rests on the finding by the District Justice that, while Mr. Fitzsimons was not remunerated for his two weeks holidays and was not allowed annual leave with pay and did not receive any pay other than what he received by way of commission, he was not at the loss during his annual leave of any commission based on premiums for the reason that premiums falling to be paid during his annual leave were collected by him in part before going on holidays, in part after returning from holidays, and in part by getting other agents of the Society to collect them for him. It is said, therefore, that if the Society were required to pay him a special two weeks pay for his annual 14 days leave, this would be tantamount to giving him 54 weeks pay for 50 weeks work, whereas the Act merely requires that a "worker" who is allowed 14 days annual leave should get 52 weeks wages for 50 weeks work. I cannot accept this argument. In the first place, I do not think it can be said, on the findings of the District Justice, that Mr. Fitzsimons did only 50 weeks work; it may have been so in terms of hours worked, but it was not so in terms of collections, book-keeping and arrangements with fellow-agents (upon terms, reciprocal or otherwise, which we can only guess). But even if it could be said, this being a criminal prosecution in which matters of proof must be established beyond reasonable doubt, that Mr. Fitzsimons did only 50 weeks work, it is no answer for the Society to say that payment of holiday money would result in his getting 54 weeks pay for 50 weeks work. That is a result which is in no way precluded by the Act. For example, a "worker" who is paid on piece-rate and who is entitled to 14 days annual leave may, through the obligement of fellow workers, have his piece-work done for him during his holidays. Could it be said that in such a case he would not be entitled to holiday pay because it would result in his getting 54 weeks pay for 50 weeks work? I think not. And I think the reason is that the duty cast on the employer is an absolute one, that is, one unqualified by financial or other side effects. What s. 10, sub-s. 2, of the Act says (and the italics are mine) is that ". . . the employer of the worker *shall pay* to the worker *in respect of the annual leave* a sum equivalent to twice the worker's normal weekly wage." The Society did not do so in the present case, and in my view it is no answer to say that if they had done so Mr. Fitzsimons would have been unnecessarily and excessively benefited, anymore than it would be a good answer for a factory owner who failed to take safety precautions prescribed by the Factories Act to say that if he had taken the precautions, a worker would be unnecessarily and excessively protected because of independent precautions taken by the worker or a third party. In my opinion this defence fails.

I turn to the Society's main line of defence, which is that the Regulations are of no effect as being *ultra vires* the Act. If this submission is correct, it clearly constitutes a good defence because, as the Minister concedes, the Act has no application to Mr.

Fitzsimons except by virtue of the Regulations. To test the validity of the submission it is necessary to examine the Act and the Regulations in some detail.

The short title of the Act is the Holidays (Employees) Act, 1961. It is in four parts. Part I is headed "Preliminary" and consists in the main of definitions, provisions enabling the Minister to enlarge or restrict the range of persons entitled to the benefits of the Act, and the repeal or amendment of certain earlier legislative provisions. Part II is headed "Public Holidays"; it defines public holdays; it specifies the rights of "workers" in respect of public holidays in terms of payment to be made to them for work done on such days or in terms of compensatory paid holidays; it makes it an offence to deprive a "worker" of these rights; and it enables the Minister to make regulations varying the periods of work which qualify a "worker" for such rights. Part III is headed "Annual Leave"; to summarise its provisions, it gives in certain circumstances to specified types of "workers" annual paid leave or payment in lieu of annual paid leave in certain cases of cesser of employment; it makes it an offence for an employer to fail to allow annual leave in accordance with the Act; and it gives the Minister power to make regulations varying in specified ways the annual leave provisions. Part IV is headed "Miscellaneous"; it deals with penal, procedural and administrative matters, all of which might fairly be described as matters which the legislature thought fit or necessary to include for the purpose of giving effect to the rights and duties created in the earlier parts of the Act.

Broadly speaking, therefore, one may say that the Act confers on "workers" certain rights in respect of public holidays and annual leave, and imposes corresponding obligations on employers in respect of those rights. It is to be noted that nobody but a "worker" is to be entitled to those rights, and "worker" is defined in s. 3, sub-s. 1, of the Act as follows:—

"3.—(1.) In this Act—

"worker" means any person of the age of fourteen years or upwards who is employed, other than a person who is—

   (*a*) one to whom articles or materials are given out to be made up, cleaned, washed, altered, ornamented or repaired or adapted for sale in his own home or on other premises not under the control or management of the person who gave out the materials or articles,

   (*b*) an agricultural worker to whom the Agricultural Workers (Holidays) Act, 1950, applies

   (*c*) the master or a member of the crew of any sea-going vessel (not being a barge or a hopper), whether publicly or privately owned, engaged in the transport of cargo or passengers,

   (*d*) a lighthouse or lightship employee,

   (*e*) a clergyman in Holy Orders,

   (*f*) a member of any religious order or community,

   (*g*) the wife, husband, father, mother, grandfather, grandmother, step-father, step-mother, son, daughter, grand-son, grand-daughter, step-son, step-daughter, brother, sister, half-brother or half-sister of his employer maintained by and dwelling in the house of his employer,

   (*h*) a person who is employed by or under the State not being—

      (i) a person so employed in an unestablished position to whom, by virtue of section 6 of the Act of 1936 [i.e. the Conditions of Employment Act, 1936], that Act applies,

      (ii) a person so employed in an unestablished position as a porter, door-keeper, messenger, night watchman, charwoman, cleaner or labourer or in other subordinate duties, or

      (iii) a person so employed in an unestablished position as an artisan or other skilled labourer,

   (*i*) employed as a fisherman, or

   (*j*) a member of any particular class of employed persons declared by an order made under this section to be an excluded class for the purposes of this section; . . ."

It will be seen, therefore, that every employed person aged fourteen years or upwards is a "worker" unless he comes within the exclusions at (*a*) to (*j*) of the subsection; and "employed" means employed under a contract of service or a contract of apprenticeship, since s. 2, sub-s. 1, of the Act says that the word "employ" means "employ, under a contract of service (whether the contract is expressd or implied or is oral or in writing) or a contract of apprenticeship, and cognate words shall be construed accordingly." The power of the Minister to effect the exclusion referred to at item (*j*) *supra* is set out in s. 3, sub-s. 2, of the Act, which is as follows:—"(2). The Minister may, whenever and so often as he thinks fit, after consultation with such Ministers of State or employers' organisations and with such workers' organisatons as he considers appropriate to be consulted, by order declare that any particular class (defined in such manner and by reference to such things as the Minister thinks proper) of employed persons shall be an excluded class for the purposes of this section, and whenever any such order is made then so long as such order is in force the class of employed persons to which such order relates shall be an excluded class for the purposes of this section."

So far there is no difficulty in identifying the persons entitled to the benefits of the Act as "workers." It is when we pass to sub-s. 3 of s. 3 of the Act that we enter the area of controversy. The relevant portion of that sub-section for the purpose of this case is as follows:—

"(3.) The Minister may, after consultation with such Ministers of State or employers' organisations and with such workers' organisations as he considers appropriate to be consulted, make regulations providing—

(*a*) that any person or any class or description (defined in such manner and by reference to such things as the Minister thinks proper) of persons shall be deemed to be a worker or workers for the purposes of this Act; . . .

Any regulations made by the Minister under this sub-section may contain such supplemental and consequential provisions or modifications of the provisions of this Act as he considers necessary for giving full effect to the regulations."

It was in purported exercise of his powers under the latter sub-section that the Minister made the Regulations in this case. Reg. 3 is in the following terms:—

"3. The following class of persons, namely, wholetime insurance agents whose ordinary remuneration is by way of commission on premiums collected by them and who are engaged under a contract for services, shall be deemed to be workers for the purposes of the Act."

Assuming that the work done by Mr. Fitzsimons under his contract with the Society was in fact "wholetime" (a fact, incidentally, which has not been found by the District Justice and which was a necessary proof in this prosecution), Mr. Fitzsimons would appear to come within the class described in Reg. 3. But it is the submission of the Society that that class, based as it is on a contract for services, is outside any class which the Minister was empowered by s. 3, sub-s. 3, of the Act to deem to be "workers" for the purposes of the Act. This submission stands or falls on the correct interpretation of the scope of the powers delegated to the Minister by that sub-section.

We have been told, by counsel for the Minister, that that sub-section was inserted as an amendment when the Bill was passing through Parliament. While that may give a historical explanation of the sub-section, and in particular of the difference in wording between it and sub-s. 2 of s. 3, it is not, as I understand the authorities, a matter I can take into account in construing sub-s. 3 of that section. I must determine the meaning of sub-s. 3 of s. 3 by the words used in it. But I must not look at these words in isolation; I must judge them by the company they keep. In other words, I must read them in the context of the Act as a whole, so as to determine what meaning and effect should be given to them for the purpose of carrying into force the general purpose or object of the Act. As I have already indicated, a perusal of the various sections shows that the legislature intended by the Act to give to certain "workers" the right to certain holiday allowances and annual leave allowances at the expense of their employers. However, this statement of the general object of the Act begs the question I have to decide, for the sub-section I am construing gives to the Minister power to extend the range of persons entitled to those benefits, and the extent of this range is precisely what I have to determine.

Counsel for the Society submits that the object of the Act may be seen more clearly by looking at its long title. I take it to be established by the modern authorities that the long title is part of the Act (see Maxwell on Interpretation of Statutes, 11th Ed., p. 41), but there are also modern authorities that say that it is not permissible to call in aid the long title for the purpose of limiting the interpretation of a statutory provision that is clear and unambiguous—see *Ward* v. *Holman* [1964] 2 Q.B. 580. But I do not think the most indulgent apologist for the draftsman would suggest that s. 3, sub-s. 3, of the Act is clear and unambiguous in its import. A literal interpretation of it would say that it empowers the Minister to deem literally *any person* to be a "worker" for the purposes of the Act; but, since the Act is confined to relations between "workers" and "employers," such a reading would be manifestly absurd. Is it then to extend to any person or class or description of persons who work for others, as independent contractors or otherwise, wholetime or part-time? Counsel for the Minister does not contend for such a wide construction, but he is unable to suggest the precise limitation of the Minister's powers.

In that state of uncertainty, I feel I am justified in drawing on the long title for such guidance as it gives on the matter. It reads as follows:—"An Act to make better provision for the allowance of holidays to employed persons and to provide for other matters connected with the matter aforesaid." In the light of the definition of "employ" and cognate words such as "employed" given in s. 2, sub-s. 1, of the Act, the long title may be correctly expanded to read as follows:—"An Act to make better provision for the allowance of holidays to persons employed under a contract of service or a contract of apprenticeship and to provide for other matters connected with the matter aforesaid." The long title so read provides a legislative statement of the purpose and scope of the Act, and it thereby gives the key-note for the interpretation of the powers given to the Minister by sub-s. 3 of s. 3 of the Act. Notwithstanding the generality of the words "any person or any class or description . . . of persons" in that sub-section, I deduce from the *ratio legis*, as indicated by the long title and the provisions of the Act read as a whole, that the scope of the general words in the sub-section is limited to persons employed under a contract of service or a contract of apprenticeship.

The principle of interpretation by which I reach this conclusion is to be found in a passage in Maxwell on Interpretation of Statutes (11th Ed.) at p. 78 which was cited with approval by Danckwerts, L.J. in *Mixnams Properties Ltd.* v. *Chertsey U.D.C.* [1963] 3 W.L.R. 38 at p. 49 of the report. That passage is as follows:—"Presumption against Implicit Alteration of Law. One of these presumptions is that the legislature does not intend to make any substantial alteration in the law beyond what it explicitly declares, either in express terms or by clear implication, or, in other words, beyond the immediate scope and object of the statute. In all general matters outside those limits the law remains undisturbed. It is in the last degree improbable that the legislature would overthrow fundamental principles, infringe rights or depart from the general system of law, without expressing its intentions with irresistible clearness, and to give any such effect to general words, simply because they have a meaning that would lead thereto when used in either their widest, their usual or their natural sense, would be to give them a meaning other than that which was actually intended. General words and phrases, therefore, however wide and comprehensive they may be in their literal sense, must usually be construed as being limited to the actual objects of the Act." Examples of the operation of these propositions are to be found in *National Assistance Board* v. *Wilkinson* [1952] Q.B.

648; *Leach* v. *Rex* [1912] A.C. 305; *R.* v. *Salisbury* [1901] 2 K.B. 225; the decision of the Supreme Court in *Daly* v. *Greybridge Co-Operative Creamery Ltd.* [1964] I.R. 497; and *Allen* v. *Thorn Electrical Industries Ltd* [1968] 1 Q.B. 487.

The principle enshrined in the passage I have cited from Maxwell seems to me to be the correct one to apply in the present case, for it is not conceivable that the legislature, having indicated that the scope of the Act was to be limited to persons employed under a contract of service or a contract of apprenticeship, should by the use of general words in sub-s. 3 of s. 3 of the Act have given the Minister power to broaden the scope of the Act to such an extent that he could, by the making of regulations, import into work-contracts made with independent contractors a series of statutory terms as to holiday allowances, the breach of which would result in criminal liability. I cannot believe that the power to effect such radical and far-reaching changes in the law of contract was intended, or should be deemed to have been intended, by a loosely drafted sub-section in an Act that has declared its purpose and scope to be otherwise.

The conclusion I have reached on principle that the Regulations are *ultra vires* is borne out by the operational implications of the Act and the Regulations. I substantiate that view by the following three examples:—

(*a*) The legislature thought it proper in sub-s. 3 of s. 3 to require the Minister before making regulations to consult with such Ministers of State or employers' organisations and with such workers' organisations as he considers appropriate. By definition these mean organisations of persons who employ or are employed under a contract of service or a contract of apprenticeship. If the legislature intended to give the Minister power to make regulations deeming persons who work under a contract for services to be "workers" for the purposes of the Act, it is difficult to see what organisations the Minister should consult with, or why consultations should be required with organisations who might have no interest in the making of the proposed regulations. On the other hand, mandatory consultation with organisations of "workers" is quite understandable if the regulations are to deal with persons employed under a contract of service or a contract of apprenticeship.

(*b*) The power given to the Minister by sub-s. 3 of s. 3 is to deem certain persons to be "workers for the purposes of this Act." He is not given power to deem persons to be "workers" for the purposes of any part or parts of the Act. He purported by the Regulations made in this case to deem the Society's wholetime agents (amongst others) to be workers for the purposes of the Act. It is conceded, however, by counsel for the Minister that Part II of the Act cannot apply to them. Many of the expressions used in Part II, and in particular the definition of a "full day's pay" in s. 9, sub-s. 13, by reference to a contract of service, show that Part II cannot be applied to the Society's wholetime agents. The result is that, under the guise of deeming them to be "workers" for the purposes of the Act, the Minister in fact deemed them to be "workers" for the purposes of only portion of the Act. To my mind, this alone would be sufficient to show that the Regulations are *ultra vires*. If a person is deemed to be a "worker," he should be capable of exercising all the rights accorded by the Act to his category of "worker." If he were to have only some of those rights, the Act would have said so. Sect. 8 sub-s. 1 (and the marginal note thereto), shows that "all workers" are to be entitled to qualify for the benefits of Part II of the Act.

(*c*) A close examination of the Act shows that it cannot be effectively operated in respect of persons engaged under a contract for services. It would make this judgment unduly long if I were to subject the Act to a detailed analysis for the purpose of proving that statement. I limit myself to pointing out that all of the following expressions are used in the Act, expressly or by necessary implication, by reference to a contract of service (or apprenticeship):—(i) "employ" and cognate words; (ii) "non-working day"; (iii) "short day"; (iv) "working day"; (v) "worker"; (vi) "domestic worker"; (vii) "non-domestic worker"; (viii) "industrial worker"; (ix) "employment year; (x) "whole holiday" (xi) "public holiday"; (xii) "compensatory holiday"; (xiii) "qualifying periods of work"; (xiv) "appointed holiday"; (xv) "full day's pay"; (xvi) "normal full working day" and (xvii) "annual leave." This catalogue—apart from any reference to the various contexts in which these expressions occur—shows that if the Minister was given power to deem a person engaged under a contract for services to be a "worker" for the purposes of the Act, many consequential amendments would be needed to make the provisions of the Act fully applicable to him. Yet, power to amend is withheld from the Minister; he is merely permitted by sub-s. 3 of s. 3 to make "such supplemental and consequential provisions or modifications of the provisions of this Act as he considers necessary for giving full effect to the regulations." This, in my view, is added proof that the legislature in enacting sub-s. 3 of s. 3 of the Act did not envisage that the Minister would have the power to extend the meaning of "worker" to cover a person engaged under a contract for services. The public-holiday benefits which apply to "all workers" under Part II are inseparable from the annual-leave benefits conferred by Part III. If a person is entitled to qualify for one he is also entitled to qualify for the other, and the common and primary qualification is that he be a "worker." The calculation of his public-holiday benefits clearly cannot be made unless he has a contract of service (see Part II *passim* and, in particular, s. 9, sub-s. 13) and the linking of the qualifications for public-holiday benefits with the annual-leave provisions is done in such a way as to show that the legislature intended both to rest on a contract of service and not on a contract for services. For example, s. 9, sub-s. 8, in referring to the periods of work necessary to qualify a "worker" for public-holiday benefits, says: "In the calculation of the qualifying periods of work defined in this subsection days of annual leave shall be included and a worker shall be deemed to have worked on each day of his annual leave the normal number of hours which he would have worked on that day under his contract of service." This sub-section, to my mind, necessarily implies that a "worker," in order to be entitled to either public-holiday benefits or annual-leave benefits, must be employed under a contract of service.

For the foregoing reasons I consider that the Regulations in question in this case are *ultra vires* and of no effect. I would answer the question put by the District Justice by saying that both summonses should be dismissed. For the reasons given by Mr. Justice McLoughlin in his judgment, I agree that the correspondence tendered in evidence in the District Court is inadmissible for the purpose of determining the correct interpretation of the Act.

Extract 12.10

NESTOR v MURPHY [1979] I.R. 326

S. 3(1) of the Family Home (Protection) Act, 1976 states:

> Where a spouse, without prior consent in writing of the other spouse, purports to convey any interest in the family home to any person except the other spouse, then, subject to subsections (2) and (3) and section 4, the purported conveyance shall be void.

"Conveyance" is defined in s. 1 to include an agreement to make a conveyance and the term "convey" is to be interpreted accordingly. The defendants were a husband and wife who jointly owned a family home. They entered into a contract with the plaintiff for the sale of the house. When they failed to complete the sale the plaintiff sought an order of specific performance. The defendants argued that the contract was void, as the husband had not obtained the prior written consent of his wife. The High Court ordered specific performance of the contract and the defendants appealed unsuccessfully to the Supreme Court. Kenny and Parke JJ. concurred in Henchy J.'s judgment.

Henchy J.

The two defendants are a married couple. Their family home is in Lucan in the county of Dublin. It is held by them under a long lease and they are joint tenants of the leasehold interest. In July, 1978, they agreed to sell their interest to the plaintiff. They each signed a contract to sell to the plaintiff for £18,500. In form it is a binding and enforceable contract. However, they refuse to complete the sale. The reason they give is that the contract is void under s. 3, sub-s. 1, of the Family Home (Protection) Act, 1976, because the wife did not consent in writing to the sale before the contract was signed. That is the net point in this claim by the plaintiff for the specific performance of the contract.

A surface, or literal, appraisal of s. 3, sub-s. 1, might be thought to give support to the defendants' objection to the contract. That sub-section states:—"Where a spouse, without the prior consent in writing of the other spouse, purports to convey any interest in the family home to any person except the other spouse, then, subject to subsections (2) and (3) and section 4, the purported conveyance shall be void." Sub-sections 2 and 3 of s. 3, and s. 4, are not applicable to this case. By reason of the definition in s. 1, sub-s. 1, the contract signed by the defendants is a "conveyance." Therefore, the argument runs, the provisions of s. 3, sub-s. 1, make the contract void because a spouse (the husband), without the prior consent in writing of the other spouse, "conveyed" an interest in the family home to the plaintiff.

The flaw in this interpretation of s. 3, sub-s. 1, is that it assumes that it was intended to apply when both spouses are parties to the "conveyance." That, however, is not so. The basic purpose of the sub-section is to protect the family home by giving a right of avoidance to the spouse who was not a party to the transaction. It ensures that protection by requiring, for the validity of the contract to dispose and of the actual disposition, that the non-disposing spouse should have given a prior consent in writing. The point and purpose of imposing the sanction of voidness is to enforce the right of the non-disposing spouse to veto the disposition by the other spouse of an interest in the family home. The sub-section cannot have been intended by Parliament to apply when both spouses join in the "conveyance." In such event no protection is needed for one spouse against an unfair and unnotified alienation by the other of an interest in the family home. The provisions of s. 3, sub-s. 1, are directed against unilateral alienation by one spouse. When both spouses join in the "conveyance," the evil at which the sub-section is directed does not exist.

To construe the sub-section in the way proposed on behalf of the defendants would lead to a pointless absurdity. As is conceded by counsel for the defendants, if their construction of s. 3, sub-s. 1, is correct then either the husband or the wife could have the contract declared void because the other did not give a prior consent in writing. Such an avoidance of an otherwise enforceable obligation would not be required for the protection of the family home when both spouses have entered into a contract to sell it. Therefore, it would be outside the spirit and purpose of the Act.

In such circumstances we must adopt what has been called a schematic or teleological approach. This means that s. 3, sub-s. 1, must be given a construction which does not overstep the limits of the operative range that must be ascribed to it, having regard to the legislative scheme as expressed in the Act of 1976 as a whole. Therefore, the words of s. 3, sub-s. 1, must be given no wider meaning than is necessary to effectuate the right of avoidance given when the non-participating spouse has not consented in advance in writing to the alienation of any interest in the family home. Such a departure from the literal in favour of a restricted meaning was given this justification by Lord Reid in *Luke* v. *Inland Revenue Commissioners* [1963] A.C. 557 when he said at p. 577 of the report:—"To apply the words literally is to defeat the obvious intention of the legislation and to produce a wholly unreasonable result. To achieve the obvious intention and produce a reasonable result we must do some violence to the words. This is not a new problem, though our standard of drafting is such that it rarely emerges. The general principle is well settled. It is only where the words are absolutely incapable of a construction which will accord with the apparent intention of the provision and will avoid a wholly unreasonable result, that the words of the enactment must prevail."

Because it is evident from the pattern and purpose of the Act of 1976 that the primary aim of s. 3, sub-s. 1, is to enable a spouse who was not a party to a "conveyance" of the family home, and did not give a prior consent in writing to it, to have it declared void, and because an extension of that right of avoidance to spouses who have entered into a joint "conveyance" would not only be unnecessary for the attainment of that aim but would enable contracts to be unfairly or dishonestly repudiated by parties who entered into them freely, willingly and with full knowledge, I would hold that the spouse whose "conveyance" is avoided by the provisions of s. 3, sub-s. 1, is a spouse who has unilaterally (*i.e.*, without the other spouse joining) purported to "convey" an interest in the family home without having obtained the prior consent in writing of the other spouse. It is only by thus confining the reach of the sub-section that its operation can be kept within what must have been the legislative intent.

I would dismiss this appeal and affirm the order for specific performance made by Mr. Justice Butler.

Extract 12.11

LAWLOR v MINISTER FOR AGRICULTURE [1988] I.L.R.M. 400

Art. 5(1) and (2) of E.C. Regulation No. 1371/84 provides for the allocation of milk quotas when a farm is sold or transferred. Art. 5(3) states that those provisions might have retrospective effect. The Regulation was implemented into domestic law by the European Communities (Milk Levy) Regulations, 1985 (S.I. No. 416 of 1985). In the course of the sale of one of the plaintiff's farms the Minister was required to apportion his milk quota, of which the plaintiff sought to retain as large a fraction as possible. The plaintiff contended that insofar as the domestic Regulations purported to give retrospective effect to the E.C. Regulation they were unconstitutional and, alternatively, that they were ultra vires because they were not made within the framework of the enabling legislation or with constitutional propriety. In the extract from his judgment, in which he upheld the validity of the Regulations, Murphy J. considered the schematic approach and its application to legislative measures which implement E.C. regulations.

Murphy J.
    . . . Attention was drawn to the appropriate canons of interpretation of E.E.C. legislation. In particular reference was made to the second edition of *Charman* and the comments to be found therein on the teleological and schematic approaches to interpretation. With respect, it seems to me that the principles of interpretation were most helpfully and authoritatively dealt with in the paper read by Professor Kutscher, the President of the Chamber at the Court of Justice in Luxembourg in 1976 on *Methods of Interpretation as seen by a Judge at the Court of Justice*. I may quote at some length a passage from page 1.36 of that paper as follows:

> It would be superfluous to point out once more what importance schematic interpretation has in the case law of the Court of Justice. Its application corresponds to the special features which characterise the legal system of the community. If this legal system takes the form of a broadly conceived plan and if it confines itself essentially to setting aims and directions as well as to establishing principles and programmes for individual sectors, and if in addition there is no legislature which fills in the framework drawn up by the treaties within a

reasonable time . . . the judge is compelled to supplement the law on his own and to find the detailed rules without which he is unable to decide the case brought before him. The judge can succeed in this task only by having recourse to the scheme the guidelines and the principles which can be seen to underly the broad plan and the programme for individual sectors. Without recourse to these guidelines and principles it is not even possible to give precise definition to the significance and scope of the general rules and concepts of which the treaties make such abundant use . . . It is plain that such a schematic interpretation which sees the rules of community law in their relationship with each other and with the scheme and principles of the plan, cannot escape a certain systemization and therefore on occasion demand that solutions of a problem be inferred by deducation from general principles of law.

It is interesting to note from his decision in *Buchanan & Co v Babco Ltd* [1977] Q.B. 208 at 213 that Lord Denning MR was equally impressed by Judge Kutscher's paper and he, Lord Denning, explained the European method of interpretation in the following terms:

They adopt a method which they call in English by strange words—at any rate they were strange to me—the schematic and teleological method of interpretation. It is not really so alarming as it sounds. All it means is that the judges do not go by the literal meaning of the words or by the grammatical structure of the sentence. They go by the design or purpose which lies behind it. When they come upon a situation which is to their minds within the spirit—but not the letter—of the legislation, they solve the problem by looking at the design and purpose of the legislature—at the effect which it was sought to achieve. They then interpret the legislation so as to produce the desired effect. This means that they fill in gaps, quite unashamedly, without hesitation. They ask simply: what is the sensible way of dealing with this situation so as to give effect to the presumed purpose of the legislation?

It is proper to say, however that the House of Lords on appeal from the Court of Appeal in *Buchanan & Co. v Babco Ltd* [1978] A.C. 141 made it clear that they did not share Lord Denning's enthusiasm for the schematic or teleological approach nor did they find any justification for incorporating it in the English legal system.

It seems to me that in construing E.E.C. regulations I am bound to apply the canons of interpretation so clearly adumbrated by Judge Kutscher in his paper and with regard to domestic legislation it does seem to me that similar principles must be applicable at least insofar as it concerns the application of Community regulations to this State. Moreover, it does seem to me that the teleological and schematic approach has for many years been adopted in this country—though not necessarily under the description—in the interpretation of the Constitution. The innumerable occasions in which the preamble to the Constitution has been invoked and in particular the desire therein expressed to promote the common good with due observance of prudence, justice and charity so that the dignity and freedom of the individual may be assured, through social order attained, the unity of our country restored and concord established with other nations in seeking to fill the gaps in the Constitution is itself an obvious example of the teleological approach. Indeed in somewhat more mundane circumstances arising in the interpretation of the Family Home (Protection Act) 1976 in *Nestor v Murphy* [1979] I.R. 326 Henchy J expressly decided that the court must adopt what has been called a schematic or teleological approach . . .

Extract 12.12

RAFFERTY v CROWLEY [1984] I.L.R.M. 350

S. 80 of the Building Societies Act, 1976 provides that:

A society shall not make a loan on the security of any freehold or leasehold estate which is subject to a prior mortgage unless the prior mortgage is in favour of the society making the loan.

The issue to be decided was whether a charge on land to secure part of the leasehold rent constituted a "prior mortgage". The plaintiff and defendant were, respectively, the vendor and purchaser of a house which was subject to a small rent reserved in the lease. The defendant argued that the covenant to pay the rent constituted a "prior mortgage" within the meaning of s. 80. The matter was considered by Murphy J. in the High Court.

Murphy J.

. . . It was successfully argued in *Provincial Building Society v Brown and Ministry of Finance for Northern Ireland* [1950] N.I. 163 that the essential characteristics of a mortgage within the meaning of what was then s. 13 of the Building Societies Act, 1894 included first the granting of an estate by the mortgagor to the mortgagee to secure the loan, secondly the right to redeem and thirdly the right to foreclose. It was accordingly held that a charge in the form of a land purchase annuity payable to the Ministry of Finance for Northern Ireland was *not* "a prior mortgage" within the meaning of s. 13 aforesaid. However, subsequent to that decision—and perhaps as a result of it—the legislature in the United Kingdom when enacting the Building Societies Act 1962 and the Oireachtas here in enacting the Building Societies Act, 1976 introduced a definition of the word "mortgage" so as to include expressly a "charge".

Reading s. 80 of the 1976 Act and extending the word "mortgage" to include a charge as required by the interpretation section how can it be said that it does not include or extend to the 1962 charge?

Counsel on behalf of the vendor plaintiff has sought to adopt a schematic or teleological approach to the Act and in particular s. 80 thereof. She says that the purpose of the Act, and in particular Part VI thereof, is to ensure that advances made by building societies are fully and properly secured for the benefit of the society and its members. That being the intent of the Act—or so the argument goes—no purpose would be served and no benefit would be achieved by preventing or prohibiting a society from lending on the security of part of the lands comprised in and demised by a lease where the owner of that part (or his predecessor) had charged it with the payment of the rent apportioned to that part as such a charge does not reduce, in any way, the value of the leasehold interest. Again, it is pointed out that the 1976 Act expressly recognises the right of a building society to advance money on the security of leasehold property. Every person holding any part of lands demised by a lease is on risk for the payment of the entire of the rent thereby reserved. Accordingly, the mutual covenants and cross-charges benefit rather than prejudice the holders of any part of leasehold land and through him any person holding a mortgage or charge on such lands. Accordingly, there is nothing to be gained and no purpose served by interpreting the words "a prior mortgage" in s. 80 so as to include cross-charges of this nature.

Whilst I have every sympathy with the case made by the plaintiff and indeed I believe that it would be in the public interest generally to uphold this construction of s. 80 of the 1976 Act I do not believe that the accepted canons of construction would permit me to support that view.

Reference was made to the decision of the Supreme Court in *Nestor v Murphy* [1979] I.R. 326 as an example of a case in which the schematic approach might be adopted. However, it appears clearly from the judgment of Henchy J, that the approach was justified so as to avoid "a pointless absurdity". Again, Henchy J. pursued "the pattern and purpose" of the legislation then under consideration where he was satisfied that by doing otherwise "would not only be unnecessary for the attainment of that aim but would enable contracts to be unfairly or dishonestly repudiated by parties who entered into them freely, willingly and with full knowledge". It would appear that the schematic approach is justified where—in the words of Lord Reid in *Luke v The Inland Revenue Commissioners* [1963] A.C. 557 at p. 577:

> To apply the words literally is to defeat the obvious intention of the legislation and to produce a wholly unreasonable result.

It is clear that by s. 80 the legislature set its face against a building society making a loan on the security of a property which was subject to *any* prior mortgage. It would have been a relatively easy task to restrict the operation of the section to cases where the prior mortgage or charge exceeded specified amounts or perhaps a particular percentage of the value of the property in question. Alternatively, what could have been done was to exclude the various categories of prior charge as was done by s. 32 of the United Kingdom Building Societies Act 1962. If that precedent did not commend itself to the draftsman he could have adopted the formula used in s. 99 of the Companies Act, 1963 which, having provided for the registration of (among other things) a charge on land wherever situate or any interest therein, goes on to provide:

> but not including a charge for any rent or other periodical sum issuing out of land.

In fact it does not require reference to examples or precedents confidently to infer that the legislature in enacting s. 80 in its existing form was conscious of that fact that it could have exempt from the scope of the prohibition certain prior mortgages or charges and deliberately chose not to do so. In these circumstances it seems to me that I am precluded from interpreting s. 80 so as to achieve an effect—however desirable—not intended by the Oireachtas.

The conclusion which I have reached is supported to some extent by the decision of Pennyquick, VC, in *Abbotspark Estate* [1972] 3 All E.R. 148. In that case the court had approved of what is known as a management scheme under the Leasehold Reform Act 1967 which imposed certain liabilities in respect of moneys on the owners of leasehold property and these liabilities by virtue of the Leashold Reform Act 1967 constituted a charge on the property. In those circumstances the learned judge commented (at page 150) as follows:

> This is an extremely serious position from the point of view of owners of the enfranchised properties. So far as I can see, on the material which has been put before me by counsel who have been thoroughly into the matter, there is no answer to the point, that is to say, if the charge under para. 3(b) of the scheme (the liability of the lessees) is not in some way postponed to any future building society mortgage, then a building society would be prohibited by s. 32 from making an advance on the property.

It appears, therefore, that, whilst the particular point was not the subject matter of controversy before the court, the learned judge was satisfied that the liability of the lessees by becoming a statutory charge on their property constituted a prior mortgage or charge within the United Kingdom equivalent of s. 80 of the Building Societies Act, 1976.

Like Vice-Chancellor Pennyquick I regard this as a very serious matter. There must be many building estates in which rents, small in themselves, are reduced still further by apportionment amongst individual assignees who have properly and correctly charged their respective interests with payment of the apportioned rent only to find themselves now precluded from obtaining an advance from a building society as a result of the charge so created. This would be an awesome consequence for the property holder and clearly a matter of the greatest possible concern to the building societies.

In the case of *Nash v Halifax Building Society and Another* [1979] 2 All E.R. 19 Browne-Wilkinson J. concluded that an advance made in breach of s. 32 of the United Kingdom Building Societies Act 1962 was not irrecoverable as the section was enacted for the protection and benefit of a society and its members. If that decision is followed here it will obviously be a considerable comfort to the building societies in relation to loans already made but clearly, the directors of building societies would incur serious responsibilities if they choose to make loans on unauthorised securities.

Having regard to the far reaching effects which this decision may have in an area of the greatest social and economic significance, I will direct the Registrar of the Courts to forward a copy of the judgment herein to the Minister for the Environment and to the Registrar of Building Societies in case it is felt that consideration should be given to making some amendment to this important legislation in the light of the conclusions expressed above.

Extract 12.13

CHARLES McCANN LTD. v Ó CÚLACHAIN [1986] I.R. 196

The Corporation Tax Act, 1976 provides for relief from corporation tax for profits which are derived from manufactured goods which are exported from the State. The appellant imported unripened bananas and subjected them to an artificial ripening process. The question in issue was whether the ripened bananas were "manufactured" goods. Carroll J., in the High Court, rejected the claim. The appellants appealed successfully to the Supreme Court. Finlay C.J. and Hederman J. concurred in McCarthy J.'s judgment.

McCarthy J.

The question of law stated for the High Court by the then President of the Circuit Court and now the subject of this appeal is "whether notwithstanding my finding of fact that the bananas were processed in this country by the appellant, I am correct in holding that the ripened bananas are not goods within the meaning of s. 54 of the Corporation Tax Act, 1976." The High Court (Carroll J.) confirmed the Circuit Court decision, and the company appeals, raising for consideration the true construction of s. 54 of the Corporation Tax Act, 1976, which, so far as relevant, reads:—

"(1). In this Part "goods" means goods manufactured within the State by the person who exports them or some of them and who in relation to the relevant accounting period is the company claiming relief under this part . . .

(3). (*a*) The definition of "goods" contained in subsection (1) shall include goods manufactured within the State which do not come within that definition and which are exported by the person who in relation to the relevant accounting period is the company claiming relief under this Part where the selling by such person of the goods so exported is selling by wholesale.

(*b*) "Selling by wholesale" in paragraph (*a*) means selling goods of any class to a person who carries on a business of selling goods of that class or who uses goods of that class for the purposes of a trade or undertaking carried on by him."

Section 58 creates an entitlement to relief from corporation tax in respect of these goods, in certain specified circumstances. These sections and a number of others, from ss. 53 to 68, form Part IV of the Act of 1976 under the heading "Profits from Export of Certain Goods."

The company imports unripe bananas from Ecuador and Colombia and, at its premises in Dublin subjects the bananas to what Carroll J. correctly described as a complex and costly process of ripening artificially by ethylene gas in specially constructed and equipped ripening rooms; a process requiring special expertise but not professional qualification. The learned President of the Circuit Court considered that the fact that the raw material for the process was imported into the State disqualified the goods exported from relief, but this view was not supported in the High Court or in this Court and, in my view, it was an incorrect reading of the section.

In the High Court, Carrolll J. cited a portion of the judgment of Henchy J. in *Inspector of Taxes* v. *Kiernan* [1981] I.R. 117 at p. 121 where he said:—

> Leaving aside any judicial decision on the point, I would approach the matter by the application of three basic rules of statutory interpretation. First, if the statutory provision is one directed to the public at large, rather than to a particular class who may be expected to use the word or expression in question in either a narrowed or an extended connotation, or as a term of art, then, in the absence of internal evidence suggesting the contrary, the word or expression should be given its ordinary or colloquial meaning . . .
>
> Secondly, if a word or expression is used in a statute creating a penal or taxation liability, and there is looseness or ambiguity attaching to it, the word should be construed strictly so as to prevent a fresh imposition of liability from being created unfairly by the use of oblique or slack language . . .
>
> Thirdly, when the word which requires to be given its natural and ordinary meaning is a simple word which has a widespread and unambiguous currency, the judge construing it should draw primarily on his own experience of its use.

I do not accept the proposition made on behalf of the company that the Act of 1976 is other than one addressed to the public generally. No doubt, most members of the public would find difficulty in understanding many of its provisions, but that is not the test. The particular class envisaged in the first rule as stated would be such as would be contemplated by the Solicitors Act, 1954, the Opticians Act, 1956, the Dentists Act, 1928, and a great variety of other specialised legislation. At first sight, it might be thought that "manufactured" is a simple word which has a widespread and unambiguous currency; closer examination, however, reveals the use of the word in many differing ways; in some instances the word implies virtual creation, in others alteration of appearance rather than make-up, of shape rather than substance. I doubt if true guidance can be obtained from the application of the third basic rule. The second is clearly to be applied and depends for its application upon there being ambiguity or doubt as to the meaning of the word, and certainly there is that. Since the decision of the High Court in this case Murphy J., in construing somewhat like legislation, the Finance Act, 1980, s. 41, sub-s. 2 (as amended by the Finance Act, 1982, s. 26 and Schedule 2 thereof) in *Cronin (Inspector of Taxes)* v. *Strand Dairy Limited* (Unreported, High Court, Murphy J., 18th December, 1985) having adverted to the judgment of Carroll J. in the instant case, and that of Lord MacDermott L.C.J. in *McCausland* v. *Ministry of Commerce* [1956] N.I. 36, expressed his own view as follows:—

> It seems to me, therefore, that one must look at the goods alleged to have been manufactured and consider what they are; how they appear, what qualities they possess, what value attaches to them. One then looks at the processs and seeks to identify to what extent that process conferred on the goods the characteristics which they are found to possess. It is obvious—as indeed Lord MacDermott pointed out (at p. 43) that the question is to a large extent one of degree. Nobody would doubt that well made and fully finished furniture would

constitute manufactured goods but it is unlikely that the ordinary man would accept that the trunk of a tree which had been felled and provided a convenient seat constituted a manufactured article.

I agree with the approach as so stated, subject to the qualification that one must also, in aid of construction of the particular word *as used in the statute*, look to the scheme and purpose as disclosed by the statute or the relevant part thereof. It is true that one may eventually put the question, as stated by Carroll J.—whether an ordinary person would attribute the word "manufacture" to the ripening process, not whether the ordinary person in the street would describe the bananas which have been subjected to the ripening process as "manufactured goods", but one must ensure that the ordinary person, as so contemplated, is one adequately informed as to those matters identified in the judgment of Murphy J. which I have cited. The scheme and purpose of the relevant part of the statute appear to me to be the very context within which the word is used and the requirements of which must be examined in order to construe it. It is manifest that the purpose of Part IV of the Act of 1976 was, by tax incentives, to encourage the creation of employment within the State and the promotion of exports—naturally outside the State—objectives of proper, social and economic kind which the State would be bound to encourage. Employment is created by labour intensive processes and exports by the creation of saleable goods. The operation described in the case stated clearly comes within both categories; in my judgment, it is then a matter of degree, itself a question of law, as to whether or not what the company has done to the raw material makes it goods within the definition in section 54. Applying that test, I am satisfied that the ripened bananas, having been subjected to the process as described, constitute a commercially different product and one within the definition.

I would allow the appeal accordingly and answer the question posed in the negative.

Extract 12.14

WEEKES v REVENUE COMMISSIONERS [1989] I.L.R.M. 165

The applicant sought judicial review of certificates of default which were issued under s. 485 of the Income Tax Act, 1967. S. 485(1) of the Act empowers the Collector General to issue a certificate to a county registrar or sheriff certifying the amount of income tax of which a taxpayer is in default. S. 485(2) provides that "immediately upon receipt of the certificate the county registrar or sheriff shall proceed to levy the sum therein certified". In the applicant's case there had been delays of between three and a half and five months in the execution of the certificates. The applicant contended that the delay invalidated the certificates.

Lardner J.
 . . . If one takes the literal interpretation for which the prosecutor contends, it seems to be an extraordinary result if the interpretation of s. 485(2) is that, if the sheriff does not immediately (by which I mean within a very short time) after receipt of the certificate execute on foot of it, his power is gone and that the power to execute no longer exists. I find it impossible to accept that in the context of this Act.

The view I take is that the section is using the words "immediately" and "shall" to indicate the point in time when the duty of the county registrar or the sheriff commences. I think that the duty expressly referred to here is a duty to act with reasonable expedition having regard to the acts to be done. It is a duty owed to the Revenue Commissioners and not, in my estimation, to the taxpayer. I am fortified in that interpretation by a passage in the judgment of Henchy J in *Kellystown Co v Hogan* [1985] I.L.R.M. 200, where he said towards the end of p. 202:

> The interpretation contended for by Kellystown, while it may have the merit of literalness, is at variance with the purposive essence of the proviso. Furthermore, it would lead to an absurd result, for moneys which are clearly corporation profits would escape the tax and, indeed, the tax would never be payable on dividends on shares in any Irish company. I consider the law to be that, where a literal reading gives a result which is plainly contrary to the legislative intent, and an alternative reading consonant with the legislative intent is reasonably open, it is the latter reading that should prevail.

In the present case it seems to me that the proposition contended for by the applicant is not in accordance with the intention of the statute or this section, and the interpretation which I have accepted seems to me to satisfy the test laid down by Henchy J. It further seems to be in accordance with the statement of McCarthy J in *C. McCann Ltd v Ó Cúlachain* [1986] I.R. 196, at p. 201 where he said that the Court must "look to the scheme and purpose as disclosed by the statute or the relevant part thereof". I agree with the statement of the law in that case.

When one turns to the actual provisions of s. 485(2), and particularly with regard to the words "shall proceed", I accept what was submitted by Mr Cooke SC on behalf of the Revenue Commissioners that it is reasonable to interpret that as meaning "shall start going about" levying the tax. I also accept that, in levying the tax, the sheriff or the county registrar has to take certain steps before actual seizure. Mr Binchy in his affidavit deposes to the steps which have been taken. He must firstly find the taxpayer and conduct an investigation into his circumstances and find out if he has any goods to be seized. He then has to make arrangements for the actual seizure, by getting people and transport and that sort of thing. This process of execution follows upon the issue of a certificate under sub-s. (1) by the Collector.

S. 485(1) states that the Collector may issue a certificate to the county registrar or the sheriff. He clearly has a discretion. He might alternatively decide to sue the taxpayer or to give the taxpayer a further time to pay, and may send a further demand notice. I consider that, by the issue of the certificate, that discretion is not terminated. In practice what happens is that the sheriff sends out a warning notice to the effect that if there is no payment within seven days or so the recipient's goods will be liable to seizure. I think that is a perfectly proper procedure, enabling the matter to be disposed of without the necessity for carrying out execution by seizure and removing goods.

It was stated by Mr Hogan on behalf of the applicant that the procedure whereby the issue of the certificate was followed by a delay of three and a half to five months was oppressive, in that it involved a threat of execution being held over the taxpayer's head. I am not persuaded that this is an argument of any substance, since at any time the taxpayer can discharge the debt due by paying the sum involved.

I have come to the conclusion that the applicant has not made out a case for judicial review, and I therefore dismiss the application, with costs to the respondents.

Extract 12.15

MURPHY v BORD TELECOM EIREANN [1989] I.L.R.M. 53

Art. 119 of the E.E.C. Treaty contains the principle of equality of pay for men and women engaged in equal work. The Anti-Discrimination (Pay)

Act, 1974 provides for equal pay where a man and a woman are engaged in "like work", which includes work of equal value. The applicant did work which was of greater value than that performed by the male employee with whom she compared herself. Initially, it was held that that did not amount to "like work" (see [1986] I.L.R.M. 483). The matter was referred to the European Court of Justice which ruled, *inter alia*, that:

> . . . Art. 119 of the E.E.C. Treaty must be interpreted as covering the case where a worker who relies on that provision to obtain equal pay within the meaning thereof is engaged in work of higher value than that of a person with whom a comparison is to be made.

The case was remitted to the High Court where Keane J. had to consider the interpretation of the 1974 Act in the light of that ruling.

Keane J.

. . . When the hearing of the case was resumed before me, counsel were agreed that the effect of the preliminary ruling was that the appellants were entitled to a determination whether the inequality of pay between them and a male employee of the respondents resulted from grounds other than sex and that such a determination must be made on the basis that the appellants and the male employee are employed on "like work". The question remained as to which of two possible courses suggested by counsel was appropriate in the light of the ruling of the Court of Justice of the EC. The first course was to remit the case to the Labour Court with a direction that the appellants' claim be determined on the basis that they and the male employee were employed on "like work" within the meaning of ss. 2(1) and 3 of the Act of 1974. The second course was to resolve the question as to whether the inequality of pay between the appellants and the male employee was based on grounds other than sex in these proceedings, subject to any directions that might be necessary as to the delivery of pleadings etc.

The following basic principles appear to be of importance in deciding which of these courses is appropriate.

1. Article 119 of the EEC Treaty is part of the domestic law of the State by virtue of s. 2 of the European Communities Act, 1972. So too is Article 177, which enables a judge of a national court to obtain a ruling on the interpretation of any article of the treaty, which ruling once obtained is binding on the national court.

2. The effect of the court's ruling in the present case is that Article 119 must be interpreted as applying to a case where a worker who relies on that provision to obtain equal pay within the meaning thereof is engaged in work of higher value than that of the person with whom a comparison is to be made.

3. The judgment of the court also reiterates what was said in *Defrenne v Sabena* [1976] E.C.R. 445, i.e. that the principle that men and women should receive equal pay for equal work, which is laid down in Article 119, may be relied on in legal proceedings by the employees concerned and must be taken into account by national courts and tribunals as a constituent part of community law.

4. The interpretation of the relevant sections of the Act of 1974 is exclusively a matter for the Irish courts.

5. The interpretation of those sections, in accordance with the canons of construction normally applied in Irish courts, has in the present case yielded a result which is in conflict with Article 119 of the Treaty as interpreted by the Court of Justice of the E.C.

6. Where such a conflict exists, national law must yield primacy to community law: *Crotty v An Taoiseach* [1987] I.L.R.M. 400. The exclusive role of the making of laws assigned to the Oireachtas by Article 15 of the Constitution has been expressly modified by Article 29.4.3 so as to enable community law to have the force of law in the State.

7. Where such a conflict arises, the national law is, accordingly, inapplicable. In the words of the Court of Justice of the E.C. in *Amministrazione della Finanze dello Stato v Simmenthal* [1978] E.C.R. 629, 644:

every national court must, in a case within its jurisdiction, apply community law in its entirety and protect rights which the latter confers on individuals and must accordingly set aside any provision of national law which may conflict with it, whether prior or subsequent to the community rule.

In the present case, counsel seemed to agree that treating the national law as inapplicable meant that the relevant provisions of the Act of 1974 were of no effect and that the rights of the appellants under Article 119 could be protected only in proceedings in this Court. Mrs Robinson SC, however, on behalf of the appellants submitted that the applicability of the national law could and should be preserved by giving a purposive interpretation to the relevant sections rather than the literal construction which would normally be demanded.

In my view, it does not follow that, if the national law is inapplicable, the rights of the appellants under Article 119 can be protected only by proceedings in this Court. The Oireachtas has provided in the Act of 1974 a statutory machinery intended to give effect to the principle of equal pay for equal work and has entrusted the arbitral role between employers and employees in this area to the Labour Court. That tribunal in discharging its statutory function is as much bound to apply the law of the community as is this court. Similarly, where national law and community law conflict, it must give precedence to community law. It is accordingly entirely appropriate in the light of the ruling of the Court of Justice of the E.C. in the present case to remit the matter to the Labour Court with a direction that the issues between the parties should be determined on the basis that the appellants and the male employee are employed in "like work". The statutory adjudication must, in other words, be arrived at by applying the relevant principle of community law enunciated by the Court of Justice of the E.C. rather than the words of ss. 2 and 3 of the Act of 1974 literally construed as our principles of statutory construction require. This seems to me entirely in accordance with the judgments of the Court of Justice in *Simmenthal* and in the present case.

There are other considerations which indicate that remitting the case to the Labour Court with such a direction is the appropriate course. The Act of 1974 is presumed to be constitutional until the contrary is shown and it is a necessary corollary of that presumption that the Oireachtas is presumed not to legislate in a manner which is in breach of rights protected under community law. Those rights already existed in our domestic law by virtue of s. 2 of the European Communities Act, 1972 when the Act of 1974 was passed by the Oireachtas. In the present case, in the light of the ruling of the Court of Justice of the E.C., this court should seek if possible to adopt a teleological construction of the relevant sections of the Act of 1974, i.e. one which looks to the effect of the legislation rather than the actual words used by the legislature.

It should be pointed out, in this context, that Mr Geoghegan SC on behalf of the respondents did not press the court at the resumed hearing to adhere to the literal construction and reject the teleological construction relied on by Mrs Robinson. There were of course practical considerations which made this a sensible course for the respondents to adopt. If, however, a party in a case such as the present were to press for a literal construction of the Act which necessitated a finding that the Oireachtas had legislated in contravention of community law and hence in a manner which appeared to violate the primacy given to community law under the Constitution, I would have thought it desirable that the Attorney General should be joined in the proceedings before that issue was resolved. In the present case, however, that course is unnecessary since, having regard to the stance adopted by the parties, a teleological construction of the sections, if such is available, should be adopted.

Such a construction was urged upon me both at the original and the resumed hearing by Mrs Robinson on behalf of the appellants. This requires reading into the wording of ss. 2 and 3(a) proviso that, in cases where the work is of unequal value and the worker doing the work of greater value is in fact being paid less than the other worker, the work is to be treated as though it were of equal value, and reading s. 3(c) as though the words "at least" appeared before the words "equal in value". Such a construction necessarily involves a departure from the ordinary and natural meaning of the words "equal in value". In the light of the interpretation of Article 119 laid down by the Court of Justice of the E.C., however, it is this approach, rather than the literal approach adopted in my earlier judgment, which must be adopted by the court.

In my earlier judgment, I indicated that this approach does not in the present case bring about a situation of equal pay for equal work, but rather one of equal pay for unequal work. It has not been contended on behalf of the appellants that the Act can be interpreted so as to enable their remuneration to be increased to a level which would reflect the superiority of their work over the work of the male employee. They have confined their claim to the raising of their remuneration to the level of the male employee. However, while this matter is not specifically addressed in the judgment of the court, I think it is implicit in their judgment that the principle enshrined in Article 119 is sufficiently respected by the national legislation if it ensures that workers of one sex engaged in work of superior value to that of work of the opposite sex are not paid a *lower* wage than the latter on grounds of sex.

I am satisfied, accordingly, that the teleological construction of the relevant sections in the present case ensures the primacy of community law and the efficacy of Article 119, as interpreted by the Court of Justice of E.C., in this State.

I should, however, add one rider. In my earlier judgment, I said that:

This teleologial or schematic approach, which was adopted by the Supreme Court in *Nestor v Murphy* [1979] I.R. 321, is not appropriate in a case such as the present where the legislature could by the use of apt language have provided for a particular situation but has failed to do so, whether intentionally or by an oversight. For the same reason, it is not possible to pray in aid the provisions of the E.E.C. Treaty or the council directive on equal pay in the absence of any ambiguity, patent or latent, in the language used by the legislature.

This passage appears to me, on further consideration, to be misleading. While it is true that the language used by the Oireachtas, literally interpreted, yields a result which is at variance with the law of the community, it does not follow, as this passage might have suggested, that the literal construction is the only construction available. On the contrary, in the light of the judgment of the Court of Justice of the E.C., it is clear that it must give way in the present case to the teleological construction, for the reasons I have already given.

In the result, the case should be remitted to the Labour Court with a direction that the applicants' claim be determined on the basis that they and the male employee are employed on "like work" within the meaning of s. 2(1) and s. 3 of the Act of 1974. Since the respondents had contended both in this court and in the Court of Justice of the E.C. for the literal construction of the section, which has now been found to be wrong, it follows that they must bear the costs of the proceedings in both courts.

Extract 12.16

FRESCATI ESTATES LTD. v WALKER [1975] I.R. 177

The Local Government (Planning and Development) Act, 1963 governs the granting of planning permission to develop land. S. 25 of the Act provides for the making of regulations and s. 26 provides that applications for planning permission should be made in accordance with the regulations.

The Act also defines the term "owner". However, the provisions which deal with applications for planning permission use the word "applicant" rather than "owner".

The defendant was granted outline planning permission to develop the plaintiffs' land. It was conceded that she was not an "owner" but that her purpose in applying for permission was to prevent the plaintiffs' proposed development of the land. The plaintiffs appealed the granting of permission to the Minister for Local Government. They also issued a summons in which they sought an injunction restraining the defendant from proceeding with her application and ordering her to withdraw it. They argued that as she was not an "owner" her application was invalid. In the High Court, Kenny J. refused to grant the injunction. He held that the application was valid, as the Act drew a distinction between "owner" and "applicant" and employed the latter term to describe those who sought permission.

The Supreme Court disagreed with Kenny J.'s interpretation. They held that although the "applicant" did not have to be an "owner", an application had to be approved by the owner. Consequently the defendant's application was invalid. However, the Court refused to grant the injunction sought by the plaintiffs as an appeal to the Minister was still pending. In the course of his judgment, with which the rest of the Court concurred, Henchy J. rejected the literal interpretation and examined the scheme of the Act. He was influenced in his decision by the fact that a literal interpretation would make severe inroads on an owner's rights in respect of the land and could make the owner subject to the criminal law.

Henchy J.
The substantive question in this case may be put shortly. Is a person who has no legal estate or interest in a property entitled to apply under the Local Government (Planning and Development) Act, 1963, for permission to develop the property?

The plaintiffs are the owners in fee simple of the property in question. Not alone has the defendant no legal estate or interest in it but the trial judge found as a fact that "she has no intention or hope of acquiring any estate of any kind in the property or of developing it." The plaintiffs' application for permission to develop it having been refused, they claimed compensation of £1,309,972 under s. 55 of the Act of 1963. So as to avoid liability for the compensation claimed, the planning authority gave the plaintiffs an undertaking on the 4th October, 1973, to grant development permission subject to certain conditions. The matter would no doubt have proceeded to a satisfactory conclusion—at least from the plaintiffs' standpoint—were it not for the intervention of the defendant who, by letters dated the 30th August and the 8th October, 1973, applied for outline planning permission to develop the property in a manner quite inconsistent with the way the plaintiffs wished to develop it. On the 28th November, 1973, the planning authority notified the grant of the outline planning permission sought by the defendant, notwithstanding the fact (now found by the trial judge) that she had no intention or hope of acquiring any estate of any kind in the property or of developing it, and that her application was made merely as part of a campaign to prevent the plaintiffs from carrying out any development of the property.

The plaintiffs lodged an appeal to the Minister against the permission notified to the defendant and, since they contend that the defendant's planning application is a nullity, they seek in the present proceedings an injunction to restrain the defendant's application and a mandatory injunction ordering her to withdraw it. The matter came before Mr. Justice Kenny as an application for those injunctions in interlocutory form. Rejecting the submission that the defendant's application was void because she has no estate or proprietary interest or right in the land, he refused the application for the interlocutory injunctions. Hence the present appeal by the plaintiffs.

Counsel for the defendant puts her case in broad and forthright terms. Conceding that his client has no special standing by virtue of any legal estate or interest, actual or prospective, in the property, he bases her claim to be entitled to apply for development permission entirely on the fact that the provisions of the Act dealing with applications for development permission (in particular, ss. 25 and 26) refer to an *applicant* and not, as in the case of certain other provisions of the Act, to an *owner* (which is specially defined in s. 2) or *occupier*.

For my part I have no difficulty in accepting that the choice of the word *applicant* and the deliberate avoidance of the use of any word or expression to suggest that the person seeking permission should have any legal estate or interest in the property show that the legislature did not intend that possession of such estate or interest by the person applying was to be necessary. The trial judge so held and I would respectfully agree.

The sweep of the argument of counsel for the defendant, however, carries with it the further submission that because no limiting qualifications are laid down by the relevant sections for an applicant, *anyone* can be an applicant for development permission. An applicant may not be debarred, the argument runs, not alone because he has no legal estate or interest in the property but also irrespective of the genuineness or otherwise of the proposed development, or whether the applicant is acting in good faith or not, or whether those with a legal estate or interest know or approve of the application, or whether other (and possibly conflicting) applications have been made or are pending. There is nothing in the Act, it is said in effect, to debar a pauper from making an application for permission for a multi-million pound development of a property which he has only read about in a newspaper.

Support for those far-reaching propositions is said to be found in the fact that development permission (except as may be otherwise provided by the permission) enures for the benefit of the property and of all persons for the time being interested therein (s. 28, sub-s. 5); so unless and until the person who has got a permission acquires the necessary interest, the permission remains merely a paper or potential benefit annexed to the land. If more than one such permission are granted, and even if they are granted without the knowledge or approval of the owner or occupier, it is argued that no harm is done to anyone because none of those permissions can be put into effect except by a person who has an interest in the property. So, it is said, the purposes of the Act of 1963 are not frustrated or diverted if applications for development permission are open to all and sundry.

That the proposition that virtually anyone may apply for permission to develop a particular property could lead to strange incongruities was shown by instances raised in the course of the argument. However, it is a matter of principle that a statute—particularly a statute like the present one which makes substantial inroads on pre-existing rights—should not be construed as intending to confer unqualified and indiscriminate rights on people generally in respect of another's property such as the right to avail themselves of the legal processes of a planning application so as to gratify what may be merely an idle or perverse whim. The long title of this Act proclaims its purpose to be ". . . to make provision in the interests of the common good, for the proper planning and development of cities, towns and other areas . . ." The powers given by the Act must be read as being exercisable in the interests of the common good and the Courts should lean against a construction which would make the exercise of such powers available to an individual for the purpose of advancing a purely personal motive at the expense of the general purpose of the Act.

Apart from the irreconcilability with the general principle of the proposition put forward on behalf of the defendant, a number of specific provisions of the Act clearly show its unsoundness. For the sake of brevity I shall confine myself to a selection of those provisions for the purpose of showing that the operation of the Act requires that an applicant for permission must have a particular degree of standing.

When an application for development permission under Part IV of the Act is made, it puts in train a scheme of inquiry, investigation and hearing leading to a quasi-judicial determination. Much of the necessary procedure is laid down by regulations made pursuant to the Act, but these I ignore in determining the scope of the Act. As Lord Diplock said in the context of another Act:—"It is legitimate to use the Act as an aid to the construction of the Regulations. To do the converse is to put the cart before the horse"—*Lawson* v. *Fox* [1974] A.C. 803, 809.

Section 25, sub-s. 1, of the Act of 1963 requires the Minister to make permission regulations and enacts that permission shall be granted on application being made in accordance with the regulations and subject to the requirements of the regulations. Sub-section 2 of that section proceeds to set out what the regulations may require from applicants. The regulations may require any applicants "to furnish to the Minister and to any other specified persons any specified information with respect to their applications" (para. c) and "to submit any further information relative to their applications (including any information as to any estate or interest in or right over land)" and "the production of any evidence to verify any particulars of information given by any applicants"—see paras. (d) and (e).

Since applications cannot be successful unless they comply with the requirements of the regulations (s. 25, sub-s. 1), the legislature must be credited with the intention of delineating the range of eligible applicants by the extent of the permitted requirements. Thus, a total stranger to the property, who has no liaison with those interested in it, could scarcely have been envisaged as a successful applicant, for normally he could not furnish the specified information (including any estate or interest in or right over the land) or produce evidence to verify particulars given as to such information.

Furthermore, when we turn to s. 9, sub-s. 1, of the Act of 1963 we find that a planning authority may, for any purpose arising in relation to their functions under the Act, require the occupier or the person receiving the rent to state in writing within a specified period particulars of the estate, interest or right by virtue of which he is an occupier or receives the rent and the name and address (so far as they are known to him) of every person who to his knowledge has any estate or interest in or right over or in respect of the property. Sub-section 2 of that section makes it an offence punishable on summary conviction with a fine not exceeding £20 for a person from whom such information is required to fail to state it within the time specified, or to make a statement in writing which is to his knowledge false or misleading in a material respect.

The effect of s. 9 is that when an application for permission to develop is made, the planning authority, in order to carry out their functions under the Act, may find it necessary to serve on the occupier or the person receiving the rent the notice referred to in sub-s. 1 of the section; if the person so served does not comply with the notice in the way specified in sub-s. 2, he will become liable to the sanction of the criminal law. If, as counsel for the defendant contends, applications for development permission may be made in multiplicity and indiscriminately by persons at large, obligations would be cast on occupiers of or persons receiving rent out of property and failure to comply with those obligations would subject such people to a fine with a liability to imprisonment in default of payment. The fundamental rule that a statute must be construed so as to keep its operation within the ambit of the broad purpose of the Act rules out such an interpretation; otherwise it would be possible for persons, by means of frivolous or perverse applications, to cause the imposition of duties and liabilities which would be wholly unnecessary for the operation of the Act in the interests of the common good.

Section 83 of the Act of 1963 provides an equally cogent reason why the Act does not envisage persons unconnected with any real interest in property or its development being allowed to apply for development permission. That section provides that an authorised person (*i.e.*, a person so authorised for the purposes of the section by the planning authority or the Minister) may enter, subject to an order of the District Court prohibiting or restricting the entry, on any land for any purpose connected with the Act and may do all things reasonably necessary for the purpose for which the entry is made and, in particular, may survey, make plans, take levels, make excavations, and examine the depth and nature of the subsoil. If the Act had to be read as allowing that degree of intrusion at the behest of *any* individual who chooses to make a development application in respect of another person's property, the constitutionality of the statute would be very much in question.

The inequities and anomalies that would follow if there is to be an unrestricted right to apply for permission to develop another person's property is shown by the terms of many provisions of the Act. For example, since the planning authority must investigate and deal with each application with sufficient care to ensure that their decision will have due regard to the development plan required by Part III of the Act, a group of people making multiple applications in respect of properties in which they have no legal interest, and which they have no intention or hope of developing, could put such a strain on the resources of the planning authority as to stifle the operation of the Act in delay and confusion. Since s. 41 requires particulars of all applications for development permission to be entered on the register (which s. 8 requires the planning authority to keep), and since s. 28, sub-s. 5, provides that a grant of permission will normally enure for the benefit of the property and all persons interested in it, the register (which incorporates documents by reference) would become encumbered with bulk and detail if applications without restriction were allowed, and consequently might prove confusing or misleading for those who would be required to consult it.

If there need never be a connexion between the applicant and those who have a legal estate or interest in the property, the period for appealing against the decision of the planning authority would be, for the applicant, one month from the *receipt* of the decision, but for others (who, if the argument on behalf of the defendant is correct, could include those with a legal estate or interest) it would be 21 days from the day of the *giving* of the decision (s. 28, sub-s. 5)—thus giving preferential treatment to someone who may be merely a meddlesome interloper. It is no answer to this complaint to say that a grant or refusal of an application for development permission cannot prejudice a subsequent application. As I have shown, the mere making of an application by a person with no legal interest can operate to the detriment of the owner or occupier. And in any case, I find nothing in the scheme of the Act that would allow interfering, if well-intentioned, outsiders to intrude into the rights of those with a legal interest to the extent of lumbering the property with unwanted grants or refusals of permission, thus cluttering the title.

To sum up, while the intention of the Act is that persons with no legal interest (such as would-be purchasers) may apply for development permission, the operation of the Act within the scope of its objects and the limits of constitutional requirements would be exceeded if the word "applicant" in the relevant sections is not given a restricted connotation. The extent of that restriction must be determined by the need to avoid unnecessary or vexatious applications, with consequent intrusions into property rights and demands on the statutory functions of planning authorities beyond what could reasonably be said to be required, in the interests of the common good, for proper planning and development.

Applying that criterion, I consider that an application for development permission, to be valid, must be made either by or with the approval of a person who is able to assert sufficient legal estate or interest to enable him to carry out the proposed development, or so much of the proposed development as relates to the property in question. There will thus be sufficient privity between the applicant (if he is not a person entitled) and the person entitled to enable the applicant to be treated, for practical purposes, as a person entitled.

As for the present case, the defendant's application was invalid and should not have been entertained for she had no legal estate or interest in the property and her application was made without the knowledge or approval of the plaintiffs who, as the owners of the fee simple, are the only persons who would be legally competent to carry out the development for which the defendant sought permission.

The procedural point has been taken that in seeking injunctions against the defendant the present proceedings are misconceived. When these proceedings were instituted on the 12th November, 1973, the decisions of the planning authority that are complained of had not yet been made. They were not made until the 23rd November, 1973. On the 30th November, 1973, the plaintiffs appealed against those decisions. There the matter still stands, with the appeal not yet heard by the Minister. Whatever may have been the validity of the plaintiffs' claim to the injunctions when the proceedings were begun, they have no right to be granted them at this stage. At the moment the plaintiffs are the appellants and the defendant is the respondent in an appeal against a decision to grant development permission. The plaintiffs have sought (a) an injunction restraining the defendant from applying for the planning permission in question and (b) a mandatory injunction requiring the defendant to withdraw her applications for that permission. However, since the planning authority has notified its decision and since the plaintiffs have appealed against that decision, the matter has passed the stage of being merely a pending application. It has matured into a decision which the plaintiffs' planning appeal has brought into the seisin of the Minister. Since the defendant ranks as respondent in that appeal, she is no longer a moving party, so she cannot be restrained in the pending proceedings by means of either the negative or the mandatory injunctions sought. For that reason I would uphold the trial judge's decision to refuse to grant the interlocutory injunctions sought.

If the order proposed by this judgment is made, it would be simply a matter for the plaintiffs to have their planning appeal heard, in which case the Minister would allow the appeal, thus negativing, on the ground of the defendant's lack of standing, the planning authority's decision. This would achieve the plaintiffs' purposes no less effectively than if the injunctions sought in this action had been granted.

Consequently, while I would decide the substantive point in favour of the plaintiffs, for the procedural reasons stated I would dismiss the appeal.

Extract 12.17

MOGUL OF IRELAND LTD. v TIPPERARY (NORTH RIDING) COUNTY COUNCIL
[1976] I.R. 260

S. 135 of the Grand Jury (Ireland) Act, 1836, as amended, provides for compensation in respect of malicious injuries and a court may award such sums "as the person or persons ought to receive for such injury or damage". In *Noblett v Leitrim County Council* [1920] 2 I.R. 143 the Irish Court of Appeal held that an award under s. 135 could include consequential losses. That decision was overruled by the Supreme Court in *Smith v Cavan and Monaghan County Councils* [1949] I.R. 322. S. 1 of the Malicious Injuries (Ireland) Act, 1853 provides for the compensation of "all damages" sustained by a person as a result of an unlawful assembly. It further provides that recovery shall be "by like application and proceedings . . . and subject to like provisions" as are provided for applications under s. 135 of the Act of 1836.

The applicants' premises were damaged by explosives which were placed by a group of armed men. In their application to the Circuit Court for compensation they proved that they suffered direct losses of over £29,000 and consequential losses amounting to £220,000. A case was stated to the Supreme Court on the question whether the applicants could recover the consequential losses under either of the statutory provisions. The majority answered in the negative, with O'Higgins C.J. and Walsh J. dissenting on the interpretation of s. 1 of the Act of 1853. The judgment of Henchy J. is interesting for its discussion of the role of precedent in statutory interpretation and its view that the Act of 1853 is part of a statutory series and must be interpreted accordingly.

Henchy J.

The question for resolution in this Case Stated was posed to and answered by the Supreme Court in *Smith* v. *Cavan and Monaghan County Councils* [1949] I.R. 322. The arguments and authorities for and against the allowance of consequential loss in a claim under s. 135 of the Grand Jury (Ireland) Act, 1836, were fully deployed in that case. The section was considered with due regard to its legislative background and its subsequent amendment and adaptation. The case was argued before a full court, whose jurisdiction to declare the law authoritatively was no less comprehensive than that of this Court. No point of substance seems to have been advanced in argument at this hearing that was not then brought to the court's attention. The court was fully aware that its task was to decide authoritatively and conclusively a point on which there had been a divergence of judicial opinion in previous cases. The court took time to consider its opinion and then decided (Maguire C.J., Murnaghan, Geoghegan and O'Byrne JJ.; Black J. dissenting) that consequential loss was not recoverable. That decision has stood unquestioned in the Courts of this State from 1949 up to now.

This Court, while affirming its general adherence to the doctrine of *stare decisis*, has asserted its freedom to depart from a previous decision, but only for "the most compelling reasons"—see *The State (Quinn)* v. *Ryan* [1965] I.R. 70, 127—or, as it was otherwise put, where the "Court is clearly of opinion that an earlier decision was erroneous it should be at liberty to refuse to follow it, at all events in exceptional cases"—*Attorney General* v. *Ryan's Car Hire Ltd.* [1965] I.R. 642, 654. Therefore, the primary consideration is whether this Court is clearly of opinion that the decision in *Smith's Case* [1949] I.R. 322 was erroneous. If the point were *res integra*, one might reach the opposite conclusion, but I do not think it is possible to assert a *clear* opinion that *Smith's Case* was wrongly decided. I do not propose to set out the arguments for or against the acceptance of the conclusion reached by the majority in *Smith's Case* but, in my opinion, the tenability of that conclusion cannot be clearly rejected in the face of its supporting reasoning—to which must be added the opinions of Holmes L.J. in *Brackley Co-operative Society* v. *Tyrone County Council* (1901) 1 N.I.J.R. & L.G.R. 146, of Sir John Ross L.C. in *Leyburn* v. *Armagh County Council (No. 2)* [1922] 2 I.R. 58 and *McKnight* v. *Armagh County Council* [1922] 2 I.R. 137, and of Kennedy C.J., FitzGibbon and Murnaghan JJ. in *Kennedy* v. *Minister for Finance* [1925] 2 I.R. 195.

A decision of the full Supreme Court (be it the pre-1961 or the post-1961 Court), given in a fully-argued case and on a consideration of all the relevant materials, should not normally be overruled merely because a later Court inclines to a different conclusion. Of course, if possible, error should not be reinforced by repetition or affirmation, and the desirability of achieving certainty, stability, and predictability should yield to the demands of justice. However, a balance has to be struck between rigidity and vacillation, and to achieve that balance the later Court must, at the least, be *clearly* of opinion that the earlier decision was erroneous. In *Attorney General* v. *Ryan's Car Hire Ltd.* the judgment of the Court gave examples of what it called exceptional cases, the decisions in which might be overruled if a later Court thought them to be clearly wrong. While it was made clear that the examples given were not intended to close the category of exceptional cases, it is implicit from the use in that judgment of expressions such as "convinced" and "for compelling reasons" and "clearly of opinion that the earlier decision was erroneous" that the mere fact that a later Court, particularly a majority of the members of a later Court, might prefer a different conclusion is not in itself sufficient to justify overruling the earlier decision. Even if the later Court is clearly of opinion that the earlier decision was wrong, it may decide in the interests of justice not to overrule it if it has become inveterate and if, in a widespread or fundamental way, people have acted on the basis of its correctness to such an extent that greater harm would result from overruling it than from allowing it to stand. In such cases the maxim *communis error facit jus* applies: see *per* Lord Buckmaster in *Bourne* v. *Keane* [1919] A.C. 815, 874; *Ross Smith* v. *Ross Smith* [1963] A.C. 280; *R.* v. *National Insurance Commissioner: Ex p. Husdon* [1972] A.C. 944.

We are concerned here with a pure question of statutory interpretation which was fully argued and answered in *Smith's Case* after mature consideration. There are no new factors, no shift in the underlying considerations, no suggestion that the decision has produced untoward results not within the range of that court's foresight. In short, all that has been suggested to justify a rejection of that decision is that it was wrong. Before such a *volte-face* could be justified it would first have to be shown that it was clearly wrong. Otherwise the decision to overrule it might itself become liable to be overruled. In my opinion, counsel for the applicants have, at most, established no more than that the interpretation for which they contend might possibly be preferred to that which commended itself to the court in *Smith's Case*. That is not enough. They should show that the decision in *Smith's Case* was clearly wrong and that justice requires that it should be overruled. They have not done so. I would therefore decline the invitation to overrule the decision in *Smith's Case*.

Counsel for the applicants argue in the alternative that the consequential loss may be recovered under s. 1 of the Malicious Injuries (Ireland) Act, 1853. Undoubtedly, the claim for direct loss is entitled to succeed under s. 1 of the Act of 1853 because the damage was caused by an unlawful assembly of six armed and masked men who overpowered security men and other employees and then blew up electrical installations. Although *Smith's Case* decided that consequential loss is not recoverable in a claim under s. 135 of the Act of 1836, there is no express decision in this State on whether consequential loss may be recovered in a claim under s. 1 of the Act of 1853. The Court of Appeal in Northern Ireland held in *Robinson* v. *Tyrone County Council* [1952] N.I. 54 that consequential loss could be recovered under that section but, as far as can be ascertained, this is the first time the point has been considered expressly by any court in this State.

The long title of the Act of 1853 is:—"An Act to extend the remedies for the compensation of malicious injuries to property in Ireland." The preamble, having recited inter alia the Act of 1836 and the Malicious Injuries (Ireland) Act, 1848, states that it is expedient to extend the benefit of the Act of 1836 to "certain cases of losses or damages sustained by persons by means of certain other unlawful, riotous, or tumultuous acts herein-after mentioned." It is to be noted that the purpose of the Act of 1853 is to extend the remedial procedure of the Act of 1836 to certain new types of acts causing losses or damages. The Act of 1848 is recited for the purpose of showing that the Act of 1853 is an extension of the cases covered by the Act of 1848. So, in order to understand the legislative pattern into which the Act of 1853 fits, it is necessary to turn to the Act of 1848. The long title of the Act of 1848 shows it to be an Act to repeal, and substitute other provisions in place of, those provisions in the Obstruction of Trade Act, 1783 (23 & 24 Geo. 3, c. 20) which provided for making satisfaction to persons injured by violent obstruction of the freedom of the corn markets and the corn trade. The preamble recites the Act of 1783 as providing that where persons unlawfully, riotously, and tumultuously assembled together wilfully and maliciously pull down, demolish etc. buildings where grain is kept, or do other specified damage, "*all damages* which shall be sustained" may be recovered by action against the chief or other magistrate of the town or city or against any one or more of the inhabitants of a parish not being a town or city. Section 2 of the Act of 1848 then proceeds to enact that "*all damages*" sustained by means of offences under the Act of 1783 are to be recovered in the manner provided in the Act of 1836 for the recovery of "*compensation* for losses or damages."

It is clear, therefore, that the Act of 1853 creates no new measure of damages. It merely extends, in regard to other kinds of damage to property, the right given by the Act of 1848 to use the procedure of the Act of 1836 for the recovery of compensation for losses or damages. There is no extra significance in its use of the expressions "compensation" (which is also to be found in both the Act of 1836 and the Act of 1848) or "all damages" (which is to be found in both the Act of 1848 and the Act of 1783). The expression "all damages" means full or unreduced damages, *i.e.*, such damages as have been suffered without reduction from them of any moneys received by the applicant on foot of an insurance of the property damaged or destroyed: see *London Assurance Co.* v. *Sainsbury* (1783) 3 Doug. K.B. 245. The use of the word "compensation" in ss. 137, 139 and 140 of the Act of 1836, in s. 2 of the Act of 1848 and in s. 1 of the Act of 1853 (each time in the same context) makes abundantly clear that the Act of 1853 was using the word to connote nothing more than what was recoverable under s. 135 of the Act of 1836. If the expressions "all damages" and "compensation" had been introduced into the malicious-injury code for the first time by the Act of 1853, they might have to be given a special meaning for the purpose of that Act. But, as I hope I have shown, their use *in pari materia* in the earlier legislation, the statement in the preamble to the Act of 1853 of the scope of the purpose of that Act, and the context in which they are used, rule out the possibility that an award under s. 1 of the Act of 1853 is to be measured differently from an award under s. 135 of the Act of 1836, namely, as covering only actual loss—which, apparently, was all that was claimed in England for similar damage under the Riot Act, 1714: see *London Assurance Co.* v. *Sainsbury* (1783) 3 Doug. K.B. 245.

Apart from reasoning based on the legislative genesis of s. 1 of the Act of 1853, the internal textual evidence provided by that section shows that its measure of damages is that laid down by the Act of 1836. Section 1 of the Act of 1853 enacts, as does s. 2 of the Act of 1848, that the damages to which it refers are to be recovered "by like applications and proceedings, and by like presentments of the grand jury . . . and subject to like traverses, and subject to like provisions, and in like manner in all respects as by [*the Act of 1836 or the County Dublin Grand Jury Act, 1844*] are provided in relation to the application for or recovery of compensation for losses or damages sustained by any person or persons . . ." I interpret those words as putting an applicant for compensation under the Act of 1853, as regards standing to claim and recover, in the same position (save as to proof of the unlawful act or offence) as that of an applicant under the Act of 1836—just as the standing of the grand jury under both Acts is also put on the same footing. Save as to the nature and quality of the act relied on, the proofs required to sustain a claim, and the grounds on which a grand jury might have rejected a claim (or part of a claim), are the same under both Acts. To quote the Act of 1853, the claims in both cases are "subject to like traverses, and subject to like provisions, and in like manner in all respects." The word "traverses" is not used as connoting denials of facts in a pleading, but in the technical sense in which it is used in the Grand Jury Acts to connote appeals against presentments. Thus, if a presentment of a grand jury had wrongfully allowed, in whole or in part, a malicious injury claim, an individual who was affected could have applied to the judge of assize for leave to traverse, *i.e.*, to appeal; on the trial of the traverse, the judge was empowered to make such order as he thought proper: see s. 138 of the Act of 1836 (which section was repealed by the Local Government (Ireland) Act, 1898) and *In re Glover* (1880) 6 L.R. Ir. 401. The correct identification of the meaning of "traverse" in this context is made by Campbell L.C. in *Noblett* v. *Leitrim County Council* [1920] 2 I.R. 143, 149 where he refers to ". . . the transfer in 1898 of the jurisdiction [*of the grand jury*] to the County Court Judge retaining the right of traverse or appeal to the Judge of Assize . . ."

The conclusion I have reached, by reference to both legislative background and textual content, as to the correct measure of compensation under s. 1 of the Act of

1853 is reinforced when regard is had to the illogical and anomalous results that would follow if compensation under that section were assessable otherwise than under s. 135 of the Act of 1836. While the terms of s. 135 of the Act of 1836 show that compensation under that section is confined to damage committed maliciously or wantonly, compensation is recoverable under the Act of 1853 for damage caused by an unlawful act (such as an act of negligence) which is not in itself a crime, provided it was committed by persons who were unlawfully, riotously, or tumultuously gathered together: *Dubtax Ltd.* v. *Dublin County Council* (1941) 75 I.L.T.R. 125; *Morrison* v. *Dublin Corporation* [1948] I.R. 424. That being so, should the legislature be credited with expressing an intention in the Act of 1853 that larger compensation might be awarded for the consequences of an act when it was committed negligently than could be recovered if it was committed maliciously or wantonly? In all reason the answer should be:—"Not unless the Act of 1853 clearly says so." In my opinion it does not.

Let me illustrate with an example the consequences of the contrary conclusion. Suppose a group of people conspire together against A. and B. They arrange that one of their number will burn down A.'s house and that the others will go to B.'s house and merely use threatening words to him. As a result of that conspiracy, A.'s house is maliciously burned down. As a result of the same conspiracy, B. is subjected to a threatening demonstration by an unlawful assembly in the course of which, through the dropping of a lighted match or some other act of negligence, his house is burned down. A. would be entitled to lay a claim for compensation under s. 135 of the Act of 1836: B.'s claim would lie under the Act of 1853. The law in those circumstances might be criticized for having stumbled into unfair discrimination if it allowed B., whose house was accidentally destroyed, to recover compensation for consequential as well as actual loss, while confining A., whose house was intentionally destroyed, to actual loss. No judicial statement has yet even hinted that such a conclusion could be drawn, and the reason I believe is because s. 1 of the Act of 1853 makes clear that the application for and recovery of compensation under that Act is to be subject to like provisions as those laid down in the Act of 1836. One of those provisions is that in s. 135 stating that the decree is to be for "such sum or sums of money as the person or persons so injured ought to receive for such injury or damage." *Smith's Case* has conclusively ruled that such decree may not include a sum for consequential loss, so I would hold that a decree made under s. 1 of the Act of 1853 is subject to the same limitation.

To sum up, compensation, whether under s. 135 of the Act of 1836 or under s. 1 of the Act of 1853, is "such sum or sums of money as the person or persons so injured ought to receive for such injury or damage." Although the sum to be awarded is described in s. 1 of the Act of 1853 as "all damages which shall be so sustained," no authority for the proposition that such compensation could include a sum for consequential loss is found until the year 1900 (*Duffy* v. *Mayo County Council*—Vanston's Local Government in Ireland; vol. 2, p. 1235) but in the following year Holmes L.J. stated (*Brackley Co-operative Society* v. *Tyrone County Council* (1901) 1 N.I.J.R. & L.G.R. 146) that in his experience damages for consequential loss had never been allowed, and he refused to award them. Accepting that this was a correct statement of the contemporaneous exposition of the Act of 1836, and in the light of its legislative background (as set out by Palles C.B. in *Ballymagauran Co-operative Agricultural & Dairy Society* v. *County Councils of Cavan & Leitrim* [1915] 2 I.R. 85), the Supreme Court in *Smith* v. *Cavan and Monaghan County Councils* overruled *Noblett* v. *Leitrim County Council* [1920] 2 I.R. 143—thus restoring what it considered to have been for many years before that decision the accepted reading of the Acts, which is that consequential loss was not recoverable.

The decision in *Smith's Case* is comparable with other decisions which give a restricted scope to a statutory measure of damages or compensation. A prime example is the artificial judicial limitation of damages awarded under the Fatal

Accidents Act, 1846 (Lord Campbell's Act). Although it is said to have been Lord Campbell's intention when introducing the Act of 1846 in parliament that it would allow damages to be awarded to cover *solatium* for personal loss, as well as pecuniary loss, and although s. 2 of the Act was, accordingly, broadly worded so as to allow the jury to award "such damages as they think proportioned to the injury resulting from such death," it was nevertheless decided by the courts that an award under the sections must not go beyond pure financial loss. When such decisions, questionable though their rationale may be, become embedded in the legal system with the passage of time, and when people have ordered their affairs on the basis of their rightness, it invariably requires an amending statute to dislodge them.

The disallowance of consequential loss in a malicious injury claim has been criticized as unjust because in certain cases the substantial loss is consequential and not actual. From the standpoint of the person who has suffered the malicious injury, such criticism is indeed justified. But, looked at from the viewpoint of the guiltless but mulcted group of ratepayers who have been chosen to bear the burden of the compensation, it has less validity. In *Noblett* v. *Leitrim County Council* Sir James Campbell L.C., in referring to the Court of Appeal's decision in that case which allowed consequential loss to be recovered, said:—"The effect of our decision may aggravate the burden upon the innocent ratepayer, but it may also afford, as the statute intended, a salutary stimulus to his efforts for the prevention of crime and for the detection of offenders." Whatever validity there may have been in that justification of such an award when the Act of 1836 was passed, it has lost much of its force today,.

The malicious injury provisions of the Act of 1836 were designed to cope with episodes of lawlessness in an agricultural, static, unpoliced and politically restive society. In the absence of the ease of movement that was to come with the development of an efficient system of roads, the building of railways, and the introduction of the internal combustion engine, most people lived out their lives in local communities and had what the legislature obviously deemed sufficient knowledge of local activities to enable them, if not to prevent crime, at least to help in apprehending those who had offended against what the statute sought to prevent or to make less common, namely, malicious acts such as burning corn, hay or straw, or killing or maiming horses or cattle. The rationale of the code is more tenuous to-day when rapid modes of travel make it less likely that the perpetrators of malicious acts will have come from the local community; when prevention and detection of crime are in the hands of a national police force and, therefore, can no longer be said to be a local communal responsibility; when explosive, incendiary, and other devices have a sophistication and destructiveness beyond anything that the legislators might possibly have envisaged in 1836; when industrialization and the growth of cities have the result that the burden of compensation is frequently shared by ratepayers who are not resident but merely rated occupiers in the area of levy; and when the basis of liability for rates is considered by many people to be anachronistic and discriminatory in some respects.

There is no doubt that the arbitrariness and inequity which its critics see in the malicious injury code (a code which one critic has suggested is, in its present form, inconsistent with constitutionally guaranteed rights: see the article by J. M. Kelly entitled The Malicious Injuries Code and the Constitution in (1969) 4 Ir. Jurist (N.S.) 221-233) would be accentuated if trading and other consequential losses resulting from such damage or destruction had also to be made good by the selected ratepayers. Although the courts have disallowed consequential loss for much the greater part of the period since the passing of the Act of 1836, yet successive legislatures, British and Irish, have refrained from making such loss recoverable; this might be said to be a sanction, if not an approval, of its irrecoverability.

Whatever view be taken of the criticisms to which I have referred, the basis for them would disappear if the legislature were to make malicious damage, actual and consequential, recoverable from the central exchequer and not from local rates. In the meantime, the law being as it was laid down in *Smith's Case*, I would answer the question in the Case Stated by ruling that the consequential loss claimed is not recoverable.

AIDS TO INTERPRETATION

Canons of interpretation establish general guidelines or approaches to interpretation. In addition there are a number of maxims, presumptions and external aids to which the courts have recourse. It should be noted that they supplement, and do not replace, the canons of interpretation. In general, they apply to particular types of legislation or to particular forms of words.

1. Maxims and presumptions

It is beyond the scope of this work to consider maxims and presumptions in any great detail, an awareness of their existence being sufficient. However, it should be noted that those involved in the drafting of legislation will probably have taken them into account and will have framed its provisions accordingly. Put another way, maxims and presumptions operate to inform the draftsman that if a particular object is sought to be achieved there might be a particular statutory formula which can be employed.

Usually maxims consist of general propositions regarding the interpretation of statutory words. In this respect they reflect legal attitudes. Maxims assist the courts in the interpretation of forms of words which appear frequently in statutes. Examples are *noscitur a sociis* which was invoked in *Dillon v Minister for Posts and Telegraphs*, Supreme Court, unreported, June 3, 1981 (Extract 12.18) and the *ejusdem generis* rule which was applied in *C.W. Shipping Co. Ltd. v Limerick Harbour Commissioners*, [1989] I.L.R.M. 416 (Extract 12.19). The effect of the maxim, *generalis specialibus non derogant* is that a subsequent general statute does not effect a repeal of a prior special statute. It was invoked in *McGonagle v McGonagle* [1951] I.R. 123 and *The People v T.*, Court of Criminal Appeal, unreported, July 27, 1988 where s. 1 of the Criminal Justice (Evidence) Act, 1924, which restricts a spouse's competence as a witness in the trial of the other spouse, was held not to repeal earlier special legislation which made the spouse competent, in certain specified cases.

In some cases a court might invoke a presumption that a particular statute, or a statute of a particular type, should be interpreted in a particular manner. For instance, it is a presumed that penal statutes should be interpreted strictly. This is based on the belief that if the Oireachtas wishes to create a criminal offence it will do so clearly and unambiguously. This presumption was adverted to in *Frescati Estates Ltd. v Walker* [1975] I.R. 177 (Extract 12.16) and *C.W. Shipping Co. Ltd. v Limerick Harbour Commissioners*, [1989] I.L.R.M. 416 (Extract 12.19). The presumption is also applied where the provision in question has a bearing on the liberty of the individual. In *The People v Farrell* [1978] I.R. 13 the Court of Criminal Appeal observed that the Offences Against the State Act, 1939, being penal legislation must be strictly construed. A similar principle of strict construction applies with regard to revenue statutes—see *Inspector of Taxes v Kiernan* [1981] I.R. 117 (Extract 12.5) *Kellystown Co. v Hogan* [1985] I.L.R.M. 200, *Charles McCann Ltd. v Ó Cúlachain* [1986] I.R. 196 (Extract 12.13). Other presumption of importance are those against retrospective effect, *Hamilton v Hamilton* [1982] I.R. 446, against extra-territorial effect, *Chemical Bank Ltd. v McCormack* [1983] I.L.R.M. 350, against unclear changes in the law, *Minister for Industry and Commerce v Hales* [1967] I.R. 50 (Extract 12.9) and of compatibility with international law, *Ó Domhnaill v Merrick* [1984] I.R. 151.

Extract 12.18

DILLON v MINISTER FOR POSTS AND TELEGRAPHS
SUPREME COURT, UNREPORTED, JUNE 3, 1981

The plaintiff was a candidate in a general election. He applied to the defendant for free postage of his election literature. His application was rejected on the grounds that the contents of his literature breached the Post Office Act, 1908 and regulations made thereunder, which prohibit the sending through the post of material which is "indecent, obscene or grossly offensive". The defendant alleged that certain statements in the plaintiff's literature were grossly offensive.

Henchy J.

The plaintiff, Andrew Dillon, is a duly nominated candidate for the forthcoming general election. He has chosen Dublin North Central as the constituency for which he is attempting to win a seat in Dáil Éireann. He is one of the founder members of a new organisation called the Young Ireland Party, but as that organisation is not registered as a political party, he will contest the election as an independent candidate.

Like all other Dáil candidates, he is entitled, subject to regulations made by the Minister for Posts and Telegraphs, to avail himself of the free postage facilities provided for by s. 50 of the Prevention of Electoral Abuses Act, 1923. That section would allow him, if he complies with its provisions and those of the regulations made thereunder, to send, free of any charge for postage, to each person on the register of electors for the constituency, one postal communication "containing matter relating to the election only" and not exceeding two ounces in weight. The Dáil Elections Free Postage Regulations, 1961 (S.I. No. 195 of 1961) set out in detail the conditions under which this right of free postage is to operate. One of those conditions is that there must be deposited in advance a specimen of the communication which it is desired to be sent free of postage charge.

The plaintiff got a brochure prepared and printed which, as he intimated to the Department of Posts and Telegraphs, he wished to have circulated free by post. Despite changes made in its original form, it has been rejected as ineligible for free postage by the Department. In the conviction that the objections taken to it are unfounded, he has instituted proceedings against the Minister for Posts and Telegraphs seeking certain injunctions. He has now applied in the High Court for an interlocutory injunction to restrain the Minister from preventing or hindering him from sending the brochure free through the post. He was unsuccessful in that application, which was one of urgency, for the election is set for the 11th of this month. He has now appealed to this Court against the refusal of that interlocutory relief, and because the matter requires to be disposed of without delay, we have expedited the hearing of the appeal and the delivery of our decision.

The argument on the hearing of the plaintiff's motion in the High Court ranged further afield than in this Court. Before us, counsel for the Minister reduced the grounds of objection to the relief sought by the plaintiff to two points: (1) that the brochure is "grossly offensive", and (2) that it contains matter other than "matter relating to the election only". Otherwise, it would appear, the Minister does not contend that the printed brochure fails to qualify for free circulation through the post.

As to the first of those objections, the Minister rests his case on certain restrictions imposed by the Post Office Act, 1908, and regulations made thereunder. Assuming (without necessarily so holding) that that Act and those regulations have application to this case, one notes that Art. 6 of the relevant regulations (The Inland Post Warrant, 1939) prohibits the posting, conveyance, or delivery by post of "any postal packet . . . having thereon, or on the cover thereof, any words, marks, or designs of an indecent, obscene or grossly offensive character". Again assuming (without necessarily so deciding) that this brochure falls within the definition of "postal packet" given in the 1908 Act, or within the more restricted definition of "postal packet" given in the 1939 regulations, I would find it impossible to hold that the brochure is debarred from the benefit of free post because of the passage in it to which the Minister takes exception. That passage, and it is the only passage relied on for the purpose of this point, runs as follows:

> Today's politicians are dishonest because they are being political and must please the largest number of people.

I am far from saying that even if the prohibition were simply against words of a grossly offensive character, I would have held that that sentence would offend against such a prohibition. And I venture to think that those who practise what is often dubbed the art of the possible would not feel grossly offended by such an expression of opinion which, denigratory and cynical though it might be thought by some, is no more than the small coinage of the currency of political controversy. Some of the most revered and successful politicians who have lived have failed, at least in the eyes of reputable historians, to align great political acumen and success with moral or intellectual honesty. A charge of dishonesty is one that rarely penetrates the epidermis of any seasoned politician.

But the embargo is not simply against words of a grossly offensive character. So I do not have to reject the Minister's objection on that ground. The embargo is against "any words, marks or designs of an indecent, obscene or grossly offensive character". That assemblage of words gives a limited and special meaning to the expression "grossly offensive character". As Stamp J. said in *Bourne v. Norwich Crematorium Ltd.* [1967] 2 All E.R. 576, 578:

> English words derive colour from those which surround them. Sentences are not mere collections of words to be taken out of the sentence, defined separately by reference to the dictionary or decided cases, and then put back into the sentence with the meaning which you have assigned to them as separate words . . .

Applying the maxim *noscitur a sociis*, which means that a word or expression is known from its companions, the expression "grossly offensive character" must be held to be infected in this context with something akin to the taint of indecency or obscenity. Much of what might be comprehended by the expression if it stood alone is excluded by its juxtaposition with the words "indecent" and "obscene". This means that the Minister may not reject a passage as disqualified for free circulation through the post because it is apt to be thought displeasing or distasteful. To merit rejection is must be *grossly* offensive in the sense of being obnoxious or abhorrent in a way that brings it close to the realm of indecency or obscenity. The sentence objected to by the Minister, while many people would consider it to be denigratory of today's politicians, is far from being of a "grossly offensive character" in the special sense in which that expression is used in the Act.

As to the Minister's second objection, that the printed brochure contains matter other than "matter relating to the election only", this complaint is founded on the inclusion in the brochure of the following sentences:

> By expressing your views on the following proposals and by voting Andrew Dillon No. 1 you will help. Please note them on a scale of 1 to 10 and add one of

your own. Then return to Drumnigh House, Portmarnock, Co. Dublin. Young Ireland Party.

The Minister does not object to the plaintiff's request for a first preference vote, but his counsel has argued that the appeal for the electors' views on the issues propounded in the manifesto contained in the brochure, coupled with a request that the elector might evaluate them in order of merit and add one of his own, goes beyond electioneering and in effect is an attempt to seek responses and support which are calculated to come to fruition, at least in part, after the election.

I am unimpressed by this objection. The embargo on the free postal circulation of matter unrelated to the election is designed to prevent candidates from abusing the privilege of free postal circulation by including matters which are extraneous to the election. What matters those are may sometimes be a highly subjective assessment. But there are areas of expression which are necessarily allied to the election. An election address or manifesto may legitimately and as a due part of the electoral process, seek to dredge up the past, cast an enthusiastic or condemnatory eye on the present state of affairs, or seek to focus attention on the future in terms of the candidate's or his party's confident projections or of what he sees as his opponents' disastrous programmes. Everything that falls within that compass—and perhaps even more—is essentially related to the election. The plaintiff is not seeking to use his brochure merely as a springboard from which to project and stimulate the future prospects of his new party and thereby to turn it to account as a gambit separate and distinct from what is conceded to be a legitimate election appeal for votes. On the contrary, he couples a request for the electors' views on his propounded issues with a request for their votes. This amounts to what might be called a consultative canvass. The requested views may indeed not come to hand until the election is over, but that is no reason for saying that such a request does not relate only to the election. The variety of possible political opinions, criticisms, projections, choices and lawful disclosures that a forthcoming election is apt to generate is a good reason why, in the interests of free democratic processes, the expression "matter relating to the election only" should be liberally construed. That is particularly so when, as in this case, the person seeking to block the free postal circulation of the plaintiff's election brochure is a member of the Dáil and whose party leader is seeking re-election to the Dáil in the same constituency as the plaintiff has chosen to contest.

I would reject the two objections taken by the Minister and allow the appeal. It has not been suggested that the plaintiff would not be entitled to the interlocutory relief sought if those objections fail. Accordingly, I would grant him a mandatory injunction until the 11th June (the date of the election) or until further order, requiring the Minister, his agents, or those who become aware of the making of this order, to accept for postage, free of charge, subject to the terms of s. 50 of the 1923 Act, the printed brochure referred to in the plaintiff's affidavit.

Extract 12.19

C.W. SHIPPING CO. LTD. v
LIMERICK HARBOUR COMMISSIONERS
[1989] I.L.R.M. 416

The applicants, who wished to operate a tug in the Shannon Estuary, sought judicial review of the respondents' refusal to issue them with a licence under s. 53(1) of the Harbours Act, 1946. That section provides for the licensing of a "lighter, ferry-boat or other small boat". The extract from O'Hanlon J.'s judgment deals with the question whether a tug is an "other small boat", which he decided in the negative applying the *ejusdem generis* rule.

O'Hanlon J.

. . . The first question which arises for determination in the present proceedings involves the construction of the provisions of s. 53 (1) of the Harbours Act, 1946, for the purpose of determining whether a tug-owner seeking to carry on his towage business within the confines of a harbour to which the Act relates, requires to be licensed by the harbour authority before it is lawful for him to do so.

The text of s. 53 (1) is as follows:—

> "53.—(1) A harbour authority may, at their discretion, issue to the owner of a lighter, ferry-boat or other small boat which such owner proposes to use or ply for hire habitually in the harbour of the harbour authority a licence authorising such use or plying for hire."

The penalty for carrying on any of these activities without a licence is the remarkably small one of a fine not exceeding £5 which may be imposed on summary conviction of an offence under the section.

The Applicant contends that the phrase, "lighter, ferry-boat or other small boat" is not sufficient or appropriate to include within its ambit a tug. A tug, it is submitted, is not a lighter or ferry-boat, nor is it *ejusdem generis* with either class of craft so as to permit it to be comprehended within the descriptive words "or other small boat".

The meaning of a similar phrase was considered by the Court of Queen's Bench, consisting of Lord Campbell CJ and Erle and Crompton JJ, in the case of *Reed v. Ingham* (1854) 23 L.J.M.C. 156, which involved a conviction for an offence under the Watermen's Act (7 & 8 Geo. 4 c. lxxv). S. 37 of the Act imposed a penalty on any person (other than a freeman of the Watermen's Company or an apprentice to a freeman or widow of a freeman) who should work or navigate "any wherry, lighter or other craft" from or to any place or places or ship or vessel within the limits of the Act. It was held, on appeal by way of Case Stated against a conviction, that the words of the section did not extend to a person who worked a steam-tug for the purpose of towing vessels on the river.

The following passage appears in the judgment of Lord Campbell CJ:—

> We are called upon to put a construction on the word "craft" in s. 37 of the 7 & 8 Geo. 4, c. lxxv. There is no doubt that it may have such a meaning there as will exclude a steam tug. The question is whether it is so used. The section involves serious consequences and interferes with the existing rights of Her Majesty's subjects. It imposes a penalty and establishes a monopoly. For these reasons, it ought to be strictly construed. Now, can we suppose the legislature intended by it to prevent any person from using a steam-tug for the purpose here specified other than a freeman of the Watermen's Company and to impose a penalty for so doing? I think this cannot be so, and that the word "craft" must be looked at together with what precedes it in order to ascertain its meaning. Now it is preceded by the words "wherry, and lighter", and must, according to the ordinary rules of construction be limited to craft *ejusdem generis* with them, which a steam tug is not. Looking to the previous act relating to the Watermen's Company (11 & 12 Will. 3 c. 21) the object seems to be to give them the sole right of carrying passengers or goods for hire, but not to extend their privilege to all sorts of vessels. If so, this steam-tug is not within the monopoly.

Erle J. said:

> He has navigated a steam tug for the purpose of moving a vessel, and the question is, whether he comes within the meaning of the words which I have stated. The whole turns on the wide term "craft". No doubt this may include a steam tug, but the ordinary rule of construction is, that where a wide term follows a narrower term, it is confined to the same class as is so specified. According to that rule, "craft" should be here confined to something of the same

kind as wherries and lighters. A "wherry" and a "lighter" are in common parlance boats plying for hire and carrying passengers or goods; "other craft", therefore, will include other kinds of boats plying for hire and carrying passengers or goods. A steam tug is clearly different. The privilege is given to the Watermen's Company for the public good, on the ground that they have gone through a certain apprenticeship, and are presumed to know how to manage wherries, lighters and such craft . . . I think a person perfectly qualified to ply with a wherry or lighter might be wholly incompetent to take charge of a steam-tug for the purpose of towing large vessels. Such a vessel is, therefore, not within the purpose for which the privilege was given, and this being a penal clause, it must be construed strictly.

It will be seen that the word "wherry" used in the statute which was under consideration in that case was equated, to all intents and purposes, with the word "ferry-boat" which is found in s. 53 of the Harbours Act, 1946, and I would consider that the words "or other small boat" are more difficult to apply in common parlance to a tug than the more general words "or other craft", which had to be considered in *Reed v. Ingham*.

I regard that decision as a useful precedent for the purposes of the present case, and I propose to construe the words of s. 53 (1) of the Act of 1946 in the same manner as did the Court of Queen's Bench in construing the Act of Geo. 4 in that case. I consider that the words "or other small boat" should be construed as being *ejusdem generis* with the specific, descriptive words which immediately precede them, and I do not regard a tug as being of the same *genus* as a lighter or a ferry-boat. It is a very specialised type of craft designed for carrying out towing (or occasionally pushing) of much larger vessels, and not for the carriage for hire of persons or goods. I agree with the submission made by Counsel on behalf of the Applicant in this case that if licensing of tugs under s. 53 had been in the contemplation of the legislature in enacting the Harbours Act, 1946, one would have expected such craft to receive special mention—as they did elsewhere in the Act (S. 49 and 2nd Schedule, Part II, par. 14). Furthermore, if it were intended to prevent tug-owners from carrying on their costly, and potentially very lucrative, operations save under licence, one would expect a more effective deterrent to be provided than the imposition of a maximum penalty of £5 for carrying on their operations in defiance of the licensing requirements of the Act.

Article 14 of the Second Schedule to the Act, taken in conjunction with s. 60, entitles a harbour authority to make bye-laws regulating the use of tugs within its area of jurisdiction, but no such bye-laws have hitherto been made.

As was mentioned in the judgment of Erle J. in *Reed v. Ingham*, a penal provision in a statute must be construed strictly, and this rule is a further constraint on giving to the terminology of s. 53 (1) of the Act of 1946 the wide interpretation necessary if the use of tugs is to be brought within its ambit.

I have, therefore, come to the conclusion that the use of tugs within the harbour area over which the Respondents are entitled to exercise their jurisdiction does not require to be licensed pursuant to the provisions of s. 53 of the Harbours Act, 1946 and the Applicant is and has at all material times been entitled to carry on its business as tug-owner in the said area without requiring the grant of such licence. The Applicant is entitled to a declaratory order in its favour to this effect . . .

[O'Hanlon J. proceeded to hold first, that the applicants were not entitled to an award of damages on the ground that the defendants had acted *bona fide* and second, that even if a licence was required by the applicants the refusal was invalid as the defendants failed to operate fair procedures]

2. External aids

It has earlier been noted that courts when interpreting a statute have recourse to other statutes which are in *pari materia* as an aid to interpretation. But, that aside, the courts traditionally were reluctant to seek assistance in material which lies outside the statute. This reluctance is evident in *Minister for Industry and Commerce v Hales* [1967] I.R. 50 (Extract 12.20) where correspondence between the Minister who initiated the legislation and a citizen was held to be inadmissible. In more recent years this reluctance has been abandoned and a variety of external materials have been examined. In *Maher v Attorney General* [1973] I.R. 140 the Supreme Court examined a commission report on which the legislation in question was based. In *Rowe v Law* [1978] I.R. 55 O'Higgins C.J., dissenting, considered the parliamentary history of s. 90 of the Succession Act, 1965 including various different drafts which had been mooted. He also took account of the marginal note to the section, although this would appear to conflict with s. 11(g) of the Interpretation Act, 1937 which prohibits account being taken of marginal notes and statute headings. The propriety of having recourse to external material is now beyond doubt. In *Bourke v Attorney General* [1972] I.R. 36 (Extract 12.21) the Supreme Court held that it was entitled to examine the *travaux preparatoires* of the European Convention on Extradition, on which s. 50 of the Extradition Act, 1965 was based. In *Wavin Pipes Ltd. v Hepworth Iron Co. Ltd.* [1982] 8 F.S.R. 32 (Extract 12.22) Costello J. held that a court could consider the parliamentary debates on the provision in question. And in *McLoughlin v Minister for the Public Service* [1985] I.R. 631 (Extract 12.23) the Supreme Court examined the explanatory memoranda which accompanied the Bill which eventually became the Act in question.

Extract 12.20

MINISTER FOR INDUSTRY AND COMMERCE v
HALES [1967] I.R. 50

The substantive aspects of this case have already been considered—see Extract 12.9. However, McLoughlin J. considered the admissibility of extrinsic evidence of the purpose of the provision. It was sought to adduce evidence of correspondence which preceded the enactment of the Act and the making of the regulation in question. That correspondence supported the contention that it was intended that wholetime insurance agents were to be brought within the scope of the Act.

McLoughlin J.

I have had an opportunity of reading the judgment about to be delivered by Mr. Justice Henchy and I concur in the conclusion at which he has arrived for the reasons stated in his judgment.

There is, however, one aspect of the case upon which I feel I should elaborate in some detail. During the argument it was stated by Mr. McCarthy, counsel for the Minister for Industry and Commerce, that s. 3, sub-s. 3, of the Holidays (Employees) Act, 1961, was introduced by the Minister during the committee stage of the Bill and especially with the intention that he would have recourse to the subsection to make regulations to apply the Act to wholetime insurance agents. Although I hold the view that this aspect of the matter is quite irrelevant to the interpretation of the subsection, as I will later explain, I think it necessary that I should state first some of the history concerning it as outlined to the Court by Mr. MacCarthy.

[His Lordship outlined the evidence concerned and continued . . .]

I have cited this history as it is relevant to the submission made by Mr. McCarthy that the Court should have regard to it in considering the proposition that, in interpreting s. 3, sub-s. 3, of the Act of 1961, the Court should, in order to evaluate the scope and object of the Act and the remedy it was designed to effect, have regard to the contemporaneous circumstances under which the sub-section was introduced into the Act; and on this point he specifically referred to the contents of the Department's letter of the 24th July, 1961, which I have already quoted, as indicating an intention by the Minister to introduce this sub-section specifically to ensure that insurance agents would be brought within the provisions of the Act. As authority for that proposition Mr. McCarthy relied on the text at p. 19 of Maxwell on Interpretation of Statutes (7th Edn.).

I quote from the 9th Edition (1946) of that text-book, at p. 22:—"Aim, Scope and Object of Act—Heydon's Case—The literal construction then, has, in general, but *prima facie* preference. To arrive at the real meaning, it is always necessary to get an exact conception of the aim, scope amd object of the whole Act; to consider, according to Lord Coke: 1, What was the law before the Act was passed; 2, What was the mischief or defect for which the law had not provided; 3, What remedy Parliament had appointed; and 4, The reason of the remedy. According to another authority 'in order properly to interpret any statute it is as necessary now as it was when Lord Coke reported *Heydon's Case* to consider how the law stood when the statute to be construed was passed, what the mischief was for which the old law did not provide, and the remedy provided by the statute to cure that mischief.' At the same time the language of a statute must not be strained to make it apply to a case to which it does not legitimately, on its terms, apply by invoking consideration of the supposed intention of the legislature." The author then refers, in the following pages, to certain cases citing instances where a history of legislation was resorted to in interpreting certain statutes and concludes at p. 29 as follows:—"The reports furnish other instances. But it is unquestionably a rule that what may be called the parliamentary history of an enactment is not admissible to explain its meaning. Its language can be regarded only as the language of the three Estates of the realm, and the meaning attached to it by its framers or by individual members of one of those Estates cannot control the construction of it."

Mr McCarthy also referred to Halsbury's Laws of England (3rd Ed.) Vol. 36, para. 580:—"If the words of a statute are ambiguous, then the intention of Parliament must be sought first in the statute itself, then in other legislation and contemporaneous circumstances, and finally in the general rules laid down long ago, and often approved, namely, by ascertaining what was the common law before the making of the Act; what was the mischief and defect for which the common law did not provide; what remedy Parliament hath resolved and appointed to cure the disease of the commonwealth; the true reason of the remedy." The notes to that paragraph, where it refers to the phrase "contemporaneous circumstances," directs the reader to pp. 409 *et seq.* of that volume from which pages I quote the following paragraph:—"620. Contemporaneous circumstances. In construing a statute it is permissible to have regard to the state of things existing at the time the statute was passed, and to the evil which, as appears from its provisions, the statute was designed to remedy. For this purpose recourse may be had to annals or histories of the period and to antiquarian researches. The state of things which may be considered includes the state of the law, and it ought generally to be assumed that Parliament knew the existing state of the law. A statute cannot, however, be construed otherwise than in its ordinary meaning in order to attain the result which it was thought would be achieved, and, if in fact an enactment proceeds on a truly erroneous view of the law, that enactment has misfired." Paragraph 622 of the same volume states:—"622. Proceedings in Parliament: reports of Commissions, etc. Even when words in a statute are so ambiguous that they may be construed in more than one sense, regard may not be had to the bill by which it was introduced, or to the fate of amendments dealt with in either House of Parliament, or to what has been said in Parliament. Reference may not be made for the purpose of ascertaining the meaning of a statute to the recommendations contained in the report of a Royal Commission or of a departmental committee or in a White Paper which shortly preceded the statute under consideration because it does not follow that such recommendations were accepted by the legislature."

Mr. McCarthy said that there is a modern liberal view that tends to indicate that the history in this case should be looked at to interpret this sub-section so as to give it the meaning he contends should be given to it in this case, but he failed to produce any authority to that effect. Even if that were so, it gives no assistance in this case. Mr. McCarthy did not dispute the general proposition of the law regarding the interpretation of statutes, as submitted by Mr. Micks and dealt with in the judgment of Mr. Justice Henchy, as to the use of the long title, that the Act must be construed as a whole and that delegated legislative power must not be *ultra vires* the statute creating the power. To give the sub-section and the Regulations the effect contended for by Mr. McCarthy would seem to me to be repugnant, and to do violence, to the intentions of the legislature as indicated by the Act construed as a whole. As against that, there is this matter of supposed evidence of the intention of the Minister in introducing the sub-section. As regards that matter, first, what has to be interpreted is not the intention of the Minister but the intention of the legislature as expressed in the Act; secondly, it should be noted that for a considerable time after the Act was passed, and therefore possibly even at the time the Act was passed, it would appear from the history that I have outlined that the Minister was under an erroneous impression (*a*) that these insurance agents were, as he was so advised, workers and non-domestic workers within s. 3, sub-s. 1, of the Act, and (*b*) that therefore the question of making regulations under s. 3, sub-s. 3, of the Act to bring them within the Act did not arise. For these reasons it is clear that such evidence of contemporaneous circumstances could not possibly assist in interpreting s. 3, sub-s. 3, of the Act even if it were admissible, which I hold not to be so.

Indeed the conclusion that such evidence is inadmissible is confirmed by the most compelling authorities. There is the case of *Salkeld* v. *Johnson* 2 Exch. 256 and I quote from the judgment of Chief Baron Pollock (delivering the judgment of the Court composed of himself, Parke B., Alderson B. and Platt B.) at p. 273 of the report:—"We propose to construe the act of Parliament, according to the legal rules for the interpretation of statutes, principally by the words of the statute itself, which we are to read in their ordinary sense, and only modify or alter so far as it may be necessary to avoid some manifest absurdity or incongruity, but no further. It is proper also to consider the state of the law which it proposes or purports to alter, the mischiefs which existed, and which it was intended to remedy, and the nature of the remedy provided, and to look at the statutes *in pari materia* as a means of explaining this statute. These are the proper modes of ascertaining the intention of the legislature; and we shall not, therefore, refer to the Report of the Real Property Commissioners, published shortly before the passing of this act, and to which it is supposed to have owed its origin, in order to explain its meaning; not conceiving that we can legitimately do so, however strongly we may believe that it was introduced in order to carry into effect their recommendation . . ." Next there is the case of *The Queen* v. *Hertford College* 3 Q.B.D. 693 in which Lord Coleridge C.J. (delivering the judgment of the Court of Appeal composed of himself, and Bagallay, Bramwell and Brett L.JJ.) said at p. 707 of the report:—"We are not, however, concerned with what Parliament intended, but simply with what it has said in the statute. The statute is clear, and the parliamentary history of a statute is wisely inadmissible to explain it, if it is not . . ." In Craies on Statute Law (6th Ed.) the cases I have referred to are cited as still being authorities. I quote from p. 128 of that work:—"It is not permissible in discussing the meaning of an obscure enactment, to refer to 'the parliamentary history' of a statute, in the sense of the debates which took place in Parliament when the statute was under consideration."—and from p. 130 of that work:—"As to reports of Commissioners it is now settled that these are inadmissible as aids to construction when the intention of a statute is in question."

If, as was said by Chief Baron Pollock, the statute should be construed principally by the words of the statute itself which we should only modify or alter so far as it may be necessary to avoid some manifest absurdity or incongruity, it would be departing very far from this canon of interpretation if we were to admit evidence of contemporaneous circumstances which would result in giving an interpretation to a section of the statute, and the regulations made under it, which would be repugnant to the intentions of the legislature as indicated by the Act in question, construed as a whole.

I would, accordingly, answer "No" to the questions set out in the Case Stated as to each of the complaints for the reasons I have given and for the reasons expressed in the judgment of Mr. Justice Henchy with which, as I have already indicated, I concur.

Extract 12.21

BOURKE v ATTORNEY GENERAL [1972] I.R. 36

Part 2 of the Extradition Act, 1965 governs extradition generally, whilst Part 3 governs extradition to the United Kingdom. S. 11 (which is contained in Part 2) and s. 50 (which is contained in Part 3) exempt from extradition a person charged with a "political offence" or an "offence connected with a political offence".

The plaintiff's extradition to the United Kingdom on a charge of assisting a prisoner to escape, contrary to s. 39 of the Prison Act, 1952 (U.K.), was ordered. The prisoner had been convicted of spying for the Soviet Union, and the plaintiff gave evidence that he acted out of sympathy for the prisoner and his beliefs. The High Court directed the release of the plaintiff. The Supreme Court dismissed the defendant's appeal with Walsh, Budd and Teevan JJ. agreeing with Ó Dálaigh C.J. In the extract from his judgment Ó Dálaigh C.J. examined the history of the European Convention on Extradition on which s. 11 of the Act was based and contrasted it with the equivalent provision in the Extradition Act, 1970.

Ó Dálaigh C.J.

. . . Article 3 of the European Convention on Extradition from which the provisions of our Act have been borrowed is in these words:—

Political Offences

1. Extradition shall not be granted if the offence in respect of which it is requested is regarded by the requested Party as a political offence or as an offence connected with a political offence.
2. The same rule shall apply if the requested Party has substantial grounds for believing that a request for extradition for an ordinary criminal offence has been made for the purpose of prosecuting or punishing a person on account of his race, religion, nationality or political opinion, or that that person's position may be prejudiced for any of these reasons.
3. The taking or attempted taking of the life of a Head of State or a member of his family shall not be deemed to be a political offence for the purposes of this Convention.

4. This Article shall not affect any obligations which the Contracting Parties may have undertaken or may undertake under any other international convention of a multilateral character.

As s. 50 of the Act of 1965 is a repetition of s. 11 which is acknowledged to be derived from Article 3 of the European Convention, we have been invited as a means of throwing light on the interpretation of s. 50 to look at the *travaux preparatoires* for the Convention. I accept that this is a valid and proper approach. Section 11 and s. 50 speak of the same things. As the Convention may be examined to discover the meaning of s. 11, it is no less legitimate for the Court to look at Article 3 and the *travaux preparatoires* in interpreting section 50. The European Convention on Extradition had its origin in a recommendation adopted by the Assembly of the Council of Europe at its 36th sitting on the 8th December, 1951. The recommendation (No. 16), which is in two parts, (*a*) asked Governments of the member states to submit their views upon the desirability of concluding a convention based on a memorandum prepared by the Secretariat-General and upon the form and content of such a convention, and (*b*) recommended the Committee of Ministers to nominate a mixed committee to be entrusted with the examination of the replies and the preparation of a draft convention.

The memorandum prepared by the Secretariat-General had this to say on the question of non-extradition for political offences:—"This principle [*i.e., non-extradition for political offences*] has been universally accepted ever since the promulgation of the Belgian law of 1833 which marks a historic turning-point in the evolution of this question. Nevertheless, certain breaches of this practice have made their appearance with the international conventions governing offences against international public order and morals. This is the case with the Convention of 1937 on the suppression of terrorism, the Convention of 1949 on Genocide, and lastly, certain laws on war crimes (*Cf.* Article 5, Clause 2 of the French law of 10th March, 1927). The non-extradition of political offenders is primarily based on the fact that the criminal nature of the act is relative, depending on the peculiar conditions obtaining in the places and institutions in which the political offences were committed. It remains to be decided to what extent this motive applies among the Members of the Council. A further ground may reside in the rule of non-intervention in the internal affairs of another country. In this respect it may be queried how the principle laid down in the European Convention on Human Rights can be reconciled with this rule. Lastly, there is the ground arising from the desirability of protecting the political refugee from the vengeance and illwill of the government he is opposing. In this connection the question arises whether the legal guarantees provided for in the Convention on Human Rights do not adequately meet the concern expressed. In any event, a number of conditions must be complied with before such exceptional action can be rejected. An initial requirement is that it shall concern Member States and countries of the Council of Europe; that such Members shall have subscribed to the provisions of the Convention on Human Rights, especially those of an optional nature contained in Article 25 and 46 of the Convention; and lastly that they shall be parties to the Protocol relating to political rights and freedoms. Even should a political offence not be deemed to warrant treatment as an exception for extradition purposes, there would still remain the question of related offences of a complex nature; that of defining the political character of the offences or the political aims of the application for extradition, all matters which are continually the subject of discussion and of conflicting, if not legally disputable solutions. Treaties as modern as that of 1930 between Germany and Turkey, and that of 1932 between Belgium and Austria leave the decision as to the political nature of the offence to the sole discretion of the State to which application is made. Furthermore, in a series of extradition treaties signed by Great Britain, the onus is on the defendant or the convicted person to prove that the application for extradition is based on political grounds, even though the offence itself may not be a political one. In the event of it proving impossible to draw up detailed regulations, an international legal body might be empowered to settle disputes, to adapt the rules to any new aspects of the question as they arise and draw up suitable and universally binding legislation."

The Belgian Law of 1833 mentioned in the memorandum of the Secretariat-General is the Law concerning Extradition (Official Bulletin, No. 77). It provided at Article 6 that:—"It shall be expressly stipulated in these agreements [*i.e., in extradition treaties*] that no foreigner may be prosecuted or punished for any political crime antecedent to the extradition, or for *any act connected with such a crime*, or for any crime or misdemeanour not provided for by the present law; otherwise all extraditions and all temporary arrests are prohibited." The origin of the expression "act connected with such crime" is identified as being itself a borrowing from Article 227 of the Belgian *Code d'Instruction Criminelle*, where the subject matter is the joinder of several counts in one indictment. Article 227 of the Code is in these terms:—"Les délits sont connexes, soit lorsqu'ils ont été commis en même temps par plusieurs personnes réunies, soit lorsqu'ils ont été commis par différentes personnes, même en différents temps et en divers lieux, mais par suite d'un concert formé a l'avance entre elles, soit lorsque les coupables ont commis les uns pour se procurer les moyens de commettre les autres, pour en faciliter, pour en consommer l'exécution, ou pour en assurer l'impunité." Beltzens' *Encyclopédie* (Code d'instr. crim. art. 227, no. 13) has the comment:—"Les terms de cette disposition ne sont pas limitatifs, mais indicatifs."

The draft article dealing with non-extradition for political offences which emerged from the work of the Committee, and which was submitted on the 17th September, 1954 (Doc. 302) bears a number of affinities with its Belgian antecedent. The draft is headed "*Political Offences*" and it reads as follows—:

1. A requested High Contracting Party may decide that extradition shall or may be refused for an act which, according to the circumstances in which it has been committed, is political or connected with a political act and committed with a view to preparing for, to ensuring the commission of, to concealing or to preventing such a political act; or when there is reason to believe from the circumstances that the extradition is requested with a view to taking action against someone for an act of a political character.
2. The following shall not be deemed political offences:
    (a) Offences in respect of which the High Contracting Parties are obliged by international conventions to institute proceedings;
    (b) attempts on the life of a Head of State or Head of Government.

The opening sentence of the draft article differs from the wording of an earlier draft in a report submitted on the 24th May, 1954 (Doc. 234) but the change thus effected is not relevant to the scope of the article.

I have already set out the text of the article as finally adopted and embodied in the Convention. It will be seen to differ very considerably from the draft proposed by the mixed committee. No significance attaches to the change of the word "act" to "offence"; but what is of significance is that the words "and committed with a view to preparing for, to ensuring the commission of, to concealing or to preventing such a political act" find no part in the Convention. These words, in the draft, qualified "act which . . . is political or connected with a political act" by requiring that the act in question should have been done with a view to preparing for, ensuring the commission of, etc., the first-mentioned political act. The Convention, as adopted, has rejected this limitation; the High Contracting Parties were satisfied that there should be simply a connection between the offence in question and the political offence. The High Contracting Parties, in my opinion, have clearly rejected the narrow limitations upon connected offence which arose from the historical background to the expression as exemplified, for instance, in the judgment of the German Supreme Court in 1933 in *Re Fabijan* [1933-34] Ann. Dig. 360 (No. 156): see Vol. 6 of the Digest of International Law at pages 823-6.

As has been stated, counsel for the defendants submitted that the formula in s. 50 of the Act of 1965 ("political offence or offence connected with a political offence") was to be equated with the expression "offence of a political character" which occurs in s. 3 of the Extradition Act, 1870. Counsel sought to effect this equation with the object of calling in aid the several decisions of the English courts, on the meaning of the formula, from *In re Castioni* [1891] 1 Q.B. 149 to *In re Extradition Act, 1870* [1969] 1 W.L.R. 12, in which latter case the authorities are to be found conveniently collected. The Act of 1870 has been repealed by our Act of 1965, save for s. 24 which deals with the power to take evidence in relation to criminal matters pending before foreign tribunals. It may be noted that s. 24 of the Act of 1870 concludes with the proviso that nothing in the section shall apply in the case of any criminal matter "of a political character." Therefore, the formula of the Act of 1870 is still of importance in our law. In *Re Castioni* Hawkins J. at p. 165 of the report adopted a definition of the expression "offence of a political character" which was to be found in Stephen's History of the Criminal Law of England (Vol II, pp. 70-71) and which referred to crimes which "were incidental to and formed a part of political disturbances." This formula, not unexpectedly, also commended itself to the author of the work, Mr. Justice Stephen who was a member of the court.

Castioni's Case was reviewed in *R. v. Governor of Brixton Prison—Ex p. Kolczynski* [1955] 1 Q.B. 540. Kolczynski was one of seven Polish nationals who sought political asylum in England. They were serving as members of the crew of a small trawler fishing in the North Sea as part of a Polish fishing fleet, and to accomplish their purpose they overpowered the captain of the vessel and the other members of the crew and thereupon brought the ship into an English port, where they were placed under arrest. The Polish Government, pursuant to a treaty of extradition made in 1932 and an Order in Council of 1934, sought the extradition of the prisoners on the ground that they had committed various extraditable offences. The Order in Council applied the provisions of the Extradition Act, 1870, to Poland with the result that extradition was prohibited if the offence in respect of which surrender was demanded was one "of a political character." The magistrate who heard the case accepted evidence that while at sea a political officer overheard and recorded the prisoners' conversations with a view to preparing a case against them on account of their political opinions. The magistrate came to the conclusion that the only object the prisoners had in mind in seizing the trawler was to leave their native country, in which they suffered an intolerable sense of frustration and oppression, and that they had achieved their object with the minimum amount of injury to person and property. He left the question whether the prisoners were entitled to the protection of the Extradition Act to the High Court through the prisoners' application for a writ of habeas corpus. It was held they were entitled to the protection of the Act of 1870 as it had been proved that the requisition was made with a view to trying them for an offence of a political character.

Cassels J., who delivered the first judgment in *Kolczynski's Case*, said at p. 549 of the report:—"The words 'offence of a political character' must always be considered according to the circumstances existing at the time when they have to be considered. The present time is very different from 1891, when *Castioni's* case was decided. It was not then treason for a citizen to leave his country and start a fresh life in another. Countries were not regarded as enemy countries when no war was in progress. Now a state of totalitarianism prevails in some parts of the world and it is a crime for citizens in such places to take steps to leave. In this case the members of the crew of a small trawler engaged in fishing were under political supervision and they revolted by the only means open to them. They committed an offence of a political character, and if they were surrendered there could be no doubt that, while they would be tried for the particular offence mentioned, they would be punished as for a political crime." Lord Goddard C.J. at p. 551 of the report observed:—"The court in *Castioni's* case were careful to say that they were not giving an exhaustive definition of the words 'of a political character'. They applied a formula taken from

Stephen's History of the Criminal Law, Vol. II, p. 71, as sufficient for the facts of
that case, and no doubt when that work was written, about 1882, no better definition could be given. No doubt the conception of what is commonly called nowadays
a 'police state' was not unknown in the middle years of the nineteenth century. One
need only recall the vigour of Mr. Gladstone's language and some of Lord Palmer-
ston's dispatches as to the state of affairs prevailing in Naples, then a part of the
Kingdom of the Two Sicilies, under the despotic rule of a monarch usually referred
to as King Bomba. But all that had passed by the time Sir James Fitzjames Stephen
wrote, though no doubt political police were still very active in Czarist Russia. The
evidence about the law prevalent in the Republic of Poland today shows that it is
necesary, if only for reasons of humanity, to give a wider and more generous
meaning to the words we are now construing, which we can do without in any way
encouraging the idea that ordinary crimes which have no political significance will
be thereby excused." Devlin J. agreed.

Kolczynski's Case is an illustration of the degree to which English law has developed since 1890 when *Castioni's Case* was decided. Notwithstanding the
development during the intervening 65 years, the formula of the Act of 1870
("offence of a political character") remains unaltered, and an offence to fall within
the British formula must still apparently have a political complexion.

The final draft proposed for Article 3 of the European Convention on Extradition, in defining the connected offences which were to be protected, in my opinion
also insisted that the connected offence should have a political character. It was not
enough that there should be a connection; it was required also that the offence (act)
should be committed with a view to preparing for, to ensuring the commission of, to
concealing or to preventing such political offence (act). That is to say, the connected
offence (act) should be of a political character. But as has already been pointed out,
the High Contracting Parties, in adopting the Convention, rejected this limitation.
The effect of the omission of the limitation is to widen the character of the connection which satisfies the requirements of Article 3. The connection need not
necessarily be of a political character. Therefore, I reject the submission that the
scope of Article 3 of the Convention is the same as that of the British formula of
1870. On the contrary, in my opinion, the true equation is between "political
offence" in the Convention and "offence of a political character" in the Act of 1870.
In my opinion the Convention has added its protection to a wide area of offences
which are not necessarily political in character but which are simply connected with
a political offence.

I would reach the same conclusion on a consideration of the terms of s. 50 of the
Act of 1965 without reference to the *travaux preparatoires* of the Convention. The
statute does not stipulate that the connected offence shall have a political complexion. The statute characterizes the first offence only: that offence must be
political. The statute does not characterize the connected offence as political. The
Court, in my opinion, should draw the conclusion that the Oireachtas left the
connection to be spelt out by the Courts in the widest possible manner.

A distinction can be drawn between "purely" political offences which, of their
very nature, are political (*e.g.*, treason, sedition, espionage) and "relative" political
offences (*e.g.*, murder) committed in the course of a rebellion. It may be noted that
the Harvard Draft Convention on Extradition (1935) 29 A.J.I.L. (Supp.) 112-3 provided that the phrase "political offense" as used in the draft included treason,
sedition, and espionage. Both the Norwegian law of the 11th June, 1908, and the
German-Turkish Extradition Treaty of 1930 exemplify both kinds of political
offence. In the first instance the wording is ". . . Extradition may not be effected for
any political offence, (or) for any ordinary offence committed in connection with a
political offence and with intent to promote the purpose aimed at by such political
offence." The German-Turkish text is more interesting. It reads:—". . . The
Contracting Parties shall not be bound to grant extradition for a political offence, or
an offence connected with a political offence and committed with a view to preparing

for, ensuring the commission of, concealing or preventing such an offence." With the insignificant difference of the use of the word "offence" for "act", this is the formula which commended itself to the mixed committee established by the Council of Europe, but which the Assembly, in adopting the Convention, rejected . . .

Extract 12.22

WAVIN PIPES LTD. v HEPWORTH IRON CO. LTD.
[1982] 8 F.S.R. 32

S. 34 of the Patents Act, 1964 governs petitions to revoke patents which have been granted earlier. The grounds on which a patent may be revoked include lack of novelty and obviousness. The crucial requirement is that the design had previously been "published". S. 2 defines "publish" as meaning "made available to the public". In the course of this case the High Court had to consider whether "public" was confined to the public in Ireland or whether it referred to the public in the State and elsewhere. Costello J. adopted the latter interpretation. His judgment is significant in that he considered the parliamentary history of s. 34 and, in consulting the Dáil Debates, for the first time in this country departed from the common law tradition of not consulting parliamentary sources. In the extract from his judgment the propriety of this approach is considered.

Costello J.
. . . "*Available to the Public*"
Hepworth refer to section 34(1)(*e*) which provides that a patent may be revoked on the ground that the invention is not new having regard to what was "published" before the priority date of the claim, and say that this subsection must be read in the light of the definition of "published" in the definition section (section 2) and means "*made available to the public* by the written or spoken word or by public use, or in any other way." They urge that the word "public" as used in section 2 means the public of this country; and that accordingly in considering novelty under subsection 34(1)(*e*) regard can only be had to what was available to the Irish public before 7 February 1969. Subsection 34(1)(*f*) must, it is said, be construed in the same way. If this argument is correct it would follow that Wavin cannot rely on the French and Belgian patents to which I have just referred.

In support of this interpretation of the section Wavin refers to the judgment of Budd J. in *Rawls and Another* v. *Irish Tyre and Rubber Services Ltd.* [1960] I.R. 11. This case was an infringement action in which the defendants sought revocation of the plaintiffs' patent on the ground, *inter alia*, that the alleged invention was obvious and did not involve any inventive step having regard to what was known or used prior to the date of the patent. Budd J. was required to consider the provisions of the Industrial and Commercial Property (Protection) Act, 1927 which did not detail, as the 1964 Act does, the grounds on which the Court can revoke a patent but which provided that "every ground on which a patent might formerly at common law have been repealed by *scire facies* shall be available by way of defence to an action of infringement and shall also be a ground of revocation under this section." He pointed out that "obviousness" having regard to what was known or used—that is, known in the sense of being common general knowledge—was one of the grounds of revocation and that he was required to consider where and in what geographical area the common general knowledge which it was alleged invalidated the patent was to be ascertained. He pointed out that "prima facie a reference to anything known or used, without territorial delineation, would . . . in an Irish statute, be deemed prima facie at any rate, to be a reference to what was known or used in this country and not to what was known or used in other countries" (p. 32);

and having considered in detail the provisions of the 1927 Act concluded that the intention of the legislature was to "legislate in patent matters in such fashion as to treat this country as a separate entity for patent purposes," and that the expression "common general knowledge" in the principle of the common law which he was required to apply must mean common general knowledge within the Republic (p. 34). And so, Hepworth say, just as the courts in deciding under the 1927 Act whether to revoke a patent on the ground of lack of novelty would consider only what was common general knowledge in this country, they should likewise in proceedings to revoke a patent under the 1964 Act consider only what was made available to the public of this country.

In support of Hepworth's contention that "publication" in the relevant subsections must refer to documents which are made available to the public of this country only Mr. Drysdale has pointed to the British Patents Act 1977 which quite explicitly provided that the concept of the "state of the art" which is used throughout the statute is to be taken to comprise matter "made available to the public (*whether in the United Kingdom or elsewhere*) by written or oral description, by use or in any other way," and submitted that had it been intended that the Irish Act of 1964 was to be construed in a like manner it would have been drafted in an equally explicit manner. It is urged that the failure to provide explicitly in the 1964 Act that "available to the public" means "available to the public in the state *or elsewhere*" signifies that the Act should not be construed in the way the English Act so clearly provides. It seems to me that the respondents could rightly claim support for this submission from the Patents Bill, 1981 which has been published in this country since the trial of this action and which adopts the phraseology of the 1977 British Statute to which I have just referred.

I can begin my interpretation of the 1964 Act by observing that, unlike the U.K. Patents Act 1949, whose title describes it as an Act "to consolidate certain enactments relating to patents," the statute I am considering is expressly entitled an Act "to make new provisions in respect of patents and related matters." The new provisions are in fact extensive; not only is the law as enacted by the 1927 Act changed but the Act departs quite significantly from the principles of patent law which had been re-enacted by the British Patents Act 1949.

In approaching an interpretation of the provisions of section 34 Mr. Murphy on Wavin's behalf asked me to look first at section 19 which establishes the grounds on which an opposition to the grant of a patent can be based and he suggested that I should compare them with grounds on which a patent can be revoked which are set out in section 34. There is, he says, a startling and quite significant difference between the two sections. I agree. In opposing the grant of a patent an opponent can plead lack of novelty or obviousness, but when he relies on a claim of prior publication in opposition proceedings the subsection explicitly provides that it must be established that the invention had been published *in the State* (subsection (1)(*b*)); and if prior user is claimed the user relied on must have taken place *in the State* (subsection (1)(*d*)). Similarly, if the obviousness of the alleged invention is called in question the Controller (or on appeal, the court) can only have regard to what was published *in the State* or user *in the State* (subsection (1)(*e*)). Quite clearly then an opponent in opposition proceedings cannot rely under these subsections on a patent which might have been available to public inspection abroad before the priority date but which had not been made available to the Irish public. Contrast this section with the provisions of section 34. No reference is made in the later section to prior publication *in the State* or prior user *in the State*. Instead provision is made for revocation if the patent was not new "having regard to what was published before the priority date" or if it can be shown that the invention was obvious and did not involve any inventive steps having regard, *inter alia*, to matter "published in the manner specified in paragraph (*e*) of this subsection"—that is, to a subparagraph which makes no reference to publication *in the State*. The omission from section 34 of references to prior publication and user having taken place "within the State" which had been included in the earlier section must have been deliberate. It can reasonably be assumed that the only purpose of the omission was to remove the limitation imposed by the words "*in the State*" and to provide that "publication" in subsections 34(1)(*e*) and (*f*) was not limited to what had been made available to the Irish public.

Support for this interpretation is to be found by considering the provisions of the British Patents Act 1949. It had obviously been found helpful to base a great deal of Irish patent law on the law as it had evolved in England both as a result of judicial decisions and statutory enactment, and the Irish Patents Act, 1964 follows in many respects the provisions of the earlier British Act of 1949. But it significantly departs from it when it deals with revocation matters. The British Act provided for revocation if the invention is not new "having regard to what was known or used, before the priority date of the claim, *in the United Kingdom*" (subsection 32(*f*)); or on the ground that the invention was obvious and did not involve any inventive step "having regard to what was known or used before the priority date *in the United Kingdom*." A deliberate intention to depart from the long established principles of law which were incorporated in the 1949 Act can be inferred from the fact that the words, "*in the State*" were omitted from the corresponding section of the 1964 Act. It seems to me, therefore, that whilst accepting that greater clarity could have been achieved had the drafting methods of the British 1977 Act been employed the 1964 Act should be construed as permitting a petitioner in revocation proceedings to rely on matters made available to the public both in the state and elsewhere.

I have reached a conclusion on the interpretation of section 34 and section 2 from a consideration of the text of the statute. However, in the course of his submissions on Wavin's behalf Mr. McCracken referred me to the parliamentary history of the Act, and I think I should refer to those submissions and my reasons for believing them to be well founded.

In a judgment which I delivered on the 13 March 1981 in *Beecham Group Ltd.* v. *Bristol Myers Company* I expressed the view that I was entitled to obtain assistance in the interpretation of section 19(1)(*e*) of the Patents Act, 1964 from the parliamentary history of the Act and I explained that I had reached this conclusion as a result of the decision of the Supreme Court in *Bourke* v. *Attorney General and Wymes* [1972] I.R. 36. Relying on this view Mr. McCracken has asked me to consider the parliamentary history of the Act which is relevant to the point I am now considering. That history discloses that a motion was moved in the Dáil during the Committee Stage of the Bill to provide that "publication" in the Act would mean "available within the State to the public by written word or public use"; in other words to provide that in revocation proceedings the court could only have regard to documents published in the State before the priority date of the impugned patent. This amendment was resisted by the Minister in charge of the Bill who indicated quite clearly that it was proposed to change the law, to adopt a concept of absolute novelty in patent matters and that a change in the law was necessary in order to keep the laws of this country in conformity with the State's obligations under international conventions (including the Council of Europe Convention on the Unification of Certain Points of Substantive Law on Patents of Invention) to which it was proposed to adhere (see *Dáil Debates* Vol. 207 columns 1644 *et seq.*)

It would be difficult to find a clearer case than this to demonstrate how the parliamentary history of an enactment can assist in ascertaining the legislative intent. In the present case I am asked to hold that by using the words "available to the public" the Oireachtas intended them to mean "available to the Irish public," but the history of the measure shows that parliament quite expressly refused to amend the Bill to give the words this meaning and quite deliberately retained the words "available to the public" so that the law could be changed, the concept of absolute novelty adopted and so that the State could undertake certain international obligations. The evidence relating to (a) the fact of the rejected amendment and (b) the reasons given for its rejection assists therefore in establishing that the words used in the statute should not be interpreted as Hepworth suggest and support the construction of the phrase which results from an examination of the text of the statute itself.

I think I should very briefly here set out the reasons by which I have concluded that in certain circumstances a court is entitled to have regard to the parliamentary history of an Act to assist in its interpretation because to avoid overburdening an already long judgment I did not state them in my judgment in *Beecham Group Limited* v. *Bristol Myers Company*. The rules for the interpretation of statutes are judge-made. As long ago as 1769 it was established in England that "the sense and meaning of an Act of Parliament must be collected from what it says when cast into law; and not from the history of changes it underwent in the House where it took its rise" (Willes, J. in *Millar* v. *Taylor* (1769) 4 Burr. 2303 at p. 2332, quoted in Cross *Statutory Interpretation* at p. 134) and this rule has been applied ever since both in England and in this country. It should, however, be pointed out that this rule is not one followed in civil law jurisdictions, or in the United States of America, or in the European Court of Human Rights. I would have felt constrained to follow it, however, particularly as it has been re-affirmed by a divisional court in this country (see *Minister for Industry and Commerce* v. *Hales* [1967] I.R. 50 in which the court refused to consider the legislative history of the Holiday (Employees) Act 1961) but for the decision of the Supreme Court in the *Bourke* case to which I have already referred.

There is no strict rule of construction which requires the court to examine only the words of the statute it is construing. In *McMahon* v. *Attorney General* [1972] I.R. 69 the Supreme Court considered the Report of a Special Committee on electoral systems which preceded the Ballot Act, 1872 on which provisions of the Electoral Act, 1923 dealing with secrecy of the ballot were based. In *Maher* v. *Attorney General* [1973] I.R. 140 the court found assistance in the interpretation of the Road Traffic Act, 1968 in the Report of a Commission which had been established to consider the law relating to driving whilst under the influence of drink.

In the *Bourke* case the Supreme Court was called upon to interpret the phrase "offence connected with a political offence" in section 50, Part III, of the Extradition Act, 1965. Part III of the Act dealt with the special arrangements for extradition between this country and the United Kingdom; Part II with extradition generally. The Act made it clear that Part II enacted as part of the municipal law of the State certain provisions of the Council of Europe Convention on Extradition signed on the 13 December 1957 and Part II contained a prohibition against extradition in respect of a political offence "or an offence connected with a political offence" (section 11). In interpreting the phrase "offence connected with a political offence" in Part III of the Act the Supreme Court took the view that as section 11 and section 50 speak of the same thing, as the Convention could be examined to discover the meaning of section 11, the court was entitled to look at the Convention for the purpose of interpreting section 50. But the court not only examined the text of the Convention for the purpose of interpreting the meaning of the phrase "offence connected with a political offence" used in section 50 of the Irish statute, it also examined the *travaux preparatoires* of the Convention. In the course of this examination it reached conclusions as to the meaning of the phrase and based these conclusions on the fact that the original draft of the Convention had been amended in the course of its consideration by the organs of the Council of Europe and on the reasons disclosed in the *travaux preparatoires* for such amendments.

In doing so the Supreme Court extended considerably the existing rules as to the use of treaties in the interpretation of statutes (*Salomon* v. *Commissioners of Customs and Excise* [1967] 2 Q.B. 306; *Post Office* v. *Estuary Radio Ltd.* [1968] 2 Q.B. 740). Parenthetically I think that it is relevant to note that not only had the House of Lords recently sanctioned the limited use of the *travaux preparatoires* of an international convention in the interpretation of a statute (see: *Fothergill* v. *Monarch Airlines Ltd.* [1980] 3 W.L.R. 209), but the Master of the Rolls, emboldened he said, by remarks of the Lord Chancellor in a debate in the House of Lords on 26 March of this year, has made use of the parliamentary history of the Employment Act 1980 for the purpose of interpreting some of its provisions (see: *Hadmor Productions Ltd.* v. *Hamilton* [1981] 3 W.L.R. 139). The arguments against the use by the courts of the parliamentary history of a statute for the purpose of its construction must apply with equal force to the history of the adoption of an international convention by an international organisation. And so, if the courts can properly look at the history of the adoption of an international convention for the purpose of ascertaining the meaning of the words used in it there would appear to be no reason in principle why in appropriate cases they should not be free when construing the words of a statute to obtain assistance from the history of its enactment by parliament. As I do not find persuasive the arguments against the use of the legislative history in the interpretation of statutes (which are helpfully brought together in the Report of the Law Commission and the Scottish Law Commission, "The Interpretation of Statutes"), as I believe I am entitled to seek asistance from the legislative history in appropriate cases, as in the present the legislative history greatly assists in construing the meaning of "available to the public" as used in the Patents Act, 1964, I have used it in support of the construction of the 1964 Act which I have already given . . .

Extract 12.23

McLOUGHLIN v MINISTER FOR THE PUBLIC SERVICE [1985] I.R. 631

Compensation for the dependents of Gardai who die from injuries which they have suffered in the course of their duties is governed by the Garda Siochana (Compensation) Acts, 1941 and 45. The applicant's husband was a Garda sergeant who, in the course of duty, was fatally injured by a gunman. The issue was whether the value of pensions and gratuities which became payable on his death should be deducted from the compensation awardable. Finlay P. stated a case for the opinion of the Supreme Court. Henchy J., in considering the interpretation of the relevant provisions, had regard to the explanatory memorandum which accompanied the Bill when it was introduced in the Oireachtas.

Henchy J.

Sergeant Patrick McLoughlin of Dunboyne, Co. Meath, was fatally injured in April 1983 when he was maliciously attacked by a gunman. At the time, he was carrying out his duties as a member of the Garda Siochana. These proceedings have been brought in the High Court by his widow and children against the Minister for the Public Service. Their claim is for compensation under the Garda Siochana (Compensation) Acts, 1941 and 1945.

The general provisions under which compensation is assessed in a case such as this are to be found in s. 10 of the 1941 Act as amended by s. 2(2) of the 1945 Act. When the case came for hearing in the High Court before Finlay P. the point was taken on behalf of the Minister that in assessing compensation there should be deducted in full the value of a pension and gratuities which became payable to the widow and children on Sergeant McLoughlin's death. The matter now comes before this Court on a case stated by Finlay P. under s. 9 of the 1941 Act seeking a ruling as to whether that submission is correct, or whether in assessing compensation, regard should be had only to the extra amount of pension that became payable in the circumstances of this case.

Under the relevant statutory provisions as to pensions, because Sergeant McLoughlin's death was due to a non-accidental injury received in the execution of his duty his widow became entitled to what is called a widow's special pension, amounting to one-third of Sergeant McLoughlin's pay at the time of his death. As well as that, each of the four infant children became entitled to what is called a children's special allowance.

Under certain other statutory provisions as to pensions, if Sergeant McLoughlin's death had not been due to an injury received by him in the execution of his duty, his widow would have been entitled to a pension amounting to one-quarter of his annual pay at the time of his death, and three of the children would have been entitled to an annual allowance. In the circumstances of this case, such pension and allowances are not payable.

Put specifically, in terms of the facts of this case, the question in the case stated is whether there should be deducted in the assessment of compensation the capital value of the pension and allowances actually paid or only the capital value of the extra pension and allowances paid in this case.

The only statutory guide as to how pensions and allowances are to be treated in the assessment of compensation is to be found in s. 10 of the 1941 Act. S. 10(3) provides that in a case such as this the judge of the High Court, in fixing the lump sum to be awarded as compensation,

> shall take into consideration the fact, if it is a fact, that the applicant is entitled (under the statutes and statutory orders and regulations relating to the pensions of members of the Garda Siochana and their dependants) to a pension, allowance, or gratuity out of public funds in respect of the death or injuries which is or are the subject of the application, but shall not regard the amount of such pension, allowance, or gratuity (if any) as a measure or standard by reference to which the amount of the compensation is to be fixed.

The difference in wording between the two parts of that provision shows that it is the *fact* of entitlement to a pension, allowance or gratuity (not the amount) that is to be taken into account.

When the 1941 Act was introduced in the Dáil as a Bill there was published an Explanatory Memorandum which contained the following passage:

> Apart from any compensation which may be payable under the terms of the Bill certain pensions or gratuities are provided under the Garda Siochana Pensions Orders in cases where members of the Force are killed or injured: for example, when a married member of the Force who has received a non-accidental injury dies as a result of the injury, his widow is entitled to a special pension equal to one-third of her husband's pay, and if there are children certain allowances are provided for them also. Any benefits conferred by the present Bill are intended to supplement, but not to replace, these existing provisions.

It seems to me that if in the present case the value of any part of the special pension and allowances were to be deducted from the compensation, the purpose of the Act (as thus declared) would be defeated, for the compensation would not supplement the existing provisions: it would replace them to some extent.

Whatever uncertainty existed as to this point when the 1941 Act was passed would appear to have been cleared up by the 1945 Act. S. 2(2) of the 1945 Act amended s. 10(1) of the 1941 Act by inserting a new para. (a) which provides that the compensation shall be such sum as the judge shall think reasonable having regard to all the circumstances of the case and that, in addition to the matters which he is required by s. 10(3) to take into consideration, he shall

> have regard to the financial loss sustained by the applicant, but in so doing shall not take into account any property (including assets of the deceased) to which the applicant has become entitled by reason of the death of the deceased.

In the absence of anything in the context narrowing its connotation, the expression "any property" (which is expressly not confined to property which was owned by the deceased) must be held to include all forms of real and personal property to which the applicant became entitled by reason of the death of the deceased. It clearly includes the special pension and allowances to which the applicants became entitled by reason of the death of the deceased. The judge is therefore debarred from taking them into account in fixing the amount of compensation.

I must confess that, at least on the facts of this case, I am unable to align s. 10(3) with s. 10(1)(a). S. 10(3) requires the judge to "take into consideration" the fact that the applicants are entitled to a pension, allowance or gratuity, but s. 10(1)(a) (as I interpret it) provides that he shall not "take into account" the pension, allowance or gratuity. Unless there is a difference (which I am unable to discern) between "take into consideration" and "take into account", there may be a want of congruity between the two provisions, but if there is, it is s. 10(1)(a) that should prevail, for it represents the later thinking of the Oireachtas, having been inserted in the 1941 Act by the 1945 Act.

I consider that the answer to the question put in the case stated should be that no part of the value of the special pension and allowances is to be taken into account in fixing the amount of the compensation.

3. Mandatory and directory provisions

In some instances a statute might provide for something to be done, an omission to do which might not be of great significance. In other words, it is not essential that the thing be done. Such provisions are considered to be *directory* rather than *mandatory*. The neglect of a directory provision does not affect the validity of other matters which are connected with it. In considering whether it is mandatory or directory the provision is examined in relation to the statutory scheme. In general, the less important the provision the greater is the likelihood that it will be held to be directory. The distinction is best seen in the Supreme Court decision in *The State (Elm Developments Ltd.) v An Bord Pleanala* [1981] I.L.R.M. 108 (Extract 12.24)

Extract 12.24

THE STATE (ELM DEVELOPMENTS LTD.) v AN BORD PLEANALA [1981] I.L.R.M. 108

Art. 36 of the Local Government (Planning and Development) Regulations, 1977 (S.I. No. 65 of 1977) provides, inter alia, that notice of an appeal to An Bord Pleanala should include the grounds on which the appeal is based. A group of residents appealed against the granting of planning permission to the prosecutors. Their notice of appeal did not set out the grounds of appeal, but it stated that they would be forthcoming in due course. In consequence, the prosecutors argued that the notice was invalid and sought an order preventing the respondents from hearing the appeal. At issue was the question whether the requirement is mandatory or directory. Griffin and Kenny JJ. concurred in Henchy J.'s judgment.

Henchy J.
Elm Developments Ltd ("the developer") applied in 1979 to Bray Urban District Council, the local planning authority, for planning permission to build a shopping centre at Quinsboro Road, Bray. The application was successful. On 8 February 1980 a notification of the decision to grant the permission issued from the planning authority to the developer. This permission was, of course, not final. Under s. 26 of the Local Government (Planning and Development) Act, 1963 (as amended by the

1976 Act), any person was entitled to appeal to An Bord Pleanala ("the Board") against the grant of the permission. However, this right of appeal is not unqualified. Certain formalities are expected to be complied with. Where (as is the case here) the permission is granted, the would-be appellant must appeal within the period of twenty-one days beginning on the day of the giving of the decision: s. 26(5) of the 1963 Act. Furthermore, under the relevant Regulations (Art. 36 of S.I. No. 65 of 1977) it is required that an appeal "shall (a) be in writing, (b) state the subject matter of the appeal, (c) state the grounds of appeal, and (d) be accompanied by a deposit of £10 as required by s. 15 of the Act of 1976".

In this case, one E. Power ("the appellant") wrote to the Board on 28 February 1980. The letter stated that on behalf of local residents and himself he wished to appeal against the grant of permission. The letter was accompanied by a deposit of £10. In every respect except one, the letter was unquestionably a valid appeal. The single questionable feature was that the letter did not state the grounds of appeal. Instead, what the appellant put in the letter was: "Full particulars of the extent and nature of our appeal will be submitted to you shortly when the residents have examined the implications of this decision in detail".

Because of the failure of the appellant to state the grounds of appeal in the letter, the developer has claimed that the "appeal" is a nullity and that the Board has no jurisdiction to hear it. To bring his point home, he sought and obtained a conditional order of prohibition against the Board, under which the Board would be debarred from hearing the appeal. But D'Arcy J. refused to make absolute the conditional order. He held that the requirement that the written appeal should state the grounds of appeal is directory rather than mandatory, and that, accordingly, the Board was entitled in the circumstancs to overlook the non-compliance with it. Keane J, in *The State (Walsh)* v. *An Bord Pleanala* (19 November 1980; unrep.), a case in which the facts were indistinguishable from those of the present case, reached the same conclusion. The sole question in this appeal by the developer against the order of D'Arcy J. is whether that conclusion is correct.

Whether a provision in a statute or a statutory instrument, which on the fact of it is obligatory (for example, by the use of the word "shall"), should be treated by the courts as truly mandatory or merely directory depends on the statutory scheme as a whole and the part played in that scheme by the provision in question. If the requirement which has not been observed may fairly be said to be an integral and indispensable part of the statutory intendment, the courts will hold it to be truly mandatory, and will not excuse a departure from it. But if, on the other hand, what is apparently a requirement is in essence merely a direction which is not of the substance of the aim and scheme of the statute, non-compliance may be excused.

An example of a truly mandatory provision is to be found in the decision of this court in *Monaghan UDC v Alf-a-Bet Promotions Ltd.* [1980] I.L.R.M. 64. The developer in that case was seeking development permission which would allow him to convert a drapery shop in the town of Monaghan into a betting office and amusement arcade. The relevant planning regulations required that a notice published by the developer in a newspaper of his intention to apply for development permission should state, inter alia, "the nature and extent of the development". The notice published by the developer in that case refered only to "alterations and improvements". By no stretch of interpretation could that be said to be indicative of the nature and extent of the proposed development. The court considered that the inclusion in the notice in a newspaper of information as to the nature and extent of the proposed development was vital to the proper operation of the statutory scheme for the grant of development permission. The veiled and misleading notice that was published was held to be a non-compliance with that mandatory provision and it could not, therefore, be excused. In the course of my judgment I said:

> I . . . feel it pertinent to express the opinion that when the 1963 Act prescribed certain procedures as necessary to be observed for the purpose of getting a

development permission, which may affect radically the rights or amenities of others and may substantially benefit or enrich the grantee of the permission, compliance with the prescribed procedures should be treated as a condition precedent to the issue of the permission. In such circumstances, what the legislature has, either immediately in the Act or mediately in the Regulations, nominated as being obligatory may not be depreciated to the level of a mere direction except on the application of the *de minimis* rule. In other words, what the legislature has prescribed, or allowed to be prescribed, in such circumstances as necessary should be treated by the courts as nothing short of necessary, and any deviation from the requirements must, before it can be overlooked, be shown, by the person seeking to have it excused, to be so trivial, or so technical, or so peripheral, or otherwise so insubstantial that, on the principle that it is the spirit rather than the letter of the law that matters, the prescribed obligation has been substantially, and therefore adequately, complied with.

The present case is the antithesis of that case, In that case it was the developer who was seeking to have the departure from the statutory requirements excused. In that case the notice in the newspaper, so far from informing the public of "the nature and extent" of the proposed development, concealed that information behind the general and undescriptive words "alterations and improvements". Local residents or local business people to whom a betting office and amusement arcade would be anathema might well have been led by the notice to think that all that was proposed was a refurbished drapery premises. Whether intentionally or inadvertently, the notice was calculated to lure interested parties into abandoning their opportunity of making representations against the grant of the permission. In the circumstances, it would have been a travesty of the statutory scheme of development control if the requirement which was departed from had been held to be merely directory.

Here it is a local resident, acting for himself and other local residents, who is said to have been inexcusably at fault in not confirming to the regulations. His letter to the Board stated that they wished to appeal and requested an oral hearing. That was an appeal in writing, as was required. The letter adequately stated the subject matter of the appeal as was required. It was accompanied by a deposit of £10 as was required. It departed from the requirements of the regulations only in not stating the grounds of appeal. But it undertook to submit those grounds shortly when the residents had an opportunity of examining the implications of the decision in detail.

The decision of a planning authority to grant a development permission, while not necessarily final, will become final if an appeal is not lodged within the time fixed by the Act. Since an extension of that time is not provided for, the requirement as to time is mandatory, so that a departure from it cannot be excused. The requirement that the appeal be in writing is so obviously basic to the institution of an appeal that it too must be considered mandatory. So also must the requirement that the written appeal state the subject matter of the appeal, for the absence of such identification could lead to administrative confusion. The lodgment of a deposit of £10 with the appeal (perhaps not necessarily physically or contemporaneously with the appeal) would also seem to be an essential part of the statutory scheme, so as to discourage frivolous, delaying or otherwise worthless appeals.

The requirement that the appeal should state the grounds of appeal seems to me to rest on different considerations. Even when the appeal contains a full statement of the grounds of appeal, that statement is not conclusive as to the grounds that will be considered on the hearing of the appeal. That is because s. 17 of the 1976 Act says this:

> The Board in deciding a reference or appeal may take into account matters other than those raised by the parties to the reference or appeal if the matters either relate to the proper planning and development of the area of the relevant planning

authority or are matters to which by virtue of s. 24(2) of this Act the Board may have regard, provided that the matters are brought to the notice of those parties and they are accorded an opportunity of making observations thereon to the Board or, in the case of an oral hearing, the person conducting the hearing.

The effect of that provision is that the Board may always treat the grounds lodged with the appeal as merely interim or provisional grounds. Even if the objector in this case had lodged a set of grounds of appeal with his appeal, the Board would be entitled to entertain further or other grounds, at any stage up to the determination of the appeal, provided those further or other grounds relate to the proper planning and development of the area, or are matters to which by virtue of s. 24(2) of the 1976 Act the Board may have regard, and provided the developer is given an opportunity of making observations thereon.

Because of that, the grounds of appeal required to be stated in the appeal are not to be equated with pleadings in court proceedings, or with a notice of appeal from one court to a superior court. They cannot circumscribe or identify the issues on which the appeal will be decided. The Board (or the person holding the oral hearing, if there is one) may go outside them. They cannot be treated with any confidence by the developer as indicative of the scope of the case he will have to meet on the hearing of the appeal. I deduce that the primary purpose of the requirement of stating grounds of appeal in a case such as this is to inform the Board as to the primary matters relied on, so that the procedure for the disposition of the appeal may be decided on. Whether that deduction be correct or not, I am satisfied that the grounds of appeal required are essentially informative. To hold that they must be given as part of, or contemporaneously with, the notice of appeal, would be to attribute a conclusiveness to them which the statute clearly shows they cannot have. I consider that the Board's practice of informing an appellant in a case such as this, who has not stated grounds in his appeal, that his appeal will not be entertained unless he submits grounds of appeal, is a correct evaluation of the place that grounds of appeal take in the statutory scheme. It would be unduly legalistic, and unfair, if laymen who may have no skill in such matters, but who may be vitally affected by the permission which they wish to appeal against, were to be shut out from appealing merely because their notice of appeal did not state their grounds of appeal, particularly when those grounds of appeal can never be anything more than an opening salvo in the appellate battle. In such circumstances, the requirement of stating the grounds of appeal is essentially informative and directory, and therefore not mandatory. When the appellant in this case furnished grounds of appeal, within a few weeks of his appeal, to the satisfaction of the Board, it did not lie in the mouth of the developer to say that he had been in any way wrong-footed or damnified, or that the spirit or purpose of the Acts and regulations had been breached. In seeking an order of prohibition against the Board, he is endeavouring to benefit from what is no more than a technical breach of a regulation, which breach has been put right by the appellant and has been therefore rightly overlooked by the Board in the interests of justice.

I am glad to find that the statutory requirement of stating grounds of appeal in an appeal under corresponding sections of the English Planning Acts was also treated as being no more than directory by a Divisional Court in *Chelmsford Rural District Council v Powell* [1963] 1 All E.R. 150 and by the Court of Appeal in *Howard v Secretary of State for the Environment* [1974] 1 All E.R. 644.

It follows from the foregoing that I would dismiss this appeal.

DELEGATED LEGISLATION

As far as interpretation is concerned we have treated legislation and delegated legislation alike, but there are some features peculiar to the latter which should, at this stage, be noted. Delegated legislation consists of instruments enacted, not by the legislative organ, but by an official, such as a minister, or a subordinate body to whom or to which law-making power is delegated by statute. By virtue of s. 15 of the Interpretation Act, 1937 such power includes a power to repeal or amend the instrument and to replace it with another. Delegated legislation, which is not local or private in character, is governed by the Statutory Instruments Act, 1947, s. 1(1) of which defines "statutory instrument" as being an "order, regulation, rule, scheme or by-law" which is made in pursuance of a statutory power. The Act provides for the printing and publishing of statutory instruments and their deposit in certain designated libraries. Delegated legislation tends to contain detailed provisions which supplement the more general provisions of the parent statute. Several reasons exist for the use of this mechanism rather than the usual legislative process. The first is that the constraints on parliamentary time would make it impossible for all necessary measures to be enacted as statutes. Accordingly, the Oireachtas is content to sketch the broad outline of the legislative scheme and to delegate its detailed implementation and application to the appropriate official or body. The comparative volume of statutes and statutory instruments can be seen from the figures for 1982 when twenty-nine (29) Acts of the Oireachtas were enacted whilst three hundred and eighty-nine (389) statutory instruments were made. Second, as the contents of delegated legislation tend to be of a technical or administrative nature it is often preferable that those who possess the appropriate expertise be given the law-making function. Thus, where a minister is given power to make regulations he or she will be advised by the relevant experts in his or her department. Moreover, in some instances power is delegated to an expert body or one on which various relevant interests are represented. Third, it is desirable that a flexible and timely response can be made to meet rapidly changing social and technical circumstances, which is not afforded by the constraints on parliamentary time.

Whilst the Oireachtas has no direct role in the enactment of delegated legislation, parliamentary control is achieved by a variety of mechanisms. In many cases the parent statute expressly retains the right of the Oireachtas, or one of its Houses, to annul, or less frequently to approve, the instruments made thereunder. Thus, the Act will provide that instruments be "laid before" one or other or both Houses of the Oireachtas, who may within a stated time annul it. In practice, however, this procedure tends to be a formality and instruments are rarely, if ever, annulled in this manner. More important are the Oireachtas Joint Committees on Legislation and the Secondary Legislation of the European Communities. The former has established a sub-committee on statutory instruments which monitors their creation. The latter, as its title suggests, concerns itself with instruments which are enacted to give domestic legal effect to obligations imposed by European Community law. S. 3 of the European Communities Act, 1972 confers extensive powers to make regulations to give domestic legal effect to European law. The European Communities (Amendment) Act, 1973 provides that regulations may be annulled by a resolution of both Houses of the Oireachtas but only if the Joint Committee recommends. Parliamentary control is supplemented by judicial control which is concerned not only with the interpretation of delegated legislation but also its validity. In this respect two factors are relevant: that the instrument was made with constitutional propriety and that it is within the terms of the parent statute. Thus, in *Lawlor v Minister for Agriculture* [1988] I.L.R.M. 400 (Extract 12.11) the argument was advanced, and rejected by Murphy J., that the European Communities (Milk Levy) Regulations, 1985 were both unconstitutional and outside the terms of the parent Act.

Article 15.2 of the Constitution vests exclusive legislative power in the Oireachtas. Accordingly, the executive lacks an inherent law-making role and, unlike its equivalents in other countries, it lacks the power to rule by decree or any similar measure. Thus, any instrument which purports to have legal effect must be based on a statutory authority. But on a literal reading of Article 15.2 any delegation of legislative power would seem to be invalid. However, the Supreme Court has recognised that delegated legislation is a feature of the legal environment and that it is not impermissible *per se* to delegate legislative power. The question is one of identifying the extent to which delegation is constitutionally permissible and the test established by the Court in *Cityview Press Ltd. v An Chomhairle Oiliuna* [1980] I.R. 381, 399 is whether:

> . . . that which is challenged as an unauthorised delegation of parliamentary power is more than a mere giving effect to principles and policies which are contained in the statute itself. If it be, then it is not authorised; for such would constitute a purported exercise of legislative power by an authority which is not permitted to do so under the Constitution. On the other hand, if it be within the permitted limits—if the law is laid down in the statute and details only are to be filled in or completed by the designated Minister or subordinate body—there is no unauthorised delegation of legislative power.

That test preserves a balance between the role of the Oireachtas as exclusive law-maker and its competence to delegate legislative power. The power to enact "principles and policies" lies within the sole preserve of the Oireachtas and if the delegation purports to confer that power on a subordinate body or official it is invalid. The test must be considered in the light of other constitutional provisions and the presumption of constitutionality. With regard to the former, the Oireachtas may not confer a power to act in breach of the Constitution. Thus, in *East Donegal Co-operative Livestock Mart Ltd. v Attorney General* [1970] I.R. 317 the delegation of a power to exempt particular individuals from the operation of the parent statute was held to be invalid as it violated the constitutional guarantee of equality in Article 40.1. And, as has been seen earlier, a post-1937 statute must where possible be interpreted in a manner which is consonant with the Constitution. In this respect, where a power is delegated in ambiguous terms the courts will construe it in as narrow a manner as is reasonably possible in order to preserve its constitutionality. This is demonstrated by the Supreme Court decision in *Cooke v Walsh* [1984] I.R. 710 (Extract 12.25) where s. 72 of the Health Act, 1970 was interpreted sufficiently narrowly to exclude an unconstitutional delegation of legislative power.

Constitutional questions aside the validity of delegated legislation is tested within the framework of the parent statute. In this context, the courts examine the terms in which the power has been delegated which is principally a matter of statutory interpretation. If the exercise of the power exceeds those terms it is said to be *ultra vires* and, therefore, the instrument is invalid. In many cases, however, the delegated power is conferred in broad open-ended terms and the question of validity is by no means self-evident. Thus, in *The State (Sheehan) v The Government of Ireland* [1987] I.R. 550 it was held that the absence of a qualification on the power to order the commencement of s. 60 of the Civil Liability Act, 1961 entitled the government to defer its implementation. But where a power is exercised the courts examine the scope of the Act, the purpose of the power, consider whether the regulation is "unreasonable" and, in some cases, review the procedure adopted in enacting the regulation. In *Minister for Industry and Commerce v Hales* [1967] I.R. 50 (Extract 12.9) the making of a regulation which purported to bring insurance agents engaged under contracts for services within the Holidays (Employees) Act, 1961 was held to be *ultra vires* as the Act was interpreted as being confined to those engaged under contracts of service. Likewise, in *Cooke v Walsh* [1984] I.R. 710 (Extract 12.25) a regulation which purported to exclude a category of persons which was otherwise fully eligible for health care was held to be in-valid, as the exclusion was beyond the authority conferred by the parent Act. In *Cassidy v Minister for Industry and Commerce* [1978] I.R. 297 Extract 12.26) the Supreme Court tested the ministerial order in question both as to the purpose which it sought to achieve and its "reasonableness". And in *Burke v Minister for Labour* [1979] I.R. 354 (Extract 12.27) the Order in question was held to be invalid due to the failure of the designated rule making body to observe basic fairness in its enactment.

Extract 12.25

COOKE v WALSH [1984] I.R. 710

In an action for damages for personal injuries which arose out of a road accident a claim was made in respect of hospital charges which were in-curred by the plaintiff. The plaintiff would ordinarily have qualified for free hospital care by virtue of the Health Act, 1970. However, Art. 6 of the Health Services Regulations, 1971 (S.I. No. 105 of 1971), which were made under s. 72 of the Act, excluded those who were injured in road accidents unless it appeared that they would not be entitled to recover damages. The defendant, who would otherwise have been required to meet the hospital expenses, contended that the regulation was both unconstitutional and *ultra vires*. In holding the power to make regulations to be constitutional the Supreme Court placed a narrow interpretation on s. 72. However, it held the regulation to be invalid as it purported to exclude from the benefits of the Act a category of persons whose exclusion was not envisaged by the Act.

O'Higgins C.J.
. . . S. 72 of the Act, under which it is agreed this Regulation purports to have been made, is in the following terms:

> 72—(1) The Minister may make regulations applicable to all Health Boards or to one or more than one Health Board regarding the manner in which and the ex-tent to which the Board or Boards shall make available services under this Act and generally in relation to the administration of those services,
>
> 2) Regulations under this section may provide for any service under this Act being made available only to a particular class of the persons who have eligibility for that service.

The defendant has challenged the validity of the regulation. He mounts this challenge on two distinct grounds. In the first place he questions whether the regulation is properly made within the powers conferred on the Minister by s. 72. Obviously, if he succeeds on this ground the regulation will be held to be *ultra vires* the Minister and on that account to be void. If, on the other hand, the regulation is held to be within the apparent authority conferred on the Minister by the section, then the court must consider whether the section itself is valid having regard to the provisions of the Constitution. It is well settled that the consideration of any question involving the validity of a statute or a section thereof should, in appropriate circumstances, be postponed to the consideration of any other question, the resolution of which will determine the issue between the parties. It is, therefore, proper in this case that the question of *ultra vires*, apart from any question of constitutionality, should first be considered. In the consideration of such question, however, the validity of the section must be presumed and it must be interpreted in accordance with the existence of such a presumption. This means that if the section is capable of being interpreted in two ways, one of which would give a meaning which is consistent with what is permitted by the Constitution and the other of which would not, that meaning which is so consistent must be adopted.

The interpretation of the section is a prerequisite to a determination of whether what purports to be done by the regulation is, in fact, within the Minister's powers under the section. What then is permitted by s. 72? The first subsection applies only to health boards and clearly relates to the manner in which these boards are to administer the health services provided for under the section. While it refers to the making of regulations "regarding the manner in which and the extent to which the board or boards shall make available services", this must not be taken as meaning that such regulations may remove, reduce or otherwise alter obligations imposed on health boards by the Act. To attach such a meaning, unless compelled to do so by the words used would be to attribute to the Oireachtas, unnecessarily, an intention to delegate in the field of lawmaking in a manner "which is neither contemplated nor permitted by the Constitution". (See this Court's judgment in *Cityview Press v An Comhairle Oiliuna* [1980] I.R. at 399). Accordingly, these words must be taken as applying only to standards, periods, places, personnel or such other factors which may indicate the nature and quality of the services which are to be made available. However, it is not so much on this subsection as on subsection (2) that reliance was placed in justification of the regulation. I again quote this subsection:

> Regulations under this section may provide for any service under this Act being made available only to a particular class of the persons who have eligibility for that service.

Here, again, it is necessary to seek a meaning for these words which absolve the National Parliament from any intention to delegate its exclusive power of making or changing the laws. Needless to say, if such a meaning is not possible then the invalidity of the subsection would be established. *Prima facie*, therefore, these words are to be interpreted in such a manner as to authorise only exclusions which the Act itself contemplates. Such exclusions may be possible in relation to particular services for persons with limited eligibility. Those with such eligibility are classified under section 46 and the Minister, by subsection (3), is given power to change or alter this classification. The obligation imposed on health boards is to provide, not all the services, but, such services as are specified, for persons with limited eligibility. While I do not find it necesary to come to a final decision in this regard it seems to me possible that regulations under the subsection could excuse a particular health board or health boards from the obligation to provide a particular service for a particular class of those with limited eligibility, while the obligation to provide that service for others with limited eligibility remained. I am, however, satisfied that the subsection is not to be interpreted as permitting by regulation the cancelling, repeal or alteration of anything laid down in the Act itself unless such is contemplated by the Act.

Having said this, I turn to what the Regulation purports to do. It, in effect, seeks to add new subsections to ss. 52 and 56 of the Act which exclude, from the benefit of these sections and the statutory entitlement thereby afforded, a category of persons whose exclusion is in no way authorised or contemplated by the Act. Included in this category must, necessarily, be persons who by the Act are given full eligibility and full statutory entitlement to avail of the services provided for by the two sections without charge. This is, in reality, an attempt to amend the two sections by Ministerial regulation instead of by appropriate legislation. In my view, the National Parliament could not and did not intend to give such a power to the Minister for Health when it enacted s. 2 of the Health Act, 1970. Accordingly, in my view, the Regulation is *ultra vires* the Minister and is void.

I wish to add that during the argument on this issue the standing of the defendant to raise these questions of validity was itself questioned. In this respect reliance was placed on the decision of this Court in *Cahill v Sutton* [1980] I.R., at p. 269. While this decision referred to a constitutional issue its reasoning could apply equally to an issue of *ultra vires*, in relation to rules or regulations made under statutory power. I am quite satisfied that the defendant has sufficient standing to raise this question of *ultra vires*. By reason of the regulation he has been asked to meet a claim in respect of hospital charges which now proves, in my view, to be unjustifed and which he could only dispute by questioning the regulation as a consequence of which these charges were imposed.

Extract 12.26

CASSIDY v MINISTER FOR INDUSTRY AND COMMERCE
[1978] I.R. 297

Under s. 22A of the Prices Act, 1958, as amended, the Minister has power to regulate the maximum prices of certain commodities including alcohol. A voluntary arrangement was relied on by which publicans agreed to give the Minister notice of proposed price increases in order to allow him to consider their reasonableness. Publicans in Dundalk refused to abide by this informal price control mechanism. Accordingly, the Minister made orders which set maximum prices for the Dundalk area by which, *inter alia*, the price of a half pint bottle of lager was set at 14p! The plaintiffs sought a declaration that the orders were invalid on the grounds that they were made for a purpose which was not authorised by the Act and that they were oppressive in their application to public and lounge bars alike. The Supreme Court upheld the validity of the orders but confined their application to public bars alone. O'Higgins C.J. and Griffin J. concurred in Henchy J.'s judgment.

Henchy J.
Price control is looked on as an essential part of the strategy of the Government in the war against inflation. In practice, control of prices operates in two ways. The Minister for Industry and Commerce, the defendant, is charged with the duty of monitoring prices; he has worked out a voluntary and non-statutory arrangement whereby suppliers of goods and services agree that they will not increase their prices or charges without prior notice to him. Advance notice of a price increase enables him to have the increase vetted. If he finds it acceptable, he allows it to go through, If he finds it unjustified, he refuses to give it his approval. In the main, the Minister's veto is accepted as the determining factor in deciding whether or not there will be a price increase.

Auxiliary to this voluntary method of price control, there is vested in the Minister by statute the power to compel prices to be held at specified levels. If, for example, a commodity is being sold, or is proposed to be sold, at an excessive price, the Minister is empowered to make a statutory instrument fixing the maximum price which may be charged for that commodity. An offence is committed if the commodity is then sold for more than the maximum price so fixed. This form of compulsory price control is allowed by the Prices Acts, 1958-1972.

In 1972 the associations representing licensed vintners were co-operating with the Minister in the voluntary control of the price of drink sold in public houses. In August, 1972, it came to the notice of the Minister that this voluntary arrangement, or gentleman's agreement, was being broken in the town of Dundalk. Drink was being sold there at increased prices of which he had got no advance notice. By letter, and by sending a representative to Dundalk to make the case against the price increases, he sought to dissuade the publicans from persisitng in charging the increased prices—but to no avail. Therefore, he turned to his statutory powers of price control. In exercise of those powers, he laid down by statutory instrument the maximum prices that could be charged for intoxicating liquor in the urban district of Dundalk. The relevant statutory instruments giving that result are No. 99 of 1973 and No. 136 of 1973; the latter merely varies the maximum prices fixed by the former. Those maximum-price orders are expressly not applicable to premises registered under the Tourist Traffic Acts, 1939-1970, (*i.e.*, hotels) and the maximum prices so fixed apply regardless of whether the drink is sold in a public bar or in a lounge bar.

The five Dundalk publicans who have brought this action against the Minister seek to have those two maximum-price orders condemned as invalid. Their claim failed in the High Court. In this appeal they seek a reversal of that decision. They base their appeal on two grounds. First, they contend that the orders are bad because they were made not for the purpose allowed by the statute (the main-tainance of the stability of prices generally) but for the unpermitted purpose of forcing the plaintiffs, and the vintners' organisation of which they are members, to comply with the non-statutory arrangement whereby proposed price increases are to be notified in advance to the Minister. Secondly, they contend that the orders are bad because of unreasonableness, in that the single scale of maximum prices laid down in them unfairly compels publicans to observe those maximum prices when the drinks are being sold in lounge bars.

The trial judge disposed of the first of those grounds by finding as follows:— "There is no evidence to suggest that the Minister was under any misapprehension as to the basis upon which he could operate the informal price control which prevailed after 1968, or that he thought that there was any legal obligation on members of the licensed trade to notify intended price increases. I have no doubt that the Minister made the order because he considered that the price increases in the Dundalk area were excessive and with a view to promoting the objects of the Prices Acts, 1958-72, by maintaining the stability of prices of intoxicating liquor in the Dundalk area." On a review of the correspondence and the oral evidence, I am satisfied that those findings were justified and could not be disturbed on appeal. The increases which the Dundalk publicans arrogated to themselves produced drink prices which were higher than those obtaining in any other provincial town and even higher than those obtaining in Dublin, where the overheads in the licensed trade are considered to be higher than elsewhere in the State. Those unwarranted increases evoked complaints from the public which the Minister could not ignore. The evidence is coercive of the conclusion that the Minister, in making these orders, was primarily concerned to restore the stability of prices that had existed in the retail drink trade before the unilateral decision of the Dundalk publicans to award themselves price increases. In other words, in making these orders the Minister was exercising his statutory powers so as to achieve the object set by the legislature.

However, I think that the Minister had a secondary purpose which is not covered by the judge's findings. It would seem from the correspondence and the oral evidence that the Minister, as well as wiping out the unwarranted price increases, hoped that the threat of making maximum-price orders would force the Dundalk publicans and their organisation to return to the system of voluntary price control. He was not authorised by statute to make maximum-price orders for such a purpose, but it seems to me clear from the evidence that this further purpose behind the making of the orders was very much a secondary or subordinate purpose. The evil which the Minister wished to eliminate by making the orders was the unwarranted increase in drink prices in the Dundalk area. Having regard to the scale of those increases, he would have been wanting in the exercise of his statutory powers if he had ignored them. It is true that in correspondence he complained of those increases as being "unauthorised price increases" and as having been made "without . . . prior approval." So they were. But for the Minister to label them as such is a far cry from proclaiming it to be his sole or primary intention to compel the Dundalk publicans to return to the system of voluntary price control. If price increases had been justifiable because of increased costs but had been made without prior notice to the Minister, there is nothing to suggest that he would have wiped them out by making maximum-price orders.

The evidence forces me to the conclusion that the primary and dominant purpose of the Minister in making these orders was to eliminate unwarranted price increases and that, while he also had as his aim the return of the publicans to the voluntary practice of not making price increases without giving him prior notice, that aim was merely subsidiary and consequential to the dominant and permitted aim. I would hold that the Minister did not act ultra vires in this respect. Where a power to legislate for a particular purpose is delegated and the power is exercised bona fide and primarily for that purpose, I consider that the exercise of the power is not vitiated if it is aimed also at the attainment of a subsidiary or consequential purpose which is not inconsistent with the permitted purpose. If the law were otherwise, many delegated powers would be unexercisable, for the permitted purpose frequently encompasses of necessity the attainment of other purposes. In my opinion the first ground of appeal fails.

The second ground of appeal was dealt with by the trial judge as follows:—"In making the order, the Minister did not prescribe a separate scale of prices for lounge bars because he was advised, and took the view, that no satisfactory formula was available to distinguish a lounge bar from a public bar. There are no minimum levels of amenity, comfort, or service which can be regarded as essential to a lounge bar. I do not think that the plaintiffs' suggestion (that the matter should be left to the decision of District Justices who would be provided with suitable guidelines) is workable. In any event, the matter falls within the legislative discretion of the Minister to reconcile the exercise of property rights with the exigencies of the common good, and it is not reviewable by this Court unless the exercise of his discretion is obviously arbitrary or capricious which it clearly is not."

The lounge bar is a well-recognised and widespread feature of the licensed trade in this country. A member of the public would probably recognize the term as meaning a secluded or segregated area, usually within or annexed to a public bar, where in consideration of prices somewhat higher than those charged in a public bar, patrons are provided with amenities such as seclusion, comfortable seating and tables and, varying from premises to premises, extras such as a carpeted floor, waiter service, television, service of food, and the like. Many licensees of public houses have concentrated on this aspect of the trade. Some licensees have spent large sums in equipping lounge bars and have committed themselves to the heavy running expenses in staffing them and supplying the services expected by those who patronise them. The proprietors have built up a valuable goodwill for their lounge bars—a goodwill that would obviously be devalued if, by reason of common maximum prices (which invariably become common minimum prices) the prices in lounge bars are reduced to those in public bars. While common maximum prices would put all public bars on an equal footing as regards gross profits on sales, it would bear hard on lounge bars where, in the absence of a maximum-price order, patrons are expected, and are willing, to pay 1p, 2p or 3p extra for each dirnk. It is not unlikely that common maximum prices would affect lounge bars by reducing employment in them, diminishing profits and lowering their capital values. Do the powers vested in the Minister allow property rights to be thus interefered with? Do the demands of statutory price control permit common maximum prices to be laid down so as to compel a licensee (as one of the plaintiffs stated in evidence would be his fate) to have to cease trading as a lounge bar?

It is clear from the evidence that the Minister considered the desirablity of fixing separate maximum prices for lounge bars as distinct from public bars. He sought legal advice on the matter. The advice he got was that it was not practicable to frame a satisfactory definition of a lounge bar. I can well understand the difficulty of drafting a comprehensive definition which would specify the minimum physical requirements of a lounge bar, but I think it was a task not beyond the competence of a properly instructed draftsman. However, I am not satisfied that a definition was necessary to effect the desired result. Many of the commonest expressions in the licensing code are left without statutory definition—*e.g.*, "bar" and "public bar." It is left to the Courts to determine the true meaning and scope of such expressions. I see no reason why a similar approach could not have been adopted in regard to lounge bars. A scale of maximum prices could have been fixed for public bars and a separate scale of maximum surcharges could have been laid down for lounge bars, it being left to the Courts to determine whether a particular area of the licensed premises qualified for this purpose as a lounge bar.

If, on the other hand, it be the legislative policy that lounge bars should no longer exist as areas of licensed premises where prices higher than those in a public bar are charged, that policy should be implemented in a statute duly made in conformity with the Constitution. The change cannot be effected by ministerial orders made under the Prices Acts. The purpose of such orders is "to maintain stability of prices generally" (s. 22A, sub-s. 1, of the Prices Act, 1958) and not to devalue or disrupt, unnecessarily or unfairly, property, trade or industry. The Minister has not been empowered by Parliament to do more than what is necessary to maintain the stability of prices generally.

The general rule of law is that where Parliament has by statute delegated a power of subordinate legislation, the power must be exercised within the limitations of that power as they are expressed or necessarily implied in the statutory delegation. Otherwise it will be held to have been invalidly exercised for being ultra vires. And it is a necessary implication in such a statutory delegation that the power to issue subordinate legislation should be exercised reasonably. Diplock L.J. has stated in *Mixnam's Properties Ltd.* v. *Chertsey Urban District Council* [1964] 1 Q.B. 214 at p. 237 of the report:—

> Thus, the kind of unreasonableness which invalidates a by-law [*or, I would add, any other form of subordinate legislation*] is not the antonym of 'reasonableness' in the sense of which that expression is used in the common law, but such manifest arbitrariness, injustice or partiality that a court would say: 'Parliament never intended to give authority to make such rules; they are unreasonable and ultra vires.'

I consider that to be the correct test. Applied here it produces the conclusion that Parliament could not have intended that licensees of lounge bars would be treated so oppressively and unfairly by maximum-price orders. If the Minister had made a maximum-price order which forbade hotel owners to sell drink in their hotels at prices higher than those fixed for public bars, it would be generally accepted that such an order would be oppressive and unfair. The capital outlay and overhead expenses necessarily involved in the residential and other features of hotels are such that to force their drink prices down to those chargeable in a public bar would in many cases be ruinously unfair. Understandably, the Minister expressly excluded the application of the Dundalk maximum-price orders to hotels. To have done otherwise would have been unreasonable. But if the orders are construed as not distinguishing lounge bars in any way, and as forcing their prices down to those of public bars, they fail unreasonably to have regard to the fact that owners of lounge bars, like hoteliers, are entitled, because of capital outlay and overhead expenses, to separate treatment in the matter of drink prices, at least to the extent of not requiring them to sell at prices which may cause them serious economic hardship. For that reason the application of the orders to lounge bars is unjustifiable.

For another reason, these maximum-price orders are inapplicable to lounge bars. They apply, be it noted, only to sales of liquor in the urban district of Dundalk; we have been told that 17 such orders have been made for other localities throughout the State. In so far as these two impugned orders apply to public bars, their object and effect is, broadly speaking, to bring drink prices in Dundalk into line with drink prices elsewhere. The combination of the statutory price control, as effected by these orders, and the voluntary price control operating elsewhere results in a general standardisation of maximum prices for drink sold in public bars. Licensees of public bars, whether the bars are inside or outside the urban district of Dundalk, cannot generally point to unequal treatment in the matter of maximum prices; but there would be unequal treatment if the orders applied to lounge bars. Licensees of lounge bars would have their prices depressed to the level of the maximum prices fixed for public bars; that would be the result if the lounge bar happened to be situated in the urban district of Dundalk. If the lounge bar happened to be situated outside that urban district, the maximum-price orders would not apply so that, in such a lounge bar, prices in excess of the maximum prices in public bars might be charged. This would amount to unfair, unequal and arbitrary treatment. It would be plainly unjust and inequitable if, merely because his lounge bar is situated within the urban district, a licensee were compelled to charge no more than public-bar prices while his competitor, who might be trading only a short distance away, is not subject to such price control because his lounge bar happens to be outside the urban district. Discrimination of that kind would be justifiable only if it were based on some distinguishing economic factor; but there is none. The distinction would rest entirely on the haphazard circumstance of different locations.

Parliament cannot have intended that the Minister would exercise in such an arbitrary and unfair way the legislative powers of price control vested in him. That being so, it must be held that the orders would be ultra vires if they were to be applied to lounge bars.

My adjudication is that the impugned orders are not invalid, for being ultra vires, in so far as they apply to public bars but that their extended application to lounge bars is not within the scope of the delegated legislative functions. If the orders had been composed in such a way that the provisions applicable to public bars could be severed from the rest, I would rule that such provisions should be severed and declared valid as being intra vires. But the orders do not lend themselves to verbal severance: they simply fix maximum prices without reference to whether they are charged in lounge bars or public bars. However, there is no reason why the orders should not be severed in the range of their application, so that they may be preserved and implemented in so far as they are intra vires, and ruled inoperable only in so far as their application would run into the area of ultra vires: see *per* Lord Halsbury L.C. in *MacLeod* v. *The Attorney-General for New South Wales* [1891] A.C. 455; *per* Lord MacDermott L.C.J. at p. 118 of the report of *Ulster Transport Authority* v. *James Brown & Sons Ltd* [1953] N.I. 79. and *per* Viscount Simonds and Lord Radcliffe at pp. 520 and 525 of the report of *Belfast Corporation* v. *O.D. Cars Ltd* [1960] A.C. 490. By the operation of what Lord MacDermott L.C.J. called "horizontal severance" in the *Ulster Transport Case*, the layer of application to lounge bars may be detached and ruled inoperable, and the underlying range of application to public bars may be given the effectiveness which its validity warrants.

Therefore, I would affirm the ruling in the High Court that the impugned orders are not invalid for being ultra vires, with the qualification that they must be construed as having no application to lounge bars. If the Minister wishes to fix maximum prices for drinks sold in lounge bars, he may do so by exercising the powers vested in him by the Prices Acts but, to be valid, any maximum-prices orders so made should not be flawed by unfair and unjustifiable discrimination.

Extract 12.27

BURKE v MINISTER FOR LABOUR [1979] I.R. 354

Joint Labour Committees (J.L.C.s) are empowered under the Industrial Relations Act, 1946 to make recommendations to the Labour Court to fix minimum wages to be paid to certain categories of workers. Unless the Court refers the proposal back to the J.L.C. it must either make an order in accordance with the proposals or refuse to make the order sought. An employer is obliged to pay the minimum rates set by the order, failure to comply with which is a criminal offence, the employer also being liable to pay arrears. A J.L.C. considered a proposal to set a new minimum wage for workers in the hotel industry to give effect to an intervening national wage agreement. The proposal did not contain an adjustment in respect of the value of board and lodging provided to workers. An amendment was tabled by the employers' representatives, which sought to have their submissions on that matter considered and adopted, but it was defeated by a vote at one of the J.L.C. meetings. At subsequent meetings it became clear that the J.L.C. would not consider the submissions although no formal vote was taken. The Labour Court ultimately made an order which implemented the J.L.C.'s proposal. The Supreme Court held that the failure to consider the employers' submission amounted to a denial of basic fairness and rendered the order invalid. O'Higgins C.J., Griffin, Parke and Kenny JJ. concurred in Henchy J.'s judgment.

Henchy J.

. . . It will be seen, therefore, that the power to make a minimum-remuneration order is a delegated power of a most fundamental, permissive and far-reaching kind. By the above provisions of the Act of 1946 Parliament, without reserving to itself a power of supervision or a power of revocation or cancellation (which would apply if the order had to be laid on the table of either House before it could have statutory effect) has vested in a joint labour committee and the Labour Court the conjoint power to fix minimum rates of remuneration so that non-payment thereof will render employers liable to conviction and fine and (in the case of conviction) to being made compellable by court order to pay the amount fixed by the order of the Labour Court. Not alone is this power given irrevocably and without parliamentary, or even ministerial, control, but once such an order is made (no matter how erroneous, ill-judged or unfair it may be) a joint labour committee is debarred from submitting proposals for revoking or amending it until it has been in force for at least six months. While the parent statute may be amended or repealed at any time, the order, whose authors are not even the direct delegates of Parliament, must stand irrevocably in force for well over six months.

In the present case the order is not challenged on constitutional grounds. What is contended is that the manner of its making has tainted it with invalidity . . . [His lordship considered the facts and continued] . . . Is an order so made valid? One of the main complaints of counsel for the plaintiffs is that the proposals for the order of 1978 should not have been forwarded by the Committee to the Labour Court for ratification until the employers' motion (that the proposals should take into account the cost to the employers of board and lodging) had been voted on. I do not consider that there is any real weight in this point. It is true that that motion was never put to a vote, but what was advocated by the motion was amply discussed at the meetings held on the 16th February, the 7th March, the 2nd May and the 11th May. It is manifest from the minutes of those meetings that a majority of the members repeatedly set their faces against the motion. The Act of 1946 empowers the Committee to adopt such procedure as is thought suitable for the discharge of their functions. It was well within the competence of the Committee to deem, as they impliedly did, that the employers' motion did not require a formal vote of rejection. The votes taken were sufficient to show that the employers' motion, after full discussion, was held unworthy of support. It has not been suggested that, if the motion had been put to a vote, any other result would have been produced. So I reject the submission that the order of 1978 is invalid for want of a formal vote on that motion.

Whether the Committee were entitled to reject the motion (as they impliedly did) in such circumstances, where the order was made without any regard to the real cost to the employers of board and lodging supplied, is another matter. To appraise this point, it is necessary to bear in mind the nature and reach of the jurisdiction that was being exercised by the Committee.

As I have earlier observed, the delegated power that was vested in the Committee was of the most extensive nature. It enabled the Committee to formulate the proposals for an order fixing minimum rates of remuneration. All the Labour Court could do was to refer the proposals back to the Committee with observations. The Labour Court is given no power of initiation or amendment. It could but make or refuse to make the order. Essentially, therefore, the order-making body was the Committee. Apart from the skeletal provisions in the second schedule to the Act of 1946 as to its constitution, officers and proceedings, the Act of 1946 is silent as to how a committee are to carry out their functions in making orders.

Where Parliament has delegated functions of that nature, it is to be necessarily inferred as part of the legislative intention that the body which makes the orders will exercise its functions, not only with constitutional propriety and due regard to natural justice, but also within the framework of the terms and objects of the relevant Act and with basic fairness, reasonableness and good faith. The absoluteness of the delegation is susceptible of unjust and tyrannous abuse unless its operation is thus confined; so it is entirely proper to ascribe to the Oireachtas (being the Parliament of a State which is constitutionally bound to protect, by its laws, its citizens from unjust attack) an intention that the delegated functions must be exercised within those limitations.

Here the Committee undertook the task of making a statutory instrument fixing minimum rates of remuneration for certain workers in the hotel industry. The representatives of employers in the hotel industry, as members of the Committee, wished the Committee to give consideration, before such an order was made, to the actual cost to employers of board and lodging supplied to workers. That was an eminently reasonable proposal. It was not possible to assess a fair and reasonable figure for minimum remuneration until a fair and reasonable assessment was made of the gross value of cash remuneration plus board and lodging. By the self-denying restraint by which the Committee debarred themselves from looking at the data necessary to determine the true cost to the employer of board and lodging, the Committee left themselves open to the charge that the consequent minimum-remuneration order may be unjust and unfair.

It is no answer to that charge to say that the Committee were following the practice adopted previously before such orders were made. Two wrongs do not make a right; but in this case there was the difference that the Committee were specifically and repeatedly asked to receive and have regard to evidence as to the cost of the benefits which the workers were getting in the form of board and lodging. Nor is it a good answer to say that, if the Committee had taken into account the true, rather than the estimated, cost of board and lodging, the figures fixed as minimum rates of remuneration would not have been materially affected. As the

Committee did not hear such evidence, it is impossible to say what effect such evidence would have had on them. Even if such evidence would have made no difference, the Committee, by rejecting it unheard and unconsidered, left themselves open to the imputation of bias, unfairness and prejudice. Such accusations, if made, would be unmerited; the members of the Committee were, no doubt, all acting in good faith and to the best of their abilities.

However, the fact is that the Committee, in formulating the proposals for the order of 1978, were acting as an unelected body, functioning behind closed doors, to produce a statutory order fixing minimum rates of renumeration; and that order could not be varied for at least six months, and non-compliance with it could lead to criminal responsibility and civil compellability. Elementary fairness required that the employers as well as the employees, both of whom were represented on the Committee, should have been allowed to present and to see consideration given to material which was crucially relevant to the question of minimum rates of remuneration.

By failing to receive and consider that evidence, the Committee failed to keep within the confines of their statutory terms of reference as those must necessarily be inferred. In other words, the order of 1978 was made in excess of jurisdiction to that extent.

I would allow the plaintiffs' appeal and declare that the Employment Regulation Order (Hotels Joint Labour Committee), 1978, was and is void in so far as it purported to substitute new minimum rates of remuneration payable to hotel workers in receipt of board, or in receipt of board and lodging, and to revoke that part of the order of 1977 which dealt with minimum rates of remuneration payable to hotel workers in receipt of board, or in receipt of board and lodging.

Chapter 13

THE CONSTITUTION AND CONSTITUTIONAL RIGHTS

The Constitution presents special problems of interpretation for Irish judges. As we have seen from Chapter 4, the Constitution empowers the High Court and Supreme Court to declare that legislation is invalid on the ground that it is in conflict with the Constitution. The Constitution has also provided these courts with opportunities to discuss the fundamental legal basis for the laws and institutions of the State. In sum, the Constitution has allowed for the development of an area of law which emphasises that the present Irish legal system is different in many respects from the system which existed in Ireland until 1922. The potential of the cases discussed in this Chapter to permeate the entire system of law which has been discussed in the preceding chapters cannot be ignored.

This Chapter does not examine the Constitution in full, but focuses instead on a selection of issues which indicate the techniques which the judges have been required to develop in interpreting the meaning of the Constitution. Further analysis may be found in the texts on Irish Constitutional Law which are available. But, it must also be noted that the Constitution was 50 years old on 29th December 1987 and to mark that anniversary a number of important publications appeared in 1988. Two in particular provide valuable insights into the origins of the 1937 Constitution and the manner in which it has been interpreted since 1937. These are Litton (ed.), *The Constitution of Ireland 1937-1987* (Institute of Public Administration, 1988) and Farrell (ed.), *deValera's Constitution and Ours* (Gill and Macmillan for R.T.E., 1988), the latter being based on the R.T.E. Thomas Davis lecture series commemorating the 50th Anniversary. Both books include contributions by lawyers and historians and contain some historical material which has only come to light in recent years.

THE STRUCTURE OF THE CONSTITUTION

The 1937 Constitution, Bunreacht na hÉireann, may be divided into two broad parts. The first of these establishes the basic structures of the institutions of State, while the other sets out a list of individual human rights which cannot be infringed by the laws which operate in the State.

We have already discussed in some detail in Chapter 4 the constitutional provisions which describe the functions of the judicial branch of government, particularly its function in relation to declaring legislation invalid on the ground that it is in breach of the Constitution itself. It is important to emphasise, however, the context within which that function takes place. Article 6.1 of the Constitution states:

All powers of government, legislative, executive and judicial, derive, under God, from the people, whose right it is to designate the rulers of the State and, in final appeal, to decide all questions of national policy, according to the requirements of the common good.

This Article represents a fundamental statement as to the nature of the governance of this State. It adopts the well recognised tripartite division of government, or separation of powers, consisting of the executive, or cabinet government; the legislative branch, consisting of the National Parliament (the Oireachtas); and the judiciary. As mentioned in Chapter 2, this division may be traced back to the French and American revolutions of the 18th Century, which of course were inspirations for the 1798 rebellion in Ireland and the subsequent struggles for independence. Other Articles of the Constitution describe in more detail how these three branches of government interact with each other, but in effect these amount to providing what has been called in the United States of America the checks and balances between the three branches. This is seen quite clearly, for example, in the important role which the judges have played in reviewing whether legislation is in conflict with the Constitution, generally referred to as constitutional judicial review.

There is a further important aspect to Article 6 which may be noted: it amounts to an assertion of the popular sovereignty of the People of Ireland, since the legitimacy of the three branches is said to derive, under God, from the People. This marks a real break from the legal system which existed in Ireland prior to 1922, and which continued to some extent to operate through the existence of the Free State. Under the former system, ultimate legal authority derived from the Crown. Article 6 makes clear that the approval of the Constitution by the People in 1937 marked the beginning of a new legal order in the State and it places an emphasis on the indigenous nature of Irish legal culture. The Constitution recognises that ultimate temporal authority comes from the people of Ireland and the institutions of the State are, in a very real sense, the creation and agents of the People. The real question which arises from this simple assertion is whether that high principle has any real practical effect.

Byrne v. Ireland [1972] I.R. 241 (Extract 13.1) established clearly that it does. Mrs. Byrne suffered severe personal injuries when she fell into a hole which had been dug by an employee of the Department of Posts and Telegraphs. The apparent bar to what was otherwise a straightforward personal injuries action was that it had been thought up to then that no action could be taken against a government Department. The reason for this was that, prior to 1922, the Crown and its government Departments were regarded as immune from legal action by virtue of what is described as Crown prerogative, that is, the position of the Crown as the sovereign source of law. Under the British Constitution, it was simply impossible to bring claims against any government Department and it required the Westminster Parliament (which is now, in effect, the source of all legal authority in Britain) to pass the Crown Proceedings Act, 1947 to alter this in certain respects. It was thought in Ireland that similar legislation was required, on the basis that in 1922 this State must have acquired the prerogative immunities which formerly existed in the pre-independence legal system. *Byrne v. Ireland* indicates clearly that this was a false view of the constitutional revolution which took place, possibly in 1922 but most certainly in 1937. The judgment of Walsh J. in *Byrne* illustrates that, since 1937, nothing can be taken for granted in relation to the legal fundamentals of the present constitutional arrangements. The result in *Byrne*, by which the plaintiff was allowed to proceed in her negligence action, marks a turning point in the Irish legal system which makes *Donoghue v. Stevenson* [1932] A.C. 562 (see Chapter 11) pale into insignificance. The outcome indicates that, under the Constitution, the judges have power to make law with broad sweeping strokes. There is no need now for a State Proceedings Act, and it would also appear that the kinds of exemptions from suit which continue to exist in Britain under its 1947 Act would probably be regarded as unconstitutional in this State.

In *Webb v. Ireland* [1988] I.R. 353, the High Court and Supreme Court affirmed the basic approach taken in *Byrne* that prerogatives (in this instance in relation to treasure trove) could not have survived the enactment of the 1937 Constitution. However, the Supreme Court, which again included Walsh J., also held that in certain instances the Constitution substituted Irish versions of the old prerogatives. The *Webb* decision indicates, therefore, that while the Constitution swept away the old regime it did not always leave a void in its place. It remains for the future, however, to determine to what extent all the old prerogatives which continue to crop up in decisions of the courts were carried over into Irish law in a different form. Some thought-provoking comments may be found in Kelly, 'Hidden Treasure and the Constitution' (1988) *10 D.U.L.J. (n.s.)* 5 and Morgan, 'Constitutional Interpretation: Three Cautionary Tales' (1988) *10 D.U.L.J. (n.s.)* 24.

PRELIMINARY ISSUES IN CONSTITUTIONAL CASES

A fundamental point emphasised in constitutional cases is that the plaintiff must be able to point to some way in which a rule of law affects her in particular. In *Byrne v. Ireland*, above, this proved no difficulty to the plaintiff. Nonetheless, in some instances constitutional actions have failed because the plaintiff has not been able to establish any personal connection with the operation of the legal rule being challenged. This 'personal connection' test is referred to as the standing rule, the requirement to establish *locus standi*. *Locus standi* is a basic test in any public law case, and constitutional law is, clearly, part of public law. In general it may be said that public law concerns the operation of any institution which is dependent on legislation or the operation of any legislative provisions by the State. Criminal law is thus also clearly part of public law. So many institutions operate under legislation nowadays that it is difficult to think of areas of purely private law. Whatever the precise scope of public law, where an individual citizen wishes to bring a constitutional case, the general rule is that *locus standi* must be established. The leading case on *locus standi* in constitutional cases is *Cahill v. Sutton* [1980] I.R. 269 (Extract 13.2). In that case, the plaintiff's inability to establish *locus standi* resulted in her constitutional argument failing completely.

Some points may be noted about the *Cahill* decision. Henchy J., who delivered the leading judgment, pointed out that the courts should be reluctant to allow the constitutional function of the courts to be used as a basis for general points of interest to be litigated. This precludes the possibility of the *actio popularis* to which he refers, by which any citizen could bring a constitutional action. This approach may also be linked to the notion that the judges prefer to engage in the resolution of real disputes, rather than hypothetical moots, a point discussed in Chapter 11 in relation to *ratio decidendi*. It also emerges in Henchy J.'s judgment in *The People v. O'Shea* [1982] I.R. 337 (Extract 13.4). Second, Henchy J. acknowledges that the legislative provision challenged in *Cahill* might not be constitutionally valid, thus indicating to the Oireachtas that it should consider amending the law in this respect. In this way, Henchy J. indicates that the primary law-making role rests, under the Constitution, with the Oireachtas. The question which might be posed here is whether the Oireachtas, which has not at the time of writing made the suggested change in the law, has failed in its primary function in this respect. Might this have been the hidden reason behind the decisions in *Byrne v. Ireland* [1972] I.R. 241 or in *deBurca v. Attorney General* [1976] I.R. 38 (as to the latter see Chapter 3)? The third point as to *locus standi* is that, in some cases, a plaintiff may merely be precluded from raising certain points in argument and not others. This was the position in *Norris v. Attorney General* [1984] I.R. 36 (Extract 13.7). Finally, it may be noted that the *Cahill* standing rule is the usual, but not invariable, rule. In *Crotty v. An Taoiseach* [1987] I.R. 713 and *McGimpsey v. Ireland* [1988] I.R. 567, constitutional actions were allowed to proceed even though the plaintiffs in those actions could not establish better standing than any other citizen; in effect these cases were as close as can be imagined to *actiones popularis*.

JUDICIAL TECHNIQUES IN INTERPRETING THE CONSTITUTION

Given the importance of the Constitution in the legal system it is not, perhaps, surprising that the courts have developed some special rules of interpretation to deal with the text. The judges have, however, not reached any form of consensus as to the circumstances in which these rules apply. There is, for example, nothing as close to the agreement which, generally speaking, applies in relation to statutory interpretation: see Chapter 12. This is hardly surprising in view of the difficulties which the Constitution presents.

The Constitution does not contain the type of narrow rules which are often to be found in a piece of legislation. This is not to minimise the problems which arise in statutory interpretation but merely to indicate the major problems created by the constitutional text which attempts, in broad terms, to describe the entire basis for the Irish legal order. We have already seen how Article 6 of the Constitution represents, in effect, the cornerstone of the whole legal system. Since Article 6 is also a legal provision, its meaning must also be explained where a case presents itself to the courts; it cannot be ignored.

Generally speaking the courts have tended to avoid a literal interpretation of the Constitution. This can be seen in *Tormey v. Ireland* [1985] I.R. 289 (Extract 13.3). The plaintiff was due to be tried in the Circuit Criminal Court. It will be recalled (see Chapter 4) that prior to the enactment of the Courts Act, 1981 the plaintiff was in effect entitled to have his case transferred from the Circuit Court to the High Court (the Central Criminal Court). S.32 of the Courts Act, 1981 removed this right of transfer, and the plaintiff argued that this was in conflict with Article 34.3.1° of the Constitution which provides for the full jurisdiction of the High Court in all matters, civil and criminal. In *Tormey*, the Supreme Court held that this provision should not be taken at face value, and that it must be read in conjunction with Article 36 of the Constitution which allows for the regulation of the jurisdiction of the courts in accordance with law. The Court held that the power of the High Court by way of what were formerly the State Side orders was sufficient to give effect to the provisions of Article 34.3.1°. Delivering the judgment of the Court, Henchy J. referred to the need to interpret the Constitution harmoniously, a rule of constitutional interpretation which he has emphasised on a number of occasions, notably in *The People v. O'Shea* [1982] I.R. 384 (Extract 13.4). The harmonious rule is, broadly, similar to the golden or contextual rule of statutory interpretation, discussed by Henchy J. in *Nestor v. Murphy* [1979] I.R. 326 (Extract 12.10). Indeed, in *The People v. O'Shea*, it is notable that Henchy J. quotes with approval the views of Black J. in *The People v. Kennedy* [1946] I.R. 517, a case on statutory interpretation, in support of the harmonious interpretation rule. And Henchy J. points in addition to the old saying that 'the letter killeth, but the spirit giveth life.'

While most legal commentators agree on the importance of the harmonious interpretation rule, it should be borne in mind that there is some disagreement as to how it is applied in particular situations, including the *Tormey* case itself. As already indicated in Chapter 4, there is a noticeable difference between the approach taken in *Tormey* and that taken in *R. v. R.* [1984] I.R. 296 in relation to a similar provision in the Courts Act, 1981. For discussion of this point see Hogan, 'Reflections on the Supreme Court's Decision in *Tormey v. Attorney General*' (1986) 8 *D.U.L.J. (n.s.)* 31.

Of course, the Constitution creates a particular problem in relation to the meaning which should be given its provisions in 1974 or 1984 or 1994. What should be the approach of the courts be to explaining the fundamental law of the State at different times? Does the Constitution's 'meaning' change over time, or does it adapt to different times and develop accordingly? In relation to legislation, the courts tend to take the view that legislation must be interpreted by reference to the date when it was enacted, and that its meaning cannot change. But, by way of contrast, judges who have formulated rules of constitutional interpretation have tended to see the basic text as an 'organic' text, whose principles have a flexibility not associated with ordinary legislation. Thus, the concept of equality before the law, protected under Article 40.1 of the Constitution, may be explained in different terms today than it would have been 50 or even 20 years ago. In this way, the Constitution is not a rigid instrument which freezes the law for all time as it existed in 1937. This view might be seen as providing the courts with another excuse for making law but it can, perhaps, be seen as a logical approach when considered with reference to an actual problem. The judgment of Walsh J. in *McGee v. Attorney General* [1974] I.R. 284 (Extract 13.6) contains one of the most important explanations of this judicial approach, and it may be said that this approach is, in general, consistent with the harmonious interpretation rule emphasised by Henchy J.

It may be said, indeed, that over the last 25 years, Walsh and Henchy JJ. have made perhaps the greatest contribution to Irish constitutional jurisprudence. This is not, of course, to say that other judges have made less of a contribution, but that in the major constitutional cases of recent years the reader will probably find either a judgment of Walsh or Henchy JJ. as a central part of that case. Nor will the reader find complete consensus between these judges in all areas. In the *McGee* case, however, it may be said that both judges interpreted the constitutional text in a manner which would, simply, have been inconceivable in 1937. Neither was prepared to freeze the document in 1937. Yet in *The People v. O'Shea* [1982] I.R. 384 (Extract 13.4), they both took up what may be regarded as equally unlikely positions. The position adopted by Walsh J. would appear to involve an overly literal interpretation of the Constitution, while that of Henchy J. would appear to involve, at least partly, an interpretation based on the intention of the People in 1937. Clearly, that approach would not have led him to the view he took in *Norris v. Attorney General* [1984] I.R. 36 (Extract 13.7). The judgment of McCarthy J. in *Norris* brings together a number of important issues in this respect, and may be read with profit on that count alone.

Finally, there is one further point which arises in relation to the interpretation of the Constitution. It first surfaced in *McMahon v. Attorney General* [1972] I.R. 69, in which the Supreme Court declared that the ballot papers which had been in use in general elections up to that time were in conflict with Article 16.1.4° of the Constitution, the provision guaranteeing a secret ballot. The Supreme Court did not deal with the question whether its decision invalidated all elections up to that time, something which would of course have created a constitutional crisis. Again in *deBurca v. Attorney General* [1976] I.R. 38, where the Court declared unconstitutional the jury system in operation at that time, the validity of convictions and sentences of imprisonment (and executions) made on foot of those unconstitutionally selected juries was not discussed. Finally, in *Murphy v. Attorney General* [1982] I.R. 241, the Supreme Court resolved the issue. Although the Court held that a declaration of unconstitutionality meant that the legislation had never been validly enacted in accordance with Article 15.4 of the Constitution, this did not have the frightening consequences conjured up by the *McMahon* or *deBurca* decisions. In *Murphy*, the Supreme Court held that ss.192 to 196 of the Income Tax Act, 1967 were invalid at the time they were enacted in 1967. These provisions had had the effect that the plaintiffs, a married couple, had paid more income tax than an unmarried couple living together. The Court held this conflicted with the guarantee to protect the Family in Article 41 of the Constitution. But the Court then held that the plaintiffs were only entitled to reclaim excess income tax payments as from the time they had initiated their constitutional action. For purely pragmatic reasons, the Court held that to allow complete retrospection to its decision was not in accordance with the overall scheme of the Constitution. It is of interest to note that the leading judgment on this point was delivered by Henchy J., and this is of course completely consistent with his harmonious interpretation rule. It does, however, indicate that the judges are quite prepared to adopt solutions in constitutional cases which, however well argued those solutions are, have a sense of policy-making which emphasises the different nature of constitutional adjudication.

THE CONSTITUTION, NATURAL LAW AND HUMAN RIGHTS

As mentioned in Chapter 2, the Constitution invokes certain concepts which are clearly derived from the philosophical-theological influences of the Judaeo-Christian tradition. This is hardly surprising since most laws enacted in England and Ireland in the last 250 years have been influenced by that tradition. Although that may be at the heart of the Irish problem, it must also be part of the solution since the vast majority of the people of Ireland accept that tradition. In any event, the Constitution strikes this note from the beginning of the text. Like the United States Constitution, Bunreacht na hÉireann acknowledges God as the ultimate source of 'all authority'. Article 6, quoted earlier in the Chapter, repeats that point, indicating that, while the People of Ireland have ultimate temporal authority, these powers derive 'under God.' Once again, such a statement is not surprising and clearly has a well-established tradition in society since the emergence of the sophisticated Greek civilization.

Philosophers have argued since then that society has a limited right to legislate, those limits being set by what the Greek philosophers called the *Natural Law*. Natural Law was developed in ancient Greece as a concept by which the moral correctness of laws could be judged. As part of natural law, the philosophers developed the concept of natural rights, which were an innate part of the human personality, individual human rights which could not be interfered with by rules developed in society. Law made by society was referred to as positive law. The argument of the natural law philosophers was that positive law could only be regarded as valid if it conformed to the basic principles of natural law. In the course of the Middle Ages, the theological philosophers, such as Thomas Aquinas, adapted the Greek natural law theory to the tenets of Christian faith. In this version of natural law, God is the ultimate source of all authority, and so the historical basis for the text of the Preamble must be seen against this background. Natural law, as explained by different writers on the subject, consists of a number of broad principles including the requirement of equality before the law as well as, to some extent, the right to own private property. In the Christian explanation of natural law, the family plays an important role also. This view is incorporated into Article 41 of the Constitution. Article 41.1.1° states:

> The State recognises the Family as the natural primary and fundamental unit group of Society, and as a moral institution possessing inalienable and imprescriptible rights, antecedent and superior to all positive law.

This provision contains a summary of much of the basis on which the natural law philosophers proceed. Article 41.1.1° 'recognises' the rights which the Family possesses. Natural law is based on the concept that no law made by society can actually confer natural rights since they already exist, or as Article 41.1.1° puts it they are antecedent and superior to positive law, that is, they existed prior to and are superior to positive law. Thus, the Constitution merely 'acknowledges' the existence of these rights. But an extremely important aspect of Article 41.1.1° is that these natural law concepts now form part of the basic law of the State; the natural law rules and principles become the basis for interpreting the Constitution. Judges have been required, therefore, to be familiar with natural law and natural rights in order to decide whether legislation is invalid. While philosophers in England, where there is no equivalent to the 1937 Constitution, may argue as to the validity of English laws having regard to natural law, the same debate in this State may become a legal debate as to the validity of laws. The fact that this can strike at central pieces of legislation is illustrated by the outcome of *Murphy v. Attorney General* [1982] I.R. 241, above, which resulted in new legislation on tax allowances for married couples, which was necessitated by the Supreme Court's view of Article 41.1.1°.

This requirement that the judges take a 'crash course' in natural law might not be so difficult were it not for the fact that there is no real agreement on the content of natural law or its precise meaning and scope. In effect, there are almost as many theories of natural law and natural rights as there are natural law philosophers. There are, of course, certain basic principles, such as those mentioned above, but beyond that the picture becomes somewhat muddied. It is not possible in the present context to point to all the difficulties which the Constitution creates for the judges in this context, and to some extent a complete understanding might require all lawyers to take a full degree course in philosophy and theology, an approach which would take lawyers back to the mediaeval approach to instruction in law. For most lawyers, however, the principles of natural law do not impinge on day-to-day practice of the law, but the *Murphy* case illustrates that it may lurk in a corner waiting to spring.

The judges have, however, dealt with the impact of the natural law in the Constitution in a series of cases since the 1960s which illustrate the complexity of the problems raised as well as the far-reaching nature of constitutional adjudication. We have chosen three cases to illustrate the development of constitutional law in this context, *Ryan v. Attorney General* [1965] I.R. 294 (Extract 13.5), *McGee v. Attorney General* [1974] I.R. 284 (Extract 13.6) and *Norris v. Attorney General* [1984] I.R. 36 (Extract 13.7).

Ryan v. Attorney General [1965] I.R. 294 was the first case in which the High Court and Supreme Court examined in any detail the provisions of Article 40.3 of the Constitution. Although the plaintiff in that case was unsuccessful in her constitutional action, both the High Court and the Supreme Court accepted that Article 40.3 acknowledged the existence of certain unspecified, that is implied, constitutional rights. These are sometimes also referred to as 'the personal rights' because of the wording which Article 40.3 itself uses, or as unenumerated rights because of the fact that no complete list of such rights exists. This was a controversial view for the courts to take. The decision, in effect, adds a second, hidden, dimension to the Constitution. In addition to the expressly stated rights in the Constitution, the *Ryan* decision indicated that other rights also existed which could be used to declare laws unconstitutional. Professor Kelly, in his book *Fundamental Rights in the Irish Law and Constitution*, 2nd ed. (Figgis, 1967) objected to this on a number of grounds. Among his arguments was that it created an unacceptable air of uncertainty to constitutional law, in that the Oireachtas might enact legislation which could be declared unconstitutional many years later on the basis that it was in conflict with a constitutional right under Article 40.3 whose existence was not known at the time of the enactment of the legislation. In addition, Kelly objected that Kenny J., the High Court judge in *Ryan*, was wrong to refer to a Papal Encyclical as a source for the Article 40.3 right which was invoked by the plaintiff in the case.

There are, of course, many problems with the view taken by the courts of Article 40.3 in the *Ryan* case. Nonetheless, despite Professor Kelly's criticisms, the courts have since the *Ryan* case proceeded to accept that decision as correct, and it is unlikely that this approach will ever be questioned. In fact, no judge has ever questioned the correctness of the *Ryan* decision. But the judges have adopted what might be called a more sophisticated approach to the application of Article 40.3 than the relatively simple grammatical approach in the *Ryan* case.

This is illustrated in *McGee v. Attorney General* [1974] I.R. 284 (Extract 13.6). As the extracts from the judgments illustrate, the Supreme Court, and in particular Walsh and Henchy JJ., accept that the decision in that case posed some conceptual difficulties. In *McGee* the Court, by a 4-1 majority, declared unconstitutional legislation making the importation of certain contraceptive devices a criminal offence. In doing so the Supreme Court clearly went contrary to the views of at least one Christian Church's teaching as to what was in conformity with natural law. In *Norris v. Attorney General* [1984] I.R. 36 (Extract 13.7), the Court, by a 3-2 majority, upheld another legislative provision which was certainly consistent with some views of Christian teaching.

The *McGee* and *Norris* decisions pose some difficulties which lie at the heart of much debate as to the purpose of the law and its relationship with morality. Since the 19th Century, there have been debates as to whether there are certain areas of activity which are not the law's business. Should the law criminalise the use of certain drugs: cannabis, opium, tobacco, alcohol? Should there be partial or total controls? The response has, of course, been varied, and the consensus on these matters is not always the same, though in most countries the response to cannabis, opium and tobacco is clear. What also of private activities involving personal relationships? These were, clearly, the issues in the *McGee* and *Norris* cases and it is, perhaps, fitting that two of the most complex cases in Irish constitutional law should involve sexual morality, an issue which is often equated with morality itself in Ireland. In both cases, the arguments which had been made by distinguished lawyers, academic and practising, as to the function of the law in the area of sexual morality, were clearly well known to the judges. In fact, that English debate, between Professor H.L.A. Hart and Lord Devlin, is not explicitly referred to by the judges in *McGee* and *Norris*. It is, however, discussed by Walsh J. as a judge of the European Court of Human Rights in his dissenting judgment in *Dudgeon v. United Kingdom* (1981) 4 E.H.R.R. 149, a decision which as was mentioned in Chapter 10 played an important support role in *Norris*. One of the ironies, perhaps, as to the use of the Hart-Devlin debate in the context of Irish constitutional law is that it took place between two lawyers who discussed the issues in the context of a legal system which is greatly influenced by the thoughts of Jeremy Bentham, who as mentioned in Chapter 2 was an opponent of the natural law theory. An insight into the Hart-Devlin debate but with an emphasis on the Irish dimension also is Clarke (ed.), *Morality and the Law* (Mercier and R.T.E., 1982), based on a Thomas Davis lecture series.

Without providing a compelete analysis of the issues raised by the *McGee* and *Norris* decisions, the following questions might be asked as you read the judgments in the cases. What is the role of a moral code, as opposed to a legal code of rules? Does this difference indicate something as to the limits of legal rules? Are there certain 'no go' areas for the law, or should the law become involved in private areas of personal activity? Is there a constitutional right to be let alone? What is the common good? What function does it play in constitutional law? Does the Constitution reflect the teachings of one particular Christian Church? Should it? Does the Constitution reject the theory of Utilitarianism? What is the position of individual human rights in relation to society? Is it possible to recognise human rights without natural law as their philosophical underpinning? Would this make a difference as to the extent of those rights? Would it limit or expand their range? Do the views of the judges on the meaning of constitutional provisions change from one case to the next? Should they? What sources do the judges use as justifications for their interpretations of the Constitution? Should the judges confine themselves to the text of the Constitution or may they use any source? Or only some? Should they use history as a source? What is the function of the courts in constitutional cases? Is there a difference between declaring the law and changing the law in this context?

Extract 13.1

BYRNE v. IRELAND [1972] I.R. 241

The plaintiff suffered personal injuries when she fell into a trench which had been dug by employees of the then Department of Posts and Telegraphs. It was clear that, in refilling the trench, those employees had been negligent and that this was the cause of the plaintiff's injuries. The defence to the plaintiff's claim was that, since the employees in question were employees of the State their actions were immune from any claim on the basis that the State had inherited the old sovereign immunity of the Crown and its servants. The Supreme Court held that such immunity was not carried over into Irish law, certainly not having regard to the position of the State as the creation of the People. The extract from Walsh J.'s judgment represents the views of four of the five Supreme Court judges.

Walsh J.:
    The plaintiff claims that when she was lawfully walking along the public highway at Bray in the County of Wicklow the footpath upon which she was walking subsided, and that this was due to the negligence and breach of duty of persons employed in the Department of Posts and Telegraphs when they had been laying installations under the footpath. The plaintiff has claimed that these persons were employees of the State and that the State is vicariously liable for their negligence. The portions of the defence relevant to this appeal are those which claim that the Court cannot exercise jurisdiction over the State as the judicial power granted by the Constitution does not of common right extend to actions against the sovereign authority. It claims further that the action, being one based on an alleged tortious act or omission, was not maintainable in law by reason of the immunity of the State against such actions as sovereign authority. It is also claimed that the action could not be maintained against the Attorney General as a representative of the State and that the representative order, which the plaintiff seeks, could not be made. By order the President of the High Court dated the 6th November, 1967, it was directed that special issues be tried by a judge without a jury.
    By the Constitution which was adopted and enacted by the People and came into force on the 29th December, 1937, the People created a State which is described in Article 5 of the Constitution as "a sovereign, independent, democratic state" and under Article 4 the name of the State in the English language is "Ireland". If the State can be sued, then in my opinion it can be sued by its official name which is "Ireland" in the English language.
    Article 6 of the Constitution provides that all powers of government—legislative, executive and judicial—"derive, under God, from the people, whose right it is to designate the rulers of the State and, in final appeal, to decide all questions of

national policy, according to the requirements of the common good". Article 46 of the Constitution provides that every proposal for an amendment of the Constitution shall, upon having been passed or deemed to have been passed by both Houses of the Oireachtas, be submitted by referendum to the decision of the People, and Article 47 provides that every such proposal for an amendment shall be held to have been approved by the People if, upon having been so submitted, a majority of the votes cast at such referendum shall have been cast in favour of its enactment into law. The preamble to the Constitution is a preamble by the People formally adopting, enacting and giving themselves a Constitution.

It appears to me abundantly clear from those provisions that the State is the creation of the People and is to be governed in accordance with the provisions of the Constitution which was enacted by the People and which can be amended by the People only, and that in the last analysis the sovereign authority is the People. This is in contrast to the position in the United States of America where Chief Justice John Marshall initially established the basic premise that the United States was created by the States and the people of the States, and not by the people separated from the States. It is also in contrast to the position which prevailed in England and now in Great Britain that the King was the personification of the State and that, even with the development of a constitutional monarchy where the distinction between the King in his public and private capacities could be perceived, no legal acknowledgement of this distinction was made with the consequence that the King, or the Crown, was and remains the personification of the State in Great Britain.

Article 6 of our Constitution, having designated the powers of the government as being legislative, executive and judicial and having declared them to have been derived from the People, provided that these powers of government are exercisable only by or on the authority of the organs of State established by the Constitution. The question which now arises for decision is whether the judicial power of government which is exercised by the judiciary through the Courts is exercisable so as to bind the State itself, one of whose organs is the judiciary.

It has already been established that the State is a juristic person capable of holding property: see *Comyn* v. *The Attorney General* [1950] I.R. 142 and *Commissioners of Public Works* v. *Kavanagh* [1962] I.R. 216. It was implicit in the judgments in those cases that the State could have been sued as such. Drummond's famous dictum that property has its duties as well as its rights is no less true in this context. Even in mediaeval England the petition of right was available for all proprietary actions in the wide sense of the term in that it lay not merely for the recovery of land but for claims for damages, for interference with proprietary rights, and also for the recovery of chattels. Not only in England but in many other countries in Europe the inviolability of property was acknowledged in law as a right superior even to that of sovereignty itself. The petition of right fell into disuse from the 15th century onwards until the 19th century during which time it was superseded by the real actions. In a very full investigation of the history of the petititon of right, Lord Sommers in the *Bankers' Case* (1700) 14 St. Tr. 1 was able to treat as precedents (for the competence of the petition of right in contract) cases in which the facts corresponded to those in modern suits in contract but which had been decided as proprietary actions. Therefore, the concept of proprietary actions lying against the State, even when the King was the personification of the State, is not a new one.

The point which arises in the present case is whether a right of action lies against the State for a wrong and, in particular, whether the State is vicariously liable for the wrongs committed by its servants. The learned High Court judge, Mr. Justice Murnaghan, who tried these issues came to the conclusion that the State is not so liable and he based his rejection of the submission on the statement in Article 5 of the Constitution that Ireland is "a sovereign . . . state". He says that "the simple statement that 'Ireland is a sovereign . . . state' is completely inconsistent with the propositions that the State is subject to one of the organs of State, the judicial organ, and can be sued as such in its own courts". This appears to me to assume that, even if the State is the sovereign authority and not simply the creation of the acknowledged sovereign authority, the People, the concept of being sued in court is necessarily inconsistent with the theory of sovereignty. In the first place I think that the learned trial judge misconstrued the intent of Article 5 if he construed it as a constitutional declaration that the State is above the law. Article 1 of the Constitution affirms that the Irish nation has the "sovereign right to choose its own form of Government". Our constitutional history, and in particular the events leading up to the enactment of the Constitution, indicate beyond doubt, to my mind, that the declaration as to sovereignty in Article 5 means that the State is not subject to any power of government save those designated by the People in the Constitution itself, and that the State is not amenable to any external authority for its conduct. To hold that the State is immune from suit for wrong because it is a sovereign state is to beg the question.

In several parts in the Constitution duties to make certain provisions for the benefit of the citizens are imposed on the State in terms which bestow rights upon the citizens and, unless some contrary provision appears in the Constitution, the Constitution must be deemed to have created a remedy for the enforcement of these rights. It follows that, where the right is one guaranteed by the State, it is against the State that the remedy must be sought if there has been a failure to discharge the constitutional obligation imposed. The Oireachtas cannot prevent or restrict the citizen from pursuing his remedy against the State in order to obtain or defend the very rights guaranteed by the Constitution in the form of obligations imposed upon the State; nor can the Oireachtas delegate to any organ of state the implementation of these rights so as to exonerate the State itself from its obligations under the Constitution. The State must act through its organs but it remains vicariously liable for the failures of these organs in the discharge of the obligations, save where expressly excluded by the Constitution. In support of this it is to be noted that an express immunity from suit is conferred on the President by Article 13, s. 8, sub-s. 1, and that a limited immunity from suit for members of the Oireachtas is contained in Article 15, s. 13, and that restrictions upon suit in certain cases are necessarily inferred from the provisions of Article 27, s. 3, of the Constitution.

It is also to be noted that Article 45 of the Constitution, which sets forth certain principles of social policy intended for the general guidance of the Oireachtas, contains an express provision that the application of those principles "shall not be cognisable by any Court under any of the provisions of this Constitution". This express exclusion from cognisance by the Courts of these particular provisions reinforces the view that the provisions of the Constitution obliging the State to act in a particular manner may be enforced in the Courts against the State as such. If, in particular cases, the State has already by law imposed on some organ of State or some servant of the State the duty to implement the right or protection guaranteed by the Constitution then, in cases of default, it may be sufficient and adequate in particular instances to bring proceedings against the person upon whom the duty has been so imposed; but that does not absolve the State, upon which the primary obligation has been imposed, from responsibility to carry out the duty imposed upon it. If under the Constitution the State cannot do any act or be guilty of any omission save through one or more of its organs or servants, it is nonetheless answerable because of the identification declared by the provisions of Article 6 of the Constitution.

The suggestion advanced in this case that the State cannot be made amenable for civil wrong stems from the English feudal concept that "the King can do no wrong". There is some authority for believing that this phrase originally meant precisely the contrary to what it now means, and that its original meaning was that the King must not, was not allowed to, and was not entitled to, do wrong. However, while for many centuries past there has been no doubt as to the meaning of the phrase "the King can do no wrong", that is a concept which differs from the concept that he was immune from suit. A great variety of devices emerged for obtaining relief against the Crown; some of these took the form of suits against the officers or agents of the King personally where no consent was necesary, and some of them took the form of suits against the King himself where it was permitted by the grant of a petition of right rather than by suing by writ. The grant of a petition of right in such a case was based precisely on the proposition that the King had acted contrary to law. In the sphere of tort the petition of right did not normally lie outside real actions. Tortious immunity was a judge-made rule. It would appear to have been based on the view that it would be a logical anomaly for the King to issue or enforce a writ against himself. The theory was that the King, as the source of all justice, was incapable of committing a wrong. But the theory was reserved for torts which lay outside the sphere of interference with proprietary rights. There does not appear to be any record of how this doctrine fared in England during the years of the republic under the Cromwellian regime. The theory at least included the safeguard, frequently of little practical worth, that the servant of the Crown was personally liable for the wrongs committed by him in the performance of his service; this was based on the presumption that the officer who committed the wrongful act did so of his own accord and was thus liable for it because the King, who was incapable of committing a wrong, could not have authorised it.

By contrast, when the doctrine of sovereign immunity was imported into the United States, the doctrine was extended to cover the officers and agents of the State and over the course of years it could be availed of even by municipal authorities. The doctrine appears to have been imported into the common law in the United States as basic to the common law without, perhaps, a proper recognition of the nature of its origin, namely, that it rested upon the King being the personification of the State and, therefore, was applied only to a person. The fact that this English theory of sovereign immunity, originally personal to the King and with its roots deep in feudalism, came to be applied in the United States where feudalism had never been known has been described as one of the mysteries of legal evolution. It appears to have been taken for granted by the American courts in the early years of the United States—though not without some question, since Chief Justice Jay in *Chisholm* v. *Georgia* (1793) 2 Dall. 419 said: "I wish the state of society was so far improved and the science of government advanced to such degree of perfection that the whole nation could in the peaceable course of law be compelled to do justice and be sued by individual citizens". In later cases the United States courts defended the doctrine of immunity on the grounds that it was vital for the efficient working of government. Mr. Justice Holmes sought to justify it in *Kawananakoa* v. *Polyblank* (1907) 205 U.S. 349, 353 by saying that "a sovereign is exempt from suit, not because of any formal conception or obsolete theory, but on the logical and practical ground that there can be no legal right as against the authority that makes the law on which the rights depends". It had also been suggested that the immunity rested on a policy imposed by necessity. In *United States* v. *Lee* (1882) 106 U.S. 196 after full historical investigations the Supreme Court of the United States reached the conclusion at p. 206 of the report:

> that it has been adopted in our courts as a part of the general doctrine of publicists, that the supreme power in every State, wherever it may reside, shall not be compelled, by process of courts of its own creation, to defend itself from assaults in those courts.

Other decisions based it on public policy. In England the enactment and operation of the Crown Proceedings Act, 1947, and in the United States the Federal Torts Act, 1945, would appear to have invalidated these rationalisations.

Under our own constitutional provisions it is the Oireachtas which makes the laws and it is the judiciary which administers them; there is no apparent reason why the activities of either of these organs of state should compel the State itself to be above the law.

That the concept of state liability is not a juristic problem is also evident from the laws of several other countries. In France prior to the revolution the principle of *le*

Roi ne peut mal faire prevailed as in the English legal theory upon the same basis of the King being the personification of the state. Since the revolutionary period the liability of the state gradually grew until finally, in the *Blanco* case of 1873, it was clearly established that the state was liable for the tortious act of its servant if it amounts to a *faute de service*, though the public servant involved may be personally liable for actions which are clearly outside the scope of his employment. In France these actions against the state for the tortious actions of its servants are heard in the administrative courts. In Germany the law developed in a somewhat similar way. Article 839 of the German Civil Code of 1896 and Article 34 of the Constitution of the Federal Republic of Germany make the state liable to a third party for the tortious activities of the state's servants in the exercise of their public functions, and these actions may be brought before the ordinary civil courts.

Many other countries in the world have imposed, to a greater or lesser extent, liability on the state for the tortious acts of public servants, and included in these are common-law countries in the British Commonwealth. Section 78 of the Constitution of the Commonwealth of Australia (appearing in s. 9 of the Commonwealth of Australia Constitution Act, 1900) provided that the legislature of Australia might make laws for conferring rights to proceed against the Commonwealth or a State in respect of matters within the limits of the judicial power. Part 9 of the Judiciary Act of 1903 permitted suits by and against the Commonwealth and the States; it gave a right to sue the Commonwealth both in contract and tort without a petition of right and laid down that:

> in any suit in which the Commonwealth or a State is party the rights of parties shall as nearly as possible be the same and judgment may be given and costs awarded on either side as in a suit between subject and subject.

Under the Canadian Petition of Right Act the Crown can be sued in the Court of Exchequer and Separate Court on petition of right in contract and tort. Although a previous limitation in tort to "public work" was abolished by the Exchequer Act, 1938, a petition of right is still required. In New Zealand the Crown can now be sued in contract and tort under the Crown Proceedings Act, 1950. Under the Crown Liability Act, 1910, the former Union of South Africa could be sued without petition of right in contract and for torts arising "out of any wrong committed by any servant of the Crown acting in his capacity within the scope of his authority as such servant". In India a distinction has been drawn between acts of State and ordinary acts done under cover of municipal law. The latter case would include the negligence of the driver of a military vehicle in the ordinary use of that vehicle, as distinct from acts arising out of the exercise of a sovereign power like that of making war for which the State would not be liable: see *Union of India* v. *Jasso* A.I.R. 1962 Punj. 315 (F.B.).

In our own context it is to be noted that the Factories Act, 1955, applies to factories belonging to or in the occupation of the State: see s. 3, sub-s. 9, and s. 118 of the Act of 1955. Section 59 of the Civil Liability Act, 1961, makes the Minister for Finance liable for the negligent use of a motor vehicle belonging to the State; that section replaced virtually identical provisions in s. 116 of the Road Traffic Act, 1961, which had replaced s. 170 of the Road Traffic Act, 1933. For an example of a similar statutory provision enacted by the Oireachtas of Saorstát Éireann, see s. 6 of the Conditions of Employment Act, 1936.

I have referred to these several different matters for the purpose of indicating that there is ample support for my view that immunity from suit for wrong is not a necessary ingredient of State sovereignty.

For many years in this country, like the American experience, the notion of sovereign immunity of the State seems to have been accepted as part of the common law, without full regard to its true origin in the common law. The confusion was increased by the fact that the King enjoyed some place under the Constitution of the Irish Free State, 1922, and by the fact that in these years the law was practised and interpreted by persons who, quite naturally, had been mostly orientated by education and practice towards a system in which this concept of sovereign immunity of the Crown held sway . . .

There is no basis, theoretical or otherwise, for a claim that the State can do no wrong or, in the particular context, that Saorstát Éireann could do no wrong; and there is no basis, in theory or otherwise, for a submission that the State cannot be made vicariously liable for a wrong committed by its officers, employees and servants in the course of the service of the State. Earlier in this judgment I have given my reasons for holding that immunity from suit is not a necessary ingredient of State sovereignty.

Several provisions of the Constitution of the Irish Free State imposed obligations upon the State and conferred rights on the citizens as against the State and a breach of these, or a failure to honour them, on the part of the State would clearly have been a wrong or a breach of obligation; it is of no consequence that the wrong or breach might not be within the recognised field of wrongs in the law of tort. In principle, a wrong which arises from the failure to honour an obligation must be capable of remedy, and a contrast between the citizen and the State in the pursuit of such a remedy is a justiciable controversy cognisable by the Courts, save where expressly excluded by a provision of the Constitution if it is in respect of obligations and rights created by the Constitution, or save where expressly excluded by law if it is simply in respect of rights or obligations created by law. To take one example, Article 10 of the Constitution of Saorstát Éireann provided that all citizens of the Irish Free State "have the right to free elementary education". In my view, that was clearly enforceable against Saorstát Éireann if no provision had been made to implement that Article of its Constitution. There are several instances in the Constitution of Ireland also where the State undertakes obligations towards the citizens. It is not the case that these are justiciable only when some law is being passed which directly infringes these rights or when some law is passed to implement them. They are justifiable when there has been a failure on the part of the State to discharge the obligations or to perform the duties laid upon the State by the Constitution. It may well be that in particular cases it can be shown that some organ of the State already has adequate powers and in fact may have had imposed upon it the particular duty to carry out the obligations undertaken by the State, but that would not mean that the State was not vicariously liable for the non-performance of its various organs of their duties.

Even if one were to adopt the concept that the State can do no wrong because, as it acts by its organs, agents or employees, any wrong arising must be attributed to them rather than to the State itself, the doctrine of *respondeat superior* would still apply. That doctrine is not invalidated by showing that the principal cannot commit the particular tort. It rests not on the notion of the principal's wrong but on the duty of the principal to make good the damage done by his servants or agents in carrying on the principal's affairs. It may well be that in many cases the appropriate organ or State, or the officer or person, charged with the particular duty could be compelled by mandamus proceedings to carry out the duty imposed including, if necessary, an order to apply to the Oireachtas for the necessary finance: see *Conroy* v. *Minister for Defence* [1934] I.R. 342, 679. However, that does not exonerate the State as the principal from the damage accruing from the failure to do so or from the damage accruing from the wrongful manner in which it was done.

Where the People by the Constitution create rights against the State or impose duties upon the State, a remedy to enforce these must be deemed to be also available. It is as much the duty of the State to render justice against itself in favour of citizens as it is to administer the same between private individuals. The investigation and the adjudication of such claims by their nature belong to the judicial power of government in the State, designated in Article 6 of the Constitition of Ireland, which is vested in the judges and the courts appointed and established under the Constitution in accordance with the provisions of the Constitution.

In my view, the whole tenor of our Constitution is to the effect that there is no power, institution, or person in the land free of the law save where such immunity is expressed, or provided for, in the Constitution itself. Article 13, s. 8, sub-s. 1 (relating to the President) and Article 15, ss. 12 and 13 (relating to the Oireachtas) are examples of express immunities. For an example of a provision for the granting of immunity, see Article 29, s. 3, by which diplomatic immunities may be granted. There is nothing in the Constitution envisaging the writing into it of a theory of immunity from suit of the State (a state set up by the People to be governed in accordance with the provisions of the Constitution) stemming from or based upon the immunity of a personal sovereign who was the keystone of a feudal edifice. English common-law practices, doctrines, or immunities cannot qualify or dilute the provisions of the Constitution: see *The State (Browne)* v. *Feran* [1967] I.R. 147. I think it is apposite to quote here the words of Murnaghan J. in *In re Tilson* [1951] I.R. 1 where he said at p. 32 of the report:

> The archaic law of England rapidly disintegrating under modern conditions need not be a guide for the fundamental principles of a modern state. It is not a proper method of construing a new constitution of a modern state to make an approach in the light of legal survivals of an earlier law.

While the King had a limited place in the Constitution of Saorstát Éireann, he had no place in the present new republican form of constitution which was enacted in 1937 and came into force on the 29th December, 1937. The present Constitution provides at Article 28, s. 2, that the executive power of the State shall, subject to the provisions of the Constitution, be exercised by or on the authority of the Government. Section 3 of that Article provides that war shall not be declared and that the State shall not participate in any war save with the assent of Dáil Éireann, except that in the case of actual invasion the section provides that the Government may take whatever steps it may consider necessary for the protection of the State and that the Dáil, if not sitting, shall be summoned to meet at the earliest practicable date. Article 29, s. 4, reserves exclusively to the authority of the Government the exercise of the executive power of the State in connection with its external relations. By Article 15 the national parliament (to be known as the Oireachtas) consists of the President of Ireland, Dáil Éireann and Seanad Éireann. Article 34 expressly reserves the administration of justice to the judges and the courts to be appointed and established under the Constitution, subject to the provision in Article 37 for the exercise of limited functions and powers of a judicial nature by other persons or bodies duly authorised by law to exercise such functions in matters other than criminal matters. The defendants have placed reliance upon the provisions of Article 49 of the Constitution. Section 1 of that Article provides as follows:

> All powers, functions, rights and prerogatives whatsoever exercisable in or in respect of Saorstát Éireann immediately before the 11th day of December, 1936, whether in virtue of the Constitution then in force or otherwise, by the authority in which the executive power of Saorstát Éireann was then vested are hereby declared to belong to the people.

This is a reference to the Constitution (Amendment No. 27) Act, 1936, which provided in s. 1 that several Articles of the Constitution of Saorstát Éireann set out in the schedule to that Act were amended, or otherwise dealt with, in the manner set out in the schedule. The Act came into force on the 11th December, 1936, and the effect of it was to remove from the Constitution of Saorstát Éireann all references to the King, the representative of the Crown, and the Governor General. In particular the effect of the changes, in so far as Article 51 of that Constitution was concerned, was to divest the King of the executive authority of Saorstát Éireann and to vest it in the Executive Council. At that date the King was Edward VIII who had abdicated from the throne of England on the 10th December. On the 12th December, 1936, the Executive Authority (External Relations) Act, 1936, came into force and it provided that the diplomatic representatives of Saorstát Éireann should be appointed on the authority of the Executive Council, and that every international agreement concluded on behalf of Saorstát Éireann should be concluded by or on the authority of the Executive Council. Section 3 of that Act provided that so long as the King recognised by Australia, Canada, Great Britain, New Zealand and South Africa as the symbol of their co-operation continued to act on behalf of those nations on the advice of their several governments for the purpose of the appointment of diplomatic and consular representatives and the conclusion of international agreements, and so long as Saorstát Éireann was associated with those nations, the King so recognised was thereby authorised to act on behalf of Saorstát Éireann for the like purposes as and when advised by the Executive Council to do so. The same section provided that, immediately upon the passing of that Act (12th December, 1936), King Edward VIII should cease to be King for the purpose of those activities and for all other, if any, purposes and that his successsor for the time being would be his successor under the law of Saorstát Éireann. The joint effect of those two Acts was to remove the King entirely from the Constitution of Saorstát Éireann, to remove from him all powers and functions in relation to the executive or other authority of Saorstát Éireann or the exercise of any of the powers of government of Saorstát Éireann, and to authorise him to act on behalf of Saorstát Éireann only when so advised by the Executive Council to do so in respect of certain matters concerned only with external relations. It is to be noted that neither of these Acts made any reference whatsover to the immunities or prerogatives of the King, if any, which existed in Saorstát Éireann on the 10th December, 1936; these Acts made no reference whatsoever to any question of succession to or transmission of these prerogatives or immunities, if any.

It is unnecessary to enquire what powers, functions, rights or prerogatives were exercisable by the King on the 10th December, 1936, in or in respect of Saorstát Éireann as, for the reasons I have already given, they did not include a right of immunity from suit in the courts of Saorstát Éireann. Therefore, the provisions of Article 49, s. 1, of the Constitution of Ireland which vested in and declared to belong to the People all the powers, functions, rights and prerogatives whatsoever exercisable in or in respect of Saorstát Éireann immediately before the 11th December, 1936, whether in virtue of the Constitution of Saorstát Éireann or otherwise, did not carry over or set up an immunity from suit. It was quite within the competence of the People in enacting the Constitution of 1937 to provide for an immunity from suit which did not exist prior to the coming into operation of the Constitution, but no such provision was made. Section 2 of Article 49 provides that save to the extent to which provision is made by the Constitution or might thereafter be made by law for the exercise of any such power, function, right or prerogative by any of the organs established by the Constitution, the powers, functions, rights and prerogatives mentioned in s. 1 shall not be exercised or be capable of being exercised in or in respect of the State, save only by or on the authority of the Government. Even assuming that such a common-law immunity from suit did exist so as to be capable of being carried over by Article 49 of the Constitution in accordance with the terms of the Article, it would become thereby the immunity of the People as distinct from the State. While the present action in its original form was an action brought against the People, the parties were changed so that it is now an action against the State and the Attorney General, and the original plea in the defence claiming the immunity of the People as the sovereign authority from such action must be read as a plea claiming such immunity on behalf of the State. In either its original form or in its present form the plea would, in my view, fail even if such immunity were vested in and belonged to the People, because there is no evidence of any authority from the Government for the assertion of any such claim and, by virtue of s. 2 of Article 49 of the Constitution, no such claim could be set up in respect of the State save only by or on the authority of the Government. It is to be noted that the same situation arose in *In re P.C.* [1939] I.R. 305, 311 where Gavan Duffy J. expressed the same view on the necessity for evidence of authority from the Government for the assertion of the claim of immunity.

Extract 13.2

CAHILL v. SUTTON [1980] I.R. 269

The plaintiff sued the defendant, a doctor, in negligence in respect of certain medical treatment she received. The provisions of the Statute of Limitations, 1957 set out various time limits within which a person must begin a claim. The plaintiff was outside the time limit specified in the Statute. She claimed that this time limit was in breach of the constitutional right of access to the courts under Article 40.3 of the Constitution. This argument was based on the point that the Statute contained no provision allowing for an extension of time for a person who did not become aware of the facts on which a claim would be based until after the expiration of the specified time limit. In the Supreme Court, it was held that she was not entitled to make this constitutional point since she had known the relevant facts relating to her claim before the expiration of the specified time limit. The Court was not willing, therefore, to allow her to make a constitutional case based on the circumstances of another person.

Henchy J.:
The issue as to whether s. 11, sub-s. 2(*b*), of the Act of 1957 is unconstitutional came before the President of the High Court in July, 1977. Sub-section 2(*b*) provides:

> An action claiming damages for negligence, nuisance or breach of duty (whether the duty exists by virtue of a contract or of a provision made by or under a statute or independently of any contract or any such provision), where the damages claimed by the plaintiff for the negligence, nuisance or breach of duty consist of or include damages in respect of personal injuries to any person shall not be brought after the expiration of three years from the date on which the cause of action accrued.

Since the plaintiff has abandoned the claim in tort, it is agreed that her claim is now one for damages for personal injuries arising from an alleged breach of a contractual duty. Section 11, sub-s. 2(*b*), imposes an absolute bar on the bringing of such an action after the expiration of three years from the date when the cause of action accrued. The plaintiff's cause of action accrued in 1968. Although she became aware in 1968 of the breach of contract which is now the basis of her claim, the action was not brought until 1972, which was some four years after the cause of action accrued. Therefore, the provisions of s. 11, sub-s. 2(*b*) clearly bar the plaintiff's claim; so much is common ground.

The case made before the President that s. 11, sub-s. 2(*b*), is unconstitutional was based on two submissions. First, it was submitted that the imposition of this time limit was a failure by the State to carry into effect the guarantee given in Article 40, s. 3, sub-s. 1, of the Constitution of Ireland, 1937, in its laws to respect and, as far as practicable, by its laws to defend and vindicate the personal rights of the citizen. Secondly, it was submitted that this time limit amounted to a failure by the State to observe the duty cast on it by Article 40, s. 3, sub-s. 2, by its laws to protect as best it may from unjust attack and, in the case of injustice done, to vindicate the life, person, good name, and property rights of every citizen. The President rejected both submissions and ruled that the challenge to the constitutionality of s. 11, sub-s. 2(*b*) failed.

The appeal now before this Court is limited to a submission on behalf of the plaintiff that the President's ruling on the issue of constitutionality was incorrect. In the course of the hearing of the appeal the question arose as to whether the plaintiff had *locus standi* such as would make it competent for her to seek a ruling that s. 11, sub-s. 2(*b*), is unconstitutional. To show how that question becomes pertinent, it is necessary to state with more particularity the complaint that it made on behalf of the plaintiff against the constitutionality of that sub-section.

Section 11, sub-s. 2(*b*), is in terms an absolute bar on the bringing of an action such as this save within three years after the accrual of the cause of action. Whereas Part III of the Statute of Limitations, 1957, provides for an extension of the periods of limitation where there is evidence of disability, acknowledgment, part payment, fraud and mistake, no such extension is allowed for a case such as this. The absolute and unqualified terms of s. 11, sub-s. 2(*b*), preclude any extension of the three-year period of limitation where the would-be plaintiff did not know, and could not have learned within that period, of the accrual of the cause of action. Therefore, it is said that the sub-section is capable of shutting out a person from a right of action before it was possible for him to learn that he was entitled to it. For that reason, it is submitted that the sub-section could be compatible with the invoked constitutional provisions only if there were attached to it a saver such as was introduced for England and Wales by the Westminster Parliament in s. 1, sub-s. 1 of the Limitation Act, 1963, whereby a plaintiff may escape the rigour of the period of limitation if, *inter alia*, he shows that the material facts relating to the cause of action:

> were or included facts of a decisive character which were at all times outside the knowledge (actual or constructive) of the plaintiff until a date which (a) either was after the end of the three-year period relating to that cause of action or was not earlier than twelve months before the end of that period, and (b) in either case, was a date not earlier than twelve months before the date on which the action was brought.

The first thing to be noted about this submission is that even if s. 11, sub-s. 2(*b*), were qualified by such a saver, it would avail the plaintiff nothing. At all material times she was aware of all the facts necessary for the making of a claim against Dr. Sutton. Her present claim is founded on breach of contract. Within weeks of the commencement of her treatment in 1968 she knew of the facts which, according to her, constituted a breach of contract, and of their prejudicial effect on her. Yet she did not bring her action within the three-year period. It is clear—indeed, it is admitted—that the plaintiff would still be shut out from suing after the three-year period of limitation even if the suggested saving provision had been included in the Act of 1957.

That being the legal predicament in which the plaintiff finds herself, the argument formulated on her behalf is not that she is unjustly debarred from suing because of the alleged statutory defect but that a person to whom the suggested saving provision would apply if it had been enacted could claim successfully in the High Court a declaration that s. 11, sub-s. 2(*b*), is unconstitutional because the suggested saving provision is not attached to it. Therefore, the plaintiff is seeking to be allowed to conjure up, invoke and champion the putative constitutional rights of a hypothetical third party, so that the provisions of s. 11, sub-s. 2(*b*), may be delcared unconstitutional on the basis of that constitutional *jus tertii*—thus alowing the plaintiff to march through the resulting gap in the statute. The question which the Court has to consider is whether such an indirect and hypothetical assertion of constitutional rights gives the plaintiff the standing necessary for the successful invocation of the third party, so that the provisions of s. 11, sub-s. 2(*b*), may be declared unconstitutional on the basis of that constitutional *jus tertii*—thus alowing the plaintiff to

Little or no help on this question is to be found in the decisions of the Courts in the early years following on the enactment of the Constitution in 1937, for it does not appear that the issue of standing was dealt with as an issue in any constitutional case before 1969. In that year the High Court had to decide in *East Donegal Co-Operative* v. *The Attorney General* [1970] I.R. 317 whether the plaintiffs (who were three co-operative societies and four individuals) had the necessary standing to question the constitutionality of certain provisions of the Livestock Marts Act, 1967. The plaintiffs contended that the Act of 1967 gave excessive and arbitrary powers to the Minister for Agriculture and Fisheries in regard to the granting and the revocation of licences to operate livestock marts. In the High Court O'Keeffe P. held that the three plaintiffs who were co-operative societies operating livestock marts, and the four individual plaintiffs (each of whom was a shareholder in a livestock mart), had the necessary standing to question the constitutionality of the statutory provisions in issue because, although none of the plaintiffs had yet been actually affected adversely by the challenged sections, those sections (assuming that they gave to the Minister the powers suggested) constituted a threat to the existence of the marts in which the plaintiffs had an interest. Understandably, that ruling was affirmed when the case came on appeal to this Court. The nub of the ruling in both courts derives from the direct threat posed by the questioned sections to the property rights of each of the plaintiffs. As the judgment of this Court put it at p. 339 of the report:

> In the present case all the plaintiffs are engaged in the type of business which is directly affected, and subject to control, by the provisions of the Act and it is the opinion of this Court that they have, therefore, a right to maintain these proceedings.

Therefore, that decision does not provide any direct authority on the point in question in this case, for the plaintiffs in that case were deemed to have the necessary standing because they were asserting their own rights as the basis of their constitutional challenge, whereas in this case the plaintiff's challenge requires her to rely not on a violation of her own constitutional rights but on the notional complaint of a hypothetical third party that his constitutional rights have not been upheld. In so far as the judgment of this Court in the *East Donegal Co-Operative Case* contains observations on the law applicable to a situation such as that, they must be deemed to be *obiter dicta*.

The general approach to the question of standing that has been adopted in other jurisdictions was described as follows in the judgment of this Court in the *East Donegal Co-operative Case* at p. 338 of the report:

> With regard to the *locus standi* of the plaintiffs the question raised has been determined in different ways in countries which have constitutional provisions similar to our own. It is unnecessary here to go into this matter in detail beyond stating that at one end of the spectrum of opinions on this topic one finds the contention that there exists a right of action akin to the *actio popularis* which will entitle any person, whether he is directly affected by the Act or not, to maintain proceedings and challenge the validity of any Act passed by the parliament of the country of which he is a citizen or to whose laws he is subject by residing in that country. At the other end of the spectrum is the contention that no one can maintain such an action unless he can show that not merely do the provisions of the Act in question apply to activities in which he is currently engaged but that their application has actually affected his activities adversely. The Court rejects the latter contention and does not find it necessary in the circumstances of this case to express any view upon the former.

It should be observed that the contrast drawn in that passage is between two widely divergent opinions or contentions and not between two opposing judicial attitudes taken up in other countries. In point of fact, in no comparable jurisdiction to which the Court's attention has been directed does either of those two polarised opinions or contentions seem to have received authoritative judicial acceptance. On the contrary, in other jurisdictions the widely accepted practice of courts which are invested with comparable powers of reviewing legislation in the light of constitutional provisions is to require the person who challenges a particular legislative provision to show either that he has been personally affected injuriously by it or that he is in imminent danger of becoming the victim of it. This general rule means that the challenger must adduce circumstances showing that the impugned provision is operating, or is poised to operate, in such a way as to deprive him personally of the benefit of a particular constitutional right. In that way each challenge is assessed judicially in the light of the application of the impugned provision to the challenger's own circumstances.

This general, but not absolute, rule of judicial self-restraint has much to commend it. It ensures that normally the controversy will rest on facts which are referable primarily and specifically to the challenger, thus giving concreteness and first-hand reality to what might otherwise be an abstract or hypothetical legal argument. The resulting decision of the court will be either the allowance or the rejection of the challenge in so far as it is based on the facts adduced. If the challenge succeeds, the impugned provision will be struck down. If it fails, it does not follow that a similar challenge raised later on a different set of facts will fail: see *Ryan* v. *The Attorney General* [1965] I.R 294 at p. 353 of the report. In that way the flexibility and reach of the particular constitutional provision invoked are fully preserved and given neccessary application.

While a cogent theoretical argument might be made for allowing any citizen, regardless of personal interest or injury, to bring proceedings to have a particular statutory provision declared unconstitutional, there are countervailing considerations which make such an approach generally undesirable and not in the public interest. To allow one litigant to present and argue what is essentially another person's case would not be conducive to the administration of justice as a general rule. Without concrete personal circumstances pointing to a wrong suffered or threatened, a case tends to lack the force and urgency of reality. There is also the risk that the person whose case has been put forward unsuccessfully by another may be left with the grievance that his claim was wrongly or inadequately presented.

It is true that a Bill that has passed through Parliament but has not been signed by the President of Ireland may be refered by him to this Court under Article 26 of the Constitution for a decision as to the constitutionality of one or more of its provisions. It is also true that in those circumstances the Court has not the benefit of a case presented by an aggrieved litigant on the basis of his personal situation, so the Court may have to decide the issue *in vacuo* by reference to abstract or projected considerations. However, that is a special and limited jurisdiction which has been specially vested in this Court by Article 26, and its existence or nature cannot be taken as inhibiting the High Court or the Supreme Court from exercising the general jurisdiction to review legislation in the manner that will most effectively give force to constitutionally guaranteed rights within the general constitutional framework. Indeed, the existence of that jurisdiction may indicate an intention on the part of the framers of the Constitution that the power of the President of Ireland to obtain such a binding advisory opinion from the Supreme Court as to the constitutionality of newly made and questionable legislation should fill the vacuum that might exist until a duly qualified litigant comes forward to challenge the constitutionality of the statutory provision in question.

There is also the hazard that, if the Courts were to accord citizens unrestricted access, regardless of qualification, for the purpose of getting legislative provisions invalidated on constitutional grounds, this important jurisdiction would be subject to abuse. For the litigious person, the crank, the obstructionist, the meddlesome, the perverse, the officious man of straw and many others, the temptation to litigate the constitutionality of a law, rather than to observe it, would prove irresistible on occasion.

In particular, the working interrelation that must be presumed to exist between Parliament and the Judiciary in the democratic scheme of things postulated by the Constitution would not be served if no threshold qualification were ever required for an attack in the Courts on the manner in which the Legislature has exercised its law-making powers. Without such a qualification, the Courts might be thought to encourage those who have opposed a particular Bill on its way through Parliament to ignore or devalue its elevation into an Act of Parliament by continuing their opposition to it by means of an action to have it invalidated on constitutional grounds. It would be contrary to the spirit of the Constitution if the Courts were to allow those who were opposed to a proposed legislative measure, inside or outside Parliament, to have an unrestricted and unqualified right to move from the political arena to the High Court once a Bill had become an Act. It would not accord with the smooth working of the organs of State established by the Constitution if the enactments of the National Parliament were liable to be thwarted or delayed in their operation by litigation which could be brought at the whim of every or any citizen, whether or not he had a personal interest in the outcome.

The Constitution has given Parliament the sole and exclusive power of making laws. The Courts normally accord those laws the presumption of having been made with due observance of constitutional requirements. If a citizen comes forward in court with a claim that a particular law has been enacted in disregard of a constitutional requirement, he has little reason to complain if in the normal course of things he is required, as a condition of invoking the court's jurisdiction to strike down the law for having been unconstitutionally made (with all the dire consequences that may on occasion result from the vacuum created by such a decision), to show that the impact of the impugned law on his personal situation discloses an injury or prejudice which he has either suffered or is in imminent danger of suffering.

This rule, however, being but a rule of practice must, like all such rules, be subject to expansion, exception or qualification when the justice of the case so requires. Since the paramount consideration in the exercise of the jurisdiction of the Courts to review legislation in the light of the Constitution is to ensure that persons entitled to the benefit of a constitutional right will not be prejudiced through being wrongfully deprived of it, there will be cases where the want of the normal *locus standi* on the part of the person questioning the constitutionality of the statute may be overlooked if, in the circumstances of the case, there is a transcendent need to assert against the statute the constitutional provision that has been invoked. For example, while the challenger may lack the personal standing normally required, those prejudicially affected by the impugned statute may not be in a position to assert adequately, or in time, their constitutional rights. In such a case the court might decide to ignore the want of normal personal standing on the part of the litigant before it. Likewise, the absence of a prejudice or injury peculiar to the challenger might be overlooked, in the discretion of the court, if the impugned provision is directed at or operable against a grouping which includes the challenger, or with whom the challenger may be said to have a common interest— particularly in cases where, because of the nature of the subject matter, it is difficult to segregate those affected from those not affected by the challenged provision.

However, those examples of possible exceptions to the rule should not be taken as indicating where the limits of the rule are to be drawn. It is undesirable to go further than to say that the stated rule of personal standing may be waived or relaxed if, in the particular circumstances of a case, the court finds that there are weighty countervailing considerations justifying a departure from the rule.

As to the instant case, it is reduced to a question whether there are such countervailing considerations. The plaintiff's complaint that s. 11, sub-s. 2(*b*), of the Statute of Limitations, 1957, is invalid on constitutional grounds is based on the fact that there is not attached to it a saver for those whose claims might become statute barred despite non-culpable ignorance of crucial facts: but the plaintiff's predicament is that her action would be statute barred even if s. 11, sub-s. 2(*b*), of the Act of 1957 had been so qualified. So she cannot be heard to say that the alleged unconstitutionality has wrought her personally any actual or threatened prejudice. Therefore, she is wanting in personal *locus standi*. Her counsel is driven to grounding her allegation of unconstitutionality on the actual prejudice that would be suffered by a hypothetical person whose action would be statute barred under s. 11, sub-s. 2(*b*), despite his non-culpable ignorance of crucial facts.

The primary rule as to standing in constitutional matters is that the person challenging the constitutionality of the statute, or some other person for whom he is deemed by the court to be entitled to speak, must be able to assert that, because of the alleged unconstitutionality, his or that other person's interests have been adversely affected, or stand in real or imminent danger of being adversely affected, by the operation of the statute.

On that test, the plaintiff must be held to be disentitled to raise the allegation of unconstitutionality on which she relies. Even if the Act of 1957 contained the saving clause whose absence is said to amount to an unconstitutionality, she would still be barred by the statute from suing. So the alleged unconstitutionality cannot affect her adversely, nor can it affect anybody whose alter ego or surrogate she could be said to be. As to such other persons, although the statute was passed in 1957, the plaintiff is unable to instance any person who has been precluded from suing for damages because of the absence from the statute of the saving clause for which she contends. Therefore, her case has the unsubstantiality of a pure hypothesis. While it is true that she herself would benefit, in a tangential or oblique way, from a declaration of unconstitutionality, in that the consequential statutory vacuum would enable her to sue, that is an immaterial consideration in view of her failure to meet the threshold qualification of being in a position to argue personally, or vicariously, a live issue of prejudice in the sense indicated.

Were the Courts to accede to the plaintiff's plea that she should be accorded standing merely because she would indirectly and consequentially benefit from a declaration of unconstitutionality, countless statutory provisions would become open to challenge at the instance of litigants who, in order to acquire standing to sue, would only have to show that some such consequential benefit would accrue to them from a declaration of unconstitutionality—notwithstanding that the statutory provision may never have affected adversely any particular person's interests, or be in any real or imminent danger of doing so. It would be contrary to precedent, constitutional propriety and the common good for the High Court, or this Court, to proclaim itself an open house for the reception of such claims.

The plaintiff's lack of standing to raise the constitutional point is aggravated and compounded by her inordinate and inexcusable delay in initiating and prosecuting her claim. Dr. Sutton died in 1980 and his personal representatives have now become defendants in this action. At this remove it would be virtually impossible for the personal representatives to defend this claim on the merits, now that Dr. Sutton has died almost 12 years after the alleged acts of negligence took place.

Apart from the fact that no case has been made out for overlooking the plaintiff's unexplained delay both in instituting and in prosecuting her claim in due time, there is no pressing constitutional need to entertain the claim that s. 11, sub-s. 2(*b*), of the Act of 1957 is invalid for the reason alleged. In the 23 years since that Act was passed, it does not appear that any would-be plaintiff has come forward claiming that s. 11, sub-s. 2(*b*), has unconstitutionally precluded him from suing. If the Court were now, on hypothetical grounds, to declare s. 11, sub-s. 2(*b*), to be invalid, it would not only allow the plaintiff to proceed with her belated claim at a time when the possibility of a fair trial has passed but it would also allow all other claims of a like nature to be revived and instituted pending a statutory replacement for s. 11, sub-s. 2(*b*), save to the extent that such claims might be barred by provisions other than those contained in that sub-section. Of course, the Courts will not be deterred by arguments of inconvenience from declaring a statutory provision invalid on constitutional grounds, provided the proceedings are properly constituted and the circumstances warrant the making of such an order.

However, the plaintiff's inability to overcome the fact that she would still be statute barred even if Parliament had not left what is claimed to be an unfair lacuna in the statute, being compounded by inordinate, unexplained and inexcusable delay and by her failure to identify any real need (either in the public interest generally or in the live interest of any specific person) to strike down s. 11, sub-s.

2(*b*), of the act of 1957, must be held to leave her disqualified from proceeding with her claim.

In the result, it is not possible to uphold the conclusion of the President of the High Court in regard to the failure of the plaintiff's claim that s. 11, sub-s. 2(*b*), of the Act of 1857 is unconstitutional: but that is due solely to the fact that the plaintiff lacks the necessary competence to make that claim. This particular defence was not raised before the President; it emerged for the first time in this Court and, because it is of the essence of this judgment, it is not possible to express either approval or disapproval of the President's reasons for his conclusion that s. 11, sub-s. 2(*b*), is not unconstitutional.

While in the cirumstances of this case the Court is unable to rule on the validity of the claim made against the constitutionality of s. 11, sub-s. 2(*b*), of the Act of 1957, it is proper to point out that the justice and fairness of attaching to that sub-section a saver such as was inserted by the British Parliament in s. 1 of the Limitation Act, 1963, are so obvious that the enactment by our Parliament of a similar provision would merit urgent consideration.

For the reasons adduced in this judgment, I would allow this appeal against the order of the President of the High Court to the extent that it declared that s. 11, sub-s. 2(*b*), of the Act of 1957 is not unconstitutional. The issue of unconstitutionality must be left undetermined. Strictly speaking, that is the only point raised in this appeal, but in my view it would follow that when this case returns to the High Court the plaintiff's claim for damages should be dismissed.

Extract 13.3

TORMEY v. IRELAND [1985] I.R. 289

The plaintiff wished to have the criminal charges against him tried in the High Court, the Central Criminal Court. He was in fact returned for trial to the Circuit Criminal Court. Under the law prior to 1981 he was entitled to elect for trial in the Central Criminal Court, but that right was removed by the Courts Act, 1981. The issue raised was whether the 1981 Act removed a matter from the jurisdiction of the High Court in a manner prohibited by the Constitution. The High Court and, on appeal, the Supreme Court, rejected the plaintiff's claim, pointing out that the High Court retained a supervisory jurisdiction to ensure that trials were conducted in accordance with constitutional requirements.

Judgment of the Supreme Court, delivered by Henchy J.:
The plaintiff has been sent forward for trial to the Dublin Circuit Court on a charge of having fraudulently converted to his own use a cheque for £9,376, contrary to s. 20(1)(iv)(a) of the Larceny Act, 1916. The result of the order of the District Court sending him forward is that his trial must take place in the Dublin Circuit Court, for, as the law now stands, he has no right to have his trial transferred to the Central Criminal Court (which is the name given by statute to the High Court when exercising such criminal jurisdiction). The nub of his complaint in the present proceedings is that the imposition on him of a trial in the Circuit Court, while withholding from him the right to a trial in the High Court, is an unconstitutionality.

The offence with which the plaintiff stands charged is clearly not a minor offence within the meaning of Article 38.2 of the Constitution. It therefore could not be tried summarily. In compliance with Article 38.5 it must be tried with a jury.

The order of the District Court sending the plaintiff forward for trial by jury in the Dublin Circuit Court was made under s. 8 of the Criminal Procedure Act, 1967, after a preliminary investigation of the offence charged. The validity of that order has not been impugned in any way.

On the passing of the Courts of Justice Act, 1924, a person sent forward for trial to the Circuit Court was entitled, in a specified class of cases and in specified circumstances, to have his trial transferred to the Central Criminal Court. The right of transfer was held to have been given by s. 54 of the Courts of Justice Act, 1924, which provided that "the Attorney General or the accused person shall be entitled on application to have any case, the maximum penalty in which exceeds one year's imprisonment or five years' penal servitude, sent forward to . . . the Central Criminal Court". That section was construed as giving an irrebuttable right to a transfer, but only in cases of the gravity specified.

S. 54 of the 1924 Act remained (apart from the special cases governed by s. 34(8) of the Finance Act, 1963) the only vehicle of transfer until it was repealed by s. 6 of the Courts Act, 1964. That section gave a new right of transfer and extended it to all cases where a person had been sent forward for trial to the Circuit Court. That right of transfer was given to both the Attorney General and the accused, and it was provided that the application for a transfer was to be granted by the relevant judge of the Circuit Court if the party making the application, not less than seven days before making it, notified the accused or the Attorney General, as the case may be, of the application. In any other case, the grant or refusal of the application was to be in the discretion of the judge and his decision was made unappealable. If there were less than seven days between the date on which the accused was sent forward for trial and the date of the commencement of the trial, it was provided that the application was to be granted.

S. 6 of the 1964 Act was the sole vehicle of transfer until it was repealed by the Courts Act, 1981. The present right of transfer is contained in s. 31 of the latter Act. The effect of the provisions of s. 31 and of the repeal of s. 6 of the 1964 Act is to abolish completely the right of transfer to the Central Criminal Court. Instead, where a person is sent forward for trial to the Circuit Court sitting other than within the Dublin Circuit, provision is made for an application for a transfer to the Circuit Court sitting within the Dublin Circuit, and the application is dealt with in the same way as an application for a transfer to the Central Criminal Court was dealt with under s. 6 of the 1964 Act. But there is now no provision for a transfer, either to another Circuit or to the Central Criminal Court, in cases where the accused has been sent forward for trial to the Dublin Circuit Court. That is the position of the plaintiff in this case. Because he has been sent forward for trial to the Dublin Circuit Court, he must stand his trial in that Court. The present statutory disposition of jurisdiction in such cases means that there is no method by which he could get a trial in the Central Criminal Court.

It is the contention of counsel for the plaintiff that this removal from him of an opportunity of having a trial in the Central Criminal Court has the effect that s. 32(1) of the Courts Act, 1981, (in so far as it repeals s. 6 of the Court Act, 1964) is inconsistent with Article 34.3.1° of the Constitution, which provides that "the Courts of First Instance shall include a High Court invested with full original jurisdiction in and power to determine all matters and questions whether of law or fact, civil or criminal".

In the High Court, the submission was also made that s. 31(1) of the Courts Act, 1981 (which has the effect that persons sent forward for trial to the Dublin Circuit Court have no right of transfer, not even to another Circuit, whereas persons sent forward for trial to a Circuit Court other than the Dublin Circuit Court have a right of transfer to the Dublin Circuit Court), is invalid because of incompatibility with the guarantee of equality before the law to be found in Article 40.1 of the Constitution. However, that submission was not pursued in this Court. The case for the plaintiff in this Court was put entirely on the contention that s. 32(1) of the Courts Act, 1981, is incompatible with Article 34.3.1° in that it deprives the plaintiff of a right to a trial in the Central Criminal Court.

The reference in the plural to "Courts of First Instance" in Article 34.2 and Article 34.3.1° shows that, despite the "full original jurisdiction" in both civil and criminal cases given to the High Court by Article 34.3.1°, the High Court is not to be the only court of first instance. More specifically, Article 34.3.4° provides that "the

Courts of First Instance shall also include Courts of local and limited jurisdiction with a right of appeal as determined by law". The central question in this case is whether the latter mandatory provision, which requires Parliament to establish courts of local and limited jurisdiction with a right of appeal as determined by law, means that the jurisdiction thus created is to be exercised concurrently with the original jurisdiction conferred on the High Court by Article 34.3.1°, or whether it means that there may be instituted a local and limited jurisdiction which may be exercised to that extent to the exclusion of the High Court.

It is to be pointed out at the outset that the terms in which original jurisdiction is vested in the High Court by Article 34.3.1° cannot be read literally. To do so would produce absurdity and bring Article 34.3.1° into conflict with other constitutional provisions. At first view it might be thought that there is given to the High Court jurisdiction to determine "*all* matters and questions", but that cannot be so, for in the nature of things there are matters and questions which are not amenable to determination by any court. They are not justiciable. Consequently, "all matters and questions" must be read as confined to "all justiciable matters and questions". But even "all justiciable matters and questions" expresses too widely the jurisdiction conferred by Article 34.3.1°, for other constitutional provisons show that an original jurisdiction in certain justiciable matters and questions shall, or may, be exercised by other courts, tribunals, persons or bodies. For example, it is implicit in Article 26 that no court other than the Supreme Court shall have jurisdiction to rule on the constitutionality of a Bill referred by the President under that Article; Article 34.3.3° debars the High Court from considering the constitutionality of a statutory provision declared constitutional by the Supreme Court in a reference under Article 26; and Article 34.3.6° provides more generally that the High Court cannot entertain any question which has been determined by the Supreme Court. Furthermore, an original jurisdiction may be exercised by courts of summary jurisdiction to try minor offences (Article 38.2), by special courts to try offences of the kind specified in Article 34.3.1°, by military tribunals to try offences against military law (Article 34.4.1°), and by persons or bodies exercising limited functions and powers of a judicial nature in matters other than criminal matters, duly committed to them under Article 37. The jurisdiction to try thus vested by the Constitution in courts, tribunals, persons or bodies other than the High Court must be taken to be capable of being exercised, at least in certain instances, to the exclusion of the High Court, for the allocation of jurisdiction would otherwise be overlapping and unworkable.

Article 34.3.3° amounts to a recognition of the fact that the High Court is not expected to be a suitable forum for hearing and determining at first instance all justiciable matters. Apart from practical considerations, it would seem not to be in accordance with the due administration of justice underlying the Constitution that every justiciable matter or question could, at the instance of one of the parties, be diverted into the High Court for trial. For example, the right given by Article 38.1 of the Constitution to provide for the trial of minor offences in the District Court must imply that it would not be open to a prosecutor or a defendant in any such case to opt for a trial in the High Court. Fundamental fairness, the right to equality before the law and compliance with the basic purpose of Article 38.2 would all seem to require that it should not be an option of one of the parties to such a prosecution to frustrate a trial in the District Court by asserting a constitutional right to a trial in the High Court.

The question whether any particular statutory vesting of jurisdiction in the District Court or the Circuit Court, to the exclusion of the High Court, is constitutionally valid cannot be determined by reliance on the provisions of Article 36 of the Constitution. That Article, after referring to the judges of the Supreme Court and of the High Court and the judges of all other courts, provides that among the matters to be regulated in accordance with law shall be "the constitution and organisation of the said courts, the distribution of jurisdiction and business among the said courts and judges, and all matters of procedure". While "the said courts" must be taken in the context to comprehend courts—such as the District Court and the Circuit Court—established under Article 34.2.1°, as well as the Supreme Court and the High Court, the powers given by Article 36 to Parliament are made expressly "subject to the foregoing provisions of this Constitution relating to the Courts". Among those foregoing provisions are the provisions of Article 34. Article 36, therefore, cannot be operated or relied on in derogation of the provisions of Article 34. It is the latter provisions, and in particular Article 34.3.1°, that have to be construed and applied for the purpose of deciding the question argued in this case.

As indicated earlier in this judgment, Article 34.3.1°, despite its unqualified and unambiguous terms, cannot be given an entirely literal construction. The rule of literal interpretation, which is generally applied in the absence of ambiguity or absurdity in the text, must here give way to the more fundamental rule of constitutional interpretation that the Constitution must be read as a whole and that its several provisions must not be looked at in isolation, but be treated as interlocking parts of the general constitutional scheme. This means that where two constructions of a provision are open in the light of the Constitution as a whole, despite the apparent unambiguity of the provision itself, the Court should adopt the construction which will achieve the smooth and harmonious operation of the Constitution. A judicial attitude of strict construction should be avoided when it would allow the imperfection or inadequacy of the words used to defeat or pervert any of the fundamental purposes of the Constitution. It follows from such a global approach that, save where the Constitution itself otherwise provides, all its provisions should be given due weight and effect and not be subordinated one to the other. Thus, where there are two provisions in apparent conflict with one another, there should be adopted, if possible, an interpretation which will give due and harmonious effect to both provisions. The true purpose and range of a Constitution would not be achieved if it were treated as no more than the sum of its parts.

The Court accepts that Article 34.3.1°, read literally and in isolation from the rest of the Constitution, supports the plaintiff's claim to be entitled to a trial in the High Court. But the court considers that such an approach would not be a correct mode of interpretation. The "full" original jurisdiction of the High Court, referred to in Article 34.3.1°, must be deemed to be full in the sense that all justiciable matters and questions (save those removed by the Constitution itself from the original jurisdiction of the High Court) shall be within the original jurisdiction of the High Court in one form or another. If, in exercise of its powers under Article 34.3.4°, Parliament commits certain matters or questions to the jurisdiction of the District Court or of the Circuit Court, the functions of hearing and determining those matters and questions may, expressly or by necessary implication, be given exclusively to those courts. But that does not mean that those matters and questions are put outside the original jurisdiction of the High Court. The interrelation of Article 34.3.1° and Article 34.3.4° has the effect that, while the District Court or the Circuit Court may be given sole jurisdiction to hear and determine a particular matter or question, the full original jurisdiction of the High Court can be invoked so as to ensure that justice will be done in that matter or question. In this context the original jurisdiction of the High Court is exercisable in one or other of two ways. If there has not been a statutory devolution of jurisdiction on a local and limited basis to a court such as the District Court or the Circuit Court, the High Court will hear and determine the matter or question, without any qualitative or quantitative limitation of jurisdiction. On the other hand, if there has been such a devolution on an exclusive basis, the High Court will not hear and determine the matter or question, but its full jurisdiction is there to be invoked—in proceedings such as *habeas corpus*, *certiorari*, prohibition, *mandamus*, *quo warranto*, injunction or a declaratory action—so as to ensure that the hearing and determination will be in accordance with law. Save to the extent required by the terms of the Constitution itself, no justiciable matter or question may be excluded from the range of the original jurisdiction of the High Court.

As to indictable offences, the combined effect of the relevant statutory provisions is that all indictable offences save those which Parliament considered to be the most serious (notably treason, genocide, certain offences under the Offences Against the State Act, 1939, murder, attempted murder and piracy), are triable in the Circuit Court, and only in the Circuit Court. The jurisdiction thus vested in the Circuit Court is local and limited and there is a provision for an appeal in all cases in which there is a conviction. In the opinion of the court, that vesting of jurisdiction in the Circuit Court is in compliance with the requirements of Article 34.3.4° and the fact that it has the consequence that such cases cannot be tried in the High Court does not amount to a violation of Article 34.3.1°. Apart from the fact that an accused person in such a case may, if convicted, seek leave to appeal to the Court of Criminal Appeal, he may in appropriate proceedings invoke the original jurisdiction of the High Court to prevent the trial being entered on or being conducted in violaton of his fundamental rights.

The plaintiff in this case has not suggested that he is in danger of being prejudiced by the mere fact of having to stand trial in the Circuit Court rather than in the Central Criminal Court. It is difficiult to see how any such prejudice could be advanced, considering that the law and procedure in both courts are the same, that the judge presiding in the Circuit Court enjoys no less independence than a judge of the High Court, and that for a trial in either Court the jury is drawn from the same jury panel.

In the judgment of the Court, the plaintiff's claim that s. 32(1) of the Courts Act, 1981 is invalid having regard to Article 34.3.1° of the Constitution fails. Accordingly, this appeal will be dismissed and the order of Costello J. affirmed.

Extract 13.4

THE PEOPLE v. O'SHEA [1982] I.R. 384

The defendant was tried in the High Court, the Central Criminal Court, on a number of criminal charges. On the direction of the trial judge, the jury found the defendant not guilty on all counts. The Director of Public Prosecutions appealed to the Supreme Court against this verdict of acquittal. The issue for the Court was whether it was possible to appeal such a verdict having regard to Article 34.4.3° of the Constitution. While the judges were prepared to accept that in general the Supreme Court had jurisdiction to hear appeals from decisions and verdicts of the High Court, there was disagreement on whether this included appeals against acquittals in criminal cases. The majority held that such appeals were within the scope of Article 34.4.3°.

Walsh J.:

I agree with the judgment which has been delivered by the Chief Justice. I have also had the advantage of reading the judgment which is about to be delivered by Mr. Justice Hederman and I agree with the conclusions and the reasoning of that judgment.

There are, however, a number of observations which I would like to add. The point at issue in this case was fully argued before this Court in *The People (Attorney General)* v. *Conmey* [1975] I.R. 341. Admittedly, that case concerned an appeal against conviction but nonetheless, in view of the provisions of the Constitution which were in issue, the question of an appeal against an acquittal was inescapable and was discussed at considerable length during the arguments in that case. In that case counsel for the Attorney General contended that there was no right of appeal at all from the Central Criminal Court to the Supreme Court but he went on to contend that, if such a right did exist in the case of convicted persons, then it equally existed in respect of persons acquitted. This latter point was strongly contested by counsel for Conmey who, while maintaining that a direct right of appeal to this Court against convicion in the Central Criminal Court did lie, sought to distinguish between a decision of that court acquitting a person and one convicting a person; and he sought to maintain that an acquittal did not amount to a decision of the court and, therefore, escaped the constitutional provision. I mention this only to point out that the matter was elaborately argued with a great wealth of authority cited on both sides—more extensive, I think, than was cited in the present case. The Court in *Conmey's Case*, among the many authorities cited, was referred to *The Queen* v. *The Justices of Antrim* [1895] 2 I.R. 603, *The State (Attorney General)* v. *Binchy* [1964] I.R. 395 and *The People (Attorney General)* v. *Marchel O'Brien* [1963] I.R. 92, and this Court has been referred to those cases in the present appeal.

After a full argument and careful consideration of the point this Court took the view in its decision in *Conmey's Case* that an appeal lay also against an acquittal by the Central Criminal Court. I have heard nothing in the present case to cause me to think that the view then taken was not the correct view.

However, as the matter has now come directly in issue a brief review of the considerations which arise may not be out of place. It is important to bear in mind that the constitutional provision in question in this case relates only to the High Court, from whose decisions it expressly confers upon this Court an appellate jurisdiction—save and to the extent to which that appellate jurisdiction is restricted or removed by the Oireachtas by a law enacted subsequent to the coming into force of the Constitution. No law whatsoever has been enacted which was expressed to be one to deal with the hearing of appeals from the Central Criminal Court to the Supreme Court. Even in the exercise of the civil jurisdiction of the High Court, the few restrictions placed on the right of appeal to the Supreme Court are made by express reference to the Supreme Court and are to be found, for example, in the provisions relating to an appeal from a decision of the High Court in respect of a consulative Case stated in the District Court where the leave of the High Court is required: see s. 52 of the Courts (Supplemental Provisions) Act, 1961. There are some other statutory qualifications on the right to appeal. See, for example, the necessity for leave of the High Court to be found in s. 40 of the Copyright Act, 1963, and in s. 57 of the Trade Marks Act, 1963. Section 34 of the Criminal Procedure Act, 1967, makes no reference whatever to any form of appeal nor to appeals as such and, furthermore, it is restricted to cases in which there have been acquittals by direction of a judge and does not refer to any other types of acquittals. Its provisions are equally applicable to the Circuit Court and to the Central Criminal Court.

The plea of *autrefois acquit* is as equally applicable to convictions in non-jury trials as it is to convictions arising from jury trials. It is a good plea in bar so long as that acquittal stands, and it implies a previous acquittal by a court of competent jurisdiction. An acquittal on the merits includes an acquittal on all legal pleas or defences, such as that a limitation period has run, and "the merits" are not confined to pleas which are morally good.

Whether it is to be regarded as a tradition or as a rule of law, the fact was that no person could be put on trial a second time in respect of an offence upon which he had been acquitted on the merits. It is unnecessary to go into the various cases which turned upon whether the second indictment was, in fact, the same cause as the one on which an acquittal had been obtained. There was not, so far as I am aware, any statutory provision to ground this practice or tradition; however, it was the law. If there had been any such statutory provision affecting trial on indictment in the High Court, it would not have survived either the Constitution of Saorstát Éireann, 1922, or the Constitution of Ireland, 1937, unless the provision had been re-enacted after the coming into force of the Constitution or was statutorily carried forward in a way which amounted to re-enactment—as many provisions were by virtue of s. 48 of the Courts (Supplemental Provisions) Act, 1961: see *Warner* v. *The Minister for Industry and Commerce* [1929] I.R. 582. Therefore, until the enactment of the Constitution of 1922 and the Constitution of 1937 respectively, the matter could not have been any more strongly reinforced than by Act of Parliament and, for the reasons I have given, even if any such Act had existed it would not have carried beyond the enactment of the respective Constitutions.

So far as acquittals on summary proceedings were concerned, there was already in existence a procedure of appeal by way of Case Stated under the Summary Jurisdiction Act, 1857. That procedure was carried forward after the enactment of each of the Constitutions and is still in force; it effectively allows an appeal to the High Court against a District Court acquittal, with a further appeal to this Court. Another example may be found in the Customs (Temporary Provisions) Act, 1945, which allowed an appeal by way of a re-hearing in the Circuit Court against an acquittal of a person charged under the provisions of the Customs Acts.

So far as jury trials are concerned, there was no appeal possible in this country, even against a conviction, until the year 1924. Can it, therefore, be said that, on the enactment of the Constitution of 1922, jury verdicts of either guilty or not guilty were unimpeachable and that this unimpeachability was an essential characteristic of the jury trial which was provided for in the Constitution of 1922? I do not think so. In the year 1924 express statutory provisions were made for appeals against convictions on indictment which, by definition, covered convictions by juries in the Circuit Court as well as the High Court. As the Circuit Court is entirely the creation of statute, to this day there is no provision for any other form of appeal against a verdict of jury in a trial on indictment in the Circuit Court. That court is not embraced in the provisions of Article 34 of the Constitution. To that extent it might be said that a person acquitted, even improperly acquitted, in the Circuit Court may be in a happier position that one improperly acquitted in the High Court. From that it might be argued that there would be an absence of equality between the condition of persons acquitted in the Circuit Court and persons acquitted in the High Court; but, if there be such, the latter condition is due to the provisions of the Constitution itself and one must not be led into the absurdity of holding, in effect, that a provision of the Constitution itself is unconstitutional because the statute law might appear to put an accused who is tried on indictment in the Circuit Court in a less unfavourable position. One might have every sympathy with the sentiment expressed by Lord Campbell C.J. in *The Queen* v. *Russell* (1854) 3 El. & Bl. 942 at p. 950 of the report: "If there be an improper conviction, it should be set aside; but I hope the same practice will never prevail in the case of an acquittal". However, the case cannot be decided upon sentiment, even if one were to ignore the oversimplification contained in the sentiment so expressed by Lord Campbell.

Jury trial in criminal cases, which is made mandatory by the Constitution save in the exceptions provided for, is a most valuable safeguard for the liberties of the citizen. It must, therefore, be permitted to operate properly. It would be totally abhorrent if a conviction which had been obtained by improper means, such as the corruption or coercion of a jury, should be allowed to stand. It should be equally abhorrent if an acquittal obtained by the same methods should be allowed to stand. If attempts to sway the verdicts of jurors by intimidation or other corrupt means were allowed to go unchecked, they could eventually bring about the destruction of the jury system of trial. Persons who are tempted to do so would think twice about it if they were faced with the possibility that such efforts on their part could negative results which they had corruptly achieved. All prosecutions on indictment are, by virtue of the Constitution, brought in the name of the people and it is of fundamental importance to the people that the mode of trial prescribed by the Constitution should be free to operate, and be seen to operate, in a manner in which the law is respected and upheld.

The examples of intimidation and corruption which I have taken are extreme examples, but it is necessary to take extreme examples to test the validity of the proposition that all acquittals by a jury in the High Court are unimpeachable.

Unlike the Circuit Court and the District Court, the High Court is not amenable to orders of certiorari and, as the Constitution in Article 34 envisages, the only way of testing its decisions is by way of appeal. Therefore, it is important to bear in mind the distinction between an appeal and an order of certiorari. The latter is essentially a procedure for challenging the jurisdiction of the court or tribunal concerned to make the order sought to be impeached. It is hedged around by certain technicalities which do not apply to appeals simpliciter. That distinction is very well illustrated in the decision of the former Supreme Court of Justice in *The State (Attorney General)* v. *Binchy* [1964] I.R. 395. In that case a distinction was drawn between a jurisdictional acquittal and an acquittal simpliciter. This distinction is essential in certiorari proceedings because certiorari is not an appeal. It is also of interest to note that the unanimous court drew attention, with apparent approval, to the instances given by Holmes J. in the *Antrim Justices Case* to indicate that there were cases where acquittals were quashed by certiorari. In the judgment in the *Binchy Case* it was stated (p. 416) quite clearly that: "To quash the present verdict of 'not guilty' would not in any real sense be to quash a verdict of acquittal". The Court, however, took the view that it had to act on the record, which did not reveal on its face that it had been a verdict directed by the judge and one which the jury was not free to give save in obedience to the judge's direction. It was the admitted fact that the jury was directed by the judge, but the Court took the rather rigid view that it could not go behind the record, though everyone knew the record was incorrect. I reserve for a future certiorari case my view on the correctness of that decision that "to go beyond such a verdict" was without precedent and that it is now too late to create one. I will content myself with drawing attention to the decision of this Court in *In re Richard Tynan* (Supreme Court—20th December, 1963) where it was held that the record in a trial on indictment included the transcript and all of the orders in the case; so an examination of them did not constitute going behind the record. It must also be recalled that the sentiments expressed by the majority of the Court in *The Queen* v. *The Justices of Antrim* [1895] 2 I.R. 603 were all referable to certiorari proceedings. The appeal contemplated by the appellant in this case is not embound by any of the constraints which hedge the procedure leading to an order of certiorari.

The reality and the acknowledged facts of the present case are that the jury was not free to consider the guilt or innocence of the respondent but was bound to obey the judge's direction to acquit him. Therefore, the judge's rulings on law are as open to examination in this case as they would be in any other appeal from the High Court.

If the view which I take in this case, (*i.e.*, that an acquittal in the Central Criminal Court may be the subject of an appeal to this Court) is the view of this Court, then the Oireachtas is free to legislate in accordance with the provisions of Article 34 of the Constitution to provide that no appeal shall lie against an acquittal or that it should only lie in particular circumstances. Under the Constitution the Oireachtas is free to legislate in any way it chooses, save where such legisaltion would be repugnant to the Constitution.

Upon the authorities cited in the judgment of the Chief Justice and in the judgment about to be read by Mr Justice Hederman, and for the reasons which I have briefly touched upon, the matter cannot fall to be determined by any pre-existing legislation (of which there is none) or by any practice or tradition. The only provision in the Constitution which is sought to be relied upon is the one which provides for trial before a jury. The respondent contends that that provision refers to a trial by a jury from whose acquittal there can be no appeal. To so hold would be to hold that the Oireachtas is not free to legislate to enable appeals or even limited appeals to be taken against verdicts of acquittal. As this argument is based wholly upon practice and tradition, it cannot prevail against the express words of Article 34 and, particularly, it cannot be construed as totally excluding the Oireachtas from legislating upon this point. For the reasons I have already stated, the unimpeachability of the verdicts of a jury is not, in my opinion, an essential characteristic of trial by jury. Trial before a jury, as prescribed by Article 38 of the Constitution, is essentially a mode of trial. However, s. 1 of the same Article requires that it must be conducted in accordance with law (*do réir dlíghidh*). That requirement is not satisfied by trials where verdicts are based of error or law or have been procured by improper means.

For the reasons I have given, I am of opinion that an appeal lies to this Court from the decision of the Central Criminal Court acquitting the respondent of the charges against him in that court.

Henchy J. (dissenting):

Does an appeal lie at the suit of the prosecution direct to this Court against a verdict of not guilty reached by a jury in the Central Criminal Court? That is the preliminary question of law that has arisen on the hearing of this appeal. It happens that in the present case the jury's verdict of not guilty was reached by direction of the trial judge, but neither counsel for the appellant (the Director of Public Prosecutions) nor counsel for the respondent have suggested that any distinction is to be drawn between a case where the jury's verdict of not guilty was entered by direction and a case where the jury's verdict of not guilty was not so directed. The question raised and argued, therefore, is as broad as I have stated it at the outset of this judgment.

While the particular circumstances of the prosecution of the respondent are not crucial to the resolution of the question thus propounded, it is not inapposite to observe that the offences with which the respondent was charged were triable on indictment in the Circuit Court, and that the respondent was returned for trial to the Circuit Court. However, after such a return for trial, the appellant intervened (as he was entitled to do under the law as it then stood) to exercise the absolute right then vested in him, regardless of the wishes of the respondent, to get a final and unappealable order from the Circuit Court transfering the trial to the Central Criminal Court. If the appellant had not got that order and the trial of the respondent had taken place in the Circuit Court, and if a jury had returned a verdict of not guilty in that court, it would be beyond argument that no appeal would lie to this or to any other court against that verdict. That is because an appellate jursdiction cannot be held to be vested in any court unless it has been conferred by either the Constitution or by a constitutionally enacted statutory provision. As I understand it to be conceded, it is impossible to point to any such conferment of an appellate jurisdiction when a verdict of not guilty is returned on the trial of an indictable offence in the Circuit Court or, for that matter, in a Special Criminal Court. Furthermore, if any attempt were to be made to reopen that verdict of not guilty, the accused could defeat such an attempt by pleading *res judicata*. He would be entitled to an irrebuttable presumption of innocence in respect of the counts on which he had been found not guilty in the Circuit Court.

When, therefore, the appellant contends that the propounded question should be answered in his favour, he is submitting that the happenstance that he got an order transferring the trial from the Circuit Court to the Central Criminal Court (which is but a description of the High Court when exercising its jurisdiction to try indictable offences) had the side-effect that he acquired a right of appeal to this Court against the verdict of not guilty which was the culmination of the trial in the Central Criminal Court. In other words, that while persons who obtain acquittals in the Circuit Court or in a Special Criminal Court in respect of similar counts cannot be subjected to an appeal, the same cannot be said of a person who is found not guilty in the Central Criminal Court. The law's protection of such a person's liberty would thus be less than that enjoyed by a person found not guilty in the Circuit Court or in a Special Criminal Court. It is a startling and novel proposition.

There is no precedent for the appeal now contended for. This Court has never heard, much less allowed, an appeal against an acquittal in the Central Criminal Court. The appellant, however, contends that we should allow his appeal against the acquittals in this case. More specifically, by his notice of appeal he claims that the trial judge's direction to the jury to bring in verdicts of not guilty was a misdirection and should be set aside, and that we should order a new trial on those counts. Were such an order to issue, it would be unprecedented in the annals of criminal law in these islands. It is against the background of such considerations that the propounded question must be set in focus.

The Conmey Case

The submission that an appeal lies direct to this Court from a verdict of not guilty in the Central Criminal Court apparently derives from dicta in two of the judgments given in this Court in *The People (Attorney General)* v. *Conmey* [1975] I.R. 341. Those dicta may be summarised thus. A jury's verdict, whether of guilty or not guilty, in the Central Criminal Court is a decision of the High Court; under Article 34, s. 4, sub-s. 3, of the Constitution it is provided that this Court shall "with such exceptions and subject to such regulations as may be prescribed by law, have appellate jurisdiction from all decisions of the High Court"; no such exception has been prescribed by law in relation to such verdicts of guilty or not guilty; ergo, an appeal lies to this Court from both a verdict of guilty and one of not guilty in the Central Criminal Court.

Leaving aside for the moment the reasoning behind that opinion, I find it necessary to explore the special features of *Conmey's Case* so as to assess the degree of authority that should be attached to that opinion. Conmey was tried jointly with one Donnelly in the Central Criminal Court on a charge of murder. The trial began on the 28th June, 1972, and lasted for 13 days. I happened to be the High Court judge who presided at the trial. At the end of the trial, the jury brought in a verdict of not guilty of murder in favour of each accused but, instead, found each guilty of manslaughter. Thereupon, I sentenced each accused to three years' penal servitude but being of opinion that it was arguable that there was an insufficiency of admissible evidence, I gave a certificate of leave to appeal to each of the convicted men "solely on the ground that the evidence was insufficient to sustain the verdict". Conmey and Donnelly each took an appeal to the Court of Criminal Appeal and their appeals, which were heard together, came before that court (Walsh, Murnaghan, and Gannon JJ.) in June, 1973. Donnelly's appeal was allowed; so his conviction and sentence were quashed.

However, by a reserved judgment given on the 31st July, 1973, the Court of Criminal Appeal dismissed Conmey's appeal. The curial part of the Court of Criminal Appeal's order was as follows:

> The Court doth dismiss the said appeal and doth affirm the said conviction and sentence. And accordingly the Court doth order that the said Martin Conmey do undergo and serve the said sentence of three years' penal servitude less by the number of days he has already served of the said sentence the same to run and be computed from the date hereof.

That order, therefore, supplanted the order of the Central Criminal Court as the effective or paramount order on which Conmey's conviction and sentence rested. So long as that order stood, it would have been idle for Conmey to appeal (even if that were possible) against the decision of the Central Criminal Court—just as it would be of no avail to seek to quash a conviction in the District Court if that conviction had been affirmed on appeal by the Circuit Court. The only way the order of the Court of Criminal Appeal in *Conmey's Case* could have been set aside on appeal would have been by means of a successful appeal to the Supreme Court brought pursuant to a certificate granted to Conmey (under s. 29 of the Courts of Justice Act, 1924) either by the Court of Criminal Appeal or by the Attorney General. As appears from the report of *Conmey's Case* (at p. 357), no application was ever made to the Court of Criminal Appeal for such a certificate; an application for such a certificate was made to the Attorney General but it was refused in June, 1974, being three years after the conviction and when the sentence had been served.

In those circumstances, the order of the Court of Criminal Appeal stood beyond the reach of any appellate jurisdiction. The only conceivable way in which that order could have been overcome would have been by bringing successful collateral proceedings in the High Court challenging its constitutional validity. The order of the High Court in such proceedings could have been appealable to the Supreme Court. No such proceedings were ever brought in the High Court.

The next procedural step taken was in October, 1974, when Conmey applied to the Supreme Court for an order, pursuant to order 107, r. 7, of the Rules of the Superior Courts, 1962, enlarging the time allowed by order 58, r. 3, of those rules for serving a notice of appeal to the Supreme Court. When that application came before the Court (O'Higgins C.J., Walsh, Budd, Griffin and Doyle JJ.), all five judges agreed that the application for the enlargement of time should not be granted. One might be pardoned for thinking that that ruling exhausted the Court's jurisdiction for, in the absence of an order enlarging the time for appealing, there was no appeal before the Court and, consequently, no basis for ruling on any of the matters intended to be raised in the proposed appeal. As the Chief Justice put it in his judgment (at p. 356 of the report):

> There is now nothing to determine, as the applicant's appeal [*to the Court of Criminal Appeal*] has been disposed of. It follows from what I have said that there can be no basis for enlarging the time as sought by the applicant, since he now has no appeal to this or any other court.

To the like effect is the following excerpt from the judgment of Mr. Justice Walsh at p. 365 of the report:

> In the absence of a certificate from the Court of Criminal Appeal or from the Attorney General permitting the applicant to take an appeal to this Court, there is now no justiciable controversy which is capable of being brought within the appellate jurisdiction of this Court.

Notwithstanding those opinions, the Court ruled on the two grounds of appeal set out in what was then a proposed notice of appeal. That notice of appeal expressed itself, primarily, to be an appeal from the decision of the Court of Criminal Appeal and, secondarily, to be an appeal against the decision of the Central Criminal Court. As I have already pointed out, the second ground could arise only if the first succeeded. The first ground rested on the contention that s. 3 of the Courts (Establishment and Constitution) Act, 1961, establishing the Court of Criminal Appeal, was inconsistent with the Constitution. The Court, in a single judgment, rejected that ground of appeal, which was the sole ground of appeal against the decision of the Court of Criminal Appeal. The report of the case does not disclose how the Court found jurisdiction to hear and determine an appeal (which was otherwise ruled invalid for lateness) from the Court of Criminal Appeal in the absence of a certificate granted under s. 29 of the Courts of Justice Act, 1924, particularly when that appeal was based on an allegation of unconstitutionality which had never been raised either in the High Court or in the Court of Criminal Appeal. However, I must assume that the Court's decision validly rejected the only complaint made against the validity of the order of the Court of Criminal Appeal. This, in effect, amounted to an affirmation of that court's approval of the conviction and sentence in the Central Criminal Court. It is difficult to see, therefore, how it could have been competent for counsel for Conmey to propound the second ground of appeal. However, the Court unanimously disposed of this ground by ruling that, as he had appealed, unsuccessfully, to the Court of Criminal Appeal, Conmey had no right thereafter to appeal to the Supreme Court.

The misapprehension as to the extent to which the case is a binding precedent derives from the fact that the Chief Justice and Mr. Justice Walsh (with whose judgments Mr. Justice Doyle agreed) expressed opinions as to what the legal position would be if either the prosecution (in the case of an acquittal) or the accused (in the case of a conviction) were to appeal direct to this Court from a decision of the Central Criminal Court. Their opinions that such appeals would lie were clearly *obiter* and not part of the *ratio decidendi*. Every judicial decision has a force binding on other courts only to the extent that it is *secundam subjectam materiam*, that is to say, when what is judicially pronounced is referrable to the facts as proved or admitted. When, however, a judge postulates a factual hypothesis and chooses to state the law he considers applicable to such speculated circumstances, he enters into the realm of what is moot and extraneous, and his pronouncements as to what the law would be if the presumed situation had come to pass has no higher standing that *obiter dicta*.

The essential facts in *Conmey's Case* were that Conmey did *not* seek to appeal direct to the Supreme Court and he was *not* found not guilty in the Central Criminal Court. Consequently, such opinions as were expressed as to what Conmey's rights would have been if he had sought to appeal direct to this Court, or as to the right of the Director of Public Prosecutions to appeal to this Court had Conmey been acquitted, are no more than peripheral observations deserving of course, all due respect but not binding on this or any other court.

The question whether an appeal lies direct to this Court from an acquittal in the Central Criminal Court will, of course, be authoritatively decided by this case. However, the question whether an appeal lies direct to this Court from a conviction in the Central Criminal Court has never been authoritatively decided. The dicta in *Conmey's Case* to the effect that such an appeal lies were not accepted by four judges of this Court in *The People* v. *Shaw* [1982] I.R. 1 on the ground that they were *obiter* and were expressed *per incuriam*, for the reason, not expressly stated in the judgment of Mr. Justice Griffin (with which Kenny J., Parke J. and I agreed), that the constitutional and other implications of such an appeal were not brought into account. That opinion in *Shaw's Case* was repeated by Kenny J. in *The People* v. *Lynch* [1982] I.R. 64. In the judgment which the President of the High Court has read in this case he considers that the opinion expressed in *Conmey's Case* that a person convicted in the Central Criminal Court may appeal direct to this Court was unnecessary for the disposition of that case.

In that state of judicial dissent and inconclusiveness, it is to be earnestly hoped that, if another seeks to appeal direct to his Court, the Director of Public Prosecutions as *legitimus contradictor* will advance a comprehensive argument against the Court's jurisdiction to hear such appeal, so that this important point will be authoritatively decided.

Does an appeal lie to the Supreme Court from all decisions of the High Court?

As I have pointed out earlier in this judgment, the argument in favour of an appeal to the Supreme Court from an acquittal in the Central Criminal Court may be encapsulated as follows. Under Article 34, s. 4, sub-s. 3, of the Constitution an appeal lies to the Supreme Court from every decision of the High Court "with such exceptions and subject to such regulations as may be prescribed by law"; an acquittal in the Central Criminal Court is a decision of the High Court which has not been excepted from such appeal; therefore, the Supreme Court has jurisdiction to hear an appeal against such a decision of acquittal.

The validity of this syllogism depends on the soundness of its major premise, *i.e.*, that an appeal lies from every decision of the High Court save those validly excepted by law. I agree that if the relevant sub-section of the Constitution is looked at in isolation and is given a literal reading, it would lend itself to that interpretation. But I do not agree that such an approach is a correct method of constitutional interpretation. Any single constitutional right or power is but a component in an ensemble of interconnected and interacting provisions which must be brought into play as part of a larger composition, and which must be given such an integrated interpretation as will fit it harmoniously into the general constitutional order and modulation. It may be said of a constitution more than of any other legal instrument, that "the letter killeth, but the spirit giveth life". No single constitutional provision (particularly one designed to safeguard personal liberty or the social order) may be isolated and construed with undeviating literalness. As Black J. graphically put it in his judgment in *The People (Attorney General)* v. *Kennedy* [1946] I.R. 517 at p. 536 of the report:

> A small section of a picture, if looked at close-up, may indicate something quite clearly; but when one stands back and views the whole canvas, the close-up view of the small section is often found to have given a wholly wrong view of what it really represented. If one could pick out a single word or phrase and, finding it perfectly clear in itself, refuse to check its apparent meaning in the light thrown upon it by the context or by other provisions, the result would be to render the principle of *ejusdem generis* and *noscitur a sociis* utterly meaningless; for this principle requires frequently that a word or phrase or even a whole provision which, standing alone, has a clear meaning must be given a quite different meaning when viewed in the light of its context.

Section 29 of the Courts of Justice Act, 1924, allows an appeal to be brought to the Supreme Court from a decision of the Court of Criminal Appeal when that court or the Attorney General has given the required certificate. In *The People (Attorney General)* v. *Kennedy* [1946] I.R. 517 such certificate was given by the Attorney General after the Court of Criminal Appeal had allowed Kennedy's appeal and had quashed the convictions and sentences made and imposed in the court of trial. The question at issue in the *Kennedy Case* was whether it was open to the Attorney General to prosecute an appeal in the Supreme Court against the acquittals recorded by the Court of Criminal Appeal. The Supreme Court held that, on the true, rather than the literal, construction of s. 29 of the Act of 1924, such appeal did not lie. The letter gave way to the spirit, the spirit being the paramount principle of *aurefois acquit* as exemplified by decisions such as those cited in the judgment which the President of the High Court has delivered in this case today.

There are a number of ways in which it can be demonstrated that, notwithstanding the wording of Article 34, s. 4, sub-s. 3, of the Constitution, the Supreme Court cannot be held to have appellate jurisdiction from *all* decisions of the High Court save those validly excepted by law. Such literalism is negated by the variety of decisions emanating from the High Court (or, for that matter, from any other court) which of their nature are incapable of being appealed. A decision of the High Court is always a decision made or pronounced or recorded (even though it may emanate from a jury) by, or on behalf of, a judge or judges of that court. But many of those decisions are administrative or quasi-administrative. Thus, for example, when the President of the High Court allocates judicial work to particular judges, decides on venues for certain cases, disposes of mundane matters such as the affairs of wards of court, and makes decisions as to the many extra-curial minutiae that attach to his office, his decisions are essentially administrative and are outside the reach of the appellate jurisdcition of this Court. Further, when a judge of the High Court, in connection with the exercise of his judicial functions, makes quasi-administrative decisions, such as in relation to the hour at which he will sit, or whether he will reserve judgment or give it extempore, or the like, such decisions are not subject to appeal. I think it will be found from a study of the decided cases that such decisions involving a purely personal judicial discretion, and not affecting the rights of the parties, are not appealable.

If, therefore, appealable decisions of the High Court are confined to purely judicial decisions made in the course of the administration of justice, are all such decisions, save those duly excepted by law, appealable to this Court? The answer is plainly and demonstrably "No".

It is, in my understanding, a fundamental of our jurisprudence that a right of appeal to a particular court requires, at the least, that there be vested in that court, by the Constitution or by statute, a right to vary in whole or in part the decision of the lower court at the instance of an appellant who is, in the legal sense, aggrieved by that decision. The appellate jurisdiction may, of course, be enlarged or be qualified in its operation by statute (such as a statute of limitation) or by rules of court or other statutory instrument prescribing procedural matters, such as the service of required notices of appeal. But subject to such exceptions or regulations, the minimum prerequisites of an appellate jurisdiction are, I believe, as I have stated them.

It will be found, however, that it is of the nature of the judicial process that certain judicial decisions are not amenable to appeal. For example, an order made *ex parte*, in the making of which nobody but the applicant for the order has a legal interest, if made to the satisfaction of the applicant, cannot be appealed. There is necessarily wanting an aggrieved appellant. Of course, if the satisfied applicant for the order later discovers that the order he got is less than satisfactory, he becomes, in a sense an aggrieved person; but his remedy is not to appeal the order he asked for and was granted but to go back to the original court and apply for an amendment of the order; if such amendment is not granted, he may then appeal that order but, otherwise, there can be no appeal.

Other examples of judicial decisions of the High Court which, of their nature, are not normally open to appeal are decisions made with the express consent of all interested parties; decisions where the parties have agreed in advance that no appeal will be taken; and certain decisions of an interlocutory or non-final nature. In the latter category stands the decision of the former Supreme Court of Justice in *The People (Attorney General)* v. *Fennell (No. 2)* [1940] I.R. 453. In that case a jury, empanelled in the Central Criminal Court to try the issue whether the accused was insane or not, had found that he was sane. When the accused sought to appeal to the Supreme Court against that finding, the Court held that, because the relevant statute did not require the finding of sanity to be recorded, that finding was not a "decision" within the meaning of Article 34, s. 4, sub-s. 3, of the Constitution. Thus the Court rejected the submission that "all decisions" should be construed literally.

Apart from intrinsically unappealable decisions, there could be cited many cases—some decided by this Court, some decided notwithstanding a constitutional appellate jurisdiction no less ostensibly comprehensive than that set out in Article 34, s. 4, of our Constitution (*e.g.*, Article 66 of the Constitution of the Irish Free State), and some decided notwithstanding comparable wide appellate jurisdictions created by statute, *e.g.* s. 24 of the Supreme Court of Judicature Act (Ireland), 1877—which shows that, in the paramount interest of the preservation of the basic principles of justice, appeals will not be entertained in certain circumstances. I do not propose to cite those cases because they have not been referred to at the Bar, but I give the following examples of decisions which have been held to be unappealable because to have allowed an appeal would have been inconsistent with the due administration of justice; where the issues are abstract or hypothetical; where the interest of the would-be appellant in the outcome is too remote; where the would-be appellant has so conducted himself, by taking benefits under the decision or by approbating it, that it would be unequitable to allow him to appeal; and where the relief sought has become moot or unnecessary by the passage of time.

The examples I have given are only a random selection from the decided cases, but I feel they show that the expression "appellate jurisdiction from all decisions of the High Court" must be read as meaning "appellate jurisdiction from all *appealable* decisions of the High Court". Such a narrowing or refinement of the literal meaning of the general words "all decisions" is dictated by the rule of interpretation expressed in the maxim *generalia specialibus non derogant*. To permit an appeal to be brought is to concede that it could conceivably be successful. But if, in reliance on the generality of the words "all decisions" (save those excepted), an appeal were to be permitted which if successful, would breach a particular constitutional right or guarantee, express or implied, the particular intention of the framers of the Constitution would not be treated (as it should be) as an exception to the intention expressed by the general words. There would thus be a departure from the principle that the Constitution must be treated as a logical whole, each provision of which being an integral component, so that it is both proper and necessary to construe any single provision in the light of the other provisions. Such an application of the doctrine of harmonious interpretation requires that the words "all decisions" be given a restricted connotation.

Appeals which would breach constitutional provisions

I do not propose to attempt to identify by classification or otherwise, the decisions of the High Court that are not appealable to this Court. Such an attempt would be a form of judicial adventurism not warranted by the particular circumstances of this case or by the range of the submission of counsel. It is sufficient for present purposes to point out that an appeal is not permissible under that provision if the allowance of it would infringe any specific or more fundamental guarantee, mandate or prohibition expressed in, or postulated by, the Constitution: see *The State (Browne)* v. *Feran* [1967] I.R. 147 at p. 159 of the report. A few examples will suffice to support that conclusion.

Article 45 provides that the directive principles of social policy set out in that Article "shall not be cognisable by any Court under any of the provisions of this Constitution". Thus, if any person were to institute proceedings in the High Court seeking to compel the State to give effect to any of the specified directives, the High Court would be bound to strike out those proceedings for want of jurisdiction. Equally, if the unsuccessful plaintiff in such proceedings were to seek to appeal to the Supreme Court against such decision of the High Court, this Court also would be bound to strike out that appeal for want of jurisdiction. The prohibition against giving cognisance to such a claim derives from the express terms of Article 45 and not from any exception prescribed by law; for "law" in Article 34, as the terms of that Article show, is used to connote a law enacted by the Oireachtas as opposed to a provision of the Constitution itself. By parity of reasoning, Article 15, s. 13, would debar an appeal to this Court against a decision of the High Court rejecting, for want of jurisdiction, a claim for damages for slander arising out of words spoken by a member of a House of the Oireachtas in that House.

A number of other examples from the Constitution could be given of instances where, despite the absence of an exception by law from the appellate jurisdiction of this Court under Article 34, s. 4, this Court would be clearly and necessarily debarred from entertaining an appeal, because of a constitutional prohibition (such as is to be found in Article 13, s. 8, sub-s. 1), or because the decision of the High Court was mandated by the Constitution as the only decision that could be given (such as an order made in the High Court pursuant to Article 40, s. 4, sub-s. 5), or because an appeal to this Court from a decision of the High Court would be inconsistent with the implementation of some particular constitutional provision, express or implied.

It is under the latter heading that I proceed to consider whether an appeal to this Court from an acquittal in the Central Criminal Court would be inconsistent with the right to trial by jury guaranteed by the provisions of s. 5 of Article 38.

Double jeopardy and the constitutional right to trial by jury

The constitutional right to trial by jury is expressed negatively in Article 38, s. 5, as follows:

Save in the case of the trial of [*specified offences, viz., minor offences, offences triable in special criminal courts, and offences triable by any court-martial or military tribunal*] no person shall be tried on any criminal charge without a jury.

This means in effect that every person charged with a major (or non-minor) offence is entitled as of constitutional right—unless the case falls into one of the excepted classes—to a trial with a jury. It is agreed that the respondent in this appeal was so entitled. This important personal right, commonly referred to as the right to trial by jury, is indicated in Article 38, s. 5, to be a right to a trial with a jury, presumably to make clear (as did Article 72 of the Constitution of 1922) that what was being delineated was essentially a right to the evolved and evolving common-law trial by jury, that is to say, a trial before a judge and jury in which the judge would preside, ensure that all conditions necessary for a fair and proper trial of that nature are complied with, decide all matters deemed to be matters of law, and direct the jury as to the legal principles and rules they are to observe and apply; and in which the jury, constituted in a manner calculated to ensure the achievement of the proper exercise of their functions, would be the arbiters, under the governance of the judge of all disputed issues of fact and, in particular, the issue of guilt or innocence.

The mandate that in normal circumstances any person charged before the ordinary courts with an offence which cannot be classified as minor must be tried with a jury was presumably included in the constitutionally guaranteed personal rights because it was the belief of the framers of the Constitution, no doubt reflecting popular opinion, that such a mode of trial would provide the individual with the best safeguard against an unfair trial or a wrong conviction. While the word "jury" is not defined in the Constitution, and while the essential attributes of the required jury trial are not specified, it is clear from the decided cases that a number of time-hallowed characteristics must be present and respected before a jury trial in conformity with the implied requirements of Article 38, s. 5, can be said to have taken place. I shall not attempt an enumeration of those indispensable requirements or attributes. I shall confine myself to saying that I am satisfied, for a variety of reasons, that a quintessential feature of the jury trial required under Article 38, s. 5, is the consequence that when that trial takes place properly within jurisdiction and results in the jury's verdict of not guilty, whether directed by the judge or not, that verdict can never again be questioned in any court by way of appeal or otherwise.

While the accused is normally entitled to a rebuttable presumption of innocence right up to the point when the jury return their verdict of not guilty, from that point onwards that presumption stands irrebuttable. So much and so immediately so, that unless the accused is being validly detained on another charge, the trial judge must order his peremptory release from custody. And after the acquitted person steps out of the courtroom and breathes afresh the air of freedom, even if it should emerge afterwards that there is fresh evidence of his guilt, even evidence provided by his own admission of guilt, he cannot be put on trial again for the offence of which he has been found not guilty by the jury. If an attempt were made to re-try him, he could successfully raise the defence known in lawyers' French as *autrefois acquit*. That means that he could raise the plea, in bar of the second trial, that he had previously been acquitted of the same offence, that in consequence the matter was *res judicata*, and that the prosecution were thus irrevocably estopped from subjecting him to such double jeopardy. Unless the prosecution were to admit that the two charges were essentially the same, a jury would have to be empanelled to try that issue, and if the jury were to hold that the two charges were the same, the plea of *autrefois acquit* would prevail and the second trial would be peremptorily stopped by the trial judge.

I am satisfied that the indissoluble attachment to trial by jury of the right after acquittal to raise the plea of *autrefois acquit* was one of the prime reasons why the Constitution of 1937 (like that of 1922) mandated trial with a jury as the normal mode of trying major offences. The bitter Irish race-memory of politically appointed and Executive-oriented judges, of the suspension of jury trial in times of popular revolt, of the substitution therefor of summary trial or detention without trial, of cat-and-mouse releases from such detention, of packed juries and sometimes corrupt judges and prosecutors, had long implanted in the consciousness of the people and, therefore, in the minds of their political representatives, the conviction that the best way of preventing an individual from suffering a wrong conviction for an offence was to allow him to "put himself upon his country". That is to say, to allow him to be tried for that offence by a fair, impartial and representative jury, sitting in a court presided over by an impartial and independent judge appointed under the Constitution, who would see that all the requirements for a fair and proper jury trial would be observed, so that, amongst other things, if the jury's verdict were one of not guilty, the accused could leave court with the absolute assurance that he would never again "be vexed" for the same charge.

If one were to scrutinise the debates in Parliament and the records of the written and spoken arguments for and against the draft Constitution in 1937, I venture to think that one would not find the hint of an opinion, either from the proponents or opponents of the Constitution, that a verdict of not guilty, emanating from a jury trial mandated by Article 38, s. 5, could be reopened by appeal or otherwise. Indeed, if such opinion had been expressed by any reputable person or body, it is to be arguably contended that the Constitution would never have been enacted by the people.

It was, I believe, a consideration of such matters that led Kenny J. to express the opinion in *The People* v. *Lynch* [1982] I.R. 1 that an appeal to the Supreme Court from an acquittal by a jury in the Central Criminal Court "would result in a far-reaching change in our law which, I am convinced, those who enacted the Constitution never contemplated and which is not in accordance with prior Irish authority".

. . . .

Constitutional and Practical Consequences of Allowing such Appeals

It needs to be stressed that the submission of the appellant is not that appeals against all acquittals by juries are permissible, but only that acquittals by juries in the Central Criminal Court should be held appealable to the Supreme Court. The narrowness of this submission means that, if accepted, it would bring into existence a class of acquitted persons who would be unjustifiably singled out for unfairly discriminatory treatment. Those acquitted in the Circuit Court or a Special Criminal Court would be immune from appeal to any court, while the comparatively small number of people who are tried and acquitted in the Central Criminal Court would be liable to an appeal to the Supreme Court. While it is only a few of the more serious criminal offences that require to the tried in the Central Criminal Court, the provisions of s. 18 of the Criminal Procedure Act, 1967, allow to be added to the indictment counts in respect of certain other offences which normally would be triable in the Circuit Court. It is possible, therefore, that out of the same set of circumstances one accused may be tried in the Circuit Court for a particular offence and another accused may be tried in the Central Criminal Court for the same offence. If it turns out that both are acquitted after identical modes of trial and on foot of essentially the same evidence, why should the person who has been acquitted in the Central Criminal Court be subject to an appeal while the person who has been acquitted in the Circuit Court would be absolutely immune from appeal?

I have heard no *reason* advanced for such unequal treatment; but the *basis* is said to be Article 34, s. 4, sub-s. 3, of the Constitution which, as I have pointed out earlier, is susceptible of this interpretation only if it is given a literal rather than a schematic meaning. In my judgment, the plainly unfair discrimination resulting from such a reading would be incompatible with the basic requirements of justice under the Constitution. There would be a conflict with the requirement in Article 40, s. 1, that all citizens shall, as human persons, be held equal before the law unless there be found between them differences of capacity, physical or moral, or of social function; and there would be a want of compliance with the guarantee in Article 40, s. 3, that the State shall by its laws, as far as practicable, defend and vindicate the personal rights of the citizen and, in particular, by its laws protect as best it may from unjust attack and, in the case of injustice done, vindicate the life, person, good name and property rights of every citizen.

But even if an appeal were held to lie to this Court from an acquittal in the Central Criminal Court, when and how would that appeal be instigated and prosecuted? As is well known, and as appears from internal evidence, the Rules of the Superior Courts were made in 1962 in the belief that no appeals lay direct to the Supreme Court from jury verdicts in the Central Criminal Court. For example, order 58 (which is the order dealing with appeals to the Supreme Court) provides in rule 2 that, when a notice of appeal is served in any cause or matter in which there has been a trial by jury, the notice of appeal shall include an application for a new trial. This is understandable and justifiable only if the rule is confined to jury trials of civil matters, for in such matters there has been transferred to this Court by statutory devolution the jurisdiction to order a new trial which was vested in the former Supreme Court by s. 96 of the Courts of Justice Act, 1924. Jurisdiction to order a retrial of an indictable offence would require to be specifically conferred by statute—just as it had to be conferred on the Court of Criminal Appeal by s. 5 of the Courts of Justice Act, 1928, notwithstanding that s. 34 of the Act of 1924 had already given that court power to make any order it thought necessary for the purpose of doing justice in the case before it. No constitutional or statutory provision has given that jurisdiction to this Court, and its bestowal would be clearly beyond the powers of the Superior Courts Rules Committee. There are, therefore, no rules governing appeals from the Central Criminal Court to this Court. This means that if such appeals were held to lie against acquittals, an acquitted person would be left to languish in a limbo of uncertainty as to his ultimate fate, for want of regulation by law of that appeal.

If this Court were to hold that it has jurisdiction to hear an appeal from an acquittal in the Central Criminal Court, and if such appeal were to succeed because, for example, this Court considered that the acquittal was unwarranted by the evidence, what order could it make? It could not order a retrial, for power to do so has been withheld from it, and if the Court were to take such power to itself, it would be unconstitutionally legislating the abolition, for a restricted class of acquitted persons, of the right to plead a previous acquittal. Nor could it substitute for the acquittal a verdict of guilty, for that would amount, in effect, to trial by judges alone in breach of Article 38, s. 5, of the Constitution. Whatever way one looks at it, the appeal contended for could result only in futility, unfairness and oppression.

Even if a retrial could be ordered, the practical consequences for the accused would be indefensible discrimination, unfairness and harassment. Whereas a retrial ordered in the case of an appeal from a conviction is a risk that is voluntarily assumed by the convicted person when he appeals, a retrial ordered in the case of an acquittal would impose willy-nilly on the acquitted person the worry and the possibly crushing expense of a retrial in which, because he would have shown his hand in the first trial, he and his witnesses could be cross-examined out of the transcript of the first trial, and the prosecution could augment the case made against him at the first trial by giving fresh evidence. However, even if the evidence at the second trial did not differ essentially from that given at the first, the jury could (or perhaps should) be told by the trial judge that in the opinion of the Supreme Court they must convict. A verdict of guilty given in those circumstances could not be said to be in any real sense the verdict of an independent jury acting under the guidance of an independent judge. On top of that, even if the verdict in the second trial turned out to be one of not guilty, the prosecution could appeal again. The acquitted person—unlike a person acquitted in the Circuit Court or in a Special Criminal Court—could be subjected not only to double but to multiple jeopardy. I find the prospect of such possible unfair and oppressive discrimination repugnant to the concept of due process inherent in the Constitution.

The Statutory Background

When the present system of appeals from decisions in trials on indictment was established by the Courts of Justice Act, 1924, the only party given a right of appeal was the convicted person, and the only court given jurisdiction to hear an appeal was the Court of Criminal Appeal. Prior to the *Conmey* decision, it seems to have been universally accepted that the system of appeals thus inaugurated, and carried over by statute into the courts which were established in 1961, implicitly acknowledged the inviolacy of jury verdicts of acquittal and, by necessary implication, excluded appeals direct to the Supreme Court from decisions of the Central Criminal Court. Appeals to the Supreme Court from the Central Criminal Court, particularly appeals against acquittals, were obviously considered to be capable of producing unconstitutional discrimination between accused persons, of like or equal standing, merely beause they found themselves in different courts. Further, the statutory scheme of appeals was considered to have established a unitary mode of appeal because the Court of Criminal Appeal is given an appellate jurisdiction which is expressed to be final and unappealable, and because the Supreme Court is allowed a part in that system only when a certificate is given under s. 29 of the Act of 1924 certifying that the decision of the Court of Criminal Appeal involves a point of law of exceptional public importance and that it is desirable in the public interest that an appeal should be taken to the Supreme Court. It was generally thought that it was only in those exceptional circumstances that the Supreme Court had a role to play in the system of appeals in criminal cases.

Whatever be the true extent of the rights of appeal of persons convicted in the Central Criminal Court, certain consequences of holding that the Director of Public Prosecutions can appeal to the Supreme Court against an acquittal in that court seem clear. Whereas a convicted person can appeal only to the Court of Criminal Appeal, and then only if he gets a certificate from the trial judge that the case is one fit for appeal or, in case of a refusal of such certificate, if the Court of Criminal Appeal on appeal from such refusal grants leave to appeal, the Director of Public Prosecutions would be free of all the statutory restrictions of the right of appeal. He would not have to apply to the trial judge or to the Court of Criminal Appeal for leave to appeal. He would have a direct access to the Supreme Court, thus acquiring a forum of appeal normally denied to a convicted person. He, unlike a convicted person, would be free of the restrictions imposed by statute and by the Rules of the Superior Courts on the mode of making, the hearing and the determination of the appeal. He would have an open, untrammelled right of appeal, subject only to such limitations as this Court in its discretion might impose. If a jury's verdict of acquittal were held to be thus inconclusive, the constitutional right to trial by jury would be an unreliable weapon in the armoury of personal liberty.

There are two further statutory provisions which in my view make the right of appeal claimed by the appellant incompatible with the place given to a jury's verdict of acquittal in the statutory scheme of things.

First, s. 34, sub-s. 1, of the Criminal Procedure Act, 1967, provides that where, on a question of law, a verdict in favour of an accused person is found by direction of the trial judge, the Attorney General (now the Director of Public Prosecutions) may, *without prejudice to the verdict in favour of the accused*, refer the question of law to the Supreme Court for determination. That would appear to be a clear statutory recognition of the inviolacy of a jury's verdict of not guilty, even when it is directed by the trial judge on a wrong interpretation of the law. If the submissions advanced in this appeal on behalf of the appellant were to prevail, the result would seem to be that he would have two separate ways of questioning the correctness of a verdict of acquittal by direction in the Central Criminal Court, one under Article 34, s. 4, sub-s. 3, of the Constitution and the other under s. 34, sub-s. 1, of the Act of 1967. A double shadow would darken a verdict of acquittal by direction, whereas similar verdicts in the Circuit Court could be questioned only under s. 34, sub-s. 2, of the Act of 1967. In the light of the Constitution, such a discrimination would have to be considered a repugnancy.

Secondly, there is s. 15 of the Criminal Law (Jurisdiction) Act, 1976, which declares that a person who has been acquitted or convicted of an offence under the law of Northern Ireland is entitled to plead his acquittal or conviction as a bar in any proceedings in this State for any offence consisting of the acts that constituted the offence of which he has been so acquitted or convicted. There we have an unequivocal recognition of the right of a person who has been acquitted of an offence in Northern Ireland to plead *autrefois acquit* if an attempt is made to put him on trial in this State for the acts in respect of which he was acquitted. It is inconceivable that an acquittal in Northern Ireland should be accorded a higher defensive value than an acquittal in the Central Criminal Court. Yet that is what the position would be if we were to entertain this appeal.

Conclusions

From the foregoing considerations I draw the following conclusions:

1. There is no binding precedent to the effect that an appeal lies direct to this Court from an acquittal by a jury in the Central Criminal Court.

2. Such an appeal is not encompassed by the appellate jurisdiction given to this Court by Article 34, s. 4, sub-s. 3, of the Constitution.

3. Such an appeal would be unconstitutional because (a) it would be incompatible with what is necessarily encompassed by the guarantee of trial with a jury set out in s. 5 of Article 38; (b) it would be in breach of the equality before the law guaranteed by s. 1 of Article 40; and (c) it would violate the guarantee in respect of personal rights and protection from injustice given by s. 3 of Article 40.

4. This appeal by the Director of Public Prosecutions against the verdicts of not guilty given by a jury in the Central Criminal Court in favour of the respondent should be struck out for want of jurisdiction.

Extract 13.5

RYAN v. ATTORNEY GENERAL [1965] I.R. 294

The plaintiff challenged the constitutionality of the Health (Fluoridation of Water Supplies) Act, 1960. This Act empowered local authorities to add specified quantities of fluorine to water supplies in the State. The Act had been introduced after the government had appointed a Consultative Council to recommend proposals for the treatment of dental caries, particularly in children. The Council recommended that specified quantities of fluorine in the water supplies would contribute substantially to the elimination of dental caries. The plaintiff claimed that the Act infringed her right to bodily integrity. Since there is no mention of such a right in the text of the Constitution, it was argued that such a right was implicit in the provisions of Article 40.3. This argument was accepted by the High Court and, on appeal, by the Supreme Court. While the plaintiff was ultimately unsuccessful in her challenge to the 1960 Act, the reasoning of the judges proved of crucial importance in the development of constitutional law.

Kenny J. (High Court):

. . . This case was at hearing for 65 days during which a great volume of scientific and medical evidence was given. This could easily lead to the belief that the High Court has jurisdiction to pass judgment on the policy and advisability of legislation and to substitute a judicial view of policy and advisability for that of the Oireachtas. The issue of the advisability or desirability of legislation is a matter for the Oireachtas only, for it has the sole and exclusive power of making laws for the State (see Article

15, 2, of the Constitution). The jurisdiction (created by the Constitution) of the High Court relates not to the advisability of legislation but to the issue whether the Act under examination contravened any provision of the Constitution or involves a violation of or interference with the rights given by the Constitution to every citizen. It is, therefore, necessary to consider the relevant provisions of the Constitution, for only in this way can the questions and issues which the Court has to determine be stated . . .

Article 40 is the first of the Articles in the part of the Constitution which is headed, "Fundamental Rights", and Article 40 is headed, "Personal Rights". The arrangement of the sections in this Article (in many ways the most important in the Constitution, for Article 5 declares that Ireland is a democratic State and what can be more important in such a State than the personal rights of the citizens) presents some problems. Section 1 gives equality before the law to all citizens as human persons. Section 2 provides that titles of nobility shall not be conferred by the State. Section 3, sub-s. 1°, provides that the State guarantees in its laws to respect, and, as far as practicable, by its laws to defend and vindicate the personal rights of the citizen, while sub-s. 2° of that section provides:

> The State shall, in particular, by its laws protect as best it may from unjust attack and, in the case of injustice done, vindicate the life, person, good name, and property rights of every citizen.

Section 4 gives the right to personal liberty. Section 5 deals with the inviolability of the dwelling-house, while in section 6 the State guarantees liberty for the exercise of the rights of freedom of expression for convictions and opinions, of peaceful assembly and the right to form associations and unions. Whatever may be the extent of the general guarantee given by section 3 for personal rights, it is difficult to understand why it was inserted between the right to equality before the law and the other specified personal rights.

The first matter to be considered on this general guarantee is whether the High Court has jurisdiction to declare an Act of the Oireachtas unconstitutional because, in the opinion of that Court, it is a breach of the guarantee by the State "in its laws to respect, and, as far as practicable, by its laws to defend and vindicate the personal rights of the citizen". I have to anticipate a later part of this judgment by saying that, in my opinion, this general guarantee relates not only to the personal rights specified in Article 40 but to those specified personal rights *and* other personal rights of the citizen which have to be formulated and defined by the High Court. In the course of his argument the Attorney General conceded that the High Court had jurisdiction to declare an Act of the Oireachtas invalid if it did not respect, and, as far as practicable, defend and vindicate the personal rights of the citizen and if, in addition, the Oireachtas had acted oppressively or in bad faith in passing the Act; but when Mr. William Finlay was making the closing speech on behalf of the Attorney General, he referred in another context to a passage in the advice given to the President by the Supreme Court in relation to the constitutional validity of the Offences Against the State (Amendment) Bill, 1940, from which it would appear that a majority of the Court were of opinion that the High Court and Supreme Court had no jurisdiction to declare an Act of the Oireachtas unconstitutional because it was a violation of the general guarantee in section 3: see *In re Art. 26 of the Constitution and the Offences Against the State (Amendment) Bill, 1940* [1940] I.R. 470. The passage (at p. 481) is:

> Article 40 deals with personal rights. Clause 3 thereof provides that the State guarantees by its laws to respect, and, as far as practicable, by its laws to defend and vindicate the personal rights of the citizen, and to protect from unjust attack and, in case of injustice done, to vindicate, the life, person, good name, and property rights of every citizen. It is alleged that the provisions of the Bill are re-pugnant to the guarantee contained in this clause. It seems to us impossible to accede to this argument. The guarantee in the clause is not in respect of any

particular citizen, or class of citizens, but extends to all the citizens of the State, and the duty of determining the extent to which the rights of any particular citizen, or class of citizens, can properly be harmonised with the rights of the citizens as a whole seems to us to be a matter which is peculiarly within the province of the Oireachtas, and any attempt by this Court to control the Oireachtas in the exercise of this function, would, in our opinion, be usurpation of its authority.

If it be assumed that advice given by the Supreme Court to the President binds the High Court in the same way as does a decision of the Supreme Court in a case between parties (and my view is that it does not), the passage does not bind me to hold that the High Court has no jurisdiction to consider the validity of an Act of the Oireachtas when it is claimed that it is a violation of the general guarantee in section 3 of Article 40, because the passage is wholly irreconcilable with the later judgment of the Supreme Court in *In re Philip Clarke* [1950] I.R. 235. In that case Mr. Justice O'Byrne when delivering the judgment of the Court said (at p. 247) in relation to the passage I have quoted in the advice of the Supreme Court:

> A passage, at p. 481, in the judgment delivered by Sullivan C.J. in *In re Art. 26 of the Constitution and the Offences Against the State (Amendment) Bill, 1940* [1940] I.R. 470 was relied upon as laying down the proposition that the Court could not consider whether a guarantee contained in the Constitution has been infringed by an Act of the Oireacthas. Such an interpretation of the passage would be inconsistent with the principle already referred to as having been laid down in that judgment. The passage must be read as a rule of prudence in the consideration of the question of express or implied repugnance, especially in matters such as those involved in the said Bill.

In my opinion, the High Court has jurisdiction to consider whether an Act of the Oireachtas respects and, as far as practicable, defends and vindicates the personal rights of the citizen and to declare the legislation unconstitutional if it does not. I think that the personal rights which may be invoked to invalidate legislation are not confined to those specified in Article 40 but include all those rights which result from the Christian and democratic nature of the State. It is, however, a jurisdiction to be exercised with caution. None of the personal rights of the citizen are unlimited: their exercise may be regulated by the Oireachtas when the common good requires this. When dealing with controversial social, economic and medical matters on which it is notorious views change from generation to generation, the Oireachtas has to reconcile the exercise of personal rights with the claims of the common good and its decision on the reconciliation should prevail unless it was oppressive to all or some of the citizens or unless there is no reasonable proportion between the benefit which the legislation will confer on the citizens or a substantial body of them and the interference with the personal rights of the citizen. Moreover, the presumption that every Act of the Oireachtas is constitutional until the contrary is clearly established applies with particular force to this type of legislation.

The next matter to be considered (though I have already said something about it) is whether the general guarantee in Article 40, section 3, relates only to those personal rights which are specified in Article 40 or whether it extends to other unspecified personal rights of the citizen. If it extends to personal rights other than those specified in Article 40, the High Court and the Supreme Court have the difficult and responsible duty of ascertaining and declaring what are the personal rights of the citizen which are guaranteed by the Constitution. In modern times this would seem to be a function of the legislative rather than of the judicial power but it was done by the Courts in the formative period of the Common Law and there is no reason why they should not do it now. A number of factors indicate that the guarantee is not confined to the rights specified in Article 40 but extends to other personal rights of the citizen. Firstly, there is sub-s 2 of section 3 of Article 40. It reads:

The State shall, in particular, by its laws protect as best it may from unjust attack and, in the case of injustice done, vindicate the life, person, good name, and property rights of every citizen.

The words "in particular" show that sub-s. 2° is a detailed statement of something which is already contained in sub-s. 1° which is the general guarantee. But sub-s. 2° refers to rights in connection with life and good name and there are no rights in connection with these two matters specified in Article 40. It follows, I think, that the general guarantee in sub-s. 1° must extend to rights not specified in Article 40. Secondly, there are many personal rights of the citizen which follow from the Christian and democratic nature of the State which are not mentioned in Article 40 at all—the right to free movement within the State and the right to marry are examples of this. This also leads to the conclusion that the general guarantee extends to rights not specified in Article 40.

In my opinion, one of the personal rights of the citizen protected by the general guarantee is the right to bodily integrity. I understand the right to bodily integrity to mean that no mutilation of the body or any of its members may be carried out on any citizen under authority of the law except for the good of the whole body and that no process which is or may, as a matter of probability, be dangerous or harmful to the life or health of the citizens or any of them may be imposed (in the sense of being made compulsory) by an Act of the Oireachras. This conclusion, that there is a right of bodily integrity, gets support from a passage in the Encyclical Letter, "Peace on Earth" (Pope John XXIII, 11th April 1963):

> Beginning our discussion of the rights of man, we see that every man has the right to life, to bodily integrity and to the means which are necessary and suitable for the proper development of life; these are primarily food, clothing, shelter, rest, medical care, and finally the necessary social services.

If then the Act of 1960 imposes the consumption of fluoridated water on the citizens and if that is or may, as a matter of probability, be dangerous or harmful to the life or health of any of the citizens, the plaintiff's right to bodily integrity would be infringed and the legislation would be unconstitutional.

At an early stage in this case the Attorney General submitted that I should not hear evidence that the fluoridation of water was dangerous. He argued that the jurisdiction to declare an Act unconstitutional on the ground that it did not respect the personal rights of the citizen could be exercised only if the Act were oppressive or had been enacted in bad faith and that this had not been pleaded. The plaintiff has, however, pleaded that the fluoridation of the public piped water supply will be dangerous. The Attorney General also relied on the fact that when the Oireachtas was considering the Act of 1960, they had before them the report of the Fluorine Consultative Council who advised that the fluoridation of the public water supply at a concentration of 1 p.p.m. was not dangerous; he said that this established that the Oireachtas was not acting in bad faith or oppressively when enacting the Act of 1960. I decided to admit the evidence because a plea that the fluoridation of the public water supply involves an element of danger seemed to me to be a plea that the Oireachtas had not respected the rights of the citizen to life and to bodily integrity. Moreover, it seems to me that a plea that the process was dangerous involved a charge that the Oireachtas had acted oppressively, for a medical process which might be dangerous would, if imposed on the citizens, be oppressive.

The next issue to be considered is whether the fluoridation of the public water supplies, even if it be dangerous, is a violation of the plaintiff's right to bodily integrity. In my opinion, it is not. The plaintiff has no legal right to a supply of piped water and the Act of 1960 does not impose any obligation on her or on the members of her family to drink or use the water coming through the piped water supply. True that water today is a necessity of life and that the plaintiff probably has a right of access to a supply of water, but this does not give her a right to a supply of water which has not been fluoridated through the piped water supply. On this ground alone the case fails. Moreover, I am satisfied that the plaintiff and any of the citizens of the State can, by the expenditure of a few pounds, remove all or almost all the fluoride ions from the water coming through the piped water supply . . .

It may be, however, that this approach is too legalistic or too narrow and because of this and because of the great volume of evidence which has been given about the risks said to be involved in fluoridating water, I propose to consider whether the fluoridation of the public water supply is or may be dangerous to the citizens of this State or to some of them.

[Having reviewed the evidence presented to the Court, Kenny J. concluded that fluoridation was not harmful, but beneficial, to health, and he dismissed the plaintiff's claim. The plaintiff appealed to the Supreme Court, which dismissed the appeal. In the course of its judgment, the Court did, however, approve of the concept of unenumerated rights—eds.]

Judgment of the Supreme Court delivered by Ó Dálaigh C.J.:
. . . The constitutionality of a statute is, in many instances, determinable by a consideration and interpretation of the terms of the statute itself without reference to evidence as to their meaning or effect. Any matters necessary to elucidate its scope in such cases are matters of which the Court can take judicial notice. In the case of this Act, however, the Court is considering a statute which uses scientific terminology, deals with a scientific procedure and requires scientific knowledge to comprehend the effect of its provisions. These are not matters which are presumed to be within the knowledge of the Court, and, accordingly, the unconstitutionality of the Act, if it be unconstitutional, cannot be determined except by reference to the particular evidence which is furnished in the case. Since evidence may differ from case to case and as scientific knowledge may increase and the views of scientists alter, the Court's determination cannot amount to more than a decision that on the evidence produced the plaintiff has, or has not, discharged the onus of demonstrating that the Act is unconstitutional. It is of importance that attention should be called at the outset to this aspect of the present case . . .

Article 40, 3, paras. 1 and 2, are as follows:

3. 1° The state guarantees in its laws to respect, and, as far as practicable, by its laws to defend and vindicate the personal rights of the citizen.

2° The State shall, in particular, by its laws protect as best it may from unjust attack and, in the case of injustice done, vindicate the life, person, good name, and property rights of every citizen.

Of the further sections of this Article, section 4 protects personal liberty, section 5 the inviolablity of the dwelling-house, section 6 freedom of expression, the right of peaceable assembly and the right to form associations or unions. These latter rights are expressly qualified in various ways. The Court agrees with Mr. Justice Kenny that the "personal rights" mentioned in section 3, 1° are not exhausted by the enumeration of "life, person, good name, and property rights" in section 3, 2° as is shown by the use of the words "in particular"; nor by the more detached treatment of specific rights in the subsequent sections of the Article. To attempt to make a list of all the rights which may properly fall within the category of "personal rights" would be difficult and, fortunately, is unnecessary in this present case.

It was Mr. MacBride's contention that among the personal rights of the individual is to be included a right to what he called "bodily integrity", and this the Attorney General intimated he was prepared to concede in the words, "a right to the integrity of the person". Neither counsel offered the Court any assistance as to what the limits of this right to bodly integrity were. Mr. Justice Kenny held that a right to bodily integrity was among the personal rights guaranteed by the Constitution, and he sought to define the right in these words:

I understand the right to bodily integrity to mean that no mutilation of the body or any of its members may be carried out on any citizen under authority of the law except for the good of the whole body and that no process which is or may, as a matter of probability, be dangerous or harmful to the life or health of the citizens or any of them may be imposed (in the sense of being made compulsory) by an Act of Oireachtas.

Mr. MacBride, however, says that the Judge's definition is too narrow and he contends that any interference with bodily constitution is a violation of the right. However, for the reasons which hereinafter appear it is unnecessary to define "bodily integrity" or the "right to the integrity of the person" or to consider to what degree and in what circumstances the State might interfere with the right, whether for the benefit of the individual concerned, the common good, or by way of punishment. The Court is not pronouncing upon Mr. Justice Kenny's definition.

[The Supreme Court did not find it necessary to discuss the extent of the right to bodily integrity since, on the evidence before it, the fluoridation of water was not harmful to health – eds.]

Extract 13.6

McGEE v. ATTORNEY GENERAL [1974] I.R. 284

The plaintiff, a married woman, had been advised by her doctor that to have any more children would seriously endanger her life. Together with her husband, she took the decision to use contraceptives to avoid further pregnancy. Her doctor advised a particular method which required her importing spermicidal jelly into the State. This was impounded by the Revenue Commissioners pursuant to the powers conferred by the Criminal Law Amendment Act, 1935, which made the importation of such material a criminal offence. The plaintiff sought a declaration that these powers were in conflict with her right to privacy. In the Supreme Court, four of the five judges held in favour of her claim. It is of note that these four judges were not in agreement on the precise source of the right to privacy, Article 40.3 being mentioned as one possible source, while Articles 41 and 42 were also suggested. Of note also is the discussion of the impact of public opinion in 1937 as a guide to interpretation of the Constitution.

O'Keeffe, P. (High Court):
. . . *Griswold* v. *Connecticut* 381 U.S. 479 (1965) was cited in support of the submissions relating to Article 40. In that case the United States Federal Supreme Court held, by a majority, that one of the fundamental rights guaranteed by the United States Constitution was the right to privacy, and that legislation making it illegal to use contraceptives was an infringement of that right. It was pointed out that the legislation did not make the sale of contraceptives illegal, but interfered with the privacy of marital relations by making their use unlawful. The majority took the view that the statutes impugned dealt with a particularly important and sensitive area of privacy—that of the marital relation and the marital home. Accordingly, in the view of the Supreme Court of the United States the legislation was unconstitutional. Whether the right to privacy in this sense is one of the personal rights guaranteed by our Constitution is a matter for consideration. In my view, one must look at the state of public opinion at the time of the adoption of the Constitution in order to determine whether the effect of its adoption was to remove from the statute book a section of the Act of 1935: see the principles of construction applied by the Supreme Court in *O'Byrne* v. *The Minister for Finance* [1959] I.R. 1. The section impugned was barely two years on the statute book when the Constitution was adopted. If the submission of the plaintiff is correct, then public opinion as to what were fundamental rights must have been such as to require that the rights guaranteed to invididuals by the Constitution were inconsistent with the continued legality of the section. I consider that the best test of the position is to be found in

the views expressed when the section was being passed into law since, in point of time, this was so close to the enactment of the Constitution by the people. I find that the section was adopted without a division, although it was technically opposed. I cannot think that this reflects a public opinion in favour of the existence of such a right of privacy as is alleged by the plaintiff to be guaranteed under the Constitution. I would further point out that the section impugned in the present case is not the same as that in *Griswold's Case*. Section 17 of the Act of 1935 does not outlaw the use of contraceptives. It forbids their sale or importation and nothing more.

In my view, the section impugned is not inconsistent with the Constitution, and the plaintiff's action fails. However, it must be made clear that this does not involve any declaration that legislation cannot be enacted by the Oireachtas which would have the effect of repealing the secion impugned. All that I decide is that the section, as it stands, is not inconsistent with the Constitution.

Walsh J. (Supreme Court):

The facts of this case are not in dispute and I do not find it necessary to recite them in any detail. The central facts are that the plaintiff is a young married woman and that the case is concerned with the impact of the provisions of s. 17 of the Criminal Law Amendment Act, 1935, upon the sexual relations between the plaintiff and her husband.

The effect of the statutory provision in question is to make it a criminal offence for any person to sell or expose, offer, advertise, or keep for sale or to import or to attempt to import into the State any contraceptive. Section 17 of the Act of 1935 invokes s. 42 of the Customs Consolidation Act, 1876, and thereby includes contraceptives among the list of prohibited imports with the result that an importation of such an article could lead to the person importing the article being prosecuted and convicted under s. 186 of the Act of 1876. For the purpose of s. 1 of the Act of 1935 the word "contraceptive" means "any appliance, instrument, drug, preparation or thing, designed, prepared, or intended to prevent pregnancy resulting from sexual intercourse between human beings". I thought it necessary to give this definition in the detail in which it appears in the Act of 1935 so as to make clear that this case is not in any way concerned with instruments, preparations, drugs or appliances, etc., which take effect after conception, whether or not they are described as or purport to be contraceptives. Whether any such article is designed to or in fact takes effect after conception is a question which in each particular case can be decided only as one of fact based on the best available scientific evidence.

The event which led immediately to the present proceedings was the refusal of the second defendants to permit the importation by the plaintiff of a contraceptive jelly for use by her in her sexual relations with her husband, with the consent of her husband, and which had been prescribed for her by her medical adviser. It does not appear to be in dispute that the article in question is a contraceptive within the statutory definition to which I have already referred.

. . . Articles 40, 41, 42 and 44 of the Constitution all fall within that section of the Constitution which is titled "Fundamental Rights". Articles 41, 42 and 43 emphatically reject the theory that there are no rights without laws, no rights contrary to the law and no rights anterior to the law. They indicate that justice is placed above the law and acknowledge that natural rights, or human rights, are not created by law but that the Constitution confirms their existence and gives them protection. The individual has natural and human rights over which the State has no authority; and the family, as the natural primary and fundamental unit group of society, has rights as such which the State cannot control. However, at the same time it is true, as the Constitution acknowledges and claims, that the State is the guardian of the common good and that the individual, as a member of society, and the family, as a unit of society, have duties and obligations to consider and respect the common good of that society. It is important to recall that under the Constitution the State's powers of government are exercised in their respective spheres by the legislative, executive and judicial organs established under the Constitution. I agree with the view expressed by O'Byrne J. in *Buckley and Others (Sinn Fein)* v. *The Attorney General* [1950] I.R. 67, 83 that the power of the State to act for the protection of the common good or to decide what are the exigencies of the common good is not one which is peculiarly reserved for the legislative organ of government, in that the decision of the legislative organ is not absolute and is subject to and capable of being reviewed by the Courts. In concrete terms that means that the legislature is not free to encroach unjustifiably upon the fundamental rights of individuals or of the family in the name of the common good, or by act or omission to abandon or to neglect the common good or the protection or enforcement of the rights of individual citizens.

Turning to the particular submission made on behalf of the plaintiff, I shall deal first with the submission made in relation to the provisions of Article 41 of the Constitution which deals with the family. On the particular facts of this case, I think this is the most important submission because the plaintiff's claim is based upon her status as a married woman and is made in relation to the conduct of her sexual life with her husband within that marriage. For the purpose of this Article I am of opinion that the state of the plaintiff's health is immaterial to the consideration of the right she claims are infringed in relation to Article 41. In this Article the State, while recognising the family as the natural primary and fundamental unit group of society and as a moral institution possessing inalienable and imprescriptible rights antecedent and superior to all positive law, guarantees to protect the family in its constitution and authority as the necessary basis of social order and as indispensable to the welfare of the nation and the State. The Article recognises the special position of woman, meaning the wife, within that unit; the Article also offers special protection for mothers in that they shall not be obliged by economic necessity to engage in labour to the neglect of their duties in the home. The Article also recognises the institution of marriage as the foundation of the family and undertakes to protect it against attack. By this and the following Article, the State recognises the parents as the natural guardians of the children of the family and as those in whom the authority of the family is vested and those who shall have the right to determine how the family life shall be conducted, having due regard to the rights of the children not merely as members of that family but as individuals.

It is a matter exclusively for the husband and wife to decide how many children they wish to have; it would be quite outside the competence of the State to dictate or prescribe the number of children which they might have or should have. In my view, the husband and wife have a correlative right to agree to have no children. This is not to say that the State, when the common good requires it, may not actively encourage married couples either to have larger famlies or smaller families. If it is a question of having smaller families then, whether it be a decision of the husband and wife or the intervention of the State, the means employed to achieve this objective would have to be examined. What may be permissible to the husband and wife is not necessarily permissible to the State. For example, the husband and wife may mutually agree to practice either total or partial abstinence in their sexual relations. If the State were to attempt to intervene to compel such abstinence, it would be an intolerable and unjustifiable intrusion into the privacy of the matrimonial bedroom. On the other hand, any action on the part of either the husband and wife or of the State to limit family sizes by endangering or destroying human life must necessarily not only be an offence against the common good but also against the guaranteed personal rights of the human life in question.

The sexual life of a husband and wife is of necessity and by its nature an area of particular privacy. If the husband and wife decide to limit their family or to avoid having children by use of contraceptives, it is a matter peculiarly within the joint decision of the husband and wife and one into which the State cannot intrude unless its intrusion can be justified by the exigencies of the common good. The question of whether the use of contraceptives by married couples within their marriage is or is not contrary to the moral code or codes to which they profess to subscribe, or is or is not regarded by them as being against their conscience, could not justify State intervention. Similarly the fact that the use of contraceptives may offend against the moral code of the majority of the citizens of the State would not *per se* justify an intervention by the State to prohibit their use within marriage. The private morality of its citizens does not justify intervention by the State into the activities of those citizens unless and until the common good requires it. Counsel for the Attorney General did not seek to argue that the State would have any right to seek to prevent the use of contraceptives within marriage. He did argue, however, that it did not follow from this that the State was under any obligation to make contraceptives available to married couples. Counsel for the second defendants put the matter somewhat further by stating that, if she had a right to use contraceptives within the privacy of her marriage, it was a matter for the plaintiff to prove from whence the right sprang. In effect he was saying that, if she was appealing to a right anterior to positive law, the burden was on her to show the source of that right. At first sight this may appear to be a reasonable and logical proposition. However, it does appear to ignore a fundamental point, namely, that the rights of a married couple to decide how many children, if any, they will have are matters outside the reach of positive law where the means employed to implement such decisions do not impinge upon the common good or destroy or endanger human life. It is undoubtedly true that among those persons who are subject to a particular moral code no one has a right to be in breach of that moral code. But when this is a code governing private morality and where the breach of it is not one which injures the common good then it is not the State's business to intervene. It is outside the authority of the State to endeavour to intrude into the privacy of the husband and wife relationship for the sake of imposing a code of private morality upon that husband and wife which they do not desire.

In my view, Article 41 of the Constitution guarantees the husband and wife against any such invasion of their privacy by the State. It follows that the use of contraceptives by them within that marital privacy is equally guaranteed against such invasion and, as such, assumes the status of a right so guaranteed by the Constitution. If this right cannot be directly invaded by the State it follows that it cannot be frustrated by the State taking measures to ensure that the exercise of that right is rendered impossible. I do not exclude the possibility of the State being justified where the public good requires it (as, for example, in the case of a dangerous fall in population threatening the life or the essential welfare of the State) in taking such steps to ensure that in general, even if married couples could not be compelled to have children, they could at least be hindered in their endeavours to avoid having them where the common good required the maintenance or increase of the population. That, however, is not the present case and there is no evidence whatever in the case to justify State intervention on that ground. Similarly it is not impossible to envisage a situation where the availability of contraceptives to married people for use within marriage could be demonstrated to have led to or would probably lead to such an adverse effect on public morality so subversive of the common good as to justify State intervention by restricting or prohibiting the availability of contraceptives for use within marriage or at all. In such a case it would have to be demonstrated that all the other resources of the State had proved or were likely to prove incapable to avoid this subversion of the common good while contraceptives remained available for use within marriage.

In my opinion, s. 17 of the Act of 1935, in so far as it unreasonably restricts the availability of contraceptives for use within marriage, is inconsistent with the provisions of Article 41 of the Constitution for being an injustified invasion of the privacy of husband and wife in their sexual relations with one another. The fundamental restriction is contained in the provisions of sub-s. 3 of s. 17 of the Act of 1935 which lists contraceptives among the prohibited articles which may not be imported for any purposes whatsoever. On the present state of facts, I am of opinion that this provision is inconsistent with the Constitution and is no longer in force.

For the reasons I gave earlier in this judgment, the prohibition of the importation of contraceptives could be justified on several grounds provided the effect was not to make contraceptives unavailable. For example, the law might very well prohibit for health reasons the importation of some if not all contraceptives from sources outside the country if, for example, there is a risk of infection from their use. No such reason has been offered in the present case and in any such instance, for the reasons already given, the law could not take other steps to see that contraceptives were not otherwise available for use in marriage.

As this particular case arose primarily out of the ban on importation, I think that, in so far as Article 41 is concerned, the declaration sought should only go in respect of sub-s. 3 of s. 17 of the Act of 1935. That does not necessarily mean that the provisions as to sale in sub-s. 1 of s. 17 cannot be impugned. If, in the result, notwithstanding the deletion of sub-s. 3, the prohibition on sale had the effect of leaving a position where contraceptives were not reasonably available for use within marriage, then that particular prohibition must also fall. However, for the moment I do not think it is necessary to make any declaration in respect of that.

So far I have considered the plaintiff's case only in relation to Article 41 of the Constitution; and I have done so on the basis that she is a married woman but without referring to her state of health. I now turn to the claim made under Article 40 of the Constitution. So far as this particular Article is concerned, and the submissions made thereunder, the state of health of the plaintiff is relevant. If, for the reasons I have already given, a prohibition on the availability of contraceptives for use in marriage generally could be justified on the grounds of the exigencies of the common good, the provisions of s. 1 of Article 40 (in particular, the proviso thereto) would justify and would permit the State to discriminate between some married persons and others in the sense that, where conception could more than ordinarily endanger the life of a particular person or persons or particular classes of persons within the married state, the law could have regard to this difference of physical capacity and make special exemptions in favour of such persons. I think that such an exemption could also be justified under the provisions of s. 3 of Article 40 on the grounds that one of the personal rights of a woman in the plaintiff's state of health would be a right to be assisted in her efforts to avoid putting her life in jeopardy. I am of opinion also that not only has the State the right to do so but, by virtue of the terms of the proviso to s. 1 and the terms of s. 3 of Article 40, the State has the positive obligation to ensure by its laws as far as is possible (and in the use of the word "possible" I am relying on the Irish text of the Constitution) that there would be made available to a married woman in the condition of health of the plaintiff the means whereby a conception which was likely to put her life in jeopardy might be avoided when it is a risk over and above the ordinary risks inherent in pregnancy. It would, in the nature of things, be much more difficult to justify a refusal to do this on the grounds of the common good than in the case of married couples generally.

. . . Both in its preamble and in Article 6 the Constitution acknowledges God as the ultimate source of all authority. The natural or human rights to which I have referred earlier in this judgment are part of what is generally called the natural law. There are many to argue that natural law may be regarded only as an ethical concept and as such is a re-affirmation of the ethical content of law in its ideal of justice. The natural law as a theological concept is the law of God promulgated by reason and is the ultimate governor of all the laws of men. In view of the acknowledgment of Christianity in the preamble and in view of the reference to God in Article 6 of the Constitution, it must be accepted that the Constitution intended the natural human rights I have mentioned as being in the latter category rather than simply an acknowledgment of the ethical content of law in its ideal of justice. What exactly natural law is and what precisely it imports is a question which has exercised the minds of theologians for many centuries and on which they are not yet fully agreed. While the Constitution speaks of certain rights being imprescriptible or inalienable, or being antecedent and superior to all positive law, it does not specify them. Echoing the words of O'Byrne J. in *Buckley and Others (Sinn Féin)* v. *The Attorney General* [1950] I.R. 67, 82, I do not feel it necessary to enter upon an inquiry as to their extent or, indeed, as to their nature. It is sufficient for the court to examine and to search for the rights which may be discoverable in the particular case before the court in which these rights are invoked.

In a pluralist society such as ours, the Courts cannot as a matter of constitutional law be asked to choose between the differing views, where they exist, of experts on the interpretation by the different religious denominations of either the nature or extent of these natural rights as they are to be found in the natural law. The same considerations apply also to the question of ascertaining the nature and extent of the duties which flow from natural law; the Constitution speaks of one of them when it refers to the inalienable duty of parents to provide according to their means for the religious, moral, intellectual, physical and social education of their children: see s. 1 of Article 42. In this country it falls finally upon the judges to interpret the Constitution and in doing so to determine, where necessary, the rights which are superior or antecedent to positve law or which are imprescriptible or inalienable. In the performance of this difficult duty there are certain guidelines laid down in the Constitution for the judge. The very structure and content of the Articles dealing with fundamental rights clearly indicate that justice is not subordinate to the law. In particular, the terms of s. 3 of Article 40 expressly subordinate the law to justice. Both Aristotle and the Christian philosophers have regarded justice as the highest human virtue. The virtue of prudence was also esteemed by Aristotle as by the philosophers of the Christian world. But the great additional virtue introduced by Christianity was that of charity—not the charity which consists of giving to the deserving, for that is justice, but the charity which is also called mercy. According to the preamble, the people gave themselves the Constitution to promote the common good with due observance of prudence, justice and charity so that the dignity and freedom of the individual might be assured. The judges must, therefore, as best they can from their training and their experience interpret these rights in accordance with their ideas of prudence, justice and charity. It is but natural that from time to time the prevailing ideas of these virtues may be conditioned by the passage of time; no interpretation of the Constitution is intended to be final for all time. It is given in the light of prevailing ideas and concepts. The development of the constitutional law of the United States of America is ample proof of this. There is a constitution which, while not professing to be governed by the precepts of Christianity, also in the Ninth Amendment recognises the existence of rights other than those referred to expressly in it and its amendments. The views of the United States Supreme Court, as reflected in the decisions interpreting that constitution and in the development of their constitutional law, also appear firmly to reject legal positivism as a jurisprudential guide.

Three United States Supreme Court decisions were relied upon in argument by the plaintiff: *Poe* v. *Ullman* (1961) 367 U.S. 497; *Griswold* v. *Connecticut* (1965) 381 U.S. 479; and *Eisenstadt* v. *Baird* (1972) 405 U.S. 438. My reason for not referring to them is not because I did not find them helpful or relevant, which indeed they were, but because I found it unnecessary to rely upon any of the dicta in those cases to support the views which I have expressed in this judgment.

Lastly, I wish to emphasise that I have given no consideration whatsoever to the question of the constitutionality or otherwise of laws which would withhold or restrict the availability of contraceptives for use outside of marriage; nothing in this judgment is intended to offer any opinion on that matter.

For the reasons I have given, I would grant the plaintiff a declaration that sub-s. 3 of s. 17 of the Criminal Law Amendment Act, 1935, is not, and was not at any time material to these proceedings, of full force and effect as part of the laws of the State.

Henchy J.:

The essential facts of this case may be summarised as follows. The plaintiff, who is aged 29, lives in the restricted quarters of a mobile home with her husband, who is a fisherman earning about £20 per week, and their four children who were born in December, 1968, in January, 1970, and (the twins) in November, 1970. Her medical history shows that during each pregnancy she suffered from toxaemia; that during her second pregnancy she developed a serious cerebral thrombosis from which she nearly died, and which left her temporarily paralysed on one side; and that during her last pregnancy she suffered from toxaemia which was complicated by hypertension. She has been advised by her doctor that if she becomes pregnant again there will be a very great risk that she will suffer a further cerebral thrombosis, which is an illness that apparently has a mortality rate as high as 26% in married women of her age and which would be apt to cause her a disabling paralysis if it did not prove fatal.

Confronted with that dire prospect, she has had to decide between sexual abstinence and the use of a contraceptive—no question apparently having arisen as to a surgical intervention. With the agreement of her husband, and having due regard to her obligations to her husband, her children and herself, she decided in favour of contraception. Because of her medical history of vascular thrombosis and hypertension, her doctor advised against an oral contraceptive and recommended instead an intra-uterine device which was to be used with a contraceptive jelly. The doctor fitted the device and gave her a small supply of the contraceptive jelly. This jelly is not made in this State, so she had to order a further supply from England. When the packet containing it was sent to her by post, it was intercepted and seized by the Customs authorities because, being a "contraceptive" as defined by sub-s. 4 of s. 17 of the Criminal Law Amendment Act, 1935, its importation is prohibited by s. 42 of the Customs Consolidation Act, 1876, as applied by sub-s. 3 of s. 17 of the Act of 1935.

In the present proceedings the plaintiff has challenged the constitutional validity of s. 17 of the Act of 1935 and has claimed that it was not carried over by Article 50 of the Constitution because it is inconsistent with certain provisions in Articles 40, 41, 42, 44 and 45 of the Constitution. The primary contention is that it trenches on her rights under sub-s. 1 of s. 3 of Article 40 which provides that: "The State guarantees in its laws to respect, and, as far as practicable, by its laws to defend and vindicate the personal rights of the citizen".

The Act of 1935, as its long title shows, is not aimed at population control but at the suppression of vice and the amendment of the law relating to sexual offences. Section 17 follows immediately on a section directed agains the practice of prostitution in public and immediately precedes a section making criminal certain acts which offend modesty or cause scandal or injure the morals of the community. The section creates a criminal prohibition in an area in which the legislature has thought fit to intervene in the interests of public morality. What it seeks to do, by means of the sanction of the criminal law, is to put an end, as far as it was possible to do so by legislation, to *the use* of contraceptives in the State. It does not in terms make the use of contraceptives a crime, but the totality of the prohibition aims at nothing less. Presumably because contraceptives are of differing kinds and vary in the ways, internal and external, they can be used, and because of the difficulty of proving their use in the intimacy of the sexual act, the section strikes at their availability. Subsection 1 of s. 17 of the Act of 1935 makes it an offence to sell, or expose, offer, advertise, or keep for sale or to import to attempt to import for sale any contraceptives. In effect, this makes it legally impossible to sell or buy a contraceptive in the State. Had the prohibition stopped there, it would have left the loophole that contraceptives could be imported otherwise than for sale. That loophole, however, is sealed by sub-s. 3, of s. 17 which makes contraceptives prohibited articles under the customs code so that their importation for any purpose, if effected with the intention of evading the prohibition, is an offence: see s. 186 of the Customs

Consolidation Act, 1876; *Frailey* v. *Charlton* [1920] 1 K.B. 147; *Attorney General* v. *Deignan* [1946] I.R. 542.

Because contraceptives are not manufactured in this State, the effect of s. 17 of the Act of 1935 as a whole is that, except for contraceptives that have been imported without the intention of evading the prohibition of importation, it is not legally possible to obtain a contraceptive in this State. It is doubtful if the legislature could have taken more effective steps by means of the criminal law to put an end to their use in the State.

It is the totality and absoluteness of the prohibition effected by s. 17 of the Act of 1935 that counsel for the plaintiff impugn as infringing what they say are her constitutionally guaranteed rights as a citizen. As has been held in a number of cases, the unspecified personal rights guaranteed by sub-s. 1 of s. 3 of Article 40 are not confined to those specified in sub-s. 2 of that section. It is for the Courts to decide in a particular case whether the right relied on comes within the constitutional guarantee. To do so, it must be shown that it is a right that inheres in the citizen in question by virtue of his human personality. The lack of precision in this test is reduced when sub-s. 1 of s. 3 of Article 40 is read (as it must be) in the light of the Constitution as a whole and, in particular, in the light of what the Constitution, expressly or by necessary implication, deems to be fundamental to the personal standing of the individual in question in the context of the social order envisaged by the Constitution. The infinite variety in the relationships between the citizen and his fellows and between the citizen and the State makes an exhaustive enumeration of the guaranteed rights difficult, if not impossible.

The dominant feature of the plaintiff's dilemma is that she is a young married woman who is living, with a slender income, in the cramped quarters of a mobile home with her husband and four infant children, and that she is faced with a considerable risk of death or crippling paralysis if she becomes pregnant. The net question is whether it is constitutionally permissible in the circumstances for the law to deny her access to the contraceptive method chosen for her by her doctor and which she and her husband wish to adopt. In other words, is the prohibition effected by s. 17 of the Act of 1935 an interference with the rights which the State guarantees in its laws to respect, as stated in sub-s. 1 of s. 3 of Article 40?

The answer lies primarily in the fact that the plaintiff is a wife and a mother. It is the informed and conscientious wish of the plaintiff and her husband to maintain full marital relations without incurring the risk of a pregnancy that may very well result in her death or in a crippling paralysis. Section 17 of the Act of 1935 frustrates that wish. It goes further; it brings the implementation of the wish within the range of the criminal law. Its effect, therefore, is to condemn the plaintiff and her husband to a way of life which, at best, will be fraught with worry, tension and uncertainty that cannot but adversely affect their lives and, at worst, will result in an unwanted pregnancy causing death or serious illness with the obvious tragic consequences to the lives of her husband and young children. And this in the context of a Constitution which in its preamble proclaims as one of its aims the dignity and freedom of the individual; which in sub-s. 2 of s. 3 of Article 40 casts on the State a duty to protect as best it may from unjust attack and, in the case of injustice done, to vindicate the life and person of every citizen; which in Article 41, after recognising the family as the natural primary and fundamental unit group of society, and as a moral institution possessing inalienable and imprescriptible rights antecedent and superior to all positive law, guarantees to protect it in its constitution and authority as the necessary basis of social order and as indispensable to the welfare of the nation and the State; and which, also in Article 41, pledges the State to guard with special care the institution of marriage, on which the family is founded, and to protect it against attack.

Section 17, in my judgment, so far from respecting the plaintiff's personal rights, violates them. If she observes this prohibition (which in practice she can scarcely avoid doing and which in law she is bound under penalty of fine and imprisonment to do), she will endanger the security and happiness of her marriage, she will imperil her health to the point of hazarding her life, and she will subject her family to the risk of distress and disruption. These are intrusions which she is entitled to say are incompatible with the safety of her life, the preservation of her health, her responsibility to her conscience, and the security and well-being of her marriage and family. If she fails to obey the prohibition in s. 17, the law, by prosecuting her, will reach into the privacy of her marital life in seeking to prove her guilt.

In *Griswold* v. *Connecticut* (1965) 381 U.S. 479 the American Supreme Court held that a Connecticut statute which forbade the use of contraceptives was unconstitutional because it violated a constitutional right of marital privacy which, while unexpressed in the American Constitution, was held to be within the penumbra of the specific guarantees of the Bill of Rights. In a judgment concurring in the opinion of the court, Goldberg J. said at p. 498 of the report:

> The State, at most, argues that there is some rational relation between this statute and what is admittedly a legitimate subject of state concern—the discouraging of extra-marital relations. It says that preventing the use of birth-control devices by married persons helps prevent the indulgence by some in such extra-marital relations. The rationality of this justification is dubious, particularly in light of the admitted widespread availability to all persons in the State of Connecticut, unmarried as well as married, of birth-control devices for the prevention of disease, as distinguished from the prevention of conception, see *Tileston* v. *Ullman* 129 Conn. 84, 26A. 2d 582. But, in any event, it is clear that the state interest in safeguarding marital fidelity can be served by a more discriminately tailored statute, which does not, like the present one, sweep unnecessarily broadly, reaching far beyond the evil sought to be dealt with and intruding upon the privacy of all married couples.

At p. 499 Goldberg J. cites with approval the words of Harlan J. in *Poe* v. *Ullman* (1961) 367 U.S. 497, 533:

> . . . the intimacy of husband and wife is necessarily an essential and accepted feature of the institution of marriage, an institution which the State not only must allow, but which always and in every age it has fostered and protected. It is one thing when the State exerts its power either to forbid extra-marital sexuality altogether, or to say who may marry, but it is quite another when, having acknowledged a marriage and the intimacies inherent in it, it undertakes to regulate by means of the criminal law the details of that intimacy.

It has been argued that *Griswold's Case* (1965) 381 U.S. 479 is distinguishable because the statute in question there forbade the use of contraceptives, whereas s. 17 of the Act of 1935 only forbids their sale or importation. This submission was accepted in the High Court. However, I consider that the distinction sought to be drawn is one of form rather than substance. The purpose of the statute in both cases is the same: it is to apply the sanction of the criminal law in order to prevent the use of contraceptives. What the American Supreme Court found in *Griswold's Case* to be constitutionally objectionable was that the sweep of the statute was so wide that proof of an offence would involve physical intrusion into the intimacy of the marriage relationship, which the court held to be an area of constitutionally protected privacy. If the plaintiff were prosecuted for an offence arising under or by virtue of s. 17 of the Act of 1935, while there might not be the same degree of physical intrusion, there would necessarily be a violation of intimate aspects of her marital life which, in deference to her standing as a wife and mother, ought not to be brought out and condemned as criminal under a glare of publicity in a courtroom. Furthermore, if she were found guilty of such an offence, in order to have the penalty mitigated to fit the circumstances of her case, she would have to disclose particulars of her marital dilemma which she ought not to have to reveal.

In my opinion, s. 17 of the Act of 1935 violates the guarantee in sub-s. 1 of s. 3 of Article 40 by the State to protect the plaintiff's personal rights by its laws; it does so not only by violating her personal right to privacy in regard to her marital relations but, in a wider way by frustrating and making criminal any efforts by her to effectuate the decision of her husband and herself, made responsibly, conscientiously and on medical advice to avail themselves of a particular contraceptive method so as to ensure her life and health as well as the integrity, security and well-being of her marriage and her family. Because of the clear unconstitutionality of the section in this respect, I do not find it necessary to deal with the submissions made in support of the claim that the section violates other provisions of the Constitution.

What stands between the plaintiff and the exercise of any constitutional right claimed by her in this case is sub-s. 3 of s. 17 of the Act of 1935. With that subsection out of the way, her cause of complaint would disappear because what she wishes to do (to import the required contraceptive by post) would then be legal as the importation, not being for sale, would not be forbidden by sub-section 1. Since s. 17 without sub.s. 3 can stand as a self-contained entity, independently operable and representing the legislative intent, sub-s. 3 is capable of being severed and declared unconstitutional. Therefore, I would allow the appeal to the extent of declaring that sub-s. 3 of s. 17 of the Act of 1935 is without validity as being inconsistent with the Constitution. In the particular circumstances of this case, I do not find it necessary to make any adjudication on the constitutionality of the remaining part of the section.

Extract 13.7

NORRIS v. ATTORNEY GENERAL [1984] I.R. 36

The plaintiff challenged those provisions of the Offences Against the Person Act, 1861 which made commission of buggery and other acts by one male with another criminal offences. His main argument was that these provisions were in breach of his right to privacy. In rejecting this claim, the Supreme Court, affirming the decision of the High Court, examined the limits which are placed by the Constitution on the extent of constitutional rights, and in particular on those protected by Article 40.3. The two dissenting judgments examine the basis for the existence of the right to privacy in more detail than in the *McGee* decision. The judgment of McCarthy J. is of significance for its discussion of the impact of public opinion in 1937 on the Court's deliberations, and this also marks a point of comparison with the *McGee* case.

O'Higgins C.J. (Finlay P. and Griffin J. concurring):
In these proceedings the plaintiff seeks a declaration that ss. 61 and 62 of the Offences Against the Person Act, 1861, and s. 11 of the Criminal Law Amendment Act, 1885, are inconsistent with the Constitution and, therefore, were not continued in force by Article 50 thereof and do not form part of the law of the State. His claim, having been considered and rejected in the High Court, has been brought to this Court by way of appeal.

The Impugned Legislation

The legislation which the plaintiff challenges provides for the criminalisation and punishment of sexual acts and conduct of a kind usually regarded and described as abnormal or unnatural. Section 61 of the Act of 1861, as amended, deals with the offence of buggery committed with mankind or an animal, and provides a maximum penalty of penal servitude for life. Section 62 of the same Act deals with associated offences, such as attempts and assaults for the purpose of committing buggery, and specifically covers indecent assaults on a male person; a maximum penalty of two years' imprisonment is provided. Section 11 of the Act of 1885 provides as follows:

> Any male person who, in public or private, commits, or is a party to the commission of, or procures or attempts to procure the commission by any male person of, any act of gross indecency with another male person, shall be guilty of a misdemeanor, and being convicted thereof shall be liable at the discretion of the court to be imprisoned for any term not exceeding two years, with or without hard labour.

It is to be noted that the offences dealt with in ss. 61 and 62 of the Act of 1861 can, in relation to mankind, be committed with or upon a male or female person, but can only be committed by a male. It is also to be noted that the offence dealt with in s. 11 of the Act of 1885 only applies to male persons, that the section applies irrespective of the ages of the male persons involved and irrespective of whether the act is committed in public or private, or with or without consent. While the impugned legislation does not expressly deal with homosexual practices and conduct, it is accepted that the effect of the three sections, taken together, is to prohibit and criminalise such conduct between male persons. No similar prohibition exists in relation to such practices and conduct between females.

The Relevant Facts

The plaintiff is now and has been, since 1967, a lecturer in England at Trinity College, Dublin. He is aged 38 and is unmarried. Although born in Leopoldville, in the former Belgian Congo, he is an Irish citizen. He has asserted in his statement of claim and in evidence that he is congenitally and irreversibly homosexual in outlook and disposition, that he is neither sexually attracted to nor has he any interest in women, that he desires a sexual relationship based on his congenital orientation and that for him any heterosexual relationship, such as that of marriage, is not open or possible.

He claims that at an early age his realisation of his own feelings and disposition, and a growing awareness of public attitudes and of the state and sanctions of the criminal law, not only caused him considerable anxiety and distress but also led to a profound nervous illness which required protracted medical care and counselling. When he recovered from his illness, he decided to declare himself publicly as a homosexual and, with other homosexual men and women, formed an association known as the Irish Gay Rights Movement, of which he became chairman. In this capacity he was interviewed on television and was given an opportunity to explain the aims and activities of the movement. He is at present involved in two similar organisations—the National Gay Federation and the Committee for Homosexual Law Reform. Although known to be a homosexual and to have indulged in homosexual activities, he has never been prosecuted, nor has any member of the organisations with which he is or has been associated. He has, however, had the experience, some time in 1976, of his cross-Channel mail being opened by the authorities, but this does not appear to have been continued.

This action has been brought by the plaintiff as an individual citizen. It is not a representative action nor one brought on behalf of the organisations or groups with which he is identified, although the fact of the existence of such groups and of people with similar dispositions, feelings and outlooks may be relevant. It is as a personal litigant seeking the relief claimed that the plaintiff's rights and standing in bringing this action fall to be considered.

Courts not Empowered to Reform the Law

In the course of his evidence at the trial, the plaintiff, on many occasions, made it clear that his purpose, in the meetings he attended, the interviews he gave and in the organisations with which he is associated, is to achieve a reform of the law by the decriminalisation of certain homosexual activities. He indicated in evidence the reforms and changes which he wished to achieve, which would provide protection for the young and incapacitated, but would free from all criminal sanctions homosexual conduct carried out in private between consenting male adults. Lest it be thought that this Court could or should consider the merits of such proposed reforms or express any view thereon, I desire to make it clear that such is not and can never be a function of this Court. The sole function of this Court, in a case of this nature, is to interpret the Constitution and the law and to declare with objectivity and impartiality the result of that intepretation on the claim being considered. Judges may, and do, share with other citizens a concern and interest in desirable changes and reform in our laws; but, under the Constitution, they have no function in achieving such by judicial decision. It may be regarded as emphasising the obvious but, nevertheless, I think it proper to remind the plaintiff and others interested in these proceedings that the sole and exclusive power of altering the laws of Ireland is, by the Constitution, vested in the Oireachtas. The Courts declare what he law is—it is for the Oireachtas to make changes if it so thinks proper.

Was this Legislation Continued in Force?

In this case we are concerned only with the question whether the items of legislation which are challenged in these proceedings have in whole or in part, been carried over or re-enacted into our *corpus juris* by the people when they enacted the Constitution in 1937. Whether they have been so re-enacted depends on whether they passed the tests prescribed by Article 50, s. 1 of the Constitution. That section provides:

> Subject to this Constitution and to the extent to which they are not inconsistent therewith, the laws in force in Saorstát Éireann immediately prior to the date of the coming into operation of this Constitution shall continue to be of full force and effect until the same or any of them shall have been repealed or amended by enactment of the Oireachtas.

The purpose of Article 50, s. 1, is to continue in force the laws which had previously operated in Saorstát Éireann, with as few exceptions as possible. The phrase "subject to this Constitution" indicates an obvious requirement that, in order to be operable in the new State, such laws must fit into the framework of, and be controlled by, the Constitution. If, by the nature of their provisions, this were not possible, such laws, on that account alone, could not be continued. Subject to the Constitution in that sense, such laws are to continue to be of full force and effect "to the extent to which they are not inconsistent therewith".

If Article 50 had provided that such laws would continue to be of full force and effect "to the extent to which they are consistent with the Constitution" would it have the same meaning and effect? In my view, it clearly would not. In such circumstances, consistency would have to be proved and in the absence of such proof the law or laws would be inoperative. However, according to the actual words used in Article 50, the law or laws in question operate unless inconsistency is established, and the onus of establishing such is placed on the person who challenges their continued validity. This is not to say that such pre-Constitution laws enjoy any presumption of consistency of constitutionality. They do not. Each such law must be examined to see what it purports to authorise or permit. If on such examination it emerges that the law permits what the Constitution prohibits or forbids what the Constitution sanctions, then inconsistency is established, and to the extent thereof the law would be declared to have ceased to have effect on the coming into operation of the Constitution.

While this case is concerned with legislation passed not by the Oireachtas or Saorstát Éireann but by the British Parliament, it has proceeded on the basis that such legislation survived the foundation of the State in 1922 and was in force as part of the laws of Soarstát Éireann immediately prior to the coming into operation of the Constitution of 1937. Accordingly, the question is whether it was continued under Article 50. If on examination of such legislation now, in the light of the Constitution as it has been interpreted and understood since its enactment, inconsistencies are established, such legislation, to the extent thereof, must be held not to have been so continued. To achieve this result, however, the plaintiff must show that such inconsistencies exist. It is not sufficient to show that the legislation is out of date, is lacking in public support or approval, is out of tune with the mood or requirements of the times or is of a kind impossible to contemplate now being enacted by Oireachtas Éireann. Unless inconsistency is established, such legislation, no matter what its defects or blemishes may be, is continued by the express terms of Article 50 "to be of full force and effect" until repealed or amended by enactment of the Oireachtas.

The Plaintiff's Case

I now turn to the manner in which the impugned legislation has been challenged by the plaintiff. In considering this challenge I will, for convenience, regard the first two sections (ss. 61 and 62 of the Act of 1861) as dealing with buggery, and the other section (s. 11 of the Act of 1885) as dealing with gross indecency.

The plaintiff contends that a continued designation as crimes of the conduct dealt with in these sections is inconsistent with the observance of certain rights which the Constitution guarantees to citizens. While the extent of his complaints varies according to the conduct and its criminal designation, it will be possible to deal with them in association with each of the constitutional provisions to which they are referable. Apart from particular provisions of the Constitution in respect of which inconsistency is alleged, the plaintiff also contends that, having regard to the development in medical and psychological knowledge of human sexual behaviour, and the greater understanding to-day of homosexuality, the designation of such conduct as criminal conflicts with the values of a society which the Constitution's preamble proclaims to be based on the "due observance of prudence, justice and charity, so that the dignity and freedom of the individual may be assured . . ." In short, the plaintiff's case is based partly on a reliance on particular Articles of the Constitution and partly on its general policy as indicated by the preamble.

I will now refer to the constitutional provisions upon which the plaintiff relies, and will endeavour to state the plaintiff's case in respect of each such provision as I understand it. These provsions are as follows:

1. Article 40, s. 1—With its qualification as to regard being had to differences of capacity, physical and moral, and of social function, this provision guarantees equality before the law for all citizens. The plaintiff contends that the prohibition, in respect of the offence of gross indecency, of homosexual conduct between male persons only, constitutes in two respects discrimination which is invidious and unfair against such male citizens who are homosexual. In the first place he contends that such a prohibition ignores the sexual conduct involved in adultery, seduction and fornication, which are outlets open to heterosexual male citizens and, on that account, puts male homosexuals in a position of inequality before the law. It is also contended that, even if it were said that homosexual citizens have different capacities from heterosexual citizens and that the law can have regard to such differences, nevertheless, the regard which the law must have is "due regard" and this could not include the designation as criminal of the very expression of the difference in capacity which is inherent in such citizens. In the second place the plaintiff says that gross indecency, as an offence, is confined to sexual conduct between males. Similar or associated sexual conduct between female citizens who

have a homosexual or lesbian disposition is not prohibited. On this account the plaintiff complains that the section creating the offence discriminates against male homosexuals solely on the grounds of their sex and in a way which is unrelated to any difference of capacity, physical or moral, or of social function. For these reasons, the plaintiff contends that s. 11 of the Act of 1885, which creates the offence of gross indecency, is inconsistent with the provisions of Article 40, s. 1, of the Constitution.

2. Article 40, s. 3—Under this provision the State guarantees to respect and, as far as practicable, to defend and vindicate the personal rights of citizens. These personal rights are not merely those rights expressly referred to in the Constitution but include also other rights, unenumerated, which call to be recognised and declared as the Constitution is construed and interpreted. The plaintiff contends that among these unenumerated rights of citizens is a right of privacy. He claims that this right, which was identified by this Court in *McGee* v. *The Attorney General* [1974] I.R. 284 is not confined to a right of marital privacy. He alleges that it encompasses, but is not exhausted by, the right of a husband and wife to privacy in their sexual relations within their marriage. He contends that it is a right which adheres to every citizen as such and which places a limit on the power of the State to control his personal conduct where neither the exigencies of the common good nor the protection of public order or morality necessitates such control. He claims that the existence of this right must be implied from the preamble when it speaks of the dignity and freedom of the individual, and its protection must be guaranteed by Article 40, section 3. Reliance was placed on the majority judgment of the Supreme Court of the United States in *Eisenstadt* v. *Baird* 405 U.S. 428 (1972) and, in particular, on a passage from the judgment of Brennan J. at p. 453 of the report. Reliance is also placed on a passage from the judgment of Budd J. in *McGee* v. *The Attorney General* [1974] I.R. 284 where he said at p. 322 of the report:

> Whilst the 'personal rights' are not described specifically, it is scarcely to be doubted in our society that the right to privacy is universally recognised and accepted with possibly the rarest of exceptions, and that the matter of marital relationship must rank as one of the most important of matters in the realm of privacy. When the preamble to the Constitution speaks of seeking to promote the common good by the observance of prudence, justice and charity so that the dignity and freedom of the individual may be assured, it must surely inform those charged with its construction as to the mode of application of its Articles.

In so far as the impugned legislation seeks to control the sexual conduct of the plaintiff and like-minded citizens, carried on in private, the plaintiff claims that it constitutes an unwarranted intrusion into his private life, and is inconsistent with the State's duty to defend and vindicate his right to privacy which is one of his personal rights as a citizen.

The plaintiff further says, with regard to ss. 61 and 62 of the Act of 1861, that the conduct thereby prohibited extends to sexual acts and conduct between husband and wife, and that in this respect these sections are inconsistent with the defence and vindication of marital privacy as is required by Article 40, section 3.

The plaintiff also claims that the prohibition of all sexual acts between consenting male adults, even if carried out in private, threatens both the physical and mental health of homosexuals like him whose congenital sexual urges and feelings dispose them, inevitably, towards such acts. He further claims that the prohibition can injure and has injured the mental and physical health of homosexuals, including the plaintiff. He therefore contends that the existence of such a prohibition with its capacity for injury to the plaintiff and others constitutes a threat to the plaintiff's right to bodily integrity, and is inconsistent with the State's duty to defend and vindicate such right in accordance with Article 40, section 3. In this regard, reliance was placed on *Ryan* v. *The Attorney General* [1965] I.R. 294 and *The State (C.)* v. *Frawley* [1976] I.R. 365. . . .

. . . . . .

Locus Standi

At this stage it is convenient to consider an objection to the plaintiff's case which has been submitted on behalf of the defendant. The objection is in the nature of a challenge to the plaintiff's *locus standi* to advance the arguments on inconsistency, or most of them, which he has advanced. The defendant's objection is based on the authority of this Court's decision in *Cahill* v. *Sutton* [1980] I.R. 369. That case dealt with the validity of s. 11, sub-s. 2(*b*), of the Statute of Limitations, 1957. The Court held that, as the challenge on validity which the plaintiff in that case put forward was based solely on the absence of a saver or proviso to the time limit laid down, which, if present, would not have preserved her claim, she could not establish that any right of hers had been infringed or threatened by the absence thereof. Accordingly, the Court held that the plaintiff lacked the standing necessary to invoke the jurisdiction of the Court to determine the question of validity raised. In the course of his judgment, with which the other members of the Court agreed, Mr. Justice Henchy said at p. 284 of the report:

> If a citizen comes forward in court with a claim that a particular law has been enacted in disregard of a constitutional requirement, he has little reason to complain if in the normal course of things he is required, as a condition of invoking the court's jurisdiction to strike down the law for having been unconstitutionally made (with all the dire consequences that may on occasion result from the vacuum created by such a decision), to show that the impact of the impugned law on his personal situation discloses an injury or prejudice which he has either suffered or is in imminent danger of suffering.

The defendant seeks to apply the reasoning of that decision to this case and says that, in so far as the plaintiff's complaint against the impugned legislation is based on an alleged inconsistency with Article 40, s. 3, and with the State's obligation to protect the right to privacy, both as a claimed personal right of his as a citizen and as marital privacy in relation to married citizens, the plaintiff lacks the necessary standing to make such complaint. As to the general right to privacy which the plaintiff claims is guaranteed to all citizens, the defendant says that, if such exists, the plaintiff cannot point to any interference therewith so far as he is concerned. He has proclaimed himself publicly to be homosexual, he has been active in organising associations concerned with homosexuals, he has spoken on television and radio, yet he has never been prosecuted nor has he been intimidated in any way, and he continues to carry out, without inteference, his normal duties as a lecturer in Trinity College, Dublin. In such circumstances, the defendant contends, the plaintiff has neither suffered nor is he in danger of suffering in any way from the legislation which he challenges and, accordingly, he cannot complain that his personal right to privacy has been threatened or endangered. As to the plaintiff's complaints that the sections of the Act of 1861 are inconsistent with the observance of marital privacy, the defendant says that it is not for the plaintiff to make such a case. Not only is he not married, but the whole thrust of the case which he makes is that, for him, and for homosexuals like him, who desire a lasting partnership in life, marriage is not open or possible. Accordingly, the defendant says that, in this respect also, the plaintiff cannot be heard to make a case which is not his nor to complain of a breach of a right which he has neither suffered nor is likely to suffer.

In my view, the defendant's objection, in so far as it applies to that part of the plaintiff's case which is based on marital privacy, is well founded and should be upheld. The basis of the plaintiff's case is that there exists in our society a significant number of male homosexual citizens, of whom he is one, for whom, sexually, the female offers no attraction, and who, desiring a stable relationship, must seek such amongst male companions of a similar outlook and disposition. For these, as the plaintiff clearly implied in his evidence (see transcript, Book 1, Q. 153), marriage is not open as an alternative either to promiscuity or a more permanent sexual relationship with a male person. This being so, it is *nihil ad rem* for the plaintiff to suggest, as a reason for alleviating his own predicament, a possible impact of the impugned legislation on a situation which is not his, and to point to a possible injury or prejudice which he has neither suffered nor is in imminent danger of suffering within the principles laid down by this Court in *Cahill v. Sutton*.

However, I do not agree with the defendant's submission that the plaintiff lacks standing to complain merely because he has not been prosecuted nor has had his way of life disturbed as a result of the legislation which he challenges. In my view, as long as the legislation stands and continues to proclaim as criminal the conduct which the plaintiff asserts he has a right to engage in, such right, if it exists, is threatened and the plaintiff has standing to seek the protection of the Court.

The Plaintiff's Case Examined

At the core of the plaintiff's challenge to the impugned legislation is the assertion that the State has no business in the field of private morality and has no right to legislate in relation to the private sexual conduct of consenting adults. It is the plaintiff's case that to attempt to do so is to exceed the limits of permissible interference and to shatter that area of privacy which the dignity and liberty of human persons require to be kept apart as a haven for each citizen. Accordingly, the plaintiff says that any legislation which purports to do so is *de facto* inconsistent with the Constitution. Apart from this, however, the plaintiff has advanced other grounds of alleged inconsistency which must be considered. I propose in the first place to deal with these other grounds and then to return to what appears to be the plaintiff's main submission.

As already mentioned, the plaintiff argues that the impugned legislation is inconsistent with Article 40, s. 1, of the Constitution in that it discriminates against male citizens who are homosexual. I understand his complaint in this respect to be confined to the Act of 1885. In case I am incorrect in this respect, however, I would like to express the view that such an argument is scarcely entertainable in relation to the impugned sections of the Act of 1861. The act which constitutes buggery can only be committed by males. It is designated as a crime whether it is committed with a male or a female. It follows that the prohibition applies to the act irrespective of whether it is committed by a homosexual or by a heterosexual male. No discrimination could be involved.

As to gross indecency, however, the prohibition only applies to such conduct between males. Does the fact that it does not apply to gross indecency between females involve a discrimination which would be prohibited by Article 40, section 1? I do not think so. The legislature would be perfectly entitled to have regard to the difference between the sexes and to treat sexual conduct or gross indecency between males as requiring prohibition because of the social problem which it creates, while at the same time looking at sexual conduct between females as being not only different but as posing no such social problem. Furthermore, in alleging discrimination because the prohibition on the conduct which he claims he is entitled to engage in is not extended to similar conduct by females, the plaintiff is complaining of a situation which, if it did not exist or were remedied, would confer on him no benefit or vindicate no right of his which he claims to be breached. I do not think that such an argument should be entertained by this Court. For the same reason, I would reject the plaintiff's complaint that there is discrimination in the fact that the laws of the State do not apply criminal sanctions to heterosexual conduct outside marriage between consenting adults.

The plaintiff has also submitted that the blanket prohibition of homosexual conduct effected by the legislation threatens his physical and mental health through frustration and disorientation arising from his congenital disposition. For this reason the plaintiff asserts that his right to bodily integrity is endangered. In my opinion this submission is not a sound one. If the legislation is otherwise valid and within the competence of the legislature to enact, it cannot be rendered inoperative merely because compliance with it by the plaintiff is difficult for, or harmful to, him due to his innate or congenital disposition. In this respect the exigencies of the common good must prevail. The plaintiff also alleges that this legislation and, in particular, s. 11 of the Act of 1885, impairs his rights of freedom of expression and freedom of association which are guaranteed by Article 40, s. 6, of the Constitution. I do not accept this submission. Freedom of expression and freedom of association are not guaranteed as absolute rights. They are protected by the Constitution subject to public order and morality. Accordingly, if the impugned legislation is otherwise valid and consistent with the Constitution, the mere fact that it prohibits the plaintiff from advocating conduct which it prohibits or from encouraging others to engage in such conduct or associating with others for the purpose of so doing, cannot constitute a breach of the Constitution.

I now turn to what I have described as the core of the plaintiff's case. This is the claim that the impugned legislation constitutes an unwarranted interference with his private life and thereby infringes his right to privacy. This claim is based on the philosophical view, attributed to John Stuart Mill, that the law should not concern itself in the realm of private morality except to the extent necessary for the protection of the public order and the guarding of citizens against injury or exploitation. It is a view which received significant endorsement in the report of the Wolfenden Committee on Homosexual Offences and Prostitution. That committee's report, furnished to the British Parliament in 1957, contained the following statement in support of its recommendation for limited decriminalisation:

> There remains one additional counter argument which we believe to be decisive, namely, the importance which society and the law ought to give to individual freedom of choice in action in matters of private morality. Unless a deliberate attempt is to be made by society, acting through the agency of the law, to equate the sphere of crime with that of sin, there must remain a realm of private morality and immorality, which is, in brief and crude terms not the law's business. To say this is not to condone or encourage private immorality.

The Wolfenden Committee had been established by the Scottish Home Office and, although it recommended (in effect) the removal of criminal sanctions from homosexual conduct when carried out in private between adult responsible males, the British Parliament was very slow to accept that recommendation and to act upon it. It was not until the Sexual Offences Act, 1967 (which was introduced as a private member's bill) that the law was changed in England and Wales; in Scotland the change was not made until the passing of the Criminal Justice (Scotland) Act, 1980. In relation to Northern Ireland, the British Parliament declined to act until compelled to do so as a result of the recent decision of the European Court of Human Rights in *Dudgeon* v. *United Kingdom* (1981) 4 E.H.R.R. 149. The caution shown by successive British Governments and Parliaments is understandable because what was proposed was a significant reversal of legislative policy in an area in which deep religious and moral beliefs were involved.

From the earliest days, organised religion regarded homosexual conduct, such as sodomy and associated acts, with a deep revulsion as being contrary to the order of nature, a perversion of the biological functions of the sexual organs and an affront both to society and to God. With the advent of Christianity this view found clear expression in the teachings of St. Paul, and has been repeated over the centuries by the doctors and leaders of the Church in every land in which the Gospel of Christ has been preached. Today, as appears from the evidence given in this case, this strict view is beginning to be questioned by individual Christian theologians but, nevertheless, as the learned trial judge said in his judgment, it remains the teaching of all Christian Churches that homosexual acts are wrong.

In England, buggery was first treated as a crime by the statute 25 Hen. VIII c. 6, having been previously dealt with only in the ecclesiastical courts. In Ireland, it first received statutory condemnation in the statute of the Irish Parliament 10 Chas. I, sess. 2, c. 20. Subject to statutory changes as to punishment, it continued to be prohibited and punished as a crime in accordance with the provisions of the Act of 1861 which were complemented by the later provisions of the Act of 1885. While those statutory provisons have now been repealed in the entire of the United Kingdom, the question in this case is whether they ceased to operate in Ireland at the time of the enactment of the Constitution in 1937.

In the course of the trial of this action in the High Court, reference was made to the Wolfenden Report, to the Kinsey Survey on homosexual behaviour conducted in the United States and to a similar survey conducted in Sweden. No such survey has been conducted in Ireland, but the trial judge, on the evidence he heard, was prepared to conclude that there is probably a large number of people in this country with homosexual tendencies. Of these, however, only a small number are exclusively homosexual in the sense that their orientation is congenital and irreversible. It is this small group (of those with homosexual tendencies) who must look to the others for the kind of relationship, stable or promiscuous, which they seek and desire. It follows that the efforts and activities of the congenital homosexual must tend towards involving the homosexually orientated in more and more deviant sexual acts to such an extent that such involvement may become habitual. The evidence in this case and the text-books provided as part thereof indicate how sad, lonely and harrowing the life of a person, who is or has become exclusively homosexual, is likely to be. Professor West in his work, *Homosexuality Re-Examined*, states at p. 318:

> Exclusive homosexuality forces a person into a minority group; cuts off all prospect of fulfilment through a family life with children and hampers participation in mainstream social activities which are mostly geared to the needs of heterosexual couples.

He goes on to talk of those, whose life centres on short-term liaisons, as facing loneliness and frustration as they lose their sexual attractiveness with advancing age. Other authors, also referred to, indicate the instability of male homosexual relations, the high incidence of suicide attempts, and the depressive reactions which frequently occur when a relationship ends (Harrison; Reid, Barrett & Hewer). These are some of the consequences which, experience has indicated, tend to follow on a lifestyle which is exclusively homosexual.

Apart from these sad consequences of exclusive homosexuality, unfortunately there are other problems thereby created which constitute a threat to public health. Professor West in his work already mentioned, which was published in a revised form in England over ten years after the decriminalisation of homosexual conduct, says at p. 228: "Far from being immune from venereal infection, as many used to like to believe, male homosexuals run a particularly high risk of acquiring sexually transmitted diseases". The author goes on to show that in the post-decriminalisation decade in Britain many forms of venereal disease (syphilis, gonorrhoea, urethritis and intestinal infection) have shown an alarming increase in males, and that this is attributable directly to the increase in homosexual activity and conduct. In relation to syphilis, the author gives this serious warning:

> A promiscuous homosexual with such a reservoir of infection can transmit the disease, in all innocence, to a whole sequence of victims before the carrier is discovered. The diagnosis at this stage is not always obvious, even when suspected, since blood tests for this infection do not usually become positive until some weeks after the primary chancre has appeared.

He might well have added that, in the case of the novice or the new entrant into homosexual activity, reticence or shame might well delay further the tracing and discovery of the carrier.

Apart from these known consquences of fairly widespread homosexual behaviour and conduct, one other matter of particular importance should be noted. This is the effect of homosexual activity on marriage. It has to be accepted that, for the small percentage of males who are congenitally and irreversibly homosexual, marriage is not open or possible. They must seek such partnerships as they can amongst those whose orientation disposes them to homosexual overtures. But for those so disposed or orientated, but not yet committed, what effect will the acceptance of such overtures be likely to have on marriage? Again, precise information in relation to Ireland is not available. One can only look to what the Wolfenden Committee said in its report (para. 55) before the changes in the law occurred in the United Kingdom:

> The second contention, that homosexual behaviour between males has a damaging effect on family life, may well be true. Indeed we have had evidence that it often is: cases in which homosexual behaviour on the part of the husband has broken up a marriage are by no means rare, and there are also cases in which a man in whom the homosexual component is relatively weak, nevertheless, derives such satisfaction from homosexual outlets that he does not enter upon a marriage which might have been successfully and happily consummated. We deplore this damage to what we regard as the basic unit of society.

That view was based on the limited experience available to the Committee prior to any changes in the law. It indicates, however that homosexual activity and its encouragement may not be consistent with respect and regard for marriage as an institution. I would not think it unreasonable to conclude that an open and general increase in homosexual activity in any society must have serious consequences of a harmful nature so far as marriage is concerned.

I have been speaking of homosexuality and of its possible consequences in accordance with what, in my view, can be gathered from the evidence in this case. What I have said can be summarised as follows:

(1) Homosexuality has always been condemned in Christian teaching as being morally wrong. It has equally been regarded by society for many centuries as an offence against nature and a very serious crime.

(2) Exclusive homosexuality, whether the condition be congenital or acquired, can result in great distress and unhappiness for the individual and can lead to depression, despair and suicide.

(3) The homosexually orientated can be importuned into a homosexual lifestyle which can become habitual.

(4) Male homosexual conduct has resulted, in other countries, in the spread of all forms of venereal disease and this has now become a significant public-health problem in England.

(5) Homosexual conduct can be inimical to marriage and is *per se* harmful to it as an institution.

In the United Kingdom the decisive factor in bringing about decriminalisation of homosexuality was the acceptance of the view advocated by the Wolfenden Committee, and repeated in this case by the plaintiff, that homosexuality was concerned only with private morality and that the law had no business in entering into that field. Whether such a view can be accepted in Ireland depends not on what was done by a sovereign parliament in the United Kingdom but on what our Constitution ordains and requires.

The preamble to the Constitution proudly asserts the existence of God in the Most Holy Trinity and recites that the people of Ireland humbly acknowledge their obligation to "our Divine Lord, Jesus Christ". It cannot be doubted that the people so asserting and acknowledging their obligations to our Divine Lord Jesus Christ, were proclaiming a deep religious conviction and faith and an intention to adopt a Constitution consistent with that conviction and faith and with Christian beliefs. Yet is is suggested that, in the very act of so doing, the people rendered inoperative laws which had existed for hundreds of years prohibiting unnatural sexual conduct which Christian teaching held to be gravely sinful. It would require very clear and express provisions in the Constitution itself to convince me that such took place. When one considers that the conduct in question had been condemned consistently in the name of Christ for almost two thousand years and, at the time of the enactment of the Constitution, was prohibited as criminal by the laws in force in England, Wales, Scotland and Northern Ireland, the suggestion becomes more incomprehensible and difficult of acceptance.

But the plaintiff says that the continued operation of such laws was inconsistent with a right of privacy which he enjoys. Here, in so far as the law and the State are concerned, he asserts a "no go area" in the field of private morality. I do not accept this view either as a general philosophical proposition concerning the purpose of law or as having particular reference to a right of privacy under our Constitution. I regard the State as having an interest in the general moral well-being of the community and as being entitled, where it is practicable to do so, to discourage conduct which is morally wrong and harmful to a way of life and to values which the State wishes to protect.

A right of privacy or, as it has been put, a right "to be let alone" can never be absolute. There are many acts done in private which the State is entitled to condemn, whether such be done by an individual on his own or with another. The law has always condemned abortion, incest, suicide attempts, suicide pacts, euthanasia or mercy killing. These are prohibited simply because they are morally wrong and regardless of the fact, which may exist in some instances, that no harm or injury to others is involved. With homosexual conduct, the matter is not so simple or clear. Such conduct is, of course, morally wrong, and has been so regarded by mankind through the centuries. It cannot be said of it, however, as the plaintiff seeks to say, that no harm is done if it is conducted in private by consenting males. Very serious harm may in fact be involved. Such conduct, although carried on with full consent, may lead a mildly homosexually orientated person into a way of life from which he may never recover. As already indicated, known consequences are frustration, loneliness and even suicide. In addition, it is clearly established that an increase in the practice of homosexuality amongst males increases the incidence of all forms of venereal disease, including the incapacitating and often fatal disease of syphilis. Surely in the light of such possible consequences, no one could regard with equanimity the freeing of such conduct from all legal restraints with the certain result that it would increase and its known devotees multiply. These, however, are not the only considerations.

There is the effect of homosexuality on marriage. As long ago as 1957 the Wolfenden Committee acknowledged, in relation to Great Britain, the serious harm such conduct caused to marriage not only in turning men away from it as a partnership in life but also in breaking up existing marriages. That was the conclusion reached as to the state of facts before the criminal sanctions were removed. One can only suspect that, with the removal of such sanctions and with the encouragement thereby given to homosexual conduct, considerably more harm must have been caused in Great Britain to marriage as an institution. In Ireland, in this respect, the State has a particular duty. Article 41, s. 3, sub-s. 1, of the Constitution provides: "The State pledges itself to guard with special care the institution of Marriage, on which the Family is founded, and to protect it against attack". Surely, a law which prohibits acts and conduct by male citizens of a kind known to be particularly harmful to the institution of marriage cannot be regarded as inconsistent with a Constitution containing such a provision.

On the ground of the Christian nature of our State and on the grounds that the deliberate practice of homosexuality is morally wrong, that it is damaging to the health both of individuals and the public and, finally, that it is potentially harmful to the institution of marriage, I can find no inconsistency with the Constitution in the laws which make such conduct criminal. It follows, in my view, that no right of privacy, as claimed by the plaintiff, can prevail against the operation of such criminal sanctions.

European Convention on Human Rights

One other argument has been advanced on behalf of the plaintiff by Mrs. Robinson. This was based on the Convention for the Protection of Human Rights and Fundamental Freedoms which was signed at Rome on the 4th November, 1950, and was confirmed and ratified by the Government on the 18th February, 1953. This Convention specifies rights and freedoms for the citizens and subscribing countries, broadly similar to the rights and freedoms enjoyed by the citizens of Ireland under the laws and the Constitution. In particular, article 8 of the Convention provides as follows:

1. Everyone has the right to respect for his private and family life, his home and his correspondence.
2. There shall be no interference by a public authority with the exercise of this right except such as is in accordance with the law and is necessary in a democratic society in the interests of national security, public safety or the economic well-being of the country, for the prevention of disorder or crime, for the protection of health or morals, or for the protection of the rights and freedoms of others.

Recently the European Court of Human Rights, which is the appropriate body to do so under the Convention, interpreted this article 8 on a complaint by Jeffrey Dudgeon, a citizen of Northern Ireland, that the legislation impugned in this action, which was then in force in Northern Ireland, interfered with his rights as a homosexual. By a majority verdict the European Court held that it did so and that, accordingly, ss. 61 and 62 of the Offences Against the Person Act, 1861 and s. 11 of the Criminal Law Amendment Act, 1885, were inconsistent with the observance of article 8 of the Convention.

Mrs. Robinson has argued that this decision by the European Court of Human Rights should be regarded by this Court as something more than a persuasive precedent and should be followed. She contends that, since Ireland confirmed and ratified the Convention, there arises a presumption that the Constitution is compatible with the Convention and that, in considering a question as to inconsistency under Article 50 of the Constitution, regard should be had to whether the laws being considered are consistent with the Convention itself. While I appreciate the clarity of her submission, I must reject it. In my view, acceptance of Mrs. Robinson's submission would be contrary to the provisions of the Constitution itself and would accord to the Government the power, by an executive act, to change both the Constitution and the law. The Convention is an international agreement to which Ireland is a subscribing party. As such, however, it does not and cannot form part of our domestic law, nor affect in any way questions which arise thereunder. This is made quite clear by Article 29, s. 6 of the Constitution which declares: "No international agreement shall be part of the domestic law of the State save as may be determined by the Oireachtas".

A similar contention was put before the former Supreme Court in *In re Ó Laighléis* [1960] I.R. 93 and was rejected. In the course of his judgment in that case, Maguire C.J. said at p. 125 of the report:

The Oireachtas has not determined that the Convention of Human Rights and Fundamental Freedoms is to be part of the domestic law of the State, and accordingly this Court cannot give effect to the Convention if it be contrary to domestic law or purports to grant rights or impose obligations additional to those of domestic law.

No argument can prevail against the express command of section 6 of Article 29 of the Constitution before judges whose declared duty it is to uphold the Constitution and the laws.

The Court accordingly cannot accept the idea that the primacy of domestic legislation is displaced by the State becoming a party to the Convention for the Protection of Human Rights and Fundamental Freedoms. Nor can the Court accede to the view that in the domestic forum the Executive is in any way estopped from relying on the domestic law. It may be that such estoppel might operate as between the High Contracting Parties to the Convention, or in the court contemplated by Section IV of the Convention if it comes into existence, but it cannot operate in a domestic Court administering domestic law. Nor can the Court accept the contention that the Act of 1940 is to be construed in the light of, and so as to produce conformity with, a Convention entered into ten years afterwards.

I agree with those views expressed by the former Chief Justice.

For these reasons, I cannot accept Mrs. Robinson's argument. Neither the Convention on Human Rights nor the decision of the European Court in *Dudgeon* v. *United Kingdom* (1981) 4 E.H.R.R. 149 is in any way relevant to the question which we have to consider in this case.

For the reasons set out in this judgment, I have come to the conclusion that the plaintiff is not entitled to the relief he claims and that this appeal should be dismissed.

Henchy J. (dissenting):

The plaintiff is homosexual in nature to the extent that his sexuality is compulsively and exclusviely directed towards members of his own sex. The present state of scientific insight into homosexuality precludes any firm conclusion as to why his particular sexual status was so formed, or any scientifically viable expectation that his exclusively homosexual orientation can be wholly or partly diverted into heterosexuality. What appears clear from the evidence is that his sexual condition was predestined from birth or from childhood rather than adopted by choice, and that the future holds no real hope that any interpersonal sexual conduct in which he may engage will be other than homosexual. Such is the plaintiff who seeks in this action to have the impugned sections expunged from our statute law on the ground that they are so irreconcilable with his personal rights under the Constitution that they cannot be said to have been carried forward into the post-Constitution era and to have been stamped with constitutional validity under Article 50 of the Constitution.

The particular personal circumstances of the plaintiff in the context of his claim are crucial for two reasons. First, to determine whether he has the standing necessary in the eyes of the law to enable him to allege unconstitutionality in the challenged sections. Secondly, even if he has that standing, to decide whether the challenged sections are so inimical to his personal human rights under the Constitution that, weighed against other and more generalised considerations expressed in or postulated by the Constitution, the scale of constitutional values and priorities should be said to preponderate in his favour.

As to the plaintiff's *locus standi*, I entertain no doubt that he is qualified to bring the present proceedings. In fact, in the amended defence delivered by the Attorney General the only plea made in this respect was that the plaintiff had no *locus standi* to allege that ss. 61 and 62 of the Offences Against the Person Act, 1861, are an unconstitutional invasion of the privacy of marriage. On that plea, I would hold with the Attorney General. It is inherent in the plaintiff's case that, as an irremediably exclusive homosexual, he will never marry. Therefore, he has no standing to argue what would in this case be abstract constitutional rights of married couples: see *Cahill* v. *Sutton* [1980] I.R. 269 at p. 283 of the report. But, as an unmarried male homosexual, the impact of the impugned statutory provisions on his personal life is so real and so palpably deleterious to his well-being that he has no difficulty in coming within the general rule as to standing, which was stated as follows in *Cahill* v. *Sutton* at p. 286 of the report:

> The primary rule as to standing in constitutional matters is that the person challenging the constitutionality of the statute, or some other person for whom he is deemed by the court to be entitled to speak, must be able to assert that, because of the alleged unconstitutionality, his or that other person's interests have been adversely affected, or stand in real or imminent danger of being adversely affected by the operation of the statute.

In this case the clear evidence of the ever-present risk of prosecution, conviction and punishment, and of the many other real or imminent risks that beset the plaintiff's life because of the effect on him of the impugned provisions, marks this case as virtually a classical example of an attack on the constitutionality of statutory provisions at the hands of a litigant who has unanswerable qualifications to mount such an attack. Apart from that, however, the trial judge has held that the plaintiff had *locus standi* to the extent I have indicated and the Attorney General has not appealed against that finding.

The second reason for focusing on the facts of the plaintiff's personal predicament is for the purpose of determining whether the impact of the impugned statutory provisions on his life discloses an incompatibility between those provisions and the rights which the Constitution must be held to have vested in him.

Notwithstanding the submission of the plaintiff's counsel to the contrary, the constitutional question that calls for resolution is unaffected by the fact that the precise statutory provisions in question in this case were held by the European Court of Human Rights in *Dudgeon* v. *United Kingdom* (1981) 4 E.H.R.R. 149 to be in breach of article 8 of the European Convention for the Protection of Human Rights and Fundamental Freedoms. That Convention, as has been held by this Court, although it has by its terms a binding force on the Government of this State as one of its signatories, forms no part of the domestic law of this State. Moreover, article 8 of the Convention has no counterpart in our Constitution. Since the constitutionality of the impugned statutory provisions is the only issue raised in this litigation, the touchstone of constitutionality must be held to reside solely in our Constitution. That does not mean that this Court is not open to the persuasive influence that may be drawn from decisions of other courts, such as the European Court of Human Rights, which deal with problems similar or analogous to that now before us. At the end of the day, subject to such influences or methods as are inherent in the judicial process, the task of the Court is to determine the actual and potential effects on the plaintiff of the impugned statutory provisions and then, having viewed those effects in the light of the invoked constitutional protections in their present-day connotation and in the context of the Constitution as a whole, to decide whether there is a repugnancy between what the statutory provisions have prejudicially done to the plaintiff and what the constitutional provisions intended him to be protected against. If such repugnancy is found to exist, the challenged statutory provisions cannot be adjudged to have survived the enactment of the Constitution.

It is not necessary to catalogue in detail the many, and mainly uncontroverted, complaints made by the plaintiff of denigratory and hurtful treatment meted out to him because of his particular sexual orientation. For example, he has been physically attacked; he has suffered verbal abuse; fear of prosecution or of social obloquy has restricted him in his social and other relations with male colleagues and friends; and in a number of subtle but insidiously intrusive and wounding ways he has been restricted in, or thwarted from, engaging in activities which heterosexuals take for granted as aspects of the necessary expression of their human personality and as ordinary incidents of their citizenship.

It is not surprising that the repressive and constricting treatment suffered by the plaintiff affected his psychological health. As an involuntary, chronic and irreversible male homosexual he has been cast unwillingly in a role of furtive living, which has involved traumatic feelings of guilt, shame, ridicule and harassment and countless risks to his career as a university lecturer and to his social life generally. Those risks are not the normal lot of the fornicator, the adulterer, the sexually deviant married couple, the drunkard, the habitual gambler, the practising lesbian, and the many other types of people whose propensities or behaviour may be thought to be no less inimical to the upholding of individual moral conduct, or to necessary or desirable standards of public order or morality, or to the needs of a healthy family life, or to social justice, or to other expressed or implied desiderata of the Constitution.

A stage was reached when the plaintiff, because of what he was suffering as a result of his homosexuality, was referred to one of Dublin's leading consultant psychiatrists. After nine months of psychotherapy the psychiatrist advised the plaintiff that, in the interests of his mental and psychological health, he should consider emigrating to a country, such as England or France, where the law takes a more liberal attitude to male homosexuals. He decided to reject this advice and to continue to live here—a decision which, according to his evidence, had the effect of transforming, to a limited extent, his fear into indignation. His subsequent public espousal of the cause of male homosexuals in this State may be thought to be tinged with a degree of that affected braggadocio which is said by some to distinguish a "gay" from a mere homosexual.

Before entering on the precise question of unconstitutionality on which this appeal turns, I should like to point out that we are not called upon in this case to express an opinion upon whether the law on this topic should be as it is or upon what the purpose of the law should be. Such considerations are for moral philosophers, legal theorists, lawmakers and the like. In a case such as the present, where the legal materials we are considering are written instruments (*i.e.*, statutory provisions on the one hand and overriding constitutional provisions on the other) and are not amenable to the judicial development or extension which would be the case in regard to unwritten or case law, we must take those legal materials as we find them. The judicial function in a case such as this is to lay the impugned statutory provisions down beside the invoked constitutional provisions and if, in the light of the established or admitted facts, a comparison between the two sets of provisions shows a repugnancy, the statutory provisions must be struck down either wholly or in part—if the test of severability laid down at p. 147 of the report of *Maher* v. *The Attorney General* [1973] I.R. 140 is applicable.

The first constitutional provision that is said to be violated by the impugned sections is Article 40, section 1. It is argued that the equality before the law thereby guaranteed is not given effect to when, as is the case, homosexual acts between male homosexuals are made criminal, while homosexual acts between female homosexuals, or deviant sexual acts (such as buggery) between married couples which would generally be considered debased and immoral, are left outside the purview of the criminal law, at least in regard to wives and when committed in private. I am unable to accept this argument. I think it implies an over-wide interpretation of the scope of that constitutional guarantee. It would be a different matter if an unwarranted discrimination had been made between males in respect of the offences dealt with by the impugned sections. But such is not the case. What the sections have done is to make certain conduct between males criminal, while leaving unaffected by the criminal law comparable conduct when not committed exclusively by males. Therein lies the reason why in my view unconstitutional discrimination under Article 40, s. 1, has not been shown. The sexual acts left unaffected are for physiological, social and other reasons capable of being differentiated as to their nature, their context, the range of their possible consequences and the desirability of seeking to enforce their proscription as crimes. While individual opinions on the matter may differ, it was and is a matter of legislative policy to decide whether a compulsion of the common good is capable of justifying the distinction drawn. I would hold that the proviso contained in the second sentence of Article 40, s. 1, makes constitutionally acceptable under that Article the line of demarcation between the acts made criminal by the impugned sections and those which the plaintiff complains are left unproscribed by the criminal law.

The second, indeed, the main ground on which it is submitted that the impugned statutory provisions are unconstitutional is that they violate an essential component of the plaintiff's right of privacy. That a right of privacy inheres in each citizen by virtue of his human personality, and that such a right is constitutionally guaranteed as one of the unspecified personal rights comprehended by Article 40, s. 3, are propositions that are well attested by previous decisions of this Court. What requires to be decided—and this seems to me to be the essence of this case—is whether that right of privacy, construed in the context of the Constitution as a whole and given its true evaluation or standing in the hierarchy of constitutional priorities, excludes as constitutionally inconsistent the impugned statutory provisions.

Having regard to the purposive Christian ethos of the Constitution, particularly as set out in the preamble ("to promote the common good, with due observance of Prudence, Justice and Charity, so that the dignity and freedom of the individual may be assured, true social order attained, the unity of our country restored, and concord established with other nations"), to the denomination of the State as "sovereign, independent, democratic" in Article 5, and to the recognition, expressly or by necessary implication, of particular personal rights, such recognition being frequently hedged in by overriding requirements such as "public order and morality" or "the authority of the State" or "the exigencies of the common good", there is necessarily given to the citizen, within the required social, political and moral framework, such a range of personal freedoms or immunities as are necessary to ensure his dignity and freedom as an individual in the type of society envisaged. The essence of those rights is that they inhere in the individual personality of the citizen in his capacity as a vital human component of the social, political and moral order posited by the Constitution.

Amongst those basic personal rights is a complex of rights which vary in nature, purpose and range (each necessarily being a facet of the citizen's core of individuality within the constitutional order) and which may be compendiously referred to as the right of privacy. An express recognition of such a right is the guarantee in Article 16, s. 1, sub-s. 4, that voting in elections for Dáil Éireann shall be by secret ballot. A constitutional right to marital privacy was recognised and implemented by this Court in *McGee* v. *The Attorney General* [1974] I.R. 284; the right there claimed and recognised being, in effect, the right of a married woman to use contraceptives, which is something which at present is declared to be morally wrong according to the official teaching of the Church to which about 95% of the citizens belong. There are many other aspects of the right of privacy, some yet to be given judicial recognition. It is unnecessary for the purpose of this case to explore them. It is sufficient to say that they would all appear to fall within a secluded area of activity or non-activity which may be claimed as necessary for the expression of an individual personality, for purposes not always necessarily moral or commendable, but meriting recognition in circumstances which do not engender considerations such as State security, public order or morality, or other essential components of the common good.

Put in specific terms, the central issue in this case is whether the plaintiff's claim to be entitled to engage in homosexual acts in private must give way to the right and duty of the State to uphold considerations of public order and morality. In my opinion the legal test by which that issue should be determined is this: where, as in this case, a pre-Constitution legislature has condemned as criminal all homosexual acts between males (ranging from acts of gross indecency, the commission of which does not require even physical contact, to acts of sodomy) and thereby blights and thwarts in a variety of ways the life of a person who is by nature incapable of giving expression to his sexuality except by homosexual acts, and who wishes to be entitled to do so consensually in private, the onus lies on the Attorney General, representing the State, if he is to defeat the individual's claim, to show that to allow him that degree of privacy would be inconsistent with the maintenance of public order and morality.

In my judgment the Attorney General has signally failed to discharge that onus. In the High Court, ten witnesses were called, all on behalf of the plaintiff. Although homosexual acts in private between consenting adults have largely ceased to be criminal in England and Wales since 1967; although in most European countries for many years the legal position has been no less liberal; although a similar degree of decriminalisation has been in force for varying periods in different jurisdictions throughout the world, including some 20 or so States in the United States of America; and although there have been many studies by experts of the social, religious and other effects of such decriminalisation; not a single witness was called by the Attorney General to rebut the plaintiff's case that the degree of decriminalisation sought by him posed no real threat to public order or morality. On the contrary, the consensus of the evidence given was that the beneficial effects, both in terms of individual fulfilment of personality and of the social, political and religious mores of the community, that would flow from a relaxation of the impugned provisions would outweigh any possible ill-effects on society as a whole.

[*The judge referred to the evidence given in the High Court, and continued:*]

The foregoing summary is no doubt an over-compressed version of the evidence given, and to that extent it probably does not reproduce many of the nuances and subtleties of the opinions expressed. But it is an indisputable fact that the evidence of all ten witnesses condemned, in one degree or another, and for a variety of reasons, the impugned sections for being repugnant to the essential human needs of compulsive or obligatory homosexuals and as not being required by—indeed, as being inconsistent with—public order and morality or any of the other attributes comprehended by the constitutional concept of the common good.

In response to this massive and virtually unanimous volume of evidence, given almost entirely by experts in sociology, theology and psychiatry, the Attorney General adduced no oral evidence whatsoever. If the matters pleaded by him in his defence were susceptible of proof, at least to the extent of disproving or casting doubt on the conclusions expressed by the plaintiff and his witnesses, it would have been well within the resources and competence of the State to adduce such evidence. But the hearing in the High Court is notable for the total absence of controverting evidence. True, efforts were made in cross-examination to get witnesses to accept contrary opinions that were said to have been expressed in the writings or pronouncements of other experts or authorities. But a close study of the evidence shows that the largely unanimous conclusions expressed on oath were essentially as I have summarised them and that they stood uncontroverted at the end of the hearing of the evidence.

What choice, then, was open to the trial judge? In my opinion, since this was an oral hearing, on oath, carried out under our adversary system (which is based on the determination, from sworn testimony, according to the required onus and level of proof of the relevant issues), where the outcome of the case depended on a judicial conclusion from the actual or potential effect on our society of specified statutory provisions or of their alternatives, when the conclusions expressed overwhelmingly supported the plaintiff's case, the trial judge was bound in law to reject the Attorney General's defence and to uphold, at least in part, the plaintiff's case. The decision of this court in *Northern Bank Finance* v. *Charlton* [1979] I.R. 149 shows that, if the judge had found the factual conclusions in accordance with the plaintiff's uncontroverted evidence, his findings could not be overturned on an appeal to this Court.

In the course of his judgment the judge said that what he had to decide was:

> . . . whether there are grounds on which the legislature, under current social conditions and having regard to the prevailing ideas and concepts of morality and the current knowledge of matters affecting public health etc., could now reasonably come to the conclusion that the acts declared unlawful are such as ought to be prohibited for the attainment of the true social order mentioned in the preamble, the implementation of the principles of social policy directed by Article 45 and the preservation of the public order and morality mentioned in Article 40 of the Constitution.

Assuming that to be a correct statement of the foundation on which the case fell to be decided, it was not open to the judge to disregard the consensus of the sworn testimony before him and, in the absence of any sworn evidence to the contrary, and relying presumably on suggestions made in the course of cross-examination and on his own intuition, to reach the conclusion that the impugned provisions, if now enacted would, regardless of their impact on the plaintiff and on those in like case, be constitutionally justifiable.

The question whether the constitutional provisions he relied on gave the necessary justification depended on a complex of expert evidential considerations—social, moral, medical and others—and, since the unrebutted consensus of the evidence was against the existence of such justification, the judge was debarred from holding otherwise. The position would be quite different if the Attorney General had chosen to present evidence to the contrary. But he decided not to, although it appears from the cross-examination that such evidence was available. As was made clear by the decision of this Court in *Ryan* v. *The Attorney General* [1965] I.R. 294, where a constitutional challenge depends on expert opinion about the actual or potential effect of questioned statutory provisions, the constitutional point must be ruled on the basis of the facts or opinions as admitted to be correct or as duly found by the judge from the evidence given. Where the evidence given is entirely to one effect, it cannot be rejected.

The learned judge (who dealt with this difficult case with commendable thoroughness), in substituting his own conclusions on the personal and societal effects of the questioned provisions, seems to have laid undue stress on the fact that the prohibited acts, especially sodomy, are contrary to the standards of morality advocated by the Christan Churches in this State. With respect, I do not think that should be treated as a guiding consideration. What are known as the seven deadly sins are anathematised as immoral by all the Christian Churches, and it would have to be conceded that they are capable, in different degrees and in certain contexts, of undermining vital aspects of the common good. Yet it would be neither constitutionally permissible nor otherwise desirable to seek by criminal sanctions to legislate their commission out of existence in all possible circumstances. To do so would upset the necessary balance which the Constitution posits between the common good and the dignity and freedom of the individual. What is deemed necessary to his dignity and freedom by one may may be abhorred by another as an exercise in immorality. The pluralism necessary for the preservation of constitutional requirements in the Christian, democratic State envisaged by the Constitution means that the sanctions of the criminal law may be attached to immoral acts only when the common good requires their proscription as crimes. As the most eminent theologians have conceded, the removal of the sanction of the criminal law from an immoral act does not necessarily imply an approval or condonation of that act. Here the consensus of the evidence was that the sweep of the criminal prohibition contained in the questioned provisions goes beyond the requirements of the common good; indeed, in the opinion of most of the witnesses it is inimical to the common good. Consequently, a finding of unconstitutionality was inescapable on the evidence.

Having given careful consideration to all the evidence, I find that the essence of the unconstitutionality claimed lies not in the prohibition, as a crime, of homosexual acts betwen consenting adult males but primarily in making that prohibition apply without qualification to consenting adult males who are exclusively and obligatorily homosexual. The combined effect of the questioned sections is to condemn such persons, who are destined by nature to be incapable of giving interpersonal outlet to their sexuality otherwise than by means of homosexual acts, to make the stark and (for them) inhumane choice between opting for total unequivocal sexual continence (because guilt for gross indecency may result from equivocal acts) and yielding to their primal sexual urges and thereby either committing a serious crime or leaving themselves open to objectionable and harmful intrusion by those who would wish to prevent such acts, or to intolerance, harassment, blackmail and other forms of cruelty at the hands of those who would batten on the revulsion that such acts elicit in most heterosexuals.

One way or the other, the impugned provisions seem doomed to extinction. Whether they be struck down by this Court for being unconstitutonal or whether they be deemed invalid elsewhere in accordance with the decision in *Dudgeon* v. *United Kingdom* (1981) 3 E.H.R.R. 149 (for being in contravention of the European Convention for the Protection of Human Rights and Fundamental Freedoms) they will require to be replaced with appropriate statutory provisions. It would not be constitutional to decriminalise all homosexual acts, any more than it would be constitutional to decriminalise all heterosexual acts. Public order and morality, the protection of the young, of the weak-willed, of those who may readily be subject to undue influence, and of others who should be deemed to be in need of protection; the maintenance inviolate of the family as the natural primary and fundamental unit of society; the upholding of the institution of marriage; the requirements of public health; these and other aspects of the common good require that homosexual acts be made criminal in many circumstances. The true and justifiable gravamen of the complaint against the sections under review is that they are in constitutional error for overreach or overbreadth. They lack necessary discrimination and precision as to when and how they are to apply.

The opinion expressed by some of the witnesses in the High Court that homosexual acts in private should be decriminalised must not be taken literally. Indeed it is likely that most, if not all, of the witnesses who gave that opinion would wish, on mature consideration, to qualify it. Even the liberalising Sexual Offences Act, 1967, which was passed in England in consequence of the Wolfenden Report, makes extensive exceptions (*e.g.*, in respect of members of the armed services, in respect of acts committed on merchant ships, and because of limitations imposed by the nature of the statutory definitions) to the immunity from prosecution granted. Similar restricting limitations have been inserted in the Homosexual Offences (Northern Ireland) Order, 1982, which was enacted for the purpose of removing the incongruity in that jurisdiction between the now-impugned statory provisions and the European Convention, as found in the *Dudgeon* decision.

I make reference to these matters to indicate that, despite my finding of unconstitutionality in the impugned sections on the ground that by their overreach and lack of precision and of due discrimination, they trench on an area of personal intimacy and seclusion which requires to be treated as inviolate for the expression of those primal urges, functions and aspirations which are integral to the human condition of certain kinds of homosexuals; save in circumstances when the common good requires otherwise, the Constitution leaves a wide range of choice to the Oireachtas in framing a law in place of the questioned provisions. Not only will the Oireachtas be empowered to make homosexual acts criminal but, for the purpose of upholding the requirements of the common good in its full constitutional connotation, it will be necessary for such legislation to hedge in such immunity from criminal sanctions as it may think fit to confer (on acts of a homosexual nature in private between consenting adults) with appropriate definitions of adulthood, consent and privacy and with such exceptions relating to prostitution, immoral exploitation, publicity, drug abuse, commercialisation, family relationships and such other matters or areas of exception as the Oireachtas may justifiably consider necessary for the preservation of public order and decency.

McCarthy J. (dissenting):

The facts underlying the constitutional questions raised in this appeal are fully set out in the judgments of the Chief Justice and Mr. Justice Henchy. The direct physical and psychiatric effects that the existence of the impugned sections of the relevant statutes have had and are having on the plaintiff scarcely require proof; but there is ample proof of it. It is a feature of modern society in Ireland that the male homosexual is scorned, denigrated and, to a degree, ostracised by a very significant section of the community; it may be that this is because of apparent effeminacy or because of the criminal guilt that attaches under the relevant sections. I am content respectfully to adopt the graphic and moving description of the problems faced by the plaintiff, and others like him, in our society, as specified by Mr. Justice Henchy in his judgment and I would add to his list of those who did not suffer such social sanctions the venal, the dishonest, the corrupt and the like.

It is not appropriate to seek to make any comparable assessment of the situation of the female homosexual—suffice it to say that no evidence was led at the trial in respect of such persons. From one's own knowledge of life in the Irish community, the situation of the female homosexual is not affected in any significant way either by the existence of the impugned sections or by contemporary mores. But I do not lose sight of the fact that ss. 61 and 62 of the Offences Against the Person Act, 1861, would appear to contemplate participation by a female in the commission of the offences, although she could not be charged as the offender, whilst s. 11 of the Criminal Law Amendment Act, 1885, has no relevance whatever to females, homosexual or otherwise; the offence of gross indecency under that latter statute can only be committed by male persons.

One does not have to be a homosexual to commit an offence under any of the three sections; it is the act or deed itself that constitutes the offence. In the case of a male homosexual, it is more likely that he, rather than a male heterosexual, will commit such an act or deed; clearly, also, the act proscribed by s. 61 may be committed by a male upon a female, who may be his wife, a feature to which I shall return. Such an act was an offence in the common-law courts by the statute 10 Chas. I, sess. 2, c. 20, and in the older form of indictment it was described as "against the order of nature, that detestable and abominable crime of buggery (not to be named among Christians)"—see 1 East P.C. 480; 12 Co. Rep. 37. In *R.* v. *Jellyman* (1838) 8 C. & P. 604 it was held that a married woman who consents to her husband committing an unnatural offence with her was an accomplice in the felony and, as such, her evidence required confirmation, athough her consent or non-consent was quite immaterial to the offence.

. . . .

[The judge considered the plaintiff's *locus standi,* and continued:]

Point of Time Governing Test of Validity

Article 50, s. 1, of the Constitution provides:

Subject to this Constitution and to the extent to which they are not inconsistent therewith, the laws in force in Saorsát Éireann immediately prior to the date of the coming into operation of this Constitution shall continue to be of full force and effect until the same or any of them shall have been repealed or amended by enactment of the Oireachtas.

Counsel for the Attorney General argues that, in applying the template of the Constitution to the impugned statues, the Court should examine the question on the supposition that the challenge to the statutes had been made immediately after the enactment of the Consitutition. Would a court, in 1938, have upheld the claim of inconsistency?

In *McGee* v. *The Attorney General* [1974] I.R. 284 O'Keeffe P. said at p. 292 of the report:

> In my view, one must look at the state of public opinion at the time of the adoption of the Constitution in order to determine whether the effect of its adoption was to remove from the statute book a section of the Act of 1935: see the principles of construction applied by the Supreme Court in *O'Byrne* v. *The Minister for Finance* [1959] I.R. 1. The section impugned was barely two years on the statute book when the Constitution was adopted. If the submission of the plaintiff is correct, then public opinion as to what were fundamental rights must have been such as to require that the rights guaranteed to individual by the Constitution were inconsistent with the continued legality of the section. I consider that the best test of the position is to be found in the views expressed when the section was being passed into law since, in point of time, this was so close to the enactment of the Constitution by the people. I find that the section was adopted without a division, although it was technically opposed. I cannot think that this reflects a public opinion in favour of the existence of such a right of privacy as is alleged by the plaintiff to be guaranteed under the Constitution.

Whilst the report of the argument of counsel for Mrs. McGee (p. 296) refers to this factor in the case, an examination of the judgments does not disclose any consensus in the Supreme Court. FitzGerald C.J., who dissented, appears to have treated the matter as a contemporaneous issue, when (at p. 300) he was dealing with the relevant facts concerning the manufacture of the particular contraceptive in question.

Mr. Justice Walsh touched on the matter at pp. 306-8 of the report of *McGee's Case*. Having quoted the provisions of Article 50, s. 1, he said:

> I have referred to the wording of s. 1 of Article 50 because, apart from being the foundation of the present proceedings, one of the submissions made on behalf of the Attorney General was to the effect that a statutory provision in force prior to the Constitution could continue to be in force and to be carried over by Article 50 even though its provisions were such as could not now be validly enacted by the Oireachtas because of the provisions of the Constitution. Stated as a general proposition, I find that this is in direct conflict with the very provisions of Article 50 and is quite unsustainable. However, in my opinion, there are circumstances in which the proposition could be partially correct.
>
> If a pre-Constitutional statute was such that it was not in conflict with the Constitution when taken in conjunction with other statutory provisions then in existence *and with a particular state of facts then existing* [*my emphasis*] and if such other statutory provisions continued in effect after the coming into force of the Constitution and the particular state of facts remained unaltered, the provisions of the first statute might not in any way be inconsistent with the provisions of the Constitution. If, however, subsequent to the coming into force of the Constitution the other statutory provisions were repealed and the state of facts was altered to a point where the joint effect of the repeal of the other statutes and the alteration of the facts was to give the original statute a completely different effect, then the question would arise of its continuing to be part of the law. In my view, Article 50, by its very terms (both in its Irish and English tets), makes it clear that laws in force in Saorstát Éireann should continue to be in force only to

the extent to which they are not inconsistent with the Constitution; and that, if the inconsistency arises for the first time after the coming into force of the Constitution, the law carried forward thereupon ceases to be in force.

The relevance of this to the present case is clear. There is no evidence in the case to indicate what was the state of facts existing at the time of the passing of the Act of 1935 and the years subsequent to it up to the coming into force of the Constitution, and even for a period after that. It appears to have been assumed, though there is no evidence upon which to base the assumption, that contraceptives were not manufactured within the State at that time or were not readily available otherwise than by sale. The validity or otherwise of a law may depend upon an existing state of facts or upon the facts as established in litigation, as was clearly indicated by this Court in *Ryan* v. *The Attorney General* [1965] I.R. 294. To control the sale of contraceptives is not necessarily unconstitutional *per se*, nor is a control on the importation of contraceptives necessarily unconstitutional. There may be many reasons, grounded on considerations of public health or public morality, or even fiscal or protectionist reasons, why there should be a control on the importation of such articles. There may also be many good reasons, grounded on public morality or public health, why their sale should be controlled. I used the term "controlled" to include total prohibition. What is challenged here is the constitutionality of making these articles unavailable. Therefore, the decision in this appeal must rest upon the present state of the law and the present state of the facts relating to the issues in dispute. Therefore, even if it were established that in 1935, 1936 or 1937, or even 1940, contraceptives were reasonably available without infringement of the law, that would not necessarily determine that s. 17 of the Act of 1935 now continues to be in full force and effect.

An examination of the judgments of Budd J., Mr. Justice Henchy and Mr. Justice Griffin in *McGee's Case* [1974] I.R. 284 does not disclose any reference to this issue. It would seem, therefore, that there is no authority binding upon me as to the manner in which I should approach this particular issue, if, indeed, it is necessary to consider it. At p. 319 of the report of *McGee's Case* Mr. Justice Walsh said:

According to the preamble, the people gave themselves the Constitution to promote the common good with due observance of prudence, justice and charity so that the dignity and freedom of the individual might be assured. The judges must, therefore, as best they can from their training and their experience interpret these rights in accordance with their ideas of prudence, justice, and charity. It is but natural that from time to time prevailing ideas of these virtues may be conditioned by the passage of time; no interpretation of the Constitution is intended to be final for all time. It is given in the light of *prevailing ideas and concepts*. [The emphasis is mine.]

In *The State (Healy)* v. *Donoghue* [1976] I.R. 325 the Chief Justice accepted that view of what the preamble conveys (for the purpose of considering the issues which arose in that case) and, before citing the above passage from the judgment of Mr. Justice Walsh in *McGee's Case*, the Chief Justice said at p. 347 of the report of *Healy's Case*:

The preamble to the Constitution records that the people "seeking to promote the common good, with due observance of Prudence, Justice and Charity, so that the dignity and freedom of the individual may be assured, true social order attained, the unity of our country restored, and concord established with other nations, do hereby adopt, enact, and give to ourselves this Constitution". In my view, this preamble makes it clear that rights given by the Constitution must be considered in accordance with concepts of prudence, justice and charity which may gradually change or develop as society changes and develops, and which fall to be interpreted from time to time in accordance with prevailing ideas. The preamble envisages a Constitution which can absorb or be adapted to such changes. In other words, the Constitution did not seek to impose for all time the ideas prevalent or accepted with regard to these virtues at the time of its enactment.

After the above passage from the judgment of Mr. Justice Walsh in *McGee's Case* [1974] I.R. 284 (quoted by the Chief Justice in *Healy's Case*) Mr. Justice Walsh continued:

The development of the constitutional law of the United States of America is ample proof of this. There is a constitution which, while not professing to be governed by the precepts of Christianity, also in the Ninth Amendment recognises the existence of rights other than those referred to expressly in it and its amendments. The view of the United States Supreme Court, as reflected in the decisions interpreting that constitution and in the development of their constitutional law, also appear firmly to reject legal positivism as a jurisprudential guide.

I respectfully adopt those observations of the Chief Justice and Mr. Justice Walsh as a correct statement of the proper judicial approach in testing the constitutionality of a statute. In a case such as the present, involving an examination of a British statute, I would refer, also, to the judgment of Mr. Justice Walsh in *The State (Sheerin)* v. *Kennedy* [1966] I.R. 379 (with which the other members agreed) where he says at p. 386 of the report:

The Oireachtas established by the Constitution is the only parliament which is, or was, subject to the provisions of the Constitution and therefore the question of determining the validity of a law having regard to the provisions of the Constitution can only refer to laws enacted by the Oireachtas established by the Constitution. All laws in force on the date immediately prior to the coming into operation of the Constitution are presumed not to be in conflict with the Constitution in force at the date of their enactment or in excess of the powers of the parliament which enacted them, but they enjoy no such presumption in respect of the provisions of the present Constitution and fall to be examined under the provisions of Article 50 of the Constitution—not as to their validity but, even assuming they were valid, as to whether or not they are inconsistent with the provisions of the present Constitution.

I find it philosophically impossible to carry out the necessary exercise of applying what I might believe to be the thinking of 1937 to the demands of 1983. It seems to me that, in this respect, the Attorney General's argument fails *in limine*—it would plainly be impossible to identify with the necessary degree of accuracy of description the standards or mores of the Irish people in 1937—indeed, it is no easy task to do so today. If one had to seek, in testing the consistency or otherwise of a pre-1922 statute or a statute of Saorstát Éireann with the Constitution, to do so by reference to the presumed attitude of the Irish people in 1937 (however difficult that might be 45 years after the enactment of the Constitution), one must postulate the concept of doing so 145 years after its enactment. Suffice it to say that the Constitution is a living document; its life depends not merely upon itself but upon the people from whom it came and to whom it gives varying rights and duties. Ten years after the decisions in *McGee* v. *The Attorney General* [1974] I.R. 284 and in *Byrne* v. *Ireland* [1972] I.R. 241, it is difficult to recall the forensic surprise they created. In my view, it passes from the realm of legal fiction into the world of unreality if the test sought to be applied is one based on some such question as: "Did the people of Saorstát Éireann in 1937 consider that the offence created by [*some Victorian statute*] should no longer be in force?" The only thing considered by those who voted for or against the Constitution in 1937 was whether or not they wanted a new Constitution. An examination of the Dáil debates on the draft Constitution does not encourage any contrary view.

The Personal Right

Articles 40-44 of the Constitution set out the "fundamental rights" of all citizens; Article 40 specifies certain personal rights but does not include any express reference to a right to privacy such as is claimed by the plaintiff to have been:

> identified by the Supreme Court in *McGee* v. *The Attorney General* and not confined to the right to marital privacy but one of the personal rights of the citizen which encompasses but is not exhausted by the right of a husband and wife to privacy in their sexual relations within marriage

see p. 9 of the plaintiff's written submissions. In his judgment in *Ryan* v. *The Attorney General* [1965] I.R. 294 Kenny J. said at pp. 312-13 of the report:

> I think that the personal rights which may be invoked to invalidate legislation are not confined to those specified in Article 40 but include all those rights which result from the Christian and democratic nature of the State . . . there are many personal rights of the citizen which follow from the Christian and democratic nature of the State which are not mentioned in Article 40 at all—the right to free movement within the State and the right to marry are examples of this.

As was stated by Mr. Justice Walsh in *G.* v. *An Bord Uchtála* [1980] I.R. 32 at p. 66 of the report:

> It is now well accepted that the view, first enunciated by my learned colleague, Mr. Justice Kenny, in the High Court in *Ryan* v. *The Attorney General* [1965] I.R. 294 and confirmed by this Court on appeal in the same case (that there are rights guaranteed by the Constitution other than those which are enumerated in the Constitution itself) is the correct view.

Mr Justice Walsh does not directly indicate what he accepts as the source of such unenumerated rights but, at p. 68 of the report of *G.* v. *An Bord Uchtála*, he cited with approval the observations of Mr. Justice Henchy in *McGee* v. *The Attorney General* [1974] I.R. 284 at p. 325 of the report:

> As has been held in a number of cases, the unspecified personal rights guaranteed by sub-s. 1 of s. 3 of Article 40 are not confined to those specified in sub-s. 2 of that section. It is for the Courts to decide in a particular case whether the right relied on comes within the constitutional guarantee. To do so, it must be shown that it is a right that inheres in the citizen in question by virtue of his human personality. The lack of precision in this test is reduced when sub-s. 1 of s. 3 of Article 40 is read (as it must be) in the light of the Constitution as a whole and, in particular, in the light of what the Constitution, expressly or by necessary implication, deems to be fundamental to the personal standing of the individual in question in the context of the social order envisaged by the Constitution. The infinite variety in the relationships between the citizen and his fellows and between the citizen and the State makes an exhaustive enumeration of the gauranteed rights difficult, if not impossible.

At p. 310 of the report of *McGee's Case* [1974 I.R. 284, Mr. Justice Walsh said:

> Articles 41, 42 and 43 emphatically reject the theory that there are no rights without laws, no rights contrary to the law and no rights anterior to the law. They indicate that justice is placed above the law and acknowledge that natural rights, or human rights, are not created by law but that the Constitution confirms their

existence and gives them protection. The individual has natural and human rights over which the State has no authority; and the family, as the natural primary and fundamental unit group of society, has rights as such which the State cannot control. However, at the same time it is true, as the Constitution acknowledges and claims, that the State is the guardian of the common good and that the individual, as a member of society, and the family, as a unit of society, have duties and obligations to consider and respect the common good of that society. It is important to recall that under the Constitution the State's powers of government are exercised in their respective spheres by the legislative, executive and judicial organs established under the Constitution. I agree with the view expressed by O'Byrne J. in *Buckley and Others (Sinn Féin)* v. *The Attorney General* [1950] I.R. 67 that the power of the State to act for the protection of the common good or to decide what are the exigencies of the common good is not one which is peculiarly reserved for the legislative organ of government, in that the decision of the legislative organ is not absolute and is subject to and capable of being reviewed by the Courts. In concrete terms that means that the legislature is not free to encroach unjustifiably upon the fundamental rights of individuals or of the family in the name of the common good, or by act or omission to abandon or to neglect the common good or the protection or enforcement of the rights of individual citizens.

At first sight, Mr. Justice Walsh's judgment seems to identify the source of these unenumerated rights not as the Christian and democratic nature of the State (*pace* Kenny J. in *Ryan* v. *The Attorney General*) but as the human personality, *pace* Mr. Justice Henchy in *McGee's Case.*

I recognise that, immediately before the passage I have just cited, Mr. Justice Walsh referred to the plaintiff's submission which invoked that portion of the preamble to the Constitution in which the people in giving themselves the Constitution, express the intention to seek "to promote the common good, with due observance of prudence, justice and charity, so that the dignity and freedom of the individual may be assured". At pp. 318-19 of the report of *McGee's Case* [1974] I.R. 284 Mr. Justice Walsh said:

> In a pluralist society such as ours, the Courts cannot as a matter of constitutional law be asked to choose between the differing views, where they exist, of experts on the interpretation by the different religious denominations of either the nature or extent of these natural rights as they are to be found in the natural law. The same considerations apply also to the question of ascertaining the nature and extent of the duties which flow from natural law; the Constitution speaks of one of them when it refers to the inalienable duty of parents to provide according to their means for the religious, moral, intellectual, physical and social education of their children: see s. 1 of Article 42. In this country it falls finally upon the judges to interpret the Constitution and in doing so to determine, where necessary, the rights which are superior or antecedent to positive law or which are imprescriptible or inalienable . . . The very structure and content of the Articles dealing with fundamental rights clearly indicate that justice is not subordinate to the law. In particular, the terms of s. 3 of Article 40 expressly subordinate the law to justice. Both Aristotle and the Christian philosophers have regarded justice as the highest human virtue. the virtue of prudence was also esteemed by Aristotle as by the philosophers of the Christian world. But the great additional virtue introduced by Christianity was that of charity—not the charity which consists of giving to the deserving, for that is justice, but the charity which is also called mercy. According to the preamble, the people gave themselves the Constitution to promote the common good with due observance of prudence, justice and charity so that the dignity and freedom of the individual might be assured. The judges must, therefore, as best they can from their training and their experience interpret these rights in accordance with the their ideas of prudence, justice and charity.

In the instant case, the Chief Justice has stated that:

> the preamble proudly asserts the existence of God in the Most Holy Trinity and recites the people of Ireland as humbly acknowledging their obligation to Our Divine Lord Jesus Christ. It cannot be doubted that a people so asserting and acknowledging their obligations to Our Divine Lord Jesus Christ were proclaiming a deep religious conviction and faith and an intention to adopt a Constitution consistent with that conviction and faith and with Christian beliefs. Yet it is suggested that in the very act of so doing the people rendered inoperative laws which have existed for hundreds of years prohibiting unnatural sexual conduct which Christian teaching held to be gravely sinful. It would require very clear and express provisions in the Constitution itself to convince me that such took place.

As I have sought to indicate in my observations under the heading of *locus standi*, [excluded from this extract – eds.] I cannot the approach based upon applying the test of the then contemporary mores to the issue of constitutionality. It must be the mores contemporaneous with the raising of the issue itself. This is in no way to question the proposition that what is termed unnatural sexual conduct is denounced by Christian teaching as gravely sinful; I have no doubt but that Christian teaching is to be found which would declare sexual conduct of the kind contemplated by s. 61 of the Act of 1861 between husband and wife to be gravely sinful; yet it seems a clear inference from the judgment of Mr. Justice McWilliam—and I, as I have already indicated, am firmly of opinion—that the section constitutes an impermissible invasion of the right of privacy in marriage.

In so far as the judgment of Kenny J. in *Ryan's Case*, in referring to the Christian and democratic nature of the State, is a relevant identification of source (cited by the President of the High Court in *The State (C.)* v. *Frawley* [1976] I.R. 365 at p. 373 and in *The State (M.)* v. *The Attorney General* [1979] I.R. 73 at p. 80), I would respectfully dissent from such a proposition if it were to mean that, apart from the democratic nature of the State, the source of personal rights, unenumerated in the Constitution, is to be related to Christian theology, the subject of many diverse views and practices, rather than Christianity itself, the example of Christ and the great doctrine of charity which He preached. Jesus Christ proclaimed two great commandments—love of God and love of neighbour; St. Paul, the Apostle to the Gentiles, declared that of the great virtues, faith, hope and charity, the greatest of these is charity (1 Cor. 13, 13). I would uphold the view that the unenumerated rights derive from the human personality and that the actions of the State in respect of such rights must be informed by the proud objective of the people as declared in the preamble:

> seeking to promote the common good, with due observance of Prudence, Justice and Charity, so that the dignity and freedom of the individual may be assured, true social order attained, the unity of our country restored, and concord established with other nations.

The dignity and freedom of the individual occupy a prominent place in these objectives and are not declared to be subject to any particular exigencies but as forming part of the promotion of the common good.

The Right to Privacy

The Constitution does not guarantee or, in any way, expressly refer to a right of privacy—no more, indeed, than does the United States Constitution, with which our Constitution bears so many apparent similarities. In the United States Constitution the right to privacy in one form or another has been founded upon the First Amendment: *Stanley* v. *Georgia* 394 U.S. 557 (1969); the Fourth and Fifth Amendments: *Terry* v. *Ohio* 392 U.S. 1 (1968); in the penumbras of the Bill of Rights:

Griswold v. *Connecticut* 381 U.S. 479 (1965)—the contraceptives case; in the Ninth Amendment: *Griswold* v. *Connecticut*; and in the concept of liberty guaranteed by the first section of the Fourteenth Amendment: *Meyer* v. *Nebraska* 262 U.S. 390 (1923).

In our Constitution a right of privacy is not spelled out. As stated by Mr. Justice Henchy in his judgment, there is a guarantee of privacy in voting under Article 16, s. 1, sub-s. 4—the secret ballot; a limited right of privacy given to certain litigants under laws made under Article 34; the limited freedom from arrest and detention under Article 40, s. 4; the inviolability of the dwelling of every citizen under Article 40, s. 5; the rights of the citizens to express freely their conviction and opinions, to assemble peaceably and without arms, and to form associations and unions—all conferred by Article 40, s. 6, sub-s. 1; the rights of the family under Article 41; the rights of the family with regard to education under Article 42; the right of private property under Article 43; freedom of conscience and the free profession and practice of religion under Article 44. All these may properly be described as different facets of the right of privacy, but they are general in nature (as necessarily they must be in a Constitution) and do not set bounds to the enumeration of the details of such a right of privacy when the occasion arises. In our jurisdiction, this is best exemplified in the *McGee Case* [1974] I.R. 284 where, whilst Mr. Justice Walsh rested his judgment upon the provisions of Article 41, Budd J., Mr. Justice Henchy and Mr. Justice Walsh [*recte* Griffin: see p. 52 of unreported judgment – eds.] relied upon the guarantees of Article 40, section 3, I would respectfully share the latter view of the true foundation for what the *McGee Case* upheld—the right of privacy in marriage.

Whilst the Constitution of the Irish Free State (Saorstát Eireann), 1922, did not as it were, isolate the fundamental rights of citizens in a manner in which the present Constitution of 1937 has done, articles 6, 7, 8, 9 and 10 of that Constitution indicate the manner in which certain rights were spelled out but, to a degree, highlight the absence of such guarantees as are contained in Article 40, s. 3, and Article 41 of the Constitution. There may well be historical reasons for these differences—a greater awareness of the need for the enunciation of fundamental rights was present during the 1930s than at the time of the negotiations for the Treaty that led to the enactment of the Constitution of the Irish Free State. At all events, since 1937, the concept of judicial dynamism in constitutional law has grown, thereby identifying more readily the role of the Courts and, in particular, this Court as the judicial organ of government, not merely by way of a supervisory jurisdiction on the actions of the legislative and executive branches of government but by way of legal interpretation—thus playing its part in "seeking to promote the common good, with due observance of prudence, justice and charity, so that the dignity and freedom of the individual may be assured . . ." as most strikingly evidenced by the decision in the *McGee Case*.

How, then, to identify the nature of the personal right of privacy? The right to privacy has been called by Brandeis J. of the United States Federal Supreme Court "the right to be let alone"—a quotation cited by the Chief Justice in this case and by Mr. Justice Walsh in his dissenting judgment as a member of the Court of Human rights in *Dudgeon* v. *United Kingdom* (1981) 4 E.H.R.R. 149. By way of definition it has brevity and clarity and I would respectfully adopt it as accurate and adequate for my purpose but, to a degree, the very definition begs the question. The right to privacy is not in issue; the issue is the extent of that right or the extent of the right to be let alone. If a man wishes to maim himself in private, may he not do so? No, because he may become a charge upon the public purse. If a man wishes to masturbate alone and in private, he may do so. If he and another male adult wish to do so in private, may they not do so? No, each commits an offence under s. 11 of the Act of 1885. If a woman wishes to masturbate in private, she does not commit an offence. If a man and woman wish together to do so in private, not being married to each other, neither of them commits an offence. In such latter circumstances, the act committed by the woman upon the man may be identical with what which another man would commit upon him, save that his partner is a woman.

I refer to these particular examples to seek to illustrate the problem that arises if a test is related to what may be generalised as compelling State interest. The term "compelling State interest" is commonly used, particularly in the United States, in cases depending on the claim to privacy. It is self evident that such interest is overwhelming in the protection of minors, persons under incapacity of one kind or another, public decency, discipline in the armed forces or the security forces and so on. But what is the test in circumstances where none of these obvious instances of compelling State interest apply? The Chief Justice has touched upon the alleged greater spread of venereal diseases but I do not accept that the State has discharged in any way a burden of proof of establishing that such a circumstance amounts to a compelling State interest. I join with Mr. Justice Henchy in the observations he has made in his judgment on the failure of the Attorney General, with all the resources at his disposal, to call any evidence whatever to displace the impressive body of evidence called on behalf of the plaintiff. Subject to the matters that I have already instanced, in my opinion a very great burden lies upon those who would question personal rights in order to justify State interference of a most grievous kind (the policeman in the bedroom) in a claim to the right to perform sexual acts or to give expression to sexual desires or needs in private between consenting adults, male or female.

The Acts of 1861 and 1885 were passed during the long reign of a British monarch whose name is identified with many human virtues—those of duty, responsibility, love of family and country and so on—but a less attractive quality of that age was the gross hypocrisy that frequently prevailed, even amongst the ranks of the legislators. Certainly, male homosexuality was known to exist on a wide scale and the Act of 1861 provided a most terrible penalty for what might well be the natural expression of such a human condition. Can the impugned sections be justified to remain on the statute book in 1983 as being consistent with or, more correctly, as being not inconsistent with the personal rights guaranteed by the Constitution?

I have read the evidence of the several distinguished witnesses who testified for the plaintiff; I have examined the cross-examination of these witnesses and the textbooks and reports to which they referred. Applying, as I do, and as Mr. Justice Henchy does, the principles to be drawn from the decision of this Court in *Northern Bank Finance* v. *Charlton* [1979] I.R. 149 on the issues as to whether or not an act or acts prohibited by the impugned sections are part of the make-up of an exclusively homosexual male and whether such prohibitions are or are not required by public order and morality or any other facet of the common good, the only conclusion to which the learned trial judge could come to on the evidence was that the plaintiff's case was established. The learned trial judge stated that the question for him to decide was:

whether there are grounds on which the legislature, under current social conditions and having regard to the prevailing ideas and concepts of morality and the current knowledge of matters affecting public health etc., could now reasonably come to the conclusion that the acts declared unlawful are such as ought to be prohibited for the attainment of the true social order mentioned in the preamble, the implementation of the principles of social policy directed by Article 45 and the preservation of the public order and morality mentioned in Article 40 of the Constitution.

Without expressing any view as to whether or not the question may be so precisely stated, in my opinion there was no evidence before the learned trial judge upon which he would hold other than that the impugned sections were not consistent with the Constitution.

I cannot delimit the area in which the State may constitutonally intervene so as to restrict the right of privacy, nor can I overlook the present public debate concerning the criminal law and arising from the statute of 1861 in regard to abortion—the killing of an unborn child. It is not an issue that arises in this case, but it may be claimed that the right of privacy of a pregnant woman would extend to a right in her to terminate a pregnancy, an act which would involve depriving the unborn child of the most fundamental right of all—the right to life itself. I recognise that there has been no argument in this case relevant to such an issue, but nothing in this judgment, express or in any way implied, is to be taken as supporting a view that the provisions of s. 58 of the Act of 1861 (making it a criminal offence to procure an abortion) are in any way inconsistent with the Constitution. There are but two judicial references to this question, if question be the appropriate word. In *McGee's Case* [1974] I.R. 284 Mr. Justice Griffin said at p. 335 of the report:

> In this context, I wish to emphasise that this judgment is confined to contraception as such; it is not intended to apply to abortifacients, though called contraceptives, as in the case of abortifacients entirely different considerations may arise.

More elaborately, in *G.* v. *An Bord Uchtála* [1980] I.R. 32 Mr. Justice Walsh said at p. 69 of the report:

> Not only has the child born out of lawful wedlock the natural right to have its welfare and health guarded no less well than that of a child born in lawful wedlock, but *a fortiori* it has the right to life itself and the right to be guarded against all threats directed to its existence whether before or after birth. The child's natural rights spring primarily from the natural right of every individual to life, to be reared and educated, to liberty, to work, to rest and recreation, to the practice of religion, and to follow his or her conscience. The right to life necessarily implies the right to be born, the right to preserve and defend (and to have preserved and defended) that life, and the right to maintain that life at a proper human standard in matters of food, clothing and habitation. It lies not in the power of the parent who has the primary natural rights and duties in respect of the child to exercise them in such a way as intentionally or by neglect to endanger the health or life of the child or to terminate its existence. The child's natural right to life and all that flows from that right are independent of any right of the parent as such. I wish here to repeat what I said in *McGee's Case* [1974] I.R. 284 at p. 312 of the report: ". . . any action on the part of either the husband and wife or of the State to limit family sizes by endangering or destroying human life must necessarily not only be an offence against the common good but also against the guaranteed personal rights of the human life in question". In these respects the child born out of lawful wedlock is in precisely the same position as the child born in lawful wedlock.
>
> The Constitution rejected the English common-law view of the position of the illegitimate child in so far as its fundamental rights are concerned. It guarantees to protect the child's natural rights in the same way as it guarantees to protect the natural rights of the mother of the child.

For myself I am content to say that the provisions of the preamble, which I have quoted earlier in this judgment, would appear to lean heavily against any view other than that the right to life of the unborn child is a sacred trust to which all the organs of governmemnt must lend their support. The right of the adult male citizen *privately* to express his sexual orientation alone or with another such person free from State interference is an entirely different matter.

The plaintiff has, further, rested his case upon alleged breach of the constitutional guarantee of equality contained in s. 1 of Article 40. Having reached the conclusion already expressed, I do not consider it necessary to examine the law in the light of that section. However, I am not to be taken as agreeing with the view that the plaintiff's argument implies an over-wide interpretation of the scope of that constitutional guarantee. Likewise, in so far as the plaintiff has rested his case on article 8 of the Convention for the Protection of Human Rights and Fundamental Freedoms and the decision of the European Court of Human Rights in the *Dudgeon Case* (1981) 4 E.H.R.R. 149, I do not consider it necessary to come to any conclusion in that regard. Apart from the limited issue of *locus standi*, my judgment depends upon the right of privacy derived from Article 40, as I have sought to explain. It may be, as some of the theological witnesses claimed, that the criminalisation of the sexual acts proscribed by the impugned sections is contrary to the law of God; I am content to hold that it is contrary to one of the fundamental rights guaranteed by the Constitution.

I join with Mr. Justice Henchy where he says:

> It would not be constitutional to decriminalise all homosexual acts, any more than it would be constitutional to decriminalise all heterosexual acts. Public order and morality; the protection of the young, of the weak-willed, of those who may readily be subject to undue influence, and of others who should be deemed to be in need of protection; the maintenance inviolate of the family as the natural primary and fundamental unit of society; the upholding of the institution of marriage; the requirements of public health; these and other aspects of the common good require that homosexual acts be made criminal in many circumstances . . . Not only will the Oireachtas be empowered to make homosexual acts criminal but, for the purpose of upholding the requirements of the common good in its full constitutional connotation, it will be necessary for such legislation to hedge in such immunity from criminal sanctions as it may think fit to confer on acts of a homosexual nature in private between consenting adults, with appropriate definitions as to adulthood, consent and privacy and with exceptions as to prostitution, immoral exploitation, publicity, drug abuse, commercialisation, family relationships and such other matters or areas of exception as the Oireachtas may justifiably consider necessary . . .

I would allow this appeal.

INDEX